BIBLE
RESEARCH

A Handbook of secular evidence, from first-
class authorities, testifying to the accuracy of
the Scriptures, together with factual information concerning the history and migrations of
the Hebrew peoples

TWO VOLUMES

II

Published by
THE COVENANT PUBLISHING CO. LTD.

First published (in loose-leaf form) 1946
Second impression, with additional material,
in two volumes, 1969
Third impression, 1972

Printed and bound by Antony Rowe Ltd, Eastbourne

BIBLE RESEARCH HANDBOOK
VOLUME II

DIGITAL REPRODUCED
BOOKS FROM OUR ARCHIVES

2005

AVAILABLE

AT

YOUR LOCAL BOOKSTORE

OR

COVENANT BOOKS
121 Low Etherley, Bishop Auckland
Co. Durham, DL14 0HA

(Please ignore references to our former
address at 6 Buckingham Gate)

TABLE OF CONTENTS
(Volume 2)

ETHNOLOGY
(Migrations—Megalithic) 572.9394; (Migrations) 572.9394; (Migrations—Phoenicia Westwards) 572.93944; (Migrations—Palestine—Europe) 572.93951; (Migrations—Palestine—Europe) 572.93951; (Scots from Scythia) 572.941; *Illustration* (Declaration of Independence).

ETHNOLOGY
(Migrations—Greece—Ireland) 572.94151; (Troy—Britain) 572.942; (Phoenicia—Britain) 572.942; (Palestine—Spain) 572.94601; (Palestine—North Africa) 572.961; (Anthropometry of Celto Saxons) 573.

ANCIENT MAPS. 912.30; *Illustrations* 74^D, 74^E, 74^F, 74^G.

MANNER AND CUSTOMS
(Irish and Scottish) 914.41.

GEOGRAPHY
(The Dead Sea) 915.569.

GENEALOGY OF JESUS CHRIST. 929.2.
(Aaronic and Davidic Successions) 929.2; *Illustration* (Genealogy of Owain Tudor) (Descent of the Frankish and Swedish Kings) 929.2.

ISRAELITE FLAGS AND DESIGNS. 929.9.
Illustration (Banners of the Tribes) 929.9.

Authority: D. Simon Evans, M.A., B.D.

IT may be a matter of surprise to many to learn that the earliest west-ward migrations of peoples introduced into the British Isles a language which had (and still contains) many important similarities with the ancient Hebrew. The Welsh language derives from languages which came to Britain with the first waves of Celtic immigration in the B.C. centuries. It can be demonstrated that, in the general structure and arrangement of words and sentences, the two languages have factors in common which suggest the possibility of a common ancestry.

POINTS OF SPECIAL INTEREST

1. The great William Tyndale, who translated the Bible into English, emphasised the close agreement that was to be found between the Hebrew and English tongues. Defending the translation of the Scriptures into English, he wrote:

   "Why thẽ mighte they not be writtẽ in the mother tonge? As yf one of us preach a good sermon, why maye it not be written? Saynt Hierom also trãslated the Bible in to his mother tonge. Why maye not we also? They will saye it can not be translated in to oure tonge it is so rude. It is not so rude as they are false lyers, for the Greke tonge agreeth moare with the English then with the Latyne. And the propirties of the Hebrue tonge agreth a thousande tymes moare with the English then with the Latyne. The manner of speakynge is both one so yᵗ in a thousande places thou neadest not but to trãslate it in to yᵉ English worde for worde whẽ thou must seke a compasse in the Latyne, and yet shalt have moch worke to trãslate it wel-faveredly, so that it have the same grace ãd swetnesse, sence and pure understandinge with it in the Latyne, as it hath in the Hebrue. A thousande partes better may it be translated in to the English then in to the Latyne." (*Obedience of a Christian Man*, by William Tyndale, 1528.)

2. The Rev. Dr. Courtenay James, M.A., B.D., Ph.D., in his *Hebrew and English—Some Likenesses Psychic and Linguistic*, has shown that the Anglo-Saxon and Hebrew languages are closely related in syntax.

3. The suggested intimate relationship between the Celtic and Anglo-Saxon tongues (which belong to the same family) and Hebrew is highly significant and deserves the closest study by scholars.

SIMILARITIES BETWEEN THE WELSH AND HEBREW LANGUAGES

By D. SIMON EVANS, M.A., B.D.

Lecturer in the Department of Welsh at the University College of Swansea

Welsh and Hebrew

For over a century comparative philologists have included Celtic within the orb of the so-called Indo-European family of languages. An Italo-Celtic language has been postulated as one of the chief dialects of Indo-European. This language split up into two branches, which in turn disintegrated into various daughter languages, most of which lie within the historical period. With Italic, of which Latin is the most important descendant, we are not here concerned. Our knowledge of primitive Celtic is very scanty, but it is safe to aver that at one time Celtic-speaking tribes occupied extensive parts of Europe. At the time of Alexander the Great, people speaking a Celtic language were to be found not only in the British Isles, but in parts of France, Spain, North Italy, South Germany, in the valley of the Danube, and as far east as Galatia. Most of these dialects have long disappeared, and so thoroughly were they supplanted on the Continent during the four hundred years of Roman rule that nothing apparently remains of their former vigour apart from a few place names, a fair number of inscriptions from France and Lombardy as well as a few individual words which lie embedded in French and other languages.

Celtic philologists must in the main be satisfied with the materials offered by the descendants of the Celtic dialects spoken in these islands, which did not suffer the ill fate of Continental Celtic. It is customary to distinguish two "insular" dialects, Goidelic, from which Irish, Gaelic and Manx are descended, and Brythonic, whose daughter languages are Welsh, Cornish and Breton. Brythonic was the language of the ancient Britons, and was spoken over the greater part of Britain before the Roman occupation. Under the Romans it ceased to be the official language and in course of time was entirely superseded by Latin in the southern and eastern parts of the country. The north and west, however, were not so thoroughly romanized, and there it persisted as the speech of the native population. But three and a half centuries of Roman occupation deeply affected its structure and vocabulary; it suffered extensive phonological and morphological changes and assimilated hundreds of words from the language of the conqueror. From this process of disintegration there evolved the three daughter languages of Welsh, Cornish and Breton. Welsh literature can be traced back as far as the sixth century. Since that period the language has remained fairly static. The languages that have had the greatest influence on it in the course of its long history are Latin and especially English. From these and other languages, such as French, Welsh has borrowed much of its vocabulary, but they have not materially affected its morphology and syntax.

The origin and history of Welsh has thus been briefly stated; such are the findings of comparative philologists. The further back we extend our investigation, the scarcer do our materials become, and the greater is our speculation. Of the hypothetical primitive Celtic we have no direct evidence; still less do we know of the influences which other languages may have had on it from time to time. There must have been such influences, but we are as yet unable even faintly to discern and disentangle the diverse threads which must have gone to the weaving of the language's structure at an early period. We know that the Celts were not the original inhabitants of these islands. Nothing is known of the language or languages of the people whom the Celts found here, but whatever they may have been, they

Serial No. 85a

were in course of time supplanted by one or other of the Celtic dialects. It is safe to assume, however, that the supplanted language did not disappear without leaving its influence on the new speech whi·h the conquered were obliged to acquire. They would probably be in the majority, and while they would find it comparatively easy to adopt the new vocabulary, it would not be so easy to abandon the time-honoured modes of expression. The late Sir John Morris-Jones, in an appendix to *The Welsh People* (John Rhys and David Brynmor Jones), pp. 617-41, tried to show that there was in Welsh and Irish evidence of pre-Indo-European syntax. He drew attention to points of similarity in syntax between the Celtic languages and Egyptian and the Berber dialects. Sir John saw in such resemblances a corroboration of the theory of anthropologists that the pre-Celtic inhabitants of Britain were of the same race as the ancient Iberians who migrated through France and Spain from North Africa. While no one would now accept Sir John's theory in its entirety (he himself disclaimed it at a later date), the view that neo-Celtic languages have assimilated non-Celtic or even non-Indo-European modes of expression cannot at this stage of our enquiry be dismissed as fantastic.

Hebrew is classified by philologists as a Canaanite dialect of the East Semitic branch of another family of languages, viz. the Semitic. Comparative philologists have been loath to accept the idea of a common origin for Semitic and Indo-European, but the question has received the attention of scholars from time to time,[1] and it is probably a field of investigation with which philologists will be concerned for some time to come. Hitherto, comparative philologists have in the main limited their investigations to the field of phonology and morphology; comparative syntax has not been so popular. Much profitable work remains to be done in this field. Whether such an investigation will yield concrete results can only be shown after the data have been collected and properly classified. Whatever may be our suppositions and conceptions of the inter-relationships of the languages of the world, old and new, and of the classification of languages into families, a comparative study of the syntax of any two known languages could certainly yield no ill results and might easily lead to further profitable enquiry. At the same time it must be granted that we are far from the position where we can on the basis of such an investigation be justified in submitting theories.

In this treatise I propose to draw attention to points of similarity in the syntax of Welsh and Hebrew, two languages, which, as I have stated, philologists regard as belonging to two different families, and which in many respects possess widely different characteristics.

The Sentence: Order

In Hebrew the normal order of the verbal sentence is: *verb, subject, object* or *complement of the verb*, e.g. וַיַּרְא אֱלֹהִים אֶת־הָאוֹר כִּי־טוֹב [2] "And God saw the light that (it was) good." But this order may be altered in various ways, mainly for the sake of emphasis. Reference may

---

[1] H. Möller, *Indogermanisch und semitisch*, 1906, *Glossarium* 1909; *Vergleichendes Wörterbuch*, 1911; *Laryngalen*, 1917.
   A. Cuny, *Études prégrammaticales sur le domaine des langues indo-européennes et chamito-sémitiques* (Publications of la Société Linguistique de Paris XIV); *La catégorie du duel les langues indo-européenes et chamito-sémitiques*. Brussels, 1930.
   Recherches sur le vocalisme et le consonantisme et la formation des racines en "nostratique". Paris, 1943.
   E. Benveniste, *Origine de la formation des noms en indo-européen.* Paris, 1935.
   Reference may also be made to an older treatise, *Indogermanische und semitische Forschungen.* Bologne, 1897, A. Trombetti.
[2] Genesis i. 4.

be made to the following types: *subject, verb* הַנָּחָשׁ הִשִּׁיאַנִי "the serpent beguiled me"; *object, verb, subject* וּמְעִיל קָטֹן תַּעֲשֶׂה־לּוֹ אִמּוֹ[2] "and a little robe his mother used to make him"; *verb, object, subject,* כַּאֲשֶׁר שִׁכְּלָה נָשִׁים חַרְבֶּךָ[3] "as thy sword has bereaved women"; *subject, object, verb,* יְדֵיכֶם דָּמִים מָלֵאוּ[4] "your hands are full of blood".

In Welsh a variety of order is found.[5] The normal order of the sentence in Hebrew is very much in evidence in Welsh also, e.g. *Dywawt Kulhwch vrthi*[6] "Quoth Kulhwch to her". (The same order is found in Irish, e.g. *Airighit didiu munter Eterscéle an teach hisin*[7] "the people of Eterscel then notice that house"). As in Hebrew, we find variations of this order. At an earlier period in the history of the language we find examples of the order, *subject verb, subject object verb, verb object subject, object verb,*[8] where it does not appear that any particular emphasis is required on any part of the sentence. However, eventually, these types were displaced by the normal order which prevails in Modern Welsh, viz. that of *verb subject object,* with the position of the adverb optional. Thus in Mod. Welsh we have, for example, *Collodd y bachgen ei gap yn yr afon,* "The boy lost his cap in the river" or *Yn yr afon collodd y bachgen ei gap,* where the adverbial phrase *yn yr afon* precedes; all the other elements in the sentence must be in the order *verb subject object.*

When emphasis was required on any part of the sentence other than the verb, the practice in Welsh (as in Irish) was to bring it to the head of the sentence with a relative clause following. Originally the word or phrase thus emphasized was preceded by the copula: *ys mi ae heirch*[8] "it is I who seek her", *Oed digawn o drwc a wnathoed duw ynni*[9] "it was sufficient misfortune which God had wrought us", *Ny bu hir y buont yny doethont y Arberth*[10] "It was not long that they were before they came to Arberth". Later the copula came to be omitted: *myfi a wyr* "(it is) I who know". The examples of this construction will be the more readily understood if reference is made to the exposition of the relative clause in Welsh. This type of sentence is known as the "mixed" sentence.

Sentences of the order *subject verb, object verb* referred to above where no emphasis was required on the subject or object were obviously influenced by the type of sentence *subject a verb,* etc., where the subject came first for the sake of emphasis. It is reasonable to assume that the two types were confused, with the result that there evolved at a fairly early period in Welsh types of order which conformed to the pattern of the mixed sentence but without the emphasis. This so-called "abnormal" order prevailed in Medieval Welsh[11] and in the early modern period. It is found abundantly in the Welsh translation of the Bible: *A'r publicanod hefyd a ddaethant i'w bedyddio*[12] "Then came also publicans to be baptized"; *Eglwysi eraill a ysbeiliais*[13] "I robbed other churches"; *Am hynny y digiais wrth y genhedlaeth honno*[14] "Wherefore I was grieved with that generation".

---

[1] Genesis iii. 13.　　[2] 1 Samuel ii. 19.　　[3] Ibid. xv. 33.　　[4] Isaiah i. 15.
[5] *The Sentence in Welsh,* Henry Lewis (The Sir John Rhys Memorial Lecture, 1942). *Bulletin of the Board of Celtic Studies,* IV. 149-52.
[6] *White Book Mabinogion* (Evans), 238b.
[7] *Togail Bruidne Da Derga,* 3 (Ed. E. Knott), Dublin, 1936.
[8] *White Book Mabinogion* (Evans), 240a.
[9] *Red Book Mabinogion* (Rhys & Evans), 137.
[10] *Pedeir Keinc y Mabinogi* (Williams), 25.
[11] *Med. Welsh* from the twelfth to the fifteenth century.
[12] Luke iii. 12.　　[13] 2 Cor. xi. 8.　　[14] Hebrews iii. 10.

Agreement of Subject and Verb in Number

In Hebrew there is less precision in the matter of agreement than there is in most other languages. There is a marked tendency to *constructio ad sensum*; hence grammatical singulars, such as collectives and words that suggest a plurality, are often joined with plural predicates. On the other hand, we find a tendency to construe with a singular verb things that resemble one another or belong to the same class. The position of the verb is another factor. When the subject precedes, agreement in number is general; when the verb comes first agreement is usual, but the verb is often in the 3rd singular with a plural subject. The explanation of this construction proposed by Semitic grammarians is that the speaker or writer in such cases has his attention fixed on the act itself; hence consciousness of the coming subject is not yet present to him, and he puts the predicate in the most general form, viz. that of the 3rd singular masculine. This construction is common with הָיָה "to be"; יְהִי מְאֹרֹת בִּרְקִיעַ הַשָּׁמַיִם[1] "Let there be lights in the firmament of the heaven".

In Welsh, from the earliest period we find that the verb stands in the 3rd singular before a plural subject, and this is the normal construction in Mod. Welsh: *Aeth y dynion adref* "The men went home"; *Canodd y clychau* "The bells rang". In the older Welsh literature examples occur where the verb agrees in number with the following subject: *cet treidin guel haguid*[2] "though grass and trees should declare"; *kychwynnassant yr yniueroed hynny*[3] "those hosts set out"; *kychwynnyssont y llu mawr hwnnw*[4] "that great host set out"; *gwelsant niuer Otgar eu meint*[5] "Otgar's retinue saw their number". In the last two examples the plural verb precedes a collective noun.

In sentences where the subject precedes the verb either with or without the particle *a* agreement in number between verb and subject is the rule: *guir deur kymynint a dur*[6] "brave men slew with steel"; *A'r guyrda a doethant y gyt*[7] "And the chief men came together". Some examples occur, however, where the verb is singular: *Gwyr a aeth Gatraeth gan wawr*[8] "The men went to Catraeth at dawn"; *E gwyr hynny a ymchwelwys a'r atteb hwnnw*[9] "Those men returned with that answer". In the mixed sentence, where the subject is the stressed element, the verb is normally in the 3rd singular with plural subject, *nyni a aeth* "(it was) we who went".

Casus Pendens

By the "Casus pendens" is meant a noun which stands at the head of a sentence with no syntactical connexion with the remainder of the sentence. Usually it is referred to later in the sentence by a pronoun or pronominal ending. In highly inflected languages like Latin or Irish, such a noun is in the nominative case; hence the term "nominativus pendens". But in languages like Hebrew or Welsh where no such distinction of form occurs, its position and the following pronominal reference are the only means we have of analysing its construction. The "Casus pendens" is of common occurrence in Hebrew: כִּי כָל־הָעֹשֶׁר אֲשֶׁר הִצִּיל אֱלֹהִים מֵאָבִינוּ לָנוּ הוּא וּלְבָנֵינוּ[10] "For all the wealth which God hath taken from our father is ours and our children's", lit. "For all the wealth . . . . *it* is to us and to our children"; וְהָאִישׁ מִיכָה לוֹ בֵּית אֱלֹדִים[11] "And the man Micah had a house of God", lit. "And the man Micah to *him* (was) a house of God"; הָאָרֶץ אֲשֶׁר אַתָּה שֹׁכֵב עָלֶיהָ לְךָ אֶתְּנֶנָּה[12] "the land on which thou liest will I give thee", lit. "the land thou liest on it to thee will I give *it*".

[1] Genesis i. 14. [2] *Bulletin of the Board of Celtic Studies*, VI. 206. 2b.
[3] *Pedeir Keinc y Mabinogi* (Williams), 31. [7]Ibid. 21. [9] Ibid. 33.
[4] *Breudwyt Ronabwy* (Richards), 9.
[5] *White Book Mabinogion* (Evans), 2496.
[6] *The Black Book of Carmarthen* (Evans), 72.
[8] *Canu Aneirin* (Williams), 4. [10] Genesis xxxi. 16. [11] Judges xvii. 5. [12] Genesis xxviii. 13.

The same construction is common in Welsh also: *a'r arglwydiaeth a gaussam ninheu y ulwydyn honno, nys attygy y gennym*[1] "and the rule we have had that year thou wilt not withhold from us", lit. "thou wilt not withhold *it* from us"; *Ryuedawt hagen da oed gennyf pei ys guelwn*[2] "I should be glad however were I to see a wonder", lit. "A wonder, I should be glad were I to see *it*"; *a holl uaranned y llys wrth y gynghor ef y treulwyt*[3] "and all the resources of the court were dispensed at his direction", lit. "and all the resources of the court, at his direction were *they* dispensed".

The Nominal Sentence

In a nominal sentence the predicate consists of a noun, adjective or adverb. Usually no motion or activity is implied, and the predicate denotes an attribute of the subject. The relation between subject and predicate may be expressed by mere juxtaposition, and sentences thus constructed may be termed Pure Nominal Sentences. (The use of the copula is probably a secondary development.) This type of sentence abounds in the Semitic languages, and Hebrew is no exception: וְזָהַב הָאָרֶץ הַהִיא טוֹב[4] "and the gold of that land (is) good"; וְאַנְשֵׁי סְדֹם רָעִים[5] "and the men of Sodom (were) wicked"; כִּי עֵירֹם אָנֹכִי[6] "because I (was) naked". The predicate can be an interrogative pronoun or particle: מִי הָאִישׁ הַלָּזֶה[7] "who (is) yonder man?"; הֲכֶלֶב אָנֹכִי[8] "(am) I a dog?"

Meillet has shown that the Pure Nominal Sentence is a feature of the syntax of Indo-European languages.[9] In Welsh it is commonly found at all periods in the history of the language, and is mostly found in gnomes and proverbs. It is a marked feature of the syntax of early Welsh gnomic poetry.[10] Here are some examples of its use: *Cyfaill blaidd bugail diog* "A lazy shepherd (is) a friend of the wolf"; *Llym awel, llum bryn, anhaut caffael clid*[11] "The wind (is) keen, the hill (is) bare, to find shelter (is) difficult"; *Driccin i mynit avonit i gniw*[12] "(There is) rough weather on the mountain, the rivers (are) surging". As in Hebrew, the predicate in Welsh may be an interrogative pronoun: *Pwy eu henw wy?*[13] "What (is) their name?", cf. Irish *Cia th' ainm-siu?*[14] "What (is) thy name?"

As in Hebrew the preposition לְ "to" is used to denote possession in such sentences, i "to" is employed in Welsh: וּלְלָבָן שְׁתֵּי בָנוֹת[15] "And Laban had two daughters"; in the Welsh translation we find "Ac *i* Laban yr oedd dwy o ferched".

Circumstantial Clause

The circumstantial clause expresses some circumstance or concomitant of the main action or statement. In some aspects it corresponds to the classical genitive or ablative absolute, but its construction is different. It includes a predicate and a subject, and is connected with the main sentence by the co-ordinate conjunction *waw*; the order normally is *waw, subject, predicate*. Thus, although the circumstantial clause is subordinate in meaning to the main sentence, it is co-ordinate with it in construction. It is often equivalent to an adverbial clause or phrase; it may also correspond in meaning to a relative clause when its predicate is nominal: וְנִבְנֶה מִגְדָּל וְרֹאשׁוֹ בַשָּׁמַיִם[16] "Let us build a tower with its head in the heavens", lit. "and its head in the heavens"; וַהֲנִקְלָה הִתְחַתֵּן בַּמֶּלֶךְ וְאָנֹכִי אִישׁ־רָשׁ[17] "it is a

---

[1] *P.K.M.* 8.   [2] Ibid. 9,   [3] Ibid. 14.
[4] Genesis ii. 12.   [5] Ibid. xiii. 13   [6] Ibid. iii. 10.   [7] Ibid. xxiv. 65.
[8] 1 Samuel xvii. 43.
[9] *Mémoires de la Société de Linguistique*, XIV. 1 f.
[10] *Early Welsh Gnomic Poetry* (Jackson).
[11] *Black Book of Carmarthen* (Evans), 89.   [12] Ibid. 91.
[13] *P.K.M.* 68.   [14] *Stories from the Táin* (Strachan), 3.   [15] Genesis xxix. 16.   [16] Ibid. xi. 4.
[17] 1 Samuel xviii. 23.

light thing to be son-in-law of the king when I am a poor man?'' lit. ''and I a poor man'';
וַיָּרָץ אִישׁ וּמַדָּיו קְרֻעִים [1] ''there ran a man with his garments rent'', lit. ''*and* his garments
rent''; אַל־תְּאַחֲרוּ אֹתִי וַיהֹוָה הִצְלִיחַ דַּרְכִּי [2] ''delay me not when Jehovah has prospered my
journey'', lit. ''and Jehovah'' etc.; מַדּוּעַ בָּאתֶם אֵלַי וְאַתֶּם שְׂנֵאתֶם אֹתִי [3] ''why are ye come to
me when ye hate me?'' lit. ''*and ye*'', etc.

A similar construction occurs in Welsh. The clause is connected with the main sentence
by the co-ordinate conjunction *a(c)*. The predicate is nominal and may be a noun, adjective,
adverb or verb-noun. *Ac oni ddylai hon, a hi yn ferch i Abraham . . . gael ei rhyddhau o'r
rhwym hwn ar y dydd Saboth?*[4] ''And ought not this woman, *being a daughter of Abraham*,
. . . be loosed from this bond on the Sabbath day?'' lit. ''and she a daughter of Abraham'';
Mair Magdalen a ddaeth y bore, a hi eto'n dywyll, at y bedd[5] ''Mary Magdalene came to
the tomb early, while it was still dark'', lit. ''and it (being) still dark''; *ac a hwy ynawr
yngolwg y Tir, y chwythodd Tymhestl o wynt gwrthwyneb*[6] ''and when they were now in
sight of land, there blew a storm of adverse winds'', lit. ''and they (being) now in sight of
land''; *Ac yn ol hynny, goueileint a dellis yndaw, o gamhet idaw attal y mab ganthaw, ac ef
yn gwybot y uot yn uab y wr arall*[7] ''And with that, anxiety seized upon him, so very wrong
it was for him to keep the boy, when he knew him to be another man's son'', lit. ''and
he knowing him to be son to another man''.

The Relative Clause

Hebrew lacks a relative pronoun, and various constructions are employed to meet this
deficiency. The form אֲשֶׁר is used to introduce a relative clause. Its origin is obscure, but
whatever its origin, its use in Biblical Hebrew is that of a connecting particle and not a
relative pronoun. Syntactically, the relative clause is an independent sentence, אֲשֶׁר merely
denoting connection with the antecedent. Take, for example, the following sentence:
כָּל־רֶמֶשׂ אֲשֶׁר הוּא־חַי [8] ''every creeping thing which is alive'', lit. ''every creeping thing *it*
is alive''. The pronoun הוּא is the subject of the clause. In English the relative pronoun
which is employed in this connection. Hebrew has nothing to correspond to *which*. What
we have, then, is antecedent + independent sentence with the connecting particle אֲשֶׁר used
to denote that the sentence is subordinate. The pronoun, which in this case is the subject
of the relative clause, is generally not expressed, הָעֵץ אֲשֶׁר בְּתוֹךְ־הַגָּן [9] ''the tree (which) (is)
in the middle of the garden''. When the relative sentence contains a verb, the subject is
expressed by the verbal inflection: וַאֲנִי יְהֹוָה אֲשֶׁר הוֹצֵאתִיךָ [10] ''I am Je. which brought thee
out'', lit. ''I am Je. *I* brought thee out''.

We find the same construction employed when the relative is objective: אֲנִי יוֹסֵף אֲשֶׁר־
מְכַרְתֶּם אֹתִי [11] ''I am Joseph . . . whom ye sold'', lit. ''I (am) Joseph ye sold *me*''. The
pronoun is often omitted: אֱלֹהִים אֲשֶׁר לֹא יָדַעְתָּ [12] ''gods whom thou hast not known'', lit.
''gods thou hast not known''.

When the relative is genitive depending on a noun in the relative clause, a pronominal
suffix is attached to that noun, thus, גּוֹי אֲשֶׁר לֹא־תִשְׁמַע לְשֹׁנוֹ [13] ''a nation whose tongue
thou shalt not understand'', lit. ''a nation thou shalt not understand its tongue''. When
the relative is governed by a preposition a pronominal form of the preposition is used in
the relative clause: הָאָרֶץ אֲשֶׁר אַתָּה שֹׁכֵב עָלֶיהָ [14] ''the land upon which thou liest'', lit. ''the
land thou liest upon *it*''.

[1] I Samuel iv. 12.   [2] Genesis xxiv. 56.   [3] Ibid. xxvi. 27.   [4] Luke xiii. 16.
[5] John xx. 1.   [6] *Drych y Prif Oesoedd* (Evans, Bangor, 1902), 42.   [7] *P.K.M.*, 24.
[8] Genesis ix. 3.   [9] Ibid. iii. 3.   [10] Ibid. xv. 7.   [11] Ibid. xlv. 4
[12] Deuteronomy xiii. 7.   [13] Ibid. xxviii. 49.   [14] Genesis xxviii. 13

After phrases and nouns of time the preposition and suffix is generally omitted: עַד
הַיּוֹם אֲשֶׁר בָּא [1] ''until the day (when) he came''; after adverbs of place an adverb is usually
inserted in the relative clause: הַמָּקוֹם אֲשֶׁר הָיָה שָׁם אָהֳלֹה [2] ''the place where his tent was'',
lit. ''the place his tent was *there*''; כָּל־הַמָּקוֹם אֲשֶׁר נָבוֹא שָׁמָּה [3] ''every place whither we
shall come'', lit. ''every place we shall come *thither*''; הָאֲדָמָה אֲשֶׁר לֻקַּח מִשָּׁם [4] ''the ground
whence he was taken'', lit. ''the ground he was taken thence''.

We find אֲשֶׁר used when the antecedent is not expressed: וַיִּשָּׁאֶר נֹחַ וַאֲשֶׁר אִתּוֹ [5] ''and Noah
was left and *they who* were with him''. When thus used it may admit of a preposition
before it: וַיֹּאמֶר לַאֲשֶׁר עַל־בֵּיתוֹ [6] '' he said *to* (him) *who* was over his house''; רַבִּים מֵאֲשֶׁר
הֵמִית בְּחַיָּיו [7] ''*more than* (those) *whom* he slew in his life''.

The demonstrative זֶה is often a relative in poetry; in this construction אֲשֶׁר is omitted.
אֶל־מְקוֹם זֶה יָסַדְתָּ לָהֶם [8] ''and *they whom* I loved are turned against me''; מֶחָה אֲהַבְתִּי נֶהֶפְּכוּ־בִי
''unto the place *which* thou hast chosen for them''; the form זוּ is oftener used, נָחִיתָ
בְחַסְדְּךָ עַם־זוּ גָאָלְתָּ [10] ''thou in thy mercy hast led forth the people *which* thou hast redeemed''.
The use of the article as relative is not uncommon, especially in later writings; אַנְשֵׁי הַמִּלְחָמָה
כָּל־הַנֶּפֶשׁ לְבֵית־יַעֲקֹב הַבָּאָה מִצְרַיְמָה [12] ''of the men of war *which* went with him''; הַהֹלְכוּא אִתּוֹ [11]
''all the souls of the house of Jacob *which* came unto Egypt''; וְהַנִּמְצָא אִתּוֹ אֲבָנִ֫ ים [13] ''and
he with whom stones were found'', lit. ''and *he* stones were found with *him*''.

The syntax of the relative in Welsh (and Irish) bears a striking similarity to the construction in Hebrew. In affirmative clauses where the relative is subject or object only do
we find a proper relative pronoun used. The form of this pronoun is Old W. *hai*, Med.
W. *ae, a,* Mod. W. *a.* The origin of these forms is obscure;[14] it may be that originally they
represent relative particles and not pronouns. But whatever their origin may be, they are in
Welsh regarded as relative pronouns: *ir serenn hai bu in arcimeir o*[15] ''the star *which* was
opposite o''; *y prifford a gerdei heb law yr orssed*[16] ''the highway that led past the mound'';
y march a rodyssei Teirnon idaw[17] ''the horse *which* Teyrnon had given him''.

When the clause is negative *a* is not used, and the construction of the clause is identical
with that of an independent negative sentence. It was introduced by *ny(t)* (later the form
na was employed, probably to denote subordination): *Nit oes yndi nep ni'th adnappo*[18]
''There is not anyone within (that) will not know thee''; *y pechodeu nys gwnaeth*[19] ''the
sins which he did not commit'', lit. ''the sins he did not commit *them*'' (*s* in *nys* represents
an infixed objective personal pronoun). The negative is found without *s* in this type of
clause: *yr hynn ny welsynt*[20] ''that (which) they had not seen''.

When the relative had some function other than that of subject or object, there was in
Welsh no form of the relative to express it. As in Hebrew, the syntax of the clause was that
of an independent sentence, and in the Old W. period we find that the relative clause

[1] 2 Samuel xix. 25.   [2] Genesis xiii. 3.   [3] Ibid. xx. 13.   [4] Ibid. iii. 23.   [5] Ibid. vii. 23.
[6] Genesis xliii. 16.   [7] Judges xvi. 30.   [8] Job xix. 19.   [9] Psalm civ. 8.
[10] Exodus xv. 13.   [11] Joshua x. 24.   [12] Genesis xlvi. 27.   [13] 1 Chronicles xxix. 8.
[14] The explanation offered in *Welsh Grammar* (Morris-Jones), 287, is not convincing.
[15] *Bulletin of the Board of Celtic Studies,* iii. 256.   [19] Ibid. viii. 140.
[16] *P.K.M.,* 9.   [17] Ibid. 25.   [18] Ibid. 4.
[20] *Llyvyr Agkyr Llandewivrevi* (Jones & Rhys), 12.
For traces of the interrogative used as relative vide *Concise Comparative Celtic Grammar* (Lewis & Pedersen), 226-7, 230. For a discussion of lenition in the verb after the negative and other preverbs in relative
clauses, *vide* p. 143.

Serial No. 85d.

immediately follows its antecedent without any connecting particle: *is mod cephitor did hanaud*[1] "it is the manner (in which) a day is obtained from it"; *is gur tum tarnetor ir loc guac*[1] "it is as an increment (that) the empty space is reckoned"; *is gurth ir serenn . . . retit loyr*[1] "it is opposite the constellation (that) the moon travels". Later we find the particles *yd, y (đ), y(†)*, employed in such connexions before the verb of the relative clause. This was probably an innovation; the particle being introduced to denote subordination. Its use is almost identical with that of אֲשֶׁר in clauses where the relative has the force of an oblique case or functions adverbially. When the clause is negative, it is introduced by *ny(t), na(d)*. I propose to illustrate the construction according as the relative is (a) genitive, (b) governed by a preposition, or (c) functions adverbially.

(a) *y wraig y bywhasai efe ei mab*[2] "the woman, whose son he had restored to life", lit. "the woman he had restored *her* son to life"; *yr un o'r teuluoedd y mesurodd ef eu pennau*[3] "one of the families whose heads he measured", lit. "one of the families he measured *their* heads"; *y drws ny dylywn ni y agori*[4] "the door which we must not open", lit. "the door we must not open *it*". (In this example the relative depends on the verb noun *agori, y agori* literally translated would mean *its opening*.)

(b) *y wlat yd hanwyf oheni*[5] "the land from which I come", lit. "the land I come from *it*"; *y gwr y mynyssit uy rodi i idaw o'm hanuod*[6] "the man to whom they would have given me against my will", lit. "the man they would have given me to *him* against my will"; *y coedyd y foasant vdunt*[7] "the woods to which they fled", lit. "the woods they fled to *them*".

(c) *gwna oet a chyfnot y del Riannon i'th ol*[8] "and appoint a time and hour (when) Rhiannon may follow thee"; *y lle y dodyssynt y mab*[9] "the place (where) they had put the boy".

In Welsh, as in Hebrew, the antecedent may not be expressed before a clause in which the relative is subject or object: *ti a wely a wneuthum i yrot ti*[10] "thou wilt see (that) which I have done for thee"; *Pilatus a'y lladawd ac a oed ygyt ac ef*[11] "Pilatus killed him and (those) that were with him". In such cases the clause may be preceded by a preposition: *Yr a rodwin i idau ef*[12] "despite (aught) that I might give him"; *madws oed ymi cael attep am a ercheis*[13] "it were high time I had an answer to (that) which I asked".

We find the demonstrative pronoun and the article used before a relative clause in Welsh also: *duw yr hwnn a rodes itt bop da*[14] "God who gave to thee every good thing"; *yeuan er hvnn anwyllyaf idav onadunt oll*[15] "John who (was) dearest to him of all of them"; *Ar ny del yn uuyd*[16] "He that comes not humbly"; *Iolune ar a beir*[17] "Let us praise him who creates". The demonstrative, however, did not develop as a regular relative pronoun in Hebrew and Welsh as it did in other languages.

Waw Consecutive

The use of the "waw consecutive" as it is called in Hebrew is well known to all who have any acquaintance with the syntax of the language. It is not only used as a co-ordinate conjunction, but is commonly employed in narrative to denote sequence. This sustained use of *waw* makes for simple and racy style, and is a marked feature of the prose narrative

---

[1] *Bulletin of the Board of Celtic Studies*, iii. 256.
[2] 2 Kings viii. 5.   [3] *Er Mwyn Cymru* (O. Edwards), 96.
[4] *P.K.M.*, 46.   [5] Ibid. 2.   [6] Ibid. 14.   [7] *Brut Dimgestow* (Lewis), 6.
[8] *P.K.M.*, 19.   [9] Ibid. 20.   [10] Ibid. 6.   [12] Ibid. 3.   [13] Ibid. 15.   [14] Ibid. 6.
[11] *Bulletin of the Board of Celtic Studies*, ix. 47.   [14] Ibid. ii. 11.   [16] Ibid. x. 29.
[17] *Black Book of Carmarthen* (Evans), 88.

of the Old Testament. Thus we have in Hebrew a series of independent sentences connected by *waw* with less subordination than in other languages, e.g. Latin. The rule governing the use of *waw* in Hebrew is quite simple; the series of events related may commence with the verb in the Perfect or Imperfect. If the first verb is Perfect all the other verbs preceded immediately by *waw* must be in the Imperfect; on the other hand, if the first verb is Imperfect, all the following verbs are in the Perfect. Here is a familiar passage from the Old Testament to illustrate the use of *waw*:[1] בְּרֵאשִׁית בָּרָא אֱלֹהִים אֵת הַשָּׁמַיִם וְאֵת הָאָרֶץ: וְהָאָרֶץ הָיְתָה תֹהוּ וָבֹהוּ וְחֹשֶׁךְ עַל־פְּנֵי תְהוֹם וְרוּחַ אֱלֹהִים מְרַחֶפֶת עַל־פְּנֵי הַמָּיִם: וַיֹּאמֶר אֱלֹהִים יְהִי אוֹר וַיְהִי־אוֹר:

וַיַּרְא אֱלֹהִים אֶת־הָאוֹר כִּי־טוֹב וַיַּבְדֵּל אֱלֹהִים בֵּין הָאוֹר וּבֵין הַחֹשֶׁךְ "In the beginning God created the heaven and the earth. *And* the earth was without form and void; *and* darkness was upon the face of the deep. *And* the Spirit of God moved upon the face of the waters. *And* God said, 'Let there be light: *and* there was light. *And* God saw the Light, that it was good: *and* God divided the light from the darkness."

While it cannot be averred that we have in Welsh any usage which corresponds in detail with the use of *waw* illustrated above, there is in the language a marked tendency towards the simple and direct style which is so distinguishing a feature of Hebrew. In narrative prose, especially the prose of the Med. period, the prevailing style is that of a series of co-ordinate sentences or clauses rather than involved sentences in the style of the period. It is later that we find the periodic style employed in Welsh; it occurs for the first time in the religious works of the sixteenth century which were almost all translations from English or Latin. However, it has never established itself in the language. Here is a passage from a Med. W. saga to illustrate this style; the recurring use of the co-ordinate conjunction *a(c)* cannot escape notice: [2]"Pwyll Pendeuic Dyuet a oed yn arglwyd ar seith cantref Dyuet. *A* threigylgweith yd oed yn Arberth, . . . , *a* dyuot yn y uryt ac yn y uedwl uynet y hela. . . . *Ac* ef a gychwynnwys y nos honno o Arberth, *ac* a doeth hyt ym Penn Llwyn Diarwya, *ac* yno y bu y nos honno. *A* thrannoeth yn ieuengtit y dyd kyuodi a oruc, *a* dyuot y Lynn Cuch i ellwng e gwn dan y coet." "Pwyll prince of Dyfed was lord over the seven cantrefs of Dyfed. *And* once upon a time he was at Arberth, . . . , *and* it came into his head and heart to go a-hunting. . . . *And* he set out that night from Arberth, *and* came as far as Pen Llwyn Diarwya, *and* there he was that night. *And* on the morrow in the young of the day he arose *and* came to Glyn Cuch to loose his dogs into the wood."

Personal Pronouns[3]

Normally the personal pronouns are employed in their full form only when they act as subject: וְאִם־דַּל הוּא "and if *he* (be) poor"; in other connexions they are attached in a fragmentary form to the word to which they are related. Thus, when the pronoun is governed by a preposition, what we have is preposition + pronominal suffix. Hebrew has no possessive pronouns, the independent pronoun being attached in a fragmentary form to the noun on which it depends.

In Welsh, personal pronouns are classified as independent and dependent.[5] The independent pronouns are employed as subject, object and nominal predicate: *mi a welais* "I saw"; *cyfarwydda fi* "direct me"; *ys ef a welais* "it is *he* whom I saw". When the personal pronoun is the subject of the verb it is often not expressed, but may be understood,

[1] Genesis i. 1-4.   [2] *P.K.M.*, 1.
[3] For its use in certain idiomatic constructions vide *Gesenius' Hebrew Grammar* (Kautzsch, 1910), 438.
[4] Leviticus xiv. 21.
[5] Vide *Welsh Grammar* (Morris-Jones), 270-82.

Serial No. 85e.

as in Hebrew, from the personal ending of the verb: *gwelais* "I saw". In Welsh (and Irish), as in Hebrew, after a preposition, the pronoun came to be agglutinated to the preposition and ultimately developed into mere inflections. There are three conjugations of prepositions, distinguished by the vowel of the 1st and 2nd personal ending; thus for the 1st sing. i. *-af*, ii. *-of*, iii. *-yf*. i. *ar* "on": Sing. 1 *arnaf*, 2 *arnat*, 3 masc. *arno*, fem. *arni*. Plur. 1 *arnom*, 2 *arnoch*, 3 *arnunt, -ynt*. ii. *rhag*: "before", Sing. 1 *rhagof*, etc. iii. *gan* "with": Sing. 1 *gennyf*, etc.

The Demonstrative Pronoun

When used as an attributive adjective, the noun on which the demonstrative depends must be preceded by the article; the following demonstrative also has the article, thus: הָאִישׁ הַזֶּה "this man", lit. "the man this one". It will be noticed that the demonstrative follows its noun When another adjective is used with the noun the demonstrative stands last: הָאִישׁ הַטּוֹב הַזֶּה "this good man", lit. "the good man, this one". In Welsh also the demonstrative follows its noun, which must be preceded by the definite article: *y dyn hwn* "this man". As in Hebrew, when another adjective is used with the noun the demonstrative stands last: *y dyn da hwn* "this good man".

The Article

Hebrew has no indefinite article. The definite article הַ is derived from a demonstrative pronoun, and it still has a demonstrative force in one or two phrases, e.g. הַיּוֹם "this day, to-day", הַלַּיְלָה "this night, to-night" (cf. Welsh *heddiw* "to-day", *henoeth, heno* "to-night"[1]). As in other languages, the normal use of the article is to make the noun determinate. Reference may be made to certain peculiar usages; in narratives the article is used with the names of persons or things which appear definite to the mind of the speaker or writer: כֹּה־אָמַר הָאִישׁ בְּלֶכְתּוֹ[2] "thus spoke a man when he went", lit. "the man"; וַתּוֹרִדֵם בַּחֶבֶל[3] "and she let them down with a rope", lit. "the rope". It is employed with vocatives, the person addressed being definite to the mind of the one addressing: דְּבַר־סֵתֶר לִי אֵלֶיךָ הַמֶּלֶךְ[4] "I have a secret errand unto thee, O King"; בֶּן־מִי אַתָּה הַנָּעַר[5] "whose son (art) thou, *young man?*" Welsh also has no indefinite article; the use of the definite article *y, yr* in the main corresponds to its function in other languages. The two peculiar usages in Hebrew illustrated above are found in Welsh also: *llyma y dryw yn seuyll ar wwrd y llog*[6] "lo, *a wren* alighting on board the ship"; the same usage occurs in Irish: *Con n-accae ni, in n-ingin cucci*[7] "He saw something, *a girl* (coming) to him". With vocative: *o'r kyghorwyr drwc*[8] "O! ye evil counsellors"; *o'r kythreul enwir*[9] "O! thou evil devil."

The Adjective

In both Welsh and Hebrew the attributive adjective follows its noun: אִישׁ טוֹב "(a) good man"; Welsh, *dyn da*. In Hebrew if the noun is definite the following adjective has the article (cf. the Greek construction) הָאִישׁ הַטּוֹב "the good man" lit. "the man the good". This is not the normal construction in Welsh, where the adjective immediately follows a definite noun: *y dyn da* "the good man": but examples occur in Med. W. where the following adjective is preceded by the article: *y chorff hy y tyner*[10] "her tender body", lit. "her body the tender"; *uy mab i y cu*[11] "my dear son", lit. "my son the dear".

[1] Vide *Concise Comparative Celtic Grammar* (Lewis & Pedersen), 222.
[2] 1 Samuel ix. 9.
[3] Joshua ii. 15.   [4] Judges iii. 19.   [5] 1 Samuel xvii. 58.   [6] *P.K.M.*, 80.
[7] *The Dream of Oengus* (Shaw), 43.
[8] *Bulletin of the Board of Celtic Studies*, ix. 328.
[9] Ibid. ix. 332.   [10] Ibid. ix. 328.   [11] Ibid. ii. 17.

The Genitive

The genitive relation is expressed in Hebrew by closely connecting the governing and governed words in a manner which has no counterpart in the classical languages. The two words together are regarded as representing one idea and consequently form an accentual unity. Therefore the chief accent falls on the second word or absolute, as it is called, while the first word is uttered as shortly as is possible in consistency with the laws of pronunciation in the language; it is referred to as being in the construct state.

There are certain aspects of this construction to which I would like to draw attention: (1) The construct never has the article; if the following absolute is definite, the whole phrase is definite: סוּסֵי הַמֶּלֶךְ "(the) horses (of) the king". When the first word is indefinite the relation is usually expressed by the preposition לְ "to" מִזְמוֹר לְדָוִד "(a) psalm of David", lit. "to David". (2) The absolute may follow an adjective in the construct state to express ideas such as "good in appearance", "great in power", etc.; נַעֲרָה טוֹבַת מַרְאֶה "a good looking girl", lit. "a girl good (in) appearance"; וְשִׁבְרֵי־לֵב "the broken-hearted", lit. "those broken (in) heart" (cf. Latin accusative of respect). (3) The construct must immediately precede the noun to which it is related; consequently two co-ordinate constructs cannot precede the same absolute. Therefore, if a noun depends on two co-ordinate nouns, the first of these is placed in the construct state with the absolute immediately following, while the second follows with a pronominal suffix referring back to the absolute and preceded by the co-ordinate conjunction; thus בְּנֵי הַשַּׂר וּבְנוֹתָיו "the prince's sons and daughters", lit. "the sons of the prince and his daughters".

In Welsh the genitive relation is expressed by placing the genitive immediately after the noun on which it depends. There is no distinction of form in either of the words, the construction being determined by position rather than form. In some respects it bears comparison with the Hebrew construction: (1) The noun on which the genitive depends cannot be preceded by the article, even though it is definite in meaning: *meirch y brenin* "(the) steeds (of) the king". If the first word is indefinite the preposition *i* "to" may be used to denote the relationship: *mab i'r brenin* "a son of the king", lit. "(a) son to the king". (2) A noun may depend on an adjective, thus limiting its meaning. The noun is usually preceded by the possessive personal pronoun referring back to the noun on which the adjective depends: *merch deg ei phryd* "a good-looking girl", lit. "(a) girl fair (in) her appearance". (3) When a noun depends on two or more co-ordinate nouns, the usual construction in Welsh is to place it immediately after the first, and the second (and third) follows, preceded by the possessive personal pronoun, referring back to the genitive and connected with it by the co-ordinate conjunction: *meibion y tywysog a'i ferched* "the prince's sons and daughters", lit. "the sons of the prince and his daughters".

The Infinitive

In Hebrew the infinitive is represented by two forms, a shorter and a longer, termed construct and absolute respectively. It is not proposed to enlarge upon their various functions here. The construct is employed in connexion with prepositions, pronominal suffixes, etc. The absolute admits neither prefix nor suffix, and in general may be said to emphasize the abstract verbal idea without reference to the subject or object of the action. Most frequently it functions adverbially with a finite verb of the same stem, and may precede or follow the finite verb.

However, examples occur where the infinitive serves as a substitute for the finite verb. This usage became more prevalent in the later books of the O.T. It is found in narrative prose when several acts are denoted in succession. The first is expressed by a finite verb, and the second (or third) by the infinitive absolute: וַיִּתְקְעוּ בַּשּׁוֹפָרוֹת וְנָפוֹץ הַכַּדִּים "they blew with the trumpets, and *broke* the pitchers"[1], וַיַּעֲלֶה שְׁלֹמֹה . . . וְהַקְטִיר "and Solomon offered sacrifices and *burnt incense*"[2], גַּם־אַיֶּלֶת בַּשָּׂדֶה יָלְדָה וְעָזוֹב[3] "the hind also calved in the field and *forsook* (it)". It is also occasionally employed when the verbal action or state is to be forcibly presented and vividly expressed. It is thus found in injunctions: זָכוֹר אֶת־יוֹם הַשַּׁבָּת[4] "remember the sabbath day".

In Welsh at all periods the verb noun can be used instead of a finite verb. Usually it occurs in a succession of co-ordinate statements with a finite verb coming first: "*Ac ar hynny at y cwn y doeth ef, a gyrru yr erchwys a ladyssei y carw e ymdeith, a llithyaw y erchwys e hunan ar y carw,*"[5] "And with that he came to the dogs, and *drove* away the pack that had killed the stag, and *baited* his own pack upon the stag." "Euthum i mewn i'r ty a *gwneuthur* cwpanaid o de,"[6] "I went into the house and *made* a cup of tea." Examples occur where no finite verb precedes: "*Ac ar hynny, kymryt gwrogaeth y gwyr a dechreu* guereskynn y wlat,"[7] "And thereupon he *received* the homage of the men, and *began* to subdue the land." The use of the verb noun to denote injunctions is not common in Welsh, but some examples can be cited: "*Dyuot* brennhin morcannhuc ygundy teliau yn lann taf," "The King of Glamorgan *must come* to the chapter house of Teilo in Llandaf."[8] "Tir gwlyb, *gadel* rycheu dwfyn y adel y dwfyr y redec ohonaw ymeith,"[9] "Marsh land, deep furrows *should be left* to allow the water to flow away from it."

Have these similarities in the syntax and modes of expression of Hebrew and Welsh any major significance? A definite statement on this question would now be premature. At this stage we must remain satisfied with the presentation of the data; further extensive investigation in the field of comparative philology is essential before the position can be clarified. That the two languages possess certain features in common cannot be denied; in both we find a certain simplicity and concreteness of thought, and neither has acquired the strict systematisation which prevails in some other languages. The Hebrew scriptures are as easily translated into Welsh as into any other I.E. language.

[1] Judges 7· 19. [2] 1 Kings 9· 25. [3] Jeremiah 14· 5. [4] Exodus 20· 8.
[5] *P.K.M.*, 1-2. [6] Ibid. 6. [7] *Storïau Hen Ferch* (Jones, Aberystwyth, 1937), 104.
[8] *The Book of Llan Dav* (Evans & Rhys, 1893), 120.
[9] *Bulletin of the Board of Celtic Studies*, ii, 13.
For infinitive as imperative in Irish *v*. Windisch, *Bezzenbergers Beitr.*, 11, 85.

Authority: Sir CHARLES MARSTON, F.S.A.

The Bible Comes Alive

Marston, Sir Charles (1867-1946). "Kt., cr. 1926; J.P., F.S.A.; Chairman of the Villiers Engineering Co. Ltd.; President of the Vic-toria Institute; K.J.St.J.; . . . Wolverhampton School; Mason College (now Birmingham University). Manufacturer, Politician, Traveller, Biblical Archaeologist. . . ." (*Who's Who*, 1946.)

The Art of Writing in the Period of Moses

A Summary of the Data Reviewed

UNTIL quite recently many Bible critics pressed the theory that the first six Books of the Bible could not have been written either by Moses or Joshua, because there was no evidence that the art of writing was in existence at that time. On this assumption, they argued that the matter contained in those books must have been handed down orally over a long period (with the inevitable error and distortion which usually accompanied such a method of transmission) and that these "traditions" were collated by some later Hebrew scribe and incorporated in the accredited Scriptures.

Archaeological discoveries in Palestine during the past twenty years have completely rebutted this theory, and have shown that the Hebrew script was positively in general use there at the time of Joshua.

POINTS OF SPECIAL INTEREST

1. The Lachish Bowl is the most important of these archaeological finds. Dr. Langdon, Oxford Professor of Assyriology, who deciphered the Sinai-Hebrew script, states that this is "the most important discovery of modern times in respect to Biblical criticism", and adds that it is "entirely believable that literature, before Moses, also existed in alphabetical script".

2. The phraseology is strongly reminiscent of that of the Old Testament.

3. Sir Charles presents a well-reasoned and acceptable argument to the effect that Moses—"learned in all the wisdom of the Egyptians", Acts vii, 22—who had himself lived for many years in the locality from which the script first emerged, taught it to his Israelite scribes during the period spent in the Wilderness.

SIR CHARLES MARSTON, F.S.A.: Extracts from his *THE BIBLE COMES ALIVE*,
6th edition revised (The Covenant Publishing Co., Ltd., London, 1944), pp. 123-126,
180-181

(Pp. 123-126.)

The next example of the Sinai Hebrew script was found the following year at Lachish on a red pottery bowl in a tomb. The letters were painted across the outside of the bowl in white paint. They looked at first sight as though they had been made in chalk, and the Expedition leaders wondered if someone was playing a practical joke on them. But the inscription proved to be even more important than that on the ewer. Several attempts to decipher it did not seem to produce very satisfactory results. Finally, in a letter to *The Times* of 5th October 1935, the late Dr. Langdon of Oxford suggested that the photograph of the inscription had been printed upside down. And that when read from left to right, which was the original direction of this script, the sentence seemed to be complete, although the last four letters are uncertain. His decipherment was: Z-D-Q-W Q-T. -Y W-(?)-Y-(?)-H. This he read "Zidqo qati we" . . . which meant, "His righteousness is my hand (or support) and . . ."

The learned Professor went on to point out that, while the language is identical with the Canaanite glosses in the Tel el Amarna Letters, which are written in the old cuneiform script, yet the phraseology is strikingly similar to that of the Hebrew Bible. And that this inscription, as well as the one on the ewer, indicates that the Hebrews had already invented the system of pointing vowels. Dr. Langdon went on to state that the discovery makes it entirely believable that literature, before Moses, also existed in alphabetical script. He wrote:

"These are not traditions handed down the ages by memory only. They were actually incorporated into written documents as early as the thirteenth century. Obviously we have here the most important discovery of modern times in respect to Biblical criticism."

. . . There is therefore no longer any doubt that this writing was in general use in Palestine after Joshua had conquered the country . . . we are face to face with the fact that, within about a century of the conquest of Canaan, a script that was employed in Sinai in the days of Moses was in general use at Lachish. The obvious suggestion is that the Israelites learned to use the script when in the Wilderness of Sinai, and brought it with them into Palestine when they conquered the country under Joshua. . . .

. . . Here is the best system of recording human speech in writing, first found in common use among turquoise miners in the centre of the inaccessible peninsula of Sinai. We ask ourselves Why among miners of all people? And why in the centre of an inaccessible land like the peninsula of Sinai? The invention of such a system was worthy of the trained imagination of a great human genius. The place of its birth some great Union Theological Seminary or College, like that recently found at Ras Shamra, the ancient city of Ugarit, in highly civilised northern Syria. Instead "illiterate folk" like miners, and an illiterate mining camp in Sinai. Sinai, the wilderness into which Moses led the twelve tribes of Israel—Moses, learned in all the wisdom of Egypt—Moses who had lived for many years in Midian, the centre of the mining fraternity. There is small need to stress the evidence. The facts speak for themselves. . . .

(Pp. 180-181.)

But what will make the Lachish discoveries so famous, is the fact that whole sentences of alphabetical writing, penned in Old Testament days, have been found for the first time. There are the white letters on the red bowl, reading "His righteousness is my hand (or support)" written little more than a century after the death of Moses. There are the Lachish Letters themselves, entirely unique documents of the time of Jeremiah. The contents of these writings testify to the authenticity of the Sacred Narrative at two periods of time seven centuries apart. They constitute outside contemporary evidence of its genuineness. Moreover, apart altogether from what their contents tell us, the mere finding of the Sinai Hebrew script, and of the Phoenician Hebrew script, are discoveries that perhaps surpass in importance, anything bearing upon the Old Testament which has been previously brought to light. . . . As education increases, those who read their translations of the Old Testament, naturally want to know more about its origin. When was it written? In what language? And through what medium has it been transmitted to this generation?

In answer to such questions in the past, some have said one thing and some another. But now two archaeological expeditions, working on two different sites, have supplied the definite answers. The Jericho Expeditions have fixed the time of Moses at 1520-1400 B.C.; the Lachish Expeditions have found the Sinai Hebrew and the Phoenician Hebrew alphabetical scripts; with evidence that certainly one, and perhaps both, were in use from these earliest days onwards. Together, these forms of writing cover the interval of times from Moses, right down to the introduction of the Assyrian Hebrew script, from which in turn our translations of the Old Testament have been made. And so the mediums employed for the transmission of Old Testament literature, from Moses to our British and Foreign Bible Society, have been identified and established; and the genealogy of the sacred writings has been traced. And it is to be further remarked, that the geographical ancestry of the Old Testament positively seems to be related to that of alphabetical writing; for the earlier books of the Bible take us to the region of Sinai, where the earliest of the alphabetical scripts has been found.

Anyone who in future suggests that the Israelites ever lacked facilities for literary expression, will be betraying his unacquaintance with modern discoveries of the first importance. All the theories of oral transmission, either of the whole, or of part, of the earlier books of the Old Testament, have of course ceased to be of any account. (*Reproduced by kind permission of Eyre & Spottiswoode Ltd. and The Covenant Publishing Company Ltd.*)

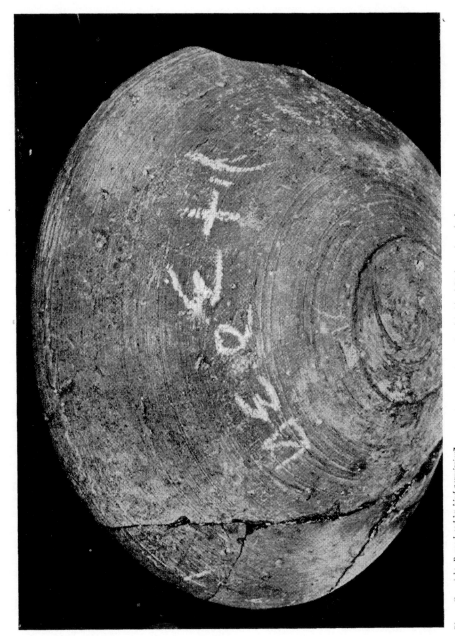

The Lachish Bowl, with Sinai-Hebrew inscription.

Serial No. 46 (to accompany Serial No. 33 [492.4).
Copyright.

Authorities:
Dr. Wm. Smith's *Dictionary of the Bible*
Dr. James Hastings' *Dictionary of the Bible*
F. R. and C. R. Conder, *A Handbook to the Bible*

The Mosaic Calendar

THE study of the sun, moon and stars has been practised by man from the most remote antiquity. The first chapter of the Bible affirms that in addition to shedding their light—the heavenly bodies were "for signs, and for seasons, and for days, and years". Modern science finds itself unable to produce any substitute method for such perfect timekeeping.

When the Israelites were detached from their Egyptian civilization, their lives were ordered by a new mode of reckoning. Both religious and secular operations became based upon the Mosaic Calendar, commencing with the New Moon of the first Passover. Festivals and Holy Days throughout the year were all related to phases of the moon—a most convenient and easily remembered practice.

A consideration of the widely differing forms of calendar which have been used by different civilizations is necessary for an understanding of Bible history and prophecy.

The function of a calendar is to adjust "the natural divisions of time with respect to each other for the purposes of civil life". The natural divisions of time are the year, the lunation, and the day, which bear no simple relationship and are generally defined only approximately in terms of the smallest of the three units. Although modern astronomers are familiar with different kinds of years to a high degree of exactitude, we need here only consider what is called the equinoctial, solar, or tropical year in its approximate value of $365\frac{1}{4}$ days, and the lunar or synodic month popularly stated as $29\frac{1}{2}$ days. It will be seen that even with these approximations there is no simple way of harmonizing whole numbers of days, months and years. In formulating a calendar for the regulation of civil life, the ancients were faced with the necessity of using the obvious basic unit of the day. Among certain scientifically-minded communities, some of the complexities of effecting a degree of harmony between the day, the lunar month, and the tropical year were accepted; but for the masses as a whole, rule-of-thumb systems were devised which, though comparatively easy to remember, quite failed to harmonize these three basic units.

Some Ancient Systems

Among the Egyptians the rule-of-thumb calendar was in fact used by the priesthood, and consisted of 12 months of 30 days each, or 360 days. An inscription of the XIIth Dynasty nomarch of Siut defines a temple day as follows: "A temple day is one-360th part of a year" (*The Cambridge Ancient History*, Vol. II [1931], chap. IX, sec. ii, p. 213). The five days difference between the religious and the civil calendar were called "over and above the year" (*ibid.*, Vol. I [1928], p. 265. In Sumeria a common month of 30 days was generally used for business purposes (*ibid.*, Vol. I [1928], pp. 165, 168, 265, 333). In ancient Greece a month of the same duration was known, and was divided into three decads (*Encyclopædia Britannica*, 13th edition, art.: "Calendar").

"A year of 360 days, containing twelve months of thirty days each, is indicated by certain passages in the prophetical Scriptures" (Wm. Smith's *Dictionary of the Bible*, art.: "Year"). Details of this calendar have been discussed in an earlier study (*Serial* No. 48 [224.5]). The month of 30 days used in the prophetical Scriptures may have been in use in patriarchal times, for the period of 150 days during which the waters of the Flood "prevailed" (*Gen.* vii. 24) may be equivalent to 5 such months, from the seventeenth day of the second month of Noah's six hundredth year when "all the fountains of the great deep" were "broken up, and the windows of heaven were opened" (*Gen.* vii. 11) to the day on which the Ark rested on dry land on the seventeenth day of the seventh month (*Gen.* viii. 4).

The Egyptian civil calendar of 365 days was a quarter-day shorter than the solar year, in 1460 of which the difference amounted to a further civil year of 365 days, and the two years again coincided. This period of 1460 solar years was known as the Sothic cycle. The error of this calendar thus amounted to one calendar year in 1460 solar years.

The Julian calendar, which took its name from Julius Caesar, was the first to use the modern Leap-year cycle; but it lost about eleven minutes on each solar year. It was abandoned in England in 1752 in favour of the more correct Gregorian calendar, which is only a modification of the Julian, which by the time of this change had lost 11 days, so that September 3 (Julian) became September 14 (Gregorian). The error of the Julian calendar is 1 day in 128 years; that of the modern Gregorian system is 1 day in 3,320 years. Both errors are ever accumulating, as in the case of the Sothic calendar. In contrast to these, as we shall see, the Mosaic calendar can never be in error, and can only change its position in the solar year by a maximum of a month.

In contrast to all of these, the Mohammedan calendar is entirely lunar and consists of 354 days.

The Mosaic Calendar

Though possessing no error, the Mosaic calendar was no more able than the other systems we have discussed to harmonize mathematically days, lunations, and solar years; but it linked them all by means of a highly practical rule.

The Mosaic calendar contained 12 months, as is clear from the following. David had 12 captains, one over each month of service (I *Chron.* xxvii). Eight months are specifically mentioned and named, among them being the twelfth: Abib, the first (*Exod.* xii. 1—xiii. 4; xxiii. 15; xxxiv. 18; *Deut.* xvi. 1); Zif, the second (I *Kings* vi. 1, 37); Ethanim, the seventh (I *Kings* viii. 2); Bul, the eighth (I *Kings* vi. 38); Chisleu, the ninth (*Neh.* i. 1; *Zech.* vii. 1); Tebeth, the tenth (*Esther* ii. 16); Sebat, the eleventh (*Zech.* i. 7); Adar, the twelfth (*Ezra* vi.

15; *Esther* iii. 7, 13). The twelfth month is mentioned as such (*Ezek.* xxxii. 1); and the latest calendar date mentioned in the Bible is "in the twelfth month, on the seven and twentieth day of the month" (II *Kings* xxv. 27).

The Bible clearly shows that each month began with a new moon: David dined with Saul on each day of the new moon, which was the first day of the month (I *Sam.* xx. 5, 18, 24, 25, 27).

The first day of each month was celebrated by a prescribed sacrificial ritual with music (*Num.* x. 10; xxviii. 11). This ceremony is frequently alluded to as the law of Moses concerning the observing of the day of the new moon, which was a holy day. The last edict of David was for the appointment of Levites for the offering of sacrifices on the first day of each month "in the sabbaths, in the new moons, and on the set feasts, by number, according to the order commanded unto them, continually before the Lord (I *Chron.* xxiii. 27–31). Solomon observed the first of the month as a holy day (II *Chron.* ii. 4; cf. viii. 12, 13). So did the great reformer, Hezekiah (II *Chron.* xxxi. 3), and the Jews after their return from Babylon (*Ezra* iii. 5; *Neh.* x. 33). The Psalms enjoin Israel to "Blow up the trumpet in the new moon, in the time appointed, on our solemn feast day. For this was a statute for Israel, and a law of the God of Jacob" (*Ps.* lxxxi. 3, 4).

Holy days ceased to be regarded with respect in Israel (*Amos.* viii. 5); and in due course the Lord declared: "Your new moons and your appointed feasts my soul hateth" (*Isa.* i. 13, 14). In conclusion it was divinely ordained that the whole calendar system should fall into disuse (*Hos.* ii. 11).

The Israelites (*Lev.* xxiii. 32), like the tribes of Germany (Tacitus, *Germania* xi), the Gauls (Caesar, *Gaul* vi. 18), the Irish (P. W. Joyce, *A Smaller Social History of Ancient Ireland*, 1906, pp. 479, 480), the Athenians (Wm. Smith's *Dictionary of the Bible*, citing Macrobius, *Saturnalia* i. 3; *Gellius Aulus* iii. 2), and other related peoples, measured their days from evening to evening. It is important to remember this when considering the beginning of the Mosaic month, which commenced with the evening of the visible new moon. This is further supported by the Hebrew word for month, which derived from the word "new": "The Hebrew *chodesh* is perhaps more distinctive than the corresponding terms in other languages; for it expresses not simply the idea of a *lunation*, but the recurrence of a period commencing definitely with the *new moon*; it is derived from the word *châdâsh*, 'new', which was transferred in the first instance to the 'new moon', and in the second instance to the 'month', or as it is sometimes more fully expressed . . . 'a month of days' (*Gen.* xxix. 14; *Num.* xi. 20, 21; comp. *Deut.* xxi. 13; II *Kings* xv. 13) . . .

". . . The commencement of the month was generally decided by observation of the new moon, which may be detected about forty hours after the period of its conjunction with the sun: in the later times of Jewish history this was effected according to strict rule, the appearance of the new moon being reported by competent witnesses to the local authorities, who then officially announced the commencement of the new month by the twice repeated word 'Mekûdash', i.e. *consecrated* . . . the recurrence of the new moon can be predicted with considerable accuracy by a calculation of the interval that would elapse either from the last new moon, from the full moon (which can be detected by a practised eye), or from the disappearance of the waning moon. Hence, David announces definitely, 'To-morrow is the new moon', that being the first of the month (I *Sam.* xx. 5, 24, 27), though the new moon could not have been as yet observed, and still less announced" (Wm. Smith's *Dictionary of the Bible*, art.: "Month").

The Exodus and the New Year

Moses was commanded of the month in which the Exodus took place: "This month shall be unto you the beginning of months: it shall be the first month of the year to you" (*Exod.* xii. 2). The day began at what we call 6 p.m. It was ordained that the Passover lamb should be selected on the tenth day of that month (*v.* 3); it was to be kept until the fourteenth day of that month (*v.* 6); it was then to be killed in the "evening", "at the going down of the sun" or close of the fourteenth (*Deut.* xvi. 4, 6). By the morning of the fifteenth all that remained of the lamb had to be burned (*v.* 10). The same night the first-born of the Egyptians were slain, and it was commanded of the Israelites that during it "none of you shall go out at the door of his house until the morning" (*v.* 22). The remaining indoors on that night was to be a perpetual observation in Israel (*vv.* 24–27). The flight of the Israelites then commenced in the daytime of the fifteenth.

The fifteenth, on which the Israelites commenced their march (*Num.* xxxiii. 3), was also the first day of eating unleavened bread. A search for leaven bread was made on the fourteenth, so that none remained for the following seven days (*Exod.* xii. 15, 16). After the Exodus the dates were commemorated perpetually in the Passover week (*Lev.* xxiii. 5–8; *Num.* xxviii. 16ff.).

The Israelites moved to the border of the Red Sea in three stages, the first "from Rameses in the first month, on the fifteenth day of the first month; on the morrow after the passover the children of Israel went out with an high hand in the sight of all the Egyptians . . . and the children of Israel removed from Rameses and pitched in Succoth" (*Num.* xxxiii. 3–6; cf. *Exod.* xii. 37). The next two stages were from Succoth to Etham (*Num.* xxxiii. 6); and from Etham to the sea (*Exod.* xiv. 1; *Num.* xxxiii. 7). The three stages measure just over thirty miles, and were covered by day and night marches: "And the Lord went before them by day in a pillar of cloud, to lead them the way; and by night in a pillar of fire, to give them light; to go by day and night" (*Exod.* xiii. 21). The duration of this march of some thirty miles is problematical; but after having crossed the sea the Israelites "went three days' journey in the wilderness of Etham, and pitched in Marah (*Exod.* xv. 22, 23; *Num.* xxxiii. 8). These three days had to be completed before the twenty-first, the day of the "holy convocation" ending the week of unleavened bread, and were therefore the eighteenth, nineteenth and twentieth. The daytime prior to the eighteenth, that is to say, of the seventeenth, must have been given over to rest and rejoicing, when "then sang Moses and the children of Israel this song unto the Lord, and spake, saying, I will sing unto the Lord . . ."; and Miriam and all the women of Israel engaged in music and dancing (*Exod.* xv. 1–21). Thus the nocturnal wind that divided the sea and permitted the Israelites to pass over was probably on the night of the seventeenth, during which the Egyptians followed and perished (*Exod.* xiv. 20–28). This leaves the day of the fifteenth, and the night and day of the sixteenth, as the three intervals of the 30-mile march, or three stages of the 10 miles each, two by day and one by night, followed by a nocturnal crossing of the sea.

From this sequence came the rule for the fixing of the seven days of the Passover; and in a similar manner rules were applied to the great feasts: "The cycle of religious feasts, commencing with Passover, depended not simply on the month, but on the moon (Joseph. *Ant.* iii. 10, § 5); the 14th of Abib was coincident with the full moon (Philo, *Vit. Mos.* iii, p. 686) . . ." (Wm. Smith's *Dictionary of the Bible*, art.: "Month"). Thus the fifteenth, sixteenth and seventeenth had nights of nearly full moon, under the light of which it was possible for Israel to march towards and across the Red Sea.

Serial No. 102*b*

The exact time of commencing the year has received much attention from scholars, who have endeavoured to discover the rule or rules governing it. It has been observed of the Mosaic calendar that: "Though the year was essentially solar, it is certain that the months were lunar, each commencing with a new moon. There must therefore have been some method of adjustment. The first point to be decided is how the commencement of each year was fixed. On the 16th day of Abib ripe ears of corn were to be offered as first-fruits of the harvest (*Lev.* ii. 14, xxiii. 10, 11): this was the day on which the sickle was begun to be put to the corn (*Deut.* xvi. 9), and no doubt Josephus is right in stating that until the offering of first-fruits had been made no harvest-work was to be begun (*Ant.* iii. 10, §5). He also states that ears of barley were offered (*ibid.*). That this was the case, and that the ears were the earliest ripe, is evident from the following circumstances. The reaping of barley commenced the harvest (II *Sam.* xxi. 9), that of wheat following, apparently without any considerable interval (*Ruth* ii. 23). On the day of Pentecost thanksgiving was offered for the harvest, and it was therefore called the 'Feast of Harvest'. It was reckoned from the commencement of the harvest, on the 16th day of the first month. The 50 days must include the whole time of the harvest of both wheat and barley throughout Palestine. According to the observations of modern travellers, barley is ripe, in the warmest parts of Palestine, in the first days of April. The barley-harvest therefore begins about half a month or less after the vernal equinox. Each year, if solar, would thus begin at about that equinox, when the earliest ears of barley must be ripe. As, however, the months were lunar, the commencement of the year must have been fixed by a new moon near this point of time. The new moon must have been that which fell about or next after the equinox, not more than a few days before, on account of the offering of first-fruits" (Wm. Smith's *Dictionary of the Bible*, art.: "Year").

More precisely, the rule was probably that the full moon of the Egyptian Passover must be commemorated annually on the fourteenth of each first month, in the best relationship to the original event with regard to the solar year; that is to say, that the full moon of Nisan might not precede the vernal equinox, for it is evident that the Egyptian Passover did not fall before the equinox. Only in this way could the divine injunction as to the time of keeping Passover be observed: "Thou shalt therefore keep this ordinance in his season from year to year" (*Exod.* xiii. 10; cf. *Lev.* xxiii. 4; *Num.* ix. 2, 3; *Deut.* xvi. 6). Josephus, commenting on the fixing of the relationship of Passover to the tropical year, says: "In the month of Xanthicus, which is by us called *Nisan*, and is the beginning of our year, on the fourteenth day of the lunar month, when the sun is in Aries, (for in this month it was that we were delivered from bondage under the Egyptians), the law ordained that we should every year slay that sacrifice which I before told you we slew when we came out of Egypt, and which was called the *Passover*; . . ." (Antiquities, Bk. III, chap. x, §5).

The Second Beginning of the Year

"The later Jews had two commencements of the year, whence it is commonly but inaccurately said that they had two years, the sacred year and the civil. We prefer to speak of the sacred and civil reckonings" (Wm. Smith's *Dictionary of the Bible*, art.: "Year"). The religious celebrations of Israel, apart from the seventh day of each week, were always on fixed calendar-dates with reference to the first month *Abib* or *Nisan*. The first month of the civil reckoning was the seventh of the sacred. Sabbatical and jubilee years began in the seventh month; and the jubilee year followed in immediate succession to the forty-ninth: "And thou shalt number seven sabbaths of years unto thee, seven times seven years; and the space of the seven sabbaths of years shall be unto thee forty and nine years. Then shalt thou cause the trumpet of the jubilee to sound on the tenth day of the seventh month, in the day of atonement shall ye make the trumpet sound throughout all your land. And ye shall hallow the fiftieth year . . .'' (*Lev.* xxv. 8–16).

It is thought by some that the civil beginning was on the Day of Atonement, which is the tenth day of the seventh month; but this is unlikely for the following reason. A beginning of the civil year on the tenth day of the seventh month would not coincide with a new moon as in the case of the religious reckoning. The sequence of feasts and holy days practically establishes the certainty that the civil year began with the new moon of the seventh month, in which such days fall on precisely the same dates as in the first month of the year; that is to say:

On the first Abib (or Nisan), the beginning of the sacred year, was a new moon heralded by the blowing of trumpets. On the first day of Ethanim (or Tisri) the seventh month, the opening of the civil year, the new moon was likewise observed as the beginning of a revival (*Neh.* viii. 2).

On the tenth Abib the Paschal lamb was selected (*Exod.* xii. 3). On the tenth Tisri was the Day of Atonement, and the ceremony of the Scapegoat (*Lev.* xvi. 29; xxv. 9).

On the fourteenth Abib was the Passover. On the fourteenth Tisri was the first day of the Feast of Tabernacles.

On the twenty-first Abib was the day of Holy Convocation, closing the week of Unleavened Bread. On the twenty-first Nisan was the last or seventh day of the Feast of Tabernacles (*Lev.* xxiii, 34, 42; *Neh.* viii. 14–18); it was followed by an eighth day of ''holy convocation''.

The basis of the civil year, which began with the seventh month (September), was agricultural, for by then all crops had been harvested and the time for ploughing had arrived. At no other time could a sabbatic year of rest be commenced without interfering with the complete cycle from ploughing to reaping: ''It is perfectly clear that this would be the most convenient, if not the necessary, commencement of single years of total cessation from the labours of the field, since each year so commencing would comprise the whole round of these occupations in a regular order from seed-time to harvest, and from harvest to vintage and gathering of fruit. . . . We can therefore come to no other conclusion but that for the purposes of agriculture the year was held to begin with the seventh month, while the months were still reckoned from the sacred commencement in Abib. There are two expressions used with respect to the time of the celebration of the Feast of Ingathering on the 15th day of the seventh month, one of which leads to the conclusion at which we have just arrived, while the other is in accordance with it. The first of these speaks of this feast as . . . , 'in the going out' or end 'of the year' (*Exod.* xxiii. 16), and the second, as . . . , '[at] the change of the year' (*Exod.* xxiv. 22), a vague expression, as far as we can understand it, but one fully consistent with the idea of the turning-point of a natural year'' (Wm. Smith's *Dictionary of the Bible*, art.: ''Chronology'').

Festivals and Holy Days

Apart from the sabbaths, which fell every seventh day, irrespective of date, festivals and holy days were fixed to monthly dates. By virtue of this fact each of such days always fell respectively in precisely the same phase of the moon from year to year. Thus the feasts of Passover, Pentecost, Tabernacles, each New Year's Day (of the civil, sacred, sabbatic, and jubilee years alike), and the first day of each month, fell respectively on different days of the week with the passage of time. The removal of Easter, which should be observed according to the law for Passover, from its fixed dates in the month to fixed days of the week occasioned much controversy in the early Christian church.

Some impression of the way in which festivals were fixed to the month may be gained from the following extract in which it is pointed out that they, as also the sabbaths, were based on cycles of seven days, weeks, months, or years: "The sacred number 7 dominates the cycle of religious observances. Every 7th day was a Sabbath. Every 7th month was a sacred month. Every 7th year was a Sabbatical year. After 7 times 7 was the year of Jubilee. The Feast of the Passover, with the Feast of Unleavened Bread, began 14 days (2×7) after the beginning of the month, and lasted 7 days. The Feast of Pentecost was 7 times 7 days after the Feast of the Passover. The Feast of Tabernacles began 14 days (2×7) after the beginning of the month and lasted 7 days. The 7th month was marked by (1) Feast of Trumpets on the 1st day. (2) Fast of Atonement on the 10th day. (3) Feast of Tabernacles from the 15th day to the 21st. The days of 'Holy Convocation' were 7 in number—2 at the Passover, 1 at Pentecost, 1 at the Feast of Trumpets, 1 at the Day of Atonement, 1 at the Feast of Tabernacles, and 1 on the day following, the 8th day. (Willis, *Worship of the Old Covenant*, pp. 190, 191)" (Hastings' *Dictionary of the Bible*, art.: "Feasts and Fasts").

Intimations of a Pre-Mosaic Calendar

There are clear intimations in Scripture that a calendar was in use in patriarchal times; but the data supplied in this source are sufficient for speculative purposes only. *Exod.* xii. 1 might be taken to imply that Moses simply gave a new beginning and added certain solemnities to a current calendar. If this be the case, we are still uninformed as to how long that system had been in use by the Israelites or the patriarchs before them. It might be thought from the Flood records that a lunar year obtained at the time of that event; and, as we have seen, from the same it might be thought that a year of 360 days was also in use: "It seems to have been the view of the writer of the first report of the Flood . . . that the oldest Hebrew year was a *pure* lunar year, containing 12 lunar months and 354 days. In *Gen.* vii. 11 (cf. viii. 14) the Flood is said to have lasted from the 17th day of the 2nd month in one year to the 27th of the 2nd month in the next year, or 1 year and 11 days. This reckoning, as Benzinger suggests (*Heb. Arch.*, p. 198), arose through the translation of a solar year into its lunar equivalent. The actual duration of the Flood was in the general Semitic tradition a year, meaning a solar year of 365 days" (Hastings' *Dictionary of the Bible*, art.: "Time").

Serial No. 102d

Published by *The National Message* Ltd.,
6 Buckingham Gate, London, S.W.1.
Copyright.

Authorities: Professors E. C. Anderson, J. R. Arnold, and W. F. Libby, of the Institute for Nuclear Studies, University of Chicago.

Archæology - A New Method of Dating

SCIENCE has come to the aid of the archæologist in computing the age of buildings, monuments, and articles which belong to the remote past. This is of particular concern to those interested in the history of Bible lands and in the migrations of Bible peoples.

Scientists now assert that, as a result of studies in nuclear fission, periods of human, animal, and vegetable remains can be dated with a very fair degree of accuracy. Thus the age of excavated sites, buildings, and graves which contain those remains can also be dated within reasonable limits.

The new principle has already been applied in connection with one important item of westward migration, namely the period assigned to the building of Stonehenge, which undoubtedly derived from eastern sources. Authorities have long been at variance on this, but the date ascribed by the astronomer, Sir Norman Lockyer (*c.* 1680 B.C.) probably holds the greatest interest. The new method confirms this date, within close limits.

It may well be that a chapter will have opened on the subject of scriptural datings, and Bible students will look forward with interest to the possible settling of many controversies.

The Science of Dating by Radioactivity Determination

Following the discovery of radioactivity by Bacquerel in 1896, a number of radioactive elements were found to exist, and their natural rates of disintegration were determined. The first radioactive elements discovered were members of the uranium chain of disintegration. The names of Lord Rutherford and Prof. Soddy are prominent among those who discovered details of the sequences of disintegration of this family; and the name of Lord Rayleigh is renowned for his investigations of the distribution of radioactive elements in the earth's crust.

As a result of researches on methane gas from Baltimore sewage, radioactive carbon was found to be a constituent of all living matter and dissolved ocean carbonates, as reported by Dr. W. F. Libby of the Institute for Nuclear Studies, and his associates, in 1946 and 1947 (*Physics Review*, 1946, vol. 69, p. 671; 1947, vol. 72, p. 931; *Science*, 1947, vol. 105, p. 576; 1947, vol. 106, p. 88).

Radioactive carbon is derived from the atmosphere where (according to Dr. Libby) it is believed to be constantly formed by the collision of cosmic ray neutrons with atmospheric nitrogen. A state of equilibrium is reached through the constant disintegration of atmospheric radiocarbon and its continual absorption in life and other cycles. The distribution of atmospheric radiocarbon has been proved to be uniform by tests carried out on samples from a variety of latitudes and countries.

Radiocarbon, the rarest of the three isotopes of carbon, is taken into living bodies through their absorption of atmospheric carbon dioxide, and enter into biological composition in proportions fixed by natural law. On death, the intake of radiocarbon ceases, and its proportion thereafter begins to diminish through radioactivity. Half of any given quantity of radiocarbon disappears in $5,568 \pm 30$ years.

The radiocarbon test may be applied to the dating of sea-shells, stalactites, and stalagmites, which form as the result of the combination of calcium salts with atmospheric carbon dioxide which has been dissolved in water. From the moment of precipitation, the radiocarbon content of the solid calcium carbonate begins to diminish at its natural rate.

The methods employed in radiocarbon dating vary and are complex chemically and physically; but in brief they afford a means of counting the number of explosions per minute registered by a specified quantity of radioactive carbon laid out in an "infinitely thin" layer. An average of readings taken gives the final result.

Although radiocarbon dating is still in its infancy, science claims that it is reliable within the limits of stated probable errors. Refinements are constantly being effected.

The value of radiocarbon dating is that it provides the archæologist with a means of dating ancient remains within known limits, for the rate of disintegration of radiocarbon, as in the case of all radioactivity, is independent of natural conditions.

Serial No. 101a.

The accuracy of modern physical methods can be relied upon within known limits, and can be re-checked. A number of careful comparative tests have been made of the accuracy of the datings obtained by means of radiocarbon assays. A specimen of cypress wood believed to be from the tomb of Sneferu at Meydum, in Egypt, when tested by the radio-carbon method of dating, was found to have an age of 4,802 ±210 years. It will be seen that this includes the known date for the tomb of Sneferu, and probably also includes the actual dates of the life-cycle for the particular wood concerned (which must have formed part of a living tree some years before Sneferu's death). Another test, on a sample of acacia wood from the tomb of Zoser, showed an age of 3,979 ±350 years as against the archæologists' dating of 4,650 ±75 years.

Other tests carried out on samples of known age have met with agreement, as in the cases of:

	Accepted age, years	Radiocarbon dating, years
A deck-board from funerary boat of Sesostris III	3,750	3,621 ±180
Wood from coffin of Ptolemaic period	2,280	2,190 ±450
Beam from tomb of Vizier Hemaka, 1st Dynasty, Sakkara	4,700—5,100	4,883 ±200
Wood from floor of a Hittite palace, Tayinat	2,625 ± 50	2,531 ±150

A most interesting synchronism was obtained when pieces of charcoal unearthed in 1950 at Stonehenge by Stuart Piggot, professor of prehistoric history at the University of Edinburgh, were sent to Dr. Libby for analysis. They showed that the samples date back to 1848 ±275 B.C. (*Daily Telegraph*, 12.5.52; and *News Chronicle*, 10.9.52). This calculation includes the date-range given on an astronomical basis by Sir Norman Lockyer, who determined that the sunrise of the summer solstice, which now takes place slightly to one side of the Stonehenge alignment, occurred directly in line with it 1680 ±200 B.C., which would have been the time when the sighting stones were placed in position (*Stonehenge* by Sir Norman Lockyer, 2nd edition, 1909, pp. 67, 68).

In a number of instances presumed archæological datings have been shown to be in error as in the case of a lump of beeswax associated with Bronze Age objects of 2,500-3,000 years' estimated age. The radiocarbon analysis showed that the beeswax was 819 ±160 years old, and was thus a late addition. Charred wood associated with Neolithic "A" material from Ehenside Tarn, Cumberland, and believed to be 4,000 years of age, was indicated by radiocarbon test to be 4,964 ±300 years old, or of greater antiquity than expected.

Serial No. 101*b*.
Published by *The National Message*, Ltd.
6 Buckingham Gate, London, S.W.1.
Copyright.

Authority: C. F. C. HAWKES, M.A., F.S.A.

The Prehistoric Foundations of Europe. To the Mycenæan Age

"Hawkes, Charles Francis Christopher; Professor of European Archæology in the University of Oxford since 1946; Fellow of Keble College since 1946; *b.* 5 June 1905; . . . entered British Museum, Dept. of British and Medieval Antiqs., 1928; Assist. Keeper 1st class, 1938; in charge of Prehistoric and Romano-British Antiqs., 1946; F.S.A. 1932; Fellow of Royal Archæological Institute . . ." (*Who's Who*, 1947.)

Bronze Age Trade between Palestine and the British Isles

ARCHÆOLOGY has established, beyond any shadow of doubt, that extensive commercial relations between Palestine and the British Isles had developed as early as 1600 B.C. Further, that works of art and utility, produced in the British Isles, were much in demand in the countries of the Middle East.

In the words of this writer: "Europe was connected, through the Ægean, with the Orient . . . A single Egyptian trade product can now appear simultaneously in the Ægean, Hungary, Moravia, Spain and Brittany, Holland, and above all in Britain. And the Baltic amber . . . appears in abundance from about this same date of 1600 in the Ægean world . . ."

POINTS OF SPECIAL INTEREST

1. The fact that there was Bronze Age trade between Palestine and Ireland ('the utmost bounds of the West') is further securely established by finds of Irish jewellery at Gaza, as mentioned by Sir Flinders Petrie.

2. Beads found in Egyptian and Ægean tombs, *c.* 1400 B.C., and at Lachish (Palestine), 1200 B.C., have their exact counterpart in precisely similar beads found in Wiltshire.

3. This writer says: "The evidence . . . points to a trade persisting over an appreciable time in the middle and aftermiddle centuries of the second millennium . . . The date of the Fall of Knossos (Crete) stands in round figures at 1400 B.C. and it is not too much to call it the turning-point of European pre-history . . . Mycenean civilisation became supreme in the Ægean . . . head and front of the achievement of the European Bronze Age."

This is of great interest to Bible students. This period was one of great moment for the Hebrew peoples and particularly for the Israelite section of the Hebrews. Most of the Israelites about this time left Egypt, under Moses. But some of the Danites broke away under Danaus and migrated to the Ægean area, playing a conspicuous part in the establishment of the Ægean civilisation (*vide* Sheet No. 41—Danite Colonies in Greece).

As stated by Hawkes, the acropolis of Mycenæ, overlooking the plain of Argos, "was the focus of the whole movement that transplanted Minoan splendour to the Greek mainland." He adds that Minoan Crete was the "inevitable half-way house between the Orient and Europe."

4. The Palestinian ports traded extensively with the Ægean (Javan) and Cyprus (Chittim) in Old Testament times.

5. It is generally accepted that the trading of this period was largely in the hands of the "Phœnicians," which term embraces not only the traders of Tyre and Sidon (some of them Canaanites) but also Israelites of the sea-faring tribes of Dan and Asher. It will be recalled that, at the commencement of the period under review, Deborah rebuked these tribes for being concerned with their shipping, when they ought to have been assisting their fellow Israelites in their struggle against Sisera (Judges v., c. 1300 B.C.).

6. The extract from the writings of Diodorus of Sicily (c. 50 B.C.), quoted hereunder, supports the evidence of other ancient writers with regard to the extensive tin trade which had developed through the preceding centuries between the British Isles and the Middle East. In his day, tin mining was evidently carried out on sound engineering lines to a considerable depth. Ictis, the island now called *St. Michael's Mount*, seems to have been used as a loading point. Significantly enough, the adjacent Cornish town of the mainland bears the Hebrew name *Marazion*.

C.F.C. HAWKES, M.A., F.S.A.: Extract from his *THE PREHISTORIC FOUNDATIONS OF EUROPE. TO THE MYCENEAN AGE* (Methuen & Co., London, 1940)

(P. 323-325.) . . . Ireland . . . had an established primacy of her own in the working of metals. And the copper for flat axes and the gold for ornaments, which we have seen reason above . . . for regarding as initially the discoveries of her megalith people, now come, with the addition of probably Cornish tin to equip the bronze-smith, into a real pre-eminence in the Early Bronze Age economics of the greater part of North-Western and Northern Europe . . . The leading ornament found in Scottish food-vessel graves is a peculiar type of multiple-string necklace of lignite or jet beads. The idea of such necklaces, ultimately Oriental, appears early in Danish amber, and jet was no doubt Britain's substitute for that precious substance, to which the North Sea trade of the megalith people must have provided the main introduction. But the form taken by the Scottish necklaces must surely be explained from the opposite quarter . . . The leading ornament of the corresponding period in Ireland was the crescentic collar of sheet gold known as the lunula. . . . Its precise antiquity is unknown; but the identity of its doubtless talismanic engraved ornament with motives found on the idol-plaques of Iberian megalithic tombs . . . points to an ultimately Iberian inspiration, with which the presence of Iberian types of lunula, e.g. in Galicia, agrees, though their exact date be unknown: the old Atlantic sea-route need not be thought wholly abandoned in the Early Bronze Age, and genuine Irish lunulæ occur in North-Western and Mid-Western France as well as once in Wales and again in Cornwall, where at Harlyn Bay, near Padstow, two were found with one of the flat axes to be noticed directly. Eastward, their distribution reaches Belgium, Hanover, and finally the islands of Denmark, between which and their Irish homeland there are three from Scotland, the homeland of the answering jet necklace, itself occurring occasionally in Ireland as well as spreading sporadically south of the Border. Obviously lunulæ and necklaces may be considered twin manifestations of the same originally Western idea. And the Baltic and Atlantic limits of the lunula distribution show the extent of an Early Bronze Age trade in Irish gold which is manifest in other forms of sheet gold-work also. The graves of the powerful immigrants from Brittany into Wessex are rich in it, in a variety of ornament-forms of which the most interesting are perhaps the gold mountings for discs of amber. For the Wessex people were rich in Baltic amber no less than in Irish gold, and when we realize that their graves may contain handled cups of amber (one from Clandon in Dorset, another actually from the Hove Barrow . . . in Sussex) as well as of native shale, and that there are several Wessex examples of the Scottish necklace-type made in amber, it becomes clear that they made a strong magnet on one flank of an Irish-Baltic trade whose richest exchange was in gold and amber . . .

(P. 327-328.) . . . The way across the Brenner Pass from Italy and the head of the Adriatic to the Danube and so to Bohemia reached the West Baltic shores down the valley of the Elbe, which a more westerly route from higher up the Danube in Bavaria also entered by way of Thuringia and the Saale. And from lower down the Danube, Moravia, and Silesia, the Vistula route to the Eastern Baltic became (though in a less degree) opened up to a similar traffic, which in due course brought into being a distinct province of Early Bronze culture centred upon East Prussia, where with imported Aunjetitz or derivative bronze types the flanged axe took on a distinctive splay-bladed 'Eastern' form. These routes were not in themselves new: they had been highways since Neolithic times; but the greatly increased tempo of Bronze Age trading-activity brought them an importance which was in effect new, for that activity was born of the fact that now the staple of material equipment was a metal whose constituents only favoured regions could supply, and whose manufacture only skilled workers could encompass, but which could under those conditions be produced in quantities great enough to supply the ever-growing demand of distant as well as home markets. And it is the distribution of the bronze goods themselves which attests both the amount of the activity and the course of its long-distance channels. Above all, the great increase in the numbers of smiths' and merchants' hoards, and their concentration in the centres and along the routes of trade, enables archæology to record at once the geography and the chronology of the process. This on the one hand: on the other, the native wealth of the shores of the Baltic, east and west alike, in the amber which was more than ever prized in the centres of metal-using civilization, furnished an inexhaustible article of exchange which made the transcontinental traffic unique in its kind, and has earned its main artery the accepted name of the Amber Route . . .

(P. 345-348.) But the graves of this rich South Hungarian district round the town of Szeged are of crucial importance. For in four graves at Szoreg and one at Oszentivan, associated with pottery in the main of Perjamos tradition, have been found little segmented beads of faience. There are also found star or rectangular beads of the same material, among a wide range of ornaments, including also Mediterranean shells, and scientific examination of this faience has shown it to be identical with that of the self-same form of segmented bead in Egypt, whence it thus appears the beads were imported. Further, segmented faience beads of this type have been found in roughly contemporary Aunjetitz graves in Moravia, at Němčice and Jirikovice, and another at Leopoldsdorf in Lower Austria, in an inhumation-grave with two gold lock-rings of Aunjetitz type, but pottery that assigns the whole to the Wieselburg culture, with its Bell-beaker and Baden traditions . . . and further points, in its white-inlaid ornament, to the influence from the Slavonian culture-area already discussed. In this period of transition from Early to Middle Bronze Age, then, imported beads from Egypt were circulating widely in the Danube basin; and this is not all. We have already spoken of trade-routes from the Aunjetitz province to the West, as well as the Amber Route to the North . . . close to that by the Lower Rhine to Britain, at Exloo in the Drenthe province of Holland, has been found a necklace comprising four of these beads and twenty-five of more or less the same shape in tin, as well as fourteen ordinary beads of amber. Here are Western or Central European tin, Northern amber, and Egyptian faience all together, and the Western ramifications of the faience bead-trade are attested by eight from a grave of the Spanish El Argar culture . . . at Fuente Alamo in Almeria, by one (of doubtful associations and relative age) from the megalithic tomb of Parc-Guren at Carnac in Brittany, and, far outweighing all in number, by at least forty from England, to say nothing of a number more from the British Isles, mainly Scotland, of different compositions and apparently later date. The latter include star forms as well as segmented, and also a quoit shape which recurs in England in normal faience in pendante form and in occasional association with normal segmented beads. Rarer varieties include spherical or near-spherical forms, and a few beads of blue glass have been reported also, which call to mind a few others from Central Europe, notably one from an Aunjetitz grave at Melk in Austria, and others, greenish and of pinched-circle shape, from another such grave at Polep in Bohemia. The associations of the British bead-finds are primarily in graves of the Wessex culture, most notably that at Aldbourne in Wiltshire that has given its name to the type of 'incensecup' it also contained . . . and a high proportion of the whole number

have occurred in or close to Wiltshire; but they also occur further afield, and also many must be of rather later date, as accompanying cremation-interments in the large cinerary urns that we shall presently find characteristic of the ensuing Middle Bronze Age in Britain, after (some even considerably after) about 1400 B.C. . . .

(P. 348.) . . . Thus the evidence so far points to a trade persisting over an appreciable time in the middle and after-middle centuries of the second millennium. And related bead-types in bone, jet, and gold, as well as the tin specimens already noticed, and the spiral-tubular bronze beads frequent in Central Europe, have a wide enough distribution in time and space to make one take a broad view of the whole matter. For indeed the segmented-bead form in general has a very long history in Egypt and the Near East generally, from long before until well after the period we are discussing, and we can only say that production rose to its height under the Eighteenth Dynasty, from just after 1600 B.C., and that the bluish glaze-colour, and far more critically the large perforation, normal to the European finds, are recorded from Abydos with a scarab of Amenhotep III (1412-1376 B.C.), and also from among the great numbers of segmented beads from Tell El-Amarna (1380-1350), whence the resemblance to Wiltshire specimens has been confirmed by spectro-graphic analysis. Finally, as closely similar beads have been dated 1200-1150 B.C. at Tell Duweir (Lachish) in Palestine. What, then, is the historical context of the connexions that the European bead-finds imply between the centre and west of our continent and the orbit of Egyptian civilization? For a satisfactory answer it is natural to turn to the Ægean, and in the first place to Minoan Crete, inevitable half-way house between the Orient and Europe.

(P. 350.) . . . All that we have said of Bronze Age trade-routes in this chapter therefore culminates in this, that from at least about 1600 B.C. onwards Europe was connected, through the Ægean, with the Orient in a commerce of a new order of significance, transcending whatever we have seen of the kind in earlier periods. A single Egyptian trade-product can now appear simultaneously in the Ægean, Hungary, Moravia, Spain and Brittany, Holland, and above all in Britain. And the Baltic amber which, with a distribution of its own almost as wide and far more abundant, was the chief precious commodity traded southward across Central Europe in the opposite direction, appears in abundance from about this same date of 1600 in the Ægean world. Further, we saw earlier that the European brⱼnze halberd might be treated as a ritual weapon and so enter the class of precious objects of exchange, and the same period has produced two halberds in Greece: one, from a grave with Minoan pottery of about 1600 at Sesklo in Thessaly, recalls to some extent at least Hungarian pattern, while the other has had closer parallels to its curved edges, straight midrib, and arrangement of rivets quoted from North Italy, and even from the far-away home of the type in Ireland. The rivets of that halberd are conical-headed in the North European manner, but they are capped with gold, and the place of its finding was the focus of the whole movement that transplanted Minoan splendour to the Greek mainland—the acropolis of Mycenæ, overlooking the plain of Argos. It was in the sixth of the famous shaft-graves, in the sepulchral treasure which also included a stone shaft-smoother of a type well known in the North and Britain; as for amber, beads of it were found in three of the others, in the fifth as many as a hundred, in the third thirty with also two spherical beads of faience. The link between Europe and the Orient has become cast in the new mould of Mycenean civilization.

(P. 356.) The date of the Fall of Knossos, closely fixed by material synchronisms with the known chronology of Egypt, stands in round figures at 1400 B.C., and it is not too much to call it the turning-point of European prehistory. That it was the Myceneans of European Greece, strong enough now in their own ships, and with the power of their own wealth behind their martial prowess, who rose against the Minoan despot and delivered the blow that brought Knossos

down, cannot indeed be proved outright. But the belief fits strikingly with facts as well as probabilities. How Egypt reacted is clear from the way in which evidence of her especial relations with Crete ceases at this time in the reign of King Amenhotep III, while the faience with his cartouche at Mycenæ seems significantly answered by his reception in Egypt of Mycenean pottery, followed as it was by two centuries of the ware's importation and use throughout the Nile Valley. The effect in Europe was that Mycenean civilization became supreme in the Ægean, standing now in its own right as the head and front of the achievement of the European Bronze Age. And in the tale of Theseus who "slew the Minotaur" and freed his country from the oppression of Minos' tribute, a great overthrow of Knossos by their countryman has come down to us as one of the most ancient memories of the Greek people. That overthrow symbolizes the winning of mastery in its own house for European civilization as against the Orient. With it the span of this book in time reaches its end. But it remains now to review the European scene of 1400 B.C. as a whole. And we shall find that the inception of the Middle Bronze Age at this time was in the main the emergence of a cultural balance, which we have already begun to see appearing, and of which the Mycenean achievement, unique as it remains, yet faithfully emphasizes the essential poise. It is the balance of the foundations of Europe.

(P. 377-378.) . . . And we have not exhausted Ireland's share of the part played in Bronze Age Europe by the British Isles. While the Irish halberd, like the flat axe, goes back to an earlier stage of our story, its Continental derivatives lasted to the Middle Bronze Age, and we have seen it appearing at Mycenæ itself; and the gold lunula was only one of the beginnings of the Irish goldsmiths' contributions to prehistoric magnificence. The 'sheet' gold-work it represents was equally that employed for the gold ornaments that we have seen make the principal glory of Early Bronze Age Wessex, and before the supervening of the heavier 'bar' work, exported already to Central Europe in late Aunjetitz times but most typical of the Middle Bronze Age, it had made its mark as far away as the Ægean also. For the gold-mounted amber disc of the Wessex graves reappears, with much other amber, in the Late Minoan Tomb of the Double-axes at Knossos; the gold pointille technique of the Breton-Wessex dagger-haft is not unknown in Mycenean Greece; and that the influence was mutual is shown by the Mycenean reminiscences in much of the other finery of the Wessex graves, in the similarity of the corrugated gold cup from Rillaton in Cornwall . . . to two from the Fourth Shaft-grave at Mycenæ, and in the copying of segmented faience beads in Irish gold—these last appearing as far along the connecting trade-routes as the Middle Rhineland. And the maintenance of these connexions in the Late Mycenean period, the Irish and European Middle Bronze Age, when the faience bead-trade still flourished, as we have seen, is further shown by the chiselled rendering of that period's soldered technique of multiple-ribbon gold-work, as seen on the ear-rings from Enkomi in Cyprus and Tell el-Ajjul in Palestine, by which the Irish smiths created not only ear-rings but the great four-leaved gold torcs which are among the acknowledged masterpeices of their craft. This is the witness of material archæology, but it is the spirit that quickeneth, and if the boat-coffin burials on both sides of the North Sea were inspired from the Orient, the Minoan-Mycenean motives in the magical carvings on the famous chalk drums from the Early Bronze Age barrow at Folkton in East Yorkshire show likewise that the spiritual potency of the Mediterranean in the far North-West was not exhausted with the inspiration of the old megalithic religion.

(Reproduced by kind permission of the publishers)

Extract from *DIODORUS OF SICILY* (translation by G. H. OLDFATHER, 1933), Book V, 1-4, 35

(1-4.)

The inhabitants of Britain who dwell about the promontory known as Belerius are especially hospitable to strangers and have adopted a civilised manner of life because of their intercourse with other peoples. They it is who work the tin, treating the bed which bears it in an ingenious manner. This bed, being like rock, contains earthy seams and in them the workers quarry the ore, which they then melt down and cleanse of its impurities. Then they work the tin into pieces the size of knuckle-bones and convey it to an island which lies off Britain and is called Ictis; for at the time of ebb-tide the space between this island and the mainland becomes dry and they can take the tin in large quantities over the island on their wagons . . . On the island of Ictis the merchants purchase the tin of the natives and carry it from there across the Strait to Galatai or Gaul; and finally, making their way on foot through Gaul for some thirty days, they bring their wares on horseback to the mouth of the river Rhone.

(35.)

. . . and not only do they go into the ground a great distance, but they also push their diggings many stades in depth and run galleries off at every angle, turning this way and that, in this manner bringing up from the depths the ore which gives them the profit they are seeking.

SIR FLINDERS PETRIE, D.C.L., F.R.S., F.B.A.: Extract from *PALESTINE AND ISRAEL* (S.P.C.K., London, 1934), p. 15

We find each year, at Gaza, gold-work from Ireland . . . dated from 2300 B.C. onward; gold-work covered with skilful granular patterns, probably from North Syria; painted pottery with spirited figures of animals . . . from regions not yet explored; daggers from Luristan . . . and carved ivory work showing Persian trade. The dominant people, who imported these, habitually used ornaments and daggers from the Caspian region. The free use of gold, even adorning children, belongs to the age before all the stream deposits of the Old World were exhausted, the time when gold was as common as it has been at Klondyke in our time. We have at the capital city and port of Gaza burst into a range of civilisations which we are only now beginning to connect with their home lands.

G. A. WAINWRIGHT, Extract from "The Coming of Iron," *ANTIQUITY* Jan.-Mar. issue, 1936, p. 24.

. . . by the 8th century, Sargon of Assyria had laid up in his storehouses 150 tons or so of good iron. His ingots were of the curious shape which 200 years later was entering Germany and France with the La Tène period of the Iron Age.

A collection of Prehistoric Irish Goldwork (*photograph by courtesy of the British Museum*).

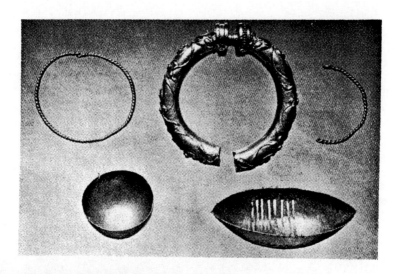

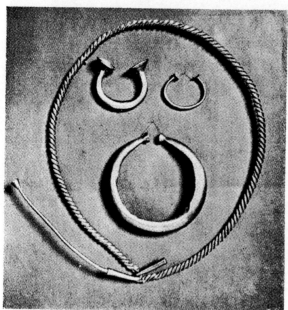

Above and left:
Prehistoric Irish Goldwork
(*photographs by courtesy of the
National Museum of Ireland,
Dublin*).

Specimens of Irish Goldwork
found at Gaza in Palestine
(*photograph by courtesy of (the
late) Sir Flanders Petrie*).

Authority: The Very Reverend J. H. HERTZ, C.H., Ph.D., LL.D., Chief Rabbi of the United Hebrew Congregations of the British Empire from 1913 to 1946.

". . . Joseph Herman Hertz was born at Rebrin, Czechoslovakia, then Hungary, on 25th September, 1872. . . . In the Jewish community he held a large number of offices, the principal of which were the presidency of Jews' College, of the Jewish Historical Society of England (1922-23), of the Conference of Anglo-Jewish preachers, of the Bayswater Jewish Schools, and of the Jewish Peace Society. He became acting principal of Jews' College in 1939. In the larger Jewish community he was president of the governing body of the Institute of Jewish Studies of the Hebrew University, Jerusalem, and a member of the board of governors of the university. . . ." (*The Times*, 15th Jan., 1946.)

Constitution of Modern Jewry

THE Jews of to-day are descended, in the main, from only two of the tribes of Israel, namely Judah and Benjamin. Reunion with the remaining ten tribes is expected by the Jews at some future date.

POINTS OF SPECIAL INTEREST

1. The statements of the Chief Rabbi, which are tersely emphatic, uphold the Old Testament record to the effect that the remnant of the Kingdom of Judah which returned to Jerusalem from Babylon under the decree of Cyrus to rebuild the Temple, comprised elements of the tribes of Judah, Benjamin, and Levi only (Ezra i).

2. A proportion of the Levites must, by inference, be with the descendants of the ten tribes.

3. Orthodox Jewry is well aware that the Jews of to-day constitute only a small part of the ancient people of Israel.

Reduced facsimile of a letter from the Chief Jewish Rabbi,
dated 18th November, 1918, to the Rev. Merton Smith

OFFICE OF THE CHIEF RABBI.

MULBERRY ST., COMMERCIAL RD., E. 1.

London,   November 18th, 1918. 567 9.

Dear Sir,

In reply to your letter of the 15th instant. I am
desired by the Chief Rabbi to state:-

1. The people known at present as Jews are descend-
dants of the tribes of Judah and Benjamin with a certain number of descendants of the tribe of Levi.

2. As far as is known, there is not any further admixture of other tribes.

3. The ten tribes have been absorbed among the
nations of the world. (See II Kings Chap. 17, more especially
vv. 22 and 23.)

4. We look forward to the gathering of all the tribes
at some future day. (See Isaiah 27, 11-12; and Ezekiel 37,
15-28.)

With the Chief Rabbi's cordial greetings,

I am, dear Sir,

Yours faithfully,

E. Buchms

Secretary.

Capt. Merton Smith.
Canadian Forrestry Corps,
Sunningdale,
Berks.

Serial No. 7.

Authority: JOSEPHUS

Antiquities of the Jews

"Josephus Flavius (c. 37-95?), Jewish historian and military commander, was born in the first year of Caligula (37-38). His father belonged to one of the noblest priestly families, and through his mother he claimed descent from the Asmonaean high priest Jonathan. A precocious student of the law. . . . *The Jewish Antiquities* . . . covers in twenty books the history of the Jews from the creation of the world to the outbreak of the war with Rome. It was finished in the thirteenth year of Domitian (93). . . ."

(*Encyclopaedia Britannica*, 13th Edition.)

ON the authority of Josephus, himself a learned Jew, it is clear that the term "Jew" (derived from the tribal name of Judah) was the appellation given to the people of the remnant of the southern two-tribed kingdom of Judah which had returned to Jerusalem from the Babylonian captivity.

POINTS OF SPECIAL INTEREST

1. The evidence of this early Jewish historian—who lived within a few centuries of the incidents he describes—refutes completely the popular fallacy that the whole, or the majority, of the descendants of the ancient people of Israel are contained in the people now known as the Jews.

2. Josephus confirms the Bible narrative as recorded in the Book of Nehemiah —the hostility of the neighbouring peoples; the division of the work of rebuilding; Nehemiah's exhortations to the Jews.

JOSEPHUS: EXTRACT FROM HIS *ANTIQUITIES OF THE JEWS* (English translation by William Whiston, A.M.; Pub. Griffin & Co.) Book XI, ch. v.

7. Now when he was come to Babylon, and had taken with him many of his countrymen, who voluntarily followed him, he came to Jerusalem in the twenty and fifth year of the reign of Xerxes; and when he had shewn the epistle to God, he gave them to Adeus, and to the other governors. He also called together all the people to Jerusalem, and stood in the midst of the temple, and made the following speech to them: "You know, O Jews, that God hath kept our fathers, Abraham, Isaac, and Jacob, in mind continually; and for the sake of their righteousness hath not left off the care of you. Indeed he hath assisted me in gaining this authority of the king to raise up our wall, and finish what is wanting of the temple. I desire you, therefore, who well know the ill will our neighbouring nations bear to us, and that when once they are made sensible that we are in earnest about building, they will come upon us, and contrive many ways of obstructing our works, that you will, in the first place, put your trust in God, as in him that will assist us against their hatred, and to intermit building neither night nor day, but to use all diligence, and to hasten on the work, now we have this especial opportunity for it." When he had said this, he gave order that the rulers should measure the wall, and part the work of it among the people, according to their villages and cities, as every one's ability should require. And when he had added this promise, that he himself, with his servants, would assist them, he dissolved the assembly. So the Jews prepared for the work: that is the name they are called by from the day that they came up from Babylon, which is taken from the tribe of Judah, which came first to these places, and thence both they and the country gained that appellation.

8. But now when the Ammonites, and Moabites, and Samaritans, and all that inhabited Coelesyria, heard that the building went on apace, they took it heinously, and proceeded to lay snares for them, and to hinder their intentions.

Authority: Sir J. GARDNER WILKINSON, F.R.S.

A Popular Account of the Ancient Egyptians

Wilkinson, Sir. John Gardner (1797-1875). "Explorer and Egyptologist; educated at Harrow and Exeter College, Oxford; lived in Egypt and Nubia, 1821-1833; made journeys of exploration; independently arrived at con-clusions respecting hieroglyphics identical with those of Champollion; F.R.S., 1833; knighted, 1839; travelled in Montenegro, Herzegovina, Bosnia, and in Italy, studying the Turin papyrus, of which he published a facsimile; works include a standard *Manners and Customs of Ancient Egyptians*, 1837." (*Concise Dictionary of National Biography*, 1930.)

The Hebrew Countenance—A Modern Fallacy

A S a result of his extensive researches in Egypt and Palestine, Sir Gardner Wilkinson became convinced that the facial characteristics which are now generally referred to as 'Jewish' (large nose, dark eyes and black hair) are of 'Syrian' (as distinct from Hebrew) origin. These non-Israelite features do not appear in the traditional portrait of the Jew of Christ's day. Wilkinson found that the Jews living in Jerusalem in the early nineteenth century were blue-eyed, often red-haired, with a "nose of delicate form and nearly straight". Their children had "the pink and white complexions of Europeans".

POINTS OF SPECIAL INTEREST

1. This facial contour and colouring, found in *modern* Syrians, is of Hittite-Armenoid origin, and was 'imported' into Jewry by large-scale prose-lyting, with consequent inter-marriage between the true Israelitish Jews and people of alien stock.
   It should be remembered that the term 'Syrian' is often used rather loosely—sometimes to denote habitat rather than race. For instance, the Bible translators have used it in respect of Jacob: "A Syrian ready to perish was my father" (Deuteronomy xxvi, 5)—an obvious allusion to Jacob's descent from Abraham, who first found a home in Syria after his call from Ur of the Chaldees.
2. In describing the fair, blue-eyed people which he saw in Jerusalem, Wilkin-son is speaking of *indigenous* Jews who were there long before the influx from the west began, following the permission granted by the Sultan in 1856 as a result of the efforts of Sir Moses Montefiore. Before that date there was only the merest handful of Jews in the Holy Land, and these were largely of true Jewish descent.
3. The statements regarding the traditional portrait of Jesus Christ, in the light of the knowledge revealed by Sir Gardner's researches, have an added interest when considered along with the description in I Samuel xvii, 42 of Christ's ancestor, David, who was "ruddy, and of a fair countenance".
4. Like many other writers, this authority uses the terms Jew and Israelite as if they are synonymous. In point of fact this practice can be misleading. The name 'Jew' (an abbreviation of the tribal name of Judah) was applied to the small remnant of the Judah kingdom—comprising frag-ments of the tribes of Judah and Benjamin, with some of the Levites—which returned from Babylonian captivity following 536 B.C. This remnant —a pitiful 50,000—was, of course, a very tiny fraction of the Israel people as a whole.
5. Belzoni's tomb is better known as the tomb of Rekmireh.

SIR J. G. WILKINSON, F.R.S.: EXTRACT FROM HIS *POPULAR ACCOUNT OF THE ANCIENT EGYPTIANS*, Vol. II, ch. viii, pp. 197-199 (Pub.: John Murray, London, 1854).

With regard to the features of foreigners resembling the Jews, it is only necessary to observe that the Egyptians adopted the same character for all the inhabitants of Syria; as may be seen in the sculptures of Karnak and other places, where those people occur, as well as in one of the sets of figures in Belzoni's tomb; and the brickmakers, far from having what is considered the very Jewish expression found in many of those figures, have not even the long beard, so marked in the people of Syria and the prisoners of Sheshonk (Shishak). They are represented as a white people, like others from Asia introduced into the paintings, and some have blue eyes and red hair, which are also given to the people of Rot-ñ-n in this same tomb. Indeed if I were disposed to think them Jews, I should rather argue it from many of these figures *not* having the large nose and dark eyes and hair we consider as Jewish types; for some of these brickmakers are painted yellow, with blue eyes and small beards. Others are red with a *rétroussé* nose.

These last may be Egyptians, or people of Pount who are represented bringing tribute in the same tomb. The fact of some having small beards, others merely the. stubble-field" of an unshaven chin, might accord with Jews as well as with the Rot-ñ-n or other northern races; but their making bricks at Thebes, and the name of Jews not being mentioned in the whole tomb, are insuperable objections.

And here I may mention a remarkable circumstance, that the Jews of the East to this day often have red hair and blue eyes, with a nose of delicate form and nearly straight, and are quite unlike their brethren of Europe; and the children in modern Jerusalem have the pink and white complexions of Europeans. The Oriental Jews are at the same time unlike the other Syrians in features; and it is the Syrians who have the large nose that strikes us as the peculiarity of the western Israelites. This prominent feature was always a characteristic of the Syrians, but not of the ancient, nor of the modern, Jews of Judæa; and the Saviour's head, though not really a portrait, is evidently a traditional representation of the Jewish face, which is still traceable at Jerusalem. No real portrait of Him was ever handed down and Eusebius, of Cæsarea, pronounced the impossibility of obtaining one for the sister of Constantine; but the character of the Jewish face would necessarily be known in those early days (in the fourth century), when the first representations of Him were attempted; and we should be surprised to find any artist abandon the style of features thus agreed upon for ages, and represent the Saviour with those of our western Jews. Yet this would be perfectly correct if the Jews of His day had those features; and such would have been, in that case, His traditional portrait.

I had often remarked the colour and features of the Jews in the East, so unlike those known in Europe, and my wish to ascertain if they were the same in Judæa was at length gratified by a visit to Jerusalem; where I found the same type in all those really of eastern origin; and the large nose is there an invariable proof of mixture with a western family. It may be difficult to explain this great difference in the eastern and western face (and the former is said to be also found in Hungary); but the subject is worthy of investigation, as is the origin of those Jews now living in Europe, and the early migrations that took place from Judæa long before the Christian era.

Authority: Dr. MAX NORDAU in a letter to the *Daily Mail* (21/8/1899).

"Nordau (originally Sudfeld), Max Simon (1848-1923), Jewish-Hungarian author, was born at Budapest on July 29, 1849, and practised medicine in his native town. He made his name by his pseudo-philosophical *Entartung* (Engl. trs. *Degeneration*, 1895), which was translated into many languages, and had a great vogue. Other works were *The Conventional Lies of Society* (Eng. version 1895), and *Biologie der Ethik* (1921). Nordau was an ardent Zionist, and took Herzl's side in wishing to accept the British Government's offer of land for a Jewish settlement in East Africa. In 1903 an attempt was made on his life by a Jew opposed to the scheme. He died on January 22, 1923.

His works include . . . some books of travel; and the critical works *Zeitgenossische Franzosen* (1901), and *Von Kinst und Kunstlern* (Leipzig, 1905)." (*Encyclopædia Britannica*, 14th Edition.)

The 'Jewish' Nose

DR. NORDAU affirms that the arched nose popularly and erroneously styled 'Jewish' is not Semitic but is of non-Hebrew origin. It occurs in modern Jewry because, in time past, the Jews 'became strongly intermingled with the Hittites'. The true Israelite nose is perfectly straight.

POINTS OF SPECIAL INTEREST

1. This statement of Dr. Nordau is of great value in that it expresses the opinion of an eminent Jew, well qualified to speak on the subject of the Jewish physical types.

2. It is important to recognise the strong Hittite infusion into Jewry, mentioned by Dr. Nordau, resulting in the introduction of completely non-Hebrew facial characteristics.

DR. MAX NORDAU: EXTRACT FROM HIS LETTER TO THE *DAILY MAIL*
dated August 21, 1899; p. 4.

(A description of the Jew, Dreyfus, after his return from Devil's Island.)

. . . Dreyfus seems to be between 5 ft. 7 in. and 5 ft. 8 in. tall . . . Dreyfus is brachycephalic; I estimate his index at eighty-three or eighty-four. The skull is not very high, the occipital bone is somewhat vaulted, and the ears are fairly long and outstanding.

Now for the face. Dreyfus is cleanly-shaved, save a short, thin moustache of indefinite colour, which, with light brown as a base, is tinged with some intermingled red and white lines. The cheeks are thin, without being actually hollow. The jaw-bones are very pronounced, the nose is not large, thin, and boldly arched. It is the nose which people style

The 'Jewish', erroneously,

for the real Semitic nose is long, thin, and perfectly straight.

The crooked nose is Armenian. The Jews only have this characteristic in a marked degree since they became strongly intermingled with the Hittites, the ancestors of the Armenians of to-day . . .

Authorities: Various

Edomite Jewry

SOME centuries after the Return from Babylon, the remnant of the Two-tribed kingdom of Judah—thenceforward known as the nation of the Jews—received a substantial infusion of non-Israelite peoples. Chief of these were the Idumeans (Edomites), who were forcibly incorporated into Jewry by John Hyrcanus, c. 125 B.C. The various tribes of Edom, particularly the Amalekites, had been bitter enemies of Israel ever since the Exodus of the latter from Egypt. Esau, their progenitor—himself a fierce, lawless man—through his Horite and Hittite wives had produced a predatory, ruthless race which ultimately, by reason of its fusion with Jewry, was destined to be an evil, disruptive force, bringing trouble and disaster to the Jewish people.

POINTS OF SPECIAL INTEREST

1. The national characteristics of the Edomites were epitomised in the Idumean Herods (I and II). The former, having seized power, exterminated the Asmonian priestly line and sought to affiliate himself to the priesthood by marrying the high priest's daughter, whom he afterwards murdered. He was subsequently guilty of one of the foulest massacres in history when he ordered the slaughter of all children under the age of two —when Christ was born.

Herod II, to whom Jesus referred as 'that fox', ordered the execution of John the Baptist, who had opposed Herod's proposed unlawful marriage to his brother's wife. This Herod, with his soldiery, mocked Jesus before returning Him to Pilate, just before the Crucifixion.

With an Idumean as king of the Jews the race of Esau achieved prominence, and, following the lead of their ruler, they were quick to oppose the new doctrine introduced by John and personified in Jesus. The Herodians vied with the Pharisees in the bitter opposition to our Lord.

Haman, too, was typical of the insensate hatred which the rejected line of Esau had for the accepted race of Israel. This Amalekite—during the sojourn in Persia of those Judahites who did not return to Jerusalem—endeavoured unsuccessfully to exterminate the latter by command of the monarch. His hatred recoiled upon himself.

3. Although the Idumeans ceased to be a separate people, the strain of Esau-Edom must have continued in Jewry right down to the present day. It seems more than probable that the factions in modern Jewry—religious Jews who follow their ancient faith, and those who have rejected their religion and resort to violence and atheism—are founded in different racial elements; the former the true seed of Israel, and the latter those who would obtain the kingdom by violence—those who "say they are Jews, and are not, but are the synagogue of Satan" (Rev. ii).

4. With regard to the incorporation into Jewry of the Iturean people, the *Jewish Encyclopædia* (article 'Iturea') says this was a "Greek name of a province, derived from the Biblical 'Jetur', name of a son of Ishmael" (comp. Gen. xxv. 15, 16). The *people* are referred to by several ancient writers, "some of whom designate the Itureans as Arabs and others as Syrians. They were known to the Romans as a predatory people, . . . and were appreciated by them for their great skill in archery. . . . The Itureans did not always possess the same land; as a nomadic people they roamed through the country". In I Chronicles v, 19-22 they are found in the lands of Reuben, Gad, and Manasseh; "in the time of the Roman conquest they dwelt in the region of Mount Lebanon . . . According to Josephus (*Ant.* xiii. 11, sec. 3), the Iturean kingdom lay north of Galilee, and in 105 B.C. Aristobulus, having defeated the Itureans, annexed a part of their country to Judea, imposing Judaism upon the inhabitants . . ." (1925 Edition).

5. So spiritually degraded was the Jewish nation during the period of its domination by the Herodians that we find Caiaphas, a Sadducee, which sect did not believe in the life after death, appointed to the high priesthood by the Romans, and sitting in judgment on Christ and condemning Him to death (Acts v. 17, xxiii. 6-10; Schaff-Herzog, *Dictionary of Religious Knowledge*, article 'Caiaphas').

A BRIEF HISTORY OF ESAU-EDOM

In order to appreciate fully the evil potentialities of the Edomite infusion into Jewry it is necessary to review the origin and history of this predatory people. Esau was elder twin brother of Jacob. He was a 'profane person' (Heb. xii. 16) who, though he valued the paternal 'blessing' (i.e. "the fatness of the earth, and plenty of corn and wine"), despised the Abrahamic 'Birthright' —which carried responsibilities as well as privileges. The terms Esau and Edom are synonymous (Gen. xxxvi). To the distress of his parents he married two Canaanite wives, although he subsequently sought to re-establish himself by taking a Hebrew woman to wife. With his descendants he left Canaan and went to live in Seir, the hilly region to the south of the Dead Sea, this territory becoming known as Edom (Gr. Idumea). The Horites were the aboriginal inhabitants, of whom Hasting's *Dictionary of the Bible* says:

"They are not explicitly said to be *rephaim*, as are the Emim and the Zamzummim, but from what there is said it is natural to infer that they were" (article 'Horites').

Young also considers that the Horites were of the race of the Rephaim.

The Rephaim (*strong*), first referred to in Genesis xiv and variously called Anakim (*giants*), Emims (*terrible*), Zamzummim (*powerful*), and Zuzims (*prominent*), were people of great stature

Serial No. 40a.

(Deut. ii). Moses' spies bewailed that descendants of these 'giants' (*Nephilim—fallen ones*) still lived in the Land of Promise, whilst the record in Deuteronomy ii declares that the enormous bedstead of Og was still in existence. Goliath, whom David slew, appears to have been one of the last of the Rephaim. In Genesis xxxvi it is stated that one of Esau's wives was Aholibamah, daughter of Anah, granddaughter of Zibeon, son of Seir—a Horite (Hastings). The text says that Zibeon was a Hivite, but verses 20 and 24 make it clear that he was a Horite. Hastings says, of this passage, "read Horite for Hivite"; whilst Young states that it is quite uncertain whether the Hebrew word 'Hivite' denotes a progenitor or a locality. Thus—in this case—it would seem that Zibeon (although a Horite by race) was a Hivite by residence. Of Esau's marriage with Aholibamah of the Rephaim, Hastings says:

"There was such a mingling of the family of Esau and his Horite connexions that the Horite name and descent was preserved" (article 'Horites').

By his Hittite wife, Adah, Esau brought another vicious strain into the race. This was particularly emphasised in Amalek, born to her son Eliphaz by Timna, a concubine, who was also probably a Horite. Small wonder that the hatred and villainy of the Amalekites was vented upon the people of Israel whenever occasion presented.

It is abundantly evident that the union of the profane Esau with the descendants of the terrible Rephaim, and with the tainted line of Canaan, the accursed son of Ham, had produced a race whose association with, and incorporation into, Jewry can only be described as calamitous. Small wonder, therefore, that Esau was rejected of God.

The burning hostility of the Edomites for Israel is apparent throughout the recorded history of the two peoples. The chief instances of this are:

1. The entirely unprovoked attack upon the Israelites after they fled from Egypt (Exod. xvii).

2. Amalek joined with Moab and Ammon during a period of Israel's weakness in the period of the Judges (iii. 13).

3. The Edomites took advantage of Judah's distress—when Nebuchadnezzar captured Jerusalem —to plunder the city and to slay the escaping inhabitants, or to deliver them up to their conquerors (Obad. 10-14).

4. The Idumeans attacked the Jews during the time of Judas Maccabeus, who was compelled to wage war against them, considerably reducing their power.

5. During the Roman siege of Jerusalem the Idumeans massacred a great number of the Jews shut up in the city, including the high priest.

JOSEPHUS: Extracts from his *ANTIQUITIES OF THE JEWS*; English translation by William Whiston, A.M. (Charles Griffin & Co., London)

Book II, ch. i, secs. 1-2

After the death of Isaac, his sons divided their habitations respectively, nor did they retain what they had before; but Esau departed from the city of Hebron, and left it to his brother, and dwelt in Seir, and ruled over Idumea . . . for Idumea was a large country, and did then preserve the name of the whole, while in its several parts it kept the names of its peculiar inhabitants.

Book III, ch. ii, sec. 1

The . . . *Amalekites* . . . were the most warlike of the nations that lived thereabout; and whose kings exhorted one another and their neighbours to go to this war against the Hebrews; telling them that an army of strangers, and such a one as had run away from slavery under the Egyptians, lay in wait to ruin them; . . . After they had sent such embassages . . . they resolved to attack the Hebrews in battle.

Book XI, ch. vi, sec. 5

Now there was one Haman, . . . by birth an Amalekite, . . . and the foreigners and Persians worshipped him . . . but Mordecai . . .

would not worship the man . . . Haman . . . determined to abolish the whole nation, for he was naturally an enemy to the Jews . . .

Book XII, ch. viii, sec. 1

. . . Judas made perpetual expeditions against these men, and endeavoured to restrain them from those incursions, and to prevent the mischiefs they did to the Jews. So he fell upon the Idumeans, the posterity of Esau, at Acrabattene, and slew a great many of them, and took their spoils.

Book XIII, ch. ix, sec. 1

. . . Hyrcanus . . . took Medaba . . . Samega, and the neighbouring places, and, besides these, Shechem and Gerizzim, and the nation of the Cutheans, who dwelt at the temple which resembled that temple which was at Jerusalem . . . which temple was now deserted two hundred years after it was built. Hyrcanus took also Dora and Marissa, cities of Idumea, and subdued all the Idumeans; and . . . they submitted to the use of circumcision, and the rest of the Jewish ways of living; at which time therefore this befell them, that they were hereafter no other than Jews.

Book XIV, ch. xv, sec. 2

Herod had now a strong army; and . . . went on for Jerusalem. . . . Antigonius, by way of reply to what Herod had caused to be proclaimed, . . . said, that they would not do justly if they gave the kingdom to Herod, who was no more than a private man, and an Idumean, i.e. a half Jew . . .

Book XV, ch. vii, sec. 10

. . . But when the king knew this thing, by his sister's information, he sent men to the places where he had the intimation they were concealed, and ordered both them and those that were accused as guilty with them, to be slain, insomuch that there were now none at all left of the kindred of Hyrcanus; and the kingdom was entirely in Herod's power, and there was nobody remaining of such dignity as could put a stop to what he did against the Jewish laws.

Book XIII, ch. xi, sec. 3

. . . Aristobulus . . . was called a lover of the Grecians; and had conferred many benefits on his own country, and made war against Iturea, and added a great part of it to Judea, and compelled the inhabitants, if they would continue in that country, to be circumcised, and to live according to the Jewish laws. He was naturally a man of candour, and of great modesty, as Strabo bears witness in the name of Timagenes: who says thus:—"This man was a person of candour, and very serviceable to the Jews, for he added a country to them, and obtained a part of the nation of the Itureans for them, and bound them to them by the bond of the circumcision of their genitals."

Extract from JOSEPHUS' *WARS OF THE JEWS*, Book IV, Ch. v, Secs. 12

NOTE: As the Roman forces approached Jerusalem, the lawless zealots—against the decision of the priesthood—had secretly admitted to the city a horde of 20,000 Idumeans who professed a desire to assist in the defence of the city and temple.

1. . . . The zealots also joined in the shouts raised by the Idumeans; and the storm itself rendered the cry more terrible; nor did the Idumeans spare anybody; for as they are naturally a barbarous and bloody nation, and had been distressed by the tempest, they made use of their weapons against those that had shut the gates against them, and acted in the same manner as to those that supplicated for their lives, and to those that fought them, insomuch that they ran those through with their swords who desired them to remember the relation there was between them, and begged of them to have regard to their common temple . . . And now the outer temple was all of it overflowed with blood; and that

day, as it came on, saw eight thousand five hundred dead bodies there.

2. But the rage of the Idumeans was not satiated by these slaughters; but they now betook themselves to the city, and plundered every house . . . they sought for the high priests, and the generality went with the greatest zeal against them; and as soon as they caught them they slew them. . . . Nay, they proceeded to that degree of impiety, as to cast away their bodies without burial, although the Jews used to take so much care of the burial of men, that they took down those that were condemned and crucified, and buried them before the going down of the sun. I should not mistake if I said that the death of Ananus was the beginning of the destruction of the city, and that from this very day may be dated the overthrow of her wall, and the ruin of her affairs, whereon they saw their high priest, and the procurer of their preservation slain in the midst of the city.

Extract from the *JEWISH ENCYCLOPÆDIA* (1925 Edition), article 'Edom'

. . . Judas Maccabeus conquered their territory for a time (B.C. 163; *Ant.* xii. 8, §§1, 6). They were again subdued by John Hyrcanus (*c.* 125 B.C.), by whom they were forced to observe Jewish rites and laws (*ib.* xiii. 9, §1; xiv. 4, §4). They were then incorporated with the Jewish nation, and their country was called by the Greeks and Romans "Idumea" (Mark iii. 8; Ptolemy, *Geography* v. 16). With Antipater began the Idumean dynasty that ruled over Judea till its conquest by the Romans. Immediately before the siege of Jerusalem 20,000 Idumeans, under the leadership of John, Simeon, Phinehas, and Jacob, appeared before Jerusalem to fight in behalf of the Zealots who were besieged in the Temple (Josephus, *B.J.* iv. 4, §5).

From this time the Idumeans ceased to be a separate people, . . .

HEINRICH EWALD: Extract from his *THE HISTORY OF ISRAEL*, English translation by J. E. Carpenter, M.A. (Longmans, Green & Co., London, 1874); Vol. V, pp. 80-82

. . . the Idumeans . . . were Israel's most bitter foes . . . we actually find them in possession of important portions of the ancient territory of Judah and Israel even so late as in the times of the Maccabees; and we shall see more clearly hereafter how hotly the doubtful contest for these districts was maintained between the Idumeans and Israel, even in these later times. They were then in possession of the whole of the southern part of the old kingdom of Judah, with the ancient capital of Hebron, up to the former territory of the Philistines to the west; but even further northeast of Jerusalem, between Jericho and the territory of the inhabitants of Samaria, now very much contracted, they occupied a tract of land extending to the Jordan, with Acrabat as its capital. . . . These old hereditary foes of Israel were still occupying that portion of the territory of which they had taken possession when Cyrus sanctioned the return, and, as far as we can tell, this monarch was by no means prepared to expel the Idumeans from the lands they had occupied and cultivated for fifty or sixty years. . . . Later on, towards the time of Nehemiah, they must have succeeded already in gaining a firm footing in Hebron, for example, and in other places to the south . . .

Extract from *EARLY ISRAEL*, by A. H. SAYCE, D.Litt., D.D., LL.D. (Service & Paton, London, 1899), p. 95

Kenaz was a grandson of Esau, and the fact that the Kenizzites shared with the Israelitish tribes in the conquest of Canaan throws light on the law of Deuteronomy which gave the Edomite of "the third generation" all the rights and privileges of a Jew. Caleb, the conqueror of Hebron, was a Kenizzite; so also was Othniel, the first of the Judges of Israel. Edomites, rather than Hebrews, were the founders of the future Judah.

Authorities: Various

The Origin of the Jewish Peoples

There is an unaccountable lack of knowledge on this subject and particularly so, having regard to the fact that the information available from instructed Jewish sources gives guidance in the clearest possible terms.

It seems to be quite taken for granted that all Jewish people are Israelites and that there are no Israelites in the world except the Jews. In point of fact, something very different is the case. The highest Jewish authorities proclaim that their community includes considerable elements of many non-Hebrew races and further, that the Jews who are descended from Israel derive from the tribes of Judah, Benjamin and Levi.

There are infusions of almost every race; white, brown, yellow and even black, for the Jews have been the most zealous of proselytisers, bringing into their fold large numbers of non-Israelites. For instance, in the 7th-8th centuries A.D., a large portion of the great Chazar kingdom, of south Russia, became proselytised to Judaism when that faith was accepted by the *chaghan* and his court.

Even before the Christian era, the Jewish nation in Palestine had received and incorporated a large infusion of Hittite-Edomite and other Canaanite stock. By the time of our Lord the first-named section (the Idumeans) had achieved the prominence in national affairs which culminated in the rise to power of the Edomite Herods. This admixture ultimately proved disastrous to the sorely split nation, the enmity to the Israelite Jews being maintained even during the final, terrible siege of Jerusalem.

By no means all modern Jews profess the orthodox rabbinical religion, for some have adopted a strongly *modernist* creed, whilst others are avowed atheists.

It is a fundamental mistake, therefore, to consider Jewry as homogeneous, either from a racial, religious, or even a cultural standpoint. There is abundant evidence to refute such an error.

Correct Use of the Term 'Jew'

The term 'Jew' (an abbreviation of *Judah*) is used very loosely and inaccurately in these days. To most people the words *Jew* and *Israelite* are synonymous, though this idea is manifestly absurd. Londoners are Britishers, but all British people are not Londoners. The highest authority has stated that those Jews who are of the Israelite race are descended almost entirely from the tribes of Judah and Benjamin. The rest of the tribes could not by any distortion be correctly termed Jews (*vide* Ser. No. 7 [572.933])

In Old Testament times only those remnants (and their descendants) of the tribes of Judah and Benjamin who had experienced the Babylonian exile were called Jews. Josephus is perfectly clear on this: "So the Jews prepared for the work: that is the name they are called by from the day that they came up from Babylon . . . and thence both they and the country gained that appellation" (Ant. xi., v. 7) (*vide* Ser. No. 17 [572.933])

The name Jew is used once only in the Old Testament with reference to the period preceding the expulsion of the Ten Tribes. This is in II Kings xvi. 6, and it is obviously a parenthetical passage added at a later time, as shown by the use of the words "unto this day". Moffatt uses the word 'Judahites'. The word is used also in reference to several other pre-Exilic occasions; in II Kings xxv. 25, II Chron. xxxii. 18, and in the record of Jeremiah. It seems plain, however, that the use of the term in these instances is due to a post-exilic compilation of records, when the name was in current usage.

The *Jewish Encyclopedia* clinches the matter with the words: "In the Old Testament the term 'Jew' appears to be applied to adherents of the worship of YHWH as conducted at Jerusalem after the Exile . . ."

The modern use is much wider in that it includes not only the descendants of the original Jews, but also great numbers of people, of many races, who have sprung from proselytes made by the Jews during the last 2,500 years. Many of the people now known as Jews are of non-Hebrew extraction.

The Kingdom of Judah

The Jewish nation derived from the kingdom of Judah. It is necessary, therefore, to consider briefly the history of this Two-tribed kingdom. After the death of Solomon, the Ten Tribes under Jeroboam broke away from the house of David (970 B.C.). The tribes of Judah and Benjamin remained loyal to Rehoboam and thenceforward constituted the southern Kingdom of Judah, with Jerusalem as the capital city. Whilst the northern kingdom fell away immediately into paganism, the Judahites maintained the worship of Jehovah in a greater or lesser degree according to the character of the reigning monarch. Faithful fragments of the Ten Tribes went over to the Judah kingdom during the reigns of the more righteous of its kings (Asa and Hezekiah in particular), rather than submit to idolatry.

The kingdom commenced to decline during the period of the evil monarch Ahaz (c. 735 B.C.) when Rezin, king of Syria, carried away "a great multitude of people". At the same time Ahaz lost a battle with the Ten Tribes in which 120,000 Judahites were slain in one day. Twenty-five years later, in the reign of Hezekiah, Sennacherib, king of Assyria, invaded, capturing all the chief towns (except Jerusalem) and deporting 200,000 people to Assyria. He handed the towns over to various Philistine petty kings. Hezekiah was left with only a remnant in his city of Jerusalem. There was a minor restoration of the nation under Josiah, but a hundred years later Nebuchadnezzar of Babylon commenced the final destruction of what remained. During the period 604-584 B.C. he removed the last residue and reduced Jerusalem to rubble.

Serial No. 56a.

Judea and Jerusalem were totally depopulated of Judahites. According to Josephus the country was left 'a desert'—in sharp contrast with the territory of the northern Ten Tribes, which had been resettled with aliens (*Ant.* X, ix. 7) (Ser. No. 24 [222.5]).

The people of the Two-tribed kingdom are correctly styled *Judahites*. They were not called Jews at that period.

The Judahite Deportations

There were thus three main deportations of the kingdom of Judah:

(1) c. 735 B.C. The Syrians took a large number of prisoners to the Damascus area. They did not remain there long, however, for several years later Tiglath-Pileser of Assyria appears to have removed them along with their Syrian captors to Kir (i.e. Upper Media, according to Josephus—*Ant.* IX, xii. 3). The Damascus territory was then resettled with people from Assyria (Ser. No. 32 [572.935]).

(2) c. 710 B.C. Probably the bulk of the Judahites, except those who found sanctuary in Jerusalem, were carried away to Assyria by Sennacherib.

(3) 604-584 B.C. Except for a small party that fled to Egypt, Nebuchadnezzar removed what was left of Judah to Babylon.

With regard to the first two deportations it may be mentioned that these captives were taken without their religious leaders and they would doubtless tend to fall away from the worship of Jehovah and to adopt the worship of the surrounding peoples, which included Israelites of the Ten Tribes. Nevertheless, there were Judahites who had remained loyal to the faith in Media at the time of the Return. Josephus calls them 'Jews' and distinguishes between them and the 'people of Israel' (*Ant.* XI, v. 2) (Ser. No. 18 [572.93951]).

The Return from Babylon

In 536 B.C., under the decree of Cyrus, king of Persia, a small remnant of the Judah kingdom returned to the tribal territories of Judah and Benjamin. Jerusalem was rebuilt and the Temple worship recommenced.

From the Books of Ezra and Nehemiah, and from the testimony of Josephus, there is accurate information as to the people who returned (Ser. No. 35 [222.7]). Of the 'congregation' of 42,360 there were only 652 Israelites who could not "shew their father's house". (Doubtless many of these were descended from the fragments of the Ten Tribes who had gone over to the Judah kingdom.) All the remainder were accounted for as being definitely of the tribes of Judah, Benjamin and Levi.

Those Who Did Not Return

It should be noted that the majority of the descendants of the exiles from the kingdom of Judah never returned from the Babylonian captivity. The Book of Esther mentions a large Judahite population scattered throughout the Persian empire, which then extended from the Ægean to India. Their number may be appreciated by reference to the record that they slew 75,000 of their detractors (Esther ix. 16). Josephus confirms the Bible record to the effect that many of the exiles did not return (*Ant.* XI, i. 2-3, and iii. 10).

There is a wealth of evidence to show that, due to the toleration often shown by the Babylonian and Persian monarchs, many of the people of Judah kept to the worship of Jehovah and that they formed religious communities wherever they settled. These are correctly termed 'Jews'. They looked to Jerusalem as the focus of their faith. It was from these communities that the devout Jews "from every nation under heaven" were subsequently drawn to Jerusalem, to hear Peter's stirring message, in which he asked them to act as missionaries of the new Gospel to "all the house of Israel" in the distant lands from which they had travelled (Acts ii. 36).

Thus it will be seen that the descendants of the Jews who did not return to Palestine formed God's point of contact with the Israelites of the Ten Tribes, also residing mainly in the provinces of the enlarged Persian empire, much of which ultimately became known as Scythia (i.e. both in Europe and Asia).

The Nation of the Jews—A Brief History

B.C. 536-A.D. 70

With the Return from Babylonia of the remnant of the Judahite kingdom, there commenced the six centuries' period of Jewish nationhood. After the decree of Cyrus, in 536 B.C., the Jews began the work of rebuilding the Temple. They were almost immediately hindered by the Samaritans, who demanded a share of the task, in view of the fact that they, too, now worshipped the God of Israel, a demand which was scornfully rejected by the Jews (Ezra iv. 3). However, Samaritan intrigues brought the work to a standstill, until some years later king Darius renewed the permission. Though the Temple was rebuilt, the wall and city of Jerusalem remained unrestored until the plea of Nehemiah produced a further permit for this express purpose, from Artaxerxes. The identity of this monarch has not been agreed upon. It has long been thought that the Bible reference in Nehemiah II is to Artaxerxes Longimanus, whose "twentieth year" (the date of the decree) fell in 445 B.C. Cogent reasons have been advanced, however, to suggest that he was not the monarch referred to and that the Artaxerxes (great shah) of Nehemiah may more likely have been Darius Hystaspes, who reigned 521-485 B.C.

From that time forward, the tiny Jewish nation was involved in endless vicissitudes. Following the fall of Persia, it became a bone of contention between the great powers of Syria and Egypt, the tide of war surging backwards and forwards for well over a century. After the death of Alexander the Great, Seleucus having appropriated the Syrian portion of the empire, Ptolemy I eventually withdrew his armies from Palestine and took with him 30,000 Jews to garrison his Egyptian frontier. Syrian supremacy was finally established in 198 B.C. by Antiochus the Great. In 168 B.C. Antiochus Epiphanes seized the opportunity to intervene in a small Jewish civil war concerning the high-priesthood. He perpetrated abominable outrages, the foremost of which was the sacrificing of a sow on the Temple altar. The Jewish religion was forbidden. This, and the general severity of the Syrian oppression culminated in the Maccabean rising. After years of struggle Simon Maccabeus established Jewish independence for a brief period. Further Syrian aggression brought relief by John Hyrcanus, who again threw off the Syrian yoke and also subdued the Edomites—traditional enemies of all Israelites—and compelled them to profess the Jewish religion, and to become incorporated in the Jewish nation (130 B.C.). During the reign of Hyrcanus the cleavage between Pharisees and Sadducees developed and became acute.

Uneasy times followed until 65 B.C. when civil war again broke out over the high-priesthood. Both sides appealed to Rome. Pompey, then ruling in Syria, entered Jerusalem without bloodshed and the land became part of the Roman Empire. Even under the Romans civil wars were frequent.

Serial No. 56b.

Then followed the period of the Herods. In 47 B.C. Antipater was made procurator of Judaea by the Romans; a rival king was set up by the Parthians, who had plundered the Holy City, but he was soon overthrown and Antipater's son, Herod the Great, became ruler in 37 B.C. During his reign the city and Temple were rebuilt (20 B.C.) and our Lord was born.

Herod's son Archelaus succeeded, but was banished in A.D. 7; his brother, Herod Antipas, to whom Jesus referred as 'that fox', succeeded him in turn.

For a few brief years the new faith of Jesus Christ and His followers agitated the scene. The Jewish resentment of Roman domination mounted and resulted in the terrible siege and destruction of Jerusalem by Titus in A.D. 70, when almost the whole of what remained of the Jewish nation was expelled and dispersed, chiefly as slaves.

Though the Jewish nation had ceased to exist, there was a final flicker of revolt in A.D. 135, when a false messiah, Bar Cochab, collected a following and raised a rebellion. This was crushed, and the last vestiges of Jewry were driven from Palestine.

The Diaspora

The *Diaspora*, or Dispersion, of the Jews was an amazing phenomenon. During the centuries following Nebuchadnezzar's destruction of Jerusalem there developed Jewish communities, still adhering to the worship of Jehovah, in every quarter of the then-known world. Religious zeal held these communities together. They were reinforced by frequent 'waves' of exiles, some forced, some voluntary, emanating from the Holy Land. The most important of the Dispersion were:

(1) The exiles of the Babylonian captivity who did not return with Ezra and Nehemiah. Large numbers of these moved rapidly into every part of the vast Persian empire (Esther viii).

There is evidence to show that Jews driven out by Nebuchadnezzar had also settled in Spain (*vide* Ser. No. 30 [572.94601]), in Georgia and Armenia. Long before the time of Christ their descendants had established organised Hellenised communities, with synagogues, in the Balkans and along the northern shores of the Black Sea (*vide* Coon's *Races of Europe*, pp. 437-8).

(2) Ptolemy I took 30,000 Jews with him when he abandoned Palestine. Jews also flocked to Egypt and North Africa under the succeeding Ptolemies. According to Ewald (Vol. V, p. 240) two-fifths of the population of the great city of Alexandria were, at one period, Jews. The Greek version of the Old Testament (Septuagint) was translated from the Hebrew (c. 285 B.C.) for the benefit of these.

(3) During the wars of the third and second centuries B.C. thousands of Jewish prisoners were made slaves and transported.

(4) Following the destruction of Jerusalem in A.D. 70 and the final rebellion of Bar Cochab in A.D. 135 the Holy Land was completely cleared of its Jewish inhabitants. These were scattered, chiefly as slaves, throughout the countries of Roman Europe: Italy, Spain, Gaul, etc.

The Jews in Palestine were, of course, well aware of the fact that there were Jewish communities all over the then-known world. They asked ". . . will He (Christ) go unto the dispersed among the Gentiles . . . ?" (John vii. 35).

In accordance with his pronouncement "to the Jew first", St. Paul invariably made for the Jewish community when visiting a foreign city.

The general movement of the Jewish people was inevitably westwards. Those in eastern lands finally found themselves, with their countless proselytes, settled mainly in the countries of eastern Europe; western Russia, Poland and eastern Germany absorbing by far the greater proportion.

Between about 1890 and the present day there has been a further westerly movement. Upwards of 3,000,000 have found homes in the Anglo-Saxon countries, particularly in the U.S.A.

Proselytes to Judaism

Following the inception of the nation in 536 B.C., the Jews became the most zealous of proselytisers and, for more than a millennium, they continued to convert individuals, communities and even nations to Judaism. The converts—and their descendants—became Jews. Jesus Christ remarked upon this trait: "Ye compass sea and land to make one proselyte . . ." (Matt. xxiii. 15). There were proselytes present at Pentecost, drawn from every country to which the Jews had been dispersed, from the Ægean to India. Doubtless many of these would be Israelites of the Ten Tribes, some of whom still resided in this same vast territory.

Whole nations became Jews by proselytism; sometimes forcibly. The Idumeans were compelled by John Hyrcanus to become Jews. The Itureans, whose kingdom lay to the north of Galilee, were also incorporated into Jewry by force (see Ser. No. 40 [572.933]).

About A.D. 700 the Chazars, a nation of Turkish origin, who had established themselves in south Russia in the preceding centuries, became Jews when Judaism was made the state religion by the chaghan and his court. This Chazar empire flourished for almost 500 years, finally becoming merged in the empire of Russia.

The Jewish faith was carried also to the coloured peoples. Their descendants to-day are to be found among the black Falashas of Ethiopia, the Moors of North Africa. the Tamils in India, and even among the Chinese.

The Alien Infusions into Jewry

It is well known that the Jews are not—and do not claim to be—a people of one race. In the opinion of Professors Huxley, Haddon and Carr-Saunders:

"... The Jews can rank neither as a nation nor even as an ethnic unit, but rather as a socio-religious group carrying large Mediterranean, Armenoid, and many other elements, and varying greatly in physical characters . . ."

"The so-called 'Jewish' nose is really Armenoid . . ." (We Europeans, pp. 152, 103).

Professor Sayce, in his Races of the Old Testament (pp. 114-5), confirms this:

"... The Jewish race is by no means a pure one. It has admitted proselytes from various nations, and at different periods in its career has intermarried with other races . . ."

Professor Ripley, in his Races of Europe, says:

"The Jews are not a race but only a people after all."

Dean Inge, in an article in the Evening Standard, dated 26th January 1939, also voiced this view. He said:

"It is clear that the Jews have taken the physical characteristics of the nations among whom they live. In other words, they have not kept their blood unmixed."

Serial No. 56c.

The Non-Israelite Infusions commenced even at the very outset of the entry into Canaan, when the tribes of Judah and Benjamin failed to drive out the Jebusite inhabitants of Jerusalem and the surrounding territory. At the time of the Return from Babylon, Ezra complained bitterly that the Jews had married outside their race. The 'strange wives' were duly 'put away', but there can be no doubt that the children of these unions would remain. It may be said that these early and comparatively small infusions could easily be absorbed in the main stock without any discernible effect, but the same cannot be said of the greater infusions of alien race, namely:

(1) At the time of Esther, when the Jews in the Persian empire achieved prominence, "... many of the people of the land became Jews; for the fear of the Jews fell upon them" (Esther viii. 17).

(2) The incorporation of the Edomite nation, in its entirety, by John Hyrcanus. It will be recalled that the Edomites held a strong Hittite strain (*vide* Ser. No. 40 [572.933]).

(3) The absorption of the Itureans.

(4) The introduction of proselytes of every nationality during the centuries immediately before and immediately following the time of Christ.

(5) The conversion to Judaism of the Chazar nation.

The sum-total effect of these vast-scale accretions to Jewry must indubitably have been to reduce the true Israelite element very considerably.

The Ashkenazim and the Sephardim

Modern Jewry is divided into two main divisions.

The ASHKENAZIM section is by far the greater. Reliable authorities have computed that not less than 90 per cent of all Jews are of the Ashkenazim. R. B. Dixon, Professor of Anthropology at Harvard University, states:

"The vast majority of European Jews and of those who have migrated thence to America and elsewhere belong to the Ashkenazim . . . they are predominantly . . . brachycephalic . . ." (*Racial History of Man*, p. 165).

Gunther, in his *Racial Elements of European History*, estimates that the Ashkenazim form nine-tenths of the Jewish world community (p. 75) which, prior to the terrible Hitler persecutions, numbered about sixteen million. Practically the whole of the Jews of eastern Europe are Ashkenazim.

The SEPHARDIM or 'Spanish' Jews, who now constitute only about 10 per cent of Jewry, claim to derive from ancestors who settled in the Peninsula and in North Africa as early as the period of Nebuchadnezzar's destruction of Jerusalem. They did not, as did the Ashkenazim, migrate through the centuries by the 'European' route. Racially they are much less mixed than the Ashkenazim or 'European' Jews, although their dispersion following the Spanish persecutions in the fifteenth century resulted in a certain amount of intermingling with the Ashkenazim and with other European and North African peoples.

Professor Dixon considers that the present Sephardic Jews of Constantinople and Jerusalem most faithfully portray the characteristics of the original stock which—he says —was 'predominantly dolichocephalic' (i.e. longheaded).

The Sephardim are further discussed in Ser. No. 30 [572.94601]).

The Language of Modern Jewry

The ancient Hebrew language commenced to fall into disuse after the expulsion of the Judahites by Nebuchadnezzar. After the Return from Babylon it began to give place to Aramaic. Although Hebrew was retained amongst the intelligentsia, even until the final dispersion, the common tongue of the Jewish people was Aramaic. At a distance from Jerusalem it was used almost exclusively (*vide* Ewald's *History of Israel*, pp. 180,181).

Jews of to-day use the language of the country in which they dwell, Hebrew being still retained for religious purposes.

Yiddish is also used. This is a jargon of several eastern European languages as developed late in the Middle Ages. It is written in Hebrew characters and it incorporates only a few elements of that ancient language, to which it otherwise bears little or no resemblance.

The Religious Position

As in the time of Christ, modern Jewry is by no means unanimous on the subject of religious faith. Though there is now no bitter strife, as with Pharisees and Sadducees, there is great diversity.

Orthodox, rabbinical Jewry still holds to the oracles of God as expressed in the Old Testament and interpreted by Talmudic and other writings. In the words of the late Chief Rabbi Hertz, orthodox Jews "look forward to the gathering of all the tribes at some future day".

The Jews still have their 'Sadducees', however. As far back as 1885 a very 'modernistic' note had been struck when, at a Pittsburg Conference, the Reform Wing of the Jewish Synagogue stated:

"We consider ourselves no longer a nation, but a religious community only; and we therefore expect neither a return to Palestine, nor a sacrificial worship under the sons of Aaron, nor the restoration of any of the laws concerning a Jewish State" (*Jewish Encyclopedia*, article: "Zionism").

Finally there is that small minority of Jews which is avowedly irreligious, unless the creed of Marxism be regarded as a religion; for the originators and leaders of Communism seem to have been drawn from the ranks of atheistic Jews. Their hatred of all forms of worship brings vividly to mind the bitter denunciation of Jesus Christ, who stigmatised a section of the Jewish leaders of His day as the brood of the serpent ("generation of vipers"). He held their kind guilty of all the righteous blood shed upon the earth since the murder of Abel (Matthew xxiii). Our Lord could only have been alluding to a continuing strain, for those to whom He was speaking could not have been personally responsible for earlier crimes. Is it possible that the evil line of Canaan introduced into Jewry by the Edomite descendants of Heth is to-day represented by the apostles of atheistic Marxism? The Risen Lord, in His message through St. John (Revelation ii) warns against the Synagogue of Satan "which say they are Jews and are not".

Our Debt to the Jews

Christians should never forget the debt which the world owes to the Jews. When the Ten Tribes deserted the worship of Jehovah, Judah remained loyal. As soon as they were able, devout elements of the deported nation of Judah left comfortable places in Babylonia to return to a devastated Jerusalem to make a fresh start under the laws of God and to build the Jewish nation. For centuries this nation battled against odds, with strife from within and without. But the oracles of God were preserved and handed on.

Though the strain of Canaan, in the person of the Jewish leaders of the day, persecuted and finally executed Israel's Redeemer, there were at the same time splendid Jews, Israelites indeed, who lived and died for the "Faith once delivered to the saints"—the first missionaries of the Gospel of Christ.

Serial No. 56d.

EXTRACTS FROM *THE JEWISH ENCYCLOPEDIA*, 3rd edition, 1925.

Article: Jew (The Word)

JEW (The Word): Up to the seventeenth century this word was spelled in Middle English in various ways: 'Gyu', 'Giu', 'Gyw', 'Iu', 'Iuu', 'Iuw', 'Ieu', 'Ieuu', 'Ieuz', 'Iwe', 'Iow', 'Iewe', 'Ieue', 'Iue' ('Ive'), 'Iew', 'Jew'. All these forms were derived from the Old French 'Giu', which was earlier written 'Juieu', derived from the Latin accusative 'Judaeum' with the elision of the letter 'd'. The Latin form 'Judaeus' was derived from the Greek 'Ιουδαῖος and this in turn from the Aramaic יהודאי, corresponding to the Hebrew יהודי, a gentilic adjective from the proper name 'Judah', seemingly never applied to members of the tribe, however, but to members of the nationality inhabiting the south of Palestine . . .

In the Old Testament the term 'Jew' appears to be applied to adherents of the worship of YHWH as conducted at Jerusalem after the Exile: it is thus used in the late Book of Esther . . .

Article: Diaspora

. . . When Ptolemy I evacuated Syria many of the Jews voluntarily followed him to his kingdom (Hecataeus, of Abdera, 14, cited by Josephus, *Contra Ap.* i. 22; *idem Ant.* xii. 1). A similar thing occurred in 198 (Jerome, *Ad Dan.* xi. 708); and under Ptolemy VI, Philometor, the son of the high priest Onias, disappointed in his expectations, betook himself with a considerable number of followers to Egypt, and there set up a rival temple to that of Jerusalem (*Ant.* xiii. 3). On the other hand, during the wars of the third and second centuries B.C., thousands of Jews were made captives and reduced to slavery, passing from owner to owner and from land to land until their enfranchisement. This enfranchisement indeed usually occurred very soon, it being precipitated by the fact that, through their unswerving attachment to their customs, they proved inefficient servants. Besides, owing to the close solidarity which is one of the lasting traits of the Jewish race, they had no difficulty in finding coreligionists who were willing to pay the amount of their ransom. The inscriptions of Delphi have preserved an instance of these enfranchisements of Jewish slaves by payment of money (Collitz, *Griech. Dialektinschr.* ii. 2,029; the amount paid was 4 minas, or about $80). The celebrated rhetorician Cecilius of Calacte was originally a Jewish slave (Suidas, *s.v.*); he was confounded by Plutarch with the questor of Verres, Cecilius Niger, who was perhaps his patron.

The Jews thus freed, instead of returning to Palestine, usually remained in the land of their former slavery, and there, in conjunction with their brethren in faith, established communities. According to the formal testimony of Philo (*Legatio ad*

Caium, § 23), the Jewish community in Rome owed its origin to released prisoners of war. The political importance which it had already acquired in the proceedings against Flaccus (59 B.C.) shows that it did not consist merely of a few captives brought by Pompey (63 B.C.), but rather of prisoners made in earlier wars—in Asia Minor, for instance. The great Jewish insurrections under Vespasian, Trajan and Hadrian, terminating, as they did, so disastrously, threw upon the market myriads of Jewish captives. Transported to the west, they became the nuclei of communities in Italy, Spain, Gaul, etc. Among these captives was the historian of the Jewish people, Flavius Josephus. Under Domitian the Jewish slaves in Rome were sold at very low prices. Even the poet Martial, whose purse was never well filled, possessed one (*Epig.* vii. 35; the interpretation, however, is uncertain). The names of many Jews found in the tumulary inscriptions in Rome betray their servile origin. To these sales of prisoners of war must be added, as further sources of the Diaspora, the deportations, more or less voluntary, effected by the various governments, either to chastise the rebels or to populate the uninhabited parts of their territories. Not to mention the great Babylonian exile, and the transportation of Jews to Hyrcania by Ochus (*Syncellus* i. 486; *Orosius* iii. 7), Ptolemy I, according to tradition, took with him to Egypt 30,000 (?) Jews in order to garrison the frontiers (*Pseudo-Aristaeus*, ed. Schmidt, p. 255; *Ant.* xii. 1). The same king compelled Jews to settle in Cyrenaica (*Contra Ap.* ii. 4). Antiochus the Great, it is said, transferred to the sparsely populated districts of Phrygia and Lydia 2,000 Jewish families drawn from Mesopotamia (*Ant.* xii. 3, 4). Tiberius sent 4,000 Jews of Rome to wage a war in Sardinia (Tacitus, *Annales* ii. 85), many of whom perished, while the survivors must have formed the nucleus of a Jewish community in that country. Many rulers, without resorting to violent measures, made successful efforts to attract Jewish colonists to the newly founded cities by conceding to them important privileges. Such was the policy, if not of Alexander, at any rate of Seleucus Nicator, Ptolemy Philadelphus, the successors of Antiochus Epiphanes (in Antioch) . . .

Besides, owing to the barrier which their deeply rooted religious observances formed around them, the Jews never became absorbed in the surrounding populations. On the contrary, an active religious propaganda, to be treated more fully later on, caused each small group of Jewish families to become the center around which numerous proselytes of other races clustered. Many of these adherents afterward fully embraced the Jewish faith. It may be said that if proselytism was not the conscious design of the Diaspora, it at all events powerfully contributed towards its consolidation and expansion. Thus, as early as the middle of the second century

B.C. the Jewish author of the third book of the *Oracula Sibyllina*, addressing the "chosen people", says: "Every land is full of thee and every sea" (*Sibyllines* iii. 271; compare I Macc. 15); and if these words contained some exaggeration, the prophecy became true in the subsequent century. The most diverse witnesses, such as Strabo, Philo, Seneca, the author of the Acts of the Apostles, and Josephus, all bear testimony to the fact that the Jewish race was disseminated over the whole civilized world (Strabo, frag. 6, cited by Josephus, *Ant.* xiv. 7, 2; Philo, *In Flaccum*, 7; Seneca, frag. 41-43, in Augustine, *Civ Dei* vi. 10; Acts ii. 9-11; Josephus, *B.J.* ii. 16, § 4; vii. 3, § 3). King Agrippa, in a letter to Caligula, enumerates among the provinces of the Jewish Diaspora almost all the Hellenized and non-Hellenized countries of the Orient (Philo, *Legatio and Caium*, § 36); and this enumeration is far from being complete, as Italy and Cyrene are not included. The epigraphic discoveries from year to year augment the number of known Jewish communities.

The following table, which is doubtless incomplete, attempts to summarize modern knowledge concerning the geography of the Diaspora, according to the literary texts and the inscriptions . . .

This gradual entrance into the fold of Judaism must have been a frequent occurrence in the first and second centuries. Juvenal refers to it in his famous words: "*Quidam sortiti metuentem sabbata patrem. Nil præter nubes et caeli numen adorant*", etc. (*Sat.* xiv. 96 *et seq.*; compare *Persius* v. 179; Tertullian, *Ad. Nat.* i. 13). The term 'metuens' itself is technical, being a translation of the Greek . . . by which the Greek texts usually designate the proselytes (Acts xiii. 16, 26, 43; xvii. 4; *Ant.* xiv. 7, § 2; compare *Eph. Epigr.* iv., No. 838, and Schurer, *Juden im Bosporischen Reiche*, p. 20) . . .

It can not be doubted that Judaism in this way made numerous converts during two or three centuries; but the statements of Josephus, Philo, and even of Seneca, who represent the whole world as rushing toward Jewish observances, must be regarded as fanciful exaggerations (*Contra Ap.* ii. 39; Seneca, in *Aug. Civ. Dei* vi. 11; Philo, *De Vita Moysis*, § 2 [ed. *Mangey* ii. 137]). At the same time, it is an indisputable fact that proselytes were found in large numbers in every country of the Diaspora. The pagan authors, struck by this phenomenon, carefully distinguish the Jews by race from the Jews by adoption (Suetonius, *Tib.* 36: "*gentis eiusdem vel simila sectantes*"; *Dio Cassius* xxxvii. 17) . . .

Article: Bosporus

A quite recent discovery of Jewish Greek inscriptions was announced Jan. 12, 1901, to the Imperial Russian Geographical Society. A young explorer, A. L. Pogodin, discovered and deciphered new inscriptions in Kertch and other places in South Russia, from which it is clearly evident that Jews settled in the Bosporus as early as the fourth century B.C., and were an important section of the Greek colony. They had their cemeteries, synagogues, and other communal institutions. In trade as well as in social life they mingled freely with the Greeks, as is evidenced by the fact that the language of the inscriptions is Greek. Other inscriptions show that, in the first century B.C., the Jews founded in the Bosporus a colony of their own. In the inscriptions of the third century of the common era Jewish religious symbols and sepulchral inscriptions are found. In the same century the Jews even took part in religious persecutions (*Budushchnost*, 1901, No. 3, p. 46).

Article: Russia

. . . Armenian and Georgian historians record that after the destruction of the First Temple . . . Nebuchadnezzar deported numbers of Jewish captives to Armenia and the Caucasus. These exiles were joined later by co-religionists from Medea and Judea . . . at the end of the fourth century there were Armenian cities possessing Jewish populations ranging from 10,000 to 30,000 . . .

Jews had lived in Georgia also since the destruction of the First Temple . . . after the capture of Jerusalem by Vespasian (70 C.E.) other Jewish exiles joined their co-religionists in Mzchet . . .

Monuments consisting of marble slabs bearing Greek inscriptions and preserved in the Hermitage, St. Petersburg, and in the museum at Feodosia (Kaffa), show that Jews lived in the Crimea and along the entire eastern coast of the Black Sea at the beginning of the common era, and that they possessed well-organised communities with synagogues. They were then already Hellenized, bearing such Greek names as Hermis, Dionisiodorus, and Heracles. In the reign of Julius the Isaurian (175-210) the name 'Volamiros' was common among the Jews of the Crimea. This was the origin of the Russian name 'Vladimir' . . .

Jews from the Crimea moved eastward and northward and became the founders of Jewish communities along the shores of the Caspian Sea and of the lower Volga . . . carrying with them a civilization more advanced than that of the native tribes among which they settled . . . After the overthrow of the Chazarian kingdom by Swyatoslaw (969), Jews in large numbers fled to the Crimea, the Caucasus, and the Russian principality of Kiev, formerly a part of the Chazar territory . . .

Article: Chazars

CHAZARS: a people of Turkish origin whose life and history are interwoven with the very beginnings of the history of the Jews of Russia. The kingdom of the Chazars was firmly established in most of

South Russia long before the foundation of the Russian monarchy by the Varangians (855). Jews have lived on the shores of the Black and Caspian seas since the first centuries of the common era. Historical evidence points to the region of the Ural as the home of the Chazars. Among the classical writers of the Middle Ages they were known as the 'Chozars', 'Khazirs', 'Akatzirs', and 'Akatirs', and in the Russian chronicles as 'Khwalisses and 'Ugry Byelyye'.

The Armenian writers of the fifth and following centuries furnish ample information concerning this people. Moses of Chorene refers to the invasion by the 'Khazirs' of Armenia and Iberia at the beginning of the third century: "The chaghan was the king of the North, the ruler of the Khazirs, and the queen was the chatoun" (*History of Armenia*, ii. 357). The Chazars first came to Armenia with the Basileans in 198. Though at first repulsed, they subsequently became important factors in Armenian history for a period of 800 years. Driven onward by the nomadic tribes of the steppes and by their own desire for plunder and revenge, they made frequent invasions into Armenia. The latter country was made the battle-ground in the long struggle between the Romans and the Persians. This struggle, which finally resulted in the loss by Armenia of her independence, paved the way for the political importance of the Chazars. The conquest of eastern Armenia by the Persians in the fourth century rendered the latter dangerous to the Chazars who, for their own protection, formed an alliance with the Byzantines. This alliance was renewed from time to time until the final conquest of the Chazars by the Russians. Their first aid was rendered to the Byzantine emperor Julian in 363. About 434 they were for a time tributary to Attila—Sidonius Apollinaris relates that the Chazars followed the banners of Attila—and in 452 fought on the Catalanian fields in company with the Black Huns and Alans. The Persian king Kobad (488-531) undertook the construction of a line of forts through the pass between Derbent and the Caucasus, in order to guard against the invasion of the Chazars, Turks, and other warlike tribes. His son Chosroes Anoshirvan (531-579) built the wall of Derbent, repeatedly mentioned by the Oriental geographers and historians as Bab al-Abwab (Justi, *Gesch. des Alten Persiens*, p. 208).

In the second half of the sixth century the Chazars moved westward. They established themselves in the territory bounded by the Sea of Azov, the Don and the lower Volga, the Caspian Sea, and the northern Caucasus. The Caucasian Goths (Tetraxites) were subjugated by the Chazars, probably about the seventh century (Lowe, *Dia Reste der Germanen am Schwarzen Meere*, p. 72, Halle, 1896). Early in that century the kingdom of the Chazars had become powerful enough to enable the chaghan to send to the Byzantine emperor Heraclius an army of 40,000 men, by whose aid he conquered the Persians (626-627). The Chazars had already occupied the north-eastern part of the Black Sea region. According to the historian Moses Kalonkataci, the Chazars, under their leader Jebu Chaghan (called 'Ziebel Chaghan' by the Greek writers) penetrated into Persian territory as early as the second campaign of Heraclius, on which occasion they devastated Albania (*Die Persischen Feldzuge des Kaisers Herakleios*, in *Byzantinische Zeitschrift*, iii. 364). Nicephorus testifies that Heraclius repeatedly showed marks of esteem to his ally, the chaghan of the Chazars, to whom he even promised his daughter in marriage. In the great battle between the Chazars and the Arabs near Kizliar, 4,000 Mohammedan soldiers and their leader were slain.

In the year 669 the Ugrians or Zabirs freed themselves from the rule of the Obrians, settled between the Don and the Caucasus, and came under the dominion of the Chazars. For this reason the Ugrians, who had hitherto been called the 'White' or 'Independent' Ugrians, are described in the chronicles ascribed to Nestor as the 'Black', or 'Dependent', Ugrians. They were no longer governed by their own princes, but were ruled by the kings of the Chazars. In 735, when the Arab leader Mervan moved from Georgia against the Chazars, he attacked the Ugrians also. In 679 the Chazars subjugated the Bulgars and extended their sway farther west between the Don and the Dnieper, as far as the head-waters of the Donetz in the province of Lebedia (K. Grot, *Moravia i Madyary*, St. Petersburg, 1881; J. Danilevski and K. Grot, *O Puti Madyars Urala v. Levediyu*, in *Izvyestiya Imperatorskave Russkavo Geografcheskavo Obshchestva*, xix.). It was probably about that time that the chaghan of the Chazars and his grandees, together with a large number of his heathen people, embraced the Jewish religion. According to A. Harkavy (*Meassef Niddahim*, i.), the conversion took place in 620; according to others, in 740 . . .

This account of the conversion was considered to be of a legendary nature. Harkavy, however (in *Bilbasov* and *Yevreiskaya Biblioteka*), proved from Arabic and Slavonian sources that the religious disputation at the Chazarian court is a historical fact. Even the name of Sangari has been found in a liturgy of Constantine the Philosopher (Cyrill). It was one of the successors of Bulan, named Obadiah, who regenerated the kingdom and strengthened the Jewish religion. He invited Jewish scholars to settle in his dominions, and founded synagogues and schools. The people were instructed in the Bible, Mishnah, and Talmud, and in the "divine service of the hazzanim". In their writings the Chazars used the Hebrew letters (Harkavy, *Skazaniya*, etc., p. 241). Obadiah was succeeded by his son Hezekiah; the latter by his son Manasseh; Manasseh by Hanukkah, a brother of Obadiah; Hanukkah by his son Isaac; Isaac by his son Moses (or Manasseh II); the latter by his son Nisi; and Nisi by his son Aaron II. King Joseph himself was a son of Aaron, and ascended the throne in accordance with the law of the Chazars relating to succession. On the whole, King Joseph's account agrees generally with the evidence given by the Arabic writers of the tenth century, but in detail it contains a few discrepancies. According to Ibn Fadlan, Ibn Dastah, and others, only the king and the grandees were followers of Judaism. The rest of the Chazars were Christians, Mohammedans, and heathens; and the Jews were in a great minority (Frahn, *De Chazaris*, pp. 13-18, 584-590). According to Mas'udi (*Les Prairies d'Or*, ii. 8), the king and the Chazars proper were Jews; but the army consisted of Mohammedans, while the other inhabitants, especially the Slavonians and Russians, were heathens. From the work *Kitab al-Buldan*, written about the ninth century (p. 121; cited by Chwolson in *Izvyestiya o Chazarakh*, etc., p. 57), it appears as if all the Chazars were Jews and that they had been converted to Judaism only a short time before that book was written. But this work was probably inspired by Jaihani; and it may be assumed that in the ninth century many

Chazar heathens became Jews, owing to the religious zeal of King Obadiah. "Such a conversion in great masses", says Chwolson (ibid. p. 58), "may have been the reason for the embassy of Christians from the land of the Chazars to the Byzantine emperor Michael. The report of the embassy reads as follows: '*Quomodo nunc Judaei, nunc Saraceni ad suam fidem eos molirentur convertere*'" (Schlozer, *Nestor*, iii. 154) . . .

The Jewish population in the entire domain of the Chazars, in the period between the seventh and tenth centuries, must have been considerable . . .

Four years later the Russians conquered all the Chazarian territory east of the Sea of Azov. Only the Crimean territory of the Chazars remained in their possession until 1016, when they were dispossessed by a joint expedition of the Russians and Byzantines . . . Many members of the Chazarian royal family emigrated to Spain. Until the thirteenth century the Crimea was known to European travellers as 'Gazaria', the Italian form of 'Chazaria'.

EXTRACT FROM *THE UNIVERSAL JEWISH ENCYCLOPEDIA.*

Ashkenazim and Sephardim

As a result of this identification of Ashkenaz with Germany, the term Ashkenazim is used to denote one of the great divisions of Jewry in contradistinction to the Sephardim or 'Spanish Jews', from whom they differ in many respects. The Ashkenazim include the descendants of the German and French Jews who after the Crusades and subsequent persecutions in Germany, and after the expulsions from France, migrated into Prussia, Poland, and other countries of northern, central and eastern Europe, as well as the majority of Jews now residing in the Americas, England, and South America. The Sephardim are the descendants of the Jews expelled from Spain and Portugal who settled along the Mediterranean Coast and those who went to Holland, South America, England and its dependencies.

About 92 per cent of all Jews or approximately 14,500,000 are Ashkenazim. Until the eighteenth

century the Sephardim were numerically superior, numbering at one time more than 50 per cent of world Jewry, but beginning with the end of the fifteenth century, after they had been expelled from the Iberian Peninsula, they mixed with the Oriental Jews of Turkey, and with Ashkenazic Jews in Bohemia, Holland, and Southern Germany, and their relative number declined rapidly. A major cause is the fact that the Sephardim in large measure lived in countries which had a high mortality rate due to unsanitary conditions. Other causes for the dwindling of the Sephardim are their pride which makes them reluctant to intermarry with the Ashkenazim, and their inability to adapt themselves to unpleasant economic restrictions as easily as their Ashkenazic brethren. It is of interest that the children of marriages between Ashkenazim and Sephardim generally prefer to become Ashkenazim.

EXTRACT FROM *ENCYCLOPÆDIA BRITANNICA*, 14th Edition, Article 'Jews'.

The Diaspora in the West

Already, before the destruction of Jerusalem, the Diaspora had been a familiar phenomenon in Europe. The prisoners captured in innumerable wars and distributed throughout the empire as slaves had been followed (if not preceded) by merchants and traders. Later writers from the period of

Augustus onwards show the extent to which Jewish practices were spread throughout the civilised world of their day. Paul found them in Greece and Italy and the infant church consistently advanced where the synagogue had blazed out the way. Indeed, it is probable that, before the Roman empire had begun to decay, Jews were present in all of its greater cities.

EXTRACT FROM *THE JEWS IN BABYLONIA IN THE TIME OF EZRA AND NEHEMIAH ACCORD-ING TO BABYLONIAN INSCRIPTIONS*, by SAMUEL DAICHES, Ph.D., Jews' College, London, 1910;
Chapter I, 'Jews in Babylonia During and Before the Exile', p. 8.

The exile, however, marks the beginning of a new period. While before the exile small numbers of Jews lived in Babylonia, after the exile naturally the Jewish population of Babylonia became very large. In spite of the returns to Palestine under Zerubabel and Ezra the number of the Jews in Babylonia steadily increased in the course of time. We meet the names of Jews in cuneiform tablets almost immediately after the beginning of the exile. But they are scarce, and they remain scarce for more than a century. We have nearly four thousand contract-tablets from the time of Nebuchadnezzar (604-561) down to the time of Darius I (521-485). But, as said, the Jewish names which we find there are not many. A sudden change comes when we reach the times of Artaxerxes I (464-424) and Darius II (424-404). In the business documents dating from the years of these two kings the names of Jews are found in great abundance. It is difficult to say whether the difference is due to the different places from which the tablets came (the first-mentioned tablets having been written in Babylon and surrounding places,

and the last-mentioned documents having been written in Nippur), or to the different times. The latter seems the more probable reason. The longer the Jews lived in Babylonia the more they entered into the social and commercial life of the Babylonians. It may, however, also be that more Jews lived in the south of Babylonia (see below, p. 10). Be this as it may, the life of the Jews in Babylonia in the time of Artaxerxes I and Darius II becomes now partly known to us through the Babylonian documents dating from this period . . . About 250 of these documents have been published by Professor Hilprecht and Professor Clay in Vols. IX and X of Series A (Cuneiform Texts) of the Babylonian Expedition of the University of Pennsylvania, under the title of "Business Documents of Murashu Sons of Nipper". The documents published in B.E. IX are dated in the reign of Darius II. And in these documents a very large number of Jewish names is found. We find these Jews as contracting parties, as officials, as agents, as servants, and as witnesses . . .

Serial No. 56g.
Published by *The National Message*, Ltd.,
6 Buckingham Gate, London, S.W.1.
Copyright.

Authorities: Various

Were the Tribes ever really Lost?

ALTHOUGH the actual term 'Lost Tribes' does not appear in Scripture, the deportation and subsequent disappearance of the vast bulk of the ancient people of Israel have been thoroughly established from both Scriptural and secular sources. Nevertheless, there still remain critics who, in order to support or contest one viewpoint or another, maintain vigorously that the Tribes were never 'lost' and, indeed, that the bulk of the Israelites probably never left Palestine at all until the final Dispersion. Though this criticism is ill-founded, there are writers of some note whose theories merit analysis. Generally speaking, the critics cling to the idea that Israel of old is today perpetuated in the people now known as Jews, and in no other people. It seems strange, therefore, that these same writers steadfastly reject the evidence of modern Jewry through its own accredited literature to the effect that the Jews themselves know full well that most of the Israelites of today are somewhere outside the Jewish fold.

A Survey of the 'Never Lost' Theories

Although most of the literature which maintains that the Tribes never became 'lost' does not bear serious examination, the works of two of the more authoritative writers may usefully be mentioned. These are *The Lost Tribes a Myth*—an extensive and scholarly work by Professor Allen H. Godbey; and *The British Israel Theory*—a somewhat anxiously written attack on the Anglo-Israel position by Professor H. L. Goudge, D.D.

Those who maintain that the Tribes never became 'lost' advance various (and often contradictory) reasons in support of their theories. The chief of these are:

(a) The bulk of the Israelites, both of the northern and southern kingdoms, never left Palestine at all until—as Jews—they were driven out by the Romans. After the Assyrio-Babylonian deportations, which removed only the ruling classes and city dwellers, the common people of both kingdoms merged, to be joined by the small band of exiles who returned from Babylon under Ezra and Nehemiah. Thenceforward the whole evolved into the nation of the Jews.

(b) Even if the Israelites were carried away to Assyria and Babylonia, the descendants of the deportees of the northern and southern kingdoms subsequently became merged by the common bond of their Jehovah worship in the vast territories of Asia and Europe over which they were scattered.

(c) There is no historical record of the separate existence of the Ten Tribes after their expulsion from Palestine.

An Examination of the Theories
Theory (a)

That the bulk of the people of the two kingdoms never left Palestine at all, but merged either before or soon after the time of the return from Babylon under Ezra and Nehemiah.

Reasons advanced in support	Rebuttal
After Jeroboam took over the northern ten tribes, many of the northerners joined Rehoboam rather than worship the false gods of the north (II Chronicles xi).	The narrative merely states that certain elements of the Ten Tribes "came to Jerusalem to sacrifice" and that they thus "strengthened the kingdom of Judah for three years".
Abijah, son of Rehoboam, after slaying 500,000 of Jeroboam's northern Israelites, captured certain of their cities and towns (II Chronicles xiii).	As was the case in the long centuries of strife between England and Scotland, the kingdoms of Israel and Judah were constantly at war, with an almost ceaseless ebb and flow of conflict. It is noteworthy that the narrative states that: "Jeroboam did not recover strength again *in the days of Abijah*". But at a later time, Pekah of Israel slew 120,000 men of Judah in one day (II Chronicles xxviii, 6).

Reasons advanced in support	Rebuttal
In the time of Asa, king of Judah, an "abundance" of the tribes of Ephraim, Manasseh and Simeon joined the southern kingdom (II Chronicles xv).	Here, again, northern Israelites joined in sacrificial worship to the True God: "They gathered themselves together at Jerusalem" with the people of Judah and Benjamin. The account does not state that they took up permanent residence in the southern kingdom. If any of them did so they would have needed accommodation, lands and positions at the expense of the people of the Two Tribes already in residence. There is no evidence of their having asked for or having received such magnanimous treatment.
In c. 723 B.C. Hezekiah sent an appeal to northern Israelites to join him in a revival of worship at Jerusalem. Although many of them refused scornfully, "divers of Asher, Manasseh and Zebulon humbled themselves and came to Jerusalem" (II Chronicles xxx).	That this appeal was made *after* the first deportation of northern Israelites is clear from the reference by Hezekiah to them as the "remnant escaped out of the hand of the kings of Assyria". Large populations from Gilead, Galilee, and Naphtali and other regions had already gone into captivity.
	Verse 1 of chapter xxxi states definitely that, after the celebrations, they returned "every man into their own cities". There is no suggestion that these northerners remained in Judah.
In c. 626 B.C., during a further religious revival under Josiah, it is recorded that certain offerings had been accepted from "Manasseh and all the remnant of Israel"—i.e. long after the last of the deportations of the northern tribes (II Chronicles xxxiv).	It would be idle to assert that every single Israelite of the northern kingdom was carried captive. Undoubtedly there would be scattered oddments who would escape the net. Indeed, it was prophesied that "gleaning grapes" should be left behind (Isaiah xxiv, 13).
The inscription of Sargon claims only 27,280 captives of northern Israel.	As recorded in II Kings xv and in the inscription of Tiglath-Pileser (Pul), the inhabitants of Gilead, Galilee and Naphtali (a very large slice of the northern kingdom) had already been deported years *before* the Shalmaneser-Sargon campaign commenced. Indeed, as mentioned above, Hezekiah described what was left of the northern kingdom as a 'remnant'. Sargon's captives were all that remained of a terrible three-year siege of the city of Samaria itself. Moreover, in the interests of prudence, Shalmaneser would undoubtedly clear the countryside as he advanced towards the capital.

Reasons advanced in support	Rebuttal
Only the ruling classes and city dwellers were deported. The bulk of the common people remained behind in the land.	There is no shred of evidence, Scriptural or otherwise, to support this assertion. It is true that, in the later case of the southern kingdom, Nebuchadnezzar left some ''of the poor of the land'' to be vinedressers. But these quickly fled to Egypt, leaving the land, as subsequently stated by Josephus, 'desert'. If northern Israel territory had not been substantially depopulated, there would have been no room for the Cutheans and other peoples which the successive Assyrian monarchs brought in to take the place of the deported northern Israelites.
The term 'Israel' refers only to those of the aristocracy, the ruling classes and warriors—arrogant and oppressive.	This can only be described as an extreme personal opinion, for which there is no support from any Scriptural or historical source. It is, of course, well known that there were non-Hebraic peoples in both the northern and southern kingdoms, who doubtless became classified as Israelites, and many of these were ''hewers of wood and drawers of water'', as prophesied. But to suggest that the bulk of the ordinary people of the land were not Israelites is straining speculation to its limit.
At the dedication of Ezra's temple sacrifices were offered: ''for all Israel, twelve he-goats, according to the number of the tribes of Israel'' (Ezra vi).	From the inception of the Aaronic priesthood it was laid down that God's blessing and guidance should on all occasions be invoked for the whole of the tribes of Israel. The regalia and ritual could not be appropriated by or adapted for any one section. The priests of the southern kingdom dared not exclude their brethren of the northern tribes from their petitions. The present-day Jewish Prayer Book still contains prayers for the Israelites of the Ten Tribes.
I Chron. ix records that some elements of the tribes of Ephraim and Manasseh are listed as inhabitants of Jerusalem.	Although appearing so early in Chronicles, this record was apparently compiled by or for Ezra at the time of the return from Babylon. It is not disputed that small numbers of these (and other) tribes had taken up residence both in Jerusalem and in Judea; but the numbers were insignificant. Those here mentioned are a portion only of a very small community containing Judahites also —the whole numbering a mere six hundred and ninety persons.

Note on Theory (a)

That there were elements of the Ten Tribes present in the Judah kingdom is not in dispute. On each occasion of a religious revival at Jerusalem devout subjects of the idolatrous northern kingdom eagerly accepted the opportunity to worship the God of their fathers. Usually they returned from Jerusalem to their homes, but there would doubtless be some who would seek permanent residence in Judah. Some idea of the proportion may be gleaned from the records of Ezra and Nehemiah to the effect that, of the 42,360 Israelites (including women) who returned from Babylon, 29,818 'men' were of the tribes of Judah, Benjamin, and priestly categories—leaving only 652 "who could not shew their father's house" (i.e. in Judah). Anna, the prophetess, of the tribe of Asher, mentioned in Luke ii, may have been descended from one of these.

Theory (b)

The exiles of both the northern and southern kingdoms, bound by the common bond of Jehovah worship, mingled together forming 'Jewish' communities in the lands of their exile.

Reasons advanced in support	*Rebuttal*
Their common system of worship would naturally tend towards a fusion in the lands of exile of the two peoples.	This most definitely was not the case. The Ten Tribes went into captivity as *pagans*. From the outset Jeroboam had substituted idolatry for the worship of Jehovah (II. Chronicles xi). Except for a few very brief periods the nation continued in the way of Jeroboam. The Ten Tribes remained pagan to the last and it was for this reason that they were finally expelled (II Kings xvii, 22–23). At the time of Ezekiel they were still unrepentant, even in exile. Dr. Goudge himself admits that if the northern Israelites did not preserve their Jehovah worship "they almost certainly would have been lost (sic) in the populations around them".
Being of a common stock, the people of the two kingdoms would cling together in their exile.	Their common ancestry did not prevent fearful wars when they were in Palestine.
	The Ten Tribes and a substantial portion of the Two Tribes (as to the latter, following the invasion of Sennacherib) were carried to Assyria. What remained of the Judah kingdom was taken to Babylonia—many hundreds of miles away. Large-scale admixture would be impossible.

Reasons advanced in support	Rebuttal
The book of Esther records that there were Jews—worshippers of Jehovah—throughout the 127 provinces of king Ahasueras, "from India even unto Ethiopia", which suggests that all Israelites had united in one system of worship.	Esther and Mordecai were both of the tribe of Benjamin. As mentioned above, the Ten Tribes went out of Palestine, as pagans, a century and a half before the expulsion of the Yahvist Judahites. By the time of Esther (c. 500 B.C.) the latter, whilst they had time to permeate the whole Persian Empire, were certainly not able to convert any large number of their kinsmen of the Ten Tribes. There is no record of any such *large scale* repentance. Such evidence as there is refutes this idea. There would doubtless be *isolated cases* of conversion to Judaism.
At Pentecost there was gathered at Jerusalem a multitude of "Jews, devout men" from the whole region from India to the Aegean—the very countries through which the exiles were dispersed (Acts ii). Peter addressed them as "Ye men of Israel".	The narrative states that these men were "Jews and proselytes". As the then race-conscious Peter addressed them all as "men of Israel", it seems likely that the proselytes were elements of the Ten Tribes converted from paganism. It is of note that the Apostle urged them to return to the distant lands from which they had come to act as Gospel messengers to "all the House of Israel".
St. Paul spoke of the whole Twelve Tribes as "instantly serving God" (Acts xxvi).	Even the Jews of Palestine could not be so described. Had they not recently crucified the Son of God? What Paul implied was that the Twelve Tribes could hope to attain the promises made by God to the fathers when all Israel should be "instantly serving God". The sense of the passage is future. Moffatt and other translators make this quite clear.

Theory (c)

There is no historical record of the separate existence of the Ten Tribes, as distinct from the Jews, following the expulsion from Palestine.

This is quite unfounded and easily disposed of. There is excellent evidence, which no competent critic would reject, from the works of an authority admirably qualified to write on the subject—Josephus, a Jewish scholar and historian, discoursing on matters of Israel's history. Writing in c. 70 A.D., he said:

" . . . There are but two tribes in Asia and Europe subject to the Romans, while the ten tribes are beyond the Euphrates till now, and are an immense multitude" (*Ant.* XI.5.2).

Serial No. 64c.

This evidence proves beyond all possible doubt that the northern Israelites, in the days of the early Church, were entirely separate and distinct from Jewry and that they were then outside Roman domination in territory somewhere beyond the Euphrates (which reaches almost to the Caucasus). Early Church writings show that many of the Apostles journeyed to all parts of this region, even as far as India, taking their message to the ''Lost Sheep of the House of Israel'' as directed by their Master, when He was with them. In this vast area they were, as mentioned by Professor Godbey (p. 145) ''primarily among Indo-Iranic peoples.''

General Note

The critics who argue that the Ten Tribes never became lost are handicapped by two erroneous premises:

(a) That all the Jews of to-day are Israelites and that there are no Israelites outside Jewry.

(b) That the Hebrews and their kindred peoples were of non-Nordic stock.

Both these premises have been shown to be wrong (vide Serial Nos. 35 (222, 7); 7, 17, 26, 28, 40, 56 (572.933); 29 (572.9353); 8 (572. 9389); 57 (572.9394).

Remarkable though it is, the critics entirely ignore the evidence of those who ought to know something about it—the Jews themselves. They, at least, are not in any doubt on the subject, as may be seen from the subjoined extracts from Jewish authorities. Perhaps Dr. Goudge would classify this evidence with his ''speculations in the more foolish literature of post-Christian Judaism''.

The evidence shows conclusively that, at the time of the final dispersion of the Jews, the Ten Tribes were, in the main, far away from Palestine, but that their existence, even if not their precise location, was at that time known to the leaders of Jewry. In the great upheavals which swept Asia and Europe they became submerged in the vast agglomeration of peoples which ebbed and flowed during the succeeding centuries. Though there was ebb and flow, the final movement of the bulk of these was inexorably westward.

There are numerous references by the prophets to the separate destinies and ultimate re-union of the northern and southern tribes, but these are outside the scope of this article.

EXTRACT FROM *JEWISH ENCYCLOPEDIA* (1925 Edition) Article "Tribes, Lost Ten".

''As a large number of prophecies relate to the return of 'Israel' to the Holy Land, believers in the literal inspiration of the Scriptures have always labored under a difficulty in regard to the continued existence of the tribes of Israel, with the exception of those of Judah and Levi (or Benjamin), which returned with Ezra and Nehemiah. If the Ten Tribes have disappeared the literal fulfilment of the prophecies would be impossible; if they have not disappeared, obviously they must exist under a different name.''

EXTRACT FROM PROFESSOR H. GRAETZ'S *HISTORY OF THE JEWS*, English Translation by
Rabbi A. B. Rhine, D.D., 1930, Vol. I, p. 146.

''The idols of Dan and Samaria and of other cities were taken to Nineveh, and the thousands of captives were scattered and settled in groups in thinly populated districts, the location of which is not definitely known, in Halah and Habor on the river Gozan, in the mountains of Media, and in Elam west of Persia. The house of Israel, that had endured for two hundred and sixty years, under the rule of twenty kings, vanished in one day, leaving no trace behind it, because it forsook its original elevating and invigorating teachings and followed the enervating vices connected with idolatry. What became of the ten tribes?

Some believed they discovered them in the far east, some in the far west. There were deceivers and visionaries who claimed to be descendants of the lost tribes. Undoubtedly the ten tribes were absorbed among the nations and disappeared.''

EXTRACT FROM LETTER BY DEAN INGE TO THE LONDON *EVENING STANDARD* (26th January, 1939).

''The Assyrians deported most of the Ten Tribes in 720 B.C. They never returned, and foreigners from the East were brought in to replace them. The Babylonians deported only the upper and middle classes, leaving the mainly Canaanite fellahin on the land.''

EXTRACTS FROM THE *JEWISH PRAYER BOOK* (1935).

(P. 44) ''O Rock of Israel, arise to the help of Israel, and deliver, according to thy promise, Judah and Israel. Our Redeemer, the Lord of Hosts is his name, the Holy One of Israel. Blessed art thou, O Lord, who hast redeemed Israel.''

(P. 253) ''And it shall come to pass on that day that a great Shofar shall be blown; and they shall come who were lost in the land of Assyria, and they that were outcasts in the land of Egypt; and they shall worship the Lord in the holy mountain at Jerusalem.''

EXTRACTS FROM THE *JEWISH QUARTERLY REVIEW*, 1888 (Vol. I) (Article by Dr. A. Neubauer).

(P. 15) ''The captives of Israel exiled beyond the Euphrates did not return as a whole to Palestine along with their brethren the captives of Judah; at least there is no mention made of this event in the documents at our disposal.''

(P. 17) ''In fact, the return of the ten tribes was one of the great promises of the Prophets, and the advent of the Messiah is therefore necessarily identified with the epoch of their redemption.''

(P. 21) ''The hope of the return of the Ten Tribes has never ceased amongst the Jews in exile. . . . This hope has been connected with every Messianic rising.''

EXTRACTS FROM *THE LIFE AND TIMES OF JESUS THE MESSIAH*, by ALFRED EDERSHEIM, M.A.Oxon., D.D., Ph.D. (Revised edition, Longmans, Green & Co., London, 1886).

(P. 8) ''In general, it is of the greatest importance to remember in regard to this Eastern dispersion, that only a minority of the Jews, consisting in all of about 50,000, originally returned from Babylon. . . .''

(Pp. 14–16) ''In what has been said, no notice has been taken of those wanderers of the ten tribes whose trackless footsteps seem as mysterious as their after-fate. The Talmudists name four countries as their seats. But, even if we were to attach historic credence to their vague statements, at least two of these localities cannot with any certainty be identified. Only thus far all agree as to point us northwards, through India, Armenia, the Kirdish mountains, and the Caucasus. And with this tallies a curious reference in what is known as IV Esdras, which locates them in a land called Arzareth, a term which has, with some probability, been identified with the land of Ararat. Josephus describes them as an innumerable multitude, and vaguely locates them beyond the Euphrates. . . .

. . . Still the great mass of the ten tribes was in the days of Christ, as in our own, lost to the Hebrew nation.''

Serial No. 64d.

Authority: BARON VON HAXTHAUSEN
Transcaucasia

"Haxthausen, August Franz Ludwig Maria, Freiherr von (1792-1866), German economist, was born in Westphalia; graduate of Göttingen university; studied land laws, and published a book on the subject in 1829; this book secured for him commission to report upon land laws of the Prussian provinces, which he did exhaustively in 1843; undertook a similar task in Russia for emperor Nicholas. Received many honours; wrote numerous books, three of them being on the people between the Black Sea and the Caspian" (Compiled from *Encyclopaedia Britannica*, 1946).

Judah and Benjamin in the Caucasus

THE view that sections of the Judah kingdom pushed rapidly northwestwards from the lands of their exile is strongly supported by the evidence of the learned traveller and writer, Von Haxthausen, who made a careful survey of the Caucasian region during the middle period of the last century.

He found that, in Transcaucasia, there were Judaic communities who claim descent from the tribes of Judah and Benjamin, some of whom, while observing the Law as given through Moses, are favourably disposed towards Christianity.

As might be expected from remnants of the royal tribe, the tradition of the Davidic kingly line is firmly maintained among these communities.

POINTS OF SPECIAL INTEREST

1. The Karaim, who claim origin from the residue of the tribe of Judah carried captive to Babylon, state that some of their people trekked as far west as Central Europe at an early period. The Karaim do not recognise the Talmud, a fact which suggests that they were little influenced by post-captivity Jewry.

2. According to Haxthausen, the Karaim claim also that their leading family was of Davidic origin through an ancestor who had been removed to Armenia at the time of Nebuchadnezzar. This Davidic descent was asserted also by the Georgian kings of the period A.D.   .

3. Another Judaic sect, the Uriani, trace their descent from exiles of the tribe of Benjamin, always closely associated with Judah. Their traditions state that they had contact with Jesus and His disciples.

4. This evidence tends to emphasise the early movements of elements of the Judah kingdom in the direction of south-east Europe. It is noteworthy that compatriots of Haxthausen, in recent years, have found Celtic-speaking communities in the same region (Ser. No. 104 [572.936313]).

5. The Uriani claim to have accepted Christ from the earliest times.

(Extracts from *Transcaucasia*, by Baron von Haxthausen; London, 1854.)

The Karaim Jews, who do not reject the ancient traditions and interpretations, but only the Talmud, live principally in the provinces of Erivan and Akhalzik. They assert their descent, pure and unmixed, from the tribe of Judah, which was led to Babylon. It is well known, they say, that in the reign of Cyrus a part returned to Judea, but another part remained after the destruction of Babylon, penetrated further north, settled in Armenia, and spread gradually to the Caucasus; passing then to the Crimea, they settled there, from whence finally colonies penetrated into Poland. They also assert that their ancestors possessed great power and authority in Armenia; and that when Christianity made its way into that country, a number of them became Christians. The most powerful family among them, the Bagratides—descended from Sarbad (of the race of David), who was sent to Armenia by Nebuchadnezzar—at first exercised a feudal sway over the province of Iberia, and had the privilege of crowning the Armenian kings; but at a subsequent period they obtained possession of the throne, and eventually of the three Georgian thrones.

The Jews of the Karaim sect are regarded as eminently honest and trustworthy, and, in contrast with the Talmudists, inspire general esteem. They have adopted the Tatar dress, and are only distinguished by their shaven faces, with narrow whiskers reaching to the chin. The language they usually speak among themselves is the Tatar. They keep aloof from the Talmudists, and regard the Mohammedans as an offset from themselves. Mohammed's instructor is said to have been a Karaim Jew, and tradition states that the prophet gave the Karaim a passport, which is recognised by all his followers, whom it commands to hold this sect in honour, and forbids ever to persecute them. They live in harmony with Christians, and regard Christ as a prophet who proceeded from their race, and whose disciples founded a new sect. Not having been in Judea in the time of Christ, they do not share the animosity usually entertained by Jews against Christians.

Serial No. 105a.

There is a small community of the Karaim Jews at Jerusalem, who maintain a connection with all the rest of their brethren, the latter regarding them as the parent community. On certain Fridays (four times a year, I was informed), the Karaim assemble on the west side of Mount Moriah, on the spot where the strains of exultation of their fathers once resounded, there to pour forth their songs of lamentation for the destruction of the Temple and the Holy City, and the dispersion of the chosen people of Jehovah (pp. 137-139).

In the district of Derbend there is said to be a sect of Jews named Uriani, who embraced Christianity, but without relinquishing their observance of the Jewish law in its full extent. They keep holy only the Sabbath-day, and adhere strictly to all the injunctions and usages of the Law, following the example of Christ, whom they acknowledge as the Messiah, and who likewise enjoined obedience to the Law. It is said that they claim to be a remnant of the Tribe of Benjamin, who during or after the Captivity moved northwards from Assyria. At the period of the birth of Christ, they assert, their scribes announced that the Messiah was born in Bethlehem, and in consequence they sent thither two of their number, named Longinus and Elias, who were received among the seventy Disciples of Christ. After the Crucifixion and Resurrection the latter returned to their brethren, taking with them the under-garment of Christ (not the seamless coat), which is still preserved and worshiped in the Cathedral of Mzcheta, near Tiflis. Longinus is said to have committed to writing the teachings of the Saviour, in a book which they assert is still in existence, or at least a transcript of it, but is preserved with great secrecy. They have no knowledge of the New Testament. It would be of the highest interest to institute a research respecting this sect, although very difficult to arrive at the truth; but how important the discovery of a book, which might in any degree form a corollary to the Gospel!

The fate of the Israelitish tribes in Assyria, it is known, still remains a matter of historical doubt; they were unquestionably dispersed throughout Asia, and a large portion penetrated to the Caucasian countries, although they are not found there in any considerable numbers at the present day. In the fifth century the king of Persia transplanted 71,000 Jewish families from the towns of Armenia to Persia (pp. 140-141).

The kings of Georgia asserted their descent from the stem of David in their public documents, which began in these terms: ''We, King of Kings, consecrated by the grace of God, absolute monarch and independent sovereign, son of Jesse, David, Solomon, and Bayrout, Lord of Seven Kingdoms, Heraclius,'' etc.

One of the most remarkable families of the Caucasian countries is that of the Princes Orbellian, who came from China in the time of the Persian king Kai-Khosru. Branches of this family went afterwards to Armenia, and are intimately connected with the history of that country. They were the Crown generals of Georgia, and next in rank to the royal family, with whom they frequently intermarried; the last Czarina of Immiretia was an Orbellian. Stephen Orbellian, Archbishop of Sianik, wrote a family history in the thirteenth century (p. 121).

Serial No. 105b.
Published by The National Message, Ltd,
6 Buckingham Gate, London, S.W.1.
Copyright.

Authorities:
William Camden, *Britannia.*
John Milton, *The History of Britain*
Sharon Turner, *The History of the Anglo-Saxons.*

Israelites—Scythians—Sacae—Saxons

IT has already been shown, beyond all reasonable doubt, that large numbers of the ancient people of Israel were removed by successive Assyrian monarchs from their Palestinian homeland and placed in the lands to the south and south-west of the Caspian Sea, in or adjoining territory which was soon to see the rise of a Scythian power. It is beyond dispute that the deported Israelites became engulfed in the constantly moving tide of Scythian peoples, which comprised elements of several races—Nordic, Alpine and Mongol.

Out of this "Scythian" sea of peoples gradually emerged important north European nations of the Christian era. In such a way came the Anglo-Saxon and kindred nations. A positive reconstruction of their migrations has been impossible owing to the fact that a connected written record no longer exists, and ethnologists have been compelled to rely on archaeology, folk-lore and saga for such gleanings of knowledge as are available. It is quite certain that there is considerable divergence of opinion among the scholars who have investigated the matter. In the past there was a marked leaning towards the view, then seemingly widely held by continental scholars, that the Saxons of old were descended from the Scythic Sacae.

It is significant that modern researches in the lands anciently occupied by these people tend to support the views of those scholars of past generations who were convinced that the Sacae of old and the Anglo-Saxons of more modern times are racially identical.

POINTS OF SPECIAL INTEREST

1. While it is impossible to trace the origin of the belief that the Saxons were descended from the Sacae, it merits consideration because it is not out of harmony with known data, and it may in fact assist in explaining them.

2. The historian Sharon Turner made a bold attempt to show that there was strong evidence in support of a descent of the Saxons from the Sacae; though modern research has revealed that some of the information he used, and also some of his conclusions, were not well founded. For instance, Herodotus' account of the relations between the Scythians and the Medes, which was considered accurate in Turner's day, is now known to have been wrong in some important respects, as has been pointed out by C. J. Gadd in *The Fall of Niniveh* (British Museum, 1923); the Babylonian inscriptions show that at least during the siege of Nineveh the Scythians, Medes, and Babylonians were allies, and not at enmity, as accepted by Turner in the light of ideas then current. This historian appears to have relied on translations of Strabo and Ptolemy now known to be inaccurate. Thus the former does not say that the Sacae made many incursions on the Cimmerians and Treres, but that "the Sacae had made incursions similar to those of the Cimmerians and Treres" (Georg. XI. viii. 4); nor does Ptolemy say that the Saxones were a Scythian people or that they were sprung from the Sakai. Other faults, born of the lack of knowledge of his day, are also evident in his work. It seems a questionable point, for instance, to support the view expressed by Camden and Milton, and possibly derived from an earlier source, that *Saxons* means 'Sons of the Sacae'; many tribal names recorded by Latin writers, for instance, ended in '—ones', as: *Aelvaeones, Saxones, Teutones, Sigulones, Vargiones*, etc., and in these cases the common suffix bears no such significance. Nevertheless, it may fairly be stated that Sharon Turner has contributed a connection of evidence that cannot be ignored in studying the problem of European origins. His case has certainly *not* been disproved by more recent researches; in fact, some of them can definitely be said to throw a favourable light on his conclusions. If his claim of identity should prove to be mainly correct, it is only just that he should be given due credit for his shrewd analysis of over a century ago.

3. Anthropological evidence, when considered in conjunction with that from linguistic and historical sources, can certainly be held to support the possibility of a connection between the Sacae and the Saxons. Prof. Hans Gunther, the German anthropologist, strongly supports the view that the Saxons and Sacae were akin, but, following the *Aryan* theory championed by Isaac Taylor (*Origin of the Aryans*, etc.) and originated by R. G. Latham, he has accepted the reverse order of descent, that is to say, that the Sacae were descended from the Saxons (see extract in Ser. No. 55 [572.9353]). Another modern authority, on the other hand, Prof. I. M. Rostovtzeff, in his *Iranians and Greeks in South Russia* (Duke University, North Carolina, 1922), whilst he does not appear to identify the Scythians or the Sacae with the Saxons, holds that there was a westward movement into Europe out of Asia, north of the Caspian, of Scythians related to the Sacians. He writes: ". . . I entirely agree with those who believe the Scythians to be of Iranian extraction, although I readily admit a strong infusion of Mongolian and Turanian blood. . . . Our information about the Ashguzai, who are the same as the Scythians, and about the Sacians; their close affinity with the Sarmatians; whose

Iranian nationality is not disputed; and the evidence of Herodotus, confirmed by archaeology, as to the religion of the Pontic Scythians . . . leave no doubt that the Scythian tribes of South Russia were Iranians, nearly akin to the Medes and Persians, but belonging to another branch of the same stock'' (p. 60). ''The Sarmatians, like the Scythians, belonged to the Iranian group of Asiatic peoples. They may have been closely akin to the Scythians; may have belonged, like them, to those Iranian peoples who were generally called Sacian, to distinguish them from the other branch of the Iranians, represented by the Medes and Persians, who were bitter enemies of the Sacians'' (p. 114).

4. The Sacae appear to have been the most outstanding of all the early Scythians; and Herodotus tells us that the Persians called all Scythians *Sacae* (Ser. No. 65 [572.9353]). This may mean either that the original Scythians or the best known of them were Sacae. Some anthropologists, such as Gunther, hold that the Sacae were Nordics. The ancient Saxons were also of this type; as were the Israelites, as has been shown (Ser. No. 57 [572.9394]). The possibility that the name Sacae was derived from Isaac has also been discussed (Ser. No. 55 [572.9353]). Pliny writes of the Sacae: ''The more ancient writers give them the name of Aramii'' (Ser. No. 55). Every Israelite had to confess that he was of Aramean descent (Deut. xxvi. 5; translated 'Syrian'). Here, then, is evidence of a possibility of a relationship between those Hebrews of the Aramean 'House of Isaac' (Amos vii. 16) and the Scythians called by the Persians *Sacae*. The Scythians first appear in history as the *Ashguzai* of the Assyrian inscriptions of Esarhaddon's time, living in regions contiguous or identical with the regions into which the captives of Israel were placed.

It is interesting to observe that Ptolemy, the Alexandrian geographer (*c.* 150 A.D.), shows in the vicinity of the Biblical Bashan a Saccaea, identified by the Rev. J. L. Porter, D.D., as the modern town of Shuka, about four miles east of Bathanyeh, the ancient *Batanis* (*The Giant Cities of Bashan*, 1891, p. 36).

5. Descent of the Saxons from the Sacae would imply a migration of the latter from their ancient lands to western Europe. It is now widely accepted that extensive migrations have taken place from Asia into Europe from the 7th century B.C. down to the time of the Hunnish invasion. As has been pointed out by Rostovtzeff, in his *Iranians and Greeks in South Russia*, there were four main waves of kindred settlers in South Russia: Cimmerians, Scythians, Sarmatians, and Goths, some of these clearly having been closely related to tribes in Asia at an earlier period. It is highly possible that some of the Sacae entered Europe north of the Caspian. It is known, for instance, as has been mentioned by Prof. W. M. McGovern, in his book *The Early Empires of Central Asia* (1939) that Alexander the Great crossed over the Jaxartes River and routed the Sacae; Greek supremacy was established over regions south of that river for many years to come, and the Sacae never again appear as a strong power in those territories, although their name was left in places that had been contacted by them, as in Sacasena. The route of the Sacae presumably took them northward, between the Sea of Aral and Lake Balkash, or eastward towards Lake Baikal, south of which we find the *Issyk-kul*, and a town *Issyk-pakte*. Chinese records indicate that the Se, or Sek (Sacae) occupied these regions, called Zungaria, in the second century B.C. It appears likely that, driven westwards from these regions, the Sacae entered Europe; in fact, it is probable that if they did not migrate early

of their own accord, the advance of the Huns, to appear on the banks of the Don in 374 A.D., compelled them to do so, as was the case with the Goths and Alans. It is logical that if they moved in advance of the Huns they would avoid conflict with Rome by passing south of the Baltic to settle in what came to be called Saxony, and eventually into the British Isles.

Among older authorities, Professor George Rawlinson and his brother Sir Henry held the view that the Scythians were *related* to the people of northern Europe, but that they were a separate branch of the parent stock whose first large increase took place in the vicinity of Armenia in the eighth or seventh centuries B.C. It was into this region that the Assyrians deported the people of ancient Israel and Syria.

6. Albinus, the Yorkshire tutor to Charlemagne, in a Latin play on words, refers to the Saxons under the name of *Saxi*, whom he calls an ancient and powerful race (Froben: *Beati Flacci Albini sev Alcuini*, 1777, tom. II, Vol. I, p. 242, lines 38-50). If the Saxons are indeed descended from the Sacae, the name *Saxi* may prove to be a valuable link between the early and late forms of the name.

7. If the belief that the Saxons are descended from the ancient Sacae be true, it has a tremendous significance for the modern British, American, and other people to whose countries people of Saxon stock have migrated, and whose origins may thus be traceable (from entirely secular sources) as far back as the Sacae of the sixth century B.C. (see Serials No. 37 [572.9355]; 55 [572.9353]) and, with a fair degree of justification, to the Israelites of the 'House of Isaac', uprooted and driven from Palestine nearly 2,700 years ago.

EXTRACT FROM WM. CAMDEN'S *BRITANNIA* (1806 ed.), Vol. I, p. 151.

CAMDEN, WILLIAM (1551-1623), English antiquary and historian, born in London, was educated at Christ's Hospital, St. Paul's School, and Oxford; became second Master of Westminster School in 1575 and headmaster 1593. Was made Clarenceux king-of-arms, 1597. Travelled British Isles extensively, and published his *Britannia* in six editions between 1586-1607. Published Annales of the reign of Queen Elizabeth, 1615, 1625 and 1627. "Seldon spoke of the *Annales* and of Bacon's *History of Henry VII.* as the only two serious works on English history up to his day." A man of enormous energy, he had many influential friends, among them Archbishop Ussher, Sir Robert Cotton, and John Selden. The Camden Society was founded in his honour, 1838 (compiled from the *Encyclopædia Britannica*, 1946).

The origin and etymology of the Saxons, like those of other nations, have been involved in fable. . . . Each of these writers adopts the opinion most agreeable to them; I mean not to controvert any of them; but that of the most learned Germans seems most probable and worthy to be embraced, which makes the Saxons descend from the Sacae, the most considerable people of Asia, and to be so called *quasi Sacasones*, q. d. *Sons of the Sacae*, and to have gradually overspread Europe from Scythia or Sarmatia Asiatica, with the Getae, Suevi, Daci and others. Nor is their opinion ill-founded, which brings the Saxons out of Asia, in which the human race had both its rise and increase. For besides that Strabo writes that the Sacae, as before the Cimeri-

ans, invaded distant regions, and called part of Armenia after their name Sacasena; Ptolemy also places the Sassones, Suevi, Massagetae, and Dahi, in that part of Scythia; and Cisnerus observes, that these people kept almost as near to one another in Europe as before in Asia.

Nor is it less probable that our Saxons come from these Saci or Sassones of Asia than the Germans from the Germani of Persia mentioned by Herodotus, which indeed themselves in some measure assert from the correspondence of language. For the very learned Joseph Scaliger tells us, *Fader, Muder, Broder, Tutcher, Band*, and the like, are still to be found in the Persian language for Father, Mother, Brother, Daughter, Band.

EXTRACT FROM THE FAMOUS JOHN MILTON'S *HISTORY OF ENGLAND* (Westley & Davis, 1835 edition), Bk. III, pages 506, 507

The Saxons were a barbarous and heathen nation, famous for nothing else but robberies and cruelties done to all their neighbours, both by sea and land; in particular to this island, witness that military force, which the Roman emperors maintained here purposely against them, under a special commander, whose title, as is found on good record, was "Count of the Saxon shore in Britain", and the many mischiefs done by their landing here, both alone and with the Picts, as above hath been related, witness as much. They were a people thought by good writers to be descended of the Sacae, a kind of Scythians in the north of Asia, thence called Sacasons, or sons of Sacae, who with a flood of other northern nations came into Europe, toward the declining of the Roman empire; and using piracy from Denmark all along these seas, possessed at length by intrusion all that coast of Germany, and the Netherlands, which took thence the name of Old Saxony, lying between the Rhine and Elve, and from thence north as far as Eidora, the river bounding Holsatia, though not so firmly or so largely, but that their multitude wandered yet uncertain of habitation.

EXTRACT FROM *THE HISTORY OF THE ANGLO-SAXONS, FROM THE EARLIEST PERIOD TO THE NORMAN CONQUEST*, by SHARON TURNER, F.A.S., R.A.S.L. (seventh ed., Longmans, London, 1852)

(Book II. Ch. i., p. 78)

Ptolemy, the Alexandrian, was the first writer whom we know to have mentioned the Saxons. By the passage in his Geography, and by the concurrence of all their future history, it is ascertained, that, before the year 141 after Christ, there was a people called Saxones, who inhabited a territory at the north side of the Elbe, on the neck of the Cimbric Chersonesus, and three small islands, at the mouth of this river. From the same author it is also clear, that the Saxons were of no great importance at this period; for in this peninsula, which is now divided into Jutland, Sleswick, and Holstein, no fewer than six other nations were stationed, besides the Saxones and the remnant of the cimbri.

(Book II. Ch. i, pp. 81-89.)

The early occupation of Europe, by the Kimmerian and Keltic races, has been already displayed. The next stream of barbaric tribes, whose progress formed the second great influx of population into Europe, were the Scythian, German, and Gothic tribes. They also entered it out of Asia. It is of importance to recollect the fact of their primeval locality, because it corresponds with this circumstance, that Herodotus, besides the main Scythia, which he places in Europe, mentions also an Eastern or Asiatic Scythia, beyond the Caspian and Iaxartes. As these new comers pressed on the Kimmerians and Kelts, their predecessors, those nations retired towards the western and southern extremities of Europe, pursued still by the Scythian invaders. This new wave of population gradually spread over the mountains, and into the vast forests and marshes of Europe, until, under the name of Germans, an appellation which Tacitus calls a recent name, they had not only reached the Rhine, but had also crossed it into France. Here Caesar found one great body firmly settled, descended from them, whom he calls Belgae; though its component states had their peculiar denominations, besides a very large force of recent German invaders, under the command of Ariovistus.

This second stock of the European population is peculiarly interesting to us, because from its branches not only our own immediate ancestors, but also those of the most celebrated nations of modern Europe, have unquestionably descended. The Anglo-Saxons, Lowland Scotch, Normans, Danes, Norwegians, Swedes, Germans, Dutch, Belgians, Lombards, and Franks, have all sprung from that great fountain of the human race, which we have distinguished by the terms Scythian, German, or Gothic.

The ancient languages of these nations prove their ancient affinity, the contiguous chronology of their first origin, and their common derivation, and afford evidence of these truths, from which every one may satisfy his doubts or his curiosity. We have works still existing in the ancient Gothic, and Saxon, as well as in the Frankish and Icelandic, in which the philologist will easily perceive their mutual relationship. The comparison of these with the modern German, Danish, Dutch, Swedish, and Flemish, will equally demonstrate the kinship between the ancient parents and their existing descendants.

The first appearance of the Scythian tribes in Europe may be placed, according to Strabo and Homer, about the eighth, or, according to Herodotus, in the seventh century before the Christian era. Herodotus likewise states, that the Scythians declared their nations to be more recent than any other, and that they reckoned only one thousand years between Targitaos, their first king, and the aggression of Darius. The first scenes of their civil existence, and of their progressive power, were in Asia, to the east of the Araxes. Here they multiplied and extended their territorial limits, for some centuries, unknown to Europe. Their general appellation among themselves was Scoloti, but the Greeks called them Scythians, Scuthoi, or Nomades.

To this judicious and probable account of Herodotus, we add the information collected by Diodorus. He says, that the Scythians, formerly inconsiderable and few, possessed a narrow region on the Araxes: but, by degrees, they became more powerful in numbers and in courage. They extended their boundaries on all sides: till at last they raised their nation to great empire and glory.

One of their kings becoming valiant and skilful in the art of war, they added to their territory the mountainous regions about Caucasus, and also the plains towards the ocean, and the Palus Mæotis, with the other regions near the Tanais. In the course of time they subdued many nations between the Caspian and the Mæotis, and beyond the Tanais. Thus, according to Diodorus, the nation increased, and had kings worthy of remembrance. The Sakai, the Massagetai, and the Arimaspoi drew their origin from them.

The Massagetai seem to have been the most eastern branch of the Scythian nation. Wars arising between them and the other Scythis tribes, an emigration from the latter took place, according to the account which Herodotus selects as in his opinion the most authentic, which occasioned their entrance into Europe. Such feuds and wars have contributed more than any other cause, to disperse through the world its uncivilised inhabitants.

The emigrating Scythians crossed the Araxes, passed out of Asia, and invading the Kimmerians, suddenly appeared in Europe, in the seventh century before the Christian era. Part of the Kimmerians flying into Asia Minor, some of the Scythian hordes pursued them; but, turning in a direction different from that which the Kimmerians traversed, they missed their intended prey, and fell unintentionally upon the Medes. They defeated the Medes, pressed on towards Egypt, and governed those parts of Asia for twenty-eight years, till Cyaxares, the king of Media, at last expelled them.

The Scythian tribes, however, continued to flock into Europe; and, in the reign of Darius, their European colonies were sufficiently numerous and celebrated to excite the ambition of the Persian monarch, after his capture of Babylon, but all his efforts against them failed. In the time of Herodotus they had gained an important footing in Europe. They

seem to have spread into it from the Tanais to the Danube, and to have then taken a westerly direction; but their kindred colonies, in Thrace, had extended also to the south. Their most northward ramification in Europe was the tribe of the Roxolani, who dwelt above the Borysthenes, the modern Dnieper . . .

As they spread over Europe, the Kimmerian and Keltic population retired towards the west and south. In the days of Caesar, the most advanced tribes of the Scythian, or Gothic, race were known to the Romans under the name of Germans. They occupied all the continent but the Cimbric peninsula, and had reached and even passed the Rhine. One of their divisions, the Belgæ, had for some time established themselves in Flanders and part of France: and another body, under Ariovistus, were attempting a similar settlement near the centre of Gaul, which Caesar prevented. It is most probable that the Belgæ in Britain were descendants of colonists or invaders from the Belgæ in Flanders and Gaul.

The names Scythians and Scoloti were, like Galli and Kimmerians, not so much local as generic appellations. The different tribes of the Scythians, like those of the Kimmerians and Gauls, had their peculiar distinctive denominations.

The Saxons were a German or Teutonic, that is, a Gothic or Scythian tribe; and of the various Scythian nations which have been recorded, the Sakai, or Sacæ, are the people from whom the descent of the Saxons may be inferred with the least violation of probability. Sakai-suna, or the sons of the Sakai, abbreviated into Saksun, which is the same sound as Saxon, seems a reasonable etymology of the word Saxon. The Sakai, who in Latin are called Sacæ, were an important branch of the Scythian nation. They were so celebrated, that the Persians called all the Scythians by the name of Sacæ; and Pliny, who mentions this, speaks of them as among the most distinguished people of Scythia. Strabo places them eastward of the Caspian, and states them to have made many incursions on the Kimmerians and Treres, both far and near. They seized Bactriana, and the most fertile part of Armenia, which, from them, derived the name Sakasina; they defeated Cyrus; and they reached the Cappadoces on the Euxine. This important fact of a part of Armenia having been named Sakasina, is mentioned by Strabo in another place, and seems to give a geographical locality to our primeval ancestors, and to account for the Persian words that occur in the Saxon language, as they must have come into Armenia from the northern regions of Persia.

That some of the divisions of this people were really called Saka-suna, is obvious from Pliny; for he says, that the Sakai, who settled in Armenia, were named Sacassani, which is but Saka-suna spelt by a person unacquainted with the meaning of the combined words. And the name Sacasena, which they gave to the part of Armenia they occupied, is nearly the same sound as Saxonia. It is also important to remark, that Ptolemy mentions a Scythian people, sprung from the Sakai, by the name of Saxones. If the Sakai who reached Armenia were called Sacassani, they may have traversed Europe with the same appellation; which being pronounced by the Romans from them, and then reduced to writing from their pronunciation, may have been spelt with the *x* instead of the *ks*, and thus Saxones would not be a greater variation from Sacassani or Saksuna than we find between French, François, Franci, and their Greek name φραγγι; or between Spain, Espagne, and Hispania.

It is not at all improbable but that some of these marauding Sakai, or Sacassani, were gradually propelled to the western coasts of Europe, on which they were found by Ptolemy and from which they molested the Roman Empire, in the third century of our era. There was a people called Saxoi, on the Euxine, according to Stephanus. We may consider these, also, as a nation of the same parentage; who, in the wanderings of the Sakai from Asia to the German Ocean, were left on the Euxine, as others had chosen to occupy Armenia. We may here recollect the traditional descent of Odin preserved by Snorre in the Edda and his history. This great ancestor of the Saxon and Scandinavian chieftains is represented to have migrated from a city, on the east of the Tanais, called Asgard, and a country called Asaland, which imply the city and land of the Asae or Asians. The cause of this movement was the progress of the Romans. Odin is stated to have moved first into Russia, and thence into Saxony. This is not improbable. The wars between the Romans and Mithridates involved and shook most of the barbaric nations in these parts, and may have excited the desire, and imposed the necessity, of a westerly or European emigration.

EXTRACT FROM THE *ENCYCLOPAEDIA BRITANNICA* (1946), article 'Scythia'

The oldest inhabitants of Scythia were the Cimmerii; some of them were nomads, while others tilled some land in the river valleys and in the Crimea, where they left their name to ferries, earthworks, and the Cimmerian Bosporus. . . . In the 7th century B.C. these Cimmerians were attacked and partly driven out by a horde of newcomers from upper Asia called Scythae; these imposed their name and their yoke upon all that were left in the Euxine steppes, but the basis of the population remained unaltered. Their tombs even occur in Bulgaria and Hungary. The new-comers brought with them new customs and a new artistic taste. About the same time similar peoples harassed the northern frontier of Iran, where they were called Saka (Sacae), and in later times Saka and Scyths, whether they were originally the same or not, were regarded as synonymous. It is difficult always to judge whether given information applies to the Sacae . . . or the Scyths. Figures of Saka appear at Persepolis.

• • • • •

At Alexandropol and Solokha in the same district were equally elaborate tombs, the latter specially rich. Another tomb in this region, Melgunov's barrow, found in 1760, contained a dagger-sheath and pommel of Assyrian work and Greek things of the 6th century.

Certain of the objects which occur in these Scythic graves are of special form typical for the Scythic area. Most interesting of these is the dagger or sword. . . . Just the same form of short sword was used in Persia and is shown on the sculptures at Persepolis; the type is no doubt oriental in origin. Another special type is the bow-case (gorytos), made to take a short curved bow and to accommodate arrows as well. Further, there is the peculiar cauldron on one conical foot, round which the fire was built, the cylindrical hone pierced for suspension and the cup with a rounded bottom. Assyrian and afterwards Greek craftsmen working for Scythic employers were compelled to decorate these outlandish forms, which they did according to their own fashion; but there was also a vigorous native style that, more than anything else, expressed the distinctive individuality of the Scyths.

EXTRACTS FROM PROFESSOR GEORGE RAWLINSON'S ESSAYS ON AND TRANSLATIONS OF THE *HISTORY* OF HERODOTUS (John Murray, London, 1858)

But no important part is played by Indo-European nations in the history of Western Asia till the eighth or seventh centuries before our era, the preceding period being occupied by a long course of struggle between the Semites and the Turanians. The Into-Europeans thus occupy, chronologically, the third place in the ethnic history of this part of Asia. . . .

It may reasonably be conjectured, as has been already remarked, that the scene of the original development of the Indo-European dialect, or at any rate of the first large increase of the races speaking this language, was the mountain district of Armenia. It is from this point that the various tribes constituting the Indo-European family may with most probability be regarded as diverging, when the straitness of their territory compelled them to seek new abodes. As Cymry, Gaels, Pelasgi, Lithuanians, Teutons, Arians, Slaves, etc., they poured forth from their original country, spreading (as we have said) in three directions, northward, eastward, and westward. Northward across the Caucasus went forth a flood of emigrants, which settled partly in the steppes of Upper Asia, but principally in Northern and Central Europe, consisting of the Celtic, Teutonic, Lithuanian, Thracian,

Slavonic, and other less well-known tribes. Westward into the high plateau of Asia Minor descended another body, Phrygians, Lydians, Lycians, Pelasgi, &c., who possessed themselves of the whole country above Taurus, and in some instances penetrated to the south of it, thence proceeding onwards across the Hellespont and the islands from Asia into Europe, where they became, perhaps, the primitive colonists of Greece and Italy. Eastward wandered the Arian tribes in search of a new country, and fixed their home in the mountains of Affganistan, and upon the course of the Upper Indus.

With the first-mentioned of these three migrations we are in the present discussion but slightly concerned. Its main course was from Asia into Europe, and the Asiatic continent presents but few traces of its progress. It is perhaps allowable to conjecture that the Massa-getæ and Thyssa-getæ (Greater Goths and Lesser Goths) of the steppe country near the Caspian were Teutons of this migration, and the Thracians of Asia Minor appear to have been an eddy from the same stream; but otherwise Asia was merely the region whence these Indo-European races issued, and their various movements and ultimate destinies belong to the ethnic history of Europe. (Appendix to Bk. I, Essay xi, paras. 9, 10).

It results from this entire investigation, that the Scythians were not Mongolians, but members of the Indo-Germanic race. Language, as Mr. Grote correctly observes, is the only sure test; and language pronounces unmistakably in favour of the Indo-European, and against the Mongol theory. The small number of Scythic words which remain to us present from thirty to forty roots capable of identification with well-known Indo-European terms. (Appendix to Bk. IV, Essay ii, para. 10).

The Scyths, as their language exhibits them, were neither Medes, nor Slaves, nor Goths, nor Celts, nor Pelasgians, but their tongue possessed affinities to the speech of all these nations. We must not therefore be led away by doubtful etymologies to identify the Scythians with any special Indo-European race. They were probably a branch of this ethnic family as distinct from all other branches as Celts, Germans, and Slaves from one another Appendix to Bk. IV, Essay ii, para. 11).

Serial No. 70d.
Published by *The National Message*, Ltd.,
6 Buckingham Gate, London, S.W.1.

Judah and Benjamin in Captivity

T HE people of the Two-tribed kingdom of Judah were carried captive to Assyria and Babylonia, in a series of deportations which extended over a period of 160 years ending some time after 584 B.C., when the final remnants were swept away following the siege and fall of Jerusalem.

THE DEPORTATIONS

The Decline of the Two-tribed kingdom commenced during the period of the evil monarch Ahaz, during whose reign it suffered disastrously. The Syrians invaded and carried away a considerable number of his people. Conflict with the Ten tribes saw 120,000 of his fighting men killed in one day's battle. The Edomites roughly handled his forces and also took captives, whilst the Philistines, taking advantage of his plight, captured many towns in the south (II Chronicles xxviii). His son Hezekiah, during a period of devotion to the worship of Jehovah, gave the kingdom a brief respite and recovered the territory yielded to the Philistines (II Kings xviii, 8), but the decline was only temporarily arrested, for he too lost a large proportion of his subjects when Sennacherib captured all the chief towns of the kingdom (except Jerusalem), deported 200,150 of their inhabitants, and handed the captured towns over to the Philistines. So reduced was Hezekiah by this time that, during the siege of his capital, the Assyrian general Rabshakeh tauntingly offered him 2,000 horses if he would produce riders for them. Final doom was pronounced upon the kingdom during the reign of Manasseh (c. 690 B.C.), "I will stretch over Jerusalem the line of Samaria" (II Kings xxi, 13). There was a further brief respite during the reign of Josiah which delayed, but did not avert, final catastrophe, for the pathetic residue of the kingdom was utterly broken and rooted out by Nebuchadnezzar during the reigns of Judah's three last kings, Jehoiakim, Jehoiachin, and Zedekiah, mere puppets of the mighty Babylonian monarch.

The Deportations were as follows:

Reign of:	
Ahaz (c. 735 B.C.)	Rezin, king of Syria, carried away "a great multitude of people" to the Damascus area of that country.
Hezekiah (710 B.C.)	Sennacherib, king of Assyria, invaded and captured all the chief towns and villages excepting only Jerusalem. He deported 200,150 of the inhabitants, presumably to Assyria, handing over their cities to various Philistine petty kings.
Jehoiakim (604 B.C.)	Nebuchadnezzar of Babylon took 3,000 of the principal people of the kingdom to Babylon.
Jehoiachin (595 B.C.)	Nebuchadnezzar deported a further 10,000 to Babylon. These were craftsmen smiths, and the pick of the fighting men.

Zedekiah (585-584 B.C.)	*First phase.* At the fall of Jerusalem all that remained of the remnant of the kingdom were removed to Babylon, with the exception of the very poorest of the population. These were left as vinedressers and husbandmen, to prevent the land from becoming a wilderness. They were quickly joined by Judahites who had fled for refuge to the neighbouring lands. This assorted community was placed under the governorship of Gedaliah, himself a Judahite. They enjoyed the produce of a bountiful harvest.
	Second phase. Almost immediately, Gedaliah was murdered, and Johanan, another prominent Judahite, assumed the leadership. Against the advice of Jeremiah, he led them to Egypt, but, five years later, their sanctuary failed them, for Nebuchadnezzar transferred them to Babylon, following a successful expedition against Egypt.

Evidence on the deportations is tabulated below:

DURING THE REIGN OF AHAZ

BIBLE NARRATIVE	SECULAR SOURCES
II Chronicles xxviii, 5 "Wherefore the Lord his God delivered him into the hand of the king of Syria; and they smote him, and carried away a great multitude of them captives, and brought them to Damascus."	
II Kings xvi, 9 ". . . the king of Assyria went up against Damascus, and took it, and carried the people of it captive to Kir. . . ."	"*Kir.* . . . A variety of conjectures have been offered on this point. . . . But the common opinion among recent commentators has been that a tract on the river Kur or Cyrus . . . is intended." (Prof. George Rawlinson in Wm. Smith's *Dictionary of the Bible* (1863 ed.).
	Josephus: "Now this king, upon the reception of those ambassadors, came to assist Ahaz, and made war upon the Syrians, and laid their country waste, and took Damascus by force, and slew Rezin their king, and transplanted the people of Damascus into the Upper Media, and brought a colony of Assyrians, and planted them in Damascus." (*Antiquities*, Bk. IX, ch. xii, sec. 3.)

BIBLE NARRATIVE | SECULAR SOURCES

II Kings xviii, 13.

"Now in the fourteenth year of king Hezekiah did Sennacherib king of Assyria come up against all the fenced cities of Judah, and took them." (See also II Chron. xxxii, 1, and Isaiah xxxvi, 1.)

II Kings xviii, 31, 32.

(The Assyrian general Rabshakeh, speaking to the besieged inhabitants of Jerusalem):

". . . Make an agreement with me by a present, and come out to me. . . . Until I come and take you away to a land like your own land, a land of corn and wine. . . ."

Josephus (*Antiquities*, Bk. X, ch. 1, sec. 1):

"It was now the fourteenth year of the government of Hezekiah, king of the two tribes, when the king of Assyria, whose name was Sennacherib, made an expedition against him with a great army, and took all the cities of the tribes of Judah and Benjamin by force; . . ."

Inscription of Sennacherib.

"I then besieged Hezekiah of Judah who had not submitted to my yoke, and I captured forty-six of his strong cities and fortresses and innumerable small cities which were round about them. . . . I brought out therefrom two hundred thousand and one hundred and fifty people, both small and great, male and female, and horses, and mules, and asses, and camels, and oxen, and innumerable sheep I counted as spoil. (Hezekiah) himself . . . I shut up within Jerusalem his royal city. I threw up mounds against him, and I took vengeance upon any man who came forth from his city. His cities which I had captured I took from him and gave to Mitinti, king of Ashdod, and Padî, king of Ekron, and Ṣilli-Bêl, king of Gaza, and I reduced his land. . . . Hezekiah . . . despatched after me his messenger to my royal city Nineveh to pay tribute . . . a heavy treasure, together with his daughters, and the women of his palace, and male and female musicians." (*Guide to the Babylonian and Assyrian Antiquities of the British Museum*, edited by Sir E. A. Wallis Budge, pp. 226-7.)

NOTE: Although Sennacherib's inscription does not actually say that he carried his prisoners away, it is clear that he did so. His words "brought out" obviously mean out of their land, for there would have been no point in merely bringing them out of their respective cities. They are mentioned as part of the spoil, which would undoubtedly find its way to the victor's capital. Furthermore, the cities of the unfortunate Judahites were handed over to the Philistines. Rabshakeh's placatory words support the view that these 200,000 captives of Judah and Benjamin were taken out of their land. He was obviously trying to persuade the people of Jerusalem to surrender and accept a similar deportation as an alternative to the certain destruction which awaited them if they persisted in their defence of the city. Professor George Rawlinson concurs in the view that the 200,000 were carried away. (*The Five Great Monarchies*, Vol. II, p. 162.)

BIBLE NARRATIVE	SECULAR SOURCES

BIBLE NARRATIVE

Jeremiah lii, 28.

"This is the people whom Nebuchadrezzar carried away captive: in the seventh year three thousand Jews and three and twenty."

Note: The seventh year of Nebuchadrezzar was the eleventh year of Jehoiakim. (See Jeremiah xxv, 1, and II Chron. xxxvi, 5.)

SECULAR SOURCES

Josephus (*Antiquities*, Bk. x, ch. vi. sec. 3).

". . . the king of Babylon . . . slew . . . Jehoiakim . . . he also took the principal persons in dignity for captives, three thousand in number, and led them away to Babylon. . . ."

Note: In the third year of Jehoiakim a careful selection of the nobility of Judah had already been taken to Babylon, Daniel among them. (Dan. i, 1-6.)

DURING THE REIGN OF JEHOIACHIN
(Also known as Coniah or Jeconiah)

II Kings xxiv, 11-15.

"And Nebuchadnezzar . . . carried away all Jerusalem, and all the princes, and all the mighty men of valour, even ten thousand captives, and all the craftsmen and smiths: none remained, save the poorest sort of the people of the land . . . those carried he into captivity from Jerusalem to Babylon." (See also II Chron. xxxvi, 9-10.)

Josephus (*Antiquities*, Bk. X, ch. vii, sec. 1).

"But . . . the king of Babylon . . . besieged Jehoiachin in Jerusalem . . . and . . . gave orders to his generals to take all that were in the city captives, both the youth and the handicraftsmen, and bring them bound to him; their number was ten thousand eight hundred and thirty-two . . . and appointed Jehoiachin's uncle, Zedekiah, to be king. . . ."

Jewish Encyclopædia (New York, 1925, article "Captivity").

"As soon as Jehoiachin or Jaconiah, who had meanwhile succeeded his father, Jehoiakim, as king, had, after a short defense, surrendered to the leaders of the Babylonian army, Nebuchnezzar ordered him, together with the most distinguished men of the land, and the most valuable treasures of the Temple and the palace, to be sent to Babylonia. . . ."

BIBLE NARRATIVE

Jeremiah xxxix, 2-10.

"And in the eleventh year of Zedekiah . . . the city was broken up. . . . Then Nebuzar-adan the captain of the guard carried away captive into Babylon the remnant of the people that remained in the city, and those that fell away, that fell to him, with the rest of the people that remained. But Nebuzar-adan . . . left of the poor of the people, which had nothing, in the land of Judah, and gave them vineyards and fields at the same time."

Jeremiah xli, 16-17.

"Then took Johanan . . . all the remnant of the people whom he had recovered from Ishmael . . . and dwelt in the habitation of Chimham, which is by Bethlehem, to go to enter into Egypt."

Jeremiah xliii, 5-7.

"But Johanan . . . took all the remnant of Judah . . . into the land of Egypt . . . to Tahpanhes." (See also II Kings xxv and II Chron. xxxvi.)

SECULAR SOURCES

Josephus (*Antiquities*, Bk. X, ch. vii, sec. 4).

"Now, in the ninth year of the reign of Zedekiah . . . the king of Babylon made a second expedition against Jerusalem, and lay before it eighteen months, and besieged it with the utmost application. There came upon them also two of the greatest calamities, at the same time that Jerusalem was besieged, a famine and a pestilential distemper, and made great havoc of them. . . ."

Ch. viii, sec. 2-6.

"Now the city was taken . . . in the eleventh year of the reign of Zedekiah . . . the general of the Babylonian king now overthrew the city to the very foundations, and removed all the people . . . all whom . . . he carried to the king of Babylon to Riblah, a city of Syria. So the king . . . himself led all the captives and Zedekiah to Babylon."

Ch. ix, sec. 1-6.

"Now the general of the army, Nebuzaradan, when he had carried the people of the Jews into captivity, left the poor, and those that had deserted, in the country; and made . . . Gedaliah . . . their governor . . . those that fled away during the siege of Jerusalem, and had been scattered over the country . . . came together from all parts to Gedaliah to Mispah. . . . Ishmael . . slew Gedaliah and . . . took captive the people that were in Mispah . . .

(continued at foot of next column)

Jewish Encyclopædia (New York, 1925, Article "Captivity").

"Another deportation took place upon the downfall of the kingdom of Judah. . . . Zedekiah, was captured and brought before Nebuchadnezzar at Riblah . . . and he was taken in chains to Babylon . . . the same year Nebuzaradan, captain of Nebuchadnezzar's body-guard, ordered that the Temple, the royal palace, and all the dwellings in the city of Jerusalem be set on fire, and that the surviving inhabitants be taken captive to Babylon. . . Now, if the figures as given in Jeremiah . . . be accepted as correct, the total number of exiles . . . will be 12,000 men, or in all 36,000 to 48,000 souls. . . . Their habitation was in the province of Babylon. . . . A number of western Semitic proper names, discovered upon inscriptions found in Nippur, have led Hilprecht to believe that many of the exiles were settled in that place. . . ."

Note: The numbers of those deported, as given in the Bible narrative, do not include the families of the men taken.

but . . . Johanan overtook him . . . and . . . took those whom he had rescued . . . and removed into Egypt . . . on the fifth year after the destruction of Jerusalem. . . . Nebuchadnezzar . . . fell upon Egypt . . . and took those Jews that were there captives, and led them away to Babylon. . . ."

THE NEW HABITAT

The evidence shows that the people of Judah and Benjamin were resettled in at least three different territories, viz:

Syria. , The "multitude" of captives taken in the period of Ahaz were carried to the Damascus area of Syria. Shortly afterwards, the people of this city were themselves subjugated by Tiglath-Pileser of Assyria and deported to Kir—a region near the Caucasus. It seems likely, therefore, that the Judahites would accompany their erstwhile captors to this locality—which is almost in Europe.

Assyria. It is a reasonable deduction that the 200,000 captives taken from the towns and villages of the Two-tribed kingdom by Sennacherib were carried—with the spoil—to Assyria, the country to which his predecessor and successor also removed their defeated enemies. This was by far the largest deportation from the Judah kingdom and it is noteworthy that the captives went to the same country as their idolatrous kinsmen of the Ten tribes, within a few years of the latter's final deportation.

Babylonia. Those taken during the reigns of Jehoiakim, Jehoiachin, and Zedekiah found exile in Babylonia, both in the capital and in other cities of that country. Archaeological research has found inscriptions of this period, bearing Judahite names which have their counterparts in the books of Ezra and Nehemiah, at Nippur, S.E. of Babylon. Tablets bearing Old Testament names have also been found at Kannu, in N.W. Mesopotamia. These have, in some quarters, been linked with the people of the Ten tribes. However, as the names there discovered betoken devout Jehovah worship, it would appear to be improbable that they are connected with the idolatrous northern kingdom. It is more likely that they refer to Judahites of the Sennacherib captivity, or (possibly) to fragments of Judah and Benjamin who were taken to Syria during the reign of Ahaz.

The record in the book of Esther discloses that there was a subsequent remarkable dispersion of the Babylonian captives throughout the whole of the Medo-Persian empire. By 520 B.C. those who had not returned to rebuild Jerusalem had become scattered over the vast territory stretching from the Mediterranean to India (Esther viii, 9). It is clear that these were Judahites and not of the Ten tribes for they are definitely named as "Jews" and, moreover, the perfidious Haman complained to his king that they still kept their own laws. The Ten tribes had long since abandoned these.

POINTS OF SPECIAL INTEREST

1. The deportation by Tiglath-Pileser of the inhabitants of the Damascus area of Syria to the region of the Caucasus provides ground for interesting study. If, as seems highly probable, the Judahites taken during the reign of Ahaz were also carried to Kir, there would be two distinct communities, Syrian and Judahite, located in that isolated, near-European territory.

2. It seems strange that the deportation by Sennacherib (the largest of them all) should have received so little attention from Bible commentators. It seems quite clear that the great majority of the people of Judah and Benjamin did not go to Babylonia at all, but followed their Ten-tribed kinsmen to Assyria.

3. The disastrous blows sustained by the kingdom of Judah during the reigns of Ahaz and Hezekiah account for its greatly reduced state at the time of Nebuchadnezzar and for the comparatively small number of captives which that king removed to Babylonia.

Serial No. 32c.

4. Nebuchadnezzar first carried away the nobility, the chief military men and the skilled craftsmen. Thus, with a minimum of effort, he rendered the kingdom incapable of further effective resistance.

5. The miserable residue which sought sanctuary in Egypt found their way, perforce, to Babylon after all.

6. Josephus makes it perfectly plain that the territory of Judah and Benjamin was completely depopulated of Israelites, and left "a desert" for seventy years (Ant. Bk. X, ch. ix, sec. 7). This contrasts sharply with the fate of the land of the Ten tribes, which was resettled with people from other parts of the Assyrian empire.

7. During the reign of Josiah—long after the Ten tribes had been carried away—there were remnants of the latter still living in their tribal territories. Manasseh and Ephraim are particularly mentioned (II Chron. xxxiv, 9). These were undoubtedly the "gleaning grapes" which Isaiah had said should be left behind (Isaiah xvii, 6).

Ten-Tribed Israel in Assyria

A SUFFICIENT weight of evidence is available—from the Bible narrative, the inscriptions of the ancient Assyrians, the early historians, and from other secular sources—to identify the regions to which the captives from the Ten-tribed kingdom were taken following their removal from Palestine by Tiglath-Pileser, Shalmaneser, and Sargon. This testimony shows that they were carried beyond the Tigris, the main bulk being settled in the country to the south-west and south of the Caspian Sea; i.e. roughly speaking, that part of modern Persia which lies to the north of latitude 35°N. and to the west of longitude 55°E.

THE DEPORTATIONS

The **Decline** of the Ten-tribed kingdom commenced *c.* 860 B.C., during the reign of Jehu. "In those days the Lord began to cut Israel short" (II Kings x, 32). Some time after 750 B.C. a pronouncement came through Isaiah: "Within three-score and five years shall Ephraim—i.e. Ten-tribed Israel—be broken that it be not a people" (ch. vii, 8). The 'breaking' was completed, in the main, when the capital city of Samaria was taken, following a three-year siege which commenced in 720 B.C. "There was none left but the tribe of Judah only" (II Kings xvii, 18) except 'gleaning grapes'—the scattered oddments that would inevitably escape the captor's net—which Isaiah had said should be left behind (ch. xvii, 6). The Ten tribes were replaced by deportees from Babylon, Cuthah, Ava, Hamath, and Sepharvaim (II Kings xvii, 24). These, mostly 'Cutheans', later became known as Samaritans. The enforced exchange of populations seems to have ceased *c.* 680 B.C., during the reign of the Assyrian monarch Esarhaddon (Ezra iv, 1-3).

Of the **two main deportations**, the first was carried out by Tiglath-Pileser. The second was commenced by Shalmaneser and completed by Sargon. The Bible accounts are tersely informative; they are supported by the Assyrian inscriptions and the testimony of Josephus, the 'Romanised' Jewish historian. This evidence is tabulated below, together with relevant extracts from the *Jewish Encyclopædia*, the latter being quoted as the informed opinion of modern orthodox Jewry.

TIGLATH-PILESER

(This monarch is referred to as 'Pulu' (Pul) in the Babylonian record.—*Encyclopædia Britannica*, 14th Edition.)

Bible Narrative

II Kings xv, 29

"In the days of Pekah king of Israel came Tiglath-pileser king of Assyria, and took Ijon, and Abel-beth-maachah, and Janoah, and Kedesh, and Hazor, and Gilead, and Galilee, all the land of Naphtali, and carried them captive to Assyria."

I Chronicles v. 26

"And the God of Israel stirred up the spirit of Pul king of Assyria, and the spirit of Tilgath-pilneser king of Assyria, and he carried them away, even the Reubenites, and the Gadites, and the half tribe of Manasseh, and brought them unto Halah, and Habor, and Hara, and to the river Gozan, unto this day."

Note.—Northern Dan would also be swept up in this campaign. Some portions of Naphtali must have been allowed to remain, for Tobit (ch. 1) mentions captives of this tribe as having been taken during the later invasion of Shalmaneser. Esdras also mentions that monarch as removing people of the Ten tribes (II Esdras xiii).

Secular Sources

Inscription of Tiglath-Pileser III (or IV)

"The towns of Gil(ead) and Abel-(beth-Maachah?) on the frontier of Beth-Omri [Samaria], the widespread (district of Naph-ta)li to its whole extent I turned into the territory of Assyria . . . The land of Beth-Omri . . . a collection of its inhabitants (with their goods) I transported to Assyria . . ." (Sayce's *Assyria*, pp. 177-178).

Josephus, 'Antiquities', Book IX, ch. xi, sec. 1

". . . But the king of Assyria, whose name was Tiglath-Pileser, when he had made an expedition against the Israelites, and had overrun all the land of Gilead, and the region beyond Jordan, and the adjoining country, which is called Galilee, and Kadesh, and Hazor, he made the inhabitants prisoners, and transplanted them into his own kingdom . . ."

'Jewish Encyclopædia', 1925 Edition, Article: Captivity

"Tiglath-pileser . . . While he annexed these borderlands of the tribes of Zebulon, Asher, and Naphtali, together with such of the eastern territory of the Jordan as belonged to Israel, he led the inhabitants of these provinces into Assyria, and established them there (II Kings xv, 29)."

SHALMANESER-SARGON

Bible Narrative

II Kings xvii, 6

"In the ninth year of Hoshea the king of Assyria took Samaria, and carried Israel away to Assyria, and placed them in Halah and in Habor *by* the river of Gozan, and in the cities of the Medes."

II Kings xviii, 11

"And the king of Assyria did carry away Israel unto Assyria, and put them in Halah and in Habor *by* the river of Gozan, and in the cities of the Medes."

Apochryphal Book of Tobit, ch. i, 1-14

". . . Tobit, . . . of the tribe of Naphthali; Who in the time of Enemessar king of the Assyrians was led captive out of Thisbe, which is at the right hand of that city, which is called properly Nephthali in Galilee above Aser . . . and I did many almsdeeds to my brethren, and my nation, who came with me to Nineve, . . . And I went into Media, and left in trust with Gabael, the brother of Gabrias, at Rages a city of Media ten talents of silver."

Ch. xiv, 14

"And he died at Ecbatane in Media . . ."

Apochryphal Book of II Esdras, xiii, 40

"Those are the ten tribes, which were carried away prisoners out of their own land in the time of Osea the king, whom Salmanasar the king of Assyria led away captive, . . ."

Note.—The record of Tobit fixes the identity of two of the cities of Media, namely Ecbatana and Rhages. It also establishes the fact that some part of the tribe of Naphtali was settled around Nineveh.

The quotation from II Esdras agrees with the evidence of Tobit to the effect that Shalmaneser removed at least some elements of the tribes in the north, before Samaria itself fell to Sargon—after Shalmaneser's death.

Secular Sources

Inscription of Sargon

"(In the beginning of my reign) the city of Samaria I besieged, I captured . . . 27,280 of its inhabitants I carried away; . . ." (Sayce's *Assyria*, p. 178).

Josephus, 'Antiquities', Book IX, ch. xiv, sec. 1

". . . the king of Assyria, . . . beseiged Samaria three years, . . . and quite demolished the government of the Israelites, and transplanted all the people into Media and Persia; . . ."

'Jewish Encyclopædia', 1925 Edition, Article: Captivity

". . . The second deportation took place after the conquest of Samaria . . . which conquest was followed by the demolition of the northern kingdom."

HALAH, HABOR, HARA, THE CITIES OF THE MEDES, THE RIVER GOZAN, THE RIVER CHEBAR

These are the ancient names of the localities to which the Ten tribes were deported, the River Chebar being the scene of the incident in which Ezekiel delivered his message to certain of the captives of the House of Israel, i.e. the Ten tribes (ch. iii, 15-17). In fixing the modern equivalents of these ancient place-names it is necessary to go back to the earliest evidence available, either directly or through the medium of modern historians who have examined this evidence. The original sources are: the Bible narrative; certain gleanings from the Book of Tobit; the Assyrian inscriptions; the record of the early historians and geographers. With regard to the last named, it must always be remembered that their geographical knowledge was not by any means precise, judged by modern standards. Thus their locations and topographical features often vary quite considerably.

The traditional theory with regard to these places, as shown on many Bible maps, is as follows:

The River Chebar:	The modern Khabur (ancient Chaboras), which enters the Euphrates in eastern Syria.
Gozan:	A tributary of the above-named Khabur. Alternatively, the region west of the Khabur known to the Greeks as Gauzanitis; so named many centuries after the deportations.
Halah and Habor:	Towns in the Khabur area.
Hara:	Harran (Charran). The Syrian city where Abraham sojourned.
The cities of the Medes:	Towns of northern Persia—not in dispute.

This view appears to have achieved acceptance on the ground of the similarity of the names Chebar and Khabur, Hara and Harran. But further evidence than this is needed; for there was another Khabur river north of the Tigris, and to this day there is a place called Chebardunge, near the River Abhar, nor far from Teheran. Furthermore, there is a town Haran (Haru or Herau) to the north-west of the Elburz mountains. On the ground of resemblance of names, these places have an equal claim. Thus other reasons must be adduced to support any theory based only upon similarity of names.

It should be borne in mind that the Assyrian monarchs—who transplanted many other nations as well as Israel—were not concerned merely with punitive measures. Had this been the case it would have been far simpler to exterminate the vanquished peoples, for mass-slayings were commonplace. The Assyrians were determined to control a vast empire of subject peoples, and they used these large-scale enforced migrations as a means of preventing possible resurgence on the part of the captive nations. Uprooted from their homelands, the patriotic urge was weakened; and the captives were occupied for many years in settling down in their new territory, though paying tribute to their conquerors.

The Assyrians usually took good care to place their captives in regions remote from their native lands. For instance, Tiglath-Pileser carried the Syrians to Kir (the River Cyrus?) (II Kings xvi, 9) near the Caucasus in the 'Upper Media' mentioned by Josephus (*Antiquities*, Book IX, ch. xii, sec. 3): "and transplanted the people of Damascus into the Upper Media, and brought a colony of Assyrians, and planted them in Damascus"; whilst according to this same authority (*Antiquities*, Book XI, ch. ii, sec. 1), the territory of the Ten tribes was repopulated with people of 'Persia and Media'. There could be no trickle back from these far-off lands, for great rivers and lofty mountain ranges would have made any such effort a pilgrimage indeed. Had the Ten tribes been taken to the places of the traditional theory, a mere local revolt would have made it an easy matter for the captives to make a bid for home—a journey of a mere 300 miles on what was the main highway of those days.

A **more critical examination** of the collated information confirms the view of many scholars to the effect that the Ten tribes were carried beyond the Tigris. Whilst it is quite possible—and even probable—that some fragments became scattered through Assyria as a whole, there is no real evidence to indicate any substantial settlement of the Ten tribes south of that river. On the other hand, there are reliable records of Ten-tribed communities northwards of Nineveh (Mosul).

An analysis of the available evidence gives the following identifications, all the places named being at such distances from Palestine as to rule out the possibility of 'back-trailing' on the part of the deportees:

Authority	Modern Equivalent
	Halah
Ewald, nineteenth century orientalist, in his *History of Israel* (1874 edition), Vol IV, p. 165.	North of Nineveh and south of Lake Van.
	Habor (Septuagint Abor)
Ewald (p. 165).	North of Nineveh and south of Lake Van.
Royal Geographical Society Map (*Proceedings*, May 1889).	Shows a town Abhar and a river of that name to the south-west of the Caspian, flowing in a south-easterly direction, and not far from Teheran.
War Office Map of the Persian Gulf, 3rd Edition (Communications Revised), 1941; Sheet 32.	Also shows this town by a river which enters into the salt lake Darya-yi-Namak.
Élisée Reclus 'The Universal Geography', Vol. IX.	Shows the above river as the Abhar.
	Hara
Royal Geographical Society Map, as above.	Show a town Harau (Hara or Herau) between the Caspian Sea and the Qizil Uzun, to the north-west of the Elburz mountains.
War Office Map, as above.	
Phillips Atlas of Classical and Scriptural Geography (compiled from D'Anville and other authorities), 1855.	Shows the above-named town as 'Hara'.
	The River Chebar
Dr. William Smith's Ancient Atlas, illustrating Old Testament and Classical Authors.	Apply the name Khabur or Chabur to a river which enters the Tigris to the north-west of Nineveh—as well as showing the other Khabur or Chabur—the ancient Chaboras which flows into the Euphrates.
Everyman's Atlas of Ancient and Classical Geography (1912 edition).	

Note.—In view of Tobit's record of Ten-tribed captives at Nineveh, this northern Khabur is infinitely more acceptable than the Chaboras, which is within comparatively easy reach of Samaria. Ewald (p. 165) concurs with this view.

Khabur (river or canal) is a name not uncommon in the Tigris-Euphrates area. The theory has been advanced that the Naru Kabaru (great canal) at Nippur, S.E. of Babylon is the Chebar of Ezekiel. But this does not reconcile easily with the prophet's narrative. Ezekiel, a Judahite priest deported to Babylon in the time of Jehoiachin, was commissioned to carry God's warning to both "houses" of Israel. The terms "house of Israel" and "house of Judah" are used in contra-distinction (ch. iv). He could easily deliver his message to the Judahites in captivity, for he resided among them. But, to enable him to address the more distant Ten tribes, he was carried by the spirit to Tel Abib, where he remained for seven days "astonished" by his remarkable experience (ch. iii). It will be recalled that certain elders of the Ten tribes subsequently journeyed to Babylonia to "enquire of the Lord" through Ezekiel (ch. xiv and ch. xx).

Authority	Modern Equivalent
Gozan	
Royal Geographical Society Map (*Proceedings*, May 1889). War Office Map of the Persian Gulf, 3rd Edition (Communications Revised), 1941; Sheet 32.	Show the River Kizil (Red) Uzun, rising to the south of Lake Urmia and discharging into the south-west Caspian.
Ewald, *History of Israel*, Vol. IV, p. 165.	Says this river is still known by the name Ozen.
Spruner's Historical Atlas of the Ottoman Empire.	Calls the same river 'Osen'.
Spruner's *Atlas Antiquus* (1865), Map No. 3.	Calls it 'Gozan'.
Phillips Atlas of Classical and Scriptural Geography (1855).	Names it 'Gozan'.
Dr. Wilhelm Sieglin's map in *Atlas Antiquus* (1893; Asia Superior; Tab. 6).	Shows town named Gauzania to the east of Lake Urmia, on a southern tributary of the Talkheh Rud, east of Tabriz.
Everyman's Atlas of Ancient and Classical Geography (1912 edition).	Shows a town of Gauzania to the north of Lake Urmia, on the north bank of the Araxes river.

The Cities of the Medes

It is generally accepted that these were cities of ancient Media (modern northern Persia). Although the Bible does not mention any of them by name, the Book of Tobit records Israelite communities at Rhages and Ecbatana (modern Teheran and Hamadan—*Encyclopædia Britannica*, 9th Edition, Vol. 34, Map No. 40).

General Note

As Ewald states (p. 165), the localities named in the Bible narrative are those to which the stream of compulsory emigration was directed in the greatest strength. Doubtless there would be forced labour for many Israelites throughout the Assyrian empire; there is archæological evidence of Israelites having lived in the ancient Mesopotamian cities of Kannu (Kanneh?) and Kara-u, although it is more likely that these were Judahites; but Northern Persia was, without doubt, the new habitat of the bulk of the Ten tribes.

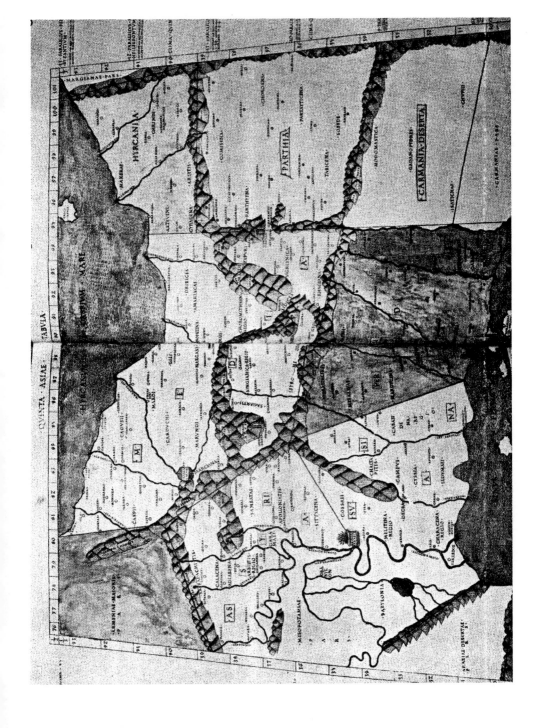

Shown overleaf is one of Ptolemy's Maps, Rome, 1490 edition, showing Gauzania, by the River Cyrus, which is shown entering the southern Caspian.

(Photo by Wallace Heaton Ltd.)   *(By courtesy of the Royal Geographic Society)*

It is known that Ptolemy, the Alexandrian geographer (*c.* A.D. 90-168), derived much of his information from earlier sources, such as the works of Eratosthenes (250 B.C.), Hipparchus (*c.* 150 B.C.), Poseidonius (*c.* 30 B.C.), and Marinus of Tyre (A.D. 70-130). Considering the age in which he lived, the manner in which Ptolemy presented his data is remarkable. He treated the earth as a sphere, dividing it into degrees of latitude and longitude, using a meridian of longitude through the Canary Islands, and 90° of latitude measured from the Equator to the Pole. In Book VI of his *Geography*, Ptolemy tabulates Gauzania as a Medean city with latitude 40 2/3°, longitude 82°, according to this system, situated on the Cyrus (Kir or Araxes) river system. In view of there being a modern *Ghazian* near the mouth of the Sefid Rud, it seems likely that the Kir and Kizil Osen, or Gozan river, were confused by the early geographers.

Authorities: Various

Who Were the Scythians?

It has been securely established that the bulk of the people of the Ten-tribed kingdom of Israel, and a substantial portion of those of the Two-tribed kingdom of Judah, were deported from Palestine during the period 734-710 B.C. to what is now north-west Persia, but known to the ancient historians as part of the vast territory which they called Scythia.

The Scythian question has profoundly puzzled historians and ethnologists, ancient and modern, and at this late period of history there would appear to be no likelihood of any solution which might achieve general acceptance. The divergence of view of accredited authorities is remarkable —and when experts disagree the layman is entitled to make his own choice. Nevertheless, in order to attempt to follow the migrations of the Israel peoples after their expulsion from Palestine, it is necessary to consider the available data on this most controversial subject, even though the evidence adduced is often conflicting as between one authority and another.

In particular, the territory originally called Scythia extended from the mouth of the Danube, northwards of the Black Sea, to the Volga. In its widest sense, however, the term embraced all lands eastwards, even as far as the borders of India and eastern Turkestan. In general, the Scythians comprised a vast agglomeration of nomadic and semi-nomadic nations and tribes of diverse origin: Nordic, Alpine, Slavonic, Mongol. Some of them were cultured and righteous; others were barbarous and foul. Their names, customs, language, and habitat changed with the centuries. The Greeks had their own classification for these peoples. The Romans used other names; whilst the Persians indiscriminately called them all Sacæ. Pliny, writing prior to A.D. 80, said: ''. . . Upon no subject that I know are there greater discrepancies among writers.'' Small wonder, therefore, that modern ethnologists disagree.

It was into this heterogeneous assortment of obscure nations and tribes that the Israel peoples disappeared from the Bible narrative. And it is out of this ethnological maze that—in one form or another—they might be expected ultimately to emerge.

Many Variants of the Name Scythian

According to the early Greek writers, the Scythians called themselves *Skolotoi*. There were many variants, however, according to the period and nationality of the record. Some of the variants, derivatives, and equivalents are listed below:

Skuthes	Suktas
Skuthai	Sughuda
Sakhi	Sagetai
Saca	Sagh
Sacæ	Sogdii
Sukhu	Sigynnæ

Note: The Behistun Rock inscription gives Suktas as the phonetic equivalent of Sogdiana.

Gimirri (meaning 'the tribes') is the Babylonian equivalent of *Scythian* and *Saka*. The *Gimirri* were also referred to as *Manda*.

The Origin of the Name

Although the name Scythian (wanderer) has been indiscriminately applied at one time or another to almost the whole of mankind anciently dwelling to the east of the Carpathians, it is becoming accepted that the term arose—and, strictly speaking, should be applied—in respect only of a definite section of the peoples so loosely included.

The origin of the name is obscure. It seems quite definite that the 'fossil' root was something like *s-k-* and that this was sometimes hardened into *s-g-*. Rawlinson considered that the word *Saka* "may perhaps be the true national appellative, whence the other names by which the Greeks knew the race were derived".

The Scythians, or Skuths, were nomadic tent-dwellers. The ancient Hebrew-Aramaic word for tent or booth was *Succoth* (S-c-th)—phonetic *Sukkah*. The Israelites also had nomadic tent-dwellers: ". . . I made the children of Israel to dwell in booths . . ." (Lev. xxiii. 43). Quite apart from the projection of the Israel people into Medo-Persia, it has been established that there had been considerable Hebrew migration in a northerly and north-westerly direction from the Tigris-Euphrates area, about the time of Abraham. It may well be that this old Hebrew word supplies the lost derivation.

This theory derives support from the Tel-el-Amarna tablets, which refer to invaders of Palestine *c.* 1400 B.C. by the name of Khabiru. Many scholars are convinced that the terms *Khabiru* and *Hebrews* are synonymous, although some of these incline to the view that the Khabiru of the tablets were non-Israelite Hebrews who probably invaded further north at or about the same time as Joshua's conquest of Canaan. Professor T. Eric Peet, Brunner Professor of Egyptology in the University of Liverpool, mentions that the tablets also refer to a people called *Sagaz*. He says: "It is hard to escape the conclusion that Khabiru and Sagaz are two names for one and the same people, and this is supported in remarkable fashion by an inscription found at Boghaz Keui, the Hittite capital in Asia Minor, in which the phrase 'Khabiru-gods' is used as an equivalent for 'Sagaz-gods' " (*Egypt and the Old Testament*, 1922, p. 117). Thus we have this fossil word *S-k-* or *S-g-* used to describe Hebrew peoples in the second millennium B.C. In the light of this it seems decidedly possible that at least some of the Scythian peoples, called by the Persians *Sacæ*, were non-Israelite Hebrews who had long preceded the Ten Tribes in their Iranian habitat.

Serial No. 55a.

Another **distinct possibility** is that the term *Skth* involves the (pre-Israelite) Hebrew name *Isaac*. The Hebrew pronunciation of this name has been variously given as *yis-khawk, zis-khawk, tsaw-khak,* and *saw-khak.* It is impossible to say dogmatically what the original Hebrew pronunciation was, but from ancient Armenian sources it is known that the pronunciation as far back as the early centuries A.D. was *sahak* (*Encyclopædia Britannica,* 9th edition, article: 'Armenian Literature'). **It is noteworthy that the s-k sound persists throughout.** By about 800 B.C. the people of the Ten-tribed kingdom of Israel were being referred to as the House of Isaac (*Beth-Sahak-,* Amos vii. 16). They had long forsaken the laws and worship of Jehovah, and would surely dissociate themselves from His name (Isra-el). It is most significant that *Sacæ* people are recorded in the same regions as those to which the *Sahak* were deported, within a generation or so of the time of the expulsion of the latter from their Palestinian homeland.

THE SACAE

Although the Persian inscriptions include all the Scythian peoples under the term *Saka,* it is clear that this ancient Persian name was used particularly with relation to a dominant group of nations of Iranian origin. This group is now usually referred to as the *Sacæ.* Their emergence into recorded history took place during the early part of the seventh century B.C.

Of the Ancient Writers:

HERODOTUS (fifth century B.C.) records that, in his day, the *Saka Humavarga* were located east and south-east of the Sea of Aral, even as far as Turkestan and the borders of India. He associates the Sacæ with the Bactrians, and says that they were at one period led by Hystaspes, son of Darius, who had married Atossa, daughter of Cyrus. By the time of the Alexandrine writers, the bulk of the Sacæ appear to have been dwelling somewhere beyond the Jaxartes.

DIODORUS (first century B.C.) says that kindred Sacæ peoples spread from the Araxes to as far west as the Don, and that they settled two remarkable colonies from Assyria and Media on the latter river, and in Paphlagonia and Pontus; further, that these colonists later became classified as *Sauromatians.*
This parallels the *Sigynnæ* migration, mentioned by Herodotus, who claimed to be colonists from Media, and who had earlier migrated westwards, as far as the Rhine (*vide* Serial No. 21[572.93951]).

STRABO (first century B.C.) states that this dominant people had conquered the whole territory from Cappadocia to far east of the Caspian. He mentions that they gave their name to Sacasene, the most fertile tract of land in Armenia.

PLINY (first century A.D.) considered that the name *Sacæ* properly belonged to that portion of the Scythian peoples whose territory originally abutted on the boundaries of Persia itself.

Of Modern Ethnologists:

TARN states that there were Sacæ both north and south of the Jaxartes about the period of Eratosthenes (*c.* 276-194 B.C.). Those south of that river were the *Dahæ, Massagetæ* and *Sacaraucæ* ". . . a huge confederacy of tribes, lords of the Caspian steppes, northward from the great Balkan mountains, to the lower Oxus and the Aral".
This author says that the Saca language has now been discovered and identified as belonging to the north Iranian group, which included the Sogdian and Parthian.

ROSTOVTZEFF mentions the Sacæ in conjunction with the Ashguzai and other Scythic peoples. He, too, considers them to have been Iranians, nearly akin to the Medes and Persians, but belonging to another branch of the stock. He is opposed to the view that the Iranians were all Mongols.

GÜNTHER says that the Sacæ were Nordics, and were spread over the whole territory from south-east Europe eastwards, as far as Turkestan, Afghanistan and the borders of India. He adds that fourth-century writers describe them as being fair or ruddy-fair and tall, and that they resembled the so-called Kelts and "Germans" of those days. This authority considers that the Medes and Persians also were Nordics.

GRANT joins the Sacæ with the Massagetæ. He states that these important peoples were ". . . like the Persians; tall, blond dolichocephs (long-heads) and they have left behind them dim traces of their blood among the Mongolised nomads of Turkestan, the Kirghiz. . . . The Sacæ were the most easterly members of the Nordic race of whom we have definite record."

General Note on the Sacæ

The old idea that the Sacæ belonged to a group of barbarous Turanian, or Mongolian, peoples, is now being generally discarded. That there were crude and barbarous Turanian peoples in the vast territory once known as Scythia is, of course, quite true. These were sometimes dominated by the Sacæ or ruled over by a Sacian aristocracy.

Strabo quotes the Athenian poet Chœrilus as saying that the Sacæ were then a nomadic shepherd people; a righteous nation.

The Sacæ of Herodotus wore trousers, and had tall, stiff caps which rose to a point. They fought with bow, dagger, and battle-axe. The last-named weapon (the *sagaris*) doubtless got its name from the Saks (or Sags) who used it so well; although there are those who think that the weapon gave its name to the users.

That the Sacæ spread both west and east from their Iranian habitat is not to be denied; nor is the fact that those who moved east were finally pressed back, inevitably westwards, by Mongol hordes from still further east, though sometimes leaving remnants behind which became absorbed in the incoming race.

There were Sacian troops—excellent fighting units—in the armies of Persia. Sacæ fought conspicuously at Arbela as allies of Darius. About a century later, tribes bearing this name subverted the Græco-Bactrian kingdom and established their rule over the entire tract between the Aral and the Indus; subsequently to be merged in the Partho-Sassanian empire and finally thrust westwards in the general movement of civilised nations in that direction.

THE MASSAGETAI

As this important people, first recorded in the region of Turkestan, were not subject to the Persia of Herodotus, he did not include them amongst his Scythic peoples. On the other hand, Diodorus and other later writers grouped them as having common origin with the Sacæ. It is now realised (as mentioned particularly by Tarn) that the term *Massagetai* means merely "the great Sak (or Sag) horde". For the purpose of this work, therefore, the Massagetai and the Sacæ are accepted as being either identical or close kindred peoples.

Serial No. 55b.

THE CIMMERIANS

Almost the first historical record of the Scythians is in respect of their descent, in the seventh century B.C., upon the *Cimmerians* (Gr. Κιμμεριοι), who then supposedly dwelt in the plains of southern Russia now known as the Ukraine. This incursion drove some of the Cimmerians westwards and others southwards, across the Caucasus into Armenia and Asia Minor, where they ravaged and plundered for about a century, before they, too, retired to the west.

Sir Henry Rawlinson, in his comments on the Behistun Rock inscription, remarked that the Babylonian equivalent of the Persian *Saka* was *Gimiri* (meaning—The Tribes) and that the identification of the Sacæ with the Cimmerians would seem highly probable (*Proceedings of the Royal Asiatic Society*, May 1849).

Dr. Eduard Meyer, Professor of Ancient History in the University of Berlin, in an article on the ancient history of Persia in the *Encyclopædia Britannica* (14th edition) concurs with this view.

Professor V. Gordon Childe, in an article on Scythia in the same encyclopædia, also inclines to the view that the Cimmerians may have been of Iranian race.

It would thus appear that this obscure people, who left their name in the *Crimea* were, like the Sigynnæ of Herodotus, precursors of the westward movement of the Sacæ peoples and that they were supplanted by a stronger section of their own kinsmen.

Rawlinson's coupling of the Cimmerians with the Gimiri of the Behistun Rock has a bearing on the movements of the deported Israelites. The name *Gimiri* (which Rawlinson considered signified *the tribes*) was the Babylonian equivalent of *saka*. It is phonetically close to *Khumri*—Omri—the name by which the Ten Tribes were known to the Assyrians. According to Dr. Pinches, this was pronounced *Ghomrí* (*see* Serial Nos. 22 [222.5]; 27 [222.5]; and 37 [572.9355]).

THE HEBREW MIGRATIONS

In assessing the movements of the Israel peoples following their expulsion from Palestine, it is important to bear in mind the continued existence of what remained of their parent stock, the Hebrews—or *Habiru*.

It is well known that there had been extensive migrations of this cultured people, about the time of Abraham, not only throughout Palestine and to Egypt, but also in a northerly direction from the Tigris-Euphrates basin (*vide* Serial No. 4 [222.11]). The idea that Abraham was a humble shepherd seeking pastures new is now quite discredited. Quite apart from the evidence of the Scriptural narrative to the effect that he was *persona grata* at the court of Pharoah and with the rulers of Canaan ("Thou art a mighty prince among us," Gen. xxiii. 6), it has been established from secular sources that the Habiru to which he belonged were highly civilised—to a degree not generally appreciated.

There seems to be a strong probability that the regions of Medo-Persia into which the Israelites were thrust, and also the ancient lands of Parthia, Bactria, Sogdiana, etc., were then peopled, at least partially, by nations deriving from the same basic stock.

WHITHER ISRAEL?

The Israelites were, in the main, deported to north-west Persia. It is certain, however, that they did not remain in the region of their first exile for any prolonged period. Whilst it is true to say that there are isolated pockets of people claiming to be descended from the

Ten Tribes still living in remote parts of that region, it is an inescapable fact that the bulk of the Israelites moved on *somewhere* within a comparatively short period of their expulsion from Palestine. The times were turbulent. Powers and nations rose and fell rapidly; grouped and regrouped. In all directions the peoples of these regions were on the move. *Somewhere* in the tossing sea of peoples called Scythian, God's people were in existence as a *nation*.

"Thus saith the Lord, which giveth the sun for a light by day, and the ordinances of the moon and of the stars for a light by night. . . . If those ordinances depart from Me, saith the Lord, then the seed of Israel also shall cease from being a nation before Me for ever." (Jer. xxxi. 35, 36.)

POINTS OF SPECIAL INTEREST

1. See Serial Nos. 10 [222.5], 11 [222.5], 24 [222.5], 27 [222.5], 29 [572.9353], 32 [572.935], for details of deportations of the Israel and Judah kingdoms.

2. The thrusting of Israel into this veritable sea of peoples is in line with Bible prophecy:

   ". . . I will sift the house of Israel among all nations, like as corn is sifted in a sieve, yet shall not the least grain fall upon the earth" (Amos ix. 9).

3. The term *Scythian* is used once only in Scripture (Col. iii. 11), where it is used antithetically to *Barbarian*:

   ". . . neither Greek nor Jew, circumcision nor uncircumcision, Barbarian, Scythian, bond nor free . . ."

4. It must be remembered that the knowledge available to the ancient historians and geographers was often vague and limited. For instance, judged by modern standards the geography of Herodotus has been frequently shown to be far from accurate. Modern ethnologists, in using the works of ancient writers, have been severely handicapped. The discrepancies of which Pliny complained have been responsible for most of the diversity of views which now prevails in the ranks of the ethnologists of to-day.

5. The meaning of the term 'Scythian' has varied greatly according to the period in which it was used. It was applied originally to the peoples dwelling in the territory between the Carpathians and the Caspian. Ultimately, however, it became the name of almost all peoples living eastwards of that territory. Thus there were so-called *European* and *Asiatic* Scythians. Ptolemy divided them into two groups: those living to the east and those to the west of the Ural Mountains.

6. According to Tarn and other writers the word 'Scythian' was really the name of a particular Iranian people in south Russia. On the other hand, Pliny states that, in his day, the name was given only to the nations dwelling to the east of the Sarmatæ and 'Germans', the latter not by any means being the same people as those to-day called by that name.

Serial No. 55c.

7. It is of interest to note that the writers whom Pliny regarded as 'ancient', called the Scythians of their acquaintance '*Aramii*' (Arameans). This would undoubtedly appear to support the opinion (mentioned above) that some of the peoples now referred to as 'Iranian' had a common origin with the Hebrews who migrated northwards from the Tigris-Euphrates region about 2000 B.C., i.e. that some of these Iranian peoples were Hebrews of pre-Israelite origin. The Israelites were Arameans.

   The Israelites would undoubtedly come into contact with, and perhaps to some extent associate and even become confused with, these 'cousin' peoples. Isaiah may have been referring to this in his prophecy of the regathering of Israel: "... Yet will I gather others to him, beside those that are gathered ..." (Isa. lvi. 8).

8. It is established from archæological evidence that some of the Scythians were 'longheads' (Nordics), whilst others were of Alpine or Mongol origin. There has been a tendency in some quarters to regard all the Scythian nations as Mongols, but many modern ethnologists now accept definitely that the most important of them were non-Mongol and that some of the Mongol nations were dominated by a non-Mongol aristocracy.

9. Fair-haired Scythians made a marauding expedition against Palestine and Egypt about 626 B.C. The town of Scythopolis in the Jordan valley possibly owes its name to their onslaught.

10. From the Behistun Rock inscription it is definite that the words *Scythian*, *Sacæ*, and *Gimirri* were different names for the same people, the last mentioned being the Babylonian equivalent, and signifying 'the tribes'. Sayce, in his *Higher Criticism and the Monuments* (pp. 451-520), gives yet another equivalent. He states that the *Manda* of Ecbatana were *Gimirri*, and therefore Scythians of classical history. He adds that the great Cyrus was a Manda.

11. There is abundant evidence that whilst some of the Iranian and Iranian-dominated portions of the Scythians moved westwards, others pushed eastwards, even as far as India and Chinese Turkestan. There are strong suggestions that Buddha was of Scythian ancestry. After maintaining themselves in this eastern territory for several centuries, these Scythians (or *Sacæ*) receded westwards before advancing Mongol hordes from still further east.

12. This 'pillar-to-post' existence of the Israel people, following their disappearance among the Scythian peoples, brings to mind the prophecy of Jeremiah: "... I will send for many fishers ... and they shall fish them; and ... many hunters ... shall hunt them ..." (ch. xvi. 16). They were indeed hunted; inevitably westwards—although some portion of them first migrated eastwards, almost to China. Attila might reasonably be called 'hunter-in-chief'. And the 'fishers' were surely the *fishers of men* who eventually covered the whole of the territory referred to by the ancients as Scythia, from the Ægean to India, i.e. among the Parthians, Medes, etc., addressed by Peter at Pentecost, when he adjured them to go back to their distant homes and assure "all the house of Israel" that Jesus was both Lord and Christ (Acts ii. 36). It is well known that some of the Apostles preached to these far-flung peoples, carrying their witness of Christ's message—even though many of their hearers and their descendants continued in pagan worship for many centuries.

13. The multitude assembled at Pentecost included 'devout men' from all parts of Scythia—in Europe and Asia. The Bible account calls them *Jews*. They may have been descendants of the Judah exiles who had become scattered throughout the Persian empire as far as India, even as early as the period of Esther, but, in view of Peter's direct reference to the House of Israel, it is equally possible that they were proselyte Jews of the Ten Tribes. Peter, at any rate, was fully aware that most of the House of Israel was then dwelling in Scythia. This agrees with the evidence of Josephus to the effect that, in his day, the Ten Tribes were "Beyond Euphrates . . . an immense multitude" (*Ant.*, Book XI, ch. v., sec. 2). It will be recalled that the Euphrates reaches right up to the Caucasus region. "Beyond Euphrates" is therefore an expression synonymous with Scythia in the widest use of the term.

The distribution of the Scythians and Northern Nomads from the geography of Herodotus,
according to E. H. Minns, Litt.D., F.B.A., in 'The Cambridge Ancient History', vol. III, map 4.
(Reproduced by kind permission of *The Cambridge University Press*).

NATIONS AND TRIBES CLASSIFIED GENERALLY AS 'SCYTHIANS' BY THE ANCIENT HISTORIANS

The ancient Greek and Roman historians have used a bewildering number of names in their descriptions of the agglomeration of peoples included in the general term 'Scythian'. The majority of these are listed below:

HERODOTUS (c. 484-425 B.C.)	STRABO (born c. 63 B.C.)	DIODORUS SICULUS (first century B.C.)	PLINY THE ELDER (23-79 A.D.)	PROCOPIUS (sixth century A.D.)
Callipidæ Alazones Aroteres Georgi Sauromatæ Sigynnæ (Bk. V, ch. ix.) Saka Humavarga (Amyrgian Scythians) } Rawlinson Saka Tigrakhuda *Note:* These were the Scythians under Persian rule at the period of Darius.	Dahæ Massagetæ Sacæ Asii Pasiani Tochari Sacarauli Aparni Xanthii Pissuri *Note:* According to Tarn, the term 'Massagetæ' means 'the Great Saca Horde'.	Sacæ Massagetæ Arimaspians Palians Napians Sauromatians 'many others'.	Sacæ Massagetæ Dahæ Essedones Ariace Rhymmici Pæsi Amardi Histi Edones Came Camace Euchatæ Cotieri Anthusiani Psace Arimaspi Antacati Chroasai Oetei Napei Palei } 'Asiatic' Scythians who, in Pliny's day, lived beyond the Jaxartes. He says that the Persians had called them all Sacæ and that earlier writers had used the term 'Aramii'. *Note:* Pliny says that the following European nations had also been loosely included as Scythians: Sarmatæ (or Sauromatæ) Hamaxobii (or Aorsi) Alani Rhoxolani Sarmatian Iazyges Daci (or Getæ) Suevi Easternæ Germans	Tetraxitæ (a branch of the Goths) Sauromatæ Melanchlænæ *Note:* Procopius lists these nations — in his day living to the north and east of the Sea of Azov— as being called Scythians at that time.

Serial No. 55e.

EXTRACT FROM *HERODOTUS* translation by Professor George Rawlinson, London, 1858, with appendices and annotations by Sir Henry Rawlinson and Sir J. Gardner Wilkinson.

"HERODOTUS (c. 484-425 B.C.), Greek historian, called the 'Father of History', was born at Halicarnassus in Asia Minor. . . . Of his trustworthiness as a historian varying opinions have been entertained . . . Cicero calls his style 'copious and polished'; Quintilian, 'sweet, pure and flowing'; Longinus says he was 'the most Homeric of historians'; Dionysius, his countryman, prefers him to Thucydides, and regards him as combining in an extraordinary degree the excellences of sublimity, beauty and the true historical method of composition'' (*Encyclopædia Britannica*, 14th edition).

(Bk. VII,, lxiv.)

The Sacæ, or Scyths, were clad in trousers, and had on their heads tall stiff caps rising to a point. They bore the bow of their country and the dagger; besides which they carried the battle-axe, or *sagaris*. They were in truth Amyrgian Scythians, but the Persians called them Sacæ, since that is the name which they give to all Scythians. The Bactrians and the Sacæ had for leader Hystaspes, the son of Darius and of Atossa, the daughter of Cyrus.

Professor Rawlinson's footnotes to the above:

⁶ In the inscription on the tomb of Darius at Nakhsh-i-Rustam, the Asiatic Scythians under Persian rule are distinguished as '*Saka Humavarga*' and '*Saka Tigrakhuda*', the former apparently designating the eastern Scythians on the confines of India; the latter, those scattered through the empire, who are known simply as 'bowmen'. According to Hellanicus, the word 'Amyrgian' was strictly a geographical title, *Amyrgium* being the name of the plain in which these Scythians dwelt. . . .

⁶ '*Saka*' is the word used throughout the Persian inscriptions. It may perhaps be the true national appellative, whence the other names by which the Greeks knew the race were derived. . . .

Later writers distinguish the Sacæ as a particular tribe of the Scythæ (Strab. xi., p. 744; Q. Curt. vii. 8 and viii. 4; Plin. H. N. vi. 17; Ptol. vi. 13, etc.).

(App. Bk. VII, Essay I, pp. 208-210.)

The Sacæ. It is very difficult to locate with any certainty the Sacæ of Herodotus. In his notices they are generally connected with the Bactrians, upon whom therefore it is natural to suppose that they adjoined, but on which side he intended to place them it is not easy to determine. Their conjunction in the list of the satrapies with certain Caspians might lead us to locate them upon the lower Oxus, and in the region between that river and the Caspian Sea (the modern Khanat of Khiva); and this position would suit exactly the notice of Hellanicus, who derives the title of Amyrgii, by which a portion of the Persian Sacæ were certainly distinguished, from a tract called "the Amyrgian *plain*", which they inhabited. But on the other hand it must be remarked first that this region has with good reason been assigned to the Chorasmians, who were certainly not Sacæ; secondly, that the Caspians, joined with the Sacans, are not those from whom the sea derived its name, and therefore may have dwelt at any distance from it; and, thirdly, that the Alexandrine geographers knew of no Sacæ south of the Oxus. The country beyond the Jaxartes is that usually assigned to them by these writers, but this cannot be the Sacia of Herodotus. It is too remote from Bactria; and besides, Herodotus assigns it to the Massagetæ, who were not Scythians, and were not subject to Persia. There remain two tracts between which our choice lies: one is the tract between the lower Oxus and the lower Jaxartes, which has been regarded above as a part of Sogdiana, but which may possibly be the Sacia of Herodotus' time. It is a low plain, like the country south of the Oxus, so as to answer the description of Hellanicus; and it approaches, if it does not adjoin, Bactria. This whole tract, however, except along the river-courses, is an arid desert, and can never have supported more than a very scanty population. The other is the region east of the Bolor range—the modern kingdoms of *Kachgar* and *Yarkand*, the most western portion of Chinese Tartary. This seems to be the Sacia of Ptolemy and Curtius; and as its eastern position and near approach to Gandaria and India accords with the place assigned to the Sacæ (Saka) in Darius's lists, it is perhaps on the whole to be preferred to the other. The western and northern portions of this region are very mountainous, but on the south and east it sinks down into a vast sandy plain or desert, which extends uninterruptedly from about longitude 75 degrees to longitude 118 degrees E. from Greenwich.

EXTRACT FROM STRABO: *GEOGRAPHY*, English translation by W. Falconer, M.A., Bohn's Classical Library (London, 1856).

"STRABO (born c. 63 B.C.), Greek geographer and historian . . . by language and education thoroughly Greek. . . . The *Geography* is the most important work on that science which antiquity has left us. . . . Judged by modern standards, his description of the direction of rivers and mountain-chains seems defective, but allowance must be made for difficulties in procuring information. . . . He had before him the results of Eratosthenes, Hipparchus and Posidonius. . . .'' (*Encyclopædia Britannica*, 13th edition).

(Bk. XI, ch. viii., pars. 1, 2, 3, 4.)

1. In proceeding from the Hyrcanian Sea towards the east, on the right hand are the mountains which the Greeks call Taurus, extending as far as India. They begin from Pamphylia and Cilicia, and stretch to this part from the west in a continuous line, bearing different names in different places. The northern parts of this range are occupied first by Gelæ, Cadusii, and Amardi, as we have said, and by some tribes of Hyrcanians; then follow, as we

proceed towards the east and the Ochus, the nation of the Parthians, then that of the Margiani and Arii, and the desert country which the river Sarnius separates from Hyrcania. The mountain, which extends to this country, or within a small distance of it, from Armenia, is called Parachoathras.

From the Hyrcanian Sea to the Arii are about 6,000 stadia. Next follow Bactriana, Sogdiana, and lastly nomade Scythians. The Macedonians gave the name of Caucasus to all the mountains which follow after Ariana, but among the barbarians the heights and the northern parts of the Parapomisus were called Emoda, and Mount Imaus; and other names of this kind were assigned to each portion of this range.

2. On the left hand opposite to these parts are situated the Scythian and nomadic nations, occupying the whole of the northern side. Most of the Scythians, beginning from the Caspian Sea, are called Dahæ Scythæ, and those situated more towards the east Massagetæ and Sacæ; the rest have the common appellation of Scythians, but each separate tribe has its peculiar name. All, or the greatest part of them, are nomades. The best known tribes are those who deprived the Greeks of Bactriana, the Asii, Pasiani (Asiani?), Tochari, and Sacarauli, who came from the country on the other side of the Iaxartes, opposite the Sacæ and Sogdiani, and which country was also occupied by Sacæ; some tribes of the Dahæ are

surnamed Aparni, some Xanthii, others Pissuri. The Aparni approach the nearest of any of these people to Hyrcania, and to the Caspian Sea. The others extend as far as the country opposite to Aria.

3. Between these people, Hyrcania, and Parthia as far as Aria, lies a vast and arid desert, which they crossed by long journeys, and overran Hyrcania, the Nesæan country, and the plains of Parthia. These people agreed to pay a tribute on condition of having permission to overrun the country at stated times and to carry away the plunder. But when these incursions became more frequent than the agreement allowed, war ensued, afterwards peace was made, and then again war was renewed. Such is the kind of life which the other nomades also lead, continually attacking their neighbours, and then making peace with them.

4. The Sacæ had made incursions similar to those of the Cimmerians and Treres, some near their own country, others at a greater distance. They occupied Bactriana, and got possession of the most fertile tract in Armenia, which was called after their own name, Sacasene. They advanced even as far as the Cappadocians, those particularly situated near the Euxine; who are now called Pontici.

(Bk. VII, ch. iii., par. 9.)

And the sheep-feeding Sacæ, a people of Scythian race, but they inhabited wheat-producing Asia; truly they were a colony of the nomades, a righteous race.

EXTRACT FROM *DIODORUS OF SICILY*. English translation by G. Booth (published by J. Davis, London, 1814).

"DIODORUS SICULUS, Greek historian . . . lived in the times of Julius Cæsar and Augustus. . . . The latest event mentioned by him belongs to the year 21 B.C. His history, *Bibliotheca historica*, 'Historical Library' consisted of forty books, and was divided into three parts. . . . Of this extensive work there are still extant only the first five books, . . . and also the eleventh to the twentieth books inclusive . . ." (*Encyclopædia Britannica*, 1946).

(Bk. II, ch. iii.)

The Scythians antiently enjoyed but a small tract of ground, but (through their valour) growing stronger by degrees, they enlarged their dominion far and near, and attained at last to a vast and glorious empire.

At the first a very few of them, and those very despicable for their mean original, seated themselves near to the river Araxes. Afterwards one of their antient kings, who was a warlike prince, and skilful in arms, gained to their country, all the mountainous parts as far as to mount Caucasus, and all the champaign country, to the ocean, and the lake Mæotis, and all the rest of the plain to the river Tanais . . . there were two brothers that descended from this king, that were remarkable for valour, the one called Palus and the other Napas. These two brothers, after many glorious actions done by them, divided the country between them, and from their own names called one part of the inhabitants Palians, and the other Napians.

Some time afterwards their posterity becoming

famous and eminent for valour and martial affairs, subdued many territories beyond Tanais.

Then turning their arms the other way, they led their forces as far as to the river Nile, in Egypt, and having subdued many nations lying between, they enlarged the empire of the Scythians as far as to the eastern ocean one way, and to the Caspian sea and the lake of Mæotis another.

This nation prospered still more and more, and had kings that were very famous; from whom the Sacans, the Massageties, and the Arimaspians, and many others called by other names derive their origin. Amongst others, there were two remarkable colonies that were drawn out of the conquered nations by those kings; the one they brought out of Assyria, and settled in the country lying between Paphlagonia and Pontus; the other out of Media, which they placed near the river Tanais, which people are called Sauromatians, who many years after, increasing in number and power, wasting the greatest part of Scythia, and rooting out all that they conquered, totally ruinated the whole nation. . . .

Serial No. 55f.

PLINY (THE ELDER): EXTRACTS FROM HIS *NATURAL HISTORY*, Bostock and Riley's translation (H. G. Bohn, London, 1855).

''PLINY, THE ELDER . . . (c. A.D. 23-79), . . . expressly quoted in the first six books of the Annals of Tacitus. . . . The scheme of his great work is vast and comprehensive . . . studied the original authorities on each subject and was most assiduous in making excerpts from their pages . . .'' (*Encyclopædia Britannica*, 13th edition).

(Bk. IV, ch. xxv.)

On nations beyond the mouth of the Danube.

On setting out from this spot, all the nations met with are Scythian in general, though various races have occupied the adjacent shores; at one spot the Getæ, by the Romans called Daci; at another the Sarmatæ, by the Greeks called Sauromatæ; and the Hamaxobii or Aorsi, a branch of them; then again the base-born Scythians and descendants of slaves, or else the Troglodytæ; and then, after them, the Alani and the Rhoxolani. The higher parts again, between the Danube and the Hercynian Forest, as far as the winter quarters of Pannonia at Carnuntum, and the borders of the Germans, are occupied by the Sarmatean Iazyges, who inhabit the level country of the plains, while the Daci, whom they have driven as far as the river Pathissus, inhabit the mountain and forest ranges. On leaving the river Marus, whether it is that or the Duria, that separates them from the Suevi and the kingdom of Vannius, the Basternæ, and, after them, other tribes of the Germans occupy the opposite sides. Agrippa considers the whole of this region, from the Ister to the ocean, to be 2,100 miles in length, and 4,400 miles in breadth to the river Vistula in the deserts of Sarmatia. The name 'Scythian' has extended, in every direction, even to the Sarmatæ and the Germans; but this ancient appellation is now only given to those who dwell beyond those nations, and live unknown to nearly all the rest of the world.

(Bk. VI, ch. xviii.)

At this spot are the altars which were raised by Hercules and Father Liber, as also by Cyrus, Semiramis, and Alexander; for the expeditions of all these conquerors stopped short at this region, bounded as it is by the river Jaxartes. . . .

(Bk. VI, ch. xix.)

Beyond this river are the peoples of Scythia. The Persians have called them by the general name of Sacæ, which properly belongs to only the nearest nation of them. The more ancient writers give them the name of Aramii. The Scythians themselves give the name of 'Chorsari' to the Persians, and they call Mount Caucasus Graucasis, which means ''white with snow''. The multitude of these Scythians is quite innumerable: in their life and habits they much resemble the people of Parthia. The tribes among them that are better known are the Sacæ, the Massagetæ, the Dahæ, the Essedones, the Ariacæ, the Rhymmici, the Pæsci, the Amardi, the Histi, the Edones, the Camæ, the Camacæ, the Euchatæ, the Cotieri, the Anthusiani, the Psacæ, the Arimaspi, the Antacati, the Chroasai, and the Œtei; among them the Napæi are said to have been destroyed by the Palæi. The rivers in their country that are best known are the Mandragæus and the Carpasus. Indeed, upon no subject that I know of are there greater discrepancies among writers, from the circumstance, I suppose, of these nations being so extremely numerous, and of such migratory habits.

PROCOPIUS: EXTRACTS FROM HIS *HISTORY OF THE WARS*, Book VIII, ch. v., sec. 5 (Loeb Classical Library, with English translation by H. B. Dewing; Heinemann, London, and Harvard University Press, Cambridge, Mass., 1914, etc.).

''PROCOPIUS, Byzantine historian, . . . of the fifth century A.D. . . . As an historian Procopius is of quite unusual merit . . . industrious in collecting facts, careful and impartial in stating them: his judgment is sound, his reflections generally acute; his conceptions of the general march and movement of things not unworthy of the great events he has recorded'' (*Encyclopædia Britannica*, 13th edition).

Now beyond the Mæotic Lake and the outlet flowing from it the first people were the Goths called Tetraxitæ, whom I have just mentioned, who in ancient times lived close along the shore of this strait; but the Goths and the Visigoths and Vandals were located far away from them as were other Gothic nations. These Tetraxitæ were called also Scythians in ancient times, because all the nations who held these regions are called in general Scythians, while a few of them had an additional designation such as Sauromatæ or Melanchlænæ or something else.

EXTRACT FROM *IRANIANS AND GREEKS IN SOUTH RUSSIA*, by M. ROSTOVTZEFF, Hon. D.Litt., Professor in the University of Wisconsin, Member of the Russian Academy of Science (Clarendon Press, Oxford, 1922).

"ROSTOVTZEFF, MICHAEL IVANOVICH; American historian; b. 70 in Russia; ed. Kiev and St. Petersburg Univs. Prof. of Classical Philology and Ancient History Univ. of St. Petersburg (Russia) 01-18; Prof. of Ancient History Univ. of Wisconsin 20-25; Prof. of Ancient History and Archæology Yale Univ. 25-39; Dir. of Archæological Studies 39-; mem. (fmr. Pres.) American Historical Asscn. . . ." (*International Who's Who*, 1943-44).

(P. 60.)

. . . I cannot dwell in detail on the hotly disputed problem of Scythian nationality. It will have been gathered from the preceding pages that I believe the Scythians to have been Iranians, although lately several high authorities, such as Geza Nagy, Minns and Treidler, have revived the Mongolian or Turanian theory, which seemed to have been completely disposed of by the judicious observations of Schiefner, Zeuss, Gutschmid, Müllenhoff and Tomaschek. It is difficult to insist on either hypothesis: decisive proofs are lacking on both sides. It has been thought that a conclusive argument in favour of the Iranian theory was furnished by the Iranian names of native or semi-native citizens of Panticapæum, Tanais and Albia. But it is forgotten that these names belong to the Roman period, and bear witness to Sarmatian, not Scythian infiltration into the Greek cities. Stress has been laid on the Mongolian physiognomy of the Scythians as represented on Bosphoran monuments of the fourth and third centuries B.C. But it must be borne in mind that the monuments give two ethnographical types: one Mongolian, as in the gorytus from Solokha, the other Indo-European, as in most of the other monuments. In spite of this I entirely agree with those who believe the Scythians to be of Iranian extraction, although I readily admit a strong infusion of Mongolian and Turanian blood. . . . Our information about the Ashguzai, who are the same as the Scythians, and about the Sacians; their close affinity with the Sarmatians, whose Iranian nationality is not disputed; and the evidence of Herodotus, confirmed by archæology, as to the religion of the Pontic Scythians . . . leave no doubt that the Scythian tribes of South Russia were Iranians, nearly akin to the Medes and Persians, but belonging to another branch of the stock. It is well known that the linguistic evidence, founded on the few Scythian words transmitted to us by the Greeks, is in no way opposed to this hypothesis. But sufficient emphasis has not been laid on the archæological evidence, which seems to me almost decisive. We have seen that very ancient monuments, which we have every reason for assigning to the Scythians, can only be explained by Iranian parallels; and that it is impossible to define the general character of Scythian art, except by connecting it with Persian art of the same period.

(P. 120.)

The Sarmatians, as described by Greek and Roman authors, did not differ greatly from the Scythians. They were Iranians . . . perhaps of purer blood than the Scythians, who had probably incorporated certain Mongolian tribes into their political and military organization.

(*Editor's Note:* This authority considers the Sauromatians and the Sarmatians to be different peoples (p. 113).)

EXTRACT FROM HANS F. K. GUNTHER'S *RACIAL ELEMENTS OF EUROPEAN HISTORY*. English translation by G. C. Wheeler (Methuen, London, 1927).

"GUNTHER, HANS. Professor. Dr. of Philosophy. Born 16.11.1891 at Freiburg, Breisgau. No religion. Studied at Universities of Freiburg and Paris; in the Department of Anthropology of the Dresden Museum of Zoology and Ethnology; in summer of 1923 independent scientific writer at Skien (Norway); autumn 1925 at Upsala (Sweden) and autumn 1926 at Lidingo (Sweden), then to Jena. In 1935 became Professor at Berlin University (translated from *Wer Ist's*—the German *Who's Who*).

(Pp. 130, 131.)

The investigations into the traces left behind them by that wide-spread Nordic people, the Sacæ (Scythians), with its many tribes, are well worthy of attention. It had been living on the steppes of south-eastern Europe, and spread thence as far as Turkestan and Afghanistan, and even to the Indus. The ancient writers (such as Polemon of Ilium, Galienos, Clement of Alexandria, Adamantios) state that the Sacæ were like the Kelts and Germans, and describe them as fair or ruddy-fair. The Scythian (Sacæ) tribe of the Alans are also described as having a Nordic appearance. Ammianus (about A.D. 330-400) calls them 'almost all tall and handsome, with hair almost yellow, and a fierce look'. Their descendants are probably the chivalrous Ossetes, who stand out among the Caucasian peoples through their tall stature and light colouring (30 per cent blond) One part of the Sacæ seems to have been merged in other Nordic waves, in the Medes and Persians; another seems to have spread as far as China and Siberia (Semireshchensk), and been lost, giving, however, energetic ruling classes to the tribes of Inner Asiatic race and Turkish speech there settled. It is believed, too, that Scythian blood has been preserved particularly among the Afghans (on this people cp. p. 151). Hildén in 1914 found a Nordic strain among the Obi Ugrians, which may suggest the Nordic Sacæ or the Nordic Tokhari. Among the Tartars there are still found to-day, 'scattered here and there, fair men with cheeks like milk and blood, who have a look of being cut off from the Swedish people'.

Serial No. 55g.

W. W. TARN, Litt.D., F.B.A., Hon. LL.D. (Edinburgh): EXTRACTS FROM HIS *THE GREEKS IN BACTRIA AND INDIA*, Part II , ch. iii., pp. 79-81 (Cambridge University Press, 1938).

"TARN, WILLIAM WOODTHORPE, Litt.D. (Camb.); Hon. LL.D. (Edin.); Fellow of British Academy; Hon. Fellow of Trinity College, Cambridge; b. 1869; . . . Educ.: Eton; Trinity College, Cambridge. Member of Inner Temple. Publications: *. . . Hellenistic Civilisation*, 1928 (2nd ed., 1930); *Hellenistic Military and Naval Developments*, 1930; *Chapters in Cambridge Ancient History*, Vols. VI, VII, IX, X; *The Greeks in Bactria and India*, 1938; articles and studies" (*Who's Who*, 1946).

The true home of nomadism was the vast Eurasian steppe, extending far to the eastward, a reservoir of peoples which, as the world then went, seemed inexhaustible. Every nomad horde had its own territory within which it moved, pasturing its flocks and herds; of various blood and speech but identical way of life, hordes easily coalesced or broke up again, though on the whole the tendency seems to have been for the greater hordes to absorb the lesser ones. This world of nomads had offshoots in more than one direction, and the offshoot which concerned Bactria was that which extended southward into the great gap between the Aralo-Caspian water system and the mountain barrier of the Pamirs and its contiguous ranges. This offshoot seems to have been entirely composed of peoples who spoke some form of Iranian; I must follow general usage and call them Iranians, but it will be understood that that refers to a common inheritance of language and customs and not to blood, which cannot be traced. Through this gap between mountain and sea the Iranian peoples had once poured southward; Medes and Persians, Bactrians and Arachosians, had long since conquered and settled the lands of the Iranian plateau, the Ariana of Eratosthenes, and had forgotten that they were ever nomads; but behind them there remained layers of the less-developed peoples of the Iranian name, still largely in the nomad stage, for whom Persians and following them Greeks used the general designation 'Saca', though Greek writers were apt improperly to call them 'Scythians', really the name of a particular Iranian people in South Russia. One of the brilliant results of the explorations of recent years in Central Asia has been the discovery and identification of the Saca language, belonging to the North Iranian group which includes Sogdian and Pahlawik (Parthian Pahlavi). The history of the Sacas, so far as they had any before the second century B.C., had consisted in a great attempt made in the seventh century B.C. to follow their kinsmen southward; it was a far-reaching effort and one or two of its details will be noticed later.

When Eratosthenes said that the Jaxartes separated Sacas and Sogdians, his statement was only true for the Chodjend district at the great southward bend of that river; for though in his day and later there were Saca peoples north of the Jaxartes, a considerable proportion of the Saca name lived to the south of it, and these were the people with whom the Bactrian Greeks were primarily concerned. Bactria's defence against the nomads, until the arrival of the Yuehchi, was a domestic matter, a defence against those backward Iranian tribes in the steppes to the west and north-west who were perpetually attracted by the rich settled lands; it was not altogether a conflict between the desert and the town, for some of the Sacas were now only semi-nomads. The peoples south of the Jaxartes who principally came in question, and of whom more will be heard later, were essentially three, the Dahæ, Massagetæ, and Sacaraucæ. The Dahæ, who originally came from the Jaxartes steppes, were a comparatively small confederacy of three tribes now living on the Caspian northward of Hyrcania and only semi-nomad; they occupied some oases, including Dihistan (which long bore their name), and though primarily horse-archers were also known as good fighters on foot. They had not appeared in Darius' province-lists, but had been subject to Xerxes; whether they were still subject to Persia when Alexander came cannot be said. Their importance to history was that one of their three tribes, the Parni, had in 248-7, according to their own reckoning, founded a kingdom in the Hyrcanian-Parthian satrapy, but when Euthydemus came to the throne there was nothing to suggest that 'Parthia' would ever be more than a local principality. The Sacaraucæ, the Sacas of 'Saca-land beyond Sogd' which Darius I had ruled, will be described later (p. 291); they occupied the country south of the Jaxartes from the Chodjend district westward toward the Oxus, but as Ptolemy knows of other Saca peoples between the lower Jaxartes and the lower Oxus the Sacaraucæ, as we shall meet them later, were probably also a confederacy of several tribes. Most important to the Greeks were the Massagetæ, whose name is now supposed to signify 'the great Saca horde'. They were a huge confederacy of tribes, lords of the Caspian steppes northward from the Great Balkan mountains to the lower Oxus and the Aral; eastward of the Aral they may or may not have extended to the mouth of the Jaxartes, westward of it they stretched northward for an unknown distance, possibly to the Aorsi at the head of the Caspian. Five of their tribes are recorded: Derbices, Apasiacæ, Attasii, Chorasmii, Augasii; and we shall meet another later. What their confederacy really meant is unknown; the tribes apparently often acted independently. Some of the Massagetæ fought on foot, which means that they were agriculturists; but the majority still led a pastoral life and fought on horseback after the universal fashion of the nomads, horse-archers led by an aristocracy of mailed warriors on mailed horses. They ruled various subject races, including primitive 'fish-eaters' in the swamps at the river mouths and along the sea shores, some of whose peculiar customs were transferred by Greek writers to their Saca overlords; and they had slain the great Cyrus and had defied Alexander.

EXTRACT FROM *THE PASSING OF THE GREAT RACE*, by MADISON GRANT, LL.B. (G. Bell & Sons, London and New York, 1921).

"GRANT, MADISON, lawyer; b. New York, Nov. 18, 1865 . . . Yale, 1887; LL.B., Columbia, 1890. . . : Admitted to Bar, 1889. Pres. N.Y. Zool. Soc. . . . Author: *The Passing of the Great Race*, 1916; . . . *The Conquest of a Continent*, 1933; also various works on zool. subjects. . . . Died May 30, 1937" (*Who Was Who in America*).

(Pp. 259, 260.)

. . . The Sacæ and Massagetæ were, like the Persians, tall, blond dolichocephs (long-heads) and they have left behind them dim traces of their blood among the Mongolised nomads of Turkestan, the Khirghizs. Ancient Bactria maintained its Nordic and Aryan aspect long after Alexander's time and did not become Mongolised and receive the sinister name of Turkestan until the seventh century. . . . The Sacæ were the most easterly members of the Nordic race of whom we have definite record. . . . Evidence is accumulating that Central Asia had a large Nordic population in the centuries preceding the Christian era. . . .

(Pp. 411, 412.)

. . . The Sacæ or Saka were the blond peoples who carried the Aryan language to India. . . . One tribe gained the most fertile tract in Armenia, which was called Sacasene after them. . . .

EXTRACT FROM *CHAMBERS' ENCYCLOPÆDIA* (New Edition, 1927)

Scythians, a nomad race of Asia known to the ancient writers. They were originally either of Mongolian or of Iranian origin—opinion is divided on the subject. . . . They moved westward and first came into historical priminence in the seventh century B.C., when they dispossessed the Cimmerians of the rule of the Russian steppes, and eventually controlled the vast treeless plain from the Danube to the Volga. . . . Some of the ancient writers indiscriminately termed Scythians all the tribes living north of the Euxine. In the seventh century B.C. some of the Scythians invaded Media. . . . About the same period (626) certain fair-haired men from the north invaded Palestine and Egypt; these have been identified with the Scythians. . . . The far-reaching influence of the Scythians began to lessen owing to pressure from the Thracians on the west and from the Sarmatians on the east, but it was not until the second half of the third century B.C. that the latter definitely superseded the Scythians, who henceforth cease to count in European history. The Scythians of Asia, however, after about 128 B.C. overran Parthea (Persia), routed several Parthian armies, and levied tribute from the Parthian kings. During the first century before and the first century after Christ hordes of Scythians, having overthrown the Bactrian and Indo-Greek dynasties of Afghanistan and India (125-25 B.C.), invaded Northern India: and there they maintained themselves with varying fortune for five centuries longer. Their kings were warm supporters of northern Buddhism; indeed an attempt has been made to show that Buddha was of Scythian descent. The Jats of India and the Rajputs have both been assigned the Scythian ancestry, Greek influence told strongly on the Scythian conquerors. Greek was even used as the official language of several dynasties in Bactria and Punjab.

EXTRACT FROM *ENCYCLOPÆDIA BRITANNICA*, 14th Edition, Article 'SCYTHIA'

SCYTHIA, originally . . . the steppe from the Carpathians to the Don. With the disappearance of the Scythæ as an ethnic and political entity, the name of Scythia gives place in its original seat to that of Sarmatia, and is artificially applied by geographers, on the one hand, to the Dobrogea, the lesser Scythia of Strabo, where it remained in official use until Byzantine times; on the other, to the unknown regions of northern Asia, the eastern Scythia of Strabo, the "Scythia intra et extra Imaum" of Ptolemy; but throughout classical literature Scythia generally meant all the regions to the north and north-east of the Black Sea, and a Scythian (*Skuthēs*) any barbarian coming from those parts. Herodotus . . . to whom, with Hippocrates, we owe our earliest knowledge of the land and its inhabitants, tries to confine the word Scyth to a certain race and its subjects, but even he seems to slip back into the wider use. Hence there is much doubt as to his exact meaning. . . .

Ethnology. Herodotus divides the Scythians into the agriculturists (Callipidæ, Alazones, Aroteres and Georgi) in the western part of the country, and the nomads with the royal Scyths to the east. The latter claimed dominion over all the rest . . . the Sauromatæ are represented as half-caste Scyths speaking a corrupt variety of Scythian. Presumably, therefore, the Scyths also spoke an Iranian dialect. . . . The settled Scythians might be, in part, the remains of this Iranian population. . . . The Cimmerians . . . who preceded the Scythians used Iranian proper names, and possibly represented this Iranian element in greater variety . . . the skulls dug up in Scythic graves throw no light on the question, some being round and some long. . . .

EXTRACT FROM *THE OLD TESTAMENT IN THE LIGHT OF THE HISTORICAL RECORDS AND LEGENDS OF ASSYRIA AND BABYLONIA*, by THEOPHILUS G. PINCHES, LL.D., M.R.A.S., 3rd Edition, 1908 (S.P.C.K.)

"PINCHES, THEOPHILUS GOLDRIDGE (1856-1934). English scholar. Born in London, he began the study of Assyrian when nineteen. Lecturer in Assyrian at University College, London, he was a recognised authority on Assyro-Babylonian literature and customs. His many works include *The Religion of Assyria*, 1906; *An Outline of Assyrian Grammar*, 1910; and *The Tablet of the Epic of the Golden Age*, 1932. He died June 6, 1934" (*Concise Universal Biography*, edited by Sir J. A. Hammerton, 1935).

(P. 339.)

That Jehu, who destroyed the house cf Omri, should be called "son of Omri" in the inscriptions of Shalmaneser II of Assyria, is strange, and needs explanation. Perhaps the successor of a king could loosely be spoken of as his son, as occupying the place of such a relative; and, as is well known, Belshazzar, in the book of Daniel, is called son of Nebuchadnezzar, which, according to the Babylonian inscriptions, he certainly was not. That Jehu may have been in some way related with Jehoram, and therefore a descendant of Omri, is possible and even probable. That he was not descended from him in a direct line is certain.

It is noteworthy that the Assyrian form of the name, Yaua, shows that the unpronounced aleph at the end was at that time sounded, so that the Hebrews must have called him Yahua (*Jehua*). Omri was likewise pronounced in accordance with the older system, before the ghain became ayin. Humrî shows that they said at that time Ghomrî.

Authorities:

(a) "Rawlinson, Sir Henry Creswicke, first baronet (1810-1895), Assyriologist; . . . deciphered the celebrated cuneiform inscription of Darius Hystaspes at Behistun, 1846; returned to England, 1855; K.C.B., 1856; M.P., Reigate, 1858-9, Frome, 1865-8; became a member of the India council, 1868; created baronet, 1891; president of the Royal Asiatic Society, 1878-81, and of the Royal Geographical Society, 1871-2 and 1874-5, contributing many valuable papers to both societies."

(b) "Rawlinson, George (1812-1902), canon of Canterbury; B.A., Trinity College, Oxford, 1838; M.A., 1841; president of Union, 1840; fellow of Exeter College, 1840; Bampton lecturer, 1859; Camden professor of ancient history, 1861-89; canon of Canter-bury, 1872; rector of All Hallows, Lombard Street, 1888; edited with brother Sir Henry C. Rawlinson . . . *The History of Herodotus*, 4 vols. 1858-60 (abridged edit. 2 vols. 1897); published *The Five Great Monarchies . . . of the Ancient Eastern World*, 4 vols. 1862-7, *The Sixth Great Monarchy* (i.e.) Parthia), 1873, *The Seventh Great Monarchy* (i.e. Sassanian or new Persian), 1876, and Histories of Ancient Egypt, 2 vols. 1881, and Phœnicia, 1889, and many kindred works; wrote life of his brother, 1898." (*Dictionary of National Biography*, 1930.)

(c) *The Sculptures and Inscriptions of Darius the Great on the Rock of Behistûn in Persia*, by L. W. King and R. C. Thompson; printed by Order of the Trustees, British Museum, 1907 (Harrison & Sons, London).

The Behistûn Rock

NEAR the village of Behistûn, in Persia, is a precipitous rock, 1,700 feet high, on the important ancient road which connected the highlands of Media with Babylon. The rock carries on its face an important cuneiform inscription of Darius Hystaspes (Darius the Great). This inscription, which was cut c. 516 B.C., records in three languages—Persian, Susian (Median), and Babylonian—the names of twenty-three provinces subject to him. In the Persian and Susian versions one of these provinces is called Scythia, the root of which is, phonetically, *Sak*. In the Babylonian text this province is called "(matû) Gi-mi-ri", translated "land of the Cimmerians". Sir Henry Rawlinson, who first copied and translated the inscription—although not disposed definitely to identify these Gimiri with the Cimmerians (Kimmerii or Cumri)—was prepared to accept the probability of a connection between them. The Behistûn Rock inscription establishes that the Sacæ lived in the land of the Cimmerians (modern north-west Persia) and that they formed part of the agglomeration of peoples known to the ancients as Scythians (or Skythians or Skuths).

POINTS OF SPECIAL INTEREST

1. Herodotus states that the Sacæ were known as Scythians. He also says: "But the Persians called them (the Amyrgian Scythians) Sacæ, since that is the name which they give to all Scythians" (Book VII, lxiv).

2. The name 'Gimiri' (which Rawlinson considers to be the Babylonian equivalent of 'the tribes') is phonetically close to 'Khumri', the name by which the Ten tribes were known to the Assyrians (see extracts from the *Guide to the Babylonian and Assyrian Antiquities of the British Museum*, 1922, p. 46, issued in Serial No. 22 [222.5] of this Handbook). According to Pinches the *kh* was pronounced -*g*.

3. The events described by the inscription generally, occurred in the regions to which the Ten tribes had been deported one to two centuries previously.

4. The root name *Sak* is also found in one of the names applied to the Ten tribes (Beth-Saac—House of Isaac; Amos vii).

5. In his *Origin of the Nations*, Professor George Rawlinson says the race called by the Assyrians Gimiri and the Greeks *Kimmerii* ravaged Asia Minor during the period 670-570 B.C. (p. 170).

Extract from *THE HISTORY OF HERODOTUS* translated by Professor George Rawlinson, M.A., assisted by Colonel Sir Henry Rawlinson, K.C.B., and Sir J. G. Wilkinson, F.R.S. (John Murray, London, 1859)

Appendix to Book IV, Essay I, footnote 1

The ethnic name of *Gimiri* first occurs in the Cuneiform records of the time of Darius Hystaspes, as the Semitic equivalent of the Arian name *Saka* (Σάκαι). The nation spoken of contained at this time two divisions, the Eastern branch, named *Humurga* (Ἀμύργιοι of Herodotus and Hellanicus), and the *Tigrakhuda* or "archers", who were conterminous with the Assyrians. Whether at the same time these *Gimiri* or *Saka* are really Cymric Celts we cannot positively say . . . But . . . the Babylonian title of *Gimiri*, as applied to the Sacæ, is not a vernacular but a foreign title, and . . . may simply mean "the tribes" . . .

Comments of Sir Henry Rawlinson, as extracted from *PROCEEDINGS OF THE ROYAL ASIATIC SOCIETY*, May 12th, 1849, p. xxi

As on the one hand, however, the termination of the name is certainly *miri* or *mirri*, while on the other, the identification of the Persian Sacæ or Scythians with the people named by the Greeks Κιμμέριοι . . . would seem highly probable, I venture . . . to read the entire name *Gimiri* . . .

THE BEHISTÛN ROCK INSCRIPTION
(parallel portions of the trilingual text)

As translated by: **L. W. King and R. C. Thompson** (*The Inscriptions of Darius the Great at Behistûn*, British Museum, 1907)

and: **Sir Henry Rawlinson** (*Journal of the Royal Asiatic Society*, 1847, p. xxvvii).

"Thus saith Darius, the king: These are the provinces which are subject unto me, and by the grace of Auramazda became I king of them:

| | KING AND THOMPSON | | RAWLINSON |
Persian	*Susian*	*Babylonian*	*Persian*
Persia	Persia	Persia	Persia
Susiana	Susiana	Elam	Susiana
Babylonia	Babylonia	Babylon	Babylonia
Assyria	Assyria	Assyria	Assyria
Arabia	Arabia	Arabia	Arabia
Egypt	Egypt	Egypt	Egypt
The (Islands) of the Sea	(The Islands of) the Sea	The (Islands) in the Sea	Those which are of the sea
Sparda	Sparda	Sapardu	Sparta
Ionia [Media]	Ionia and Media	Ionia [Media]	Ionia
Armenia	Armenia	Armenia	Armenia
Cappadocia	Cappadocia	Cappadocia	Cappadocia
Parthia	Parthia	Parthia	Parthia
Drangiana	Drangiana	Drangiana	Zarangia
Aria	Aria	Aria	Aria
Chorasmia	Chorasmia	Chorasmia	Choriasmia
Bactria	Bactria	Bactria	Bactria
Sogdiana (phonetic: Suguda)	Sogdiana (phonetic: Šuktaš)	Sogdiana	Sogdiana
Gandara	Parruparæsana	Paruparæsanna	
Scythia (phonetic: Saka)	Scythia (phonetic: Šakka)	The land of the Cimmerians (phonetic: Gi-mi-ri)	The Sacæ
Sattagydia	Sattagydia	Sattagydia	The Sattagydes
Arachosia	Arachosia	Arachosia	Arachosia
Maka	Maka	Maka	The Mecians

twenty-three lands in all."

The Behistûn Inscription.
View of Columns I-IV of the Persian Text at Behistûn, from ledge below the inscriptions.

The Behistûn Inscription.
General view of Darius and the rebel leaders.

Serial No. 47 (to accompany Serial No. 37 [572.9355]).
Copyright.

Authorities:

Prof. I. M. ROSTOVTZEFF,
Iranians and Greeks in South Russia.

Baron VON HAXTHAUSEN,
Transcaucasia.

The Westward Trek – Israel linked with the Caucasus

THE movements of nations and tribes during the late centuries B.C. and the early centuries A.D. were so sporadic and involved that modern ethnologists have great difficulty in establishing the identity or habitat of any of them with certainty. For centuries the position—particularly in the Near and Middle East—was so fluent that any one locality might have been occupied by totally different peoples within the space of a few generations.

The general final movements of most of this agglomeration of peoples were, without doubt, in a westward direction from the vast, indeterminate Eurasian territory northwards and eastwards of the Black Sea, anciently known as Scythia.

The student of Bible history is particularly concerned with accumulating evidence which tends to throw light upon the movements of the Israelites after their removal from Palestine to the Caspian area of Media. Of outstanding interest is the testimony of modern authorities to the fact that Israelitish customs survive in the Caucasus regions, furnishing a sure indication that Israelites passed that way in the westward trek from Media, the land of their deportation.

Who were the Scythians?

This subject is extensively dealt with in Serial No. 55 [572.9353].

The Sarmatians

According to Diodorus Siculus (Serial No. 55 [572.9353]), the Sarmatians were a people who came "out of Media". Confirmation of his statement may be found in the Hittite and Assyrian patterns displayed in worked-metal remains of Sarmatian culture discovered in south European Russia. Though there is divergence of opinion as to the racial classfication of the many tribes of Sarmatians, the main point of interest is that some of them, at least, came from the region into which the Israelites were thrust. They undoubtedly played a part in the later history of the Roman Empire, by which time some of them had established themselves on the lower Danube. Professor Rostovtzeff points out that Sarmatian archaeology shows much that is traceable to Assyro-Babylonian, Persian, and Egyptian origins.

The Ossetes—their Israelitish customs

The Ossetes—a people who now reside in the Caucasus region—are descended from the Alans, who were the strongest and most numerous of the Sarmatian tribes. The earliest reference to the Alans is *c.* A.D. 35 when according to Josephus, they occupied the Kuban valley. Later they lived in the Don and Dniester regions. Finally, "the Hun invasion swept them from the steppe, but they took refuge in the Caucasus and were probably settled in their present territory in the 5th and 6th centuries" (*Enc. Brit.* 1946).

Baron Von Haxthausen visited the Ossetes in 1843 and has left an account of their manners and customs. These are clearly traceable to a mixture of Israelitish and pagan civilisations of pre-Christian period. Their mixed rites are strongly reminiscent of the corrupt religion of Israel (particularly the northern tribes) at the time of their deportation to Media. The prophet Elijah is much venerated by the Ossetes. Some of them still continue with sacrificial forms of worship, even though most of them are Christians of the Greek church.

Caucasus Gaelic

It is worthy of note that, in support of Haxthausen, some of his countrymen in the German Army in the Second World War found villages tucked away in the high Caucasus whose inhabitants spoke "Gaelic as their native language" (J. A. Rennie, *In the Steps of the Clansmen*, Rich & Cowan, London, 1951, p. 18).

Proof of Contact

The ancient peoples mentioned probably contained elements of several races and it does not necessarily follow from the similarity of customs and language that they were descended from Israelites, though doubtless many of them were. What *has* been established, beyond doubt, is that some Israelites at a period before the end of the first century A.D. circulated for a time in the territory between the Caucasus and the lower Danube, leaving their manners and customs behind. It has also been established that, at the present date, there lives in the Caucasus a community of people who use a form of the Gaelic language, thus confirming contact between their ancestors and the ancestors of the ancient Gaels of Britain.

Serial No. 104a.

Modern Europeans

There can be no doubt that most of the culture of the nations of modern Europe came across the continent from the Near and Middle East by way of what was once known as Scythia. Just as in the ancient past contemporary cultures influenced each other, so in modern times nations and peoples often have many factors in common, whilst retaining individual traits.

EXTRACTS FROM *IRANIANS AND GREEKS IN SOUTH RUSSIA*, by I. M. ROSTOVTZEFF (Clarendon Press, Oxford, 1922).

"ROSTOVTZEFF, MICHAEL IVANOVICH; American historian; b. 70 in Russia; ed. Kiev and St. Petersburg Univs. Prof. of Classical Philology and Ancient History Univ. of St. Petersburg (Russia) 01-18; Prof. of Ancient History Univ. of Wisconsin 20-25; Prof. of Ancient History and Archæology Yale Univ. 25-39; Dir. of Archæological Studies 39-; mem. (fmr. Pres.) American Historical Asscn. . . ." (*International Who's Who*, 1943-44).

The Sarmatians, like the Scythians, belonged to the Iranian group of Asiatic peoples. They may have been closely akin to the Scythians; may have belonged, like them, to those Iranian peoples who were generally called Sacian, to distinguish them from the other branch of the Iranians, represented by the Medes and Persians, who were bitter enemies of the Sacians. That the Sarmatians were of Iranian extraction has been definitely established by the study of the Ossetian language: the Ossetians are known to be descended from the Alans, the strongest and most numerous, as we shall see, of the Sarmatian tribes. Ossetian, although it contains an admixture of heterogeneous elements, is unquestionably an Iranian tongue, nearly related to Persian. . . .

Whence came this Neo-Iranian wave, which re-enacted the story of the Cimmerians and the Scythians? We have little information about the history of Central Asia in that tangled and difficult period, the Hellenistic. Chinese records speak of an important movement during the Ts'in and Han dynasties: Mongolian tribes were pushed westward by the vigorous defence of the Chinese frontier, and by the construction of the Limes which we know as the Great Wall of China. This movement probably displaced a number of Iranian tribes in Central Asia and in Turkestan, who turned northward and westward, as the Scythians had turned before them, and made for western Siberia and the Ural and Volga steppes to the north of the Caspian: the southern road being barred by the kingdom of Parthia. I have no doubt that the events which took place in Central Asia during the third and second centuries were much less elementary and more complicated than the Chinese sources make them out. . . . This much we can already affirm, that the flow of Sarmatian tribes towards the South Russian steppes was due to the political and economic condition of Central Asia between the fourth and the second centuries B.C.: a symptom of which was a movement of Mongolian tribes towards the west, and a corresponding movement of Iranians (pp. 114, 115).

A noteworthy change has taken place in the arms. The Scythian sword—the acinaces with its characteristic sheath and hilt—is nowhere found. It has been supplanted by a long sword with a remarkable hilt, a type which was also adopted, in the first century, by the citizens of Panticapaeum. . . . The only parellels, as far as I know, are the swords of the second Assyrian empire, the hilts of which are surmounted by a knob of bone or bronze, and some Chinese swords of the Han period. The Scythian gorytus is also absent: indeed the part played by the bow and quiver is much less important than in the Scythian graves. The lance seems, with the sword, to have been the favourite weapon of the warriors buried in the tumuli of the Kuban. The scaled corselet was replaced, towards the end of the first century, by the corselet of ring-armour; and a helmet, often conical, is sometimes found in such tombs as have not been despoiled.

The horse-trappings are no longer the same as in Scythian tombs . . . instead round phalarae, of silver or gold, with embossed ornaments, usually geometric, sometimes in an animal style, but in an animal style which is not Scythian, and which recalls the corresponding styles of the second Assyrian empire and of archaic Ionia. The normal material of the horse-trappings is silver: the silver phalarae are often gilt. Here also we notice a return to Oriental tradition, to the tradition of the late Assyrian period, in which the bridles were commonly decorated with round phalarae of metal. It is in these tombs that we find the first stirrups. . . .

Still more important is the complete change in the forms of the gold ornaments sewn to clothing and shrouds. In the East, at all periods, clothes had been ornamented with metal plaques sewn on to the material. . . . The Kuban graves have yielded hundreds of garment plaques, but never of a type known from the Scythic tombs. . . . All these shapes belong to the Oriental repertory: exactly the same plaques have been found in Assyria: the same ornaments appear later in Sassanian and Arabic art. . . (pp. 129, 130).

The torcs are massive and rude. . . . The mirrors are no longer of bronze, like the Scythian mirrors. . . . Both shape and alloy are purely Asiatic, and are widespread in Asia, especially in Central Asia and in China. . . .

The Kuban polychromy is very closely akin to the Persian goldsmith's work which is represented by the Oxus treasure in the British Museum and by finds from Susa in the Louvre. The processes, the principles, the shapes are the same, but the Kuban work is ruder and more primitive. . . .

The group of Kuban graves which I have described is by no means isolated. Similar graves occur in most parts of the South Russian steppes, and we find a flourishing development of the same civilization in western Siberia. The most remarkable parallel to the Kuban culture appears in the valley of the Don. . . . (pp. 132, 133, 134).

The whole civilization was Iranian; in part it was directly based on the productions which marked the last period of cultural development in Babylonia and Assyria. . . . (p. 141).

Setting out from Central Asia, the Sarmatians moved both westward, occupying the steppes of the Ural region; and northward, to the Siberian steppes. . . . (p. 143).

Far from being destructive barbarians, the Sarmatians were a fresh wave of Iranian conquerors, who brought to Europe the new achievements of Iranian culture in the home of the Iranian people. Like their predecessors, the Scythians, the Sarmatians did not aim at abolishing the centres of Greek civilization. They fought with the Greeks, but never because they were bent on destroying or subduing the Greek cities. . . . They contrived to make their way into the Greek cities and to Iranize them almost completely. . . . (p. 146).

EXTRACTS FROM *TRANSCAUCASIA*, by BARON VON HAXTHAUSEN (London, 1854).

"HAXTHAUSEN, AUGUST FRANZ LUDWIG MARIA, Fre herr von (1792-1866), German economist, was born in Westphalia; graduate of Göttingen university; studied land laws, and published a book on the subject in 1829; this book secured for him commission to report upon land laws of the Prussian provinces, which he did exhaustively in 1843; undertook a similar task in Russia for emperor Nicholas. Received many honours; wrote numerous books, three of them being on the people between the Black Sea and the Caspian" (compiled from *Encyclopædia Britannica*, 1946).

The houses are all arranged on the same plan. First there is an open hall, with a threshing-floor on one side, upon which the corn is trodden out by oxen, not threshed by a machine as amongst the Georgians. There is something quite German in this custom of having the threshing-floor inside the house: with all the other Caucasian tribes which I visited, it is in the open air, in or near the villages. From the hall you enter a large dwelling-room, terminating in a kind of wooden chimney, with a square aperture in the roof. The hearth is placed beneath this opening, upon the ground, between two large stones: over it, fastened to a cross-beam is an iron hook, from which hangs a kettle, precisely similar to those in the peasant's cottages of Westphalia and Lower Saxony. The stalls for the milch-cows are on each side of the dwelling-room, that they may be under the eye of the mistress, who, as in Westphalia, can overlook them from the fireplace. There are no windows in the houses, only small square openings. The wooden chair assigned to the head of the family is always placed beside the hearth; it is either three-legged, with a round back carved and ornamented, or stands upon four legs connected by cross-pieces, which form a back and arms. In one house I saw also a sofa-shaped bench, about five feet long, prettily carved. Against the walls stand three-legged benches, which, when required for use, are brought to the fireplace beside the arm-chair; these are, however, only for the men; the women, including even the mistress, almost invariably seat themselves on the floor. The Ossetes never sit crosslegged, like the Orientals, but always upon chairs, benches, or blocks of wood. They have also low three-legged tables, which I have never seen amongst any of the other Caucasian tribes, who even at their meals merely spread a car-

Serial No. 104b.

pet on the ground. Iron fire-shovels and tongs lay on the hearth, and a roasting-spit with four long forks rested on a three-legged stand and was turned. A kneading-trough, hollowed out of the trunk of a tree, and a churn, resembling those used in the north of Germany, were placed on one side of the fireplace. When the churn is used, it is placed obliquely upon a rocking-stand of wood, and shaken about till the butter is ready. Butter made from cream in this way is not found among any of the other Caucasian tribes, nor even among the Russians, whose butter is merely a sort of grease prepared from the cream.

I observed cradles, quite different from those in other parts of the Caucasus, but similar in form to European ones. The Ossetes are, I believe, the only Caucasians who have bedsteads; these are frequently placed in a niche, and together with the beds, bolsters, and coverlets, exactly resemble those we have in Europe. Even in Russia, the peasants stretch themselves out on the stove, a bench, or the ground, where they spread out their pillow and coverlet; whilst in the houses of the nobility, in the interior of the country, bedsteads are unknown; the beds are laid at night upon sofas, and removed in the morning.

On shelves fastened to the wall beside the hearth are placed the cooking utensils, of copper and iron, with vessels of wood, glass, and even earthenware, which is purchased at Tiflis; all are bright and clean, showing the pride taken in them by the Ossetian housewife. The Ossetes, like the Germans, brew beer from barley, and give it the same name; the other Caucasians hardly know of its existence; even the Russians have only the *quas*, a sort of drink resembling beer. They use drinking-horns like those of the Georgians, and, to my astonishment, wooden beercans, and on particular occasions wooden beakers, exactly like those used from time immemorial in Germany. Their festive customs likewise have quite a German character. The beaker, fresh filled with beer, is passed from one guest to another; and after each has quaffed, he says, "I drink to your good health!" While one is drinking, the rest sing an ancient drinking-song, accompanied by a clapping of hands:

"Banas! na kuchta furesti:
Denoason fameste:
Banas! banas! banas!

the word *banas* being repeated until the person sets down the beaker.

Among the agricultural implements, the plough struck me as being quite different in construction from all others I had observed among the Caucasians: it resembles the Mecklenburg hoeing-plough. I noticed also here the common German hoe, which I had not seen elsewhere. My companion, Prince Paul Lieven, who travelled through Vladikaukas before he rejoined me at Kertsch, penetrated into the interior of the country, passing through several villages of the northern Ossetes, where he made many characteristic sketches: some of these represent mediaeval towers and fortresses, which indicate traces of a power and a chivalrous age concerning which history is silent. The farms in the highest mountain districts are even now quite like castles; whilst those in the valleys are mere log-houses. Those on the hills are built of stone, and surrounded by a wall, with a lofty tower in the centre three stories high: the lowest story is assigned to the cattle; in the middle one, which is reached by a staircase on the outside, reside the family; and in the top story are kept the stores. At the very top a watchman is placed, who announces all strangers, friends or foe. The walls of these buildings are remarkably compact and firm, although no mortar or cement is used in their construction. In the court-yard there are several houses, and invariably one set apart for guests (pp. 386-390).

The remarkable similarity between the customs of the Ossetes and the Germans has been observed by preceding travellers. Were some German traveller to visit the Ossetes, reside among them, study their habits and customs, and collect their traditions, the results would probably be of great interest, and throw light on the early history of the Germanic race (p. 393).

The majority of the Ossettes are nominally Christians, and belong to the Greek Church; but there are some dwelling on the Circassian frontier who are Mohammedans; neither Christianity nor Mohammedanism however appears to make much impression on them: they are in fact semi-pagans, indeed some are wholly and avowedly heathens. They offer sacrifices of bread and flesh upon altars in sacred groves; of these the most famous is in the interior of the country, not far from the village of Lamadon; it was originated by the Nards, an ex-

tinct tribe, supposed to have been Jews. The cave of the prophet Elijah (Asilja-leget), the guardian and patron of the Ossetes, is in this grove. Profound peace reigns around it; the shepherds pasture their flocks in silence, and neither turmoil, strife, nor rapine dare disturb the calm of these holy precincts. Once, says the legend, a holy man was taken prisoner and carried off to a strange country in the west; when an eagle, bearing him aloft over high mountains and broad seas, deposited him here, and he passed the remainder of his life in performing religious service in the cave of Elijah. This service became hereditary in his family. The eldest descendant dressed in a coat of his own weaving, once a year ascends the sacred rock alone, and having entered the cave, offers up a mystic sacrifice. No one else is permitted to approach: an attempt to climb the rock would be punished with blindness, and instant death would be the penalty for entering the cave. The interior is said to be composed of emerald; in the centre stands an altar of rock, bearing a golden goblet filled with beer. As soon as the priest enters, he receives the gift of prophecy for the ensuing year. If the beer is agitated in the goblet and runs over, there will be peace and an abundant harvest; but if the beer does not move, there will be war and famine. On the following day a great banquet, to which every one in the neighbourhood contributes, is held in the village of Lamadon, and there the priest of Elijah makes known the events of the coming year.

The Christian Ossetes likewise frequently present sacrifices and thank-offerings, consisting chiefly of flesh, fish, and bread, on ancient altars in caves and sacred groves, and sometimes on large artificial mounds of stones. Before the caves of Elijah (for there are several, that which I have just mentioned being the most celebrated), goats are slain, and their skins hung upon lofty trees. The Christian festivals are religiously observed, when sacrifices are offered. At Easter a sheep is killed; the flesh is handed round by the oldest person present, while a prayer is recited; the bones and skin are then burned. Different sacrifices are appointed for all the great festivals; on New Year's day a pig is slain, at Easter a sheep or lamb, at Michaelmas an ox, at Christmas a goat. There are four Saints to whom particular veneration is paid—the prophet Elijah, the archangel Michael, St. Gregory, and St. Nicholas. On the first day of the week, called *Chatzawibon* (Lord's day), and on the seventh, called *Shabate*, the Ossetes wear no covering upon their heads; they do not however distinguish these days by any strictly religious observances. Monday and Friday they consider unpropitious for entering upon an undertaking—a superstition which also exists widely in Europe. These customs exhibit a singular mixture of Christianity and Judaism: if the tradition be correct that the Nards were Jews, the introduction of many of these practices may be attributed to them (pp. 395-398).

Persons struck by lightning are considered sacred,

and are buried on the spot where they died, amidst universal rejoicing and shouts of "O Elei, eldar Tschoppe!" (O Elijah, Lord of the rocky mountain!). It is supposed that the prophet Elijah has taken them immediately to himself. The grave becomes a resort of pilgrims, and a black goat-skin is hung beside it, similar to those in front of the caves of Elijah (p. 400).

At the same time, the strictest ideas of the rights of marriage prevail among the Ossetes. Every child born in marriage, even if proved to be by incest or adultery, is considered a legitimate offspring, in name, succession, and inheritance. A woman who has borne children cannot, after the death of her husband, marry again out of the family: she has been purchased, and is their property. The father or brother of the deceased may marry her, which indeed the Ossetes consider a matter of duty, a point of honour: they look upon it as a continuation of the first marriage, which is indissoluble. The children of the second marriage rank as children of the first, and inherit the name and property in the same manner. This idea is carried out still further. If the deceased husband has left no brother or father surviving, and the widow is thus obliged to remain unmarried, she is not on that account prevented from living with other men; and any children which may result from such connexions are considered the legitimate offspring of the first marriage. We had an example before us: our hostess was a widow, and had three daughters by her deceased husband; he had been dead five years, but she was now nursing a child less than twelve months old. This boy was the heir to the farm, bore the husband's name, and supplanted in the inheritance the daughters born in wedlock, who received nothing of their father's property, but would be eventually sold for the profit of this bastard. This indeed had already occurred in the case of the eldest daughter, thirteen years of age, whose betrothed explained these particulars to us with the most perfect naïveté (pp. 403, 404).

The custom and the law of blood-revenge prevails among both nobles and freemen; and it is remarkable that there are also courts of arbitration and expiation, precisely like those which formerly existed in Germany. If a murder be committed, any relative of the victim is entitled, and indeed obliged, to take revenge, and slay the murderer or one of his family; this accomplished, he goes to the grave of his kinsman and exclaims, "I have revenged thy blood and slain thy murderer!" A man who has killed any member of a powerful family often passes years without stirring out of doors; for the avenger is not permitted to enter the house of the murderer; if, however, the latter has no family to shelter him, he usually enters the service of some noble who is sufficiently powerful to protect him. In one instance which was related to me, blood-revenge was carried on between two families for several generations, until both were almost exterminated; at length they

agreed to take two orphan children, one from each family, and slay them together upon an old sacrificial altar; after which a lasting reconciliation was effected. In cases of murder or manslaughter, the injured party is always at liberty to refuse any offer of atonement, and to demand blood-revenge. Frequently however, especially in recent times, the case is referred to a court of arbitration, in which it is customary to tax the wounds of a man who has been killed, at twice the amount for those of one who has recovered, the rate being in proportion to the rank of the family. Compensation for wounds and injuries which are not fatal is fixed by these courts. Formerly it was a prevalent custom for a murderer to pay a fixed price for a certain time to the family of the murdered man, say for a year, during which time the blood-revenge remained dormant (pp. 407, 408).

The physiognomy, figure, and whole outward appearance of the Ossetes form a perfect contrast to the surrounding Caucasian tribes, especially the Georgians, who are characterized by a tall slender figure, a noble bearing, regular features, aquiline nose, finely formed mouth, dark complexion, black eyes and hair, in short exhibiting the truest type of form and beauty. The Ossetes, on the other hand, are short and thick-set, being rarely above five feet four inches in height, and have broad, haggard features, usually blue eyes, and red or light brown hair (p. 413).

A parricide draws upon himself a fearful popular revenge: he is shut up in his house, with all his possessions, surrounded by the populace, and is burned alive. The reverence for their ancestors is remarkable; they consider no oath more sacred or binding than swearing by the graves of their forefathers. If a man has received injury from another, and can obtain justice by no other means, he generally brings his injurer to reason by threatening to disturb the ancestors of the latter in their graves. At the head of each village is an Elder, elected or hereditary, who is also willingly obeyed; he is the arbitrator in minor disputes, and the leader in feuds and warlike expeditions (p. 415).

A mythological tradition of the Scandinavian Germans says, that the later divine race of the Asae emigrated hence with their people northward; but the accredited story informs us that, in the great wanderings of the Teutonic races, especially the Goths, these peoples migrated north to the foot of the Caucasus, established themselves there, and founded a powerful kingdom, from which they were afterwards expelled by Eastern races, the Huns, and driven towards the West. The only certain fact is, that some of them remained in these parts. Many of the Goths settled in the mountains of the Crimea, and traces of them existed there until a recent period. It is indeed possible, that a branch of this Teutonic race may have settled permanently among the mountains of the Caucasus (p. 417).

Serial No. 104c.

Published by The National Message, Ltd.,
6 Buckingham Gate, London, S.W.1.

Authorities: Various

Danite Colonies in Greece

PIONEERS of the tribe of Dan established colonies in and about the islands and coastal areas of Greece about the time of the Exodus and in the succeeding centuries. The earliest of these, breaking away from the main body of Israelites, moved in from Egypt, to be followed by later migrations from the tribe after the entry into Canaan. The Danites were a maritime people, their ships engaging in the extensive trade between the ports of the eastern Mediterranean and the western world, as it was then known.

POINTS OF SPECIAL INTEREST

1. In his blessing Jacob said that Dan should be "a serpent by the way". In addition to being the origin of one of the Danite emblems, this phrase was prophetically descriptive.   A serpent leaves a trail which can be followed. In their migrations this tribe registered their passing permanently by naming places, rivers, etc., "after the name of Dan their father".

   In Jacob's pronouncement "Dan shall judge his people, as one of the tribes of Israel", there is a strong inference that a time would arrive when this tribe should be controller of its own affairs. The dominant spirit of the Danaans is certainly in line with this.

2. Moses' blessing "he shall leap from Bashan" was also prophetic, for the northern limits of Bashan reached as far as Mount Hermon, which was also the limit of northern Dan—one of Dan's 'jumping-off' places.

3. The Greek gods (deified ancestors) were developed by the colonisers "from the south and east". There is surely a strong resemblance between the story of Heracles and the feats of the mighty Samson—a Danite of whom even the renowned Danaans of Greece might well be proud.

4. In view of the popular belief that all the 'Phœnicians' were of Canaanite stock, the seafaring activities of the tribe of Dan cannot be too strongly emphasised. The traders from Palestinian ports during the first millennium B.C. should, strictly speaking, be divided into two groups—the Phœno-Israelites and the Phœno-Canaanites; although the two plied their trade in such close association that their actual commercial operations are indistinguishable from each other. As early as the time of Solomon the ships of Israel ranked equally with those of Tyre and Sidon.

DAN IN PALESTINE

Dan (*Judge*) was the fifth son of Jacob, by Bilhah (Rachel's maid). His only recorded son was Hushim—also known as Shuham.

When the Israelites entered Canaan, Dan—one of the largest of the tribes—found itself in difficulty as to living space. Amorites still remained in parts of the allotted territory and, in places, these proved too strong to be ejected. In consequence, six hundred Danite pioneers made an expedition to the Sidonian hinterland in the north, near Mount Hermon, where they appropriated the city of Laish and laid the foundations of a large Danite settlement which they named Dan "after the name of Dan their father".

The Danites were mariners. After her victory over Sisera, Deborah reproached the whole tribe for being concerned with their ships when they should have been helping to combat Israel's common enemy. The then important harbour of Joppa was in Danite territory. Although now largely silted up, it was once one of the most important ports on the Mediterranean. The timber for the Temple was floated in rafts to Joppa, which was undoubtedly Solomon's chief maritime base. This port also handled a good deal of the Tarshish trade, as witness Jonah's attempted voyage; though the ship he chose was obviously a 'foreigner', for the crew asked him his nationality. Dan's sea-trading propensities are also alluded to in Ezekiel's message to Tyre, where Danite commerce is associated with that of Javan (the Ionian coastlands).

The people of Dan appear generally to have held themselves somewhat aloof from their fellow Israelites. The only person of prominence mentioned in Scripture was the mighty Samson. Aholiab, a Danite, was chief assistant to Bezaleel in the construction and ornamentation of the Tabernacle and its appurtenances, whilst—singularly enough—Hiram, the renowned overseer of the work of building and embellishing Solomon's Temple, was of Danite descent on his mother's side, though his father—a resident of Tyre—was of the tribe of Naphtali.

Dan was 'brigade' leader in Israel's wilderness camp and on the march. The brigade, comprising the three tribes of Dan, Asher, and Naphtali, pitched on the north side of the square, under "the standard of the camp of Dan" (Num. ii). The eagle and serpent are the emblems ascribed to this tribe.

THE DANAUNA,

From the records of Rameses III, as given by Hall in his *Ancient History of the Near East*, 1902 (p. 381), it is learned that a collection of marauding peoples, including the Danauna and Pulesti, moved down towards Egypt from the Ægean, through Palestine. Cotterell, in his *Ancient Greeks* (p. 26), is prepared to accept the Danauna as Danaans. Hall, who dates this movement about 1200 B.C., says that the Pulesti were undoubtedly the Philistines (p. 71). He also would have been prepared to accept the Danauna as Danaans but for the fact that the Tell el Armarna letter No. 151 describes the former as a tribe of Canaan. Hall himself, however, admits that these Danauna were not a purely Canaanitish tribe (p. 176). From all of which it may reasonably be inferred that they were a tribe dwelling in Canaan who were not Canaanites —which is precisely true of the Danites, who entered Canaan under Joshua at the same period as that given for the movement towards Egypt. Thus the Danaans of Greece seem to have been here confused with their kinsmen, the Danites of Canaan.

It should be remembered that the period 1200 B.C. was one of troublous times for Israel. For their sins God "sold them into the hands of the Philistines, and into the hands of the children of Ammon" (Judges x. 7). The Danites would certainly fall under the yoke of their neighbours, the Philistines, and be compelled to play a part in the military and naval operations of the latter. Hence their presence as 'Danauna' with the Philistines in the southward surge towards Egypt.

THE DANITE MIGRATION FROM EGYPT TO GREECE

The eponym Dan is found to be a root-name applied to some of the most famous sections of the ancient Greeks and their leaders. The derivatives of this name include Danaus, Danæ, Danaans, Danoi, Danaoi, Danaids.

Serial No. 41a.

CONCLUSION

As early as 1852, Dr. R. G. Latham, a well-known ethnologist of his time, identified the Greek Danaans as the tribe of Dan. His words form a very masterly conclusion to this matter:

"Neither do I think that the eponymus of the Argive *Danai* was other than that of the Israelite tribe of Dan; only we are so used to confine ourselves to the soil of Palestine in our consideration of the history of the Israelites, that we treat them as if they were *adscripti glebæ*, and ignore the share they may have taken in the ordinary history of the world. Like priests of great sanctity, they are known in the holy places only—yet the seaports between Tyre and Ascalon, of Dan, Ephraim, and Asher, must have followed the history of seaports in general, and not have stood on the coast for nothing. What a light would be thrown on the origin of the name *Pelop*-o-nesus, and the history of the *Pelop*-id family, if a *bona fide* nation of *Pelopes*, with unequivocal affinities, and contemporary annals, had existed on the coast of Asia! Who would have hesitated to connect the two? Yet with the Danai and the tribe of Dan this is the case, and no one connects them" (*Ethnology of Europe*, p. 137).

HECATEUS OF ABDERA. Translation of an Extract from Muller's comments on his fragments; from *FRAGMENTA HISTORICORUM GRÆCORUM*, Vol. II, p. 385

Hecatæus therefore, tells us that the Egyptians, formerly, being troubled by calamities, in order that the divine wrath might be averted, expelled all the aliens gathered together in Egypt. Of these, some, under their leaders Danaus and Cadmus, migrated into Greece; others into other regions, the greater part into Syria. Their leader is said to have been Moses, a man renowned for wisdom and courage, founder and legislator of the state. Afterwards many Mosaic institutes followed.

Extract from *DIODOROUS OF SICILY*, by G. H. OLDFATHER, 1933; Book I, Sec. xxviii, 1-5.

Now the Egyptians say that also after these events a great number of colonies were spread from Egypt all over the inhabited world. To Babylon for instance, colonists were led by Belus, who was held to be the son of Poseidon and Libya; and after establishing himself on the Euphrates river he appointed priests, called Chaldeans by the Babylonians, who were exempt from taxation, and free from every kind of service to the state, as are the priests of Egypt;[*] and they also make observations of the stars, following the example of the Egyptian priests, physicists, and astrologers. They say also that those who set forth with Danaus, likewise from Egypt, settled what is practically the oldest city of Greece, Argos, and that the nations of the Colchi in Pontus and that of the Jews, which lies between Arabia and Syria, were founded as colonies by certain emigrants from their country; and this is the reason why it is a long-established institution among these two peoples to circumcise their male children, the custom having been brought over from Egypt. Even the Athenians, they say, are colonists from Sais in Egypt . . .

HERODOTUS: Extract from Book V, 58

Now the Phœnicians who came with Cadmus . . . introduced into Greece upon their arrival a great variety of arts, among the rest that of writing, whereof the Greeks till then had, as I think, been ignorant. And originally they shaped their letters exactly like all the other Phœnicians, but afterwards, in course of time, they changed by degrees their language, and together with it the form likewise of their characters. Now the Greeks who dwelt about those parts at that time were chiefly the Ionians. The Phœnician letters were accordingly adopted by them, but with some variation in the shape of a few, and so they arrived at the present use, still calling the letters Phœnician, as justice required, after the name of those who were the first to introduce them into Greece.

[*] On the exemption of the priests of Egypt from taxation cp. chap. 73; on the Chaldæans, cp. Book 2, 29f.

According to Thucydides (*Peloponnesian War*, Bk. I, ch. 1) the earliest immigrants to Greece were called Pelasgians. Danaus, who later arrived with his followers from Egypt, commanded that all should be called Danaans (*Strabo* 5, 2, 4). Hecateus of Abdera, a Greek historian of the early third century B.C., records that there had been an expulsion of 'aliens' from Egypt and that some of these, under their leaders Danaus and Cadmus migrated into Greece, though the greater part followed Moses. Confirming this, Diodorus Siculus states that those who left Egypt with Danaus settled in Argos, and that—according to contemporary belief—Athens also was colonised from Egypt. Strabo says that the Danaans colonised the regions round about Lemnos and Imbros; also that some of them sailed from those islands with Tyrrhenus to the region of Italy neighbouring the Tyrrhenian Sea, their descendants becoming known as Etruscans (5.2.2.; 5.2.4.; 6.2.2.). In his *History of Greece* (p. 18), Dr. William Smith says that of all the heroic families of Greece, none was more heroic than the Danaans of Argos.

That Greece was colonised from Egypt was a fact so well accepted in ancient times that Herodotus, writing in the fifth century B.C., purposely omitted to give an account of it.

Herodotus (II, 49) says that Cadmus was a Tyrian, and the classical writers agree that he introduced the letters of the alphabet to Greece. Herodotus called him a 'Phœnician', as the Greeks called most of the dwellers in Palestine by that name. Tyre was close to northern Dan, which provided a substantial portion of the pioneering mariners of those days. Danites—and other Israelites—resided in Tyre.

The 'Phœnician' historian Sanchoniathon, who is reputed to have lived before the Trojan war, in the fragments of his writings which have survived furnishes a strong indication that the Greek and Phœnician deities were based on ancestor worship and were of Hebrew origin. His genealogies ascend to Kronos (*Saturn*), whom (he says) "the Phœnicians call Israel" (Cory's *Ancient Fragments*, 1876, pp. 21-22). He recites further that Kronos had a son Ieoud (*Judah*).

Gladstone, in his *Juventus Mundi* (pp. 36-42), traces the origin of the name Danaoi to approximately 200 years before the Trojan war, i.e. to about 1300 B.C. Though he does not identify the Greeks with Dan, he suggests that an original tribe of Danaans may have existed with an Egyptian origin, and dynastic line, in Danaus.

In his *Oldest Civilisation of Greece*, Hall, though recognising the Greek claim to an origin in the "south and east"—mentioned by Gladstone in his preface to Schliemann's *Mycenæ*—dismisses it on the ground that:

> "No bullheaded god or deity to whom bulls were sacred is known among the Semites" (p. 230).

This argument itself falls to the ground, however, when it is realised that the Israelites (whom Hall himself calls Semites) tried to reintroduce the bull-worship they had known in Egypt, when they compelled Aaron to make the calf of gold. The Greeks had no Moses to purge their idolatry: hence signs of bull-worship among the early Greeks.

THE LACEDÆMONIANS (SPARTANS)

There is good evidence to the effect that the Lacedæmonians (Spartans) were Israelites. Josephus has recorded an exchange of letters between a remnant of this section of the ancient Greeks and the Jews in Palestine during the period of the Maccabees, in which the Israelite descent of the Lacedæmonians is definitely established (Josephus' *Antiquities*, Bk. XII, iv, 10 and 1 Mac. xii). The seal affixed to the Lacedæmonian letter bore the Danite emblems, eagle and serpent. It is worthy of note that the same heraldic device of the tribe of Dan is described in Homer's *Iliad* as appearing over the contending armies during the siege of Troy: a clear indication at least that the emblems were recognised as having national significance in the eyes of the foremost classical writer of ancient Greece (Bk. XII, lines 216-249).

According to Herodotus (I, 56), the Lacedæmonians were of Doric blood—so called from Dorus, son of Hellen. As it has been clearly established that the Lacedæmonians were Danites, it follows that the Dorians must have been Hebrews. Herodotus states that the Lacedæmonians claimed that their laws were brought from Crete by Lycurgus (I, 65).

Scriptural References

Joshua xix, 47

"And the coast of the children of Dan went out too little for them:"

Judges i, 34

"And the Amorites forced the children of Dan into the mountain: for they would not suffer them to come down to the valley:"

Judges xviii, 1-29

". . . the tribe of the Danites sought them an inheritance . . . and . . . six hundred men appointed with weapons of war . . . went up . . . and came unto Laish, . . . it was far from Zidon, . . . by Beth-rehob. And they built a city, and dwelt therein. And they called the name of the city Dan, after the name of Dan their father, . . ."

Judges v, 17

". . . why did Dan remain in ships? Asher continued on the sea shore, and abode in his breaches."

II *Chronicles* ii, 16

"And we will cut wood out of Lebanon, . . . and we will bring it to thee in floats by sea to Joppa; and thou shalt carry it up to Jerusalem."

Ezekiel xxvii, 19

"Dan also and Javan going to and fro occupied in thy fairs:" (*Note:* Javan represents Ionians—Young.)

Genesis xlix, 16-17 (Jacob's blessing)

"Dan shall judge his people, as one of the tribes of Israel. Dan shall be a serpent by the way, an adder in the path, that biteth the horse heels, so that his rider shall fall backward."

Deuteronomy xxxiii, 22 (Moses' blessing)

". . . Dan is a lion's whelp: he shall leap from Bashan "

Authority: JOSEPHUS

Antiquities of the Jews

"Josephus Flavius (c. 37-c. 95?), Jewish historian and military commander, was born in the first year of Caligula (37-38). His father belonged to one of the noblest priestly families, and through his mother he claimed descent from the Asmonæan high priest Jonathan. A precocious student of the law. . . . The *Jewish Antiquities* . . . covers in twenty books the history of the Jews from the creation of the world to the outbreak of the war with Rome. It was finished in the thirteenth year of Domitian (93). . . ." (*Encyclopædia Britannica*, 13th Edition.)

Spartan Hebrews

THE Lacedæmonian Greeks, whose chief city was Sparta, discovered that they were of Abrahamic stock. They sent greetings of kinship to the Jews in Palestine. These were later acknowledged by the Jewish high priest Jonathan.

POINTS OF SPECIAL INTEREST

1. The Spartan section of the ancient Greek people was of the Hebrew race.

2. Both Jews and Lacedæmonians acknowledged this, although the latter for a long time had lost sight of the fact.

3. Support for Josephus' record is to be found in the Apocrypha (I Macc., xii).

4. The seal on the Lacedæmonians' letter bore an eagle with a serpent in its talons. Both the eagle and the serpent are stated to be emblems of the Israelite tribe of Dan. According to the *Jewish Encyclopædia* (articles 'Dan' and 'Flags'), the tribal symbol of Dan was a serpent (see Gen. xlix, 17). Adam Clarke, in his *Commentary on Numbers ii*, refers to both the serpent and the eagle being given as the emblems of Dan (Vol. I, p. 631). The learned Jewish scholar of the Cromwellian period, Aben Ezra, as cited by Thomas Fuller, B.D., in his *Pisgah Sight of Palestine*, quotes the eagle as representing the tribe of Dan. Thus the Spartans had preserved their Israel heraldry, though they had temporarily forgotten their ancestry during the centuries which had elapsed since leaving their Palestinian homeland.

JOSEPHUS: Extracts from his *ANTIQUITIES OF THE JEWS*, English translation by Ralph Marcus, Ph.D., Professor of Semitic Philology and Jewish Institute of Religion Lecturer in Semitic Languages, Columbia University (Loeb Classical Library, London, and Harvard University Press, Cambridge, Mass., 1943)

Book xii, iv, § 10

At that time there had begun to reign over Asia Seleucus, surnamed Soter, who was the son of Antiochus the Great. And then also died Hyrcanus' father Joseph, who had been an excellent and high-minded man and had brought the Jewish people from poverty and a state of weakness to more splendid opportunities of life during the twenty-two years when he controlled the taxes of Syria, Phœnicia, and Samaria. And death also came to his uncle Onias, who left the high priesthood to his son Simon. When he too died, his son Onias became his successor in office, and it was to him that the Lacedæmonian king Areios sent an embassy with a letter, of which the following is a copy: "Areios, king of the Lacedæmonians, to Onias, greeting. We have come upon a certain document from which we have learned that the Jews and Lacedæmonians are of one race and are related by descent from Abraham. It is right, therefore, that you as our brothers should send to us to make known whatever you may wish. We also shall do this, and shall consider what is yours as our own, and what is ours we shall also share with you. Demoteles, the courier is bringing this letter to you." The writing is square. The seal is an eagle holding fast a serpent.

Book xiii, v, § 8

Jonathan . . . sent envoys . . . to visit the Spartans on their return from Rome . . . on their return journey they came to Sparta and delivered to them the letter which they had received from Jonathan, of which the fol-

lowing is a copy: "Jonathan, high priest of the Jewish nation, and the senate and council of priests to their brothers, the ephors and senate and people of Lacedæmon, greeting. . . . When in former times there was brought by Demoteles to Onias, who was our high priest, from Areius, your king, a letter, of which a copy is appended, concerning the kinship which exists between us and you, we gladly received the letter and showed ourselves kindly disposed toward both Demoteles and Areius, although we needed no such evidence since the kinship had been made certain through our sacred writings. . . ." And the Lacedæmonians received the envoys in a friendly manner, and after making a decree concerning a friendly alliance with the Jews, sent them on their way.

EXTRACT FROM APOCRYPHA
(I Maccabees, xii)

5. And this is the copy of the letters which Jonathan wrote to the Lacedæmonians: . . .

7. There were letters sent in times past unto Onias the high priest from Darius, who reigned then among you, to signify that ye are our brethren, as the copy here underwritten doth specify. . . .

11. We therefore at all times without ceasing, both in our feasts, and other convenient days, do remember you in the sacrifices which we offer, and in our prayers, as reason is, and as it becometh us to think upon our brethren. . . .

Authority: TACITUS

History

Tacitus, Cornelius (c. 55-120 A.D.), lived through reigns of Nero, Galba, Otho, Vitellius, Vespasian, Titus, Domitian, Nerva and Trajan; probably died near close of reign of Claudius; eminent pleader at the Roman bar; son-in-law of Julius Agricola, promoted by Vespasian, Titus, and Domitian, to rank of praetor, by A.D. 88; consul in A.D. 97. Was held in high regard by his friend Pliny. The *Histories*, originally in twelve books, brought the history of the empire from Galba in A.D. 69 down to the close of Domitian's reign in A.D. 97. "In the fragment of the fifth book we have a curious but entirely inaccurate account of the Jewish nation, of their character, customs and religion, from a cultivated Roman's point of view, which we see at once was a strongly prejudiced one." (Compiled from the *Encyclopaedia Britannica*, 1946.)

Myceneans and Israelites

THERE is evidence that Crete possessed a high civilisation possibly as early as Egypt itself, as is indicated by archaeological finds of both pre-Dynastic and Dynastic types in that island.

Crete also had early contacts with Greece and Asia Minor, where many finds testify to the fact, and as is indicated in the similarity of the place-names, etc. There were, for instance, towns named Mycenae in both Crete and Greece; and a Mt. Ida was to be found both near Troy and near the Cretan Mycenae.

The civilisation of Cretan Mycenae, in particular, bore striking resemblances to that of the Hebrews.

According to a curiously garbled account by the Roman historian Tacitus, the "Jews" were "natives of the Isle of Crete", who derived their name from that of Mt. Ida (Judah), well known in ancient history and mythology. This story might well be considered fantastic were it not for the fact that archaeological data, as revealed by the late Sir Arthur Evans, proves that a most intimate cultural link existed between the Myceneans and the Israelites.

It is evident that, although Tacitus had obviously absorbed an inexplicably false impression as to the origin of the Israelites, there is a substantial element of truth underlying his story.

Data from Ancient Sources

Whatever may have been the sources of Tacitus' data, the Jews were not, of course, as is stated in one of his accounts, "natives of the isle of Crete"; but this inaccuracy certainly does not provide grounds for disregarding his story. Egyptian, Jewish and Greek writers have testified that at some time before the Exodus a colony of Israelites left Egypt and proceeded to Greece. The Greek account, as given by Diodorus of Sicily and Hecataeus of Abdera has been given in an earlier serial (Ser. No. 41 [572.938]). An Egyptian version of the same story as given by Manetho has been preserved by Josephus (Contra Apion. Bk. I, 26). The Apocrypha (I Mac. xii) contains correspondence that passed between the Greeks and the Jews, the latter of whom accepted the Abrahamic origin of the former. If such widespread testimony agrees on the matter of an Israelitish colonisation of Greece, we should not be surprised to find indications, even though somewhat distorted in the course of history, that these same people also colonised Crete, which is a natural stopping-point en route. Such an indication is provided by Tacitus, whose narrative, if it stood altogether unsupported, might be considered as of no value; however, archaeological data furnish corroborative evidence and prove conclusively that the early Israelites and the Mycenaeans of Crete possessed cultures that had much in common. Additional support for the identification of the Mycenaeans with the Israelites is to be found in classical history and mythology, which trace important elements of Greek civilisation back to Crete, Egypt, and Phoenicia.

Common Factors in Mycenean and Israelitish Cultures

Many features of the archaeology of Cretan Mycenae have attracted the attention of antiquarians; in particular, the striking similarity of its religious elements to those of

Israel has received special mention by the famous authority on Cretan archaeology, Sir Arthur Evans, in his *Mycenean Tree and Pillar Cult.*

Mycenean religion abounds in Biblical motives. One of the most prominent of these is the fig tree. This symbol is one of the oldest and one which is commonly used in the Bible story. The fig tree provided the first covering for nakedness (Gen. iii, 7), and features prominently in the parables of Jeremiah concerning Judah (Jer. xxiv), as also in our Lord's parable concerning the Jewish nation (Luke xiii, 6-9; Matt. xxi, 18-22; Mark xi. 12-26; Matt. xxiv, 32, 33). The good and bad figs of the former, and the barren fig tree of the latter, portray the conditions of the respective portions of the *House of Judah.* So strongly does this religious motive appear in Mycenean archaeology that Sir Arthur Evans writes of the "traditional sanctity of the fig tree" in its religious scenes. He observes that in associated mythology the gift of Demeter was a "Sacred Fig" which stood beside the tomb of Phytalos; that fig leaves appear as sacred types on coins of Kameiros in Rhodes and Carian Idyma; that Dionysius was worshipped under the form of a fig tree in Laconia; that where Gaia sought to ward off the bolts of Zeus from her son Sykeas a fig tree is said to have sprung up; and that the tree had a primitive religious sanctity in the Peloponnese (p. 6).

The horned altar of the Myceneans was identical with that of the Israelites. It will be recalled that in Israel the horns of the altar were repeatedly smeared with sacrificial blood (Ex. xxix, 12; Lev. iv, 7, 18, 25, 30, 34; viii, 15; iv, 9; xvi, 18; etc.). Adonijah, fearing the wrath of Solomon, sought sanctuary by grasping the horns of the altar (I Kings i, 50, 51), as also did Joab (I Kings ii, 28).

Sacred doves, trees, and pillars were common features of Mycenean religion, in which Sir Arthur Evans discovered "the constant combination of the sacred tree with pillar or domen'' (p. 8). The association of sacred trees and pillars with the religion of Israel and in turn with the British Isles has already been dealt with (Ser. Nos. 60, 76, [572.9394]); and in this latter connection Sir Arthur Evans has observed: "In the Druidical worship of the West, the tree divinity and the Menhir or stone pillar are associated in a very similar manner, and lingering traditions of their relationship are still traceable in modern folklore. To illustrate indeed this sympathetic conjunction of tree and pillar we have got to go no further afield than the borders of Oxfordshire and Warwickshire. Beside the prehistoric stone fence of Rollright the elder tree still stands hard by the King stone, about which it is told that when the flowery branch was cut on Midsummer Eve, the tree bled, and the stone 'moved its head' '' (p. 8).

Perhaps the most striking connection between the sacred pillars of Mycenean religion and that of Israel is the name by which they were known—*baetylae*—which is clearly derived from a Semitic source. Jacob's stone on which he had his vision became "Bethel", or the "House of God".

A racial connection with Israel would indeed explain many remarkable features of Cretan history and mythology—why, as in Palestine, where there was a river Jordan, there was in Crete a river Jardanus; why, as in the case of Moses on Mt. Sinai, the Cretan lawgiver Minos "would go up every nine years, as it appears, to the cave of Zeus, tarry there, and come back with commandments drawn up in writing, which he alleged were ordinances of Zeus" (Strabo X. iv. 8); and why Tacitus asserted that the names of the Judaeans and Ida (the sacred mountain of Crete) were identical.

Mycenean architecture portrays no temple images in human form (p. 25); this finds a parallel in the religion of Israel, which forbade the making of graven images (Ex. xx, 4; Lev. xxvi, 1; etc.). It was not until the time of Daedelus that human statuary first appeared in religious connections, as is indicated by the name *Daedelae* (Wm. Smith's *Dict. of Greek and Roman Biography and Mythology*).

The sacred groves, eventually used by Israel for idolatrous purposes, have a parallel in Mycenea, and in related mythology. The oaks of Dodona were sacred to Pelasgic Zeus; the sacred plane tree of Zeus Agamemnon stood by the Castalian spring; there was the plane of Helena at Sparta; and that of Menelaos at Kaphyae in Arcadia. The oak woods of Mount Lykaeos were the shrine of Arcadian Zeus. Near Gortyna and Theren, near Knossus, were sacred plane trees; a grove of holy cypresses stood by the ruins of the "house of Rhea" near Knossus; and before the cave of Zeus on Mt. Ida stood a sacred black poplar (p. 29).

The many affinities of Mycenean religion to the Semitic are so striking that Sir Arthur Evans wrote of this "community" that it seems to go "beyond the natural parallelism for which a similar stage of religious evolution might naturally account" (pp. 32, 33). Tacitus' account, however, definitely indicates that a Judahite population lived in Crete at an early time, and that the Idean name is none other than that of Judah; this explanation would far more easily account for the remarkable "community" that in fact exists between Mycenean and Israelitish religious motives.

Mythological and historical sources indicate that important elements of the Greeks had come from Egypt and Crete. Herodotus (I. 56) informs us, for instance, that the Lacedaemonians were of Doric blood, receiving this name from Dorus the son of Helen. Under Dorus the Lacedaemonians lived at the foot of Olympus, and some of them, migrating, became known as Macedni, or Macedonians. Sparta was in Lacedaemonia, and it is interesting to note that the Lacedaemonians claimed that Lycurgus brought their laws from Crete (*Herod.* I, 65). Herodotus further says that according to "the common Greek accounts", "the chiefs of the Dorians are really genuine Egyptians" (VI. 53); and that "almost all the names of the gods came into Greece from Egypt. My inquiries prove that they were all derived from a foreign source, and my opinion is that Egypt furnishes the greater number'' (II. 50).

It is clear that Tacitus associates the deities Saturn and Jupiter, who are intimately connected with the early king-lines of classical civilisation, with the Israelites; this in turn harmonises with the accounts of Herodotus and others, who tell us that most of the gods of the Greeks were of Egyptian origin. ''The gods of the popular religions'', says Cicero, in his *Tusculan questions*, ''were all but deceased mortals advanced from Earth to Heaven''.

Diodorus of Sicily several times refers to the Egyptian origin of the gods of mythology; he writes: ''And since Egypt is the country where mythology places the origin of the gods . . . we shall begin our history with the events connected with Egypt'' (I. ix, 6); ''Cadmus, who was a citizen of Egyptian Thebes . . .'' (I. xxiii, 4); ''Moreover, certain of the rulers of Athens were originally Egyptians, they say . . .'' (I. xxviii, 6); ''In general, they say, the Greeks appropriate to themselves the most renowned of both Egyptian heroes and gods, and so also the colonies sent out by them'' (I. xxiii, 24).

By means of many such connections it would appear reasonably certain that mythology preserves corrupted accounts of the pre-Exodus migrations of certain bodies of restive Israelite pioneers from Egypt to the Aegian; and that Cretan archaeology throws a confirmatory light on this fact.

EXTRACT FROM *THE HISTORY* OF TACITUS, Bk. V. sec. 2 (Everyman Library Series, 1932 ed.)

Being now to relate the progress of a siege that terminated in the destruction of that once celebrated city, it may be proper to go back to its first foundation, and to trace the origin of the people. The Jews, we are told, were natives of the isle of Crete. At the time when Saturn was driven from his throne by the violence of Jupiter, they abandoned their habitations, and gained a settlement at the extremity of Libya. In support of this tradition, the etymology of their name is adduced as a proof. Mount Ida, well known to fame, stands in the isle of Crete: the inhabitants are called Idæans; and the word, by a barbarous corruption, was changed afterwards to that of Judæans. According to others, they were a colony from Egypt, when that country, during the reign of Isis, overflowing with inhabitants, poured forth its redundant numbers under the conduct of Hierosolymus and Juda. A third hypothesis makes them originally Ethiopians, compelled by the tyranny of Cepheus, the reigning monarch, to abandon their country. Some authors contend that they were a tribe of Assyrians, who for some time occupied a portion of Egypt, and, afterwards transplanting themselves into Syria, acquired in their own right a number of cities, together with the territories of the Hebrews. There is still another tradition, which ascribes to the Jews a more illustrious origin, deriving them from the ancient Solymans so highly celebrated in the poetry of Homer. By that people the city was built, and from its founder received the name of Hierosolyma.

Serial No. 81b,
Published by *The National Message*, Ltd.,
6 Buckingham Gate, London, S.W.1.
Copyright.

Authority: HERODOTUS

History

"Herodotus (c. 484-425), Greek historian, called the 'Father of History', was born at Halicarnassus in Asia Minor. . . . Of his trustworthiness as a historian varying opinions have been entertained. . . . Cicero calls his style 'copious and polished'; Quintilian, 'sweet, pure and flowing'; Longinus says he was 'the most Homeric of historians'; Dionysius, his countryman, prefers him to Thucydides, and regards him as combining in an extraordinary degree the excellences of sublimity, beauty and the true historical method of composition." (*Encyclopaedia Britannica*, 14th Edition.)

ACCORDING to Herodotus the Cappadocians, who later play an important role in the New Testament record, were known to the ancient Greeks by the name of Syrians. They had been subject to the Medes, and were now within the empire of Persia.

POINTS OF SPECIAL INTEREST

1. When Peter made his famous Pentecostal speech there were Cappadocians present in the multitude, whom he addressed as "Ye men of Israel" (Acts ii). His first Epistle (I Peter i, 1) "to the strangers (Gr. *diaspora*) scattered throughout Pontus, Galatia, *Cappadocia*, Asia and Bithynia" was addressed to people who were obviously of Israelite descent (I Peter ii, 9-10).

2. Portions of ten-tribed Israel had been deported to "the cities of the Medes" at the time of the Assyrian conquest of Northern Israel (II Kings xvii and xviii) in 721 B.C.

3. As Herodotus states that the Cappadocians had Median connections, and as Peter writes to these people as those Israelites whom the prophet Hosea had said should become "Lo-Ammi" (I Peter ii, 10, and Hosea i, 9) it is reasonable to infer that this particular section of the dispersion of Israel had entered Asia Minor from Media, the territory west and southwest of the Caspian Sea.

HERODOTUS: EXTRACT FROM HIS *HISTORY*, Book I, Ch. 72. (English translation by Canon George Rawlinson, M.A.) (JOHN MURRAY, London, 1858)

The Cappadocians are known to the Greeks by the name of Syrians. Before the rise of the Persian power, they had been subject to the Medes; but at the present time they were within the empire of Cyrus, for the boundary between the Median and the Lydian empires was the river Halys. This stream, which rises in the mountain country of Armenia, runs first through Cilicia; afterwards it flows for a while with the Matiêni on the right, and the Phrygians on the left: then, when they are passed, it proceeds with a northern course, separating the Cappadocian Syrians from the Paphlagonians, who occupy the left bank, thus forming the boundary of almost the whole of Lower Asia, from the sea opposite Cyprus to the Euxine. Just there is the neck of the peninsula, a journey of five days across for an active walker.

HERODOTUS: EXTRACT FROM THE *APPENDICES* TO ABOVE TEXT, Essay ix, sec. 2, p. 574 (By George Rawlinson, M.A., late fellow and tutor of Exeter College, Oxford; assisted by Col. Sir Henry Rawlinson, K.C.B., and Sir J. G. Wilkinson, F.R.S.)

East and south-east of Armenia, extending from the *Kur* (Cyrus) on the north to the vicinity of Isfahan on the south, was Media, divided (like Armenia) into two provinces, Media Magna and Media Atropatênê. Media Atropatênê lay towards the north, being interposed between Armenia and the Caspian, and including within it the rich and fertile basin of Lake *Urumiyeh*, as well as the valleys of the *Aras* (Araxes) and the *Sefid Rud*, and the low countries of *Talish* and *Ghilan* on the shores of the sea, thus nearly corresponding with the modern province of *Azerbijan*. Hence Media Magna extended eastward to the Caspian Gates near Mount Demavend, following the line of Elburz, and being separated from the Caspian by a portion of Hyrcania, now *Mazanderan*. On the west, the Assyrian plain formed the boundary, Media here lying along Zagros, and reaching southwards to about the 32nd parallel, where Persia adjoined upon it. Eastward Media was bounded by the Great Salt Desert, which extends across Iran from lat. 35 degrees to lat. 30 degrees. The entire country was thus eight degrees (550 miles) long, and from 250 to 300 miles broad.

Authorities: Various

The Nordic Hebrews

Until fairly recent years a true assessment of the racial origin of the Hebrews has been almost impossible, owing to the long-prevailing obses- sion that the present-day Jewish people accurately reproduce the racial characteristics of ancient Hebrew forbears.

Now that abundant proof has been found to show that the Jews of to-day contain elements of many races and are, in the main, not true Hebrews at all, the racial origin of these ancient people becomes an open question, and it may usefully be enquired "Who were the Hebrews?" without displaying what would once have been considered an abysmal ignorance of self-evident facts.

The *Habiru* first became prominent, in the Middle Euphrates area, in the centuries prior to 2000 B.C. By the time of Abraham they had pushed colonies northwards and westwards, through Persia, Palestine and Egypt. Some of these pioneers moved further westwards, through North Africa and Spain, reaching even as far as Britain. To those who remained behind, the land of Palestine was known as *Amurru* (the land to the West) and its occupants, whether Canaanite or Hebrew, were Amorites (westerners).

Thus, in addition to the other nations of Canaan, there were in Pales- tine 'Amorites' who were descended from Ham—the Amorites of the Bible —and also Hebrew descendants of Shem—the Amurru—who, together with the Israelites who followed them, became the Amorites described as such by modern ethnologists.

It can be shown conclusively that these Hebrew-Amorites were of the racial type now known as *Nordic*. In the words of the *Encyclopædia Britannica*, these dwellers in Palestine were "a race much more like the northern Europeans" than the type which has popularly been termed 'Semitic'.

SEMITE RACE—A MISNOMER

Great confusion of thought has arisen through the indiscriminate misuse of the term *Semitic*. It is popularly considered that there is, and always has been, a Semite race. The Arabs and the modern Jews (and therefore the ancient Hebrews) have been awarded this racial classification by authorities who should have shown more care. As mentioned by Gunther, in his *Racial Elements of European History* (p. 74), and by other authorities, there is no such thing as a Semitic race; there are only Semitic-speaking peoples, showing varying racial compositions. There is a Semitic *language-group*, but that is a very different matter. It should be noted that some authorities have used the name Semite to describe people whom they admit were of Hamitic descent. It cannot be too strongly emphasised that—in its correct usage—the term *Semitic* denotes linguistic and not racial attributes. *The true understanding of the movements and development of the Hebrew peoples has been completely clouded by its persistent misuse.*

THE AMORITES

As this name has often been used rather loosely by modern authorities, it is very necessary to have a correct appreciation of its full meaning. The word *Amorite* is used first in the Bible in Genesis x, where it is stated that Canaan, son of Ham, begat Sidon and Heth. Then follows a list of tribes who sprang from Canaan: Jebusites, Amorites, Girgasites, Hivites, Arkites, Sinites, Arvadites, Zemarites and Hamathites. It is probable that these names were not patronymics, but were geographical terms. Thus, the Jebusites mentioned in Genesis x were those descendants of Canaan who had settled in the city of Jebus (Jerusalem). Similarly, the Arkites resided in Arca, the Hamathites in Hamath, and the Zemarites in the place to this day called Sumra. The term Hivite would also be geographical.

Thus the Biblical term *Amorite* was applied to those descendants of Canaan who resided in a portion of the territory known to the people of the Euphrates basin as *Amurru* (Mar-Tu, the land to the West) many centuries before the Israelites entered the Promised Land. But the term *Amurru* was not used consistently, for a Hebrew resident of Palestine might be called either a Canaanite or an Amorite by a dweller in ancient Babylonia (*vide Cambridge Ancient History*, Vol. I, 1929, p. 230), for usage varied with time.

But the "Amorites" so called by modern archæologists were something far greater than the comparatively small number of the Hamitic people using that name, mentioned in Scripture as sharing Palestine with numerous other tribes. According to modern research, an "Amorite" race originated in the area of the Middle Euphrates. About the time of Abraham (*c.* 1900 B.C.) they had gained control of the whole of Babylonia and had pushed out pioneering colonies over Palestine and even as far as Egypt. Many authorities consider that the Hyksos who controlled Egypt for a period were of this dominant race. It is clear that descendants of Canaan and Amoritic Hebrews had dwelt together in Palestine for centuries. Prof. R. B. Dixon, in his *Racial History of Man* (1923), p. 172, mentions that in the period 2500 B.C.-1500 B.C. the population of Palestine consisted primarily of 'Mediterranean' and 'Caspian' peoples.

It will be recalled that the Ammonites and Moabites, who dwelt to the east of the Jordan, derived from Hebrew parents who moved in from the Euphrates area at the same time as Abraham.

It has been securely established that large sections of a highly civilised race moved westwards and northwards from Babylonia about 2000 B.C. (Serial No. 4 [222.11]). Some authorities call these migrating people *Habiru* or *Hebrews*, other authorities name them

Amorites; whilst some writers have used the term *Unman-Manda*, although this name is usually associated with people of the same race who became prominent in Medo-Persia at a much later date. The language of the *Amurru* was "an earlier stage of the Hebrew language". The Ras Shamra Tablets show that people using archaic Hebrew had lived in southern Palestine as early as 2100 B.C. (Serial No. 50 [222.1]).

There is thus good ground for believing:

(*a*) That the Amorites of the Bible were of Hamitic descent (i.e., they were Canaanites).

(*b*) That they were thus named because they lived in the territory of *Amurru* and not because of any racial affinity with the people known to modern ethnologists as "Amorites".

(*c*) That the "Amorites" so called by modern authorities (using the word in a strictly ethnological sense) were first found in the Tigris-Euphrates basin and gradually moved westwards at, or about, the time of Abraham.

(*d*) That these "Amorites" were, in fact, none other than a branch of the Hebrew or kindred peoples who had migrated from their homeland to what Babylonians generally then called 'the land to the West'.

THE HEBREWS WERE NORDICS

The sub-joined evidence shows that the people whom some authorities call *Hebrews* and others *Amorites* were of that section of the human race now known as *Nordic*.

Professor Coon:

"The Sumerians, who lived over five thousand years ago in Mesopotamia are almost identical in skull and face form with living Englishmen."

Professor Sayce

says that the 'Amorites' of Palestine were tall, handsome people, with white skins, blue eyes and reddish hair, having all the characteristics of the white race. He quotes support from Sir Flinders Petrie to the effect that they were fair-haired 'long-headed' people. Professor Sayce states that captives taken by Shishak of Egypt, at the time of Rehoboam, from Israelite cities, are depicted on the walls of the temple of Karnak. They are 'Amoritic' as opposed to the so-called 'Jewish' type.

This authority also traces these 'Amorites' via North Africa, Spain and Western France as far as the British Isles. He says that their 'cromlechs', which can be seen in Palestine, particularly on the east side of the Jordan, mark their westerly migration. The skulls found in these cromlechs are dolichocephalic (long-headed).

Encyclopædia Britannica:

"Egyptian illustrations of the New Kingdom show the Palestine Amorites to have been a race much more like the northern Europeans than the Semites; long-headed, with blue eyes, straight nose and thin lips . . ."

It is now becoming accepted that the Amoritic-Hebrew migrations reached as far north-west as the British Isles possibly before the Israelites entered Palestine after their Exodus from Egypt.

WHAT OF THE ISRAELITES?

It has been clearly demonstrated that the physical type now erroneously termed 'Jewish' is definitely non-Hebraic (Serial Nos. 26, 28, 40, 56 [572.933]). Who, then, were the Israelites racially?

It is quite obvious that, if the Hebrews were Nordics, so also were the Israelites, for the latter derived from the former. The world in general has been so obsessed by the idea that the Jews of to-day represent the true Hebrew type that the error dies hard. It is only in recent years that modern research has established beyond doubt the fact that the so-called 'Jewish' type is something very different from the ancient Hebrew.

Professor Sayce, Sir Gardner Wilkinson and other authorities have shown from the Egyptian sculptures that the people now referred to as "Amorites" were typical of the inhabitants of the cities of Israel at the very time when the Israelites had been a united nation, at the highest peak of their power and prosperity under David and Solomon. *Obviously* these captives must have been mainly Israelites, though possibly there were non-Israelite Hebrews among them. Professor Sayce himself remarks that the so-called 'Jewish' (Hittite) physiognomy is conspicuous by its absence in this period.

The captives depicted by the ancient Egyptians on the temple walls of Karnak were *Nordics*. They were captured in Israelite cities (I Kings xiv and II Chron. xii). Some authorities call them Amorites: other authorities call the same people Hebrews. The Bible says they were Israelites.

All three descriptions are correct. But the Bible term is the most definitive. They were *Israelite* Hebrews.

"THE LIGHT OF THE WORLD"

*(From the original painting in Keble College Chapel
by Holman Hunt)*

ANCIENT RACES PORTRAYED ON THE EGYPTIAN MONUMENTS

(*Key and note next page*)

No. 1. Three Amorite heads from the top of the pylon of the Ramesseum, time of Ramses II.

No. 2. Head of a Pulista, or Philistine, from the court of Medînet Habu, time of Ramses III.

No. 3. The king of the Hittites, with pigtail, from the façade of Medînet Habu, time of Ramses III.

No. 4. Hittite head from the Great Hall of Karnak (north side), time of Ramses II.

No. 5. Three Hittite (?) heads from the top of the pylon of the Ramessium. The reading of the name is not quite certain.

No. 6. Three small Hittite heads from the Great Hall of Karnak (south side), time of Ramses II.

No. 7. Head of the chief of Ganata or Gath from the temple of Shishak, the contemporary of Rehoboam, at Karnak. The type is Amorite.

No. 8. Head of the chief of Judah-melech or Jehud-ham-melech, "Jehud of the king" (probably the Jehud of Josh. xix. 45), from the temple of Shishak, at Karnak. The type is Amorite.

(From A. H. Sayce, *Races of the O.T.*, 1925 ed., by kind permission of the Lutterworth Press.)

Note: Distinction should be made between *ethnic* and *geographical* names. The king of the Hittites is clearly of Armenoid appearance. But the chief of Ganata or Gath, in Rehoboam's time—one taken prisoner in Shishak's invasion—quite probably was an Israelite, for David had broken the Philistine power and Solomon had consolidated the control. The 'Philistine' of Ramses III period (1215-1184 B.C.) is also during Israel's occupation of Philistia; at this time also the bulk of the Canaanite Amorites had been driven out and their territory occupied by Israel for "three hundred years" (Judges xi. 19-26). Even the alleged 'Amorite' of Ramses II period (1558-1491 B.C.) may have been Hebrew, for the Habiru had long been in the land.

THE TESTIMONY OF HOLMAN HUNT, O.M., D.C.L.

This artist, world-renowned for his pictures of the Saviour, went to great pains to obtain a correct appreciation of the complexion and facial contour of the true Israelitish Jews. He realised that the typical 'western' Jews were—in the main people of mixed race. In addition, therefore, to consulting with some of the foremost authorities of his day on the races of the East, Holman Hunt went in person to Jerusalem in order to see for himself the type of the true Jew.

It must be remembered that at that time (1854) there were only a very few Jews in Palestine—in fact, only the merest handful. This was actually a few years before Sir Moses Montefiore obtained the permission of the then Sultan for a limited number of Jews to settle in Palestine, and the better part of a century before the British conquest in 1917 opened the way to the large-scale immigration of 'western' Jews.

The Jews whom the artist saw and interviewed were descendants of ancestors who had been dwelling in the Holy Land from time immemorial—possibly from soon after the expulsion which followed the rebellion of Bar Cochab in A.D. 135.

The point is that Holman Hunt, supported by the opinion of reliable authorities of his day, satisfied himself that he had found the true Jewish type, and that the Jews of that type were 'fair'—in fact, they were of the classification now known as *Nordic* and far removed in appearance from the type popularly known as 'Jewish'.

It is remarkable that the artist himself was frequently hailed as a 'Jew' by the non-Jewish inhabitants of Palestine. The views expressed by him find support in the writings of Sir Gardner Wilkinson, also a famous traveller in Bible lands (Serial No. 26 [572.933]).

EXTRACT FROM *ENCYCLOPÆDIA BRITANNICA*, 1946 Edition, Article 'AMORITES'

The Amorites as known from the Bible . . . as a pre-Israelite people in Canaan, and also as the inhabitants of two trans-Jordan kingdoms . . .

The non-biblical material has markedly increased our knowledge and has also complicated it. Egyptian illustrations of the New Kingdom show the Palestinian Amorites to have been a race much more like the northern Europeans than the Semites: long-headed, with blue eyes, straight nose and thin lips. Even the royal name *Akvaruvāsh*, the reputed contemporary of the ancient king Narâm-Sin of Akkad (about 2530 B.C.), in the Hittite copy of an inscription of the latter, seems to be Aryan or Indo-European . . .

Another impression is gained from the Babylonian material of the earliest period, where "west" . . . and "the land of the Amorites" (*Amurru*, ideogr. *Mar Tu*) were of identical meaning. The Amorites were inhabitants of a territory lying west of Babylonia . . .

The motherland of these peoples was the region of the Middle Euphrates . . . About 2057 B.C. . . . Sumu-abum founded the Amorite kingdom of Babylon. Hammurabi, his fifth successor . . . united the whole of Babylonia under his sway (1925 B.C.) . . .

Meanwhile the Amorites had settled in the west of Lebanon and in the mountainous parts of Canaan, and perhaps even ruled Egypt for a short time. It is, in fact, probable that the foreign domination of Egypt, the so-called Hyksos (c. 1800-1580 B.C.), is connected with the wanderings of this Amorite people. . . . On the other hand, Bauer's careful researches have led him to an underestimation. According to him, *Amurra*, meaning the land to the west, or "the west", is a geographical term . . .

There is a rich but scattered abundance of material on the language of the Amorites. . . . From this it is seen that the language represents an earlier stage of the Hebrew language.

EXTRACT FROM *THE RACES OF EUROPE*, by PROFESSOR C. S. COON (Macmillan, New York, 1939), pp. 83, 110-112

"COON, CARLTON STEPHENS, anthropologist; . . . A.B. magna cum laude, Harvard, 1925, A.M., 1928, Ph.D., 1928; . . . Field work and anthrop. research, N. Africa, Balkans, Ethiopia, Arabia, 1925-34, discovering remains Neanderthal man, N. Africa, 1939; instr., later asst. prof., asso. prof. anthropology, Harvard . . . Editor: Dixon Memorial Volume for Peabody Museum (Harvard), 1943 . . ." (*Who's Who in America*, 1946-47.)

It can be shown that Sumerians who lived over five thousand years ago in Mesopotamia are almost identical in skull and face form with living Englishmen, and that predynastic Egyptian skulls can be matched both in a seventeenth-century London plague pit . . .

The Long Barrow population formed a distinct, homogeneous type; one different from any which, to our knowledge, had previously inhabited the British Isles since the days of Galley Hill; and one which cannot be duplicated, except as an element in a mixed population, anywhere on the western European continent. One is, therefore, led to conclude that the Megalithic cult was not merely a complex of burial rites which diffused without visible carriers; and also that the bearers of this complex avoided mixture by coming by sea.

In looking for related populations of equal age, we may eliminate at once the smaller, less dolichocephalic branches of the Mediterranean race proper, including the Danubian. A few individual crania in Neolithic Spain and Italy would qualify, but none of the series from these countries. The standard Egyptian crania, as groups, are all too small, as is the single lady from Greece. In one particular feature, the nasal index, the Long Barrow people resemble the Egyptians more than most of the more northerly Mediterraneans, for the Long Barrow crania are leptorrhine . . .

A true and valid similarity, however, may be found between the English Long Barrow series and the early skulls from el'Ubaid in Sumeria, which, whether belonging to the fourth or the third millennium B.C., are in either case older than their British counterparts. The only difference which prevents identity, is that the Mesopotamian faces and noses are somewhat longer.

EXTRACT FROM *SOME SOURCES OF HUMAN HISTORY*, by PROFESSOR SIR W. M. FLINDERS PETRIE (S.P.C.K., London, 1922), pp. 54-56

"PETRIE, SIR (WILLIAM MATTHEW) FLINDERS (1853-1942), English Egyptologist . . . He took an early interest in archæological research, and between 1875 and 1880 studied ancient British remains at Stonehenge and elsewhere; . . . In 1880 he began a long series of important surveys and excavations in Egypt. . . . Much of this work was done in connection with the Palestine Exploration Fund . . . was appointed Edwards professor of Egyptology at University College, London . . . was knighted in 1923. He resigned his professorship in 1933 and from 1932 to 1938 excavated in Palestine. Sir Flinders died July 28, 1942, at Jerusalem." (*Encyclopædia Britannica*, 1946 edition.)

The history of Palestine cannot be traced further than the Neolithic cave sanctuaries of about 3000 B.C. In these caves the bodies were burned, and over them were piled the infant sacrifices of the Canaanite worship. Little has yet been traced of this age. The Amorite age which followed it is the most original and distinctive period of the country. The Semitic Amorites seem to have been akin to the Hyksos migration, which streamed down Syria into Egypt. They had brought much of civilisation with them from Babylonia, and they developed a high ability in metal work, so that their products and their artists were eagerly sought by the Egyptian conquerors about 1500 B.C. The Amorite had pressed on an older population, and it was his fusion of race with the native Canaanite that produced the high civilisation which the Egyptians met. The distinctive sign of the Amorite is the stone pillar worship. He set up those rough stone pillars, as high as ten feet or more in the older sanctuaries, in a row, of sometimes as many as eight. They were the centre of worship, altars were placed between them for offerings, and this national worship of the high places continued, largely partaken of by the Israelites, till the Captivity. The sacred pillars or tall conical stones are figured on Roman coins of Syrian shrines: the Gabal or stone of Emesa was brought to Rome with great pomp by the crazy orgiastic Syrian priest who ruled the Roman world; and in the present time I have found a conical stone placed on a shelf, in a little weed-grown enclosure in a Syrian village. How far this system of rows of sacred stones may be linked with the West we cannot yet discriminate. The Amorite civilisation received a great shock in the repeated raids of Egypt, 1500-1160 B.C. It was also being largely affected there by the Egyptians, the Cretan, and the Cypriot works which flowed into Syria. Thus it became modified, and passed into the nondescript Levantine style, which was taken up by the Phœnician Brummagem workers, and spread over the Mediterranean.

EXTRACT FROM *THE HITTITES*, by PROFESSOR A. H. SAYCE (The Religious Tract Society, London, 1925), pp. 16-19

SAYCE, ARCHIBALD HENRY (1845-1933). ' British Orientalist . . . was educated at Bath and at Queen's College, Oxford, becoming a fellow in 1869. From 1891 to 1919 he was professor of Assyriology at Oxford. Although his conclusions have been modified (e.g. in chronology and transliteration) by the work of other scholars . . . it is impossible to overestimate his services to Oriental scholarship. . . . .He was a member of the Old Testament Revision company (1874-84), deputy professor of Comparative Philology in Oxford (1876-90), Hibbert lecturer (1887), Gifford lecturer (1900-2).'' (*Encyclopædia Britannica*, 14th edition.)

The Hittites and Amorites were therefore mingled together in the mountains of Palestine like the two races which ethnologists tell us go to form the modern Kelt. But the Egyptian monuments teach us that they were of very different origin and character. The Hittites were a people with yellow skins and "Mongoloid" features, whose receding foreheads, oblique eyes, and protruding upper jaws are represented as faithfully on their own monuments as they are on those of Egypt, so that we cannot accuse the Egyptian artists of caricaturing their enemies. If the Egyptians have made the Hittites ugly, it was because they were so in reality. The Amorites, on the contrary, were a tall and handsome people. They are depicted with white skins, blue eyes, and reddish hair, all the characteristics, in fact, of the white race. Prof. Petrie points out their resemblance to the Dardanians of Asia Minor, who form an intermediate link between the white-skinned tribes of the Greek seas and the fair-complexioned Libyans of Northern Africa. The latter are still found in large numbers in the mountainous regions which stretch eastward from Morocco, and are usually known among the French under the name of Kabyles. The traveller who first meets with them in Algeria cannot fail to be struck by their likeness to a certain part of the population in the British Isles. Their clear-white freckled skins, their blue eyes, their golden-red hair and tall stature, remind him of the fair Kelts of an Irish village; and when we find that their skulls, which are of the so-called dolichocephalic or "long-headed" type, are the same as the skulls discovered in the prehistoric cromlechs of the country they still inhabit, we may conclude that they represent the modern descendants of the white-skinned Libyans of the Egyptian monuments.

In Palestine also we still come across representatives of a fair-complexioned blue-eyed race, in whom we may see the descendants of the ancient Amorites, just as we see in the Kabyles the descendants of the ancient Libyans. We know that the Amorite type continued to exist in Judah long after the Israelitish conquest of Canaan. The captives taken from the southern cities of Judah by Shishak in the time of Rehoboam, and depicted by him upon the walls of the great temple of Karnak are people of Amorite origin. Their "regular profile of sub-aquiline cast", as Mr. Tomkins describes it, their high cheek-bones and martial expression, are the features of the Amorites, and not of the Jews . . .

It is clear, then, that the Amorites of Canaan belonged to the same white race as the Libyans of Northern Africa, and like them preferred the mountains to the hot plains and valleys below. The Libyans themselves belonged to a race which can be traced through the peninsula of Spain and the western side of France into the British Isles. Now it is curious that wherever this particular branch of the white race has extended it has been accompanied by a particular form of cromlech, or sepulchral chamber built of large uncut stones. The stones are placed upright in the ground and covered over with other large slabs, the whole chamber being subsequently concealed under a tumulus of small stones or earth. Not unfrequently the entrance to the cromlech is approached by a sort of corridor. These cromlechs are found in Britain, in France, in Spain, in Northern Africa, and in Palestine, more especially on the eastern side of the Jordan, and the skulls that have been exhumed from them are skulls of men of the dolichocephalic or long-headed type.

EXTRACT FROM *THE HIGHER CRITICISM AND THE MONUMENTS*, by PROFESSOR A. H. SAYCE (S.P.C.K., London, 1894)

(Pp. 353-354)

From the time of Thothmes III it was usual to crown the oval cartouche in which the name of the conquered locality was written with the head and shoulders of a typical representative of its population. The prisoners brought back to Egypt served as models, and the Egyptian artists drew their outlines with almost photographic fidelity. Now it is remarkable that the heads which surmount the names of Shishak's conquests in Palestine are the heads of Amorites, and not of Jews. They reproduce the features of that fair-skinned, light-haired, blue-eyed, and long-headed Amorite race with which the earlier monuments of Egypt make us familiar. Nothing can be more unlike the Jewish type as we see it in the

tribute-bearers of Jehu on the Black Obelisk of Nineveh, or as we are familiar with it to-day. It is evident that in the days of Shishak and Rehoboam the old Amorite race was still strong in the south of Judah. Outside Jerusalem and the more important fortresses it must have been the prevailing type. In no other way can we account for its having been selected by the sculptors of Shishak to typify the population of the kingdom of Judah, to the entire exclusion of any other type . . .

(P. 355.)

The blond Amorite race was widely spread . . . In short, the mountainous country of Palestine was largely in the hands of Amorite tribes . . .

EXTRACT FROM *UR OF THE CHALDEES*, by SIR LEONARD WOOLLEY, 6th Edition
(1929) (Charles Scribner's Sons, New York)

"WOOLLEY, SIR (CHARLES) LEONARD. Kt., cr. 1935; M.A. Oxon, Hon. D.Litt. Dublin; Hon. LL.D. St. Andrews; Hon. A.R.I.B.A.; Major G.S.P.R. Directorate, 1939-43; . . . b. 17 April 1880 . . . Asst. Keeper Ashmolean Museum, Oxford, 1905-7; Excavations at Corbridge, 1906-7; Excavating in Nubia for the Eckley B. Coxe Jnr. Expedition, 1907-11; Oxford University Expedition to Nubia, 1912; British Museum excavation at Carchemish, 1912-14; Archæological work in Sinai for the Palestine Exploration Fund, 1914 . . . Excavations at Tel el Armarna for Egypt Exploration Society, 1921-22; Excavations at Ur, 1922-34; Excavations . . . near Antioch, Syria, 1936-37 . . ." (*Who's Who*, 1946.)

(P. 117.)

. . . I have already said that we do not quite know who the Sumerians are; tradition would make them come from the East; the study of their bones and skulls shows that they were a branch of the Indo-European stock of the human race resembling what is called Caucasian man, a people who in stature and in appearance might pass as modern Europeans rather than as Orientals.

EXTRACTS FROM *ABRAHAM, RECENT DISCOVERIES AND HEBREW ORIGINS*, by SIR LEONARD WOOLLEY (Faber & Faber), 1935

(Pp. 291-292.)

c. 2278 After the conquest of the Guti Ur-Nammu, governor of Ur, sets himself up as king and establishes the Third Dynasty of Ur. The great imperial age of Ur is continued by Dungi (2260), Bur-Sin (2213), Gi-mil-Sin (2204) and Ibi-Sin (2195). During this time, the first appearance of Amorites amongst the population of southern Mesopotamia, these being probably the Habiru or Hebrew immigrants, employed as herdsmen.

(P. 164.)

. . . The Kirkuk tablets prove that the population of Nuzi was largely composed of Amorites or Hurrians who may be blood-relations of the Habiru or Hebrews . . .

EXTRACT FROM AN ADDRESS by W. HOLMAN HUNT, O.M., at a Lecture in Exeter Hall, London, on 2nd May 1900; from *God and Greater Britain*, by the Rev. Robert Douglas, M.A. (pub.: James Nisbet & Co., London), 1902

(Pp. 183-187.)

. . . The question is why, in my picture of "The Light of the World" and later pictures of the Saviour and of the Jews connected with him, I represented them of what, in general terms, may be called a fair complexion, and not strikingly like the Jew as we know him in the West? In the case of the first picture, which I finished and exhibited in 1854, it was an important point to me to leave no doubts in the spectator's mind that the figure represented was intended as a spiritual representation of the Saviour. I had to consider, therefore, whether I should follow the traditional type adopted by painters, a figure with grey or blue eyes and chestnut hair, or whether I should represent Him of the type generally known to us as the Jewish. From all that I could discover at the time I saw no reason to depart in respect of complexion from the traditional type, and I therefore with no further question represented the Saviour of the traditional complexion. In the later picture, "The Finding of the Saviour in the Temple", I had to represent not the spiritual Saviour but the human Christ; and as I wanted to avoid any traditional treatment that was not justified after the closest observation, I took pains to consult every authority I could that would prepare me for my Eastern work. Amongst other books that I studied diligently was Sir Gardner Wilkinson's *Ancient Egyptians*, . . .

. . . I had the additional advantage of speaking to people before I left England, of speaking to great authorities who had lived in the East, like Sir Henry Layard, who was a great friend of the Jews, and other travellers who had been in other parts of the East, and they all agreed in saying that the general type of the Jew, as they found him in the East, was fair. When I arrived in Egypt I observed with the greatest diligence, and found that their observations were supported by the facts before my eyes. Going further into Jerusalem, I looked with great attention at all the Jews I found there, and although there were a certain proportion dark, and who were readily recognisable to an Englishman as Jews, there were some, the greater number, who were fair, and who might have passed without being so recognised. Well, I made it my business to attend the services in all the synagogues, and I chose the models that I wanted for my work more for their picturesqueness and beauty than with any desire to make them resemble the Jews of the West. When I brought my picture home, many people expressed surprise at the fact that many of the figures were not strikingly like Jews as they knew them in England; but I found that people who had been in the East defended me, and before long the picture was admitted to be in that respect quite correct. Now, before committing myself to this treatment I felt that it was very necessary indeed to try, if possible, to arrive at some conclusion as to what the type and complexion of the ancient Jew was. All of you here will probably be prepared for the fact, that while the Bible is so frank and so exact in its history of people, it spends no words at all upon the outer aspects of its heroes, however important they are. We get no description of Abraham, none of Jacob, nor with two exceptions, and then incidentally, of any of the characters in the Bible. This observation applies to the Gospel history also. We know what Socrates was like, we know what Plato was like fairly well; we know what Alcibiades was like; and even of others of whom there are no busts, we have a general idea of their appearance from the descriptions; but we have not any description of Jesus Christ, of whom, if of any being, other than Jewish historians would certainly have given exact accounts. Incidentally I said there were exceptions, and these, in my opinion, are important. Isaac is not described, but while Jacob is not described, Esau, his brother, is reported as being "red and hairy". . . . There is a long gap before any other person is incidentally described; but we come to a most important character in David, and of him it was said that he was fair—taking our version—and ruddy, but in the original it is "fair and red-haired". These are very important pieces of evidence about the complexion of the original Jews, because a perfectly dark race does not have fair children. Persons called dark in England often have fair children; but a person of pure Asiatic or African type never has fair children. The children are as dark when they are born as they are in adult years. Now we must remember that the Jew was a stranger in the land; he was unlike the people about him; and from the beginning of the history to the end, he is always spoken of as belonging to a peculiar people, that is to say, that he was different from the people about him. You find this corroborated by the fact that when Abraham's son grew up old enough to be marriageable, he called Eliezer to him and made him swear that he would go back to his own cradle-land, Padan-Aram, and find him a wife of his own race; for he said, "What shall it profit me if my son marry a daughter of Canaan?" And then we find

Eliezer bringing back Rebecca for Isaac to marry. Now, when his sons grow up, Isaac has evidently become an invalid, and Rebecca is very anxious about the one son she has the greatest affection for, and she says, "What will it profit me if my son marry a daughter of Heth?" and she sends him back also to Padan-Aram to find a wife of his own race. Now for the most part the people about them were dark people, not dark in the English sense merely, but with dark blood and the characteristics of a dark race. You may assume that there was some outward mark of difference, and I think the facts lead us to conclude that this outward mark of difference was that they were a fairer people than those about them. When the history of the patriarchs is at an end, we come to the time of the establishment of the Israelites as a nation, and we find that intermarriage with the women of the country they are invading is forbidden so strictly, that it is considered high treason, and is visited with death. Moses ordained that, and you will find throughout the later history this was always remembered by the leaders of the nation . . . a great many of the Jews of the Herodian time were merely Idumeans, and they of course called themselves Jews.

I might also mention another fact, and it is this, that if a traveller were to arrive at Jerusalem on a Saturday or Sunday afternoon, outside Jerusalem, under the shadow of the wall, he would find some few hundreds of fair women sitting who had come out to take the air, these being days on which business cannot be conducted; and if he had come straight from England he would naturally ask, "Who are these fair women?" when to his surprise he would be told that they were Jewesses. As an example of the general recognition of the characteristic fairness of the Jewish type in Palestine, I would add that frequently when as a young man travelling about the country, at a season when no European tourists were in the land, the boys of a town dancing about would salute me with cries of "Iud", "Iud", meaning "Jew".

EXTRACT FROM *THE CAMBRIDGE ANCIENT HISTORY*, Vol. 1 (1928) (article by R. A. S. Macalister, Litt.D., F.S.A., Professor of Celtic Archæology, University College, Dublin)

(P. 230.)
The most important political term, however, is Martu or Amor (Amurru): it is specifically the western land, and Amor is also the name of its deity. Sometimes the term is applied to the whole region west of the Euphrates; but later it is restricted further west, and includes the Lebanons and Damascus, as distinct from the coastland of Canaan. But it is never used consistently. A strong Amorite chief could extend his sway . . .

Ibid (article by S. A. Cook, Litt.D., Cambridge).

(P. 182.)
By the 'Semites' is generally understood the group of peoples known as the Aramæans (Syrians, etc.) in the north, the Babylonians and the Assyrians in the east, the Arabs in the south, and the Phœnicians, Hebrews, Moabites, etc., in the west. They are the inhabitants of the region bounded by the Taurus and the mountains of Armenia and Iran, the Persian Gulf, the Indian Ocean and the Red Sea, Egypt, and the Mediterranean.

(Pp. 184-185.)

The problem of this term now becomes acute. The term 'Semite' is more convenient than accurate, and is derived from Shem, a son of Noah, the hero of the Deluge (Gen. ix-xi). In an elaborate genealogical table many divisions of the world as formerly known are traced back to Noah's three sons, with the result that each division stands in some more or less intelligible relationship to the rest. This method of reckoning geographical, ethnical or political divisions has always been in vogue and recurs, for example, in Hesiod's genealogy of 'Hellen' (the Hellenes), the son of Deucalion (also the hero of a Deluge), who is the father of Dorus (Dorians), Aeolus (Aeolians), and Xuthus, the father of Ion (Ionians) and Achæus (Achæans) . . . The narrative in its original form told how Canaan was cursed and condemned to be the servant of Shem, whereas Japheth is very favourably recognised as Shem's protégé. The genealogy represents Canaan as the 'father' of certain Phœnician cities and of Heth, the latter being not necessarily the Hittites of Asia Minor, but later offshoots in Palestine. Canaan's territory is from Sidon to south Palestine and the east of the Dead Sea; and it includes the Amorites and other peoples who are regularly spoken of as pre-Israelite . . .

(Pp. 185-186.)

. . . Feelings of relationship can express themselves in genealogical form and differently at different times; hence Shem may have had diverging meanings, just as was the case with Amor (the Amorites), Heth (the Hittites), and many another name . . .

The best-known Semitic languages are the Akkadian (sometimes used as a convenient term for the practically identical Babylonian and Assyrian dialects), Canaanite (a term to include Phœnician, Hebrew, Moabite, etc.), Aramæan (Syriac, etc.), and South Arabian (Minæan and Sabæan). Their close interrelation resembles that among the members of the Romance or of the Teutonic sub-divisions of the Indo-European family. But the linguistic, ethnical and cultural boundaries are not similar. Semitic languages have been adopted by invaders (Kassites, Philistines, etc.); Armenians and Jews despite a noteworthy physical similarity spoke entirely distinct languages . . .

(Pp. 192-193.)

. . . In this way five epochs have been distinguished, the latest being the Mohammedan movement of the seventh century A.D. The first invasion would date about the fourth millennium B.C., occupying Mesopotamia and North Syria. About the middle of the third millennium will come the Canaanites and a modification ('Amorite') of the Semitic element in Mesopotamia. A thousand years later the Aramæan wave, a vast movement, brings the Hebrew and related peoples (Edom, Moab and Ammon), and fills the north as far as the Taurus mountains. Again, after another millennium, a fourth invasion is responsible for the Nabatæans and for later settlers, e.g. the Lakhmids and Ghassanids of the east and west respectively.

Serial No. 57.g

Authorities: Various

Early Hebrew Colonies in the British Isles.

THE existence and movements of the main body of the Hebrews have almost invariably tended to be overlooked by Bible students, who naturally have focussed their attention more particularly on the history of the Israelites, though these were, in fact, originally quite a small section of the Hebrew peoples. It is, nevertheless, most essential that the migrations of the parent stock of the Israelites should be kept in mind if the Bible record of race origins and race movements is to be reconciled with the researches of modern ethnologists.

It has already been shown that the Hebrews were of the *Nordic* race, though linguistically they have usually been classified with the group of peoples which have been termed *Semitic*.

In the present article first-class evidence is submitted to show that some of the Hebrews moved westwards from Bible lands via the Mediterranean and Atlantic coastlands, to reach the British Isles as colonists about or not long after 2000 B.C.

Irrefutable testimony of migrations from Palestine, Trans-Jordan and Sinai to these shores is found in the trail of stone monuments—menhirs, dolmens, stone-circles, etc.—which marks an unmistakable path between these widely-separated points.

There is good reason to believe that the religion of the British Druids, in its original form, resembled closely the patriarchal worship of Abraham and the earlier descendants of Shem who, under various names, played a notable part in the advancement of ancient civilisation.

The migration to Britain of these early Hebrew colonists blazed the trail for later waves of immigrants and laid a foundation for the virile community which was destined ultimately to develop into the unique group of English-speaking peoples which has done so much for the civilisation of modern times.

Loose Terminology

A correct understanding of the movements of peoples in and from Bible lands has, until the present century, been almost impossible owing to the fact that the terms used to describe those peoples have been so ambiguous and so carelessly and indiscriminately applied as to render it highly difficult to follow their movements. In particular the consistent misuse of the term *Semite* has thrown investigators "off the track". Until quite recently it had been generally considered that this was a racial term, involving a conglomeration of "Arab" peoples with hooked noses. It is now realised that the so-called Semitic nations comprised elements of several races whose languages were related; just as the term *Indo-European* denotes a group of peoples, in different ethnic categories, whose languages have a common base—the so-called "Aryan".

The terms *Phœnician, Amorite, Hittite* and *Hebrew* have been equally sadly misused (*vide* Serial No. 57 [572.9394] and Serial No. 58 [572.93944]). A brief glossary of these terms in their correct usage may be useful.

Phœnician. An ancient Greek term, used to describe peoples who dwelt, and who had dwelt, in Palestine, Syria and Asia Minor during the first two millennia B.C. These peoples included Canaanites, Hebrews and Israelites, the last-named having, of course, derived from the Hebrews.

Racially, the so-called *Phœnicians* embraced both Nordic and Mediterranean elements. Linguistically they have been divided into *Semitic* and *Indo-European* groups. Some of the Semites were Nordics, whilst the Indo-Europeans were probably not all Nordic.

Semites. Peoples of several racial types whose habitat was the Bible lands in general—Palestine, Syria, Arabia—and who spoke related languages called *Semitic*. It is worthy of note that there are authorities who now feel that these Semitic languages were actually evolved by "Aryan" peoples who had sojourned in Sumeria possibly as early as the fourth millennium B.C.

Amorites. (*a*) An indigenous *Canaanite* people residing in Palestine at and before the period of the Exodus.

(*b*) A Semitic-speaking people, now shown to have been Nordics, and close kinsmen of the *Habiru* who had moved from the Tigris-Euphrates area, about 2000 B.C. to *Amurru*—the land of the West (Palestine).

Hittites. (*a*) *Hatti*—stated by Weill (p. 92) to be pre-Indo-European, indigenous peoples of *Asianic* stock. Their Armenoid physiognomy is reflected in modern Levantine peoples, and is often erroneously referred to as "Jewish".

(*b*) Archæological research into the great "Hittite" civilisation which centred on Boghaz Keui, in Asia Minor, has revealed that an Indo-European aristocracy had, long before the Israelites entered their Promised Land, imposed its culture upon the native *Hatti* (who possibly were the same people as those Hittites whom the Bible calls "children of Heth").

The Indo-Europeans spoke a totally different language (Nesite) from that of the indigenous Hittites. Waddell is quite positive that the Indo-European section of the Hittites (whom he names "Catti") was of the Nordic race and this view is held by other.modern authorities.

Serial No. 60a.

Hebrews. According to Scripture, the Hebrews were the descendants of Eber, great-grandson of Shem. (The terms *Semite* and *Shemite* are by no means synonymous—for instance, the Canaanites, who mostly were descendants of *Ham*, have been classified as "Semites"). Thus the Hebrews were only a portion of the great Shemite race. Their original language is now the subject of some controversy. Though most authorities hold that they spoke a language now called *Semitic*, some scholars have expressed the view that their parent tongue was related to the Indo-European. The *Habiru* of secular record have been positively identified with the Hebrews of the Bible.

The Language Problem

It cannot be too strongly emphasised that similarity of language is not a *proof* of racial kinship. Conversely, because peoples now speak different languages it does not by any means follow that they are necessarily of different ethnic types. There are many examples of this. For instance, the coloured people of the U.S.A. lost their own languages within a few score years of leaving their native lands. Though they now speak English, they are not racially akin to the Celto-Saxons and though they would not now be able to converse with their long lost kinsmen in Africa and elsewhere, they are still Negroid in the ethnological sense.

On the other hand, similarity of language is proof positive of *contact* between races, and may therefore be used to *support* acceptable evidence of racial affinity.

When Experts Differ

It must be stressed most positively that there is great divergence of view among the authorities who have written about the migrations of ancient man. It is probably true to say that no two of them agree on all points. On some fundamental matters the opinions of authorities with the highest credentials are diametrically opposed, and frequently they are highly critical of each other. When experts disagree it is the layman's privilege to accept the opinions which support his case and, where Scripture is involved, the Bible-lover is entitled to quote the evidence of the authorities whose views align themselves with the Bible record.

The Cradle of Civilisation

There are divergent schools of thought as to the place of origin of civilisation as we know it. A considerable section of modern scholarship has concluded that civilisation first arose in the Tigris-Euphrates basin. A second school is of opinion that it was on the banks of the Nile that culture commenced. A third theory is that the "civilising" element of mankind spread from an original homeland in the more northerly parts of the ancient world —eastern Europe or western Asia.

Tradition comes down generally on the side of those authorities whose researches have led them to hold that civilisation arose in the Tigris-Euphrates basin, and Christians have gladly availed themselves of their testimony, although they have readily agreed that civilisation spread almost immediately to the Nile valley, where it progressed on lines somewhat similar to that of Sumeria. Those who hold that the "civilisers" originated in the north would seem to have more difficulties to explain away than their opponents. In reviewing this matter, however, it must be borne in mind that the Bible itself is by no means explicit in defining the lands in which Noah and his descendants *first* settled. The Ark came to rest on the mountains of Ararat (*creation*). This locality may have been in fairly close proximity to Sumeria. On the other hand, it may have been at a great distance from Bible lands. The record says that some of Noah's descendants journeyed from the East (margin: or east-wards) and came to the land of Shinar, this having from ancient times been identified as Babylonia. On the other hand, some traditions have associated Mount Ararat, in Armenia, with the Ark's resting place. Thus the geographical terms mentioned in the 10th chapter of Genesis should be construed in the light of positive evidence only and not identified with a particular area merely on long-held traditional beliefs. There are many who feel that the Adamic world lay far to the east, in the region of the Hindu-Kush mountains, and that the first settlements of the families of Noah were made in the vast area between there and the Caspian Sea, where their cities may still lie buried. This view would not necessarily be unscriptural.

Whether or not the "civilisers" *originated* in the northern lands, Indo-European migrants undoubtedly left a northern habitat and broke in at a very early period (*c.* 2000 B.C.) not only on the so-called "Semites" of Bible countries, but also on the indigenous peoples of Asia Minor, Crete, and the Ægean. These invaders were the Indo-Europeans. Their period of residence in northern homes (doubtless of centuries) had produced a virile and dominant group, speaking languages which had a common "Aryan" base, which, according to Waddell (p. xi) derived originally from Sumeria. They appear to have had little difficulty in subduing the southern peoples and imposing their own culture. The most advanced of these invaders were those of the Nordic section. Under various names (Hatti or Khatti, Mitanni, Kassites, Achæans, Dorians, Amorites, Habiru) they had founded empires in Sumeria, Asia Minor, and the Ægean before Abraham left Ur. It is considered by some authorities that the Hyksos or "Shepherd kings" (who dominated Egypt during a period ending in *c.* 1830 B.C.) were the rulers of a section of these same irresistible Indo-Europeans, who had overthrown (for a time at least) the might of Egypt.

Shem and Japhet

In the light of the most recent research the Bible student should find less difficulty in understanding the record of Scripture in relation to the spread of population after the Flood. It will be recalled that God blessed the line of Shem and entrusted to it His high mission; whilst Japhet was made a "protégé", "dwelling in the tents of Shem". After Babel, which appeared to be the metropolis of the Noahic community, the peoples were scattered and much of the "scattering" must have been in a northerly direction. The Bible narrative shows that the Hamites seem to have moved off generally in the direction of Syria, Canaan, and Egypt; thus those who went north would be of Shem and Japhet. There is certainly no Scriptural reference to the effect that they were in any way *tied* to a particular area. Some of them doubtless remained behind in Babylonia. After some centuries of exile some urge or circumstance impelled large numbers of them to head back southwards. Doubtless their return was hotly disputed by many who were their long-lost blood relatives. But the invaders prevailed. In the Tigris-Euphrates area there arose the "Amorite" regime, in which Hammurabi was conspicuous. At Boghaz-Keui, in Syria, there emerged the so-called "Hittite" civilisation, though the native *Hatti*, whose name it bore, were merely a subject race.

The chief point at present to be noted is that the Hebrews, or Habiru, from which Abraham and his descendants sprang, were a portion only of a Shemite (not Semite) aris-tocracy, a large section of which appear to have sojourned for centuries in the northland. In passing, it may be observed that, about the time of Abraham, there wás a pronounced drift back northwards (Serial No. 4 [222.11]), and thus, when the Israelites were finally deported to the Caspian area (*c.* 740-720 B.C.) doubtless they found themselves amongst kinsmen (however distant) who had not been contaminated with the foul religions and diseased humanity of Canaan. God had said, "I will cleanse their blood."

Serial No. 60b.

Early Hebrew Colonies in Bible Lands

The Hebrews, or Habiru (also called Arameans) were obviously pioneers and colonisers. There is evidence of this from both Scriptural and secular sources. When Terah took Abraham and Lot from Ur they went first to Haran in Syria, where they lived until the death of Terah. The fact that there were Hebrews in Syria, even before the period of Abraham, is confirmed by a reference in the Boghaz Keui records of the so-called Hittite civilisation of which Indo-Europeans were the overlords. Haran was within the bounds of this ancient empire. Weill links these early Hebrew settlers definitely with those who subsequently moved southwards into Canaan. It will be remembered that the descendants of Lot (Moab and Ammon) settled in Trans-Jordan. The progeny of Esau (Edom) was so hopelessly intermingled with indigenous Canaanite stock that they should not be classified as true Hebrews.

There is evidence also from the Ras Shamra Tablets (Serial No. 50 [222.1]) which shows that Hebrews who had moved into South Palestine before 2100 B.C. had later migrated northwards to the Syrian coastal area by *c.* 1400 B.C.

There can be no doubt whatever that the virile Hebrews were in advance of the indigenous peoples both in culture and in active endeavour. They were equally acceptable to the Amorite people of Hammurabi (their close kinsmen), the Indo-Europeans of Boghaz Keui, or the ruling classes of proud Egypt. Abraham, it will be recalled, was *persona grata* at the court of Pharaoh and was regarded by the Hethites of Hebron as "a mighty prince among us". There can be no reasonable doubt that these enterprising and cultured people (already shown to have been Nordics) were akin to the most advanced of the Indo-Europeans who swept southwards to dominate the countries of the Near and Middle East about or before the period of Abraham.

In view of this record of pioneering adventure, there should be no surprise occasioned by the production of modern evidence to the effect that these spirited Hebrews pushed colonies westwards to the utmost bounds of the then-known world.

The Westward Trail of the Stone Monuments

That such a people did push westwards is amply demonstrated in the record of imperishable stone. From Palestine, Syria, Trans-Jordan and Sinai there stretches a trail of ancient stone monuments (the first of which appear to have been built not later than the early part of the 2nd millennium B.C.) via the Mediterranean and Atlantic coasts to the British Isles and beyond. It is clear that stone monuments of various types were erected by the Hebrews themselves, and that at a later period the sacred function of such structures, whether as pillars of "witness", or altars, etc., was perverted by their being adopted in the idolatrous religions of Canaan, so strongly condemned by the Prophets. The evidence which follows shows that, not only does the trail exist, but also that the dolmens, menhirs, and stone circles at either end of the trail are substantially similar:

EXTRACT FROM *HETH AND MOAB* by C. R. Conder, R.E. (1885).

". . . even with such knowledge as we possess it appears clear that the dolmen-building races most probably belonged to some ancient Asiatic stock slowly spreading westwards into Europe—a course of migration which has been firmly established in the case of the Indo-European races through philological discovery" (p. 202).

". . . long before the Law of Moses existed the fathers of the Hebrew race seem to have used the same stone monuments which were subsequently condemned in consequence of the cruel and shameless rites with which they were connected in Canaanite paganism" (p. 272).

EXTRACT FROM *ANCIENT HISTORY FROM THE MONUMENTS: SINAI*, by Major H. S. Palmer, of the Royal Engineers (S.P.C.K., 1878.)

"The remains thus described are nearly identical in character with those which in England and Scotland are commonly called Druidical circles" (pp. 102-103).

EXTRACT FROM *CENTRAL AND EASTERN ARABIA*, by W. G. Palgrave (1865).

". . . there is little difference in the stone wonder of Kasseem and that of Somersetshire, except that the one is in Arabia, the other, though the more perfect, in England" (p. 252).

Professor R. Rice-Holmes, in his *Ancient Britain and the Invasions of Julius Caesar* (p. 83) confirms the existence of the great trail of dolmens from Syria to North Africa, through Spain to Western Europe. He states that these erections are undoubtedly the work of a tall, blond, dolichocephalic race.

Dean Stanley, in his *Sinai and Palestine*, 1866 (p. 277), pointed out that stone circles in Britain find their counterpart in the land of Israel.

Professor L. A. Waddell, in the extract subjoined, confidently mentions these monuments as evidence that the "Phœnicians" had established themselves in Britain.

Sir Norman Lockyer (extract appended) says that the folklore and traditions associated with the monuments indicate a close connection between the ancient British and the Semitic civilisations.

Professor A. H. Sayce in his book *The Hittites* says that a dolichocephalic race, akin to the 'Amorites', was responsible for the chain of cromlechs reaching from Britain, through Spain and North Africa, to Palestine (p. 19).

After consideration of this cumulative testimony it must surely be agreed without reservation that the rude stone monuments of Britain have their counterparts in the Bible countries where the Hebrews first originated.

The British Druids

Julius Caesar and many other ancient historians have paid tribute to the culture and learning of the British Druids. There has been much controversy with regard to the origin of this mysterious priesthood, and a good deal of fanciful literature has been written concerning them. Some authorities have expressed the opinion that they were indigenous to the countries of north-west Europe. This view, however, does not harmonise with Scripture, and the Bible-lover will be content to accept the outlook of those authorities who state that the Druids moved in with the earlier waves of immigration from the east. Whether or not they actually erected the stone circles such as Stonehenge, it seems to be accepted that they certainly used them for religious purposes. Though there is evidence that corruption of a serious nature befouled the Druidic worship of the Continent, it seems that, in the main, the ritual and worship of the British Druids was of a high order. Stukeley, who made a wide investigation of the whole question over two hundred years ago, did not hesitate to assert that, in his view, the true Druidism was introduced into Britain from Bible lands about the period of Abraham, and that it undoubtedly derived from the original undefiled religion of the patriarchs. It will be remembered that the line of Shem had been entrusted with the oracles of God. At the time of Abraham the True Faith was certainly perpetuated in the circle of the mysterious Melchizedek, who doubtless was associated with the line of Shem. Though the Druidic religion was originally and generally pure in Britain, there is positive evidence that the religion of Canaan was practised in some parts of the British Isles at a very early date. The ritual of *Beltane* or Bel-fire is itself proof of this. It may be that these practices had preceded the first Hebrew colonisation, having been brought in by the so-called Iberians. On the other hand, it may have been introduced by later "Phœnician" Canaanites—or even by "Phœno-Israelites" who had deserted the worship of Jehovah.

Be this as it may, there are credible authorities who assert that the original religion of the British Druids was so in harmony with that of Christianity that the early Christian missionaries who arrived in Britain in the first and second centuries found a sympathetic foundation on which to build the new Faith.

The First Inhabitants of the British Isles

There is fairly general agreement among authorities that the first civilised inhabitants (apart from scattered aboriginal inhabitants of the Stone Age), of the British Isles were a rather small statured, dark-haired people of the "Mediterranean" type—long-headed, narrow browed. Though some authorities consider them to have been "aborigines" of the Stone Age period, others are of the opinion that they, too, had moved in from eastern lands, and this latter view is certainly more in line with Scripture.

These early inhabitants became known to later historians as *Iberians*, though this description may well be misleading, for it is highly probable that the term had passed westwards from the original Iberia (south of the Caucasus) through the Spanish Peninsula, which also bore this name. Thus, though the phrase "dark Iberian" has passed into modern currency, it should be regarded with suspicion on several counts for, as mentioned by Trevelyan, these early inhabitants were of several races, not all of them dark-haired. He adds, moreover, that these so-called Iberians were "no mere savages".

It has been demonstrated that the so-called *Phœnicians*, whose trading ports and settlements were pushed westwards during the first and second millennia B.C., comprised both Hebrew and Canaanite elements. In the later period of the "Phœnician" Golden Age there were also strong elements of the Hebrew sub-race—the Israelites (Serial 58 [572. 93944]). It will be recalled also that Canaanite tribes fleeing from Joshua established themselves as far west as Tangier (Serial 9 [572.961]). It has been shown that there was an extensive trade between the countries of the Levant and the British Isles from c. 2000 B.C. onwards (Serial 49 [571.3]) and Serial 45 [386.0936]), and it would appear that a very early migration of "Canaanites" travelling by the same route as Joshua's victims reached the British Isles in considerable strength *before* the arrival of the Hebrews, and that it was these "Mediterranean" Canaanites (who had doubtless sojourned for a period in Spain) who thus became known as Iberians, in the same way that the modern dwellers in Saxony became known as Saxons, though they are not racially akin to the people whose name they carry.

During the whole of the second millennium B.C. and during the early part of the first, there arrived colonies, small at first, of what Waddell calls *Hitto-Phœnician Catti*. He links them positively with the Nordic Amorites and the Indo-Europeans who swept southward into Bible lands.

The trail of stone monuments shows that these more cultured immigrants were "tall, blond dolichocephs" from Bible lands. Sayce is emphatic in this, and Sir Norman Lockyer's investigation from the point of view of astronomy confirms it. There is strong reason to believe that these enterprising people who arrived in the British Isles up to 2,000 years before the time of Julius Caesar were mostly Hebrews. Stonehenge, Avebury, and a host of other ancient circles, associated with the British Druids, stand as testimony to the fact that the race who erected them originated in Palestine, Syria and Sumeria—the "jumping-off" point of the ubiquitous Hebrews.

Blazing the Trail

The evidence adduced supports the Scriptural inference that of the selected line of Shem, the Hebrews in particular had been chosen to serve in the capacity of pioneers of civilisation and to blaze the trail to the western lands where, in the fulness of time, an important section of the race was to grow to full stature, to be used as a vehicle whereby progress and enlightenment should be radiated to the world at large. Thus, although the first arrivals in the British Isles seem to have been *Mediterranean* Canaanites who had sojourned for a period in the Iberian peninsula, the first "civilisers" were the *Nordic* Hebrews. Adventurers of this ubiquitous aristocracy established trading posts and settlements which later became bases not only for further waves of their own people but also in later centuries for their offspring, the Israelites, who, in contingents small and great, followed from time to time in their wake—to Egypt, where some elements of their parent stock had been in residence since the time of Abraham; back to Canaan, where Habiru incursions had helped to destroy the hold of the Egyptian overlords "who knew not Joseph"; in exile to Medo-Persia, where Hebrew and other kindred peoples, long resident there, provided associations more wholesome than the corruptions of Canaan. Most interesting of all, Israelites arrived by devious routes in the far-off *Isles of the West*, so frequently mentioned by the Prophets, to find that their pioneering Hebrew kinsmen had already paved the way for the large-scale immigration which was to continue for more than a thousand years, bringing into Britain wave after wave of invaders—Celts, Angles, Saxons, Jutes, Danes, Normans, etc., now known most positively to have been of the same basic racial stock. Though there undoubtedly remain quite appreciable elements of "Mediterranean" and "Alpine" origin in certain parts of these islands, and even though these two strains are present in some small degree in many of the inhabitants at large, it is a fact accepted by modern ethnologists that the population of the British Isles as a whole is predominantly Nordic.

Thus, the "tall, blond dolichocephs" who commenced their westerly movement from Bible lands 4,000 years ago were ultimately reassembled in the Isles of Britain. The Hebrews, who had performed their pioneering function, became merged with their kindred the Israelites. The smaller numbers of Mediterraneans have, to a large extent, remained as identifiable entities in some of the more westerly regions of Britain and in southern Ireland, though the movement of peoples caused by the Industrial Revolution has produced a certain amount of admixture with the predominating Nordics.

Serial No. 60d.

EXTRACTS FROM *PHŒNICIA AND WESTERN ASIA* by RAYMOND WEILL (George G. Harrap & Co. Ltd., London, Toronto, Bombay, Sydney, 1940. Translated by Ernest F. Row).

"WEILL, RAYMOND, D.Litt.; French egyptologist; b. 74; ed. École Polytechnique.
Has conducted excavations in Egypt, Sinai and Jerusalem; Pres. Société Française d'Égyptologie; Prof. of Egyptology at École des Hautes Études 20– and of Oriental History at the Sorbonne 31–; awarded several prizes of Inst. de France . . ."
(*The International Who's Who*, 1945–46.)

Chapter I: Phœnicia: Its Geographical Setting, Configuration, and Towns

(Pp. 15–19.)

The scope of the name "Phœnicia" may have changed through the centuries before the classical period, and we have known for some years that about 1300 B.C. as far up as Latakieh, a long way to the north of Aradus, there was an important national centre of a people who were Phœnician in all their characteristics. This was not a colony, but the real primitive Phœnicia was far more widely extended than in the Greek acceptation of the name. And even in Greek tradition itself we can follow the gradual narrowing of the term in its later stages.

In the great variety of city legends among the Greeks we constantly note the appearance of the memory of founders who came from distant lands. Among these traditional heroes are Cecrops, founder of Athens, who came from Egypt, and Inachus, who arrived in Argos with an Egyptian or Libyan colony and whose successors were dethroned, several centuries later, by Danaus, coming also from Egypt. The descendants of the latter were in their turn dispossessed by Pelops, son of Tantalus, king of Phrygia and father of Atreus in the legend of Mycenæ. And there was also Cadmus, founder of Thebes, the brother of Phœnix, the Phœnician *par excellence*.

So we find Egypt, Libya, and Phrygia (north-west Asia Minor) in company with Phœnicia itself. And in legendary tradition it seems that all these countries were related. Similarly, too, Cadmus and Phœnix are shown as brothers of Thasos (in the Ægean) and Cilix (Cilicia), or else Cilix is one of the many sons of Phœnix, whose name thus seems to stand for the regions of north-west Asia Minor as well as for the islands of the neighbouring sea.

We learn also, in another direction, that Phœnicia is a name for Caria, and therefore for south-west Asia Minor, and also that Phœnicia is Colchis (Black Sea, between the Caucasus and Armenia), and therefore north-east Asia Minor. It results from this that the name *Phœnicia* covered the four corners of Asia Minor as well as the islands, and meant, in the primitive Hellenic use of the term, no less than the entire extent of the Ægeo-Asianic world.

But the Cadmus and Phœnix of the legends stand also in very close relationship to Sidon, so we have to acknowledge that, on the whole, *Phœnicia* was at the beginning of Hellenic times a very wide term, covering the whole of the seas and the Ægean world, including the Asianic coasts and those of the Gulf of Syria. . . .

These developments are curiously similar: *Keftiu* to the Egyptians in 1500 and *Phœnicia* to the primitive Hellenes meant the entire Creto-Aegeo-Asianic world, after which the two names were restricted in their application, but the divergent points of view of Greek and Egyptian geographers met again a few centuries before the Christian era and were concealed anew in the designation of the classical Phœnicia. Had there not been this agreement, the reasons determining such a development are difficult to explain precisely, but the kind of identity between the two words, as shown by history, is particularly strange.

In the latter part of the second millennium, none the less, and, as we shall see, at Ras-Shamra about the year 1300, the greater Phœnicia, limited later to the south, would seem to have been still existent and active in Northern Syria. We shall return later to the history of Ras-Shamra. . . .

Chapter II: Syro-Palestine in the Third Millennium

(Pp. 25–30.)

The Egyptians at the beginning of the Pharaonic period—say at the time of the 1st dynasty, about the year 3000—had a foothold in Asia already: they had settlements and made expeditions into the Sinaitic peninsula and the land of Palestine proper. During the Old Empire, about 2600 or 2500, they are found installed at Byblus, then the coastal stronghold of central Phœnicia. . . .

. . . But it is necessary here to glance at the conditions of primitive Hebraic history. We say *Hebraic* and not *Israelite*. When the Israelites left the southern desert to enter Palestine they were only a small clan, a very restricted portion of a much larger collection of peoples who carried out this immigration or conquest: they took part in a general movement. This happened in about the fourteenth century. This great assemblage of Semitic peoples coming up from the south-east were called, in the Biblical tradition that retained very clearly the memory of their arrival, *Aramæans*, and, preferably, *Hebrews*. Among them were *Ammon*, *Moab*, who were to establish themselves to the east of the Dea Sea, *Edom* on the southern confines of Judea, *Israel*, who followed the others and lagged behind, and lastly some other groups such as *Amalek*, who were never to succeed in emerging from the nomadic or semi-bedouin state. Edom had arrived very early. And in a note of very great value that has been preserved by chance (Genesis xxxvi. 20–30) the Bible describes the people who occupied Se'ir before the arrival of Edom, in the form, naturally, of a genealogy, connected with the ancestor Se'ir himself. He had seven sons, of whom *Lotan* was the eldest, and *Hori* was the son of Lotan. Here, then, we have the two names of peoples which had passed into Egyptian geography. But at the same date as the Biblical sources of information *Hori* held a clearly predominant position among his relations, so that the Bible describes his family as *Horites, sons of Seir*. Such was the population of southern Palestine in pre-Hebraic times, say about 1600 or 1500, according to the evidence of the Bible itself. It is understandable, then, that in earlier centuries these peoples and names were those which the Egyptians met and recorded at first, and the only ones they still knew during the Middle Empire, in the first centuries of the second millennium. . . .

(P. 29.)
. . . among the Semites of the primitive Syro-Palestinian region that we have just been considering, there was community or close affinity of speech, and that is the very definition of Semitism; . . .

Chapter III: Semites and other Races in Hither Asia in the Third Millennium

(P. 35.)
Such, then, was the appearance of the Syro-Palestinian world in the earliest days, say down to the third or the second millennium. Only for the third millennium, however, is the picture entirely accurate. For the succeeding one it lacks reference to certain new arrivals, the Indo-Europeans, who began to come from about the year 2000. But the arrival of the Indo-Europeans was a phenomenon of enormous extent, covering the greater part of the area of Hither Asia and Mediterranean Europe. . . .

Chapter VII: Coming of the Indo-Europeans: Kassites, Mitannians, and Hittites (2000–1500)

(P. 83.)
The Indo-Europeans were a *linguistic group*, exactly as the Semitic group was, and as different as the Semites both from the Sumerians and from the peoples of the primitive "Asianic" group. The Indo-European languages, already greatly differentiated in the classical period (say during the first millennium), were at that time the Celtic in Gaul and neighbouring countries, the Latin and other Italiot tongues of the peninsula, the Greek around the Ægean Sea, the Germanic on the continent north of Italy, the Slavonic to the north of the Hellenic area, the Armenian, and, finally, the Sanskrit in India.

The whole of linguistic Europe to-day is Indo-European. Germany is Germanic, England is Germano-Celtic, and pure Celtic is preserved in Ireland as well as in the Breton of French Lower Brittany. French is a mixture of this Celtic, which once covered the whole of Gaul, with Latin, and Italian is more closely akin to Latin. . . .

(P. 95.)
. . . It is quite natural that after the beginning of the Indo-European period, after 2000, such movements and migrations were accomplished just as easily, and it is understandable that Indo-European intrusions from north to south affected Syro-Palestine and led to settlements as far as the extreme south. This penetration of Syro-Palestine was, moreover, parallel to the great Indo-European arrival on the middle Euphrates—that of the Mitannians—and the two invasions were very probably connected with each other. The presence of an important Indo-European element in Syro-Palestine is made entirely clear by the documents relating to this country which we shall find in Egypt, in the first period of the New Empire, the fifteenth and fourteenth centuries, and the information they provide is of capital importance for our purpose. It should be explicitly stated that these documents dating from after the year 1500 are undoubtedly valid for a period appreciably earlier. . . .

Serial No. 60e.

Chapter VIII: Egypt, Syro-Palestine, Mitanni, and the Hittites, from the Middle Empire to the Middle of the Fourteenth Century

The Habiru

(Pp. 120-121)

Before leaving this period it is necessary to a proper understanding of the history of Syro-Palestine in the fourteenth century of Amenhotep III and IV, to direct our attention to the *barbarians* or *brigands* who infested the country at that time and to whom the Amarna Letters make constant reference.

According to these documents there took place in Canaan an intrusion of foreign, warlike peoples who insinuated themselves by fair means or foul among the peoples and cities. The letters of Rib-Addi of Byblus recur insistently to the danger of their presence and their aggressions, and the princes of many other cities wrote in a similar strain.

These invaders were called *Habiru*, the reading of the name, which presents a difficult problem in Akkadian cuneiform, being confirmed by a reference to the same people in the Boghaz Keui documents. They do not, however, appear in quite the same guise in the land of Hatti as at Amarna. In Syro-Palestine they were formidable men of war, generally dreaded by the letter-writer, who complains to the king of Egypt that they have taken some neighbouring city and are threatening him, or else that they have made common cause with some hostile king in the vicinity, or, again, that such-and-such a nearby enemy has taken them into his service. We thus get a clear picture of the procedure of these intruding "barbarians"—obtaining concessions by force, serving as mercenaries when needed, and as conquerors when absolutely necessary. Their name appears to be connected with an old Semitic root meaning *attached, contracting, i.e. mercenary* or *confederate,* perhaps *associated*—exactly what the Greco-Roman world was to understand by *barbarians*. In Hatti, where in some writings appear "the gods of the Habiru", the people thus designated are of a different kind. They are established sedentaries, one element of the population like the others, undoubtedly the same immigrants as in the Canaanite land, but arriving long before and becoming settled. There is mention in Hatti also of certain personages called "So-and-so the Habiru",

the title appearing to represent a kind of feudal rank. This same appellation, with the same meaning, is met with also in Babylonia proper in the second half of the millennium, particularly around 1400, and later, about 1080. . . .

(Pp. 122-123)

Now Israel, a small clan of the great Aramæan family, was also one clan among many others in the great family of the *Hebrews* (*Ibri*, plur. *Ibrim*), on which point the genealogical facts are quite clear: in Genesis x, 21, we have "Shem also, the father of all the children of *Eber*" (see also vv. 22-24). In the Israelite story of the Canaanite wars later on (Joshua, Saul, etc.) the name *Hebrew* often appears, and in such circumstances as to denote a whole of which Israel was only a part, while other clans, friends and enemies of Israel were also called *Hebrews*. It is noticeable besides that in the Biblical account this name *Hebrew* is applied to the people of Israel only when it is non-Israelites who are speaking. We shall not dwell here on this very remarkable point, but confine ourselves to the fact that *Aramæans* and *Hebrews*, according to the preceding argument, were the same unit. And then the Habiru of all the cuneiform texts are also this same people, provided only that the words *Ibri* in the Bible and *Habiru* in the cuneiform writings are one and the same vocable. After long years of discussion this identity of the vocables is to-day regarded as certain. Important results follow from it, both for the Habiru in general and for the history of Israel and the Biblical tradition. . . .

This throws a flood of light on the history of Israelite origins and makes admirably clear the circumstances of the arrival of the Israelites and their occupation of Palestine between the fourteenth century and the twelfth. For obviously if the Habiru of Amarna were not the Israelites themselves they were their cousins. Among all the other Hebrew clans it was these Amarna Habiru who threatened everything and made themselves a place everywhere, from one end of Syro-Palestine to the other. . . .

Chapter XII: Phœnician Expansion and Mediterranean Colonization (Tenth to Sixth Century)

(Pp. 179, 180)

The city of Tyre, whose influence was predominant in the great maritime area from about 1000 onwards, had important colonies in Cyprus—Citium, Idalium, Lapethus, etc.—where she was soon in competition with the Greeks of Asia Minor, their rivalry being particularly keen in the eighth and seventh centuries. Generally speaking, the Phœnicians occupied the south coast and the Greeks the rest of the island.

At Rhodes, much further to the west, and therefore in a much more Hellenic atmosphere, the Tyrians had the settlements of Ialysus and Camirus. Phœnician action in this quarter was checked by the Greeks and soon ended in a kind of stoppage or equilibrium. Phœnician activity is seen also, though to a smaller extent, on the Pamphylian coast, in Crete, and in the Sporades and Cyclades.

In Egypt a colony is known near Memphis called

the *Field of the Tyrians*, at the time of the Saïte kings.

In Sicily the principal Phœnician settlements on the north coast—Panormus (Palermo), Soluntum (Solonte), etc.—belong to the early period. (Later on we shall find these names reappearing for a long time in the history of Carthaginian domination and its struggles for the possession of Sicily.)

In Malta the Phœnicians possessed Gaulus (Gozo), and far to the west, halfway between Tunis and Sicily, the important station of Pantelleria. There were stations also on the south coast of Sardinia and in the Balearic Islands, notably at Iviça, where the Carthaginians settled in 650.

On the north coast of Africa was a regular group of places in what is now Tunisia around the principal centre, Carthage, whose foundation may go back, as we have seen, to the end of the ninth century. Nearby were Hadrumetum, and Utica on the Gulf of Carthage. The latter city was the earliest of the

Tyrian settlements on this coast, dating probably from about 1100.

On the European coast was Marseilles, founded about 600.

Finally, in the extreme west, were Gadir (Gades, Cadiz) at the mouth of the Guadalquivir, dating from the ninth or eighth century, and on the same Atlantic coast, west of the Straits, the famous Tartessus (the Biblical *Tarshish*), the name containing the same root as that of Tarsus in Cilicia, whose people were no doubt its first colonizers. In this country we shall find the Phœnicians in competition in the seventh and sixth centuries with the Phocæan Greeks, particularly in the region of Malaga.

After the sixth century, as we have said, the hegemony of Carthage replaced that of the old eastern metropolis in the Great Sea. We shall relate the history of this later on.

EXTRACT FROM *NEW LIGHT ON THE MOST ANCIENT EAST* by PROFESSOR V. GORDON CHILDE (Kegan, Paul, Trench, Trubner, London, 1935 edition)

"CHILDE, Professor V. Gordon, D.Litt.; D.Sc.; F.B.A.; F.R.A.I., F.S.A.; F.S.A. Scot.; University Professor of Prehistoric European Archæology, and Director of Institute of Archæology, London, since 1946 . . . B.Litt. 1916; first class honours in Literæ Humaniores, 1917; Private Secretary to the Premier of N.S.W., 1919–21; travelled in Greece, Balkans, and Central Europe; Librarian to Royal Anthropological Institute, 1925–27. Professor of Prehistoric Archæology, Edinburgh, 1927–1946 . . ." (*Who's Who*, 1948.)

(Pp. 1-3)

Barely a thousand years ago Scotland and the rest of northern Europe were still sunk in the night of illiteracy and barbarism. A thousand years earlier and history's light shines upon our dark continent merely from a few points on the shores of the Mediterranean. And in the next millennium these points flicker out one by one until only the ghostly radiance of heroic myth lights up the storied walls of Troy and Tiryns. . . .

. . . But one thread is clearly discernible running through the dark and tangled tale of these prehistoric Europeans; the westward spread, adoption, and transformation of the inventions of the Orient. And it is from a study of objects of Oriental type found, imported, or copied, in the cultural provinces of Europe that we may hope to define in more than purely relative terms the age of the several cultural groups recognized in illiterate Europe before the middle of the first millennium B.C.

For on the Nile and in Mesopotamia the clear light of written history illumines our path for fully fifty centuries and looking down that vista we already descry at its farther end ordered government, urban life, writing, and conscious art. There in the Ancient East, too, some episodes at least in the

great drama of the conquest of civilization are enacted on the open stage. The greatest moments— that revolution whereby man ceased to be purely parasitic and, with the adoption of agriculture and stock-raising, became a creator emancipated from the whims of his environment, and then the discovery of the metal and the realization of its properties—have indeed been passed before the curtain rises. Yet even so, we are so much nearer the beginnings on the banks of the Nile and the Euphrates that we have better hope of understanding those most momentous advances there than from a scrutiny of kitchen-middens on the Baltic or of shell-heaps on the Scottish coasts. And frequently the data from the Orient serve as a written commentary upon European prehistory. Some of the peoples of Oriental antiquity were close kinsmen to the neolithic inhabitants of parts of Europe or descendants of the race of palæolithic hunters who had lived there before. From the Oriental kinsmen of our barbarian ancestors may we not expect to learn something even of the spiritual life of the latter? May not the practices of the Orient, glossed by literary texts, throw light on contemporary usages in silent Europe?

EXTRACT FROM *HISTORY OF ENGLAND* by PROFESSOR GEORGE M. TREVELYAN (Longmans Green & Co. Ltd., 1945 edition).

Early Man: Iberian and Celt

(Pp. 6-7)

. . . It is thus that we must account for the variety and the present location of the races that were mingled in Britain so long ago. Cornwall, Wales and the Highlands of Scotland are inhabited by the oldest stocks: we call them, to-day, 'the Celtic fringe' of the island. But most of them are pre-Celtic—as also are the Irish. The Celts, late comers into western Europe, were tall men, fair or red-haired, who entered Britain and Ireland only a few hundred years before the coming of Julius Cæsar. The bulk of those whom we miscall 'Celts' are for the most part dark-haired people whose ancestors had been in the island thousands of years before the red Celt was ever heard of. They were the folk whom Matthew Arnold in his poem describes as 'dark Iberians', coming down, 'shy traffickers', to chaffer with the Phœnician traders on the shore.

We may conveniently speak of these pre-Celtic peoples, collectively, as 'Iberians', though in fact they consisted of many different races, not all of them dark-haired. Some 'Iberian' blood probably flows in the veins of every modern Englishman, more in the average Scot, most in the Welsh and Irish. The Iberians were no mere savages. . . .

The Levant was the cradle of European civilization. The inhabitants of Mesopotamia, Egypt and Crete, in days before Tyre, Athens or Rome, evolved agriculture, metal-craft, shipbuilding and many other of the arts of life. Such Promethean secrets, starting on their journey from South and East, handed on from trader to trader and from tribe to tribe ever northward and westward across the forests of barbarous Europe, or travelling more quickly by merchant galleys round the Pillars of Hercules, reached at last those half fabulous 'tin islands' in the mists and tides of the northern seas.

The trade of Britain with the Levant, or rather of the Levant with Britain, is far older than the Celtic Conquest. English jet found in Spain is believed to date from 2500 B.C., and Egyptian beads found in England from about 1300 B.C. So early, perhaps much earlier, the Mediterranean traders had discovered the British islands with their wealth of pearls and gold, to-day long exhausted, and their metals, not yet at an end. . . .

(P. 9)

. . . Many of the centres of this ancient civilization —Stonehenge perhaps—were placed on sites agriculturally barren, but once famous for the best flints or for surface gold, tin or copper, long since exhausted. . . .

. . . From the seventh to the third centuries before Christ, the Celtic tribes, originally occupying North-Western Germany and the Netherlands, were moving across Europe in many different directions. In the first centuries after Christ the Teuton tribes, starting from homes rather further to the East, were destined to move over much the same ground in much the same manner; but between the folk-wanderings of Celt and of Teuton was to be interposed the great event of the Roman penetration north of the Alps.

(P. 10)

The Celts, in their earlier day, showed as much vigour in migration as any race that came after them. One great body settled in France and became an important element in the racial content of the Gaulish nation. A southern wing settled in the valley of the Po, put an end to the Etruscan hegemony in Italy, and about 387 B.C. sacked Rome, when the geese were said to have saved the Capitol. Others pushed into Spain, others into the Balkans. During the same centuries a northern wing of this great world movement overran our island and imposed Celtic rule and language on its inhabitants. The Celtic invaders of Britain came in successive tribal waves, kindred indeed but mutually hostile and each with a dialect of its own. Erse, Gaelic, and Welsh are still extant variations of the tongues which they and the Iberians evolved. Wave after wave of Celts, each entering Britain by the lowlands of south and east, slaughtered, subdued or chased across the island not only the Iberians but such of their own kinsfolk as had preceded them; many of the pursued, as on all occasions in Britain, found refuge in the mountains to north and west.[1]

At least two big waves of Celtic invasion can be distinguished: first the Gaels or Goidels, still found in Ireland and Scotland, some of whom may have come over as early as 600 B.C.; secondly the Cymri and Brythons still found in Wales. Among the Brythonic peoples were the Belgæ and other tribes whom Cæsar found spread over Southern England; they were closely related to the Gauls beyond the

---

FOOTNOTE 1.—Professor Chadwick appears to think that the Celts who came to Britain at various times, probably from Belgium, Holland and N.W. Germany, were (like the Anglo-Saxons after them) practically one race, but that they acquired different cultures and developed different dialects of Celtic, according to the varying dates of their crossing the sea, or the variations of their subsequent history and contact with the natives.

Channel. These Britons seem to have been already settled in the island that is still called by their name, at the time when Pytheas, the Greek traveller from Marseilles, recorded his visit to the 'Pretanic isle' in the days of Alexander of Macedon.

The Celts who overran so much of Europe in the last six centuries before Christ were tall, light-haired warriors, skilful in ironwork, which was then re-placing bronze, and in arts and crafts of their own, much admired by modern archæologists. Such was the outfit, at any rate, of the later among the Celtic invaders of Britain. The fair-haired Celts imposed themselves as an aristocracy on the conquered tribes throughout Britain and Ireland. In the end the races mixed, but what proportion the Celtic bore to the old Iberian blood it is impossible to say. . . .

(Reproduced by kind permission of the Publishers)

EXTRACT FROM *PHŒNICIAN ORIGIN OF BRITONS, SCOTS AND ANGLO-SAXONS* by PROFESSOR L. A. WADDELL, LL.D., C.B., C.I.E. (Williams & Norgate Ltd., London, 1925)

"WADDELL, LAURENCE AUSTIN (Lt.-Col.), C.B., C.I.E., F.I.S., F.R.A.I. . . . b. 1854 . . . Glasgow University (M.B., C.M., with highest honours, 1878) . . . Professor of Physics and Chemistry, Calcutta Medical College; and Editor 'Indian Medical Gazette', Calcutta (6 years) . . . discovered, in 1896, the Lost Birthplace of Buddha, and many famous ancient classic sites, which he excavated; explored Tibet and its Buddhism; later Professor of Tibetan, University College, London; trav-elled in Burma, China, Japan, North America, Egypt, Mesopotamia, Syria-Phœnicia, and the Himalayas . . . Tibet Mission to Lhasa, 1903–04 . . . Hon. LL.D., Glasgow, 1895; . . . Hon. Correspondent Indian Archæological Survey . . . Author of . . . articles on Tibet in 'Encyclopædia Britannica'; various publications on archæological, geographical and ethnographical explorations. . . . Died 1938. (*Who Was Who*.)

(Pp. 363-364.)

We have found, by a mass of concrete attested facts and other cumulative confirmatory evidence, that Civilization properly so-called is synonymous with Aryanization; and that it was first introduced into Britain in the Stone Age, about 2800 B.C., or earlier, by Hitto-Phœnician "Catti", or Early Gothic sea-merchants from the Levant engaged in the Tin, Bronze and Amber trade and industries, who were Aryans in Speech, Script and Race—tall, fair, broad-browed and long-headed. Of the leading clan of Aryans, they bore the patronymic of Barat or "Brit-on", and, settling on the island of Albion, conquering and civilizing the dusky aborigines therein, they gave their own patronymic to it, calling it "Barat-ana" or "Brit-ain" or "Land of the Barats or Brits".

There were several successive waves of immigration of this Aryan Catti-Barat civilizing stock from the coast of Asia Minor and Syria-Phœnicia by way of the Mediterranean into the British Isles; and the different sections of that Aryan civilizing race called themselves variously Muru or Martu ("Amorite"), Cymr, Somer or Cumber, Barat or Briton, Goth or Gad, Catti, Ceti, Cassi, Xat or Scot, or Sax or Sax-on.

Their descendants continued to be the ruling race therein until modern times, excepting the Roman period, though even then several sections continued to maintain their independence in Wales, Cumbria, Scotland and Ireland. The later invaders, Jutes, Angles, Saxons, Norse, Danes and Normans were merely kindred North Sea colonists of the same Aryan racial Catti or Gothic stock; while the minor immigrations of batches of Belgians and others from the Continent into South Britain, mentioned by Cæsar, do not appear to have been racially Aryan. . . .

(Pp. 365–366.)

. . . The Early Aryan Gothic invaders and civilizers are seen to have been essentially a race of highly-civilized ruling aristocrats; and relatively few in numbers in proportion to the aboriginal population of the country. In physical type they were of the Aryan race, that is to say, tall-statured, fair-complexioned, with blue or greyish eyes, broad-browed and long-headed, as opposed to the small-statured, dark-complexioned, narrow-browed, and long-headed Pictish "Iberian" aborigines of the Stone Age, and the fringe of somewhat superior-cultured Stone Age race of medium-sized, fair-complexioned, broad-browed, but round-headed Slavonic or Germanic Huns, the beaker-using men of the "Round Barrows," who came from the Baltic and Germany. . . . Anterior to the arrival of Brutus about 1103 B.C. the Catti-Phœnician occupation of Albion appears to have been only very partial and sporadic with little intermixing with the aborigines. These early "prehistoric" exploiters of the Tin, Copper, Gold and Lead mines, and Jet and Amber trades, appear to have been floating colonies of merchant seamen and adventurers, who at first occupied strategic islets or peninsular seaports off-lying the chief native trade marts or mines, such as the Phœnicians usually selected for defensive purposes in most of their early colonies, on the model of Tyre, Sidon, Acre, Aradus, Carthage and Gades (or Cadiz). Of such a character are Ictis or St. Michael's Mount, Wight, Gower, the Aran isles off Galway, Dun Barton, Inch Keith, etc. Later they established themselves inland in the hinterland of their ports, as evidenced by their Stone Circles and other rude megalith monuments, which were chiefly, as we have seen, in the neighbourhood of their mines, or near their flint-factories for the manufacture of high-quality stone implements for their mines and miners, when Bronze was still too precious to spare. And these Early Phœnician pioneer exploiters of the mineral wealth of Albion do not appear to have attempted any systematic Aryanization or colonization of the country, or to have settled there with their wives and families to any considerable extent. What early civilization the aborigines of Albion then received was mainly through being employed in the mines and workshops of the Phœnicians.

. . . In this way the subsequent intermarriage of individuals of a relatively pure Aryan type would tend to enhance and fix the predominance of the Aryan blood strain introduced into Britain by the Britons, with all the superior intellectual endowments for progress which the Aryan type stands for. . . .

(P. 382.)
. . . That the British have inherited the sea-faring aptitude and adventurous spirit of the Aryan Phœ-nicians appears obvious. Whether they in the same degree reflect, and have profited by, the ancestral monotheistic Religion, is not quite so plain. And yet, I think, there is something to be said in favour of an affirmative on this question, too. . . .

EXTRACT FROM *STONEHENGE AND OTHER BRITISH STONE MONUMENTS ASTRONOMIC-ALLY CONSIDERED* by SIR NORMAN LOCKYER, K.C.B., F.R.S. (Macmillan & Co. London, 2nd edition, 1909)

"LOCKYER, SIR JOSEPH NORMAN (1836–1920), English astronomer . . . on the foundation of the Royal College of Science he became director of the solar physics observatory and professor of astronomical physics. Eight British Government expeditions for observing total solar eclipses were conducted by him between 1870 and 1905. . . . He was made a F.R.S. in 1869, received the Rumford medal in 1874, and was vice-president of the Society 1892–93. He was president of the British Association in 1903, and contributed papers to the Royal Society and Royal Astronomical Society." (*Encyclopædia Britannica*, 14th edition.)

(P. 32.)
With regard to the equinoctial year, the most complete account of the temple arrangements is to be found in Josephus touching that at Jerusalem. The temple had to be so erected that at the spring equinox the sunrise light should fall on, and be reflected to, the worshippers by the sardonyx stones on the high priest's garment. At this festival the first barley was laid upon the altar.

But this worship was in full swing in Egypt for thousands of years before we hear of it in connection with the Jews. It has left its temples at Ephesus, Athens, and other places, and with the opening of this year as well as of the solstitial one with the custom of lighting fires is associated, not only on hills, but also in churches. . . .

(P. 236.)
. . . My investigations have strongly suggested, to say the least, that there were men here with knowledge enough to utilize the movements of the sun and stars for a temple, and no doubt practical purposes before 2000 B.C., that is, a thousand years before Solomon was born, and at about the time that the Hecatompedon was founded at Athens. . . .

(P. 252.)
I propose in this chapter to bring into juxtaposition the various British and Semitic-Egyptian practices which we have so far considered.

I confess I am amazed at the similarities we have come across in the first cast of the net; we have found so much that is common to both worships in connection with all the points we considered separately. I will, for convenience, deal with the various points seriatim. . . .

(P. 472.)
I have already shown that the May year and the solstitial year had temples sacred to them in Egypt. I may now add that in the Egyptian temples we found one set for the northern stars, the equivalents of Arcturus and Capella, and another set for the southern stars, among them α Centauri. One of the most recent results of this enquiry has been that we have found a number of avenues, *not circles*, in Brittany and in different parts of Britain, *not in Cornwall*, the equivalents of the Egyptian temples aligned to the southern stars. . . .

(P. 478.)
It is interesting to note that, while the astronomical side of the inquiry suggests a close connection with Egyptian thought, the folklore and traditions, when studied in relation with the monuments, indicate a close connection between the ancient British and the Semitic civilizations. . . .

This work if subsequently confirmed by other investigators, has the double advantage of supplying us pretty accurately with the date of erection of the monuments and of indicating the methods of observing the movements of the sun and stars employed in Britain in prehistoric times; and if risings and settings were so abundantly utilized—for utility as well as priest-craft was certainly at the bottom of it—in Britain four thousand years ago, the remarkable testimony to the knowledge and wisdom of the "Druids" given by Cæsar and Pomponius Mela two thousand years nearer their time is now seen to be amply justified.

EXTRACT FROM *ABURY* by WILLIAM STUKELEY, 1743 edition.

(Pref. p. i.)

When I first began these studies about the Druid antiquities, I plainly discern'd, the religion profess'd in these places was the first, simple, patriarchal religion.

(P. ii.)

And our *british* Druids had no images. And whatever we find in history, that looks like idolatry in them, is not to be referr'd to the aboriginal Druids, but the later colonies from the continent.

Likewise I have open'd a large communication between the patriarchal family, of Abraham particularly, and of the first planters of the coasts on the ocean of Spain, Gaul, Germany and Britain.

(P. iv.)

Her God's ancient people the *Jews* are in the easiest situation, any where upon earth; and from hence most likely to meet with that conversion design'd them. And could we but reform from the abominable publick profanation of the sabbath and common swearing; we might hope for what many learned men have thought; that here was to be open'd the glory of Christ's kingdom on earth.

(P. 5.)

That our Druids were so eminently celebrated for their use of groves, shews them to have a more particular relation to Abraham, and more immediately from him deriving the usage. . . .

(P. 53.)

By the best light I can obtain, I judge our Tyrian Hercules made his expedition into the ocean, about the latter end of Abraham's time; and most likely 'tis, that Abury was the first great temple of Britain, and made by the first Phœnician colony that came hither; and they made it in this very place on account of the stones of the gray-weathers, so commodious for their purpose.

EXTRACTS FROM *STONEHENGE* by the same author, 1740 edition.

(P. 2.)

. . . we assert, that there is very much reason to believe these famous philosophic priests came hither, as a Phaenician colony, in the very earliest times, even as soon as Tyre was founded: during the life of the patriarch Abraham, or very soon after. Therefore they brought along with them the patriarchal religion, which was so like Christianity, that in effect it differ'd from it only in this; they believed in a Messiah who was to come into the world, as we believe in him that is come. Further, they came from that country where Abraham liv'd, his sons and grandsons; a family God almighty had separated from the gross of mankind, to stifle the seeds of idolatry; a mighty prince, and preacher of righteousness.

DOLMENS FROM THE HOLY LAND TO THE BRITISH ISLES

1. Near Heshbon
(Transjordan)

2. On Mt. Gilboa

3. West of Heshbon

4. In Galilee

5. Near Heshbon

6. Trans-Jordania

7. Algeria

8. Portugal

9. Spain

10. France

11. Holland

12. Ireland

13. Wales

14. Cornwall

15. Scilly Isles

SOURCES OF ILLUSTRATIONS

1. Col. C. R.Conder, *Syrian Stone Lore*, 1886, p. 44.
2.   ,,   ,,   ,,   p. 43.
3.   ,,   *Palestine*," 1889, p. 144.
4. Palestine Exploration Fund, *Thirty Years' Work in the Holy Land* (1865–1895), pub. 1895, p. 83.
5. Col. C. R. Conder, *Heth and Moab*, 1885, p. 196 (facing).
6. J. Fergusson, *Rude Stone Monuments*, 1872, p. 441.
7.   ,,   ,,   ,,   p. 402.
8.   ,,   ,,   ,,   p. 389.
9.   ,,   ,,   ,,   p. 385.
10.   ,,   ,,   ,,   p. 344.
11.   ,,   ,,   ,,   p. 309.
12.   ,,   ,,   ,,   p. 183.
13.   ,,   ,,   ,,   p. 168.
14. Godfrey Higgins, *The Celtic Druids*, 1827, p. lix (facing).
15.   ,,   ,,   ,,   p. 37.

Authorities: Col. C. R. Conder, *Palestine*
            G. Schumacher,   *Across the Jordan*

The Stone Trail from Palestine

IT is established beyond doubt that a trail of stone circles and monuments, well over 2,000 years old, marks a path from Bible Lands via North Africa and the Spanish Peninsula to the British Isles and the Scandinavian countries. It is clear that these stones were erected by a cultured people of great pioneering ability.

Stones were particularly prominent in the ritual and symbology of the ancient Hebrew people: the Bible makes frequent reference to this. There are good reasons for believing that these time-defying monuments follow the westward trail of a people whose God was the God of Shem and Melchizedek; of Abraham, Isaac and Jacob.

The Biblical Aspects of Megalithic Culture

Megalith: (Greek: *megas,* "great"; *lithos,* "a stone") a huge stone.

Stones have been used from time immemorial for numerous purposes, by almost, if not every, race of mankind. According to need, to their abilities, and to materials available, men have used stones of various sizes in worked or unworked form from prehistoric times to the present. The working of stones has been accomplished in several ways, depending partly upon the nature of the stone itself, and partly upon the tools and methods used: chipping, cutting or hewing, and grinding are among the most common ways of shaping stone that have been used from earliest times.

The ways in which stones have been utilised are sometimes so peculiar that their discovery in certain associations has been taken as indicative of the existence of a unique culture in which they play an integral part. The existence of a singular culture is deemed to be discernible in finds of so-called "megalithic" monuments, a name given to erections of one or more large stones, often unhewn, in a manner soon to be discussed.

Megalithic monuments are widely scattered over the Old World in particular; they seem to mark the movement of a particular culture, as already stated. Much speculation has centred on the question of whether this culture has been carried from place to place by a particular people, or whether it has been transmitted from one people to another through contact. It is accepted by some that megalithic culture originated with a certain people, but there seems to be uncertainty as to the identity of that people. It may be that some peoples adopted megalithic culture from its originators, but of this there is no certain proof. It seems fairly certain, for instance, that the Israelites, and even the Patriarchs who preceded Israel, made use of megalithic culture, and there is an open question as to whether that culture was native to the Hebrews or whether they adopted it as some believe.

Some of the greatest fields of megalithic structures are to be found in the territory of ancient Israel, especially in Trans-Jordanian territory, and there are strong indications that they were used by the Israelites at least for idolatrous purposes. A line of mega' ic structures of a type found in great numbers in the land of Israel, extends eastwards across Asia to China and Korea, and westwards through the Mediterranean littoral, to Spain, France the British Isles and the Scandinavian countries. This long line of monuments seems to imply the movement of something more than the culture that they represent. It seems hardly likely that this culture passed from tribe to tribe over so great a distance; rather, it seems more probable that these monuments testify to the migration of a single people to whom they were native and who erected them in the course of their movements. A question of great interest is as to whether the people who thus left these monuments were or were not Hebrews; and there are strong indications that they were such, especially in the case of the megalithic monuments in the land of Israel that have long been known to the Arabs as "kubûr beni Israîl",—"graves of the children of Israel," and when other evidence concurs with this testimony. Many features, such as the fact that certain Israelitish communities in China still make use of megalithic monuments in their age-old ceremonies of a Biblical character, support the view that the existence of such structures in other lands may well point to the Hebrew origin of the people using them. If indeed the Palestinian structures are monuments of the children of Israel, the long trails of such monuments to China and Korea on the other hand, and to the Atlantic coasts of Spain, France, and the British Isles and Scandinavian countries on the other, may constitute good evidence of the movement of the Hebrews, or in particular, Israelites, to such places.

Serial No. 76a.

A consideration of the writings of various authorities will show something of the diversity of opinions as to who were the originators of megalithic culture. The late Professor Sayce associated them with what he called "Amorites", whose "physical characteristics are those of the Libyan neighbours of the Egyptians on the west, the forefathers of the fair-skinned and blue-eyed Kabyles or Berbers who inhabit the mountains of northern Africa to-day. Anthropologists connect these Libyans with the Kelts of our own islands. At one time, it would seem, a Kelto-Libyan race existed, which spread along the northern coast of Africa to western Europe and the British isles.

"Wherever they went, the members of the race buried their dead in rude stone cairns or cromlechs, the dolmens of the French antiquarians. We find them in Britain and France, in the Spanish peninsula, and the north of Africa. They are also found in Palestine, more especially in that portion of it which was the home of the Amorites. The skulls found in the cairns are for the most part of the dolichocephalic or long-headed type; this too is the shape of skull characteristic of the modern Kabyle, and it has been portrayed for us by the Egyptian artists in the pictures of their Amorite foes" (*Early Israel*, 1899, pp. 70-72: cf. *The Hittites*, 1925, pp. 16ff.).

Conder, as we shall see, would ascribe megalithic structures a "Turanian" origin; whilst Professor C. S. Coon of Harvard University, associates these monuments with a "Long Barrow" population with "a true and valid similarity" found in "the early skulls from al 'Ubaid" (a town about four and a half miles north-west of Ur).

Dr. J. L. Myers, Wykeham Professor of Ancient History, Oxford, writing in *The Cambridge Ancient History* on megalithic origins, observes: " ... it is not possible to speak of a 'megalithic-people', but only of a megalithic-culture and a social structure imposed by its originators on the natives among whom they came" (Vol. I, 1928, p. 98). Professor T. E. Peet and Dr. Thomas Ashby, writing in the same *History*, state: "We are thus left with the theory of an actual migration or migrations to account for our phenomena, and it cannot be denied that this hypothesis, daring though it may seem, and incapable of proof on our present data, avoids many of the difficulties inherent in the two other explanations which have been put forward" (Vol. II, 1931, p. 599).

Whatever may have been the origin of megalithic culture, there are strong associations between it and the Hebrews, which may well be indicative of a solution to our interesting problem.

It is more than coincidence that the route of the Megalithic peoples, whose monuments can be traced from Palestine to Britain, is the same as that of the so called-Phoenicians, and the Kelto-Libyan "Amorites". How surprising, but logical, it would be to discover that they were one and the same people.

Menhirs, Stone Circles, Dolmens, Cairns, Mounds, all appear to have been constructed by the Hebrews; the Bible has numerous references to their erection in patriarchal times. Jacob set up as a pillar and anointed the stone upon which he had his visions at Bethel calling it "God's house" (Gen. xxviii: 18, 22). On the occasion of his covenant with Laban, he "took a stone, and set it up for a pillar. And Jacob said unto his brethren, Gather stones; and they took stones, and made an heap: and they did eat there upon the heap" (Gen. xxxi: 45, 46). Here we see that Jacob engaged in setting up two of the most common types of ancient monuments with which we are concerned—the single standing stone of witness, and the cairn, or collection of single stones by a multitude of witnesses. On the occasion of a later visit to Bethal, Jacob raised yet other monuments in the form of an altar to "the God of Bethel", and a "pillar" of witness upon which he poured a drink offering (Gen. xxxv: 7, 14).

The Mosaic law provided for the construction of unhewn stone altars (Exod. xx: 25; Deut. xxvii: 5), many samples of which are to be found in the Holy Land, as we shall see shortly.

Israel was instructed to erect a pylon of "great stones," to "plaister them with plaister" and to engrave the law thereon, in Mount Ebal (Deut. xxvii: 1-4; Joshua viii: 31ff.). On Israel's crossing the Jordan dryshod, Joshua ordered the construction at Gilgal of a twelve-stoned cairn, or circle—it is uncertain which—of stones taken from the dry bed of the river (Joshua iv: 3). The name Gilgal has been the subject of a certain amount of speculation, for the name means a circle or wheel; "gal" means also a heap; and it is tempting to think that these stones were either the centre of a sacred circle, or were placed in a circle to mark a sacred area. In the Jordan itself were placed twelve stones which remained as a national memorial until the chronicler's day, one authority has suggested these twelve stones served as the foundations of a multi-span bridge). Joshua and "all Israel with him" destroyed Achan, and all his family and his possessions, after which "a great heap of stones," possibly sealed with an earth covering, was raised over their remains in the valley of Achor (Joshua vii: 25, 26). Joshua constructed a great cairn over the remains of the king at Ai (Joshua viii: 29ff.). The last recorded act of Joshua was to set up a great stone beneath an oak, as a witness to the covenant of Israel to serve the Lord (Joshua xxiv: 26). Absalom set up a pillar of witness, and was later buried under a cairn (II Sam. xviii: 17). Samuel set up a stone of witness called Ebenezer, near Mizpeh (I Sam. vii: 12).

With respect to the numerous references to megalithic monuments and heaps of stones, it is worth noting Jeremiah's instruction to scattered Israel to "set thee up waymarks, make thee high heaps" (Jer. xxxi: 21), in the course of her migrations. This seems to have been an instruction to continue an already long-established custom.

No consideration of megalithic monuments constructed in patriarchal times should be left without some observation of the allied custom of venerating sacred trees—in particular, the oak—for megalithic monuments and sacred oaks will occupy our attention in ensuing pages.

Jacob hid his family's goods and treasures under the oak which was by Shechem; Rebekah's nurse, Deborah, was buried "beneath Beth-el under an oak" (Gen. xxxv: 4, 8). Joshua, as we have seen, "took a great stone, and set it up there under an oak, that was by the sanctuary of the Lord (Joshua xxiv: 26) in Shechem, possibly the one beneath which Jacob buried his family's treasures. The angel of the Lord appeared to Gideon beneath the oak in Ophrah (Judges vi: 11), where there was also a stone which served as an altar upon which Gideon's offering was made (Judges vi: 21). The "man of God" found the prophet "sitting under an oak" (I Kings xiii: 14). The bones of Saul and his sons were laid "under the oak in Jabesh" (I Chron. x: 12).

The original commemorative consecration of all these objects gave way to obscenities loudly condemned by the prophets. Ezekiel prophesied the end of Israel's profanities "when their slain men shall be among their idols round about their altars, upon every high hill, in all the tops of the mountains, and under every green tree, and under every thick oak, the place where they did offer sweet savour to all their idols" (Ezek. vi: 13). A profusion of these monuments is indicated. Hosea (iv: 13) utters a similar denunciation of the rites practised in the erstwhile sacred sites.

The way seems to be clear to accept the implicit truth of the native tradition concerning the Hebrew origin of what have been termed the Kelto-Libyan tribes of North Africa. The rise of their civilisation may furnish us with the dates of that Stone Age culture with which we are concerned, and which extended from Palestine, across North Africa, through Spain, western France, and into Britain and Ireland.

One of the most remarkable features of the Megalithic monuments is the remarkable similarity of some of those most widely separated, which feature affords a most valuable check on the movement of the culture of which they are an expression, if not of the movement of the people themselves.

EXTRACT FROM *PALESTINE*, by MAJOR C. R. CONDER, R.E. (George Philip and Son), 1889, pp. 142-157

Conder, Claude Reignier (1848-1910), Colonel, Royal Engineers, Altaic scholar, and Palestine explorer; born in Cheltenham. In 1872 took charge of survey in Palestine, and had surveyed greater part of country west of Jordan when murderously attacked and injured by Arabs in 1875; survey completed by Kitchener. Maps on scale of one inch to one mile and seven volumes of Memoirs published, 1880, "It may be fairly claimed," wrote Sir Walter Besant, "that nothing has ever been done for the illustration and right understanding of the historical portions of the Old and New Testaments since the translations into the vulgar tongue which can be compared with this great work." In 1881 Conder surveyed and mapped much of the country east of Jordan. He wrote voluminously on biblical antiquities; and with his father wrote *Handbook to the Bible*.

(Compiled from *The Dictionary of National Biography*).

The most remarkable feature of our work was the systematic examination of the rude stone monuments, of which we catalogued some seven hundred in all. They were known to exist east of Jordan, but it was not, I think, expected that they would prove more numerous in this region than anywhere else except in Tunis; and the contrast with their absence in Western Palestine is very remarkable.

Rude stone monuments are found in many parts of Asia, in Europe, and in North Africa. They occur from Norway to Tunis, and from India to Ireland, and they still present many curious problems to the antiquarian. These questions have been complicated by the utilitarian suggestions of writers, who ignore the folklore which is so closely interwoven with the history of these remains. It appears, I think, clear, first, that the rude stone monuments are of very high antiquity, having probably been erected in most, if not in all cases, by the early Turanians, who in Asia, North Africa, and Europe preceded the Aryans and the Semites, and who are called by modern students Iberians even in our own islands; and, secondly, that no study of these remains can be considered complete which ignores the beliefs concerning them surviving among the peasant populations of the regions where they occur.

Rude stone monuments are known in Arabia, and have been found near Lake Van and in Persia, in the Crimea and east of the Black Sea. They occur in Greece, in Cyprus, and in Phoenicia. There is, therefore, no reason for surprise at their discovery in Galilee, in Bashan, Gilead, and Moab. The only curious fact is their absence in Samaria and in Judea. There are some peculiarities, such as the occurrence of orientated avenues, of talyots or bilithons, of single stones outside circles, and of ring marks on rocks, familiar in our own land, but not as yet noted in Syria. I confine my remarks, there-

fore, to the Syrian remains, including *Menhirs*, or erect stones, whether single or in groups, circles or alignments; *Dolmens*, or monuments with a flat stone table; *Stone Circles*, *Disc Stones*, and *Cup-hollows*, all of which are exemplified in Moab.

It is clear that a stone may be placed on end for more than one purpose, though that purpose is generally monumental. Some enormous stones near 'Ammân, I believe, marked boundaries. Standing-stones have also been used to record events, like the Moabite Stone or the modern gravestone. Stones and stone pillars, or even cairns and heaps, have been used as memorials of a visit to some shrine, and are still so used. Other erect stones in Greece, in Chaldea, in Phoenicia, and in India are idols and lingams, worshipped as containing a spirit. In every case the explorer must consider the most probable reason for the erection of the stone. In Greece such stones—afterwards sculptured as terminal figures—marked boundaries, or were sacred emblems. Such boundary-stones occur also in Babylonia, and sacred stones are also mentioned in Chaldean temples. Jacob and Saul and other Hebrew heroes erected such memorials, and the pagan Arabs bedaubed them with blood, and offered to them their babes and daughters, and swore by them as sacred emblems.

In some cases burial at the foot of such a stone may possibly mark a human sacrifice, as, for instance, at Place Farm, in Wiltshire, where a skeleton was found by a *menhir* in the centre of a circle; but no sepulchral remains are found by or under the majority of these monuments. In all countries where they occur they are remarkable for a rounded or pointed top, which resembles that of later obelisks. In India the lingam stones are worshipped, and peasants rub against them. In some rural districts maidens lean against them, expecting to see a future husband. Marriages were often celebrated by such stones. The

Greystone, by the Tweed, witnessed marriages, where bride and bridegroom joined hands through a hole in the stone. Oaths were sworn at these stones in France to a late date; and the oath of Woden was sworn by men who joined hands through the stone. In Sardinia great stones with holes occur at the tombs called Giants' Graves, and also form the entrance to a circle called *cuisses de femme*. I have never found such holed stones in Syria, but a pair occur in Cyprus, which I think, from their size, not likely to have belonged, as some suppose, to an oilpress.

These standing-stones were often anointed with oil, with blood, or with milk. Libations of milk were poured through a stone in the Western Isles. Alexander anointed with oil the pillar on the grave of Achilles, as Jacob anointed the stone of Bethel, or as the Arabs smeared their *ansâb* with blood. The lingam stones in India are still anointed with ghee, and stone circles are splashed with blood. In Aberdeenshire water was believed to spring from a hollow in the top of a sacred stone; in Brittany the *menhirs* were believed to go to the river to drink. Such monuments are also wishing-stones, such as Dhu esh Sher'a, a black stone at Petra, or the Hajr el Mena ("stone of desire"), which we found in Moab. To some prayers for rain have been offered. Breton *menhirs*, and others in India and in Somersetshire, are said to represent wedding-parties turned to stone; others in the Khassia Hills are adored as ancestors by tribes which burn the dead. The stones of Allât, 'Azzi, and Hobal at Taif—still shown—were once adored as deities by Arabs, as were those of Asaf, and Naila, and Khalisah near Mecca.

Such instances out of many which have been collected show that the idea of a "Holy Stone" is no theorist's dream. Those who see in these monuments only gravestones or boundry-marks have not fully studied the facts of the case.

One curious feature of such stones I have not seen noticed. In Gilead I found a fallen *menhir* with a hollow artificially made in the side, as though to put something into the stone. At Kit's Cotty-house I found similar holes in the side stones. At Stonehenge I found them in some instances even larger. No doubt many other cases are known. The holes are not water-worn, but have been rubbed as though by fingers or arms thrust constantly into the stone. They are not lewis holes, and they were made after the stones were erected. Probably they were enlarged, like the hole in the pillar in the Church of St. Sophia in Constantinople, by countless visitors putting their fingers into the same hole.

The great alignments of Brittany and of Dartmoor are well known, though the reason for their erection is doubtful. In Moab I found one place where such a collection of standing-stones exists. It is called El Mareighât, "the smeared things," and stands on the plateau north of the great valley of Callirrhoe. There is a rude circle of *menhirs* at the site, with a trilithon or dolmen on one side. It surrounds a knoll on which

is a group of *menhirs*, the tallest being six feet high. To the east is a large *menhir*, which has been hewn to a rounded head and grooved horizontally, and between this and the circle is an alignment consisting of several rows of shorter *menhirs*, running north and south. The hills close by are covered with fine specimens of dolmens, many of which I measured.

It is impossible to regard this monument as sepulchral. The stones stand, like many in India and elsewhere, on the bare rock. The circle resembles many found in other lands; and the wild tribes of Western India still sacrifice a cock at such circles, smearing the stones with its blood; while the Khonds adore the sun in similar circles, the tallest *menhir* being on the east. In Mecca, the Kaabah was once surrounded by seven such stones, which also were smeared with blood. I believe the Mareighât circle to be an ancient temple, and the dolmen which faces the central group on the west to be probably an altar facing the sun rising behind the stones, while the alignments appear to consist of memorial stones erected by visitors to the shrine—just as the Moslem pilgrim still erects his stone *mesh-hed* or "memorial" in the neighbourhood of any shrine.

What has been said of erected stones or *menhirs* equally applies to what are called dolmens in France, or cromlechs in England, namely, stone tables raised on other stones. Such monuments also may have been erected for many purposes—as huts, as tombs, and as altars. Any hasty generalisation will certainly fail to account for every case. Unfortunately, the great authority of the late Mr. Fergusson, and his wide acquaintance with such subjects, have led recent writers to neglect many important facts not mentioned in his works, and to speak of dolmens as ancient tombs with a degree of dogmatism which shows that their own researches have not been very widely extended. After examining seven hundred examples of these monuments in Moab and Gilead, I have come to the conclusion that the sepulchral theory is often quite untenable, though we cannot deny that such rude blocks were often piled up to form huge cists or chambers hidden beneath mounds, and intended to hold either the corpse or the ashes of the dead. Sepulchral chambers—dolmens, if you will—under mounds are widely found; but a trilithon on bare rock, not so covered, is clearly unfitted for a tomb, especially when it is not large enough to cover even the body of a child. Moreover, the stone table is sometimes supported by flat stones on the rock; and observers who have found bones under dolmens have not always proved that they are original interments. Nothing is more indestructable than an earthen mound, and in many cases in Moab it was certain that no mound had ever covered the stones. There was nothing but hard rock to be found, and no cairn had ever existed to fulfil the purpose of a mound.

Again, I say, we must turn to local superstitions in order fully to understand the use of trilithons and dolmens. Wild as are the legends, they preserve what was once the religion of the dolmen-building tribes. In the Talmud we find mention of such a monument as connected with idolatrous worship in the second century A.D., the trilithon being in this case placed in front of a *menhir*. In 1872 I found such a monument on Gilboa, and another example has since been found in Bashan, while a similar combination is also known in one instance in Sweden. At the temple of Demeter in Arcadia, Pausanias mentions a trilithon called the Petroma, by which the Greeks swore, and under which they kept a certain sacred book, which was yearly read by a priest. At Larnaca, in Cyprus, a dolmen is said to exist in a chapel, and in Spain one is found in the crypt of a Church of St. Miguel in the Asturias, and another in a hermitage. The modern Arabs beyond Jordan use miniature dolmens, generally on the west side of the circles round the graves of their chiefs, as little tables on which to place offerings to the spirits of the dead.

Dolmens are also connected with the old ceremony of "passing through", which is observed in India as well as in our own islands. St. Willibald, in the eighth century, speaks of Christians squeezing between two pillars in the church on Olivet; and as late as 1881 the Moslems in Jerusalem squeezed between two pillars in the Aksa Mosque. Near Madras, the Hindus used to crawl through the hole in a sacred rock. In Ripon Cathedral, "threading the needle" was a similar rite. Children were also passed through ash and oak trees, and through hoops, or dragged through holes in the ground and under door-sills. At Craig Mady, in Stirlingshire, the newly wedded used to crawl through a dolmen. In the Jordan Valley, near the Jabbok, and again in Bashan, dolmens exist having a hole in the end-stone, and many are surrounded by a circle of stones in both districts, as also were some Celtic dolmens. On the dolmens in Ireland, called "beds of Diarmed and Grain," youths and girls used to deposit gifts of corn and of flowers. The Cyprus girls, according to Cesnola, in like manner visit the *menhirs* pierced with holes, and place in them offerings of jewellery, lighting candles before them,— which illustrates a previous remark as to these holes in the stones. There is a curious monument in the Jordan Valley, with a stone hollowed into a sort of arch a yard in diameter, through which it would be easy to crawl. From such notes it is clear that dolmens are intimately connected with ancient superstitious practices. The crawling through was always believed either to cure sickness or to ensure good fortune, and the dolmen has often been used as an altar.

After making measured drawings of about a hundred and fifty dolmens in Moab, I was able to obtain some general results. In some cases the top stone is raised only a foot from the ground, and in others the trilithon is so small that it would not serve as anything but a table or seat. Some examples on the hillsides consisted of a table stone resting on the rock at one end, and on a single side stone at the

other. In others the table was supported by horizontal stones. In most cases it was slightly tilted, and in very few were the stones even roughly hewn in shape. Not only could we never find any trace of sepulture, or of a grave beneath, but often the size precluded the idea that the dolmen could have been either a hut or a tomb. In other cases a sort of box was formed which could have held a body, but it was not covered by any mound. The general purpose seemed clearly to be the production of a flat table-like surface.

It may, however, appear strange that if these dolmens occur in such numbers at one site, they should be regarded as altars;[1] but we must not forget the story of Balaam and Balak. Visiting in succession three mountain-tops, whence the enchanter was bid to curse Israel, he addresses Balak in each case in the words, "Build me here seven altars." And on each of these mountains we found groups of dolmen still standing.

A curious circumstance in connection with dolmens is that they usually occur near springs and streams. The groups in Moab were all so placed, just as Kit's Cotty-house stands near the Medway, or Stonehenge above the Avon, or like the dolmen near a sacred spring in Finisterre. *Menhirs* also, as we have seen, are similarly connected with water and with rain.

There is, perhaps, a simple reason for this circumstance. Stonehenge was near a British village, and the rude tribes which built the dolmens no doubt, like all early migrants, settled round the natural waters of the country. But it is also not impossible that water was required in connection with rites at the dolmen altars.

Another very interesting observation was the occurrence of cup-hollows—artificial pittings, in some cases connected by well-marked artificial ducts or channels—in the table stones of the dolmens. These cup-hollows were, in some cases, quite as well formed as any that I have seen in England. I found one very unmistakable example on the Holy Rock on Mount Gerizim, where, it is said, by the Samaritans, to mark the site of the laver in the court of the Tabernacle.

I am not aware that any accepted theory has been formed about these hollows; but they are often found on high tops and on or near dolmens. We must not forget that wild tribes of Asia and of Europe have always attached great virtue to the healing power of dew, especially the dews of spring-time. Perhaps dew may have been collected in these hollows and used for superstitious rites.

---

[1] The following are the principal groups which I drew and measured:—

El Maslubiyeh, south of Nebo	..	..	150	examples
El Mareighat, farther south	..	..	150	,,
El Kurmiyeh, west of Heshbon	..	..	50	,,
Tell Mataba' and neighbourhood	..	..	300	,,
Ammân, in Mount Gilead	..	..	20	,,

In some cases rows of these monuments exist almost touching each other on the hillsides.

Two other classes of rude stone structures in Moab have still to be mentioned. The first of these is the class of great circles with walls made by heaps of stones piled up like cairns. These I have never found elsewhere, though they recall the earthen mounds which form circles in England, sometimes surrounding menhirs or dolmens, and sometimes I believe used as meeting-places or courts of justice. A splendid specimen occurs on a spur at Hadânieh above a great spring on the slopes near Mount Nebo. Inside this circle, as a precaution against thieves, I set up my whole camp and stabled my horses. Hadânieh means "sepulture," and a small circle outside the great structure here surrounds the grave of an Arab chief. The great circle is 250 feet across, the walls are thirty to forty feet thick and some five feet high, and a smaller wall inside divides the area unequally. There is an enormous cairn on the hill above about three-quarters of a mile away on the east.

Another circle of equal size was found by Lieutenant Mantell on the south slope of Mount Nebo, and east of Ammân two more about sixty feet in diameter. Yet another occurs at Kom Yajuz, measuring 200 feet across, and we visited two others of nearly the same size. To one of these the name El Mahder applies, which is radically the same word as Hazor, "the enclosure." There is nothing to show the age or object of these works, which must have entailed considerable labour, as they are so much larger than the circles of stones which the Arabs now build up round the graves of their chiefs.

The last class of monuments consists of great disc stones, which resemble mill-stones, but are much too large to be used for such a purpose. One of these, in the Jordan Valley, lies flat, like a mighty cheese, by a thorn tree, and measures eleven feet across. It is called "the dish of Abu Zeid," an Arab legendary hero, who is said to have heaped it with rice and with a whole camel as a feast to his allies. It weighs probably some twenty tons. Another example stands on end in a ruined village, and is 9½ feet in diameter. A third, on a prominant hill, surrounded by dolmens, also stands up like a wheel, and is six feet across, without any hole in the centre.

The origin of these monuments is also very uncertain, but we must not forget that one of the towns of Moab mentioned on the Moabite Stone and in the Bible was called Beth Diblathaim, which means "the house of the two discs" (or "cakes"). Mill-stones are common enough in Syrian ruins, as are the pillars of olive-presses, but no explorer who is familiar with these is likely to confound them with the great menhirs and disc stones which have been here described.

Such were the monuments which we discovered and described east of Jordan, and I have only to add a few words on the important questions of their age and distribution.

As regards age, these monuments—dolmens and menhirs—were erected apparently by a people who

had little mechanical power. Very rarely are the stones shaped, however roughly, and the dolmens are hardly ever on the hill-tops, but on slopes where they might be easily formed by dragging the stones down-hill, and sliding the cap-stones on to their supports. Probably the people that erected them was unable to sculpture or to write. In other countries such monuments are of high antiquity, and there is no reason why they should not be very ancient in Syria.

As regards distribution, these monuments are absent in Judea and Samaria. There is one example on Gilboa, and five or six in Upper Galilee, one of which is called "the stone of blood". I have seen near Jeba, north of Jerusalem, what might be a fallen dolmen, and have found what might be cup-hollows, but more probably these were mortars scooped in the rock in which gleanings of the fields were crushed. East of Jordan there are such hollows, used for making gunpowder, not connected with dolmens. The surveyors, who found so many dolmens in Moab, found none at all south of Galilee. In Moab, Gilead, and Bashan they are more numerous than anywhere else in Western Asia, as at present known.

In a previous chapter I have noticed that pottery statuettes, found in abundance in Phoenicia, are almost unknown in Palestine proper, and have suggested the reason. The same reason holds good, perhaps, as regards the rude stone monuments. They may very probably have once existed, and may have been purposely destroyed. Israel was commanded to "smash" the menhirs of the Canaanites, to "upset" their altars, and to destroy their images. These commands Josiah, the zealous king of Judah, is recorded to have carried into practice. May not this, I would ask, be the true reason for their disappearance? The Greeks and the Romans would not have so acted, and dolmens still stand close to the Roman city of 'Ammân. The Arabs, who left them east of Jordan, and who regard them as "ghouls' houses," would not have destroyed them west of the river. Josiah and Hezekiah did not penetrate beyond Jordan. At Dan many of these monuments seem to have been purposely overthrown. It seems to me therefore probable that the absence of such monuments, like the absence of sculptures and of pottery images, is best explained by supposing their destruction in the time of the reforming kings of Judah. It seems to me also that the existing monuments, though not impossibly erected by Nabatheans or other pagan Arabs, are very probably the surviving work of Canaanite tribes, as are very certainly the hieroglyphic inscriptions of Northern Syria. The age so claimed for these remains is not equal to that of some of the monuments of Egypt and of Chaldea, which represent a more advanced civilisation, and the presence of dolmens on the slopes of Nebo cannot but recall the altars which Balak, king of Moab, is said to have erected on that mountain.

EXTRACT FROM *ACROSS THE JORDAN*, by GOTTLIEB SCHUMACHER, (Richard Bentley & Son), 1886

Schumacher, Gottlieb, German archaeologist. Conducted important archaeological surveys in Holy Land. In 1885, surveyed a portion of the Jaulan. 1886, further survey across the Jordan and researches in Southern Palestine and about Acre; published *Across the Jordan*. 1887, Researches in and about Caesarea and 'Acca. 1888, discoveries in Galilee and at Caesarea; published *The Jaulan* and *Names and Places in the Old and New Testament, and their Modern Identifications*. 1890, Notes from Galilee,

Northern 'Ajlun ("Within the Decapolis"). In a strip of land 26 miles long by 5 broad, "Herr Schumacher, found as many as 63 places and names, as against seven in the best maps of the country, and (which is perhaps his most important piece of work) Herr Schumacher has been able to restore the City of Tiberias to its ancient greatness." (Compiled from *Thirty Years' Work In the Holy Land*, 1865-1895, a record and a Summary of the Palestine Exploration Fund.)

When the great number of dolmens found in this field, and their lying in such close proximity each to the other in considered in connection with the general characteristics noted above, it is difficult to avoid the conclusion that these dolmens were built originally as burial-places. The covered chamber elevated above the ground, and shut in by slabs, was the first beginning of a sarcophagus; and the body was laid, facing the rising sun, with its head in the west,— as is proved by the orientation of the main axis, the double heading, and the greater width of the western end. Since the greater number of the dolmens measured from 12 to 13 feet in length (those of from 7 to 8 feet being comparatively rare), it is possible that they were intended to contain two bodies each, in a line, unless it is deemed preferable to resort to the hypothesis 'that there were giants in those days.'

Mr. Guy le Strange, who visited this dolmen-field some months after my discovery of it, chanced to find one or two dolmens now for the most part in ruins, but in which he observed a small opening about 2 feet in diameter (being sufficiently large to crawl through), and of a roundish shape, pierced in the eastern end slab. Circular openings of this kind have been found in dolmens in other parts of the world; but I do not know that any have been noticed

before in the Syrian specimens, and on the occasion of my first visit to this field I failed to observe them.

Standing on one dolmen, I counted round me over 160 of these monuments; and I compute that from two to three times that number would scarce suffice for the sum-total of all the dolmens found in this district.

A great many of these dolmens have already been opened by the natives, with a view of searching them for treasure, but hitherto without result, as they informed me; to the Arabs they are known by the name of *Kubûr Beni Israîl*—'the graves of the children of Israel.' (PP. 66-68).

During a second visit to the region lying between 'Ain Hamâtah and 'Ain Dakkar, I made the discovery that the dolmen-field of the 'Kubûr Beni Israîl' spreads over a far greater extent of ground than I had at first supposed. A more thorough examination of the volcanic mounds round Jamleh and Khurbet Hamâtah shows that the summit of the greater number of the Tells is crowned by a fallen dolmen, the stones of which have been re-arranged by the Bedawin to serve as sheepfolds. Some, however, remain intact and are in their original condition of perfect dolmens. (PP. 68, 69).

EXTRACT FROM *RACES OF EUROPE*, by PROFESSOR C. S. COON OF HARVARD UNIVERSITY (Macmillan, N.Y., 1939)

The Long Barrow population formed a distinct, homogeneous type; one different from any which, in our knowledge, had previously inhabited the British Isles since the days of Galley Hill; and one which cannot be duplicated, except as an element in a mixed population, anywhere on the western European continent. One is, therefore, led to conclude that the Megalithic cult was not merely a complex of burial rites which diffused without visible carriers; and also that the bearers of this complex avoided mixture by coming by sea. (Pp. 110-111).

A true and valid similarity, however, may be found between the English Long Barrow series

and the early skulls from al'Ubaid in Sumeria, which, whether belonging to the fourth or the third millenium B.C., are in either case older than their British counterparts. The only difference which prevents identity is that the Mesopotamian faces and noses are somewhat longer. (p. 112).

It can be shown that Sumerians who lived over five thousand years ago in Mesopotamia are almost identical in skull and face form with living Englishmen, and that predynastic Egyptian skulls can be matched both in a seventeenth century London plague pit, and in Neolithic cist graves in Switzerland. (P. 83).

EXTRACT FROM Dr. J. L. MYERS, WYKEHAM PROFESSOR OF ANCIENT HISTORY, OXFORD, writing in the *CAMBRIDGE ANCIENT HISTORY*, vol. I. (1928), p. 98

But the individuals buried in these tombs vary in type, so that it is not possible to speak of a 'megalith-people', but only of a megalithic culture and a social structure imposed by its originators on the natives among whom they came. In the British Isles, these are more or less pure descendants of Aurignacian and other old long-headed stocks. In Scandinavia and the whole north-western area of the Continent, they are the tall massive long-headed folk who had apparantly been developing there since the dispersal of the Cro-Magnon and Solutrean hunters; they seem to be an early offshoot of the 'Tumulus people' of southern Russia, and are the ancestors of the present 'Nordic' blondes.

EXTRACT FROM PROFESSOR T. E. PEET, DEPARTMENT OF EGYPTOLOGY, LIVERPOOL UNIVERSITY, AND Dr. THOMAS ASHBY, D.Litt., F.S.A., writing in the *CAMBRIDGE ANCIENT HISTORY*, vol. II (1931), p. 599

We are thus left with the theory of an actual migration or migrations to account for our phenomena, and it cannot be denied that this hypothesis, daring though it may seem, and perhaps incapable of proof on our present data, avoids many of the difficulties inherent in the two other explanations which have been put forward. If we accept this theory, the source of such a migration becomes a matter of interesting speculation. Some writers prefer an eastern, others a northern origin, while others again would suggest north Africa. There are certain considerations, in favour of this last view, while the entire lack, hitherto, of any megalithic monuments that can be with any certainty assigned to an early date is no proof to the contrary. If, indeed, the megalithic area were coterminous with that of the Mediterranean Race, or a portion of it, the problem would be simplified. Italian and Mediterranean neo thic civilization might then have been brought over from north Africa by a first migration; while megalithic archtecture might have come with a second migration at the end of the neolithic age.

The distribution of these monuments is not inconsistent with a migration theory. Those of western Europe all lie along a possible sea route, occuring as they do in Malta, Lampedusa (those of south-eastern Italy must be an offshoot), Sardinia, Corsica, the Balearic Islands, Spain, Portugal, France, the British Isles, Belgium, Denmark, south-west Sweden, and the German shores of the Baltic; whereas the centre of Europe is almost entirely free from them (a solitary example has been recorded in Savoy). An eastern group is found in Bulgaria, the Crimea, the Caucasus, Syria, Palestine, Persia, India and Japan; and for these it might be necessary to postulate a separate origin.

EXTRACT FROM *OUR WORK IN PALESTINE*, published by the PALESTINE EXPLORATION FUND, 1873, p. 282 ff.

As the Sinai Survey Expedition had left one little piece of the Peninsula unexplored . . . On the way they found numerous *nawâmis* . . . The word itself is the plural form of *namus*, a mosquito house, the tradition being that the Children of Israel built them as a protection against a plague of mosquitoes with which they were visited. They are found in many places of the Peninsula of Sinai, and are of two kinds: first, circular houses about ten feet in diameter, built of unhewn stone, and covered with a carefully constructed dome-shaped roof, the top of which is closed by a large slab of stone, and the haunches, or sides, are weighted to prevent them from springing out; the entrance being by a low door, two feet high. There can be no doubt about their having been human dwellings; indeed, in one, charred wood and linen were found on what had once been the hearth. They exactly resemble the *bothan* (shielings) of the Shetland Islands, and the chambers discovered in the large caverns at Clava, near Inverness. Some few had a spiral path running round the outside, and were almost identical in their construction with the *talayot*, or so-called ancient watch-towers found in the Balearic Islands.

The second, and perhaps more ancient, kind consists of large stone circles, some a hundred feet in diameter, having in the centre a cist covered with a heap of large boulders. In the cists were found human skeletons. Beside the sepulchral rings, or cairns, traces were found of the deserted buildings of the silent occupants of these tombs. They are a collection of circles, enclosed within rudely heaped walls—the stones employed being of precisely the same size and character as those used in the construction of the sepulchral rings. 'Who can say', asks the Professor, 'that it was not on this very blackened earth before me that longing Israel was tempted to sin, and ate the offerings of the dead?' Most of their camps were found at the foot of Jebel el Ejmeh. The walls were not more than three feet high, composed of large boulders carefully packed together. Within was a series of very large circles communicating with one another. The Morocco Arabs . . . construct *exactly such camping grounds as the ruins now standing under Jebel el Ejmah*. There can be little doubt that these are the Hazeroth, or field enclosures, used by the pastoral people mentioned in the Bible.

Serial No. 76.e
Published by *The National Message*, Ltd.,
6 Buckingham Gate, London, S.W.1.

Authority: P. A. O. NEYMO, *Similitudes; or The Israelites, The Scotch and The Irish.*

Stone Monuments: Similarity of Israelitish and Irish Customs

AMONG the survivals of the ancient past, the customs and traditions attached to existing cairns and other stone monuments of Ireland find remarkable parallels in the Bible record. The similarities are such that they cannot be attributed to mere coincidence, and are indicative of some intimate relationship between the peoples of the two lands in some remote period.

ADDITIONAL MATERIAL

Our authority, whose book published a century ago is all but forgotten today, has rendered an invaluable service in calling our attention to many similarities between the lives of the Israelites and the Irish. Further selections from his work are to be found in *Serial No.* 110 [D.D.C. 914.41].

EXTRACTS FROM *SIMILITUDES; or, THE ISRAELITES, THE SCOTCH AND THE IRISH* (Second Edition), by P. A. O. NEYMO; printed at the Office of the *Galway Express*, Galway. A first edition only of this work is listed in the British Museum catalogue: 10390,aaaa.14 (1850?).

The day appointed for conducting the bride to the house of her husband, and generally called the "hauling home", arrived in due course, and accompanied by a friend I set out early. On the way, we turned into a shady, green lane, to see the grave of a "Saint Lawrence". I had heard that all who passed that way brought in their hands a small white stone, and threw it in the grave as an evidence of acquittal from some crime of which the saint had been accused. Having reached the end of the lane, climbed over a style near a well, known as "St. Lawrence's", and passed through a rich green field to another covered with broad low rocks, I perceived something white, which, on approaching, I found to be a large square hollow, almost filled with little white stones about the size of a hen's egg. I could never account for its not being quite filled up, having for hundreds of years received daily accessions. Even while I was standing beside it two women came, each throwing in a white stone and then kneeling down. One was comfortably dressed, and wore a scarlet "Galway cloak", the other was covered from her head to her feet in a patch-work quilt, reminding me of the commandment given, through Moses, by the Lord to the Israelites—"And if the man be poor, thou shalt not sleep with his pledge. In any case, thou sha!t deliver him the pledge again when the sun goeth down, that he may sleep in his own raiment and bless thee.''

It strikes me as being a singular coincidence that in olden times amongst eastern nations a white stone was presented to an individual acquitted of a crime of which he might have been accused, as a ''witness of his absolution from the charge''.

Similar to the grave of St. Lawrence is another which I have seen about four miles from the village of Clifden. It is close by the shore of Lake Lannan on a rising ground under the shade of trees. In general the waves make sweet music in that sheltered spot, but there are seasons when the waves, rolling in with a mighty sound, sweep over the grave of St. Lannan, and in their return carry out to the depths many of the little white stones and the secret of the falsely-accused saint.

In ancient times there was another use made of white stones, but I do not know that it was ever adopted by the Irish. A stone was cut lengthwise into two equal parts, and being each engraven with the name of an individual, they were exchanged between two who had contracted for each other a friendship through the courtesies of hospitality. On subsequent occasions they, or their descendants, by whom the symbol was recognized, gave or received hospitality on comparing the two tallies. They were called ''tesseræ'', and we find in the custom a beautiful illustration of the passage, ''To him that over-cometh will I give a white stone, and in the stone a new name written, which no man knoweth, saving he that receiveth it.''

Quite different in appearance and signification from the hollows or graves, partially filled with white stones, are the cairns, or ''memorial heaps'', so common in countries inhabited by Jews or Celts, where they were raised in witness of memorable events, for perpetuating solemn compacts, and as memorials of the dead.

When peace was restored between Laban and Jacob, and they met face to face in the valley—Mount Gilead being covered with the rich tents of the wives and the household of Jacob, and with his ring-streaked and speckled and grisled cattle, and with all his goods which he had gotten in Padan-aram, and to which Laban would lay claim—they agreed to make a covenant and leave a memento of it to all generations. ''Let us make'', said Laban, ''a covenant, I and thou; and let it be for a witness between me and thee. And Jacob took a stone and set it up for a pillar; and Jacob said unto his brethren, 'gather stones', and they took stones and made an heap''. ''And Laban said, this heap is a witness between me and thee this day. Therefore was the name of it called Galeed.'' Here was a cairn in ''memory of a compact''; and about three hundred years afterwards, some miles eastward of the same place, there was raised a cairn as a ''memento of a

solemn event'', when Joshua said to the children of Israel, ''Pass over before the ark of the Lord your God into the midst of Jordan, and take up every man of you a stone upon his shoulder, according to the number of the tribes of the children of Israel: that this may be a sign among you. And the children of Israel did so as Joshua commanded, and took up twelve stones out of the midst of Jordan, as the Lord spake unto Joshua, according to the number of the tribes of the children of Israel, and carried them over with them unto the place where they lodged, and laid them down there.''

As ''memorials of the dead''—not only the loved and lamented, but those who have died the felon's death—cairns were also raised by the Israelites, who took ''Achan the son of Zerah, and the silver, and the garment, and the wedge of gold, and his sons and his daughters, and his oxen, and his asses, and his sheep, and his tent, and all that he had: and they brought them into the valley of Achor.'' ''And all Israel stoned him with stones, and burned them with fire, and after they had stoned them with stones, they raised over him a great heap of stones, unto this day.'' And we know that though Absalom's sudden and violent death was not according to any previous sentence of judgment pronounced against him, but merely the result of the circumstances of a fierce battle yet they took him ''and cast him into a great wood, and laid a very great heap of stones upon him'', in remembrance of his unnatural rebellion.

Of the cairns in Ireland, ''commemorative of events'' there is one in the County of Down, about three miles from Hilltown, concerning which the tradition is, that several hundred years ago the inhabitants of that place coveted the flocks and herds, and the riches generally, which they knew the people of the County of Louth possessed in abundance. Accordingly they met at the place now known as Clonduff, and having entered into a solemn covenant to hold faithfully together and neither forsake nor betray each other, but through good or ill stand or fall side by side, they set out, each man on his going away casting a stone on the place where those had stood whom they had selected from amongst themselves to be their chiefs. In this way a cairn of immense size was formed, near to which on their return from Louth they raised another, which affords an example of a cairn, heaped in ''memory of the dead''.

Under several chiefs, and one who was supreme, chosen by lot, according to the usual course adopted under such circumstances by the ancient Irish, they marched to Warrenpoint, and there embarking in small wicker boats covered with the skins of animals, they fearlessly rowed across to the other shore, where the inhabitants, dwelling in peace and security, were unprepared to meet them, and fled, leaving their homes to be plundered. After a few days they rallied, armed themselves, and returned just in time to catch the spoilers entering their little vessels laden with booty. A fierce conflict followed;

the Downshire men were beaten, and their captain slain. As soon as they saw him fall they flung away the last remnants of their spoil, and lifting up the body of their leader took it to their boats. It is said that the number who returned were but very few, and these laid the remains of their chief in a deep grave, which they opened near the "cairn of covenant", having first burned the body, except the heart, which they placed in an urn, now in the possession of the Marquis of Downshire. They covered the grave with earth, and then each man cast a stone on it, but more than two-thirds of the men having fallen in Louth the heap is small compared to that gathered before their departure.

The Irish also raised cairns whenever anyone died a violent death, or wherever a felon had been buried unless his grave was within the precincts of a prison. In ancient times they even perpetuated the memory of disastrous events by cairns: for instance, every town or village in Ireland called Tallaght, or Tallagh, was once the scene of a pestilence, and the houses may, some of them, be formed of the stones of the cairn: "Tallagh" being only an abbreviation of "Tamleacht", or "the plague monument".

Cairns by the road-side are nowhere so common as in Ireland, and it is unusual to see a peasant pass one by without adding to the heap by throwing a little stone on it. If the person whose memory it is intended to perpetuate has been murdered, prayers are always offered up for the soul's repose; but should the body of a felon rest beneath, unless he died for rebellion, which is regarded as a misfortune rather than a crime, only a short ejaculation, "May God rest his soul", follows the sharp click of the little stone which falls amongst the heavy load already on his bosom.

I have heard of heaps of stones in other lands which it has puzzled antiquarians to account for satisfactorily; and Chardin describes a number of them which he saw on the side of a road in Persia, formed of large circles of hewn stone, the inhabitants of the place affirming that they have been there since Caous, who are described as a race of giants, made war in Media, and held a council in that place—it being their custom that every officer should bring with him a great stone to serve him instead of a chair. "What I wonder at most," says the traveller, "after observations of these stones, is this, that they are so big that eight men can hardly move one, and yet there is no place from whence they can be imagined to have been fetched, but from the next mountains, which are six leagues off."

This is very wonderful, and wise men are unprepared with any reasonable solution of the difficulty. Taking it, therefore, simply as it is told by the natives, and regarding it as the work of giants, who could carry on their necks rocks of a ton weight, like our own Faunma-cool, who, the old legend tells us, amused himself occasionally throwing boulders weighing twenty hundred-weight into the air, and

catching them on his hand as they fell; yet what claim has this wild eastern road to create interest, or please our imagination, or awaken our heart's sympathies like the strange picturesque road in our own beautiful "Land of the West", with its long line of curious cairns, and their touching history—not of giant's strength and power; not of man in his might; but of man in the helplessness of death; of man in his living weakness as we meet with him in everyday life? (pp. 136-146).

Through this wild pass the feet of many generations have worn a rough and rugged road, as one after another some member of the human family has been borne through to the last resting place in the old church-yard. Painful and dangerous as this road is, there is no choice but to take it for any funeral train leaving any of the widely-scattered houses in the district; and as they slowly and cautiously wend their way, the lifeless body, in its simple unadorned coffin swaying to and fro as friend after friend and neighbour after neighbour relieve each other, bearing it on their shoulders, they pause occasionally to take breath, and to gather fresh strength for the fulfilment of their melancholy duty. At such times the coffin is lowered and laid on the rocks, the women gather round, and the echoing mountains send their heart-rendering keen far out over the sea. On moving on every one throws a little stone into the chamber between the boulders where the body had been laid, offering up a prayer for the soul of the departed. In this way have been formed the cairns in the Pass of Salruck, and at one or either of them, all funeral processions now make their momentary stand.

I am reminded by this subject of the superstitions with regard to "foot-prints" and "handmarks" in stones and rocks, so universal amongst the Israelites, the Scotch and the Irish.

Of all the countries on the earth, it is said Palestine has the richest store of such relics. In the mosque of Saint Omar at Jerusalem, is a stone bearing the print of the Angel Gabriel's fingers and the prophet Mahomet's foot; and in the church which crowns the Mount of Olives, is preserved a fragment of rock imprinted with the mark of our Saviour's foot while in the act of ascension. Sir John Mandeville describes many others—such as a rock on Mount Sinai impressed with the figure of Moses; a rock in the valley of Jehoshaphat retaining the footsteps of the ass on which Christ rode into Jerusalem, a rock at Gethsemane marked with the print of His hand; and a rock near Nazareth imprinted with His footsteps. Travellers in the seventeenth century were shown in Jerusalem "the house of Annas, where our Saviour being hurried with violence down a steep place, to prevent falling He laid hold of the corner of a wall, where there is a place in one of the stones fit for a man's hand, which the monks think a great miracle; and Simon the Pharisee's house, where there is a stone with the print of a foot which they say our Saviour made when He stood to pardon Mary

Magdalen her sins; and St. Stephen's gate, and, a little out of the city, the place where Stephen was stoned: and the monks fancy that there is the print of his hands, face, and knees when he fell down''. Ibn Batuta, an Arabian traveller of the fourteenth century, says, that ''outside of Damascus on the way of the pilgrimage is the Mosque of the Foot, which is held in great estimation, and in which is preserved a stone having upon it the print of the foot of Moses.''

This superstition is to be met with in Scotland in every district from Maidenkirk to John-o'-Groat's. According to old Andrew Symson, ''Kirkmaiden in Galloway is so called, because the kirk is fourticated to the Virgin Mary, the print of whose knee is fabulously reported to be seen on a stone, where she prayed somewhere about a place in this parish called Mary Port, near to which place there was a chapel long since, but now wholly ruined''. In our Lady's Kirk in South Ronaldsha, in Orkney, Brand saw ''a stone lying about four feet long and two feet broad, but narrow and round at the two ends; upon the surface of which stone is the print of two feet, concerning which the superstitious people have a tradition that Saint Magnus when he could not get a boat on a time to carry him over Pightland Firth,

took this stone, and setting his feet thereupon, passed the firth safely, and left this stone in this church, which hath continued here ever since''. Martin adds, ''that others have this more reasonable opinion, that it has been used in former time for delinquents, who were obliged to stand barefoot upon it by way of punishment''.

Top of Noth, in Strathbogie, Dr. Hibbert speaks of ''a lofty upright stone on the westerly flank of the hill, connected with which is a monstrous traditional story, of its having been placed there by a giant, the print of whose heel in it is still visible''. In Stratherne, the marks of Saint Fillan's knees are shown in a rock on which he used to kneel in his frequent devotions. In Glenalmond tourists are taken to see ''a stone on which are the marks of the people's feet, and the hoofs of horses, cows, and sheep''. And a ballad of Galloway assures us, that

''Tho' the Brownie o' Blednoch be gane,
The mark o' his feet's left on mony a stane.''

The popular legend of the building of Stonehenge shows that a similar superstitious belief maintains in England. (pp. 149-153).

Serial No. 111*b*.
Published by *The National Message*, Ltd.,
6, Buckingham Gate, London, S.W.1.
Copyright.

Authorities: Various

Mariners of Israel

Christians in general are more or less familiar with the military exploits of the ancient people of Israel, but very few realise that some of these same Israelites also played an important part in the extensive maritime enterprises of those far-off days. It is, none the less, true to say that Israelite merchant mariners, particularly of the tribes of Dan and Asher, had a substantial share of the sea-faring trade between the western world and Palestine during what has been termed the Phoenician Golden Age.

Once again, a proper appraisal of the ancient history of Bible lands has been clouded and confused by loose terminology. In this instance the offending word is *Phoenician*—a name applied by the Greeks and Romans from Homer's time onwards, to the dwellers in the coastal strip of Palestine, irrespective of race; and more particularly used to describe the sea-traders who operated from Palestinian seaports in the early part of the first millennium B.C., carrying a wide range of merchandise between the ports of the eastern Mediterranean and the most distant shores of the then known world: even as far as Britain.

It can be shown most definitely that the people whom the Greeks called 'Phoenicians'—but who did not themselves use that term—comprised elements of several peoples, the chief of these being Canaanites (using the name in its Biblical sense), Hebrews, and Israelites. It is significant that the trade of Phoenicia reached the peak of its importance during the period of Israel's greatest ascendancy, and that its decline commenced with the disappearance of the great bulk of Israel from the Holy Land.

PHOENICIA AND THE PHOENICIANS

The territory of Phoenicia had varying limits according to the period reviewed. Procopius stated that, at one time, the southern limit extended to the boundary of Egypt (*History of the Wars*, Bk. IV, cap. x). Generally, however, it is considered as being the narrow coastal strip (not many miles in depth) extending from the region of Latakia in the north to Carmel in the south.

The term 'Phoenician' was applied by the ancient Greeks to the merchant mariners who traded from the seaports of this coastal strip of Palestine. *Phoenike* was 'the land of the red men' or 'the land of the purple' (Mommsen). The dwellers in Phoenicia did not, however, describe themselves thus. They were Canaanites, Hebrews, or Israelites, according to their various origins. The two first-named had been long in the land when the Israelites arrived. Sidon, grandson of Ham, is reputed to have founded the city bearing his name in 2750 B.C.; Tyre also claimed its foundation from the same period. In this connection Herodotus wrote that the first colonisers of Phoenicia were located originally on the Persian Gulf (the Red Sea, according to Rawlinson: I. 1; II. 44; VII. 89). Trogus considered that they had moved in from the Dead Sea area (Justin xviii: 3: 3). The Ras Shamra and Tel-el-Amarna tablets reveal that Hebrew invaders established themselves in Phoenicia before the time of the entry of the Israelites into their Promised Land.

Modern authorities have evinced various views on the racial characteristics of the Phoenicians. Rawlinson, like many others, calls them *Semitic*, but admits that this is really not a racial but a linguistic classification. Ripley (*Races of Europe*, pp. 387-389) and Waddell (whose painstaking researches may not lightly be brushed aside) both claim them as Nordics, of a totally different racial type from the modern Jews. Though the Hebrew and Israelite sections conform to this Nordic classification (Serial No. 56 [572.933]), it would be going too far to say that *all* the Phoenicians were Nordics, especially when one considers the physical make-up of such well-known examples as the Carthaginian Hannibal and also the Moorish type which has survived in the Iberian Peninsula until the present day.

CANAANITES AND ISRAELITES SIDE BY SIDE IN PHOENICIA

In the division of Canaan by lot, under Joshua, the whole of the country as far north as Sidon was apportioned among the tribes. The coastal towns of Sidon, Tyre, Akka and Dor are particularly mentioned as being awarded to the tribes of Asher and Manasseh. It is definite, however, that some localities were never occupied at all by the tribes, and others only partially so. The Bible record makes it clear that the Israelites came to some sort of unauthorised 'live-and-let-live' arrangement with the existing inhabitants, possibly because the task of complete conquest seemed too formidable. The narrative positively states that the cities of the Phoenician seaboard and the immediate hinterland were not cleared of their inhabitants and that, in these areas, the Israelites "dwelt among the Canaanites, the inhabitants of the land" (Judges i).

It will be remembered that the tribe of Dan forcibly colonised a portion of the Sidonian hinterland when they found their own territory too small. This territory—only about twenty miles from Tyre—they also named Dan, though it was not actually part of their tribal allotment (Judges xviii). It is of interest to note that Hiram, the renowned overseer in the work of building and embellishing Solomon's Temple, a resident of Tyre, was of Danite descent on his mother's side, though his father was of the tribe of Naphtali, whose territory also lay very close to that of Tyre (I Kings vii: 13; II Chron. ii: 14).

ISRAEL'S SEAMEN

There can be no reasonable doubt that a goodly proportion of the seafaring merchants of ancient times popularly referred to as 'Phoenicians' were Israelites of the tribes of Asher, Dan and Manasseh, whose territory marched and mingled with that of Tyre and Sidon. As mentioned by Dr. Latham, a well-known ethnologist of the last century: "The seaports between Tyre and Ascalon . . . must have followed the history of seaports in general, and not stood on the coast for nothing." Solomon's 'Tarshish ships' operated from these bases along with those of Hiram, carrying merchandise to every part of the then known world (I Kings x).

The concern of Dan and Asher for their shipping earned a rebuke from Deborah when these two tribes failed to do their part in the war against Sisera (Judges v). Ezekiel, recounting the former glories of Tyre, mentions the Danites as having a part in the trade of that world mart, in conjunction with Javan (the Aegean area).

The Danaans of ancient Greece, who settled in Argos after their arrival from Egypt, furnish a glimpse of the seafaring propensities of this pioneering tribe. It is more than possible that the classical *Voyages of Argo* were stories based upon actual adventures of Danite sea-rovers (Serial No. 45 [386.0936] and Serial No. 41 [572.938]).

ACCORD BETWEEN ISRAEL AND PHOENICIA

Generally speaking, there was a remarkable degree of co-operation between the Israelites and the people of Tyre and Sidon. At the period of David and Solomon this was particularly noticeable. The first Temple owed much to 'Phoenician' assistance in men and material. The merchant fleets of the two peoples worked together. The royal houses intermarried:

This accord arose doubtless from two causes:

(a) Hebrews—close kinsmen of the Israelites—had settled in Syria from a period long preceding the entry into Canaan of the latter.

(b) The live-and-let-live policy, already mentioned, had resulted in a considerable mingling of the several peoples in the territory under the dominion of Tyre and Sidon. There would be large numbers of their citizens who had blood ties with the peoples of the neighbouring Israelite tribes.

'PHOENICIAN' COLONIES IN THE WEST

Colonies, settlements and trading posts were established by the 'Phoenician' traders throughout the Mediterranean and beyond the Pillars of Hercules, to the limits of navigation as then known. In many of these places Hebrew, Israelite, or Canaanite pioneers had already blazed the trail. As early as the time of the Exodus Danaus had led a section of the Danites to the Aegean area (Serial No. 41 [572.938]). At the same time Cadmus, a so-called 'Phoenician' stated to have been a citizen of Egyptian Thebes—who was probably of Hebrew extraction—had taken a band of followers from Tyre also to Greece. Agenor and

Phoenix also led colonies from Phoenicia to Greece. Hordes of Canaanites expelled by Joshua fled to the North African coastal areas, reaching as far west as Tangier.

The more important of these western colonies were:

Tarshish

According to Strabo (I. 48) this important Hebrew-Israelite colony was established soon after the Trojan War. It was located in what is now South-West Spain, in the country at the mouth of the river Guadalquiver. There was a considerable Israelite colony in Tarshish probably at the time of Solomon, and certainly as early as the destruction of his Temple. Phoenicia and Tarshish engaged in a substantial reciprocal trade (Serial No. 39a [222.5] and Serial No. 30 [572.94601]).

Carthage

This Canaanite colony, founded in 1213 B.C. according to Philistus (Euseb. *Can.* No. 803), was truly a second Tyre. Procopius records that Gergasites, Jebusites and other Canaanite tribes, fleeing from Joshua, established themselves in Libya. With later arrivals from Tyre, they made Carthage a centre of great importance. Procopius calls these Canaanites 'Moors'. After a long period under Roman domination they resisted Vandal incursions and ultimately dominated North Africa and Spain (Serial No. 9 [572.961]). As remarked by Mommsen, the parent cities in Phoenicia declined in importance as Carthage rose. The noble families and trading firms moved west, to pastures new. The word *Punic*, a derivative of *Phoenician*, was a Roman term. Even in Christian times the Libyan farmer called himself a Canaanite (Mommsen).

Gades

(or Gadeira—modern Cadiz) is reputed to have been founded *c.* 1100 B.C. It quickly became an important half-way house in the east-west trade route.

Ictis

(probably St. Michael's Mount, Cornwall), loading port for Cornish tin. Strabo records that in his day (*c.* 50 B.C.) tin mining had been developed on sound engineering lines. The Cassiterides, or Tin Islands, of ancient record are generally held to be the Scillies (Serial No. 49 [571.3] and Serial No. 39 [222.5]).

It is of interest to note that the town adjacent to ancient Ictis is still known as Marazion.

GENERAL CONCLUSIONS

One cannot escape the strong conviction that the tremendous maritime enterprise of the so-called 'Golden Age' of Phoenicia sprang directly from the commercial possibilities brought about by the westward movement of colonists from the older lands of the Middle East. Hebrews, Canaanites and Israelites seemed to vie with each other in their pioneering endeavours. Sometimes they appeared to settle down side by side in the new settlements. Their early trails often appear to be inextricably confused—a source of great difficulty for the modern investigator who tries to unravel the tangle.

Of supreme interest to the Bible lover, however, is the fact that some portion at least of God's ancient Israel played a dominant role in the early maritime accomplishments which paved the way for the subsequent development of Western Civilisation.

Serial No. 58b.

EXTRACT FROM *STRABO* (Loeb Classical Library, translation by H. L. Jones, Ph.D., LL.D.; Heinemann, London, 1929)

"STRABO (born *c.* 63 B.C.), Greek geographer and historian . . . by language and education thoroughly Greek. . . . The *Geography* is the most important work on that science which antiquity has left us. . . . Judged by modern standards, his description of the direction of rivers and mountain-chains seems defective, but allowance must be made for difficulties in procuring information. . . . He had before him the results of Eratosthenes, Hipparchus and Posidonius" (*Encyclopaedia Britannica*, 13th edition).

(I.i.4.)

As for the people of the west, Homer makes plain that they were prosperous and that they lived in a temperate climate—doubtless having heard of the wealth of Iberia, and how, in quest of that wealth, Heracles invaded the country, and after him the Phoenicians also, the people who in earliest times became masters of most of the country (it was at a later date that the Romans occupied it).

(III. ii. 13, 14.)

In the first place, the expeditions of Heracles and of the Phoenicians, since they both reached as far as Iberia, suggested to Homer that the people of Iberia were in some way rich, and led a life of ease. Indeed, these people became so utterly subject to the Phoenicians that the greater number of the cities in Turdetania and of the neighbouring places are now inhabited by the Phoenicians. Secondly, the expedition of Odysseus, as it seems to me, since it actually had been made to Iberia, and since Homer had learned about it through inquiry, gave him an historical pretext; and so he also transferred the *Odyssey*, just as he had already transferred the *Iliad*, from the domain of historical fact to that of creative art, and to that of mythical invention so familiar to the poets. For not only do the regions about Italy and Sicily and certain other regions betray signs of such facts, but in Iberia also a city of Odysseia is to be seen, and a temple of Athene, and countless other traces not only of the wanderings of Odysseus, but also of other wanderings which took place thither after the Trojan War . . . the wanderings of Aeneas are a traditional fact, as also those of Antenor, and those of the Henetians; similarly, also those of Diomedes, Menelaus, Odysseus, and several others. So then, the poet, informed through his inquiries of so many expeditions to the outermost parts of Iberia, and learning by hearsay about the wealth and the other good attributes of the country (for the Phoenicians were making these facts known), in fancy placed the abode of the blest there, and also the Elysian Plain. . . .

The Phoenicians, I say, were the informants of Homer; and these people occupied the best of Iberia and Libya before the age of Homer, and continued to be masters of those regions until the Romans broke up their empire.

(I. iii. 2.)

. . . Again, the maritime supremacy of Minos is far-famed, and so are the voyages of the Phoenicians, who, a short time after the Trojan War, explored the regions beyond the Pillars of Heracles and founded cities both there and in the central parts of the Libyan sea-board. As to Aeneas, Antenor, and the Enetians, and, in a word, the survivors of the Trojan War that wandered forth into the whole inhabited world—is it proper not to reckon them among the men of ancient times? For it came about that, on account of the length of the campaign, the Greeks of that time, and the barbarians as well, lost both what they had at home and what they had acquired by the campaign; and so, after the destruction of Troy, not only did the victors turn to piracy because of their poverty, but still more the vanquished who survived the war. And, indeed, it is said that a great many cities were founded by them along the whole sea-coast outside of Greece, and in some places the interior also.

(XVII. iii. 15.)

Carthage was founded by Dido, who brought a host of people from Tyre. The colonisation proved to be so fortunate an enterprise for the Phoenicians, both this at Carthage and that which extended as far as Iberia—I mean the part of Iberia outside the Pillars as well as the rest of it—that even to this day the best part of continental Europe and also the adjacent islands are occupied by Phoenicians; and they also gained possession of all that part of Libya which men can live in without living a nomadic life. From this dominion they not only raised their city to be a rival of Rome, but also waged three great wars against the Romans. Their power might become clearly evident from the last war, in which they were defeated by Scipio Aemillianus and their city was utterly wiped out. For when they began to wage this war they had three hundred cities in Libya and seven hundred thousand people in their city. . . .

(IX. ii. 3.)

Be that as it may, Boeotia in early times was inhabited by Barbarians. . . . Then the Phoenicians occupied it, I mean the Phoenicians with Cadmus, the man who fortified the Cadmeia and left the dominion to his descendants. Those Phoenicians founded Thebes in addition to the Cadmeia, and preserved their dominion, commanding most of the Boeotians until the expedition of the Epigoni. On this occasion they left Thebes for a short time, but came back again. And, in the same way, when they were ejected by the Thracians and the Pelasgians, they established their government in Thessaly along with the Arnaei for a long time, so that they were all called Boeotians. . . .

(VII. vii. 1.)

. . . if one reasons from the traditions themselves: Pelops brought over peoples from Phrygia to the Peloponnesus that received its name from him; and Danaus from Egypt; whereas the Dryopes, the Caucones, the Pelasgi, the Leleges, and other such peoples, apportioned among themselves the parts that are inside the isthmus—and also the parts outside, for Attica was once held by the Thracians who came with Eumolpus, Daulis in Phocis by Tereus, Cadmeia by ` the Phoenicians who came with Cadmus. . . .

EXTRACT FROM *HISTORY OF PHOENICIA,* by PROFESSOR GEORGE RAWLINSON, M.A.
(Longmans, Green & Co., London, 1889); pp. 49-58

"RAWLINSON, GEORGE (1812-1902), English scholar and historian . . . the younger brother of Sir Henry Rawlinson . . . was elected to a fellowship at Exeter College in 1840, of which from 1842 to 1846 he was fellow and tutor. He was ordained in 1841; was Bampton lecturer in 1859, and Camden professor of ancient history from 1861 to 1889. . . . His chief publications are his translation of the *History of Herodotus* (in collaboration with Sir Henry Rawlinson and Sir Gardner Wilkinson), 1858-60; *The Five Great Monarchies of the Ancient Eastern World,* 1862-67; *The Sixth Great Oriental Monarchy* (Parthian), 1873; *The Seventh Great Oriental Monarchy* (Sassanian), 1875; *Manual of Ancient History,* 1869; *Historical Illustrations of the Old Testament,* 1871; *The Origin of Nations,* 1877; *History of Ancient Egypt,* 1881; *Egypt and Babylon,* 1885; *History of Phoenicia,* 1889; *Parthia,* 1893." (*Encyclopædia Britannica,* 13th edition.)

The Phoenician people are generally admitted to have belonged to the group of nations known as Semitic. This group, somewhat irrelevantly named, since the descent of several of them from Shem is purely problematic, comprises the Assyrians, the later Babylonians, the Aramaeans or Syrians, the Arabians, the Moabites, the Phoenicians, and the Hebrews. A single and very marked type of language belongs to the entire group, and a character of homogeneity may, with certain distinctions, be observed among all the various members composing it. The unity of the language is threefold: it may be traced in the roots, in the inflections, and in the general features of the syntax. The roots are, as a rule, bilateral or trilateral, composed (that is) of two or three letters, all of which are consonants. The consonants determine the general sense of the words, and are alone expressed in the primitive writing; the vowel sounds do but modify more or less the general sense, and are unexpressed until the languages begin to fall into decay.

It is primarily on account of their language that the Phoenicians are regarded as Semites. When there are not historical grounds for believing that a nation has laid aside its own original form of speech, and adopted an alien dialect, language, if not a certain, is at least a very strong, evidence of ethnic character. Counter-evidence may no doubt rebut the prima facie presumption; but in the case of the Phoenicians no counter-evidence is producible. They belong to exactly that geographic zone in which Semitism has always had its chief seat; they cannot be shown to have been ever so circumstanced as to have had any inducement to change their speech; and their physical character and mental characteristics would, by themselves, be almost sufficient ground for assigning them to the type whereto their language points.

There is a far closer analogy between the Palestinian group of languages—Phoenician, Hebrew, Moabite, and the Assyro-Babylonian, than between either of these and the Aramaic.

From Thasos in the East, where Herodotus saw "a large mountain turned topsy-turvy by the Phoenicians in their search for gold", to the Scilly Islands in the West, where workings attributable to them are still to be seen, all the metalliferous islands and coast tracts bear traces of Phoenician industry in tunnels, adits, and airshafts, while manufactured vessels of various kinds in silver, bronze, and terra-cotta, together with figures and gems of a Phoenician type, attest still more widely their manufacturing and commercial activity.

Without a chart, without a compass, guided only in their daring voyages by their knowledge of the stars, these bold mariners penetrated to the shores of Scythia in one direction; to Britain, if not even to the Baltic, in another; in a third to the Fortunate Islands; while, in a fourth, they traversed the entire length of the Red Sea, and entering upon the Southern Ocean, succeeded in doubling the Cape of Storms two thousand years before Vasco di Gama, and in effecting the circumnavigation of Africa.

It is also curious and interesting that the Phoenicians should have been able to ingratiate themselves with another most exclusive and self-sufficing people, viz. the Jews. Hiram's friendly dealings with David and Solomon are well known; but the *continued* alliance between the Phoenicians and the Israelites has attracted less attention. Solomon took wives from Phoenicia; Ahab married the daughter of Ithobalus, king of Sidon; Phoenicia furnished timber for the second Temple; Isaiah wound up his prophecy against Tyre with a consolation; our Lord found faith in the Syro-Phoenician woman; in the days of Herod Agrippa, Tyre and Sidon still desired peace with Judaea, "because their country was nourished by the king's country".

"MOMMSEN, THEODOR (1817-1903), German historian and archæologist, was born on Nov. 30, 1817 at Garding, in Schleswig. After being educated at Kiel he devoted himself to the study of Roman law and antiquities. . . . He was appointed in 1848 professor of civil law at Leipzig. . . . Becoming professor at Zurich, Mommsen wrote exhaustive monographs on Roman Switzerland, and began to work on his *Roman History*, the three volumes of which appeared between 1854 and 1856. . . . In 1854 the Berlin Academy made him chief editor of a *Corpus* of all extant Roman inscriptions. . . . Mommsen also found time to write two larger works *The History of Roman Coinage* and the *Römisches Staatsrecht*, a profound analysis of Roman constitutional law, and *Römisches Strafrecht*, on Roman criminal jurisdiction. . . . He was one of the founders of the *Preussiche Jahrbücher*, and for many years a member of the Prussian Parliament. . . . Mommsen died at Charlottenburg on Nov. 1, 1903." (*Encyclopædia Britannica*, 14th edition.)

(Pp. 131-132.)

Their native seat was the narrow border of coast bounded by Asia Minor, the highlands of Syria, and Egypt, and called Canaan, that is, the 'plain'. This was the only name which the nation itself made use of; even in Christian times the African farmer called himself a Canaanite. But Canaan received from the Hellenes the name of Phoenike, the 'land of purple', or 'land of the red men', and the Italians also were accustomed to call the Canaanites Punians, as we are accustomed to speak of them as the Phoenicians or Punic race.

The land was well adapted for agriculture; but its excellent harbours and the abundant supply of timber and of metals favoured above all things the growth of commerce; and it was there perhaps where the opulent eastern continent abuts on the wide-spreading Mediterranean so rich in harbours and islands, that commerce first dawned in all its greatness upon man. The Phoenicians directed all the resources of courage, acuteness, and enthusiasm to the full development of commerce and its attendant arts of navigation, manufacturing, and colonization, and thus connected the east and the west. At an incredibly early period we find them in Cyprus and Egypt, in Greece and Sicily, in Africa and Spain, and even on the Atlantic Ocean and the North Sea. The field of their commerce reached from Sierra Leone and Cornwall in the west, eastward to the coast of Malabar. Through their hands passed the gold and pearls of the East, the purple of Tyre, slaves, ivory, lions' and panthers' skins from the interior of Africa, frankincense from Arabia, the linen of Egypt, the pottery and fine wines of Greece, the copper of Cyprus, the silver of Spain, tin from England, and iron from Elba.

(Pp. 142, 143.)

The flourishing of Carthage was accompanied by a parallel decline in the great cities of the Phoenician mother-country, in Sidon and especially in Tyre, the prosperity of which was destroyed partly by internal commotions, partly by the pressure of external calamities, particularly of its sieges by Shalmaneser in the first, Nebuchodrossor in the second, and Alexander in the fifth century of Rome. The noble families and the old firms of Tyre emigrated for the most part to the secure and flourishing daughter-city, and carried thither their intelligence, their capital, and their traditions. At the time when the Phoenicians came into contact with Rome, Carthage was as decidedly the first of Canaanite cities as Rome was the first of the Latin communities.

But the empire of Libya was only half of the power of Carthage; its maritime and colonial dominion had acquired, during the same period, a not less powerful development.

In Spain the chief station of the Phoenicians was the primitive Tyrian settlement at Gades (Cadiz). Besides this they possessed to the west and east of it a chain of factories, and in the interior the region of the silver mines; so that they held nearly the modern Andalusia and Granada, or at least the coasts of these provinces. They made no effort to acquire the interior from the warlike native nations; they were content with the possession of the mines and of the stations for traffic and for shell and other fisheries; and they had difficulty in maintaining their ground even in these against the adjoining tribes. It is probable that these possessions were not properly Carthaginian but Tyrian, and Gades was not reckoned among the cities tributary to Carthage; but practically, like all the western Phoenicians, it was under Carthaginian hegemony, as is shown by the aid sent by Carthage to the Gaditani against the natives, and by the institution of Carthaginian trading settlements to the west of Gades. Ebusus and the Baleares, again, were occupied by the Carthaginians themselves at an early period, partly for the fisheries, partly as advanced posts against the Massiliots, with whom furious conflicts were waged from these stations.

In like manner the Carthaginians already at the end of the second century of Rome established themselves in Sardinia, which was utilized by them precisely in the same way as Libya.

PHOENICIA, in ancient geography, the name given to that part of the seaboard of Syria which extends from the Eleutherus (Nahr el-Kebir) in the north to Mt. Carmel in the south, a distance of rather more than two degrees of latitude. These limits, however, were exceeded at various times; thus, north of the Eleutherus lay Aradus and Marathus, and south of Carmel the border sometimes included Dor and even Joppa. The harbours which played so important a part in antiquity are nearly all silted up, and, with the exception of Beirut, afford no safe anchorage for the large vessels of modern times. Sidon, Tyre and Aradus, though now connected with the mainland, were built originally upon islands; the Phoenicians preferred such sites, because they were convenient for shipping and easily defended against attack.

The chief towns of ancient Phoenicia, as we know of them from the Amarna tablets (15th century B.C.) and from Egyptian, Assyrian and the Old Testament documents, were the following: Acco (now Acre or 'Akkā, Judg. i. 31), Achzib (now ez-Zīb, *ibid.*), Ahlab (in Assyrian Mahalliba, *ibid.*)—three towns on the coast south of Tyre, Kānāh (Josh. xix. 28), Tyre (Phoen. Sōr, now Sūr), Zarephath or Sarepta (I Kings xvii. 9 [now Sarafand]), Sidon (now Saidā), Berytus (Biruta in Egyptian, Birūna in the Amarna tablets, now Beirut), Byblus (in Phoen. and Hebr. Gebal, now Jebeil), Arka, 80 m. north of Sidon (Gen. x. 17, now 'Arkā), Sin (Assyr. Siannu, *ibid*), Simyra (Gen. x. 18, now Ṣumrā), Marathus (now Amrīt) not important till the Macedonian period, Arvad or Aradus (in Phoen. Arwād, now Ruād, Gen. x. 18; Ezek. xxvii. 8, 11), the most northerly of the great Phoenician towns.

EXTRACT FROM *THE WESTMINSTER ATLAS TO THE BIBLE*, edited by G. E. WRIGHT, Associate Professor of Old Testament, McCormick Theological Seminary, and F. V. WILSON, Professor of New Testament Literature and History, McCormick Theological Seminary; with an introduction by W. F. Albright, Professor of Semitic Languages, Johns Hopkins University (S.C.M. Press Ltd., London, 1946, p. 53; The Westminster Press, U.S.A., 1945)

In full harmony with the physical features of the region, Phoenicia was never part of Israel. Even the golden age of Israelite expansion under David and Solomon saw no attempt to conquer or control this region. Nor did the interest of the city-states of Phoenicia lead them to make any serious attempt to master the country to the east, although they usually controlled the coast as far south as Mount Carmel, and at one time took over certain border villages of Galilee (I Kings 9: 11). Phoenicia faced west; her life was centered in sea trade; her expansion was achieved by founding numerous colonies as outposts for her life and commerce. Most noted of these was Carthage.

The chief cities of Phoenicia were Sidon and Tyre. The former was more prominent in the second millennium B.C., but the latter, situated in Old Testament times on an island just off the coast, had outstripped her northern neighbor by the time of the Hebrew monarchy. Tyre was a city of unusual strength. Shalmaneser V, Sennacherib, Esarhaddon, Asshurbanapal, and Nebuchadnezzer failed in attempts to capture it. Alexander the Great had to spend seven months before he succeeded in taking it by building a great causeway from the mainland to the island.

By reason of manifold contacts and wide expansion, Phoenicia became the middleman of the ancient world for the distribution of cultural possessions. She is given credit for having carried the alphabet from Asia to Greek lands. She was also famous for her articles of merchandise and extensive trade, so well described in Ezek., ch. 27. Her purple dyes, made from the murex shells found along her shores, were widely known and eagerly sought. Excavation has shown that the famous Phoenician ivory work was used in the Samaria of Ahab as well as in other countries. . . .

EXTRACTS FROM *THE PHOENICIAN ORIGIN OF BRITONS, SCOTS AND ANGLO-SAXONS*,
by L. A. WADDELL, LL.D., C.B., C.I.E. (Williams and Norgate, Ltd., London, 1925)

"WADDELL, LAURENCE AUSTIN (Lt.-Col.), C.B., C.I.E., F.I.S., F.R.A.I.... b. 1854 ... Glasgow University (M.B., C.M., with highest honours, 1878) ... Professor of Physics and Chemistry, Calcutta Medical College; and Editor 'Indian Medical Gazette', Calcutta (6 years) ... discovered, in 1896, the Lost Birthplace of Buddha, and many famous ancient classic sites, which he excavated; explored Tibet and its Buddhism; later Professor of Tibetan, University College, London; travelled in Burma, China, Japan, North America, Egypt, Mesopotamia, Syria-Phoenicia, and the Himalayas ... Tibet Mission to Lhasa, 1903-04 ... Hon.LL.D., Glasgow, 1895; ... Hon. Correspondent Indian Archæological Survey ... Author of ... articles on Tibet in 'Encyclopædia Britannica'; various publications on archæological, geographical and ethnological explorations. ... Died 1938." (*Who Was Who.*)

FROM THE PREFACE

In the course of my researches . . .to which I have devoted the greater part of my life, and my entire time for the past sixteen years—I ascertained that the Phoenicians were *Aryans* in race. That is to say, they were of the fair and long-headed civilizing "Northern" race, the reality of whose existence was conclusively confirmed and established by Huxley. . . . Thus the daring Phoenician pioneer mariners who, with splendid courage, in their small winged galleys, first explored the wide seas and confines of the Unknown Ancient World, and of whose great contributions to the civilization of Greece and Rome classic writers speak in glowing terms, were, I found by indisputable inscriptional and other evidence, *not Semites as hitherto supposed, but were Aryans in Race, Speech and Script. They were, besides, disclosed to be the lineal blood-ancestors of the Britons and Scots*—properly so-called, that is, as opposed to the aboriginal dark Non-Aryan people of Albion, Caledonia and Hibernia, the dusky small-statured Picts and kindred "Iberian" tribes. . . .

In one of these inscriptions, a bi-lingual Phoenician inscription in Scotland of about 400 B.C., . . . its author, in dedicating a votive monument to the Sun-god Bel, calls himself by all three titles, "Phoenician", "Briton" and "Scot"; and records his personal name and native town in Cilicia, which is a well-known ancient city-port and famous seat of "Sun-worship" in Asia Minor.

This British-Phoenician prince from Cilicia is, moreover, disclosed in his own inscription in Scotland to be the actual historical original of the traditional "Part-olon, king of the Scots", who, according to the Ancient British Chronicles of Geoffrey and Nennius and the legends of the Irish Scots, came with a fleet of colonists from the Mediterranean and arrived in Erin, after having cruised round the Orkneys (not far distant from the site where this Phoenician monument stands) and colonized and civilized Ireland, about four centuries before the Roman occupation of Britain. And he is actually called in this inscription "Part-olon" by a fuller early form of that name.

This uniquely important British-Phoenician inscription, whilst incidentally extending back the existence of the Scots in Scotland for over eight centuries beyond the period hitherto known for them to our modern historians, and disclosing their Phoenician origin, at the same time rehabilitates the genuineness of the traditional indigenous British Chronicles as preserved by Geoffrey of Monmouth and Nennius. These chronicles, although formerly accorded universal credence in Britain and on the Continent up till about a century ago, have been arbitrarily jettisoned aside by modern writers on early British history, obsessed with exaggerated notions of the Roman influence on Britain, as mere fables. But the genuineness of these traditional chronicles, thus conclusively established for the period about 400 B.C., is also now confirmed in a great variety of details for other of these traditional events in the pre-Roman period of Britain.

This ascertained agreement of the traditional British Chronicles with leading ascertained facts of pre-Roman British History wherever it can be tested, presumes a similarly genuine character also for the leading events in the earlier tradition. This begins with the arrival of "King Brutus-the-Trojan" and his "Briton" colonists with their wives and families in a great fleet from the Mediterranean about 1103 B.C., and his occupation, colonization and civilization of Albion, which he then is recorded to have called after himself and his Trojan Briton followers "Brit-ain" or "Land of the Brits", after dispossessing a still earlier colony of kindred Britons in Albion. All the more so is this pre-Roman-British tradition with its complete king-lists and chronicles probably genuine, as the Ancient Britons, properly so-called, are now found to have been accustomed to the use of writing from the earliest period of their first arrival in Albion or Britain. And the cherished old British tradition that Brutus-the-Trojan and his "Britons" hailed from the Mediterranean coast of Asia Minor is in agreement with the fact that King Part-olon "the Briton" actually records his native land as being also on the Mediterranean coast of Asia Minor. And this tradition is now confirmed by the discovery that many of the pre-historic gravings and inscriptions on the rocks and monoliths in Britain are of the Trojan type.

. . . These clues lead us from Britain back to the Phoenician and Hittite homeland of the Aryan

Phoenician Britons in Syria, Phoenicia and Asia Minor of St. George of Cappadocia (and England), and there offer us the solutions to most of the long-outstanding problems in regard to the origin of the Ancient Britons and the source and meaning of our ancestral British folklore, national emblems and patron saints. . . .

Linguistically, we now find that the English, Scottish, Irish, Gaelic, Cymric, Gothic and Anglo-Saxon languages and their script, and the whole family of the so-called "Aryan" languages with their written letters, are derived from the Aryan Phoenician language and script through their parent, the "Hittite" or Sumerian; and that about fifty per cent of the commonest words in use in the "English" Language to-day are discovered to be Sumerian, "Cymrian" or Hittite in origin, with the same word-form, sound and meaning. This fact is freely illustrated in these pages, as critical words occur incidentally as we proceed. And it is found that the English and "Doric" Scottish dialects preserve the original Aryan or "Sumerian" form of words more faithfully than either the Sanskrit or Greek. The Phoenician origin of the ancient sacred "Ogam" script of the pre-Christian monuments in the British Isles is also disclosed.

In Religion, it is now found that the exalted religion of the Aryan Phoenicians, the so-called "Sun-worship", with its lofty ethics and belief in a future life with resurrection from the dead, was widely prevalent in early Britain down to the Christian era. . . .

Geographically, the topography of the "pre-historic" distribution of the early Aryan Phoenician settlements throughout Ancient Britain is recovered by the incidence of their patronymic and ethnic names in the oldest Aryan place, river and ethnic names in relation to the prehistoric Stone Circles and monuments, before the thick upcrop of later and modern town and village names had submerged or obscured the early Aryan names on the map. The transplantation by the Phoenician colonists of old cherished homeland names from Asia Minor and Phoenician colonies on the Mediterranean is also seen. The Phoenician source and meaning of many of the ancient place, river and mountain names in Britain, hitherto unknown, or the subject of more or less fantastic conjecture by imaginative etymologists, is disclosed. And a somewhat clearer view is, perhaps, gained of the line of Phoenician seaports, trading stations and ports of call along the Mediterranean and out beyond the Pillars of Hercules in the prehistoric period. . . .

Amongst the many minor effects of the discovery of the Aryan racial character of the Phoenicians and their merchant princes now disclosed, it would appear that the beautiful painting by Lord Leighton which adorns the walls of the Royal Exchange in London, portraying the opening of the Trade era in Britain, now requires an exchange of complexions between the aborigines of Albion and the Phoenician merchants, as well as some slight nasal readjustment in the latter to the Aryan type.

. . . the new-found historical evidence suggests that the modern Aryan-Britons or British, more fully than the other descendants of the Phoenicians, have inherited the sea-faring aptitudes and adventurous spirit of that foremost race of the Ancient World; and that the maritime supremacy of Britain, under her Phoenician tutelary Britannia, has been mainly kept alive by the lineal blood-descendants of these Aryan Phoenician ancestors of the Britons and the Scots and Anglo-Saxons.

(Reproduced by the kind permission of LUZAC & COMPANY, LTD.)

Serial No. 58e.
Published by *The National Message*, Ltd.,
6 Buckingham Gate, London, S.W.1.
Copyright.

Authority: JOSEPHUS.

Antiquities of the Jews

"Josephus Flavius (c. 37-95?), Jewish historian and military commander, was born in the first year of Caligula (37-38). His father belonged to one of the noblest priestly families, and through his mother he claimed descent from the Asmonaean high priest Jonathan. A precocious student of the law . . . *The Jewish Antiquities* . . . covers in twenty books the history of the Jews from the creation of the world to the outbreak of the war with Rome. It was finished in the thirteenth year of Domitian (93). . . ." (*Encyclopaedia Britannica*, 13th Edition.)

IN describing an incident which took place about 485 B.C. the Jewish historian makes mention of contact between the Jews in Babylon and their fellow Israelites then in Media. He asserts that the vast bulk of ten-tribed Israel, who had by then increased to "an immense multitude, and not to be estimated by numbers", were in his day located in the territory which he describes as "beyond Euphrates" and outside the sphere of Roman domination.

POINTS OF SPECIAL INTEREST

1. According to Young, the term Asia was anciently used to designate the north-western peninsula of the Asiatic continent (i.e. Asia Minor).

2. The statement of Josephus to the effect that ten-tribed Israel were beyond the Euphrates accords with the evidence of the writer of the Book of II Esdras, who relates that the ten tribes had left the "multitude of the heathen" (in Media), and had crossed the head-waters of the Euphrates in a journey of eighteen months' duration, to a country which he named Arsereth.

   Thus they were: (1) Outside the Roman Empire.
   (2) Beyond the upper reaches of the Euphrates.
   (3) An eighteen months' journey (on foot) from their captivity habitat in Media, on the south-west of the Caspian Sea.

   This would place them in Europe, in or beyond the countries on the more northern coasts of the Black Sea—known to the ancients as Scythia. It is worthy of note that there are "Jews" who claim to be descended from Ten-Tribed Israel, in modern Daghestan and the Caucasus regions generally. (*Jewish Encyc.* 1925 ed.). There is also a river Sereth in modern Roumania.

3. Although he emphasises that the vast bulk of the ten tribes remained in Media whilst the remnant of the tribes of Judah and Benjamin returned from Babylon to Jerusalem, Josephus records that there were some who had journeyed to Babylon, with the intention of proceeding to Jerusalem to join the Jews in the Holy City. Anna, the prophetess, of the tribe of Asher (mentioned in Luke ii, 36) was possibly a descendant of one of these fragments of the ten tribes who had thus voluntarily mingled themselves with the Jews.

JOSEPHUS: EXTRACT FROM HIS *ANTIQUITIES OF THE JEWS* (English translation by William Whiston, A.M.; Pub. Griffin & Co.) Book XI, ch. v.

2. When Esdras had received this epistle, he was very joyful, and began to worship God, and confessed that he had been the cause of the king's great favour to him, and that for the same reason he gave all the thanks to God. So he read the epistle at Babylon to those Jews that were there; but he kept the epistle itself, and sent a copy of it to all those of his own nation that were in Media; and when these Jews had understood what piety the king had towards God, and what kindness he had for Esdras, they were all greatly pleased; nay, many of them took their effects with them, and came to Babylon, as very desirous of going down to Jerusalem; but then the entire body of the people of Israel remained in that country; wherefore there are but two tribes in Asia and Europe subject to the Romans, while the ten tribes are beyond Euphrates till now, and are an immense multitude, and not to be estimated by numbers.

EXTRACT FROM THE APOCRYPHA (*II ESDRAS xiii*)

40. Those are the ten tribes, which were carried away prisoners out of their own land in the time of Osea the king, whom Salmanasar the king of Assyria, led away captive, and he carried them over the waters, and so came they into another land.

41. But they took this counsel among themselves, that they would leave the multitude of the heathen, and go forth into a further country, where never mankind dwelt,

42. That they might there keep their statutes, which they never kept in their own land.

43. And they entered into Euphrates by the narrow passages of the river.

44. For the most High then shewed signs for them, and held still the flood, till they were passed over.

45. For through that country there was a great way to go, namely, of a year and a half: and the same region is called Arsareth.

46. Then dwelt they there until the latter time. . . .

Note.—The Dariel Pass, in which the modern Georgian Military Road has been constructed, is a natural pass. This route has been used from ancient times by numerous people passing from Armenia northwards. Bordering this pass is Mount Zion, a clear indication that some Israelites used this route.
Serial No. 18.

Authority: HERODOTUS

History

Herodotus (c. 484-425), "Greek historian, called the 'Father of History,' was born at Halicarnassus in Asia Minor. . . . Of his trustworthiness as a historian varying opinions have been entertained. . . . Cicero calls his style 'copious and polished';

Quintilian, 'sweet, pure and flowing'; Longinus says he was 'the most Homeric of historians'; Dionysius, his countryman, prefers him to Thucydides, and regards him as combining in an extraordinary degree the excellences of sublimity, beauty and the true historical method of composition." (*Encyclopaedia Britannica*, 14th Edition.)

A T the time of Herodotus, the inhabitants of the territory to the north of the Danube (Ister) were known as the Sigynnae. Dressing like Medes, and skilled in chariot warfare, they claimed to be colonists from Media.

POINTS OF SPECIAL INTEREST

1. There is clear evidence of a migration from the region of the Caspian to the Black Sea area and beyond. The period of this race movement must have been shortly before Herodotus' own time—about, or not long before, 500 B.C.

2. In a footnote to this text from Herodotus, Rawlinson states:"'The Sigynnae of Europe are unknown to later historians and geographers. Apollonius Rhodius introduces them into his poem as dwellers upon the *Euxine* (vi. 320), and his scholiast calls them. ἔθνος Σκυθικόν. Curiously enough, Strabo, whose Sigynni (or Siginni) are in Asia near the Caspian, tells the same story, as Herodotus, of their ponies (xi. p. 757). . . . Perhaps the Sigynnae retained a better recollection than other European tribes of their migrations westward, and Arian origin." J. L. Myres identifies them with the Sequani who dwelt near the Rhine, and were known to the Romans in the first century B.C. (*Encyc. Brit.* xiv. ed. arts. "Sigynnae," "Sequani.")

3. In the light of Herodotus' evidence and Rawlinson's statement, it would appear that these people were an "advance guard" of a much larger movement of tribes. They seem to have been pioneers in the Trans-Danubian country which the historian describes as a "wilderness."

4. The skill in chariot warfare brings to mind the masterly use of this weapon by the Celtic peoples, of whom Boadicea and her Britons were heroic examples.

HERODOTUS: EXTRACT FROM HIS *HISTORY*, BOOK V, CHAPTER 9. English translation by Canon George Rawlinson, M.A.; (Pub.: John Murray, London), 1859.

As regards the region lying north of this country no one can say with any certainty what men inhabit it. It appears that you no sooner cross the Ister than you enter on an interminable wilderness. The only people of whom I can hear as dwelling beyond the Ister are the race named Sigynnae, who wear, they say, a dress like the Medes, and have horses which are covered entirely with a coat of shaggy hair, five fingers in length. They are a small breed, flat-nosed, and not strong enough to bear men on their backs; but when yoked to chariots, they are among the swiftest known, which is the reason why the people of that country use chariots. Their borders reach down almost to the Eneti upon the Adriatic Sea, and they call themselves colonists of the Medes; but how they can be colonists of the Medes, I for my part cannot imagine. Still nothing is impossible in the long lapse of ages. Sigynnae is the name which the Ligurians who dwell above Massilia give to traders, while among the Cyprians the word means spears.

Authorities: Various

Scotland and Scythia

THERE is a considerable amount of traditional support for the view that there were movements of peoples from Scythia to the British Isles in the centuries preceding the Roman occupation.

A particularly interesting exhibit in this connection is the Scottish *Declaration of Independence*—a document of A.D. 1320 bearing the seals of the Scottish barons in Parliament, which contained an address to Pope John XXII on the matter of the antiquity and rights of the Scottish nation.

This recites that the nation of the Scots had come to the British Isles from Asiatic Scythia, via the Mediterranean, having sojourned for a long period in the Iberian peninsula.

Of special note is the fact that the section of the Scots to which the Declaration relates is associated in this document with the ancient people of Israel, by reference to the claim that Scottish wanderers left Spain for the Isles of Britain 1,200 years after the Exodus from Egypt.

Of interest also is the claim to an unbroken succession of 113 monarchs of their own royal line.

POINTS OF SPECIAL INTEREST

1. In the past, scholars have tended rather to class this document along with other "monkish fables" alleged to have gained currency during the Roman Catholic supremacy. In the light of more recent research, however, the record has achieved credence in some authoritative quarters as genuine tradition.

2. After all, the signatories of the Declaration lived over 600 years nearer the time of the incidents referred to. In A.D. 1320 there were numerous ancient records in existence, which were subsequently lost.

3. Though this wave of immigration appears to have been classified as 'Celtic' it is significant that their kinsmen, the early Anglo-Saxons (e.g. Hengist and Horsa), also claimed ancestry in Scythia.

4. Many authorities accept that the term "Scot" derives from *Scyth*.

EXTRACT FROM OXFORD *NEW ENGLISH DICTIONARY*, 1888.

Scyth . . . a Scythian. . . .
1480. Caxton *Descr. Scot.* (1520) 1/1 Scottes ben called as it were scythes for they came out of Scicia . . . 1596 Spenser *State Irel.* Wks. (Globe) 632/2 The old English also which there remayneth have gotten up their cryes Scythian-like. . . . And herein lyeth open an other manifest proof that the Irish be Scythes or Scotts. 1871 P. Smith *Anc. Hist. East.* xxiii. §12 (1881) 473. The *Sacae* of Greek writers on Persian affairs are simply Asiatic Scyths.

THE SCOTTISH DECLARATION OF INDEPENDENCE

Latin written on parchment in a document now in the Register House in Edinburgh. This ancient document, described by Register House officials as "probably our most precious possession," is dated A.D. 1320 and bears the seals of the Scottish barons assembled in Parliament under Robert Bruce.

TRANSLATION FROM THE *SCOTS MAGAZINE*, April 1934, pp. 16-18.

To the Most Holy Father in Christ, our Lord the Lord John by Divine Providence of the Holy Roman and Catholic Church Supreme Pontiff. . . . We know, Most Holy Father and Lord, and from the chronicles and books of the ancients gather, that among other illustrious nations, ours, to wit the nation of the Scots, has been distinguished by many honours; which passing from the greater Scythia through the Mediterranean Sea and Pillars of Hercules and sojourning in Spain among the most savage tribes through a long course of time, could nowhere be subjugated by any people however barbarous; and coming thence One thousand two hundred years after the outgoing of the people of Israel, they, by many victories and infinite toil, acquired for themselves the possessions in the West which they now hold after expelling the Britons and completely destroying the Picts, and, although very often assailed by the Norwegians, the Danes and the English, always kept themselves free from all servitude, as the histories of the ancients testify. In their kingdom one hundred and thirteen kings of their own royal stock, no stranger intervening, have reigned, whose nobility and merits, if they were not clear otherwise, yet shine out plainly enough from this that the King of Kings even our Lord Jesus Christ, after His passion and resurrection, called them, though situated at the uttermost parts of the earth, almost the first to His most holy faith, nor would He have them confirmed in this faith by any one less than His first Apostle, although in rank second or third, to wit, Andrew the most meek the brother of St. Peter, whom He would have always preside over them as their Patron. . . .

THE SCOTTISH DECLARATION OF INDEPENDENCE
Facsimile of original document in the Register House at Edinburgh

[Photo by courtesy of George J. Hughes, Bridge of Allan

The Scottish Declaration of Independence, addressed to Pope John XXII, and signed by the Scottish Barons in Parliament in Arbroath Abbey, April 1320. Now in Register House, Edinburgh.

Serial No. 61b.

Authority: The Rev. GEOFFREY KEATING, D.D., *The History of Ireland.*

The Scoto-Milesian Royal House of Ireland

ACCORDING to Irish traditions transmitted to us in writing in the early centuries of the Christian era, the Scoto-Milesian royal house of Ireland, from which our present Queen is descended through her Scottish ancestors, came from Egypt, where it originated in a union of a Milesian prince with a princess called ''Scota'' and described as a ''daughter'' of the then-ruling Pharaoh. The traditions state that the Israelites were also in Egypt at that time and that the events recorded were connected with the building of a certain ''tower''.

Some details of the story are so precise that, distorted as it is in its present form, the epoch concerned can be identified as that of Jeremiah's stay at Tahpanhes, where he had taken the daughters of the king of Judah and placed them under the protection of Pharaoh Hophra whose death is clearly alluded to in the Irish records, and whose ''daughter'' Scota was conceived to be.

Various data indicate in no uncertain manner that this princess was in fact one of the daughters of the king of Judah and that our present royal house which descends from her through the Scottish kings is thus the House of David.

The Origin of the Scot-Milesian Royal House according to Keating

Keating's *History of Ireland from the Earliest Period to the English Invasion* is an attempt to produce, from a confusion of surviving historical materials, a coherent history of Ireland from its earliest ages. His sources of reference, a number of which have been lost since he wrote, provide information that is invaluable even in its strangely distorted and sometimes contradictory setting.

The distortions and contradictions of the ancient legends may be attributed to a number of factors. It is evident that at an early age, as already mentioned (Ser. No. 109 [398.22]), monkish editors both endeavoured to make the records of Ireland fit into their own conceptions of world history, and failed to preserve the proper order of the various family and tribal histories before them; their efforts in this respect are apparent by reason of attached false and conflicting synchronisms with Bible history, chronology, genealogies, etc. Thus according to Scottish compilations, the *Lia Fail*, or Stone of Destiny came to Ireland with the Milesians; but according to the Irish story it came with the Tuatha De Dananns, an earlier people.

Although Keating endeavoured to solve the many complex problems thus involved, he was unable to do so. In particular, his story of the origin of the Scoto-Milesian royal house of Ireland, which he has tried to render both intelligibly and faithfully, is, as it stands, quite absurd; but certain details of it contain kernels of truths which can be identified in known history, and the correct setting of his story can be established thereby. As a result, little room can remain for any serious doubt as to the Davidic origin of the Scottish royal line.

The Prelude to the Scoto-Milesian Invasion

The following is an epitome of Keating's history of Ireland prior to the arrival of the Milesians:

It is said that Ireland, which in various writings and periods has been known by no fewer than fourteen different names mentioned by Keating, was inhabited even before the Flood: "Some of our Shenachies say that three daughters of the wicked Cain were the first that dwelt in Ireland" (p. 105). "Banba" was the name of one of these women, who gave it to the island. Another legend says three fishermen discovered Ireland before the Flood; and yet another, that Kesair, daughter of Bith, son of Noah, who had refused him entry into the Ark, arrived in Ireland forty days before the Flood, bringing a colony with her. Keating found it hard to believe how these tales came down to us and wrote: ". . . and, moreover, I cannot conceive how our antiquaries could have obtained those accounts of persons that arrived in Ireland before the Flood, if it were not from those aerial demons who were their fairy followers in Pagan times, or, unless they had found them engraved upon some rocks, that remained after the Flood had subsided" (p. 109).

Ireland, we are told, was depopulated by the Flood, and humanity was preserved from extinction by the survival of the family of Noah, among whom the world was divided, as we read in an ancient Irish poem which translated thus:

> "In Asia Shem fixed his seat,
> Cham and his children dwelt in Afric,
> The noble Japhet and his sons
> Were they that dwelt in Europe" (p. 105).

Thus was determined the Japhetic origin of the Irish, as also of many of the nations of northern Asia. We are not told how the Irish bards obtained their detailed extra-Biblical information; nevertheless it was written that:

> "Thirty sons of famous deeds
> Sprang from Cham, Mac Noah,
> Seven-and-twenty sprang from Shem
> And fifteen from Japhet" (p. 105).

The History of Ireland after the Flood

The first visitation, which was not a colonisation, of Ireland after the Flood was, according to a poem that began thus: "I found in the Psalter of Cashel . . .", by an expedition commissioned by an eastern ruler; it returned with specimens of the island's vegetation:

> "Adna, son of Bith the wise,
> A warrior sent by Nin Mac Peil,
> First came our Eri to explore
> And pull the grass of Fidh-Inis" (p. 113).

Nin Mac Peil, we are later told, was a name given to Ninus, son of Belus.

The first colonization of Ireland was by Partholanus, A.M. 1978, 300 years after the Flood, in what Keating reckoned to be "the two-and-twentieth year before the birth of Abraham"; although he admits that other authorities would make it a thousand years after the Flood and still in Abraham's time, which is an "impossible" opinion. Partholanus led a colony to Ireland from "Migdonia", or the "Middle of Greece"; but his colony in due course perished from a plague, leaving no descendants.

The second colonization was by the Nemedians, after the island had lain waste for thirty years following the aforementioned plague. These Nemedians were distant kinsmen of the Partholanians, and likewise descended from Japhet. In this period the Fomorians, African "mariners of the race of Cham" or Ham (p. 124) invaded and oppressed the Nemedians, but were eventually overthrown; the Nemedians, fearing the return of the Fomorians, deserted Ireland and went to various parts of Greece.

The third colonization was by the Fer-Bolgs, descendants of the Nemedians who had fled to Thrace. This return was 217 years after the Nemedians had first arrived in Ireland (p. 128). Their five leaders "effected their landing in Ireland in one week, viz. Slangi on Saturday at Inber-Slangi; Gann and Sengann on the Tuesday after, at Irrus-Domnan; (in Mayo) Genann and Rudraide on the next Friday, at Tract-Rudraide" (p. 130).

Kingship really began in Ireland under the Fer-Bolgs, of whom Keating writes: "Thirty-six years was the duration of the Fer-Bolg rule in Ireland. Before them no person possessed the island that could be properly called a king of Ireland" (p. 131).

The fourth colonization was by the Tuatha-De-Dananns, another branch of the Nemedians. Some antiquarians, says Keating, claimed that these came from the north of Europe; others, from Athenian territory after a series of disastrous battles with the "Syrians", and brought with them the Stone of Fate, or *Lia Fail*. It is said the Dananns held Ireland for 197 years (p. 146).

The last, and fifth conquest of Ireland before the time of Christ, was by the Milesians, concerning whom the following extracts have been selected from Keating.

EXTRACTS FROM *THE HISTORY OF IRELAND FROM THE EARLIEST PERIOD TO THE ENGLISH INVASION*, by the Reverend GEOFFREY KEATING, D.D.; John O'Mahony's translation, New York, 1866.

"But the most celebrated Irish historian is certainly Geoffrey Keating (c. 1570-1646), who is at the same time the greatest master of Irish prose. He travelled up and down Ireland examining all the ancient records, and compiled a history of Ireland down to the Norman Conquest. Its value for the scholar lies in the fact that the author had access to many important sources of information now lost, and has preserved accounts of events independent of and differing from those contained in the Four Masters. In addition to the history and a number of poems, Keating is also the author of two theological works in Irish which are models of Irish prose" (*Encyclopaedia Britannica*, 1946).

Fenius Farsa, having become king of Scythia, determined to acquire a perfect knowledge of the various languages that had sprung long before his time from the confusion of tongues at the Tower of Babel, which Nimrod, through pride, had spent forty years in erecting; for, from the time of Adam until the confusion of tongues at the Tower, there had been but one universal language known amongst mankind. This language is called Goir-Tighern (*Gor-teeyern*), as the bard tells us in the following verse:

> "Goir-Tighern, that tongue was called,
> Used by the gifted sons of God,
> And by all great Adam's seed,
> Ere Nimrod reared his fatal Tower."

This language the Latin writers call the "Lingua Humana", i.e. the Human Language. But when Nimrod, with his kindred, were attempting to erect the Tower, their language was confounded, in order to prevent their finishing the structure which their pride had prompted them to begin; and the original language, received from Adam, was taken from all that were concerned in building it. It was, however, retained by Heber, the son of Selah, and by his tribe, and, from him, it has been called Hebrew.

The principal motive that induced Fenius to go dwell on the plain Shenaar with his school, was in order that he might there be constantly in intercourse with those whose native language was the Hebrew, and thus, that both himself and his school might obtain a full and perfect knowledge of that tongue. But, when Fenius had, as we have mentioned, resolved upon becoming a perfect master of those various tongues, he dispatched, at his own expense, seventy-two persons of learning to the several countries of the three parts of the world that were then inhabited. These he commanded to remain abroad seven years, so that each of them might learn the language of the country in which he was to reside, during that time. Upon the return of these men to Scythia at the end of the seven years, Fenius set out with them to the plain of Shenaar, bringing with him a great number of the Scythian youth,

Serial No. 113b.

having left his eldest son, Nenual, to rule in his stead, as the poet relates in the following duan:

> Fenius set out from Scythia
> With his great host—
> A glorious hero, wise and learned,
> Strong, triumphant.
> There was but one tongue in the world
> When they began it—
> There were full twelve tongues and thrice twenty
> When they were scattered.
> A great school of learning formed sage Fenius
> For every science—
> A divine hero, sage and learned
> In all language.

Our Shanachies tell us that sixty years had passed, from the building of the Tower of Babel to the time when Fenius came southward with his school, from Scythia, to the plain of Senaar, as a poet thus recounts:

> "Thrice twenty well-told years had passed,
> ('Tis thus our sages tell the story),
> When Fenius from the north came down,
> Since haughty Nimrod reared his tower."

Fenius then founded a school for the various languages on the plain of Senaar, near a city which the Book of Drom-Snecta calls Athenae, as the bard thus tells us:

> "On Senàr's plain, when the Tower was strown,
> The earliest school was held;
> There sages taught in every tongue—
> To Athens thence has science sped."

Hither all the youth of the neighboring countries came to receive instruction in the various tongues, from him and his professors. The three sages that held the chief direction of this great school were Fenius Farsa, from Scythia; Gaedal, son of Ethòr, of the race of Gomer, from Greece; and Caei, the Eloquent (or the Just), from Judea, or Iar, son of Nemha, as others call him, and as the bard thus relates:

"The names of those three learned sages
To you I quickly can reveal—
Gaedal, the son of the worthy Ethòr,
Fenius, and Iar the son of Nemha."

Another poet records the names of these sages thus:
"Fenius, sage of the flowing tongue,
Gaedal and Caei of truthful words,
Were the three chiefs of this scholar band,
That followed the true paths of the authors."

These three inscribed the alphabets of the three principal languages upon wooden tablets, namely: the Hebrew, the Greek, and the Latin. Thus we are informed by Kennfaela, the learned in the Uraicept, or Grammar, which he wrote in the days of St. Columbkille. The same author says that Nin mac Peil, or Ninus, son of Belus, son of Nimrod, was monarch of the world at that time; and he further informs us, that it was about this time that Niul, son of Fenius Farsa, was born; and that Fenius continued twenty years president of the school, in order that his son might become perfectly skilled in the various languages. As, according to some of our historians, it was in the forty-second year of the reign of Ninus, son of Belus, that this great school was established by Fenius Farsa on the plain of Senaar, I judge that he continued there for ten years of the reign of Ninus, and ten years after that king's death, before he returned to Scythia; for, all historians agree, that he spent twenty years presiding over his school, previous to his return to his kingdom" (pp. 153-156).

When Niul had spent a long time in teaching the public schools in Scythia, the fame of his learning and wisdom had gone forth into all countries, insomuch that Pharaoh Cingris, king of Egypt, induced by the fame of his knowledge, sent to invite him to Egypt, in order to get him to instruct the Egyptian youth in the sciences, and in the various tongues, as the poet tells us in the following *rann*:

"The fame had reached King Forond,
With great glory,
Of Niul Mac Fenius, who knew all
The tongues of mankind."

Niul then came to Egypt with Pharaoh's messenger, and that king bestowed upon him the land called Capaciront, or Campus Cirit, near the Red Sea. He gave him, also, his own daughter, Scota, in marriage, as Gilla-Kaemhan tells us, in the poem that begins with the line "Gaedal Glas, from whom the Gaels are sprung":

"He then went into Egypt,
And reached the potent Forond,
And married Scota, not scant of beauty,
The lovely child of generous Forond."

When Niul had thus married Scota, he established schools at Capaciront, and therein disseminated the sciences, and the various languages, amongst the youth of Egypt. It was there that Scota gave birth to Gaedal, son of Niul.

It may, perhaps, appear strange to some people, that Niul, who was the fifth in descent from Japhet, should have lived in the time of Moses, when a period of seven hundred and ninety-seven years had elapsed from the Deluge to the time that Moses took upon him the leadership of the children of Israel. But my answer to them is, that it is not incredible that Niul might have lived some hundred years; for, in those days, men lived a long time. For instance, Eber, or Heber, son of Salah, the fourth in descent from Shem, son of Noah, lived four hundred and sixty years, and Shem himself, who lived for five hundred years after his son Arphaxad had been born, as we read in the eleventh chapter of Genesis: therefore, it is not incredible that Niul should have lived from the forty-second year of the reign of Ninus, son of Belus, to the time of Moses, as we have mentioned; and it is still less to be wondered at, that Niul should have lived up to that time, if we may believe Marianus Scotus, who says that it was three hundred and thirty-one years after the Deluge, when the language of mankind became confounded at Babylon. Now, as we have already said that Niul was not born for a considerable time after that confounding of the tongues at Babylon, we may give credit to what the authors of the history of the Scotic nation say of the age in which he lived, and believe them as to the fact of his having been really born contemporary with Moses in Egypt.

But, to return to Niul; it was during the time that this sage dwelt at Capaciront, near the Red Sea, and after his wife, Scota, had given birth to Niul, that the children of Israel escaped from Pharaoh, and marched to the Red Sea, when they pitched their tents not far from the residence of Niul. When Niul had been told that the Israelites were in his neighbourhood, he went to meet and have discourse with them, so that he might learn who they were. Aaron met him outside the camp, and told him of the children of Israel's adventures, and of Moses, and of the testifying miracles wrought by God upon Pharaoh and his host, by reason of the bondage of the Israelites. Upon this Niul and Aaron formed a friendship and alliance. Niul asked the Israelite if his people had enough of food and provisions with them, and at the same time told him, that all the corn and wealth he possessed himself were at the service of the fugitive host. The night then came on, and Aaron returned to Moses, and informed him of the offers made to him by Niul. Niul likewise went home to his own people, and told them all that he had heard concerning the Children of Israel (pp. 159-162).

Others do, however, assert that Gaedal's mother was called Scota, because his father Niul was of the Scotic race from Scythia, where, according to them, it was the custom to call women after their husbands. You must now understand, that this woman was not the same Scota who was the wife of Galamh, called Miledh of Spain, and who bore him six sons.

For the mother of Gaedal was the daughter of Pharaoh Cingris—the same that held the Israelites in bondage; but the Pharaoh whose daughter was married to Miledh, was the fifteenth Pharaoh after him, and he was styled Pharaoh Nectonibus.

But Niul now informed Moses, that the anger of Pharaoh Cingris would be directed against himself for the welcome he gave to the Children of Israel. Then Moses said to him, "Come thou with us, and when we shall have reached the land which God has promised us, receive thou a portion thereof; or, if thou wilt, we shall give up the fleet of Pharaoh into thy hands to embark thereon, and remain at sea until it be seen how it shall end between Pharaoh and our host." Niul adopted the latter counsel.

A thousand armed men were then sent to seize the fleet, and it was delivered into his hands. He then embarked thereupon and thence witnessed the deeds of the ensuing day, to wit, the opening of the sea before Moses and the Children of Israel and its closing up after they had passed, upon Pharaoh and his host, by which the latter were all drowned. They amounted to three score thousand foot and fifty thousand horse, as we are informed by Ectgus O'Cuanain, Arkinnech (archdeacon), of Roscrea, in the following verse, taken from the duan that begins thus—"O, man that believest not truth:"

"There, sixty thousand men on foot,
With fifty thousand cavalry,
A storm of the strong Red Sea
Engulphed all right suddenly."

We have mentioned above, that it was in the seven hundred and ninety-seventh year after the Flood that Pharaoh was thus overwhelmed with his host.

Now, when Niul had seen Pharaoh and his forces thus drowned, he continued to dwell in the country himself; for he felt no longer afraid, after the destruction of that king. There his children and progeny grew, until they were fit to bear arms. Niul died some time after this, and Gaedal, son of Niul, and his mother, took possession of his territories.

After this, a son was born to Gaedal, in Egypt, and he was named Esru; and again, in progress of time, a son was born to Esru, and he called him Sru, and they continued to hold the same territory, and to dwell therein.

As to the Egyptians, another Pharaoh, styled Intur, or An Tuir, took possession of the sovereignty upon the drowning of Pharaoh Cingris in the Red Sea. In like manner was every king that reigned over Egypt called, also, Pharaoh, from the time of the above-mentioned Pharaoh Cingris, so drowned, down to Pharaoh Nectonibus, the fifteenth king after Cingris, who was called Pharaoh (pp. 164, 165).

Pharaoh Intur and the Egyptians, in time, remembered their old grudge to the descendants of Niul and the family of Gaedal, namely, their resentment for

Serial No. 113c.

the friendship the latter had formed with the Children of Israel. They, then, made war upon the Gaels, who were thereby compelled to exile themselves from Egypt. With this account Thomas Walsingham agrees, in the book called Hypodeigma, where he states that, "When the Egyptians had been drowned in the Red Sea, those of their countrymen who survived, drove out a certain chieftain of the Scythian nation, who lived among them, that he might not assume sovereignty over them. Banished with his tribe he came to Spain, where he resided many years, and where his posterity grew numerous, and that thence he came at last to Ireland."

Know, reader, that this chieftain was Sru, son of Esru, son of Gaedal, and not Gaedal himself, notwithstanding the false assertion of Hector Boethius; and also, in contradiction to the modern English writers, who suppose that it was Gaedal himself, that led the migration to Spain; for, according to the truth of Irish history, which we should rather trust to in this matter, it is a fact that it was in Egypt that Scota, daughter of Pharaoh Cingris, gave birth to Gaedal; and in that land he resided until his death. Nor, as others assert, was it from Greece that he had come thither, but from Scythia. And although the author we have just quoted, does assert that it was to Spain that the Gaelic prince, mentioned above, had come, yet the fact was not so, for it was to Scythia that he went; and it was the fifteenth generation from him, namely, Bratha, son of Degatha, that first reached Spain. Here follows a quotation from the antiquary, Gilla-Caemhan, in proof that it was Sru, son of Esru, that was leader in this emigration from the land of Egypt:

"Sru, son of Esru, son of Gaedal,
Grandfather of our learned host,
'Twas he from home that wended northward
Over the Red Sea's stormy wave.

"Four vessels then contained his household
Upon the Red Sea's stormy wave;
The number in each wooden dwelling
Was four and twenty wedded pairs"
(pp. 166, 167).

Some historians tell us that there were four hundred and forty years, from the drowning of Pharaoh in the Red Sea, until the arrival of the Children of Miledh in Ireland; so a bard relates in the following lay: . . . (p. 167).

However, according to the computation made in the Book of Invasions, there were but three hundred years, less by seventeen, from the time that Moses took the command of the Children of Israel in Egypt, until the sons of Miledh invaded Ireland; . . . (p. 168).

Hector Boethius asserts, in the third chapter of his History of Scotland, that Eber and Erimhon were the sons of Gaedal. But this cannot be true, for Cormac Mac Culinan tells us, in his Chronicle, that Gaedal was the cotemporary of Moses. . . .

Here follows the pedigree of Galamh, called Miledh of Spain, or Milesius, according to the holy King Cormac Mac Culinan:

GALAMH, son of	TATH, son of
BILI, son of	EOGAMHAN, son of
BREOGAN or BREGAN, son of	BEOGAMHAN, son of
BRATHA, son of	EBER SCOT, son of
DEGATHA, son of	SRU, son of
ARCADH, son of	ESRU, son of
ALLOID, son of	GAEDAL GLAS, son of
NUADATH, son of	NIUL, son of
NENUAL, son of	FENIUS FARSA, son of
FEBRIC GLAS, son of	BAATH, son of
EBER GLUN-FINN, son of	MAGOG, son of
LAMFINN, son of	JAPHET, son of
AGNON, or ADNON, son of	NOAH.
	(p. 183).

Some historians say that it was from Biscay, that the sons of Miledh set sail for Ireland, from a place that is called Mondaca, near the mouth of the River Verindo. The reason why they think so is, because Miledh was king of Biscay after he had been driven by the overwhelming force of foreign invaders, from the heart of Spain into that country, which was secure from foreign attack by its numerous forests and hills and natural strongholds. But this is not the common opinion of our own historians, who tell us, that the Milesian invaders set out on their expedition from the Tower of Breogan in Gallicia. And this latter account I consider to be the true one. For we read in the Book of Conquests, that it was at the Tower of Breogan, they first formed the resolution of sending Ith to explore Ireland, and that it was there that Lugaidh, the son of Ith, landed when he returned from Ireland with his father's dead body, to exhibit it to the sons of Miledh and to the descendants of Breogan. For this reason, I am of opinion that they set sail for Ireland, from that same place, Miledh having died a short time before. Her husband being thus dead, Scota came to Ireland with her children, as Spain was then a bone of contention between the natives and the many foreign tribes, who had come from the north of Europe to conquer that country (pp. 194, 195).

Now, eight of the chieftains of the Milesian host perished at sea, by the Druidic enchantments of the Tuatha-Dè-Dananns, namely, Ir, at Skelg Michil; Arannàn, who fell off the mast, and Donn, who was drowned, with five other chiefs, at the Sandhills. Eight noble ladies, also, had now fallen; two of these had been lost with Donn, namely, Buan, the wife of Bili, and Dil, the daughter of Miledh, who was both the wife and the sister of Donn; Skèni, the wife of Amirghin, was drowned at Inber Skèni, and it is from her that the estuary in Kiarraide (Keeree), which we have just named, has been called; Fial, the wife of Lugaidh, son of Ith, died through shame, because her husband had seen her naked, as she was coming in from swimming, and from her that estuary has been called Inber Fèli ever since; again, Scota and Fàs were slain in the battle of Sliabh Mis; two others died also, to wit, the wives of Ir and of Murthemni, son of Breogan. And these are the eight ladies and the eight chiefs, of the host of the Children of Miledh, that were lost, from their first arrival in Ireland, until they fought the battle of Talti.

Here follow, according to the Book of Conquests, the names of the seven most noble women that came to Ireland with the sons of Miledh; Scota, Tèa, Fial. Fàs, Libra, Odba and Skèni (pp. 202, 203).

Such is the alleged and incredible history of Ireland prior to the arrival of the Milesians. It would, however, be inexcusable to cast it away as of no value, for concealed therein are vital truths which can be clearly discerned. Before showing how the period and events of the Milesian invasion of Ireland, as here recorded, can be related to known history, we shall, in our next *Serial*, see how this same story has come down to us in one of the sources used by Keating, namely, the famous *Leabhar Gabhala*, or *The Book of Conquests*.

Authority: The *Leabhar Gabhála*, or the *Book of the Conquests of Ireland*.

Egypt in the Traditions of the Royal Irish

THE tradition that the Scoto-Milesian royal house of Ireland, from which Queen Elizabeth II is descended, originated in a union between a Milesian chieftain and Scota, "daughter" of a Pharaoh of Egypt, has been preserved in its greatest length by the two contemporary Irish historians of the 17th century: Geoffrey Keating and Michael O'Cleirigh.

A previous study contains extracts from the legends as they have been handed down by Keating; and we now present O'Cleirigh's version of the same story.

Since the sources from which these two writers derived their information have disappeared, their writings are now invaluable, not only to the student of Irish history, but also of Bible prophecy concerning the removal of the *House of David* to, and its re-establishment in, "the mountain of the height of Israel" (*Ezek*. xvii, 23).

THE LEABHAR GABHÁLA'S ERRORS

The defects of the following extracts will be obvious to the reader, especially where supposed Biblical connections have been introduced into the story, as in the cases of the chronology dated from Adam and related to the Flood; of the erroneous identification of the "tower" as that of Babel or Nimrod; of the unfortunate Pharaoh who is wrongly said to have perished in the Red Sea at the time of the Exodus; of Moses and Aaron; etc. Genealogies also appear, which further complicate the true story behind the legend. But through the confusion created by early monkish editors may be discerned episodes in the history of the Milesian community in Egypt in the time of the XXVIth Dynasty. As we shall see in a following *Serial* the story relates to the murder of Hophra, while he rested in his boat in the year 566 B.C., and to the rise of his general and successor, Aahmes (Amosis, Amasis, or Ameniris), whose name was confused with that of Moses.

EXTRACTS FROM THE *LEABHAR GABHÁLA, or the BOOK OF THE CONQUESTS OF IRELAND* the recension of Micheal O'Cleirigh, Macalister and MAC NEILL'S translation, University College, Dublin.

MICHAEL CLERI, or CLEIRIGH, was an Ulster man by birth, and a Franciscan Frier, who being well skilled in the language and Antiquities of his country, was sent from Louvain into Ireland by Hugh Ward (who was then employed in writing and collecting the Lives of the Irish Saints) to enquire after old manuscripts, and other helps to that work. He performed this task with indefatigable pains for about fifteen years . . . he compiled digested and enlarged three Treatises of History, or rather purged them from their Errors by collating together many manuscripts, the same having been before written by antient authors.

. . . The third treats of the first Planters of Ireland, of the successive Conquests of it from the Flood by different Nations, of the Succession of the Kings of Ireland during such time, of their Wars and Battles, and of other publik Transactions and Events of the Island from the year 278 after the Flood to the Year of Christ 1171. This Book is called *Leabhar Gabhaltas*, or, *the Book of Conquests*. These three Treatises are yet remaining in manuscript. . . . He died in 1643 (The *Works* of Sir James Ware concerning Ireland; 1745 ed., vol. II, pp. 117, 118).

122. Since we have told of the occupation of Ceasair first, who took Ireland before the flood, and of the four occupations which took it after the flood, of the seed of Aitheacht, son of Magog, son of Japhet, son of Noe—these are the four occupations: Partholon, Neimhedh, Fir Bolg, Tuatha Dé Danann —it is right for us to tell next of the seed of the son who was eldest of the children of Magog, namely, Baath and his seed, who took Grecian Scythia, the patrimony of the children of Magog; thereafter went to Egypt; again to Scythia; thence to the Gaethlaighe; after that to Spain; thence to Scythia; to Egypt; to Spain again; and thence to Ireland; and how they took it against the Tuatha Dé Danann; and the tale of the kings who took Ireland of them, one after another, with their number of years from Eremon to Mael-Shechlainn Mor, son of Domhnaill.

124. As for Magog, son of Japheth, he lived in Grecian Scythia. Five sons had Magog: Baath, Ibath, Barachan, Emoth, and Aithecht. Of the seed of Aithecht were the conquests we have related, except Cesair's only. Baath the first son of Magog, his son was Fenius Farsaidh. This Fenius was one of the three principal chiefs who were at the building of Nimrod's Tower. Fenius had two sons, Naenbal and Nel. This Naenbal, his father Fenius left in authority over Scythia behind him, when he himself was going to the Tower. As for Nel, the other son of Fenius, he was born at the Tower. He was learned in the various languages that were separated at the Tower, for till then there was none but the primitive language, Hebrew, only. . . .

125. . . . and there Nel was instructed in the learning of all languages till he was learned and famous before the nobles in their territory at large. When the king of Egypt, Pharaoh Cingcres, heard that he was thus, he invited him to him on account of the greatness of his knowledge, skill, and learning. Nel comes at that invitation, and after being a while in Egypt, the Pharaoh, that is the king of Egypt, gave him his daughter Scota to wife, besides a heritage and land. Then Scota bore a son to Nel, Gaedheal Glas his name. There are three names from which the seed of that Gaedheal are surnamed, Fenius, Scota, and Gaedheal. Feni is their name from Fenius; Scots from Scota, daughter of the king

of Egypt, who was Nel's wife, and Gaedhil from that Gaedheal, son of Niul, son of Fenius Farsaidh.

· · · ·

127. Now Nel lived southward in Egypt, in Capachirunt [Pi-Hahiroth, *Exodus* xiv. 2], on the shores of the Red Sea, which is called the *Mare Rubrum*. That was the time when the Children of Israel escaped from the Egyptian bondage wherein they were with Pharaoh; so they reached the land where was Nel, son of Fenius, on the border of the Red Sea. Nel goes to them to ascertain who they were; so Aaron, son of Amram, brother of Moses, met him on the outskirts of the hosts. They talk each with the other. Aaron tells him their own adventures, and the manifest miracles that God wrought through Moses in the land of Egypt, on account of the bondage of the people of Israel; among them were the ten revealed plagues which were brought upon them, whereby multitudes perished. Aaron and Nel made a covenant and friendship between themselves after that. Nel thought it a grief of mind all the intolerable trouble that had been inflicted upon them, and the greatness of the necessity in which they were; and he promised to divide with them all the goods in his power, so long as they should be in his neighbourhood. Then they part.

· · · ·

130. After that Nel said to Moses: "Pharaoh will come to us and oppress us in punishment for our friendship towards you, and the welcome we have given you, and because we have not persecuted and restrained you." "Come with us, with thy whole people," said Moses, "if you will, and remain permanently with us, and when we reach the land that God hath promised us, you will get a share in it; or, if you prefer, we will give you some of Pharaoh's boats, so that they may be at your command to flee before the Egyptians, till you know how we and they shall separate one from the other".

131. They agreed that the ships should be in their possession, as though it were the children of Israel who should steal them from Pharaoh, in order that the Egyptians should not find seaworthy equipments behind them to overtake them. Nel went with all his people on the sea in the aforesaid boats that night, till he should know how the hosts would separate from one another on the morrow; and they were on

Serial No. 114a.

the strait of the sea till the sons of Israel departed dryfoot through the Red Sea, and till Pharaoh, with his troops, were drowned in attempting to hinder them. This is the tale of those who were drowned there; six hundred chariot fighters, fifty thousand horsemen, and two hundred thousand footmen. When Nel saw that fate of Pharaoh with his people he returned again to his own estate, for he put every fear from him once the Egyptians were drowned thus; and he lived there till his death.

132. Gaedheal Glas, son of Nel, took the rule and strong headship of the aforesaid estate, Capachirunt, after his father's death. A son was born afterwards to Gaedheal in Egypt, Easru was he. He was nourish till he could bear arms, and he took the same principality after his father's death. That Easru had a princely son, Sru his name. He excelled the warriors of his time in valour and heroism. Easru died after a season, and his son Sru takes the principality after him.

. . . . .

133. There were five kings over Egypt from the time of Pharaoh Cingcris till then. These are their names:

Pharaoh Cerres	12 years
Pharaoh Armadis	5 ,,
Pharaoh Rameses	60 ,,
Pharaoh Amenoses	40 ,,
Pharaoh Amenomes	28 ,,

After that Pharaoh Tures took the rule of Egypt, and when he obtained strength and power, and when his warriors became numerous, he remembered their hostility and unfriendliness against the seed of Nel, son of Fenius, in the matter of the treaty and covenant that Nel formed with the Children of Israel, before they went through the Red Sea, and how he took the ships of Pharaoh with him, and did not give rapine and pursuit to the Children of Israel like everyone else. There grew up thence frays and contentions between them on both sides, so that the men of Egypt drove Sru and his son, Eber Scot, with the whole of their people, out of Egypt.

134. They advance, accordingly, on the sea to their native fatherland, Scythia. Scota, the daughter of Pharaoh Cingcris, mother of Gaodhal Glas, was with them in her old age. Fifty ships their tale, twenty-four couples in each ship. They sail thereafter to the Red Sea, to the island of Taprobane, around Sliabh Riffe northward, till they reached Scythia. After their landing in that country Scota, the daughter of Pharaoh, died among them.

135. He who was king of Scythia on their arrival at that time was Noenbal, son of Baath, son of Noenbal, son of Fenius Farsaidh. Sru, son of Easru, died after that, and Noenbal died of plague of one night. Then the seed of Noenbal, son of Fenius, and

the seed of Nel fought about the rule of the country, until Eber Scot took the kingdom from the children of Noenbal by means of his might. He was the first king of Scythia of the race of Nel. King Eber Scot fell after that by Noenius, son of Noenbal, son of Baath, son of Noenbal, son of Fenius Farsaidh.

136. Beoamain, son of Eber Scot, had a blood-feud for his father against the same Noenius, so that there arose violent battles and many combats between them; so Beoamain took the kingdom by strength of fighting from Scythia to the shore of the Caspian Sea. Beoamain fell thereafter in the battle of Etarnadh by Noenius, and he himself took the kingdom thereafter, till he fell at the hand of Ogamain, son of Beoamain. Ogamain takes the kingdom afterwards till he died a natural death. Reffill, son of Noenius, takes the kingdom after that, till he fell by Tai, son of Ogamain, for the sake of the kingdom. Tai, son of Ogamain, son of Beoamain, took the kingdom till he fell by Reffloir, son of Reffill. There arose a contest between that Reffloir, and Agnomain, son of Tai, son of Ogamain, for the sake of the kingdom, and they were four years in that contest, till Reffloir fell at last by Agnomain.

137. That Reffloir, son of Reffill, had two good sons, Noenbal and Reffloir. These arose together against Agnomain, son of Tai, for the sake of the kingdom, so that there was no peace between them. Many battles and combats took place between them, one against the other, so that the children of Reffloir, son of Reffill, at last drove their kinsman Agnomain, son of Tai, with all his people, out of Scythia. These are the chieftains he had: Eber, son of Tai, his brother; Elloth, Laimhfhind, and Glas, the three sons of Agnomain; Caicher the druid, and Cing, the two sons of Eber, son of Tai. Thirty ships their tale, threescore in each ship, of which one score were women.

138. Then they voyaged till they reached the island of the Caspian Sea. They stay a year in it. Agnomain died there. After that they go to the sea of Libis; a journey of six summer days were they rowing thither from the island of the Caspian. They find a beautiful pleasant island there, Coronis its name; they stay a year and a quarter there. Glas, son of Agnomain, died in the end of that space. After that they sail on the sea.

139. These were their chieftains: Elloth and Laimhfhind, the two sons of Agnomain; for this reason was he called Laimhfhind, because burning lamps were not brighter than his hands in the night at the rowing; Cing and Caicher, the two sons of Eber, son of Tai. It was Caicher who found a remedy for them against the singing of the mermaids, while they were in the strait of the Caspian Sea. . . .

140. When they were delivered from the music of the mermaids by the advice of Caicher, they sailed at length to the great Northern Ocean, and were for a space of a week drifting on it, suffering hunger and thirst, till they reached the northern point of Sliabh Riffe. They find there a well with the taste and satisfaction of wine, so that they took their fill from it till they were intoxicated and merry. They sleep after that, and they were in that place three days and three nights, till Caicher said to them, prophesying to them, "*I aill Ara*"; that is, "we shall not tarry till we reach the noble island of Ireland". "In what place is 'Ireland'?" said Laimhfhind. "Farther from us than Scythia; and not ourselves will reach it but our children, after three hundred years."

141. After that they sail on the sea till they reached the Gaethlaighe; they stay in that land. A noble son was born to Laimhfhind, son of Agnomain, there, namely, Eber Whiteknee. Another son was born to Elloth, son of Agnomain, Eber the Black his name. In one and the same time were born those boys, at the Gaethlaighe. They were the great-grandson of that Eber Whiteknee, son of Laimhfhind, namely, Noenel, son of Febri Glas, son of Aghnon the White, son of Eber Whiteknee, and the grandson of Eber the Black, son of Elloth, son of Agnomain, namely, Taithechta, son of Tetrech, son of Eber the Black, who were in joint rule in the Gaethlaighe. Three hundred years were the seed of Gaedheal in the Gaethlaighe, from the time when Laimhfhind, son of Agnomain, came into it, till Brath, son of Death, left it.

142. Then that Brath, son of Death, son of Erchaidh, son of Elloth, son of Nuadha, son of Noenel, son of Febri the Green, son of Agnon the White, son of Eber Whiteknee, son of Laimhfhind, son of Agnomain, proceeded from the Gaethlaighe over sea, after the death of his ancestors. Forty ships his tale. They sail to Crete, to Sicily, keeping Europe on the right, till they reached Spain. These were their chieftains then: Brath himself; Occe and Uicce, the two sons of Elloth, son of Noenbal, son of Neimhedh, son of Elloth, son of Oghamain, son of Tothechta, son of Tetrech, son of Eber the Black, son of Elloth, son of Agnomain son of Tai, son of Oghamain; Mantan, son of Caicher, son of Ercadh, son of Caomtecht, son of Soet, son of Mantan, son of Caicher the Druid, son of Eber, son of Tai, son of Oghamain.

143. Three battles were won by them after they reached Spain; a battle against the Toisiona, a battle against the Bachra, and the third battle against the Lombards. A plague fell out among them after that, so that two ships' crews of them died, headed by the chiefs Occe and Uicce, except ten who escaped, headed by the two sons of the aforementioned chieftains, namely, En son of Occe, and Un son of Uicce.

Serial No. 114*b*.

144. A son was born to Brath, son of Death, afterwards in Spain, Breoghan his name. He was nourished till he was able to bear arms. Brath died after a while, and Breoghan takes the princedom after him. There arose strifes and discords, quarrels and disputes between the various races of Spain and the tribe of Gaedheal, so that many battles and skirmishes were fought between them. However, it was Breoghan with his soldiers and people who were victorious in every battle-combat, and theirs was the victory, so that those tribes of Spain were submissive to them at last.

145. Afterwards a city was founded by Breoghan in Spain, Brigantia its name, and a tower was built by him in front of it, which is called Breoghan's Tower. A pleasant delightful dwelling, and a place for watch and outlook was that. Children were born of that Breoghan in Spain afterwards; these are their names: Bregh, Cuala, Cuailnge, Blad, Fuad, Muirthemne, Eble, Nar, Ith, and Bile.

. . . . .

148. After Golamh, son of Bile, completed all learning, as we have related, and when he came to the age of manhood, he reflected that it was no credit or honour to him that he had no knowledge or acquaintance with his native home and his kin-brethren in Grecian Scythia, or acquaintance with or travel in other countries besides. He sought leave of his kin and tribesmen to go on that journey, and they gave him leave to go on a free visit to Scythia . . .

150. He who was king over Scythia then was Reffloir, son of Nem, of the seed of Noenbal, son of Fenius Farsaidh. When they took harbour he enquired of them whence they were. . . . After a while the king considered that it was fitting for him to betroth a beautiful marriageable daughter he had to Golamh, on account of his nobility and his learning, his strength and his valour. . . .

. . . . .

151. Then Golamh assumed strength and great power among the Scythians, till he was all but stronger in the country than King Reffloir. . . . The hostility of Reffloir towards his son-in-law grew and increased at last, so that he could not refrain from challenging him to single combat. . . .

152. Having left Reffloir on his deathbed, so that he died of the gashes of that wounding afterwards, envy and great hatred filled most of the chiefs and nobles of the land in general against Golamh and his people, on account of that deed which he had done; so they rose with one mind against him, and put him out and drove him with his people from Scythia. As for Golamh, he went a-sailing with all his people, and left the king's daughter with him, and took his two sons away. Forty ships with their crews, and with their fitting champions, that was their tale. They sailed round Asia, south-east to the island of Taprobane; they stay three months there. Three months besides had they on the sea till they reached

Egypt. Pharaoh Nectonebus was king óf Egypt when they came, and he was hospitable to Golamh, on account of his renown and his glory, and the friendship of their ancestors to one another once on a time.

· · · · ·

154. Now Golamh lived in Egypt after that, and receives an estate therein, and he took Scota, daughter of Pharaoh, to him to wife. That Pharaoh Nectonebus was the thirty-second Pharaoh who took the kingdom of Egypt after the Pharaoh who was drowned in the Red Sea. Now ''Pharaoh'' was the name of every king of them, one after the other, from the first king whose name was Pharaoh to the last king; as ''Caesar'' is the surname of every king in Rome, and ''Ptolemy'' of every king in Alexandria. That is a sign of honour to the kings. These are the names of the kings who took Egypt between those two Pharaohs, with the time they spent in the kingship:—

Pharaoh Cerres	15	years
Pharaoh Armades	5	,,
Pharaoh Rameses	60	,,
Pharaoh Amenoses	40	,,
Pharaoh Amenomes	28	,,
Pharaoh Tures	7	,,
Pharaoh Daremandis	26	,,
Pharaoh Senres	40	,,
Pharaoh Thustus	9	,,
Pharaoh Oschorus	7	,,
Pharaoh Esinachus	9	,,
Pharaoh Esimes	25	,,
Pharaoh Sessonchus	21	,,
Pharaoh Pissamus	40	,,
Pharaoh Bachor	47	,,
Pharaoh Etheops	12	,,
Pharaoh Silvicus	15	,,
Pharaoh Etheops	20	,,
Pharaoh Etheops Memess	22	,,
Pharaoh Stapantes	7	,,
Pharaoh Encheprus	6	,,
Pharaoh Necha	8	,,
Pharaoh Assanet	9	,,
Pharaoh Nechot	6	,,
Pharaoh Asmutes	12	,,
Pharaoh Huprisis	30	,,
Pharaoh Ameniris	42	,,
Pharaoh Amartes	6	,,
Pharaoh Nefritis	6	,,
Pharaoh Anchoris	12	,,
Pharaoh Mutes	1	,,
Pharaoh Nectonebus	18	,,

—he was the king that Golamh found.

155. Now Golamh stayed eight years in Egypt with his father-in-law. Scota, daughter of Pharaoh, bore him two sons by one birth, Emer the White and Amergin their names. . .

156. When their education was finished thus, this is the resolution that Golamh came to, to leave Egypt and go to his own race to Spain, by the advice of his wife and his people. They bid farewell thereafter to the king and the nobles of Egypt. They went on the sea, as many ships as they had leaving Scythia, and Scota, daughter of Pharaoh, with them. They sail to the Red Sea. There arose a great storm against them, so that they were drifting till they reached the island of Taprobane. They stayed a month in it. After that they went on beyond Albania, westward, to the point of Sliabh Riffe northward, till they reached Thracia. They stay there till Scota brought forth one of her children there; Ir his name. They rowed thence till they reached the Gaethlaighe Meotacda [Maeotis]. A year were they passing those coasts, by reason of all the wandering that fell to their lot. They took rest for a space in the Gaethlaighe. Another son was born to Golamh in that place, Colptha is he. They went at last till they reached Germany; they make a halt in it.

· · · · ·

158. Golamh sails after that with his people over the river Rhine, past Gallia, to Crete, to Sicily, to Valencia (?), to Brigantia, till they reached Southern Spain, Northern Spain, and thence to Three-cornered Spain. Thursday, as far as regards the day. . . .

159. Scota, daughter of Pharaoh, bore two of her children in Spain after that, Eremhon and Erannan, the two youngest of the children of Golamh. . . .

160. . . . A valiant soldier was Golamh in those battles, and by him was every battle won on his enemies in turn, so that for that reason was the name ''Miledh'' given him; so that it stuck to him in everyone's mouth from that out, although Golamh was his first name.

· · · · ·

171. As for the sons of Mil, they sailed in a great expedition on the sea to Ireland, and did not pause in their course till they saw at a distance the island from the sea. And when they saw Ireland, their warriors made a contention of rowing and sailing to their utmost in their eagerness and anxiety to reach it; so that Ir son of Mil advanced a wave before every ship by reason of his strength and his valour. So Eber Donn son of Mil, the eldest of them, was jealous and said:—

"It is no good deed
Ir 'fore Ith to proceed"—

that is, before Lughaid son of Ith, for Lughaid had the name Ith. Then the oar that was in the hand of Ir split, so that Ir fell backwards on the thwart so that his back broke in two there; so that he died in the following night, and they preserved his body so long as they were on the sea, till they buried it afterwards in Sceillic of Iorrais Deiscert of Corco Duibhne. Sorrowful were Eremhon, Eber Finn, and Aimirgin at the death of their brother; and they said, as it were out of one mouth, it was right that Eber Donn should not enjoy the land about which he was envious for his brother, that is of Ir.

172. The sons of Mil Advanced to a landing in

Inbher Stainghe. The Tuatha Dé Danann did not suffer them to come to land there, for they had not held parley with them (?). They made, by their druidry, that it appeared to the sons of Mil that the region was no country or island, territory or land at all, in front of them. They encircled Ireland three times, till at length they took harbour in Inbher Scene; a Thursday, so far as regards the day of the week, on the day before the Calends of May, the seventeenth day of the moon; *Anno Mundi* 3500.

Authorities: Various

The Historical Basis of the Legendary Origin of the
Scoto-Milesian Royal Line

IT has now been conclusively demonstrated that Irish legends concerning the origin of the Scoto-Milesian dynasty that reigned at Tara are related to the history of Egypt during the period of the XXVIth Dynasty, when Milesians are known to have garrisoned Tahpanhes at the very time that the prophet Jeremiah and the "king's daughters" were in sanctuary there.

The legends relate that while the Milesians were in Egypt, one of their chieftains married a princess named Scota, said to be Pharaoh's "daughter"; and that from this union the kings of Tara were descended. This marriage is said to have occurred during the reign of a Pharaoh who was "drowned" in the "Red Sea". It has been shown that this particular ruler was Hophra, Jeremiah's benefactor, who was murdered in his boat in 566 B.C.

These and other relevant data indicate in no uncertain manner that the princess concerned was one of the daughters of the king of Judah; and that from her the ancient kings of Tara, the Scottish kings descended from them, and our present Royal House of Britain, are therefore to be identified with the House of David.

Origin of the Scoto-Milesian Legends

The original sources of the legendary history of Ireland before the time of Christ are quite unknown; at most, only the names of some intermediate writers or works of unknown authorship have been preserved. The time at which one, at least, of the unknown compilers of earlier material wrote is indicated by a comment which has come down in the *Leabhar Gabhala*, where we read: "Now 'Pharaoh' was the name of every king of them, one after the other, from the first king whose name was Pharaoh to the last king; as 'Caesar' is the surname of every king in Rome, and 'Ptolemy' of every king in Alexandria" (sec. 154). This change of tense, from "was" to "is" may be taken to imply that the writer of this text was under the impression that the Ptolemies, who reigned 323-30 B.C., and the Caesars, whose rule commenced with Augustus, 63 B.C. to A.D. 14, were still in power; he therefore may have written about the first century B.C. or soon after, certainly not earlier.

It is evident that monks of the early Christian era considerably altered and added to the materials at their disposal, and in this way did much harm. The detailed extracts contained in *Serials Nos.* 113 and 114 (D.D.C. 572.941) will serve to give the reader some idea of the state of the Irish legends that have come down to us, and to show that it is quite impossible to accept them as they stand, for the following reasons, among others: (1) The Milesians had not appeared, at least as such, at the time of the Exodus as maintained in the legends. (2) The tower of Babel, Shinar, the Exodus, and various individuals mentioned, could not have been contemporary, as stated in the same legends. (3) The alleged genealogical connections with the family of Noah could not possibly be as brief as those given, even if it be allowed that the recorded events happened at the time of the Exodus, when in fact they did not. (4) The longevities ascribed to the individuals concerned in the early stages of the Milesian story are false, for they call for individuals (i.e. Fenius and his son Nel) having lived some hundreds of years each. (5) A number of other details of the legends are out of keeping with the facts of history, as in the mention of Latin as one of the three chief languages of the world at the time concerned.

The True Setting of the Milesian Legends

The legends of the Milesian invasion of Ireland really begin with the period of the XXVIth Dynasty, when Carians and Ionians, of whose regions Miletus was the chief city, settled in Egypt as traders, and were employed as mercenaries. Their chief trading centre was Naucratis, on the western side of the Nile Delta; and they are particularly mentioned as having provided the garrison for the fortress of Tahpanhes from the time of Psammetichus I to Hophra inclusive. *The Cambridge Ancient History* informs us: "The first settlement of the Greek traders from Miletus is said by Strabo to have been made 'in the time of Psammetichus', which should mean about 650 B.C.; but it is probable that the phrase is but a vague one, and can be stretched to cover the preceding half-century or more, and that 'the Fort of the Milesians' may have been built at least as early as 700, if not still earlier (about 750), even before the time of Tefnakhte, whose power must have been due largely to wealth derived from the trade with Greece" (Vol. III, 1929, p. 291).

Herodotus (II, 152) preserves a strange tale of how the Milesians came to find favour in Egypt: they were the "brazen men" who chanced to arrive in Egypt from Caria and Ionia just in time to help Psammetichus gain the throne. *The Cambridge Ancient History* states that: "Psammetichus developed the use of his 'brazen men' by establishing camps of

Serial No. 115a.

them, one at Marea near Kanobos, the other on the opposite eastern border of the Delta, the 'tents' which became the important Ionian settlement of Daphnae (Tahpanhes, the modern Tell Dafnah or Defenneh)'' (*ibid.*, p. 292).

The fortress built by Psammetichus at Tahpanhes has been described by Petrie (*Ser. No.* 63 [224.2]); it lasted until the opening of the reign of Aahmes, about which time it was abandoned to the Babylonian king Nebuchadnezzar who, according to the prophecy of Jeremiah, camped on the site during his Egyptian campaign.

According to the Irish traditions, as we have seen in the two preceding *Serials*, it was during the period of the Milesian settlement in Egypt that a certain Pharaoh Cingris and his hosts perished in the Red Sea. This particular ruler, it can be demonstrated, was none other than Hophra, for Keating states in his *History of Ireland*: ''As to the Egyptians, another Pharaoh, styled Intur, or An Tuir, took possession of the sovereignty upon the drowning of Pharaoh Cingris in the Red Sea. In like manner was every king that reigned over Egypt called, also, Pharaoh, from the time of the above-mentioned Pharaoh Cingris, so drowned, down to Pharaoh Nectonibus, the fifteenth king after Cingris, who was called Pharaoh'' (p. 165). The lists of Egyptian rulers, by Eusebius and Africanus, show that there were, at least according to the former, whether they were right or wrong, fifteen Pharaohs from Aahmes II (Ameniris, Amasis, or Amosis) to Nectonibus inclusive. Hophra then stands equated with Cingris (see *Ser. No.* 116 [572.941]).

The *Leabhar Gabhala* tabulates the names of thirty-two Pharaohs; and this list is evidently derived from sources used by Eusebius and Africanus, as the many similarities show. It will be seen in the comparative tabulation in *Serial* No. 116 that the Irish list is itself in error by omitting Psammuthis and the eight Persian rulers mentioned by Eusebius and Africanus; but nevertheless the statement that fifteen Pharaohs followed the unfortunate ruler who perished at sea to, and including, Nectonibus is correct.

Much light is thrown on the reign of Hophra (Apries) by the inscriptions. His own troops, ''returning home from a disastrous expedition to Cyrene, suspected that they had been betrayed in order that Apries, the reigning king, might rule more absolutely by means of his mercenaries, and their friends in Egypt fully sympathized with them. Amasis, sent to meet them and quell the revolt, was proclaimed king by the rebels, and Apries, who had now to rely entirely on his mercenaries, was defeated and taken prisoner in the ensuing conflict at Momemphis'' (*Encyclopædia Britannica*, 1946, art.: ''Amasis II'').

Hophra (Apries) also had experienced difficulty with some of his mercenaries, who, feeling that they had a grievance, mutinied in their station at Elephantine which was under a commander named Nesuhor, and ''planned to migrate to Upper Nubia, to a region called Shas-heret. Nesuhor succeeded in dissuading them and delivered them to Apries, who accordingly punished them'' (J. H. Breasted, *Ancient Records of Egypt*, 1906, Vol. VI, pp. 506, 507). Nesuhor's own inscription concerning this event reads: ''For ye rescued me from an evil plight, from the mercenaries [Libyans], Greeks, Asiatics, and foreigners, who had it in their hearts to . . . , and who had it in their hearts to go to Shas-heret. His majesty feared because of the evil which they did. I re-established their heart in reason by advice, not permitting them to go to Nubia, (but) bringing them to the place where his majesty was; and his majesty executed their [punishment] (*ibid.*, p. 508).

Hophra either escaped or was released from his confinement. In any case, Aahmes in due course, in his third year of co-regency, found that Hophra had gathered Greek mercenaries and had become assertive. An inscription of this period tells of news brought to

Aahmes by a messenger: "Apries, he has sailed [southward . . .] ships of . . . , while Greeks without number are coursing through the Northland . . . They are wasting all Egypt; they have reached Malachite-Field, and those who are of thy party flee because of them" (*ibid.*, p. 511). The inscription goes on to tell of the resultant action: "Said his majesty: 'Ye shall fight tomorrow! Every man to the front!' His majesty mustered his infantry and his cavalry. . . . His majesty mounted upon his chariot; he took arrows and bow in his hand, [he arrived] at . . . , he reached Andropolis, the army jubilating and rejoicing on the road." "His majesty fought like a lion, he made a slaughter among them, whose number was unknown. Numerous ships [took] them, falling into the water, whom they saw sink as do the fish" (*ibid.*, p. 512). The battle ended with Hophra's being strangled while he rested in his boat; Aahmes' inscription reads: "He (Amasis) saw his favourite fallen in his . . . which he had made before the water" (*ibid.*, p. 512) (see also *Ser. No.* 91 (2 24.2)).

The death of Hophra thus took place amidst heavy losses at least among his own supporters. It is interesting to speculate as to whether some of the Greeks, feeling that they had been unjustly punished following their disaffection at Elephantine, worked out their grudge against Hophra when an opportunity to dispose of him presented itself, for having done so they joined Aahmes, were withdrawn from Tahpanhes, which was accordingly abandoned, and stationed at Memphis. It was at this time, 566 B.C., that Nebuchadnezzar, in an inscription of his 37th year, states that he fought Aahmes and his Ionian troops; the fragmentary record reads as follows: "In the 37th year of Nebuchadrezzar king of Babylon (the troops) of Egypt to do battle came . . . (Ama)su, king of Egypt his troops (levied) . . . ku of the city of Putu-yawan . . . a distant land which is in the midst of the sea . . . many . . . which were in Egypt . . . arms, horses, and . . . he levied for his assistance . . . before him . . . to do battle" (*Cambridge Ancient History*, Vol. III, p. 304).

The Irish Version of the Battle

The Irish legends, as we have seen in the two previous *Serials* (Nos. 113 and 114 [572.941]), record heavy losses in connection with the death of the Pharaoh who perished "in the Red Sea", or more correctly, at the hands of his own troops after his defeat on the Nile in "the vicinity of Sais" (J. H. Breasted, *Ancient Records of Egypt*, 1906, Vol. IV, p. 509).

It is possible that another incident has also influenced the Irish legends. Herodotus (II, 158) records that Necho II engaged in canal-building or -repairing activities in which 120,000 perished. Some knowledge of this disaster, which occurred in the vicinity of the modern Wady Tumilat, and between the Nile and the Red Sea, may have been confused by the early scribes with the final struggle between Hophra and Aahmes, for, as we have seen, our two Irish versions state in the one case, that 256,000, and in the other, that 110,000, perished in the "Red Sea". This confusion was evidently still further increased by the mistaking of the name of Aahmes, or Amosis, for that of Moses; hence in the Irish story all the events of the period concerned are said to have been at the time of the Exodus of Israel, when large numbers of Egyptians perished in the Red Sea, but nearly a millennium too early for our story. The recorded dialogue between "Moses" and Nel may well contain a vital clue to the existence of a conspiracy between Aahmes or Amosis and the Milesians against Hophra. A factor favourable to this supposition is the fact that it is known that after the death of Hophra the Milesians were transferred to Aahmes' forces.

The death of Hophra and the abandonment of Tahpanhes, followed by Nebuchadnezzar's occupation of that fortress in the same year, naturally marks the extreme limit of the stay of Jeremiah and the "king's daughters" there. It is in the period of Hophra that the mysterious "daughter" of Pharaoh is said to have married the Greek prince Neleus, from whom the kings of Tara descended. The presence of the Greek garrison and the daughters of the king of Judah in Tahpanhes at the same time, supplies us with elements of an equation in a manner that is practically self-suggestive.

The Irish King-List

The appearance of Cingris' name in the Irish legends as predecessor of the fifteen Pharaohs from Nectonibus is an error not difficult to explain. He is the first Acencheres of Josephus' *Contra Apion* (i, 15), and the Achencheres or possibly the Achoris, Athoris, or Cenchres of Eusebius. In any case he was a predecessor of Cherres or Acherres, the second Acencheres of Josephus, whose 8th year was equated by Eusebius with the Exodus and the 81st of Moses—an error followed well into the Christian era: Gregory of Tours, for instance, in his *History of the Franks*, wrote: "Cenchres, who was overwhelmed in the Red Sea . . ." (O. M. Dalton's trans., 1927).

Another factor that firmly establishes the identity of the Pharaoh of the Irish legends who died at sea, is that it is said in his days a certain "Nin mac Peil, or Ninus, son of Belus, son of Nimrod", "monarch of the world at that time", held rule. Nin mac Peil's 42nd year is mentioned in connection with the founding of a certain "great school" "on the plain of Senaar" by Fenius Farsa the Milesian (Keating, *History of Ireland*, p. 156). "Nin mac Peil", or "Ninus, son of Belus", is a reference to the Babylonian kings in general, who, on ascending the throne, "took the hands of Bel" according to an ancient custom, thereby becoming "sons" of the god. Castor, in writing of his digest of the Canon of the "kings of the Assyrians", which began with the mythical Belus, says: ". . . since we have no certain tradition respecting the length of his reign, we have merely set down his name, and commenced the chronological series from Ninus; and have concluded it with another Ninus, who obtained the empire after Sardanapallus . . ." (Cory, *Ancient Fragments*, 1876, p. 91). It may not be possible to say who was Castor's second Ninus; but the Irish mention of the 42nd year for the period concerned ties us down to Nebuchadnezzar, who reigned 43 years, and who, in a certain oration referred to by Abydenus, spoke of "Belus my ancestor" (*ibid.*, p. 71).

It was in the reign of Nebuchadnezzar that Necho attempted to reopen the canal from the Nile to the Red Sea, losing 120,000 men in the effort (Herodotus (II, 158)), probably as part of an aggressive or defensive campaign against the Babylonian monarch. As already mentioned, Nebuchadnezzar's own inscriptions of his 37th year, 566 B.C., have been found in the Suez area; this was the year of the death of Hophra, and may well mark the abandonment of Tahpanhes under commands issued by Aahmes, the Pharaoh *An Tuir* of the Irish legends.

End of the Greeks in Egypt

In covering the history of the period under consideration, *The Cambridge Ancient History* states: "To depose a Pharaoh was a serious matter, and had Apries submitted to his sentence he might have died in his seclusion at Sais. In 567-566 (Amasis's third year), however, he fled secretly from his palace, summoned the mercenaries to his aid, and a battle ensued at Momemphis, in which he was defeated. According to the official inscription of Amasis recording the event, he was afterwards slain by his own men when he was sleeping in the cabin of his *dahabiyah*. He was then buried with full regal pomp by Amasis, 'that the enmity of the gods might be removed from him'. Like Ikhnaton before him, Apries was the enemy of the gods. But he was absolved at his death.

"Amasis ascended the throne as the enemy of the Greeks, but he was too clever either to retain this character wholly, or to become too friendly to them, at all events at first. He chose a middle way. In order to placate popular sentiment he abolished the freedom which the Greeks had possessed of going where they liked in the country, and confined them to the 'treaty port' of Naucratis, abolishing Daphnae, transferring its civil inhabitants to Naucratis, and making a *synoikismos* there of all the Greeks in Egypt (about 566-565 B.C.) . . . he knew that he might have to depend for his personal safety on the fidelity of a foreign guard, and that the Greeks knew more of the outer world than the Egyptians did. So, after the death of Apries, instead of abolishing the mercenaries at Daphnae, he brought them to Memphis, where they were probably added to those of Apries's guard who survived, and had murdered their master to ensure the favour of the new king (566)" (Vol. III, p. 303).

By the end of Aahmes' reign the Medo-Persian power had appeared as a threat to Egypt, which in due course fell in the reign of his successor Psammetichus III to Cambyses, who was the first foreign conqueror to be fully "legitimized" in the eyes of his new subjects as a Pharaoh, "taking the Egyptian royal name and titulary, wearing in Egypt the Egyptian royal costume, and mounting the Egyptian throne" (*The Cambridge Ancient History*, Vol. III, p. 311). With the conquest by Cambyses the Greek relations with Egypt were severed for many years to come, and in due course the Persians conquered Miletus itself in 494 B.C., slaying and deporting its inhabitants.

The Irish traditions quoted in earlier *Serials* produce claims, supported by alleged genealogies, for the descent of the Scottish kings who ruled at Tara, from Scota and Milesian Neleus. Egyptian history provides no clue as to the identity of Scota; but from the Bible we know that the daughters of the king of Jerusalem, after the fall of that city in 584 B.C., had been removed to Tahpanhes, the very fortress known to have been garrisoned by Milesians at that time. By becoming wards of the Egyptian court, these princesses of the House of David might possibly be termed "daughters" of Pharaoh by adoption. Formal adoption of women of noble standing as priestesses was fairly common at this time. Inscriptions have been deciphered recording the adoption of the following princesses: Shepnupet I, daughter of Osorkon of the XXIIIrd Dynasty, adopted Amenirdis I, daughter of Kashta of the XXVth Dynasty; Amenirdis I adopted the daughter of Piankhi, Shepnupet II, who in turn adopted Nitocris, daughter of Psammetichus I of the XXVIth Dynasty; Nitocris adopted the daughter of Necho, Enekhnesneferibre (Breasted, p. 480). Of the adoption stela of Nitocris, J. H. Breasted writes:

"This document has thrown a flood of light on the dynastic connections in the Ethiopian and Saitic period, and its discovery was especially welcome, in view of the paucity of contemporary monuments from this age. It may be described as a decree of adoption and property-conveyance. It records the adoption of Nitocris, the daughter of Psamtik I, by a Shepnupet, daughter of Taharka, the Divine Votress, or sacerdotal princess, at Thebes. Shepnupet transfers all her property to Nitocris, and the purpose of the adoption was that the family of Psamtik I might legally gain control of this property, as well as the position which it entailed at Thebes" (*Ancient Records of Egypt*, Vol. IV, p. 477).

Serial No. 115c.

"The adoption of Nitocris, and the similar adoption of her predecessor, Shepnupet, as well as the adoption of Amenirdis by the same Shepnupet, render it clear that this was the usual method of succession in the Ethiopian and Saitic periods, and much simplifies the royal family connections of the time. Already, as early as 1885, Erman had noticed that Nitocris was but the adoptive mother of Enekhnesneferibre" (*ibid.*, p. 478).

Such adoptions were a matter of conciliatory policy throughout the period of the XXVIth Dynasty: "The whole land was peaceful under the rule of Amasis. The Ethiopians never troubled him, and Thebes was long ago reconciled to northern rule by the continued policy of adoption of the king's daughters by the priestess-ruler of the city of Amon" (*Camb. Anc. Hist.*, III, 307).

Despite the foregoing, the Irish legends may still appear somewhat incongruous in asserting that a Milesian leader married a "daughter" of Pharaoh. A similar union with foreign nobility is recorded in the Bible: Solomon married a daughter of the then-ruling Pharaoh (1 *Kings* iii: 1). Herodotus tells us a Persian story that when Cambyses requested the hand of a daughter of Amasis in marriage: "There was a daughter of the late king Apries, named Nitetis, a tall and beautiful woman. Amasis took this woman, and, decking her out with gold and costly garments, sent her to Persia as if she had been his own child" (iii: 1). Herodotus admits some doubts concerning the accuracy of this story, and says that according to the Egyptian account, it was Cyrus who sent for the daughter of Hophra, and that Cambyses was her son (iii: 2). Aahmes himself "married a Cyrenian Greek, Ladice. Policy dictated to the king friendship with the Greeks" (*Camb. Anc. Hist.*, III, 304). At least it may be said that the Irish traditions are not out of keeping with the history of the period concerned.

The formal adoption of the last survivors of the *House of David* might have been regarded by Hophra as giving a legitimate claim to their throne, and a just cause for ousting its Babylonian overlord and claiming Palestine as the proper lasting possession of Egypt. But neither Hophra nor his successors were ever able to gain Palestine before their land was conquered by Persia and all their aspirations, especially with regard to the Holy Land, collapsed. In any case the throne of David vanished from Egypt.

The scribes of a later period would naturally come to think of a princess from Egypt as a "daughter" of Pharaoh, especially if they were unaware of her family origin. The circumstantial evidence from traditions, manners and customs, already produced in earlier *Serials* mentioned, together with more to come in following *Serials* (116 and 117), strongly favours the identification of Scota as a daughter of the king of Jerusalem; and the descent of the kings of Tara, through that connection, from the House of David.

Authority: The *Leabhar Gabhala*, or the *Book of the Conquests of Ireland*

Hophra, the Pharaoh of the Irish Exodus

MANY distortions that appear in the Irish records concerning the time of origin of the royal house of Tara may be removed through a co-ordination of the *Leabhar Gabhala's* tabulation of Pharaohs with the king-lists of Eusebius and Africanus, and with the further data supplied by the Irish legends as a whole. This co-ordination clearly establishes Hophra as the Egyptian ruler of what the Irish scribes would have us believe to have been the period of the Exodus, in whose time the royal house of Tara is said to have originated through the union of a Milesian prince with a so-called 'daughter' of this Pharaoh.

The Comparative Tabulation of Ancient and Modern Lists

The following tabulation shows the king-list from the *Leabhar Gabhala* (Ser. No. 114 [572.941]) alongside the lists from Eusebius, Africanus, and modern authorities. It is evident that the Irish series bears a remarkable resemblance to the lists of Eusebius in particular, yet with important differences which suggest that it was derived from yet another ancient source now lost, but possibly even older, as indicated in *Ser.* No. 115 [572.941], where is shown the synchronism between the reigns of Nebuchadnezzar, king of Babylon, and Hophra, the Egyptian ruler who preceded the stated fifteen Pharaohs of whom Nectonebus was the last.

Known Dynasty & Ruler (XXII & XXV contemporary)		Læabhar Gabhala		Eusebius						Africanus	
				Canon		Armenian Version		Syncellus			
XVIII											
Amenhotep III	31			Orus	37	Orus	28 (38)	Orus	35 (38)	Orus	37
Amenhotep IV	18			Achencheres	12	Achencheres	16	Achencherses	16	Acherres	32
Ra-smenkh-ka	8			Athoris	9					Rathos	6
		(Cingris)		Chencheres	16						
Tut-ankh-amen	9			Acherres	8	Acherres	8	Acherres	8	Chebres	12
Ay	13	Cerres	15 (12)	Cherres	15	Cherres	15	Cherres	15	Acherres	12
Horemheb	4	Armades	5	Armais (Danaus)	5	Armais	5	Armais	5	Armesis	5
Ramessu I	2			Ramesses (Aegyptus)	68	Ramesses	68	Ramesses	68	Rameses	1
				Amenophis	40	Amenophis	40	Menophis	40	Amenophath	19
XIX											
Seti I	9			Sethos	55	Sethos	55	Sethos	55	Sethos	51
Ramessu II	67	Rameses	60	Rampses	66	Rampses	66	Rampses	66	Rapsakes	61 (66)
Menephtah & Seti II	8	Amenoses	40	Amenophis	40	Amenephthis	8 (40)	Amenephthis	40	Amenophthis	20
										Ramesses	60
Amenmeses	—	Amenomes	28	Amendes	6	Ammenemes	26	Ammenemnes	26	Ammenemes	5
Si-ptah & Tausert	6	Tures	7	Thuoris	7	Thuoris	7	Thuoris	7	Thuoris	7
XX											
				←———(12 Kings, not named)———————→							

| Known Dynasty & Ruler (XXIV & XXV contemporary) | Leabhar Gabhala | | Eusebius | | | | | Africanus | |
			Canon		Armenian Version		Syncellus			
XXI										
	Daremandis	26	Smendis	26	Smendis	26	Smendis	26	Smendes	26
Nes-ba-tata	Senres	40	Pseusennes	41	Psusennes	41	Psusennes	41	Psusennes	46
			Nephercheres	4	Nephercheres	4	Nephercheres	4	Nephelcheres	4
	Thustus	9	Amenophis	9	Amenophthis	9	Amenophthis	9	Amenophthis	9
	Oschorus	7	Osorchor	6	Osochor	6	Osorchor	6	Osochor	6
	Esinachus	9	Psinaches	9	Psinnaches	9	Psinaches	9	Psinaches	9
	Esimes	25	Psusennes	35	Psusennes	35	Psusennes	35	Psusennes	35
XXII										
Sheshanq I	21	Sessonchus	21	Sesonchosis	21	Sesonchosis	21	Sesonchosis	21	Sesonchosis	21
Uasarkon I	36			Osorthon	15	Osorthon	15	Osorthon	15	Osorthon	15
Takerat I	25									N.N.	
Uasarkon II	28									N.N.	25
Sheshanq II	–									N.N.	
Takerat II	25			Takelothis	13	Takelothis	13	Takelothis	13	Takelothis	13
Sheshanq III	52									N.N.	
Pamay	4									N.N.	42
Sheshanq IV	37									N.N.	
XXIII											
Pedusabast	23			Petubas	26	Petubastis	25	Petubastis	25	Petubates	40
Uasarkon III	14			Osorthon	9	Osorthon	9	Osorthon	9	Osorcho	8
		Pissamus	40	Psammes	10	Psammus	10	Psammus	10	Psammus	10
										Zet	31
XXIV											
Bakenranef	6	Bachor	47	Bocchoris	44	Bocchoris	44	Bocchoris	44	Bokkhoris	6

Known Dynasty & Ruler (XXIV & XXV contemporary)		Leabhar Gabhala		Eusebius						Africanus	
				Canon		Armenian Version		Syncellus			
XXV											
				Sabakon	8	Sabakon	8	Sabakon	8	Sabakon	8
Sabataka	12	Silvicus	15	Sebichos	12	Sebichos	12	Sebichos	12	Sebichos	14
Taharka	27	Etheops	20	Tarakus	20	Tarakos	20	Tarakos	20	Tarkos	18
Tanutamen	6	Etheops Memess	22	Ammeres	12	Ammeses	12 (18)	Ammeres	12		
XXIV (cont'd)											
Tafnekht II		Stapantes	7	Stephinathis	7	Stephinathis	7	Stephinathis	7	Stephinates	–
Nekau-ba		Encheprus	6	Nechepsus	6	Nechepsos	6	Nechepsos	6	Nechepsos	6
Nekau I		Necha	8	Nechaus I	8	Nechus I	6 (8)	Nechao I	8	Nechao I	8
XXVI											
Psamtek I	54	Assanet	9	Psammetichus	44	Psammetichos	44	Psammetichos	45	Psammetichos	54
Nekau II	16	Nechot	6	Nechao II	6	Nechaus II	6	Nechao II	60	Nechao II	6
Psamtek II	5	Asmutes	12	Psammuthis	17	Psammuthis	17	Psammuthis	17	Psammuthis	6
Uah-ab-ra	19	Huprisis	30	Vaphres	25	Vaphres	25	Uaphris	25	Uaphris	19
Amasis II	44	Ameniris	42	Amasis	42	Amosis	42	Amosis	42	Amosis	44
Psamtek III	—									Psammecherites	½
XXVII											
				←———— 8 named Persian rulers of Egypt ————→							
XXVIII		Amartes	6			Amyrtaeus	6	Amyrtaios	6	Amyrteus	6
XXIX											
		Nefritis	6	Nepherites	6	Nepherites	6	Nepherites	6	Nepherites	6
		Anchoris	12	Achoris	12	Achoris	13	Achoris	13	Achoris	13
				Psammuthis	1	Psammuthis	1	Psammuthis	1	Psammuthis	1
				Nepherites	1/3	Muthes	1	Nepherites	1/3	Nephorites	1/3
		Mutes	1			Nepherites	1/3	Muthis	1		
		Nectonebus	18	Nectanebus	18	Nectanebes	10	Nectanebus	10	Nectanebes	18

(Eusebius' and Africanus' figures from Baron C. J. J. von Bunsen
Egypt's Place in Universal History, 1868 ed.)

Serial No. 116b

Authority: *The Annals of Clonmacnoise*

How the Ancient History of the Irish came to be Distorted

THE *Annals of Clonmacnoise* contain useful information as to the origin of the Royal House of Tara through the union of a Milesian prince with a so-called "daughter" of a Pharaoh, who may be identified as Hophra, of the XXVIth Dynasty, when Carians and Ionians were extensively settled and employed in Egypt.

The erroneous association, by the early Irish scribes, of Nebuchadnezzar with the mythical Belus, son of Ninus, and father of the Semiramis of Eusebius' tradition, is evident in the *Annals*, where, through this mistake, an attempt has been made to place the origin of the Royal House of Tara over a thousand years too early in history. In trying to accommodate the records at their disposal to this enormous stretching of history, the early scribes added numerous obviously fanciful details.

The removal of Eusebius' false chronology and Assyrian king-list together with other imaginative material from the Irish legends, leaves them in a greatly improved condition and much nearer their original state, the form of which can be discerned by comparison with the known history of Milesian relations in Egypt during the period of the XXVIth Dynasty, when the Scoto-Milesian Royal House of Tara traditionally originated.

Eusebius' false Chronology and Assyrian King-List in Irish Legend

The chronology followed by the early editors to whom we are indebted for the transmission of Irish legends, was that of Eusebius of Cæsarea (c. 265-339 A.D.); in the case of the *Annals of Clonmacnoise*, this fact is clearly implied in the opening paragraph where his name appears.

Eusebius followed a false king-list to which, even before his time may have been attached something of a pretended chronology. Lists of names from Assyrian tablets may have provided a basis for this false system (*Transactions of the Society for Biblical Archæology*, Vol. III, [1874], p. 365; *Proceedings of the Society for Biblical Archæology*, Vol. III [1881], p. 37). Eusebius' list goes back through the legendary queen Semiramis, who reigned, according to him, nearly 2000 B.C.

Beloe, in his notes to Herodotus' *History*, mentions that Semiramis is variously placed by different ancient writers: Syncellus says she lived 2177 B.C.; Helvicus, 2248; and Philo Biblius, c. 1200. Herodotus, on the other hand, far earlier than any of these writers, says that she preceded another famous Babylonian queen, Nitocris, mother of Labynetus, and thought by some commentators to have been wife of Nebuchadnezzar, by five generations. Of all these, Herodotus is doubtless nearest the mark, for the name of Sammuramat (Semiramis) was long ago discovered on an Assyrian tablet, where she is mentioned as the wife of the predecessor of the Pul or Tiglath-Pileser of the Bible (J. W. Bosanquet, *Transactions of the Society for Biblical Archæology*, Vol. II [1873], p. 156).

It thus appears that Eusebius' Assyrian king-list and its chronology are quite false and should be removed from the Irish material which has been severely distorted in order that it might be accommodated to them.

The reason for Eusebius' chronology and Assyrian king-list being attached to Irish legends is evident when we realise that the name given to Nebuchadnezzar in Irish, *Nin mac Peil* (see *Ser.* No. 115 [572.941]) was confused by early scribes with that of Ninus, the legendary first king of Babylon whose name heads the list from Eusebius. Events of Irish history which occurred in Nebuchadnezzar's period or were dated in reference to it, were transported, in great confusion, to times many centuries too early—to the days of Nimrod, Shinar, the Exodus of Isræl, &c.

The discovery and removal of the false framework upon which the original Irish legends have been stretched and distorted, leaves us with material bearing clear indications of their original shape, and relating to the dynastic history of the Royal House of Tara from the time that it originated in Egypt through the union of a Milesian prince with a so-called "daughter" of Pharaoh in the time of Hophra, when Jeremiah the Prophet and the "king's daughters" (Jer. xliii, 6) were almost certainly in residence with the Milesians in their fortress of Tahpanhes.

According to the *Annals*, Ireland was first colonised by settlers led by the woman Keassar; but they all perished in the Flood, after which came the successive waves of Partholanians, Nemedians, Fer Bolgs, Dananns, and Milesians.

EXTRACTS FROM THE *ANNALS OF CLONMACNOISE, FROM THE CREATION TO A.D. 1408*; translated into English by CONELL MAGEOGHAGAN, A.D. 1627; edited by the Rev. DENIS MURPHY, University Press, Dublin, 1896.

From the Editor's *Preface*

These Annals have, in later times at least, usually gone by the name of the "Annals of Clonmacnoise". In the book itself there is nothing to show why it should be called by this name. No doubt it gives a special prominence to the history of those parts of the country on both sides of the Shannon bordering on Clonmacnoise. . . . Frequent mention is made of St. Queran, who was not only the founder of Clonmacnoise, but the patron saint of the men of Connaught. . . .

Nor is there any clue to the author's name throughout the work. He is said to be "an authentic author and worthy prelate of the Church, that would say nothing but the truth," "a great Latinist and Scholler", yet "he could not get his penn to name the Kings of England or other foraigne countryes by their proper names but by such Irish names as he pleased to devise out of his own head". He was Irish too, if we may judge from his sympathies shown. . . .

The original work was in Irish. The translator more than once refers to "the ould Irish book out of which he wrote". . . .

The original was supposed to be in the possession of the family of Sir Richard Nagle some fifty years ago, a descendant, by his mother's side, of the translator. . . .

The names of the severall authors wch I have taken for this booke

Saint Colum Kill, saint bohine, Collogh O'More Esqr, Venerable Bede, Eoghye O'Flannagan arch dean of Ardmach and Clonfiachna, Gillernew Mac Conn ne mboght, archpriest of Cloniuckenos, Keilachar Mac Coñ alȝ Gorman, Eusebius Marcellinus, Mc Oylyne. O'Mulchonrye and Tanaige O'Mulconrye, 2 professed Chroniclers.

Memorandum

from Adam untill the Deluge there were yeares	1656
from the Deluge untill Abrahams tyme	0292
from Abr. untill the Departing out of egypt	0500
from the Departing out of Egypt untill the building of the temple of Sollomon	0480
from the building of the Temple untill the Captiuity in Babylon	0410
from the returne from the Captiuity untill the Machabees tyme	0432
from the Machabees tyme untill Herods, &c	0134

(Page 10)

Ireland long time after the flood lay wast untill about the Yeare after the Creation of the World 1696 and after the flood 313 yeares in the 21 year of the age of the Patriarck Abraham and alsoe in the 1st yeare of the Raigne of Semiramis then monarches of the world in Assiria.

Bartholeme a Gretian Born of Morea and his 3 sonns Rowrye, Slaynge, and Laughlen fleeing out of Greece for Murderinge his one father & mother execrablie to help one of his friends and kindsmen to the Gouernment of that Kingdom landed in Ireland with such as followed him about the 17th of May in the same yeare and there continued with such as Descended of him 269 yeares, whereof he gouerned himself 30 years after all which time spent all that then Remayned aliue of them to the number of 9008 persons from the first Monday in May untill the next Monday after Dyed of a suden Infection upon the playnes of · Moynealta. It was called Moynealta, Because all the foule in the kingdome for the most part Gathered themselves there to shunn themselves.

. . . hee and his sones made manye plaines by cutting Down the woods, wch after did turn the contry to great good, and was the only thinge worthe the memory that was don in that second Inhabitation of Ireland, Dureinge wch time of 269 yeares, that is to say from the 12th of Semiramis Raigne to the 33rd of Baleus the second there Raigned in Assiria Being the first monarch and Monarch 8 Monarches wch was first begun by Nibroth sonn of Chus, who was son of Cham, who was sonne of Noeh.

Ireland after the death of Bartholeme and his People was 30 yeares waste and desolate dureinge which time Assiria was Gouerned by too Monarches, that is to say, Baleus Secundus, 19 yeares, and Altades, 11 yeares.

Culloch O'More sayeth that it was waste but the said 30 yeares onely; the first of the before Recited monarchs was Semiramis who Rayned 30 yeares, Sameas Nimas 38 yeares, Arius 30 yeares, Araleus 40 yeares, Baleus 30, Armarkes 30, Bellochus 30 and Baleus Tertius 33 yeares.

Here endeth the Second Inhabitacon of Ireland and Followeth the Third, Which is of Clanna Nevye and Ffirvolge

In the Later end of the Raigne of the said Altades, came Neuie McAgamemnon with his foure sonns Into Ireland out of Greece, his sonnes names alsoe were Sdarne, Jaruanell, the Prophett, Fergus Leahdearg, who had a son called Brittan the Balde, of whome all Welshmen are Descended, and Anynn wch people Ruled Ireland 382 yeares. During wch time there Gouerned in Assiria 13 Monarches wch were Altades 21 yeares, Manillus 30, Spartus 40, Ascatades 41, Amintas 45, Belochas Junior 52, Belopares 30, Sphereus 20, Mancaleus 30, Mamillus 30, Lamprides 32, Sorares 20, and Lampares 18.

Starna McNevie fought a Greate Battle in Dalriada against Conyn(ge) McFewer 7 yeares after their comeing. Conyngs tower was besieged both by sea and land with 60000 men, that is·to say 30000 by sea And soe many more by land, and in the end was Gotten by ffomores And destroyed. These ffomores were a sept Descended from Cham the sonn of Noeh, that there liued by pyracy . . .

. . . In the End after longe strife and continuall vexeation such as were of most account of them were Driuen out of the country by the said troblesom sept of ffomores and went Back againe to Greece where they continued the space of 50 yeares or thereabouts. Dureinge wch time of 50 yeares there Raigned in Assiria two Monarches wch were Lampares 12 yeares, and Pannias 38 yeares. At the end of wch time they being overlayed by the exactions of the Gretians, and Desirous also to recouer theire naturall contry which at the first they did quitly posses without strife or Interuption, and soe did Enjoy the same for the space of 37 yeares after under the rule of nine Kings. This sept were called ffiruolge, there were 5 Brothers that were theire Chieftains, the sonnes of Dela mcLoich that first Diuided Ireland into fiue partes . . . (pp. 12-15).

* * * * *

. . . upon them came in the people called Twathy De Dannan out of Greece too, Being a Braunch of the same stock that ffirvolge were of and were kinsmen. Dureinge the time of ffirvolge which was 37 yeares, there Raigned in Assiria 3 monarchs to witt Pannias 7 yeares, Sosarmus nineteen yeares and Mitreus 11 yeares. Twany de danaan after they had spent much tyme abroad in learneinge nigromancy Magicke, and other Diobolicall artes wherein they were exceedingly well skilled, and in these Dayes accounted the Cheefest in the world in that profession, Landed in the west part of Connaught. ffirvolge hearinge of theire comeing made towards them, and meeting them in a greate plaine called Moytoyrey in Connaught, fought wth them, where ffirvolge was ouerthrone and one Hundred thousand of them slaine with their said King Eochy mc Eirche, which was the greatest slaughter that euer was hard of in Ireland at one meeteinge.

Here Endeth the 3rd Inhabitation of Ireland and Followeth the Fourth Which is of Twany de Danann.

The Contry being thus conquered by Twany de Danann one Newae was their first kinge and lost his Arme in that great Battle of Maytory, whch by the coning skill of his surgion and goldsmith whose names were Dyan Kight and Credyn, which were passing skilfull in their profession, as it did well apeare by the wonderfull cure they did, for they made a siluer hand and put on theire King which serued for all Interprises and purposes, and thereof he was called Nwae with the siluer hand . . . (pp. 16, 17).

* * * * *

Long before this Time Neale or Nioule McFenius ffearsy ancestor of Clanna Miley from Scithia came to Egypt and there liued under the Gouernment of Pharao, and when the Israellites were in Discord with the Egiptians they landed at the place neare the Red Sea called Capacyront. This Neale came to converse with them and to know whoe they were that Landed in that place. Then Aaron the High Priest of the Jewes told him that they were Jewes, and how his Brother Moyses by the Helpe of God Brought diuers pleagues on the Egyptians for their abuses &c. Then Neale and Earon falling into more friendly familiarity & Conuersation together, Neale asked him whether the Israelites had any victuals, whereunto Earon Replied & told him that they had but very little, for they came then from the Captivity and Bondage of the Egyptians, soe as it were Impossible for them to haue but little sustenance. You shall command whatsoeuer I haue, said Neale & shall haue wheat and wine at yr pleasure . . .

After all which past Neale conplayned to the Isaraellites how odious he would groe with Pharao for using any friendship with the Israellites. Moyses, Aaron, and the rest Requested Neale with his whole familie and followers to goe with them, and that if God did please to giue them the promised land they would giue them a good share thereof, & use him thenceforward no worse then one of themselues, or if he pleased to bark with them they would prouide some place for him on the seas Remote from the power of pharao, where he might quitely Remaine untill he had seen the finall end Between the Egyptians and the Isaraelites. Then they apoynted 3000 souldiers under Neale with command as admirall of theire fleete. Neale sayled Back to the place where the Egiptians were Drowned in the Red Sea, where he found certainely that pharao himself, together with 60,000 footmen and 50,000 horsemen were Droned soe as there escaped none of the said number undrowned but one man whose name was Fasteus. Neale seeinge the Death of Pharao and his armye sheaked off all his feare and Determined to stay thenceforth in the Kingdome and to possese his share thereof for him and his posteritye for euer, soon after Neale Dyed, his sonne Gathelus succeeded in his place, whoe accordinglye possessed the same until he Dyed and had issue Essrue, sonn of the said Gathelus, which Essre had alsoe a sonne called Srue who was sonn of Neale. Neale mac Fenius Farcy was sonn of Japhett, who was sonn of Noeh, whoe was son of. . . .

Of the Comeing of the Sonns of Miletus of Spaine to this Kingdom: of the ouerthroe they gave to the Twany de Danan. Of the joynt raigne & diuision of Ireland between the two brothers Hermon & Heber, & how they squared amongue themselves, and consequently how Herminn slew Heber and Raigned himselfe as sole monarch of the Kingdom.

The most part of our Ireish Cronacles agree that the sonns of Miletus came to this land in the beginning of the destruction of Troy, & that Hermon and Heber sons of the said Miletus Raigned together joyntly when Agamemnon with his Gretians came to that Destruction. The occation of theire coming is as followeth. In the yeare after the flood 1245 being about the 12th yeare of the Raigne of Dauid king of Israel & Judea, Gallo the sonn of Billus king of Scythia after surnamed Miletus of spaine for his manye and great exployets, heareing of the great wars wch the Egyptians held then with theire neighbouring contryes, being before in some Displeasure at home for the strife that grew Between him and his Kinsman for the kingdom of Scithia & being alsoe himself much given to warr, ambitious of honour & Desirous to encrease his name (as the manner of his contry was) passed out of Scithia with a number of his friendes, kinsmen & ffollowers into Egypt, where he was no sooner arriued then well entertained by the Egyptians, & in short time after did soe well aquite himself in theire seruice, that he was made Generall of theire armies & withall married the Daughter of Symedes then the Greatest prince in Egypt or Pharao as they did then commonly call theire monarch, his other Daughter was after married to Solomon, King of Jerusalem. This Symedes or Symenides by other authors is called alsoe Silagh & became soe great & mighty, that he had in his army 1200 chariots, 60,000 Horses, and 400,000 footmen.

After the Death of king Solomon & alsœ after the Departure of Gallo out of Egipt he entred with the same into the city of Jerusalem, Ransacked the cittye spoiled the Jews, & carried away all their Treasure & Jewells with him into Egipt. Some few years before this was don, when Galle saw that his father-in-law was quiete at home and could command his neybours abrood, & after that Dwelt in Egypt 6 years or somewhat more, he tooke leaue of his friendes there and wth a number of his Depend^ts did pass on Towards Parthia & encamped at the foot of a great Hill (which for good lookes sake he called after his wife's name Scota), at length after a long & wearisome jorney; when he had been tossed too and froe for the space 2 of years he was wind-driuen into Portugall 126 years after that king seased to rule that kingdom; Gargoris, surnamed Meliola for his skill in making of Hony being the last of them. Spaine was Diuided into Prouences amongst the princes thereof, soe it was much the sooner Brought under by Gallo who in less than one yeare ouerthrew the Spaniards in sundry fights, and cheefly in 3 great batles, after which victoryes, his wife Scota, Pharao his Daughter dyed. You are to understand (to make the History more manifest) that Gallo was thrice married; first in Scithia to Seang Rifflar his Daughter, a great Prince in Scithia, by whom he had two sonns Begotten in Scithia which were called Don and Heragh Feura. Secondly to Scota Pharao's Daughter (as is afore said) by whome he had alsoe 4 sonns borne unto him in Egipt, that is to say Heber the white, Avirgin, Ire, and Colp with the sword; thirdly to Savia, the Daughter of Nicicorus, then the cheefest of Spaine, by whom he had likewise 2 sonnes which were Borne in Spaine, wch were called Heremon and Herenan, and by that marriage he had great quiteness in Spaine all his lifetime after.

In process of time being well multiplied in numbers, he Remoued some of his company into Biscaie, then called Colteberia, where they did Edifie Brigantia and aded thereto a great Tower that was named of the builder Breons Tower, for soe Galloes grandfather was called Breowen, & soone after some of them came into Ireland. . . . (pp. 19-23).

. . . & soe leaueing Gallo well settled in Spaine 40 of the chiefest of them in 30 shipps made towards Ireland, Galloes 8 sons being of the number, and the greatest in authoritye & Reputac̄on; but being come towards the shore about the 17th of May 2934 and the yeare before the birth of our Sauiour Jesus Christ the sonn of God 1029 as Collogh O'More setteth forth who was a uery worthy Gentleman and a Great searcher of antiquities, but Philip O'Sulivan in his printed book Dedicated to Phillip the 4th King of Spaine, sayeth that they came in the yeare before the birth of our Saviour 1342 which is from this present year 1627 the number of 2966 yeares, Laestheness being then the 33rd monarch of the Assirians, they were kept of a long time from Landing for Twathy de Danan that were then Ruler of Ireland did use such witchcrafts, sorcerye, and other magick arts and Incantations that thereby they Did procure such tempest, stormes, and continuall contrary winds, that Diuers of the principle of them as Donn, Ire, and fferanan, three of the Brothers, were lost & Drowned, wth others of the best sort to the number of 100 besides Gentlewomen, Gentlemen, & others of less Reckoning . . . (p. 25).

After the Landing of the sonns of Miletus & Receaveing such Losses, they made forwardes towards Taylten where they met with Twathy de Danan & fought with them & after a cruel and bloody Bataile which lasted almost from morning untill night twathy De Danan were ouerthrone to theire utter Destruction, where m^e Quoill, m^cKeght and m^cGrenie theire 3 Kings with their three wivs Ery, Fodla, and Banva were slain. (p. 26).

. . . . . .

These Twathy de Danan ruled in Ireland for the space of 197 years, under the Gouernment of 9 Kings, During wch time Gouerned in Assiria seuen Emperors or Monarchs, to wit Mitreus 15 yeares, Tulanes or Tantanes 22 yeares, Tarileus 40 yeares, Thineus 30 years, Dercilus 40 yeares, Euphalus 30, and Loasthenes 12 yeares.

Soon after this Conquest made by the sonns of Miletus theire Kinsmen and friendes, they Diuided the whole Kingdome amongue themselues in manner as followeth: But first before they landed in this land, Tea the daughter of Louthus, that was wife of Heremon, Desired one Request of her husband & kinsmen, wch they accordingly Granted, wch was, that the place shee would most like of in the kingdom should be for euer after called after or by her name, And that the place soe called should be euer after the principle seat of her Posteritie to liue in, and upon their landing she chose Leytrym which is since that time called Taragh, where the Kings pallace stood for many yeares after, and which she caused to be called Tea-mur, mur in Irish is a town or pallace in English, and being joined to Tea maketh it to be the town, pallace, & house of Tea. The south part was for 6 of them, whereof Heber the white, Louthus son of Ithus, Ehan m^cVga, Un m^cUga, Chahir, & fulmann were the number. The north part was allotted for 7 of them, who were Aeremon, Ebricke McIre, Avirgin, Goisdean, Seaga, Sorge, and Souarge. Heber the white was king of the south, and Heremon king of the north (pp. 27, 28).

Authorities: Various

The True Orientation of Early Irish Legends:
The Prophet Jeremiah a Central Figure

IT is now possible to ascertain something of the enormous damage done to the pre-Christian history of Ireland by indiscreet ecclesiastics who "stretched" the historical materials at their disposal by as much as a millennium or more and endeavoured to synchronise them with Eusebius' fabulous Assyrian chronology and king-list. The removal of this false material from the legends, some of which have been proved to identify people and events of the period of the XXVIth Dynasty of Egypt, leaves them in a much improved state, and bearing many indications as to how they may be further co-ordinated.

When deprived of the false chronology and attempted synchronisms of the early Irish ecclesiastics, the traditions of the seemingly different invasions of Ireland can be shown by their own internal evidence to relate in the main to but a single conquest—that of the Milesians. Thus the Partholanians, Nemedians, Fer Bolgs, and Dananns, instead of having invaded Ireland before the Milesians did so, as the legends tell us in their present distorted form, were themselves branches of the Milesians. This fact is of the utmost importance with regard to the old Irish legend that the *Lia Fail* was brought to Ireland by the Tuatha de Dananns.

It can also be established that the prophet Jeremiah receives paramount mention in these Irish legends, where he is alluded to both as a fugitive in Egypt after the fall of Jerusalem and subsequently as a prominent figure in the story of the Milesian colonisation of Ireland.

Eusebius the Basis of Christian Irish Chronology

Two sources of legend are particularly valuable in establishing that the king-lists and chronology of Eusebius were used by those who brought the earliest Irish materials together. The comparative tabulations of *Ser. No.* 116 [572.941], clearly show that the *Leabhar Gabhala* followed his lists; and the names of the kings of "Assyria" listed in the *Annals of Clonmacnoise* (*Ser. No.* 117 [572.941]) are derived from the same authority.

It is curious that in respect of his list of Pharaohs, Eusebius is a valuable authority, at least as having some correspondence to the known names of rulers and order of their succession; in contrast, his list and chronology of the Assyrian rulers is completely false. His Egyptian list, because it preserves the succession from the XXVIth to the XXIXth Dynasties inclusive, has proved to be invaluable as a part of the Irish tradition, the truth of which it helps to establish. But the mythical Assyrian list (exposed as useless in *Ser. No.* 117 [572.941]), has served the opposite of a good purpose in its being incorporated in the Irish story, for with the aid of that list the name of *Nin mac Peil*, i.e., Nebuchadnezzar (*Ser. No.* 115 [572.941]), of the native tradition, was equated with that of Ninus the mythical son of Belus according to Eusebius. In keeping with the fantastic "stretching" of history thus necessitated, the fortress or "tower" of Tahpanhes, celebrated in the days of Nebuchadnezzar, was, thanks to a convenient imagination on the part of the Irish editors, described as Nimrod's tower, that was to say, the Tower of Babel, which stood, as they would have us believe, about Abraham's time. Other events and people of Hophra's period were also removed far back in time, but, by reason of coincidence of circumstances, were placed at the time of the Exodus—Hophra, who was murdered in his boat in the course of a naval action, was made the Pharaoh of the Exodus who was supposed to have perished in the Red Sea; Aahmes, called Amosis by Eusebius, became Moses; and a third person, *Iar*, whose name appears repeatedly in variant forms, was declared to be "Aaron the High Priest of the Jewes". The identity of this *Iar* is a subject of great interest, as what follows will show.

A Single Invasion Transformed into Several

Stripped of their pretended synchronisms with Eusebius' false chronology, the Irish legends of the so-called invasions or conquests of Ireland show distinct signs of requiring simplification, for with the aid of that erroneous system of dating, a single colonisation of Ireland, the Milesian, was made to appear as several. The evidence calling for the reduction of these several alleged settlements of Ireland into one is obvious:

(1) The pretended invasions of Ireland were successively by Partholanians, Nemedians, Fer Bolgs, Tuatha De Dananns, and Milesians. The Fomorians, who are said to have fought both the Nemedians and Fer Bolgs in Ireland, although at times in control of the country, are for some reason not numbered among the invaders of Ireland, possibly because they represented the authochthonous, or at least a strange population called African pirates.

Partholanus, we are told in the *Leabhar Gabhala* (sec. 22), "came from his native land, that is, from Sicily of the Greeks, a-fleeing from the kin-murder that he had wrought; namely, killing his father and his mother." The Partholanian story is clearly a variant of that of the eponymous ancestor of the British, Brutus the Trojan, with which it has been confused. Even the mention of *Sicily* is not incongruous, for Brutus was of a Trojan family dwelling in Alba, in Latium, where the Siculi at one time settled.

Serial No. 118*a*.

The Partholanians are stated by Keating, who presumably derived his information from the *Psalter of Cashel*, to have been descended from "Partholan, son of Sera, son of Sru, son of Esru, son of Framant, son of Fathacta, son of Magog, son of Japhet" (Keating, p. 114); essentially the same information is found in the *Leabhar Gabhala*, where we find the descent: Partholon, Sear, Sru, Easru, Bramant, Athect, Magog, Japheth (sec. 21). But these names enter into the genealogy of the Scoto-Milesian kings, where we find Sru, son of Esru, son of Gaedal Glas, and so on, through Nel, Fenius, Baath, Magog (Keating, see *Ser. No.* 113 [572.941]). A further indication that the so-called Partholanians were in fact none other than a branch of the Milesians is to be found in the statement by Keating (p. 119) that the four sons of Partholan: Er. Orba, Ferann and Fergna, had the same number of namesakes among the sons of Miledh; although the *Leabhar Gabhala* traces the Partholanians, Nemedians, Fer Bolgs, and Dananns from Aithect, son of Magog and brother of Baath the father of Fenius (sec. 124). In the *Annals of Clonmacnoise* (p. 12), the people of Wales and Scotland are made the descendants of Miletus' nephew Lauthus; while this same authority elsewhere makes the Welsh to be the descendants of Briotan, Brittan the Bald, Britan Mael, or Brian Mael, son of Fergus Redside, son of Newie McAgamemnon (p. 14; cf. Keating, pp. 126, 127). This Agamemnon appears in the *Leabhar Gabhala* as Agnoman, father of Neimhedh (from whom the Nemedians), and son of Pamp, son of Tai, son of Ser, son of Sru, son of Eassru (sec. 42).

Further proof that the Partholanians were in fact Milesians is found in Keating's statement (p. 127) that the holy Cormac Mac Culinan, in his *Psalter of Cashel* says that "it is from this same Britan that the island Britannia or Great Britain has received the name which it bears to the present day: and the records of Ireland agree with him in this, according to the *duan* which begins—"Adam, parent, source of hosts'.

> " 'The stainless Britan passed over the sea,
> Generous son of Fergus Lethderg,
> All the Brethnaigh of victorious fame
> From him are, without falsehood, sprung.'

"Another bard bears out the same fact, where he says—

> " 'Britan Mael, the son of princes,
> Noble the trunk whence he spread;
> The son of the Red-sided Chief from Leg-Magh,
> From whom all the Brethnaigh are sprung.' "

Curiously enough, Keating then goes on and attempts to discredit the story of Brutus the Trojan.

Such then, is the evidence showing that the story of Brutus the Trojan has been attached to the descendants of the Milesian Brittan who is said to have settled Wales; and that the Partholanian story is really a distortion of a portion of Milesian history.

(2) The Nemedians, according to the internal evidence of the Irish legends, were also Milesians. Nemedh, says Keating (p. 121), was "son of Agnaman, son of Pamp, son of Tath, son of Sera, son of Sru, son of Esru . . . ." This is a Milesian descent; and in confirmation of this, as also of the descent of the Fer Bolgs and Dananns from the Milesians, Keating says: "It is at Sru, son of Esru, that the genealogies of Nemedh and Partholan separate; and at Sera that the generations of the Fir-Bolgs, Tuatha-De-Dananns and the

sons of Miledh or Milesians diverge from one another" (p. 122). Yet another version of the story states that Nemedh was from Adla, son of Partholan (ibid.); which still upholds the close relationship of Partholanians and Nemedians.

(3) The Fer Bolgs are clearly stated to have been Nemedians. Traditionally, some of the Nemedians, finding life insufferable with the Fomorians, returned to Greece and were there enslaved. In due course, as Fer Bolgs, they returned to Ireland. Their identity is thus the least difficult of solution, and by reason of this connection they are also Milesians.

(4) The Dananns, far from being in Ireland before the Milesians, according to the traditions when stripped of Eusebius' chronology and its attachments, derived from a descendant of the Milesian colonists of that island.

An indication that the Danann name, contrary to the late and mutilated form of the tradition as it has descended to us, was later than the Milesian, is preserved in the *Annals of Clonmacnoise*, which, after having mentioned the purported invasion of the Dananns, state: "Long before this Time [i.e. the Danann invasion of Ireland.—ED.]. Neale or Nioule McFenius ffearsy ancestor of Clanna Miley from Scithia came to Egypt and there liued under the gouernment of Pharao" (p. 19). We have established this period as having been during the XXVIth Dynasty (*Ser. Nos.* 115 & 116 [572.941]). The Dananns must therefore date after this time; and confirmation of this development is found in Keating, where the Dananns are stated to have been a branch of the Nemedians, who, as we have seen, were in turn Milesians: "The Tuatha-De-Dananns are the progeny of the third Chieftain of the race of Nemedh, who had emigrated from Ireland after the demolition of the tower of Conaing. They are descended from Ibaath, son of Beothach, son of Iarbanel the Prophet, son of Nemedh" (p. 135).

The Tuatha De Danann name, we are told by the *Leabhar Gabhala*, was of late origin, and derived from one who, "Dona, daughter of Dealbaeth, son of Oghma, son of Ealathan, was mother of Brian, Iucharba, and Iuchar, and they are called the three gods of Dona; from them are the Tuatha De Danann called; for Tuatha De was their name till those arrived among them, and Tuatha De Danann was. their name afterwards" (sec. 103). Tuatha De Danann, says Macalister, means "Peoples of the Goddess Danu" (*Tara*. p. 89)— although he would have Danu to have been a mythical deity. The earlier name, Tuatha De, would simply mean "People of God", as in a corresponding manner *Ceili De* (Culdees) means "companions or vassals of God" (*Chambers' Encyc.*, 1950). The Irish version of this is: "They were called Tuatha De; that is, they considered their men of learning to be gods, and their husbandmen non-gods, so much was their power in every art and every druidic occultism besides. Thence came the name, which is Tuatha De, to them" (*Leabhar Gabhala*, sec. 90; cf. Keating, p. 140).

This Dona was, according to the genealogies given, of the royal Milesian line, for her descent is stated as follows: "Dana, daughter of Delbaeth, son of Elathan, son of Niadh, son of Indae, son of Allae, son of Tath, son of Tabarn, son of Enda or Enna, son of Bathach, son of Ibaath, son of Beothach, son of Jarbanel, son of Nemedh" (Keating, p. 140).

The Tuatha De Danann, or more properly, the Tuatha De, were the people who are credited by the *Annals of Clonmacnoise* with having brought the *Lia Fail* to Ireland (see extract in Ser. No. 109 [398.22]). Since the Dananns were Milesians it is thus clear that the *Lia Fail* was the sacred stone of the royal Scoto-Milesians.

(5) The Milesians are the original of the alleged Partholanians, Nemedians, Fer Bolgs, and Dananns of Irish legend. Yet another confirmation of this fact is to be found in the

Serial No. 118*b.*

statement that: "It is at Sru, son of Esru, that the genealogies of Nemedh and Partholan separate; and at Sera that the generations of the Fir-Bolgs, Tuatha-De-Dananns and the sons of Miledh or Milesians diverge from one another. All these nations spoke the 'Scot-Berla' or Scottish tongue. . . ." (Keating, p. 122).

Only in this unity of the peoples named is it possible to comprehend some of the peculiarities of the ancient genealogies, as, for instance, in the following, by Keating from the *Book of Drom-Snecta*: "This states that Magog had three sons, namely, Baath, Ibaath, and Fathacta. From Baath descended Fenius Farsa, the ancestor of the Gaelic nation. From Ibaath sprang the Amazons, Bactrians, and Parthians; and from Fathacta came Partholan, who was the first colonizer of Ireland after the Deluge, as well as Nemedh, son of Agnaman or Adnaman, and, consequently, the Fer-Bolgs, and Tuatha-De-Dananns, as we have mentioned above, in giving an account of their conquests of the island" (pp. 147, 148). Here the name Magog is the cause of confusion, for it is evidently a monkish distortion of the name of McAgamemnon, which in turn is from that of Agnamon which already appears in the foregoing. Once the name of the son of Agnamon was made Magog, it was, of course, easy to pretend that Amazons, Bactrians, and Parthians were related to the Milesians. Similar repetition is found elsewhere, as in the case of Keating, where a play on names is found: "And this is the reason why those of the posterity of Fathacta, son of Magog . . . namely, Partholan, son of Sera, with his people; Nemedh, son of Agnaman, from whom the Nemedians have their name; the Fer-Bolgs and the Tuatha-De-Dananns, are all named Scythian Greeks (Gregaigh Scitia), because Scythia was the land from which they had first migrated in the beginning; and I likewise think, that the reason why the posterity of Gaedal, son of Niul, son of Fenius Farsa, are more especially called Scots, is because it was this Fenius Farsa here mentioned, and his descendants, that obtained the sovereignty of Scythia. . . . On this account Niul enjoined his posterity to name themselves after Scythia, and to keep alive the memory of their original home, by forever calling themselves Scots; . . ." (Keating, pp. 151, 152).

Another play on Agnaman's name appears in the *Leabhar Gabhala*, where, again through the attachment of the prefix "mac" it has been converted, with the assistance of Eusebius' false chronology, into Magog: "Since we have told of the occupation of Ceasair first, who took Ireland before the flood, and of the four occupations which took it after the flood, of the seed of Aitheacht, son of Magog, son of Japhet, son of Noe—these are the four occupations: Partholon, Neimhedh, Fir Bolg, Tuatha De Danann—it is right for us to tell next of the seed of the son who was eldest of the children of Magog, namely, Baath and his seed, who took Grecian Scythia, the patrimony of the children of Magog; thereafter went to Egypt; again to Scythia; thence to the Gaethlaighe; after that to Spain; thence to Scythia; to Egypt; to Spain again; and thence to Ireland; . . . (sec. 122).

(6) The Antedeluvian settlers of Ireland, though not of importance to our study, possibly have been brought into the traditions through a chronological displacement. The name of Nuadh or Newie may have been equated with that of Noah, and hence one of the former's female descendants, Ceasair, has been made to appear as having arrived in Ireland, *before* the Flood be it noted, for no members of her party are recorded in the Bible as having survived that event—hence the necessity of their having been drowned! (See *Ser. No.* 113 [572.941]).

The story of the giving of her name to Ireland by the legendary Banba, one of the "three daughters of the wicked Cain" (*Ser. No.* 113) is evidently similarly derived from the Danann story, for one of the three wives, each of whom gave her name to Ireland, of

McKoyll, McKight, and McGreny, was Banva, the others being Foala and Eri (*Annals of Clonmacnoise*, p. 17; *Leabhar*, sec. 173).

The exploration of Ireland after the Flood by Adna, son of Bith, in the time of Nin Mac Peil (*Ser. No.* 113) is seemingly more properly a reference to the time of the one who bears the latter name in Irish legend—Nebuchadnezzar, as we have seen.

Iar the Prophet

Legends of the alleged invasions of Ireland are characterised by frequent mention of a central figure whose name appears in variant forms. However confused the setting may have become, the repeated appearance of his names among those of the purportedly different waves of conquerors of Ireland is further evidence that those invaders constituted in fact but one people—the Milesians, and that the emphasis on and continual appearance of the name of *Iar* and its variants point to the existence of a very real person whose identity can be established.

(a) *The Partholanian Story*. The name of Iar does not appear in association with the Partholanians, for, as we have seen, they were a late branch of the Milesians.

(b) *The Nemedian Story*. The genealogy of *Iar* is given, by Keating, as descending from Nemedh, of whose invasion of Ireland we read, in terms of the chronology of Eusebius: "The course Nemedh took in his voyage to Ireland from Scythia, was. . . The following was the strength of his fleet and the number of his host, to wit, thirty-four ships, with a crew of thirty in each ship. The leaders of these were Nemedh and his four sons, Starn, Iarbanel the Prophet, Anind and Fergus Leth-derg (Fergus of the Red Side)" (Keating, p. 122). This "Iarbanel the Prophet" is further mentioned in the Nemedian story as having been father of Beothach, who in turn was father of Ibath (Keating, p. 126).

Among the fantastic distortions of the *Annals of Clonmacnoise* we read of the person of *Iar* in the same connection: "In the Later end of the Raigne of the said Altades, came Neuie McAgamemnon with his foure sonns Into Ireland out of Greece, his sonnes names alsoe were Sdarne, Jaruanell, the prophett, Fergus Leahdearg, who had a son called Brittan the Balde, of whom all Welshmen are Descended, and Anynn wch people Ruled Ireland 382 yeares" (p. 14).

In the *Leabhar Gabhala* we read that Iarbanel the Prophet was a Nemedian chief, which may provide the basis for his being counted a "son" of Nemedh: "Now as for Neimhedh, he had four chiefs with him, Starn, Iarbanel the Prophet, Fergus Redside, and Ainnian. They were four sons of Neimhedh" (sec. 44). This same authority also mentions "Semeon son of Iarbonel son of Neimhedh" (sec. 53); but elsewhere (sec. 67) this Semeon is made "son of Erglan son of Beoan son of Starn son of Neimhedh," and Iarbanel is made father of Beothach, as in Keating (see 2 above).

(c) *The Fer Bolg Story*. The Fir Bolgs, as a reputed late branch of the Nemedians, need not concern us here. The person of *Iar* only enters ancestrally into their story.

(d) *The Danann Story*. Iar figures in the genealogy of the Dananns; this further indicates that the tales of the various invasions of Ireland all belong to but one people, the Milesians.

As already stated this identification of the Dananns as Milesians brings the *Lia Fail* legends into harmony with the legendary origin of the Scoto-Milesian royal house, for this sacred stone is said to have been brought to Ireland by the Dananns, yet it was fated to be the property of the Milesians. In this connection we read: "It was also called the Stone of Fate, for it was its destiny, that a man of the Scotic nation, that is, of the blood of Miledh of Spain, should possess the sovereignty of that country wherein it should be placed" (Keating, p. 137).

Keating quotes lines from the Danann history of the *Leabhar Gabhala* in which Iarbanel the Prophet is mentioned:

> "The Fair Iarbanel, a prophet true,
> Was son of Nemedh, son of Adnaman—
> To this gray hero, mighty in spells
> Was born Beothach of wild steeds" (p. 138).

In one account, the Dananns are said to have descended from this Iarbanel or Jarbanel: "Some antiquaries say, that the nation, of whom we are now treating, were called Tuatha-De-Danann from Brian, Iuchar and Iucharba, the three sons of Dana, daughter of Delbaeth, son of Elathan, son of Niadh, son of Indae, son of Allae, son of Tath, son of Tabarn, son of Enda or Enna, son of Bathach, son of Ibaath, son of Beothach, son of Iarbanel, son of Nemedh" (p. 140).

Iarbanel the Prophet is also mentioned in the *Leabhar Gabhala* in an alternative genealogy of Ned through the Dananns: "The children of Elathan, son of Dealbaoth, son of Ned, son of Iondae, son of Alldae, son of Tai, son of Tabarn, son of Enna, son of Baath, son of Iobath, son of Beothach, son of Iarbanel the Prophet, son of Neimhedh, son of Agnoman, were Bres, Elloith, Daghda, Dealbaeth, and Oghma" (sec. 100). Another genealogy through Iarbanel appears as follows: ". . . It is, however, an opinion of other historians, as is clear in the *Dindsenchas* of the same carn, that the father of Bres was of the Tuatha De Danann themselves—that is Bres, son of Elathan, son of Dealbaeth, son of Ned, son of Iondae, son of Tai, son of Tabarn, son of Enna, son of Baath, son of Ibath, son of Beothach, son of Iarbanel the Prophet, son of Neimhedh, son of Agnamon, etc." (sec. 106). The famous Nuadha Silver-Arm is also traced to Iarbanel: "Nuadha Silver-Arm, son of Eachtach, son of Eatarlamh, son of Ordan, son of Iondae, son of Alldae, son of Tai, son of Tabarn, son of Enna, son of Baath, son of Ibath, son of Beothach, son of Iarbanel the Prophet, son of Neimhedh; twenty years was he in the kingdom, till he fell at the hand of Balor of the Mighty Blows, in the battle of Magh Tuiredh of the Fomhoire" (sec. 107).

(e) The Milesian Story. Iarbanel the Prophet is also a figure of the Milesian story, in which he is stated by Keating, on the basis of an ancient poem, to have been one of the three learned men in the "school" established by Fenius Farsa in Egypt after the abandonment of "the Tower" of Tahpanhes: "The three sages that held the chief direction of this great school were Fenius Farsa, from Scythia; Gaedal, son of Ethor, of the race of Gomer, from Greece; and Caei, the Eloquent (or the Just), from Judea, or Iar, son of Nemha, as others call him . . ." (pp. 155, 156). The prophet's name is further modified until, in a detailed account of his conversation with the Milesian Nelius, it becomes "Aaron", and his person is equated with that of the great high priest who was brother of Moses! The story of this "Aaron" is such an obvious distortion of events which in the original tradition belonged to the period of the XXVIth Dynasty, that it deserves special consideration; and its correct repositioning helps to reveal a vital equation.

"Aaron the High Priest of the Jewes", the Siege of Jerusalem, the two "Daughters" of Pharaoh, and the XXVIth Dynasty Milesians

The name of Iar, son of Nemha, from Judea, Iarbanel the Prophet, or Jaruanell, was by the Irish monks further anglicised, if such an expression may be used, until it took the familiar English form, Aaron, of the well-known Hebrew name. The metamorphosis of persons that accompanied this change may be explained by the fact that the materials at the disposal of the early Irish editors evidently indicated that the one to whom the name *Iar* or its variants belonged had some sacerdotal connection not only with the Holy Land, but also with the city of Jerusalem at the time of its fall during the period of the XXVIth Dynasty, and more particularly, with the Milesian chieftain Neleus in the days of Hophra and Nebuchadnezzar.

With the events of Milesian history in Egypt firmly fixed to the period of the XXVIth Dynasty, we may now re-examine what the Irish legends have to say in certain respects of this time. From the extracts published in earlier *Serials*, we have seen how the Milesian Neleus came into contact with "Israelites", who, unlike the people bearing that name at the time of the Exodus, appear, according to the internal evidence of the legends themselves, to have been *entering* Egypt and not, as the monkish editors would have us believe from their distorted versions of the story, *leaving* it.

Through (*a*) their adoption of Eusebius' fantastic Assyrian king-list and chronology of the Assyrians: (*b*) their equation of the death of Hophra in his boat with the believed drowning of the Pharaoh of the Exodus in the Red Sea; (*c*) of the identifying of the name of Hophra's rival and successor, Amosis, with that of Moses; the Irish ecclesiastics found themselves in a position (*d*) to make the priestly figure of the prophet *Iar*, by reason of an obvious similarity of name and events, none other than Aaron, brother of Moses, and high priest of Israel!

The *Annals of Clonmacnoise* go yet further in supplying vital information via the way of distortion. Not only is the fantastic identification of "Aaron the High Priest of the Jewes" with *Iar* from Judea, otherwise called Iarbanel the Prophet, put forward, but he is joined to the fall of Jerusalem—which event, as part of the tradition, must perforce belong to the period of the XXVIth Dynasty and therefore can be none other than the destruction of that city by Nebuchadnezzar in 584 B.C. This association is of the highest significance.

After the fall of Jerusalem, Jeremiah and the "king's daughters" (*Jer.* xliii: 6) proceeded to Tahpanhes in Egypt, where they found sanctuary with the Milesian garrison which secular records tell us was stationed there. Being of a sacerdotal family, Jeremiah may properly be described as a priest, and as such, and as a prophet also, he must have been a doubly distinguished figure of the fugitive party at Tahpanhes. By reason of these factors there can be no doubt that the legendary *Iar* from Judea, both priest and prophet, who arrived among the Milesians of Tahpanhes during the reign of Hophra was none other than Jeremiah.

In further confirmation of this identity we find in the confused *Annals of Clonmacnoise* tradition of the Milesian history, mention of two "daughters" of Pharaoh. The early Irish editors, by means of Eusebius' false chronology, tried to remove these two "daughters" to the period of Solomon, whom one of them is said to have married. It was convenient to this invention that Solomon "took Pharaoh's daughter" to wife (I *Ki.* iii: 1). But the second "daughter" of Pharaoh is said to have married a Milesian, as we have seen. This Milesian

Serial No. 118*d.*

synchronism again ties the events concerned to the period of the XXVIth Dynasty, the only period in which the Milesians were settled in Egypt.

In the quaint *Annals of Clonmacnoise* the Milesian Neleus becomes Gallo; and of his union with Pharaoh's daughter, and of her sister's alleged marriage to Solomon we read: ". . . he was made Generall of theire armies & withall married the Daughter of Symedes then the Greatest prince in Egypt or Pharao as they did then commonly call theire monarch, his other Daughter was after married to Solomon, King of Jerusalem. This Symedes or Symenides by other authors is called alsoe Silagh & became soe great & mighty, that he had in his army 1200 chariots, 60,000 Horses, and 400,000 footmen. After the Death of king Solomon & alsoe after the Departure of Gallo out of Egipt he entred with the same into the citty of Jerusalem, Ransacked the cittye spoiled the Jews, & carried away all their Treasure & Jewells with him into Egipt. . . ." Seemingly an attempt has here been made to equate the siege of Jerusalem in Nebuchadnezzar's time with Shishak's invasion of the land of Israel shortly after the reign of Solomon as mentioned in the Bible; but the name Symedes or Symenides is itself strong confirmation of the correctness of our development, for the Horus name of Aahmes was Smen-Maät (E. A. Wallis Budge, *The Book of the Kings of Egypt*, 1908, vol. II, p. 86), which is clearly the original of the Irish form of the name. If we consider the fact that Aahmes and Hophra were co-regents from 588-566 B.C., we need not be surprised to find later historians referring to the "Pharaoh" of the period by the names of either of these two individuals. Such appears to be the case in the Irish records, for "This Symedes or Symenides, by other authors is called alsoe Silagh"—this Silagh is a possible translation of Hophra's Golden Horus name, *Suatch-Taui* (Budge, *ibid.*, p. 85).

As we have seen, this story cannot be removed out of the period of the XXVIth Dynasty of Egypt, and it is therefore the account of the siege of Jerusalem under Nebuchadnezzar, and of the ultimate removal to Egypt of certain precious articles, possibly the regalia, and the *Lia Fail*, the legendary Jacob's Pillow, which was in due course taken to Ireland by the *Tuatha De* or "People of God". The two "daughters" of Pharaoh may be equated with the "king's daughters" from Jerusalem, who became wards of the Egyptian court, and as explained in *Ser. No.* 115 [572.941], may have been formally adopted by the Egyptian royal family in accordance with custom and for the purpose of gaining additional claims to the sovereignty of the Holy Land.

An additional confirmation worth noting at this point is in the name of Jeremiah's scribe, Baruch (*Jer.* xliii: 6), who accompanied him to Tahpanhes. In keeping with the appearance of the prophet's name in Irish tradition, we find also that of Simeon Brec, a typically Hebrew name, son of Starn, son of Nemedh (Keating, p. 126). In the *Leabhar Gabhala* Simeon or Semeon is made son of Erglan, son of Beoan, son of Starn, son of Neimhedh (sec. 67); or son of Iarbonel, son of Neimhedh (sec. 53). From this Semeon Brec descended those who returned to Greece and subsequently became known as Fer Bolgs (Keating, pp. 127, 129; *Leabhar*, sec. 76).

Quite independent traditions may throw some light on the movement of the House of David to Spain and thence to Ireland in the Milesian period. It is a Jewish tradition (see *Ser. No.* 30 [572.94601]) that members of the House of David reached Spain in Nebuchadnezzar's time; and an old tradition of the Irish that they were descended from David, whose harp had become their national emblem, was preserved in the Middle Ages by the father of the famous astronomer Galileo (*Ser. No.* 109 [398.22]).

It is even possible that Jeremiah himself reached Ireland, for the name of *Iar* or *Iarbanel* the Prophet appears prominently as that of an alleged "son" of Nemedh, as we have seen, among those of the colonisers of Ireland. Here, however, we may be upon more speculative ground, for the traditions in some cases say that the royal line remained for some time in Spain. Such a difference may not involve contradiction, for it must be borne in mind that two royal lines may have sprung from the two "daughters" of Pharaoh. Some such factor may lie behind the subsequent conflicts between the two main royal families of Ireland; and a late attempt to unify the stories of these two lines may account for some of the confusion that is found concerning the early king-lists of the Irish.

The main point that has been established is that, despite all other uncertainty, there are reasonable historical grounds for identifying the Royal House of Tara, and our present British royal family descended from it, as none other than the *House of David* which was removed from Jerusalem under the hand of the prophet Jeremiah, and perpetuated in the descendants of the "king's daughters" (*Jer.* xliii: 6).

Serial No. 118*e*.

Authorities: Various

Greek-Israelites in Contact with Ancient Ireland

GREEK authors affirm that the Athenians, to whom the island of Delos was sacred, had maintained contact with the people of ancient Ireland.

The Athenians reputedly derived from an Israelitish colony which, leaving Sais in Egypt, under the leadership of Cecrops, settled in Attica near the hill of the Acropolis, where Athena is said to have planted the olive tree long afterwards to be seen there.

Native Irish histories tend to confirm this friendship, for they relate that the Greeks did in fact colonise Ireland. These and other sources provide substantial evidence of contact with ancient Ireland and furnish a strong indication of its early settlement by wandering Israelites.

It has been observed by students of Irish antiquities that certain Israelitish customs and traditions are to be found in Ireland, which certainly require some explanation. These findings may therefore be of the greatest importance in this respect.

Literary Sources on Ancient Ireland

A perusal of Irish literature reveals an amazing confusion of historical and imaginative details that have defied the most painstaking attempts to clarify them. It is clear from the native records that, beginning at a very early time, Ireland was colonised by successive waves of immigrants who came from distant lands which cannot always be identified with ease. Such claims for the antiquity of Irish civilisation receive a measure of confirmation from independent archaeological discoveries which show that at least as far back as the Bronze Age, imported cultures, and probably also, waves of settlers who introduced them, contributed, in successive periods, to the creation of a well developed society.

Unfortunately it is not yet possible to synchronise the native histories, as they have come down to us, with archaeological discoveries that can be dated by means of modern comparative methods. The ancient records have suffered almost irreparably at the hands of over-zealous and insufficiently learned ecclesiastics who, not content to leave documents as they found them, set about to edit them as they saw fit. It needs little more than a cursory survey of the surviving material to reveal that monkish editors, desirous of joining their island history to that of the Bible, in which they believed the beginnings of the histories of all peoples are to be found, set about to effect a junction in the absence of material vitally necessary for so doing. The joining was accomplished in a simple manner by stretching the existing histories, as is all too apparent in fantastic and conflicting longevities ascribed to various individuals of the earliest period, and in the extending of king-lists until only confusion remains. In such circumstances it is difficult to tell what is original and reliable historical material, and what has been added or altered by later monkish editors. As they have come down to us, the native histories relate that some of the ancestors of the settlers of Ireland were acquainted with Moses and Aaron, were present to witness, but did not partake in, the Exodus, and had many other remarkable experiences. The chronologies and longevities in such accounts are clearly fantastic, and if anything, tend to cast discredit on the whole story. But it would be unjust to cast away these histories as worthless, or as having no foundation in fact.

It so happens that classical literature is of assistance in studying the antiquities of Ireland, for it throws much light on the authenticity of the native histories as we now have them. The works of various Greek and Roman writers contain mention of Ireland and its people. Although the information to be gathered from these sources leaves much to be desired, it is of the greatest value for the periods concerned, and it does, in fact help to provide a framework of reference to which existing Irish literature may be fitted.

Ireland in Classical Liturature

Scholars have written much, and inconclusively, on the supposed origins and meanings of the different names by which Ireland was known to the ancients. The learned eighteenth century antiquarian, Sir James Ware, concisely reviewed the sources in which these different names appear, without labouring unnecessarily upon speculations as to their origin. He wrote:

"This Island, in old times the Habitation of Variety of Colonies drawn out of Britain, Scythia, Iberia, Germany and Gaul, was known to the Antients principally by two Names, i.e. *Hibernia*, or *Ibernia* and *Scotia*. Hibernia (so *Ceasar*, *Pliny*, *Solinus*, *Tacitus*, *Orosius* and others call it) the most remote Country of all *Europe* to the West, is derived either from the Word *Hiar*, which among the *Irish* signifieth the West, or Western Climate, as *Camden* thinks, or from the *Iberians*, who were formerly settled there: From whence possibly *Antoninus* in his Itinerary hath taken occasion to give the Name of *Hiberione* to this Island, and in *St. Patrick's* Epistle to *Coroticus* it is twice called Hiberione, and once *Hiberia*. From either of these Fountains, the Names Ierne [as it is called by *Claudian, Strabo,* and *Stephen of Bizantium*] *Iouernia* [by *Ptolomy*] *Iuverna* [by *Solinus*] *Iris* [by *Diodorus Siculus*] *Bernia* and *Overnia* [by *Eustathius,*] and the *Irish* word, *Eri,* seem to flow; by all which Names *Ireland* was also in former ages known. For it is probable that these Authors, meeting with the Name of an Island called, *Eire,* or *Eri,* and not understanding any derivation or meaning of the Word, gave it such Shape in their Phrase, as each particular Person thought most agreeable to the Ear, or as pleased his Fancy best. Nor am I singular in this Conjecture . . . The same may be said of *Iernis,* a Name by which *Ireland* is mentioned in the antient Poem of the *Argonauticks,* written by *Orpheus*; not the antient *Orpheus* of *Thrace,* who flourished (according to *Suidas*) eleven Ages before the *Trojan* War; but by *Orpheus* of *Crotona,* who (according to the same *Suidas*) was cotemporary with *Pisistratus* the Tyrant, who died in the 63rd *Olympiad,* that is, about the Year of the World 3422, and 526 Years before Christ: and (by the way) it is observed by Archbishop *Usher,* that even the Romans cannot produce so early a Testimony of their Name. From the Word, *Eri,* an *Irishman* is called *Erigena*; and so in antient times *John Scotus,* an old writer of the 9th Century, was commonly called, *Erigena*" (*Works,* 1745 ed., vol. II, pp. 1, 2).

By far the earliest reference to Ireland is to be found in the above mentioned poetry by some thought to be a forgery, but by others attributed to Orpheus. Admittedly the existence of Orpheus has been denied; at times he is made a deity. His name is mentioned by Ibycus, about 530 B.C.; and Pindar (522-443 B.C.) speaks of him as the father of song. Traditionally an Orpheus was a member of the Argonautic expedition upon which so much speculation has centered as to the course it followed. Ware has identified the Orpheus with whom we are concerned with a much later period, in the sixth century B.C.

According to Diodorus Siculus (IV,lvi, 3), the Argonauts sailed up the Tanais, transported their ship to a river flowing northward into the sea, and thence they sailed home via Cadiz. A voyage up the Dnieper (Borysthenes), followed by a transportation across to the Vistula would seem more likely, and it may be that this, rather than that mentioned by Diodorus, was the route taken.

It has been observed by the learned Dr. R. G. Latham, that even if the doubt as to the origin of this poetry attributed to Orpheus be allowed: ''No reason for excluding these lines lies in the fact of their being forgeries. Provided that they were composed before the time of Caesar, the authorship matters little. If, as is the common practice, we attribute them to Onomacritus, a contemporary of Miltiades, they are older than Herodotus'' (*Ethnology of the British Islands,* 1852, p. 40).

In the disputed lines, the ship *Argo* is supposed to have said:
" For now by sad and painful trouble
Shall I be incompassed, if I go too near the *Iernian Islands,*
For unless, by bending within the holy headland,
I sail within the bays of the land, and the barren sea,
I shall go outward into the Atlantic Ocean."
(*ibid.* p.39).

The above are equivalent to lines 1181ff. of *Les Argonautiques D'Orphée,* in the French translation by Georges Dottin (1930), in which the Argonautic expedition is given as 1263-1256 B.C., and the Trojan war as 1189-1180 B.C. on the basis of Eusebius (*Introduction,* p. xi).

Whatever may have been the source of our quotation, we have in it a mention of not later than the 6th century B.C., to a voyage into the vicinity of Ireland nearly a century before the fall of Troy. Such a voyage should not be regarded as altogether unlikely. It must be recalled that some explanation is necessary for the appearance, mentioned by the late Sir Flinders Petrie, of Irish gold in Gaza, in southern Palestine, from about 2300 B.C. onwards (see extract and illustration in Ser. No. 49 [D.D.C. 571.3]).

Aristotle, born in 384 B.C., though by no means the next to refer to Ireland, retains the name Ierne. His quaint description of what lay beyond the Pillars of Hercules, the modern Straits of Gibraltar, contains a misinterpretation of data. Herodotus (iv. 42) had earlier recorded that Africa had been circumnavigated by Phoenician-manned ships which returned through the Pillars long before his time; and it would seem that Aristotle's account confuses a voyage to India via the South Atlantic with the northerly journey to Britain. Aristotle's account states:

"In this sea are situated two very large islands, the so-called British Isles, Albion and Ierne, which are greater than any which we have yet mentioned and lie beyond the land of the Celts. (The island of Taprobane opposite India, situated at an angle to the inhabited world, is quite as large as the British Isles, as also is the island called Phebol which lies over against the Arabian Gulf). There is a large number of small islands round the British Isles and Iberia, forming a belt round the inhabited world, which, as we have already said, is an island. The width of the inhabited world at the greatest extent of its mainland is rather less than 40,000 stades, so the best geographers say, and its length about 70,000 stades. It is divided into Europe, Asia, and Libya" (*De Mundo*, chap. 3; Forester's trans., 1931).

Aristotle's words do not necessarily indicate that he conceived the earth to be flat. Strictly speaking, the known world of his day was, as he says, an island, for the mainlands of Asia, Africa, and Europe, formed but a single mass of land surrounded by sea. It is possible that he believed that the world was spherical, for Eratosthenes (276-196 B.C.; see Ser. No. 74 [D.D.C. 912.30]) not only accepted this view, but gave the earth a circumference of 250,000 stadia (25,000 miles). This, in view of the fact that Ptolomy utilised much earlier maps, seemingly Tyrian, based on a treatment of the earth as a sphere, indicates that the spherical form had been known long prior to the time of Aristotle, who was in all probability aware of the matter. But when we stop to consider the precision with which the British Isles were mapped by the ancients, it is evident that the geographical knowledge of Aristotle, and the later Greeks generally, with regards the distant west, was already in a state of decline.

The writings of the geographer Strabo, born in Pontus in 64 or 63 B.C., illustrate this decline, for when writing of Ireland, he had of necessity to cite Pytheas, Eratosthenes, and others, for sources of information. In view of the deficiency of, and errors in, his own knowledge, his presumption in criticising earlier sources as he does, is surprising; he says:

"Next, in determining the breadth of the inhabited world, Eratosthenes says that, beginning at Meroe and measuring on the meridian that runs through Meroe, it is ten thousand stadia to Alexandria; and thence to the Hellespont about eight thousand one hundred; thence to the Borysthenes five thousand; then to the parallel circle that runs through Thule (which Pytheas says is a six days' sail north of Britain, and is near the frozen sea) about eleven thousand five hundred more . . .

However, with one exception, let all the distances of Eratosthenes be granted him—for they are sufficiently agreed upon; but what man of sense could grant his distance from the Borysthenes to the parallel of Thule? For not only has the man who tells about Thule, Pytheas, been found, upon scrutiny, to be an arch-falsifier, but the men who have seen Britain and Ierne do not mention Thule, though they speak of other islands, small ones, about Britain; and Britain itself stretches alongside of Celtica with a length about equal thereto, being not greater in length than five thousand stadia, and its limits are defined by the extremities of Celtica which lie opposite its own. For the eastern extremity of the one country lies opposite the eastern extremity of the other, and the western extremity of the one opposite the western of the other; and their eastern extremities, at all events, are near enough to each other for a person to see across from one to the other—I mean Cantium (Kent) and the mouths of the Rhine. But Pytheas declares that the length of Britain is more than twenty thousand stadia, and that Cantium is several days' sail from Celtica; and in his account both of the Ostiminians and of what is beyond the Rhine as far as Scythia he has in every case falsified the regions" (*Geography*, i. 4; H. L. Jones' trans.).

"And yet the voyage from Celtica to the north is nowadays called the remotest voyage to the north; I mean the voyage to Ierne, which island not only lies beyond Britain, but is such a wretched place to live in on account of the cold that the regions on beyond are regarded as uninhabitable. And Ierne is not farther from Celtica, they say, than five thousand stadia; so that about thirty thousand stadia all told or perhaps a few more, would represent the breadth of the inhabited world" (*Geography*, ii, l).

"Now Pytheas of Massilia tells us that Thule, the most northerly of the Britannic Islands, is farthest north, and that there the circle of the summer tropic is the same as the arctic circle. But from the other writers I learn nothing on the subject—neither that there exists a certain island by the name of Thule, nor whether the northern regions are inhabitable up to the point where the summer tropic becomes the arctic circle. But in my opinion the northern limit of the inhabited world is much farther to the south than where the summer tropic becomes the arctic circle. For modern scientific writers are not able to speak of any country north of Ierne, which lies to the north of Britain and near thereto, and is the home of men who are complete savages and lead a miserable existence because of the cold; and therefore, in my opinion, the northern limit of our inhabited world is to be placed there" (*ibid.* ii, 5.)

Strabo proceeds to accuse the Irish of gross immorality, but shows sufficient restraint to admit; "I am saying this only with the understanding that I have no trustworthy witnesses for it", which may mean only that he had read or heard some exaggerated travellers' tales, or had passed on a misinterpretation of native communal customs which were not necessarily as offensive as they had been made to appear.

Strabo's disdainful treatment of Pytheas, in particular, who claimed to have travelled the length and breadth of Britain, and whose account rings true, is only equalled by his presumption in fancying himself as a critic on the subject. Why, for instance, should the omission of any mention of Thule, which is seemingly Iceland (see Ser. No. 74 [D.D.C. 912.30]), by those who had seen Britain and Ierne in any way discredit Pytheas' account of it? Or why should not the journey from Celtica to Britain take several days, despite the fact that the one is visible from the other? The duration of such a journey depends entirely upon the distance apart of the points of departure and arrival, upon the winds, and not least in the vicinity of the Straits of Dover, upon the currents. Modern authorities indicate that these Straits first appeared about 5000 B.C., so that in the centuries B. C., they were much narrower than now, had much more violent currents, and may have been unsafe for navigation. Furthermore, although Strabo was correct in saying in effect that one could see across the Channel, he was in error in making the Rhine join the sea at the nearest point to Britain. The 'length' of 20,000 stadia given to Britain, may have been intended as a circumference.

Strabo's distorted ideas of Ireland are perhaps eclipsed by the almost complete lack of knowledge of that land on he part of the Romans. The silence of the great Caesar on the subject may indicate how little he knew of it. His invasion of Britain does not seem to have increased his knowledge of what lay beyond the Irish sea; and his sole reference to this could have been improved upon by reference to earlier Greek writings. Caesar's only reference to Ireland is an indirect and misleading one. In describing the outline of Britain, he says:

"The island is triangular in its form, and one of its sides is opposite to Gaul. One angle of this side, which is in Kent, whither almost all ships from Gaul are directed, [looks] to the east; the lower looks to the south. This side extends about 500 miles. Another side lies towards Spain and the west, on which part is Ireland, less, as is reckoned, than Britain by one-half; but the passage [from it] into Britain is of equal distance with that from Gaul. In the middle of this voyage is an island, which is called Mona; many smaller islands besides are supposed to lie [there], of which islands some have written that at the time of the winter solstice it is night there for thirty consecutive days. We, in our inquiries about that matter, ascertained nothing, except that, by accurate measurements with water, we perceived the nights to be shorter there than on the continent" (*Gaul*, v, 13).

The occupation of Britain by Roman forces seems to have added nothing of value to their knowledge of Ireland. Tacitus, writing of Agricola's penetration into North Britain, makes his only, and probably a somewhat boastful, reference to Ireland, on which Roman soldiers were never able to set foot:

"In the fifth summer, Agricola made an expedition by sea. He embarked in the first Roman vessel that ever crossed the estuary, and having penetrated into regions till then unknown, he defeated the inhabitants in several engagements, and lined the coast, which lies opposite to Ireland, with a body of troops; not so much from an apprehension of danger, as with a view to future projects. He saw that Ireland, lying between Britain and Spain, and at the same time convenient to the ports of Gaul, might prove a valuable acquisition, capable of giving an easy communication, and, of course, strength and union, to the provinces disjoined by nature.

"Ireland is less than Britain, but exceeds in magnitude all the islands of the Mediterranean. The soil, the climate, the manners and genius of the inhabitants, differ little from those of Britain. By the means of merchants resorting thither for the sake of commerce, the harbours and approaches to the coast are well known. One of their petty kings, who had been forced to fly from the fury of a domestic faction, was received by the Roman general, and, under a show of friendship, detained to be of use on some future occasions. I have often heard Agricola declare that a single legion, with a moderate band of auxiliaries, would be sufficient to complete the conquest of Ireland. Such an event, he said, would contribute greatly to bridle the stubborn spirit of the Britons, who, in that case, would see, with dismay, the Roman arms triumphant, and every spark of liberty extinguished round their coast" (*Agricola*, xxiv).

The decline in first-hand knowledge of the later Greeks on the subject of the British Isles is not difficult to explain. In an earlier age, we are told, the Phoenicians had traded with this region, and Greek mariners were seemingly also familiar with it; but with the weakening of their nations, communications with the distant west dwindled and finally ceased when Rome destroyed Carthage in 163 B.C. We know, for instance, that prior to the sixth century B.C., the Greek city of Miletus in Asia Minor had become "the most powerful maritime and commercial place; its ships sailed to every part of the Mediterranean, and even into the Atlantic ... The period during which Miletus acquired this extraordinary power and prosperity, was that between its occupation by the Ionians and its conquest by the Persians, 494 B.C." (Wm. Smith's *Dictionary of Greek and Roman Geography*). The decline of the Greeks as a power, and the ultimate cessation of all trade and communications between the eastern Mediterranean and the Atlantic resulted in the great deterioration of their knowledge which we are now considering.

Diodorus Siculus, writing about 49 B.C., like Strabo, relied upon earlier accounts of the distant west. He made use of information passed on by Hecataeus, (who wrote about the time of Alexander the Great), as well as of materials handed down by other writers. Diodorus, following Hecataeus, calls the people of what we may reasonably assume to be Ireland, Hyperboreans, for a reason that he makes clear, and states that they were friendly towards the Greeks, from which it must be implied that there had been intimate contacts between the two peoples. Diodorus states:

". . . we feel that it will not be foreign to our purpose to discuss the legendary accounts of the Hyperboreans. Of those who have written about the ancient myths, Hecataeus and certain others say that in the regions beyond the land of the Celts there lies in the ocean an island no smaller than Sicily. This island, the account continues, is situated in the north and is inhabited by the Hyperboreans, who are called by that name because their home is beyond the point whence the north wind (Boreas) blows; and the island is both fertile and productive of every crop, and since it has an unusually temperate climate it produces two harvests each year. Moreover, the following legend is told concerning it: Leto was born on this island, and for that reason Apollo is honoured among them above all other gods; and the inhabitants are looked upon as priests of Apollo, after a manner, since daily they praise this god continuously in song and honour him exceedingly. And there is also on the island both a magnificent sacred precinct of Apollo and a notable temple which is adorned with many votive offerings and is spherical in shape. Furthermore, a city is there which is sacred to this god, and the majority of its inhabitants are players on the cithara; and these continually play on this instrument in the temple and sing hymns of praise to the god, glorifying his deeds.

"The Hyperboreans also have a language, we are informed, which is peculiar to them, and are most friendly disposed towards the Greeks, and especially towards the Athenians and the Delians, who have inherited this good will from most ancient times. The myth also relates that certain Greeks visited the Hyperboreans and left behind them their costly votive offerings bearing inscriptions in Greek letters. And in the same way Abaris, a Hyperborean, came to Greece in ancient times and renewed the good will and kinship of his people to the Delians. They say also that the moon, as viewed from this island, appears to be but a little distance from the earth and to have upon it prominences, like those of the earth, which are visible to the eye. The account is also given that the god visits the island every nineteen years, the period in which the return of the stars to the same place in the heavens is accomplished; and for this reason the nineteen year period is called by the Greeks the 'year of Meton'. At the time of this appearance of the god he both plays on the cithara and dances continuously the night through from the vernal equinox until the rising of the Pleiades, expressing in this manner his delight in his successes. And the kings of this city and the supervisors of the sacred precinct are called Boreades, since they are descendants of Boreas, and the succession to these positions is always kept in their family" (Bk. II, xlvii, 1-6, C. H. Oldfather's trans.).

Several features of Diodorus' account deserve mention. It is certainly much more impartial and accurate than the story given by Strabo. It leads us to believe that the 19-year soli-lunar cycle, discovered by the Greek astronomer Meton and introduced in Athens in 432 B.C., was observed in Ireland. If so, it is evident that this particular detail of information was derived from Ireland some time after the knowledge of the Metonic cycles had been conveyed thither.

Some form of optical instrument seems to have been in use in Ireland prior to the time of Diodorus' sources. It is interesting to speculate as to what form this instrument possessed; and crude though it may have been by modern standards, its achievement must be regarded as remarkable for its time. Some connections may also be seen between the Boreades, the "supervisors of the sacred precinct" and the *Bardic* office.

The rites of Apollo, supposed to have been observed by these Hyperboreans, deserve some mention. The gods of Greek mythology, according to the Greeks themselves, were mainly of Egyptian origin. Herodotus informs us that:

"Almost all the names of the gods came into Greece from Egypt. My inquiries prove that they were all derived from a foreign source, and my opinion is that Egypt furnished the greater number" (ii, 50).

The Greeks, unlike the Egyptians, paid divine honours to heroes, as we are informed by Herodotus in the same passage. In fact, Cicero, in his *Tusculan Questions*, informs us that: "The gods of the popular religions were all but deceased mortals advanced from earth to heaven". It would seem that we may regard Apollo in some such light; his original is evidently to be found in Egypt, "the country where mythology places the origin of the gods" (*Diodorus Siculus*, I, ix, 6).

Important communities of the Greeks may be identified as Israelitish, as in the cases of those of the Lacedaemonians, whose capital was Sparta (Ser. No. 8 [D.D.C. 572.9389]), the Milesians, whose royal family came from Crete, and was evidently of Judah (Ser. No. 81 [D.D.C. 579.93918]), the Trojans (Ser. No. 83 [D.D.C. 572.942]), and the people we now consider, the Athenians, the chief people of Attica (Ser. No. 41 [D.D.C. 572.938]). It is not surprising therefore, that the origin of the Greek gods is traceable to Egypt, where the Israelites had developed from a small clan into a numerous people "more and mightier" (*Ex.* i. 9) than the natives of that land.

The attributes of Apollo are essentially those of Moses. There were at least four Apollos, three of whom derived their name from the original, who excelled in: "all the fine arts, of medicine, music, poetry, and eloquence, of all which he was deemed the inventor. He had received from Jupiter the power of knowing futurity, and he was the only one of the gods whose oracles were in general repute over the world . . ." (Lempriere's *Classical Dictionary*).

The original of the Apollo legend indicates that like Moses, he was a native of Egypt, for: "The tradition that the son of Latona was born on the floating island of Delos, is taken from the Egyptian mythology, which asserts that the son of Vulcan, which is supposed to be Orus, was saved by his mother Isis from the persecution of Typhon, and entrusted to the care of Latona, who concealed him in the islands of Chemnis . . ." (*ibid.*).

It is to be recalled that, in a parallel fashion, Moses, as a child, was saved from the Egyptian persecution by being set afloat.

Apollo, like Moses, slew a man, and then left his country, for Diodorus informs us that after a musical contest, Apollo slew the pipist Marsyas, in consequence of which he "laid away the lyre and pipes as a votive offering in the cave of Dionysus, and becoming enamoured of Cybele joined in her wanderings as far as the land of the Hyperboreans" (iii. 59).

Apollo was in later times confused with the sun; he was tutelary god of the Athenians, and was commonly "represented with a crown of rays on his head" (Lempriere). This also finds a parallel in the case of Moses: "And it came to pass, when Moses came down from mount Sinai with the two tables of testimony in Moses' hand, when he came down from the mount, that Moses wist not that the skin of his face shone while he talked with him. And when Aaron and all the children of Israel saw Moses, behold, the skin of his face shone; and they were afraid to come nigh him . . . And till Moses had done speaking with them, he put a vail on his face. But when Moses went in before the Lord to speak with him, he took the vail off, until he came out. And he came out, and spake unto the children of Israel that which he was commanded. And the children of Israel saw the face of Moses, that the skin of Moses' face shone: and Moses put the vail upon his face again, until he went to speak with him" (Ex. xxxiv: 29-35).

A further indication that the original Apollo may have been Moses, is to be seen in his rites as described, in particular, by Homer:

"The host to expiate next the king prepares,
With pure lustrations, and with solemn prayers.
Wash'd by the briny wave, the pious train
Are cleansed; and cast the ablutions in the main.
Along the shore whole hecatombs were laid,
And bulls and goats to Phoebus' (Apollo) altars paid;
The sable fumes in curling spires arise,
And waft their grateful odours to the skies.
The army thus in sacred rites engaged . . ." (*Iliad*, Bk. 1; Pope's trans.).

"Then near the altar of the darting king,
Disposed in rank their hecatomb they bring;
With water purify their hands, and take
The sacred offering of the salted cake;
While thus with arms devoutly raised in air,
And solemn voice, the priest directs his prayer:
"God of the silver bow, thy ear incline . . ."

And now the Greeks their hecatomb prepare;
Between their horns the salted barley threw,
And, with their heads to heaven, the victims slew:
The limbs they sever from the inclosing hide;
The thighs, selected to the gods, divide:
On these, in double cauls involved with art,
The choicest morsels lay from every part.
The priest himself before his altar stands,
And burns the offering with his holy hands,
Pours the black wine, and sees the flames aspire;
The youths with instruments surround the fire:
The thighs thus sacrificed, and entrails dress'd,
The assistants part, transfix, and roast the rest:
Then spread the tables, the repast prepare;
Each takes his seat, and each receives his share.
When now the rage of hunger was repress'd
With pure libations they conclude the feast;
The youths with wine the copious goblets crown'd,
And, pleased, dispense the flowing bowls around;
With hymns divine the joyous banquet ends,
The paeans lengthen'd till the sun descends:
The Greeks, restored, the grateful notes prolong;
Apollo listens, and approves the song" (*ibid.*).

This sacrificial ritual, repugnant to the Egyptians, is clearly Mosiac, as comparison with the Pentateuch will show. In both the Greek and Hebrew sacrifices we find the slaying of bulls and goats, and meat and drink offerings which, when rendered, were consumed (see Num. xviii, xxviii; Deut. xii; etc.); and among both peoples was a priestly class serving identical functions. Such then, were the rites of Apollo which Greek authors would have us believe were observed anciently by the Hyperboreans.

Boreas, whose name was given to the North Wind, beyond whose home the Greeks conceived the people of Ireland to live, was much venerated by the Athenians, who "dedicated altars to him, and to the winds, when Xerxes invaded Europe. Boreas changed himself into a horse, to unite himself with the mares of Dardanus, by which he had mares so swift, that they ran or rather flew over the sea, without scarce wetting their feet" (Lempriere). Such, evidently, is the manner in which the movement of a Trojan colony into northern realms was entered in the pages of the mythology of the Greek mysteries.

It is evident from Greek writers, that a friendly relationship existed between the Hyperboreans and the people of Delos and Athens in particular. Pindar, who, according to Suidas, was born in the third year of the 65th Olympiad, or 522 B.C., played upon the imagination with good effect by associating the voyage to the land of the Hyperboreans with mystery:

"Neither by ships nor by land canst thou find the
wonderous road to the trysting-place of the Hyperboreans" (*Pythian Odes*, x. 30; Sandy's trans.).

Pausanius, the Greek traveller of the second century A.D., several times mentions the Hyperboreans, and states that they had sent offerings to Delos:

"At Prasiae is a temple of Apollo. Hither they say are sent the first-fruits of the Hyperboreans, and the Hyperboreans are said to hand them over to the Arimaspi, the Arimaspi to the Issedones, from these the Scythians bring them to Sinope, thence they are carried by the Greeks to Prasiae, and the Athenians take them to Delos" (*Attica*, xxxi, 2).

This account would seem to indicate that there was a mainland colony of Hyperboreans; but Herodotus, in his earlier enquiries into this matter, was unable to trace such, although he admits that Ariteas says they "extended to the sea" (iv. 13), and were among the most northerly of nations. Herodotus writes:

"Of the Hyperboreans nothing is said either by the Scythians or by any of the other dwellers in these regions, unless it be the Issedonians. But in my opinion, even the Issedonians are silent concerning them; otherwise the Scythians would have repeated their statements . . ." (iv. 32).

Herodotus gives an account, rather similar to that of Pausanius and possibly the forerunner of it, of how the Hyperboreans sent offerings to Delos, seemingly long before his time, which may explain his lack of exact knowledge on the subject:

"But the persons who have by far the most to say on this subject are the Delians. They declare that certain offerings, packed in wheaten straw, were brought from the country of the Hyperboreans into Scythia, and that the Scythians received them and passed them on to their neighbours upon the west, who continued to pass them on until at last they reached the Adriatic. From hence they were sent southward, and when they came to Greece, were received first of all by the Dodonæans. Thence they descended to the Maliac Gulf, from which they were carried across into Eubœa, where the people handed them on from city to city, till they came at length to Carystus. The Carystians took them over to Delos, without stopping at Andros; and the Tenians finally brought them to Delos. Such, according to their own account, was the road by which the offerings reached the Delians. Two damsels, they say, named Hyperoché and Laodicé, brought the first offerings from the Hyperboreans; and with them the Hyperboreans sent five men, to keep them from all harm on the way; these are the persons whom the Delians call 'Perpherees,' and to whom great honours are paid at Delos. Afterwards the Hyperboreans, when they found that their messengers did not return, thinking it would be a grievous thing always to be liable to lose the envoys they should send, adopted the following plan:—they wrapped their offerings in the wheaten straw, and bearing them to their borders, charged their neighbours to send them forward from one nation to another, which was done accordingly, and in this way the offerings reached Delos" (iv. 33).

"The damsels sent by the Hyperboreans died in Delos; and in their honour all the Delian girls and youths are wont to cut off their hair" (iv. 34).

"They add that once before, there came to Delos by the same road as Hyperoché and Laodicé, two other virgins from the Hyperboreans, whose names are Argé and Opis. Hyperoché and Laodicé had come to bring to Ilithyia the offering which they laid upon themselves, in acknowledgment of their quick labours; but Argé and Opis came at the same time as the gods of Delos [Apollo and Diana], and are honoured by the Delians in a different way. For the Delian women make collections in these maidens' names, and invoke them in the hymn which Olen, a Lycian, composed for them; and the rest of the islanders, and even the Ionians, have been taught by the Delians to do the like. This Olen, who came from Lycia, made the other old hymns which are sung in Delos. The Delians add, that the ashes from the thigh-bones burnt upon the altar are scattered over the tomb of Opis and Argé. Their tomb lies behind the temple of Diana, facing the east, near the banquetting-hall of the Ceians" (iv. 35).

Other items might be quoted from early sources; but the foregoing will suffice to show that there was a very real belief among the Greeks that at one time friendly contacts had obtained between themselves and the distant Hyperboreans, who, according to Diodorus, were an island people, seemingly to be identified with the Irish.

The evidence on the whole indicates that Ireland had been colonised by people either from Greece, or with Greek affinities, before the time of Herodotus. The native Irish histories, in turn, relate that a people from Greece colonised their country; so that there is a measure of agreement on the subject, despite the fact that much remains to be clarified.

Serial No. 93e.

Published by The National Message, Ltd.
6 Buckingham Gate, London, S.W.1.

Authorities:

JOHN MILTON, *The History of Britain.*
JOHN STOW, *Annales of England.*

ACCORDING to the firm ancient legends, transmitted both by British and by Continental writers, a Trojan colony, led by one Brutus, settled in the British Isles not long after the fall of Troy, and established the line of early British kings from which the famous Caractacus and Boadicea were in due course descended.

The British version of these legends was handed down by Geoffrey of Monmouth (*d.* 1154 A.D.). Although his account has been described as a forgery by later writers, as pointed out by the Elizabethan antiquary Stow, the Brutus story was current long before Geoffrey's time, so that whatever may have been added by him in the way of imaginative detail, at least he did not invent the basic tradition.

Historical and mythological accounts of the Trojans indicate a strong original racial connection with the Hebrews. There is little doubt that adventurers of several Israelite tribes, Dan and Judah in particular, were involved in the wars of classical literature, which were the prime cause of Brutus' westward journey.

POINTS OF SPECIAL INTEREST

1. Certain phases of Trojan history, such as the story of the destruction of Troy as given by Homer, have received the widespread attention of scholars. It is unfortunate that other aspects of that history, concerning the origin and dispersal of these people, have been given much less serious consideration. Classical genealogies, for instance, convey important information concerning the relationship of the Trojans to the people of Crete and Greece. A number of excellent reference works, such as Wm. Smith's *Dictionary of Greek and Roman Biography and Mythology*, and *Dictionary of Greek and Roman Geography*, the Oxford *Companion to Classical Literature*, and Lempriere's *Classical Dictionary*, will be found to be of great value in any study of our subject.

2. While it is impossible to obtain exact agreement in all respects of classical genealogies, they point to the common origin of important elements of Greek, Trojan, and Cretan peoples, especially where king-lines are concerned. Dardanus, son of Zeus, established Dardania (*Iliad*, xx. 248), a district north-east of Troy; and from his grandson Trōs, were named both the city of Troy and the district of the Troad. The following genealogy is derived from the Oxford *Companion to Classical Literature*:

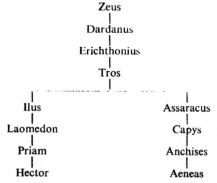

3. The Dardanians are referred to as early as the time of Ramses II (1558–1491 B.C.), when, as one of the confederacy of *Luka* (Lycians), *Pidasa* (Pisidians or Pedasians?), *Masa* (Mysians), *Dardenui* (Dardanians), *Iliunna* (?), *Kalikisha* (Cilicians), and *Mushant* (?) (*Cambridge Ancient History*, Vol. II, p. 281), they attacked Egypt as allies of the Hittites, the controlling elements of whom appear to have descended originally from Heth, son of Canaan, a distant kinsman of the Hebrews.

4. The Trojan war was a struggle between kindred peoples. Agamemnon, king of the Greek Mycenae, led the expedition against the Trojan Dardanians to recover Helen, the wife of his brother Menelaus, king of Sparta, or Lacedaemon, whose people claimed to be of Israelitish origin (Ser. No. 41 [572.938]). The following genealogy of these Greek kings is also taken from the Oxford *Companion*:

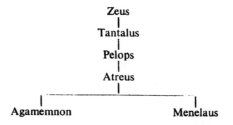

```
              Zeus
               |
            Tantalus
               |
             Pelops
               |
             Atreus
               |
      |------------------|
  Agamemnon          Menelaus
```

5. From the heights of Mt. Ida, above Troy, Zeus, said to have been born in a cave of the mountain of the same name in Crete, was stated to have observed the investment of the city by the forces under Agamemnon, king of Mycenae, which was also the name of a Cretan city. The name of Ida has been coupled by Tacitus with that of the Judaeans, who derived from the Biblical Judah (Ser. No. 81 [572.93918]).

6. Various details of circumstantial evidence appear to lend their support to the legend of the Trojan settlement of Britain. Ancient Irish accounts relate that a Partholanus, whose life was in important respects similar to that of Brutus, reached our islands at a very early date. Caesar's *Commentaries*, which tell of a people called Trinobantes (*Gaul*, v. 20), who lived in the vicinity of what are now Middlesex and Hertfordshire, seem to bear out the story of the Trojans' having founded Troja Nova, later called Trinovantum, and eventually London. The many archaeological discoveries of Roman and earlier times at Bath, the Roman *Aquae Sulis* (Sol being the counterpart of Minerva) might also be considered as favourable to the tradition of its having been founded by Bladud, a descendant of Brutus. The skilful employment of chariots by the British is also reminiscent of the Trojan use of this ancient weapon of war, as was observed by Diodorus of Sicily in the first century B.C.

7. According to the Trojan legend, the British Isles derived their name from Brutus, the leader of the expedition which established a settlement in these islands. The late Professor L. A. Waddell has pointed out that the name derived from that of a powerful people of Phoenician origin, the "Great Barats" (*Mahā Bārata*), a branch of which people, moving from their Phoenician homeland, established a great empire south of the Himalayas. Professor Waddell writes of . . . " 'The Great Barats' (*Mahā Bārata*), in regard to the prehistoric world-wide civilising conquests of the *Panch* or 'Phoenicians', the greatest ruling clan of the Aryan *Barats* or *Brihats*, who, as we shall find, were the ancestors of the '*Brits*' or *Brit-ons*, our own ancestors" (*Phoenician Origin of Britons, Scots and Anglo-Saxons*), 1925, p. 2).

EXTRACT FROM JOHN MILTON'S *HISTORY OF BRITAIN* (*The Prose Works of John Milton*; Westley and Davies, London, 1835, Bk. I).

MILTON, JOHN, after Shakespeare the greatest English poet, was born in Bread Street, Cheapside, on December 9th, 1608. . . . Milton is one of the poets respecting whose place in literature there has been least question, whether as regards the literature of their own country or that of the world. . . . After Homer there is no poet to whom the sublime is so much a native element. . . ." (*Chamber's Illustrated Encyclopaedia*, 1904).

Hitherto the things themselves have given us a warrantable dispatch to run them soon over. But now of Brutus and his line, with the whole progeny of kings, to the entrance of Julius Caesar, we cannot so easily be discharged; descents of ancestry, long continued, laws and exploits not plainly seeming to be borrowed, or devised, which on the common belief have wrought no small impression; defended by many, denied utterly by few. For what though Brutus and the whole Trojan pretence were yielded up; (seeing they who first devised to bring us from some noble ancestor, were content at first with Brutus the consul; till better invention, although not willing to forego the name, taught them to remove it higher into a more fabulous age, and by the same remove lighting on the Trojan tales in affectation to make the Britain of one original with the Roman, pitched there:) yet those old and inborn names of successive kings, never any to have been real persons, or done in their lives at least some part of what so long hath been remembered, cannot be thought without too strict an incredulity.

For these, and those causes above mentioned, that which hath received approbation from so many, I have chosen not to omit. Certain or uncertain, be that upon the credit of those whom I must follow; so far as keeps aloof from impossible and absurd, attested by ancient writers from books more ancient, I refuse not, as the due and proper subject of story. The principal author is well known to be Geoffrey of Monmouth; what he was, and whence his authority, who in his age, or before him, have delivered the same matter, and such like general discourses, will better stand in a treatise by themselves. All of them agree in this, that Brutus was the son of Silvius; he of Ascanius; whose father was Eneas a Trojan prince, who at the burning of that city, with his son Ascanius, and a collected number that escaped, after long wandering on the sea, arrived in Italy. Where at length by the assistance of Latinus king of Latiam, who had given him his daughter Lavinia, he obtained to succeed in that kingdom, and left it to Ascanius, whose son Silvius (though Roman histories deny Silvius to be the son of Ascanius) had married secretly a niece of Lavinia. She being with child, the matter became known to Ascanius. Who commanding his "magicians to inquire by art, what sex the maid had conceived", had answer, "that it was one who should be the death of both his parents; and banished for the fact, should after all, in a far country, attain the highest honour." The prediction failed not, for in travail the mother died. And Brutus (the child was so called) at fifteen years of age, attending his father to the chase, with an arrow unfortunately killed him.

Banished therefore by his kindred, he retires into Greece. Where meeting with race of Helenus king Priam's son, held there in servile condition by Pandrasus then king, with them he abides. For Pyrrhus, in revenge of his father slain at Troy, had brought thither with him Helenus, and many others into servitude. There Brutus among his own stock so thrives in virtue and in arms, as renders him beloved to kings and great captains, above all the youth of that land. Whereby the Trojans not only began to hope, but secretly to move him, that he would lead them the way to liberty. They allege their numbers, and the promised help of Assaracus a noble Greekish youth, by the mother's side a Trojan; whom for that cause his brother went about to dispossess of certain castles bequeathed him by his father. Brutus considering both the forces offered him, and the strength of those holds, not unwillingly consents.

First therefore having fortified those castles, he with Assaracus and the whole multitude betake them to the woods and hills, as the safest place from whence to expostulate; and in the name of all sends to Pandrasus this message, "That the Trojans holding it unworthy their ancestors to serve in a foreign kingdom had retreated to the woods; choosing rather a savage life than a slavish: if that displeased him, that then with his leave they might depart to some other soil."

As this may pass with good allowance that the Trojans might be many in these parts (for Helenus was by Pyrrhus made king of the Chaonians, and the sons of Pyrrhus by Andromache Hector's wife, could not but be powerful through all Epirus) so much the more it may be doubted, how these Trojans could be thus in bondage, where they had friends and countrymen so potent. But to examine these things with diligence, were but to confute the fables of Britain, with the fables of Greece or Italy: for of this age, what we have to say, as well concerning most other countries, as this island, is equally under question. Be how it will, Pandrasus not expecting so bold a message from the sons of captives, gathers an army; and marching towards the woods, Brutus who had notice of his approach nigh to the town called Sparatinum (I know not what town, but certain of no Greek name) overnight planting himself there with good part of his men, suddenly sets upon him, and with slaughter of the

Greeks pursues him to the passage of a river, which mine author names Akalon, meaning perhaps Achelous or Acheron; where at the ford he overlays them afresh. This victory obtained, and a sufficient strength left in Sparatinum, Brutus with Antigonus, the king's brother, and his friend Anacletus, whom he had taken in the fight, returns to the residue of his friends in the thick woods; while Pandrasus with all speed recollecting, besieges the town. Brutus to relieve his men besieged, who earnestly called him, distrusting the sufficiency of his force, bethinks himself of this policy. Calls to him Anacletus, and threatening instant death else, both to him and his friend Antigonus, enjoins him, that he should go at the second hour of night to the Greekish leagre, and tell the guards he had brought Antigonus by stealth out of prison to a certain woody vale, unable through the weight of his fetters to move him further, entreating them to come speedily and fetch him in. Anacletus to save both himself and his friend Antigonus, swears this, and at a fit hour sets on alone toward the camp; is met, examined, and at last unquestionably known. To whom, great profession of fidelity first made, he frames his tale, as had been taught him; and they now fully assured, with a credulous rashness leaving their stations, fared accordingly by the ambush that there awaited them. Forthwith Brutus divided his men into three parts, leads on in silence to the camp; commanding first each part at a several place to enter, and forbear execution, till he with his squadron possessed of the king's tent, gave signal to them by trumpet. The sound whereof no sooner heard, but huge havock begins upon the sleeping and unguarded enemy, whom the besieged also now sallying forth, on the other side assail. Brutus the while had special care to seize and secure the king's person; whose life still within his custody, he knew was the surest pledge to obtain what he should demand. Day appearing, he enters the town, there distributes the king's treasury, and leaving the place better fortified, returns with the king his prisoner to the woods. Straight the ancient and grave men he summons to council, what they should now demand of the king.

After long debate Mempricius, one of the gravest, utterly dissuading them from the thought of longer stay in Greece, unless they meant to be deluded with a subtle peace, and the awaited revenge of those whose friends they had slain, advises them to demand first the king's eldest daughter Innogen in marriage to their leader Brutus with a rich dowry, next shipping, money, and fit provision for them all to depart the land.

This resolution pleasing best, the king now brought in, and placed in a high seat, is briefly told, that on these conditions granted, he might be free; not granted he must be prepared to die.

Pressed with fear of death, the king readily yields; . especially to bestow his daughter on whom he confessed so noble and so valiant: offers them also the third part of his kingdom, if they like to stay; if not, to be their hostage himself, till he had made good his word.

The marriage therefore solemnized, and shipping from all parts got together, the Trojans in a fleet, no less written than three hundred four and twenty sail, betake them to the wide .ea: where with a prosperous course, two days and a night bring them on a certain island long before dispeopled and left waste by sea-rovers, the name thereof was then Leogecia, now unknown. They who were sent out to discover, came at length to a ruined city, where was a temple and image of Diana that gave oracles: but not meeting first or last, save wild beasts, they return with this notice to their ships; wishing that their general would inquire of that oracle what voyage to pursue.

Consultation had, Brutus taking with him Gerion his diviner, and twelve of the ancientest, with wanton ceremonies before the inward shrine of the goddess, in verse (as it seems the manner was) utters his request, "Diva potens nemorum," etc.

Goddess of shades, and huntress, who at will
Walk'st on the rolling sphere, and through the deep
On thy third reign the earth look now, and tell
What land, what seat of rest thou bidd'st me seek,
What certain seat, where I may worship thee
For aye, with temples vow'd, and virgin choirs.

To whom sleeping before the altar, Diana in a vision that night thus answered, "Brute sub occasium solis," etc.

Brutus, far to the west, in th' ocean wide,
Beyond the realm of Gaul, a land there lies,
Seagirt it lies, where giants dwelt of old,
Now void it fits thy people; thither bend
Thy course, there shalt thou find a lasting seat,
Where to thy sons another Troy shall rise;
And kings be born of thee, whose dreaded might
Shall awe the world, and conquer nations bold.

These verses originally Greek, were put in Latin, saith Virunnius, by Gildas a British poet, and him to have lived under Claudius. Which granted true, adds much to the antiquity of this fable; and indeed the Latin verses are much better, than of the age for Geoffrey ap Arthur, unless perhaps Joseph of Exeter, the only smooth poet of those times, befriended him. In this, Diana overshot her oracle thus ending, "Ipsis totius terrae subditus orbis erit"—That to the race of Brute, kings of this island, the whole earth shall be subject.

But Brutus guided now, as he thought, by divine conduct, speeds him toward the west; and after some encounters on the Afric side, arrives at a place on the Tyrrhene sea; where he happens to find the race of those Trojans, who with Antenor came into Italy; and Corineus, a man much famed, was their chief: though by surer authors it be reported, that those Trojans with Antenor were seated on the other side of Italy, on the Adriatic, not the Tyrrhene shore. But these joining company, and past the Herculean Pillars, at the mouth of Ligeris in Aquitania cast anchor: where after some discovery made of the place, Corineus, hunting nigh the shore with his men, is by messengers of the king Goffarius Pictus met, and questioned about his errand there. Who not answering to their mind, Imbertus, one of them, lets fly an arrow at Corineus, which he avoiding, slays him: and the Pictavian himself hereupon levying his whole force, is overthrown by Brutus, and Corineus; who with the battle-axe which he was wont to manage against the Tyrrhene giants, is said to have done marvels. But Goffarius having drawn to his aid the whole country of Gaul, at that time governed by twelve kings, puts his fortune to a second trial; wherein the Trojans, overborn by multitude, are driven back, and besieged in their own camp, which by good foresight was strongly situate. Whence Brutus unexpectedly issuing out, and Corineus in the meanwhile, whose device it was, assaulting them from behind from a wood, where he had conveyed his men the night before: the Trojans are again victors, but with the loss of Turon a valiant nephew of Brutus: whose ashes, left in that place, gives name to the city of Tours, built there by the Trojans. Brutus finding now his powers much lessened, and this yet not the place foretold him, leaves Aquitain, and with an easy course arriving at Totness in Devonshire, quickly perceives here to be the promised end of his labours.

The island, not yet Britain but Albion, was in a manner desert and inhospitable; kept only by a remnant of giants, whose excessive force and tyranny had consumed the rest. Them Brutus destroys, and to his people divides the land, which with some reference to his own name he thenceforth calls Britain. To Corineus, Cornwall, as now we call it, fell by lot; the rather by him liked, for that the hugest giants in rocks and caves were said to lurk still there; which kind of monsters to deal with was his old exercise.

And here with leave bespoken to recite a grand fable, though dignified by our best poets: while Brutus, on a certain festival day solemnly kept on that shore, where he first landed, was with the people in great jollity and mirth, a crew of these savages breaking in upon them, began on a sudden another sort of game, than at such a meeting was expected. But at length by many hands overcome, Goemagog the hugest, in height twelve cubits, is reserved alive, that with him Corineus, who desired nothing more, might try his strength; whom in a wrestle the giant catching aloft, with a terrible hug broke three of his ribs: nevertheless, Corineus enraged, heaving him up by main force, and on his shoulders bearing him to the next high rock, threw him headlong, all shattered, into the sea, and left his name on the cliff, called ever since Langoemagog, which is to say, the giant's leap.

After this, Brutus in a chosen place builds Troja Nova, changed in time to Trinovantum, now

London: and began to enact laws; Heli being then high priest in Judaea: and having governed the whole isle twenty four years, died, and was buried in his new Troy. His three sons, Locrine, Albanact, and Camber, divide the land by consent. Locrine had the middle part Loegria; Camber possessed Cambria, or Wales; Albanact, Albania, now Scotland. But he in the end by Humber king of the Hunds, who with a fleet invaded that land, was slain in fight, and his people drove back into Loegria. Locrine and his brother go out against Humber; who now marching onward, was by them defeated, and in a river drowned, which to this day retains his name. Among the spoils of his camp and navy, were found certain young maids, and Estrildis above the rest, passing fair, the daughter of a king in Germany; from whence Humber, as he went wasting the sea coast, had led her captive: whom Locrine, though before contracted to the daughter of Corineus, resolves to marry. But being forced and threatened by Corineus, whose authority and power he feared, Guendolen the daughter he yields to marry, but in secret loves the other: and ofttimes retiring, as to some private sacrifice, through vaults and passages made under ground, and seven years thus enjoying her, had by her a daughter equally fair, whose name was Sabra. But when once his fear was off by the death of Corineus, not content with secret enjoyment, divorcing Guendolen, he makes Estrildes now his queen. Guendolen, all in rage, departs into Cornwall, where Madan, the son she had by Locrine, was hitherto brought up by Corineus his grandfather. And gathering an army of her father's friends and subjects, gives battle to her husband by the river Sture; wherein Locrine, shot with an arrow, ends his life. But not so ends the fury of Guendolen; for Estrildis, and her daughter Sabra, she throws into a river; and, to leave a monument of revenge, proclaims that the stream be thenceforth called after the damsel's name; which, by length of time, is now changed to Sabrina, or Severn.

Fifteen years she governs in behalf of her son; then resigning to him at age, retires to her father's dominion. This, saith my author, was in the days of Samuel. Madan hath the praise to have well and peacefully ruled the space of forty years, leaving behind him two sons, Mempricius, and Malim. Mempricius had first to do with the ambition of his brother, aspiring to share with him in the kingdom; whom therefore, at a meeting to compose matters, with a treachery, which his cause needed not, he slew.

Nor was he better in the sole possession, whereof so ill he could endure a partner, killing his nobles, and those especially next to succeed him; till lastly, given over to unnatural lust, in the twentieth of his reign, hunting in a forest, he was devoured by wolves.

His son Ebranc, a man of mighty strength and stature, reigned forty years. He first, after Brutus, wasted Gaul; and returning rich and prosperous, builded Caerebranc, now York; in Albania, Alclud, Mount Agned, or the Castle of Maidens, now Edinburgh. He had twenty sons and thirty daughters by twenty wives. His daughters he sent to Silvius Alba into Italy, who bestowed them on his peers of the Trojan line. His sons, under the leading of Assaracus their brother, won them lands and signiories in Germany; thence called from these bretheren, Germania; a derivation too hastily supposed, perhaps before the word Germanus, or the Latin tongue was in use. Some who have described Henault, as Jacobus Bergomas, and Lassabeus, are cited to affirm, that Ebranc, in his war there, was by Brunchildis, lord of Henault, put to the worse.

Brutus, therefore, surnamed Greenshield, succeeding, to repair his father's losses, as the same Lessabeus reports, fought a second battle in Henault, with Brunchild, at the mouth of Scaldis, and encamped on the river Hania. Of which our Spencer also thus sings:

Let Scaldis tell, and let tell Hania,
And let the marsh of Esthambruges tell
What colour were their waters that same day,
And all the moor twixt Elversham and Dell,

With blood of Henalois, which therein fell;
How oft that day did sad Brunchildis see
The Greenshield dyed in dolorous vermeil, etc.

But Henault, and Brunchild, and Greenshield, seem newer names than for a story pretended thus ancient.

Him succeeded Leil, a maintainer of peace and equity; but slackened in his latter end, whence arose some civil discord. He built, in the North, Cairleil; and in the days of Soloman.

Rudhuddibras, or Hudibras, appeasing the commotions which his father could not, founded Caerkeynt or Canterbury, Caerguent or Winchester, and Mount Paladur, now Septonia or Shaftesbury: but this by others is contradicted.

Bladud his son built Caerbadus or Bath, and those medicinal waters he dedicated to Minerva; in whose temple there he kept fire continually burning. He was a man of great invention, and taught necromancy; till having made him wings to fly, he fell down upon the temple of Apollo in Trinovant, and so died after twenty years reign.

EXTRACT FROM JOHN STOW'S *ANNALES OF ENGLAND*, 1614.

STOW, JOHN (c. 1525-1605), English historian and antiquarian. His first work, published in 1561 was *The Woorkes of Geffrey Chaucer, Newly Printed With Divers Addicions Whiche Were Never in Printe Before.* In 1565, this was followed by his *Summarie of Englyshe Chronicles*; and in 1580 by his *Annales, or a Generale Chronicle of England from Brute Until the Present Yeare of Christe* 1580. His best known work, the *Survey of London*, was published in 1598, and is "of unique value from its minute account of the buildings, social condition and customs in the time of Elizabeth". Stow was a friend of Archbishop Parker; was poor all his life, and was authorized by James I to appeal for alms in 1604 (compiled from the *Encyclopaedia Britannica*, 1946).

The Law of God forbiddeth us to receive a false report, and the law of Histories is, that wee ought to publish no falsehood, nor dissemble any truth If in anything this ought to be observed, it ought to bee in the preservation of those monuments which do set forth the memorie of our ancestors, the honour of our ancient Fathers, the mercies of God upon our country, and his judgements warning us what to follow and avoide: this excellent use of ancient stories we are deprived of, by those who when they have laide hold upon some one or two mistakings in the life of some one man, doe by and by not only denie that there was any such man, but dash and cashire a whole succession of Princes and the consenting testimonies of many learned and worthy historians. The example hereof is in Brute the first king of this Monarchy, who in that age when almost all the world, especially Europe, ran doting in desire of the Trojan or Italian ancestors, some writers fabled to be the sonne of Silvius, descended from Aeneas, and that he killed his father and came by Oracle to Britaine: these things learned men finding different to the Romayne Story, some left out of the Pedigree of the British kings. Nuberigensis maketh a solemne invective against Galfridus one of the penmen of that Chronicle speaking as may appeare more of spleene than of judgement. The most learned and dilligent Antiquary master Cambden for his own censure doth not denie the person of Brute but relateth the opinion of others. John of Whethamsted the first of whom I read of in the yeare 1449 setteth down some exceptions taken to the particular narrations of Brute, namely that he was the son of Silvius and that he killed his father and such like. Pollidor Virgill is the onely man I find, upon those particular exceptions although he confessed those things to be regestred, Per duos egregios historicos, yet hee rejecteth the whole history of Brute and his successors: by the same reason that he may reject all ancient histories, and himselfe deserveth to be rejected for his many fabulous narrations, as also Nuberigensis otherwise called William Petit, who hath not a fewe, who wrote bitterly against the historie of Jeffrey of Monmouth but never wrote a word against Henry of Huntingdon that wrote of the same things before the publication of Jeffries booke: his malice against the Britaines was, because being an earnest suitor for a Bishopricke in Wales, he was rejected by David Apowen then Prince of Wales. This Nuberigensis lived in the yeare 1165 and was the first that wrote against the Brittish history, but I do not stand to confute or answere their objections for it is alreadie done at large by

Sir John Price in the defence of Brittishe hystory, and briefly by maister doctor Powell in his Epistle prefixed to Ponticus, and most gravely and judiciously by master Lambert in his Perambulation of Kent, to me it shall suffice to write that the first that I finde directly to oppugne the history of Brute, is John of Wethampsted not two hundredth years agoe, and I do not read of many of our owne that agree with him, but Polidor, Bodin and other strangers, who may well be excused for their ignorance in British Antiquities and deserve not to be laid in ballance to counterprize the authoritiee of so many learned authors of our country, who with joynt consent have affirmed the British history, whose names, or so many of them as have come to my knowledge I have here set downe to be perused of such as desire to be satisfied.

Gildas Sapiens cited by Cestrensis Ponticus, Sir John Price and others, or as some call him Nennius.

Thomas Archbishop of Yorke in the time of William the Conqueror cited by Fox in his Booke of Monuments, ex Chronico Sigebuti.

Henry Huntingdon, stiled by Polidor, Egregius Historicus in other bookes but especially in his booke de origine Britanorum cited by maister Lambert.

Mathew of Paris a most wise, faithfull, and learned historian saith of Monmouth that he did translate the Britishe history into latine.

Mathew of Westminster in floribus nameth Brito for Brutus calling him the son of Ilicion descended from Javan, which pedigree is also found in Gildas

and the ancient British histories as it may appear by Sir John Price.

Giraldus Cambrensis who carped at Galfridus and yet followeth the historie of Brute.

Ranulfus Cestrensis, Alfredus cited in Polichronicon and Sir John Price.

Fasciculus Temporam, Johannes Anglicus, Honeden.

Geruasius, Simon Dunelmesis.

Petrus Lantoft about the time of Edward the second or Edward the third.

An ancient Chronicle in French verse, these three I sawe in the studie of Sir Robert Cotton a most learned judicious and diligent Antiquary.

Alanus ab Insulis in prophetias Merlin, Ponticus Virrumnius.

Sir John Price in defensione Britanicae Historie, Johannes Baleus in Centurys, John Leyland, John Copgreave, Robert Kelway in his reports of Law, Bolio 191, speaketh of Mulmutius the British king.

Fabian Graston, Lanquet, Cooper, Stow, Hollingshead, and maister Lambert in his perambulation of Kent, and many others (page 2).

But if neither these observations nor the traditions of the Britons from age to age, which never faild to keepe memory of Brute nor the authorities alledged, then let such as will search further read the ancient Chronicles of Italy, France, Spaine, and Germany, or the Cosmography of Sebastian Munster, Macrobius or Aeneas Silvius otherwise called Pyus Secundus in his Bohemyan history. . . . (pages 2, 3).

EXTRACT FROM THE REV. THOMAS MOORE'S *HISTORY OF DEVONSHIRE*, 1620, p. 61.

Fabulus as this narrative is on the face of it, and fit only to be thrown among the rubbish of similar stories abounding in ancient chronicles, still, say Sheringham and others, it ought not to be condemned altogether; it may contain truth, mixed with fable: nor was it the invention of Geoffrey, for the most ancient writers on British affairs have delivered similar narratives. Such, moreover, was the opinion concerning their origin, universally prevalent among the Britons at the time of the Saxon invasion. Henry of Huntington, a contemporary with Geoffrey, affirms, that he "found these things in diverse histories". Sigebertus, a Frenchman, about one hundred years before Geoffrey, mentions the chief exploits of Brutus, and asserts that all these events were related in the ancient

histories of Britain; and the whole, he concludes, agrees with what is observed by Bede, that the ancient Britons came from Armorica, which, the story says, was named Brittany from Brutus, and that from thence this island received its name. Nennius also, who lived about the ninth century, relates the history of Brutus, and affirms that he had taken it from the Roman annals, the chronicles of the Holy Fathers, and the histories of the Scots and Saxons, as well as from the traditions of his ancestors, and from the monuments of the ancient inhabitants of Britain. To all this it may be added, that the Cambro-Britons affirm that they sprung from Brutus the Trojan, who had three sons, of whom Cambrus reigned in the west, whilst Brutus himself gave his name to the whole island.

Serial No. 83*d*.
Published by *The National Message*, Ltd.,
6 Buckingham Gate, London, S.W.1.
Copyright.

Authorities: Various

Israel, Tyre and Britain

THE Scriptures emphasise the friendly relationship which usually existed between the nation of Israel and the people of Tyre, the chief city of what the Greeks and Romans called *Phoenicia*. Hiram of Tyre provided Solomon with skilled workmen and materials for the building of the Temple. In return, Solomon presented Hiram with twenty cities of Galilee. "Judah, and the land of Israel", became Tyre's "merchants", and provided some of the materials and workmen for the construction and maintenance of the Tyrian fleet.

Through the medium of the fleets of Tyre and Israel ("ships of Tarshish"), the Israelites may confidently be regarded as having had direct knowledge of the people, land, and products of Britain. Though the great seaport of Tyre was cosmopolitan in the widest sense of the word, it is clear that the main population was Canaanite, with a generous admixture of Israelites and other Hebrew peoples.

Phoenicians and Israelites

The connections between the Phoenicians and the Israelites are much closer than has been realised. Both used the language of Canaan; and this undoubtedly indicates intimate association. Professor George Rawlinson, the translator of Herodotus, has remarked:

"It is primarily on account of their language that the Phoenicians are regarded as Semites. When there are no historical grounds for believing that a nation has laid aside its own original form of speech, and adopted an alien dialect, language, if not a certain, is at least a very strong, evidence of ethnic character. Counter-evidence may no doubt rebut the *prima facie* presumption; but in the case of the Phoenicians no counter-evidence is producible. They belong to exactly that geographic zone in which Semiticism has always had its chief seat; they cannot be shown to have been ever so circumstanced as to have had any inducement to change their speech, and their physical character and mental characteristics, would, by themselves, be almost sufficient ground for assigning them to the type whereto their language points" (*History of Phoenicia*, 1889, p. 52).

The Phoenicians are said by Herodotus to have come from the shores of the Erythræan Sea (Bk. i. 1; and vii. 89); this also was the case with the Hebrews.

Traditionally, the first king of Phoenicia, Agenor, was descended from Kronos, called Israel in Porphyry's version of Sanchoniathon, a Phoenician sage supposed to have lived before the Trojan period:

"For Kronus (or Saturn), whom the Phoenicians call Israel, and who after his death was deified, and instated in the planet which bears his name, when he was king, had by a nymph of the country, called Anobret, an only son, who, on that account, is Styled Iecud" (Cory's *Ancient Fragments*, 1876, pp. 21, 22).

From Saturn also descended the Greek, Trojan, and Milesian royal lines through Judah (Serial Nos. 8 [572.9389]; 41 [572.938]; 81 [572.93918]; 88 [929.2]).

The absence of reference by Greek and Roman writers to Israel by name, despite the fact that they mention the post-captivity Jews on various occasions, is highly significant. When referring to the land of Canaan, which Israel occupied, the Greeks and Romans called its people Phoenicians, or equivalents of that name. Classical references to the Phoenicians and their famed exploits may therefore be taken as applying in fair measure to Israel. The words of the historian Mommsen with regard to the Phoenicians are interesting in this respect:

"Their native seat was the narrow border of coast bounded by Asia Minor, the highlands of Syria, and Egypt, and called Canaan, that is, the 'plain'. This was the only name which the nation itself made use of; even in Christian times the African farmer called himself a Canaanite. But Canaan received from the Hellenes the name of Phoenike, the 'land of purple', or 'land of the red men' and the Italians also were accustomed to call the Canaanites Punians, as we are accustomed still to speak of them as the Phoenicians or Punis race." (History of Rome, 1913 ed., Vol. II, Bk. iii, ch 1, p. 131).

It is indicated by the prophet Ezekiel (chaps. xxvii, xxviii) that the prosperity of Tyre was interdependent with that of Israel. These nations rose and fell together; and in adversity the bonds of friendship continued between that part of Israel that remained in the Land, the Jews, and the survivors of Tyre and Sidon. Professor Rawlinson has observed that: "Hiram's friendly dealings with David and Solomon are well known; but the *continued* alliance between the Phoenicians and the Israelites has attracted less attention." He points out that Solomon took wives from Phoenicia (I *Ki*. xi. 1); Ahab married the daughter of Ithobalus, king of Sidon (I *Ki*. xvi. 21); Phoenicia furnished timber for the second Temple

Serial No. 92a.

(*Ezra* iii. 7); Isaiah wound up his prophecy against Tyre with a consolation (*Isa.* xxiii. 15–18); it was a Syro-Phoenician woman in whom our Lord found faith when there was unbelief among the Jews (*Mark* vii. 26–30); and that "in the days of Herod Agrippa, Tyre and Sidon still desired peace with Judea 'because their country was nourished by the King's country' " (*Acts* xii. 20).

The Phoenician Fleet: A Key Factor in the Ancient World

There can be no doubt that the so-called Phoenicians were a highly cultured· and powerful people possessing the finest naval power of their day, with an empire that included coastlands and islands of the Mediterranean and the Iberian peninsula. The extent to which the ancient powers were dependent upon the Phoenicians for maritime transport, even when Tyre itself was in decline, is freely admitted, even by modern writers: "To the great powers, Phoenician ships were indispensable; Sennacherib, Psammetichus and Necho, Xerxes, Alexander, all in turn employed them for their transports and seafights" (*Encyclopaedia Britannica*, 1946 art.: 'Phoenicia').

We are told that as late as the time of Cambyses (529–522 B.C.), Persia was unable to undertake the reduction of Carthage in Crete because the Phoenicians refused to transport that monarch's force against their kinsmen (*Herod.* iii. 19). In effect, conquest of the then known world could not be accomplished without the assistance of the Phoenicians.

Some indication of the place held by the Phoenicians as a sea power may also be gathered from Herodotus' statement concerning the Persian fleet at the battle of Marathon: "On board every ship was a band of soldiers, Persians, Medes, or Sacans. The Phoenician ships were the best sailers in the fleet, and the Sidonian the best among the Phoenician" (vii. 96).

We are indebted to Herodotus for a record of a remarkable voyage undertaken by Phoenicians about 600 B.C. He says that Pharaoh ordered a number of ships manned by Phoenicians to circumnavigate Africa (Libya, as it was called). This they did, returning in the third year through the Pillars of Hercules (Strait of Gibraltar), and reporting that the sun had been on their "right hand" (*Herod.* iv. 42); throughout the voyage, which accords with such a journey.

Herodotus states that Spain, or Iberia, possessed great natural wealth, especially in silver, which was transported throughout the ancient world in Phoenician ships (v. 35). Later writers who possessed a better knowledge of the distant west than did Herodotus record that the Phoenicians extensively settled Spain and had trading contacts with regions beyond. Strabo states that the Phoenicians became masters of Spain:

"As for the people of the west, Homer makes plain that they were prosperous and that they lived in a temperate climate—doubtless having heard of the wealth of Iberia, and how, in quest of that wealth, Heracles invaded the country, and after him the Phoenicians also, the people who in earliest times became masters of most of the country (it was at a later date that the Romans occupied it)" (I. i. 4).

Strabo also relates, among other things, that according to Timosthenes, Calpé, formerly called Heracleia, in Spain, was an old Phoenician port founded by Hercules, and that there the early city walls and docks were still to be seen (III. i. 7). Calpé was also the name of the northern of the two "pillars" standing on either side of the Strait of Gibraltar. Strabo writes:

"In the first place, the expeditions of Heracles and of the Phoenicians, since they both reached as far as Iberia, suggested to Homer that the people of Iberia were in some way rich, and led a life of ease. Indeed, these people became so utterly subject to the Phoenicians that the greater number of the citizens in Turdetania and of the neighbouring places are now inhabited by the Phoenicians. Secondly, the expedition of Odysseus, as it seems to me, since it actually had been made to Iberia, and since Homer had learned about it through inquiry, gave him an historical pretext; and so he also transferred the *Odyssey*, just as he had already transferred the *Iliad*, from the domain of historical fact to that of creative art, and to that of mythical invention so familiar to the poets. For not only do the regions about Italy and Sicily and certain other regions betray signs of such facts, but in Iberia also a city of *Odysseia* is to be seen, and a temple of Athene, and countless other traces, not only of the wanderings of Odysseus, but also of other wanderings which took place thither after the Trojan War . . . the wanderings of Aeneas are a traditional fact, as also, those of Antenor, and those of the Henetians; similarly, also those of Diomedes, Menelaus, Odysseus, and several others. So then, the poet, informed through his inquiries of so many expeditions to the outermost parts of Iberia, and learning by hearsay about the wealth and the other good attributes of the country (for the Phoenicians were making these facts known), in fancy placed the abode of the blest there, and also the Elysian Plain . . .

The Phoenicians, I say, were the informants of Homer; and these people occupied the best of Iberia and Libya before the age of Homer, and continued to be masters of those regions until the Romans broke up their empire" (III. ii. 13, 14).

Such evidence indicates that a considerable Phoenician population was to be found in Spain; and that there must have been continuous trade with the land of Canaan.

Phoenician Carthage

North African Carthage was by far the most famous colony of the Phoenicians. It is believed that the Phoenicians had early "commercial relations with the Libyan tribes who inhabited the district which forms the modern Tunis. In the 16th century B.C. the Sidonians established a trading station called Cambe or Caccabe. Near Bordj-Jedid, unmistakable traces of this early settlement have been found" (*Encyclopaedia Britannica*, 1946, art.: 'Carthage'). Carthage itself was founded by a Tyrian settlement traditionally led by Elissa or Dido (meaning 'fugitive'), daughter of the Tyrian king Mutton I, fleeing from her brother Pygmalion about 850 B.C. At the time of the First Punic War the population of the city is said to have numbered about a million. "The destruction of Tyre by Nebuchadrezzar in the first half of the 6th century, enabled Carthage to take its place as mistress of the Mediterranean. The Phoenician colonies founded by Tyre and Sidon in Sicily and Spain, threatened by the Greeks, sought help from Carthage. The Greek colonization of Sicily was checked, while Carthage established herself on all the Sicilian coast and the neighbouring islands as far as the Balearic Islands and the coast of Spain" (*Encyclopaedia Britannica*, 1946, art.: 'Carthage').

Some impression of the maritime prowess of the Phoenicians in the western Mediterranean may be gathered from Herodotus' statement that Hamilcar, son of Hanno, king of Carthage, led an army of "three hundred thousand men, Phoenicians, Libyans, Iberians, Ligurians, Helisycians, Sardinians, and Corsicans" into Sicily (vii. 165). Thus throughout the Mediterranean, either from their native ports of Tyre and Sidon, or from North African Carthage, the Phoenicians held naval supremacy from at least the time of Solomon until the end of the Second Punic War.

The Tin Islands: The Cassiterides

Several references by classical writers from the time of Herodotus onwards show that the Phoenicians traded with the British Isles, a part of which, at least, was called the Cassiterides. The route so involved does not necessarily call for greater navigational skill than in the case of journeys to many points within the Mediterranean itself, for the voyage to Britain can be performed without passing out of sight of land, which cannot be said of journeys to Crete, Cyprus, and many other islands of the Mediterranean. It would appear however, that the Phoenicians did not hesitate to venture far into the open sea as and when required, as is clearly indicated by evidence of the Phoenician maps utilised by the geographer Ptolemy, who is known to have derived his materials from Marinus of Tyre. Two remarkable features of these maps are that Britain and Ireland are fully outlined, with many topographical and ethnic names; and that the prime meridian of longitude for the whole series of these maps of the then known world lies in the Canary Islands (see Serial No. 74 [912.30]).

While it is widely agreed that the Phoenicians reached the Cassiterides, there is some divergence of opinion as to what part of the British Isles, if any, their name indicates. The view expressed in the *Encyclopaedia Britannica* is as follows:

"From Gadeira (Punic *Gādēr*, Lat. *Gades*, now Cadiz), the Sidonian ships ventured farther on the ocean and drew tin from the mines of north-west Spain or from the richer deposits in the Cassiterides; i.e., the Tin Islands. These were discovered to be, not a part of Britain as was imagined at first, but a separate group by themselves, now known as the Scillies; hence it is improbable that the Phoenicians ever worked the tin-mines in Cornwall" (1946 ed.).

If it be granted that the Phoenicians worked tin in the Scillies, it is evident that they were also familiar with Britain, (which is within sight of those islands), and on which a landfall was the more likely first to have been made after a crossing of the Channel or the Bay of Biscay. From the standpoint of practical navigation, it is unlikely that early navigators, in attempting to reach the Scillies from the coast of France or Spain, would endeavour to sail to them directly by dead reckoning, for the risk of missing the islands and sailing on into the Atlantic would be sufficient to cause mariners deliberately to choose to make a landfall well to the east on the south coast of Britain, and thence turn towards the desired destination. It is entirely probable that the south coast of Britain was used by the Phoenicians for provisioning, if for nothing else, in the course of their voyages to the Scillies.

The Phoenicians were less in doubt as to the location of the tin islands than were the Greeks and Romans who followed them. Neither of the latter were able to identify the Cassiterides to their own satisfaction, for the vicinity lay beyond their known world, as is clear from several sources as in the case of Herodotus, whose words are eloquent in their negations:

"Of the extreme tracts of Europe towards the west I cannot speak with any certainty, for I do not allow that there is any river, to which the barbarians give the name Eridanus, emptying itself into the northern sea, whence (as the tale goes) amber is procured; nor do I know of any islands called the Cassiterides (Tin Islands), whence the tin comes which we use. For in the first place the name Eridanus is manifestly not a barbarian word at all, but a Greek name, invented by some poet or other; and secondly, though I have taken vast pains, I have never been able to get an assurance from an eye-witness that there is any sea on the further side of Europe. Nevertheless, tin and amber do certainly come to us from the ends of the earth" (iii. 115).

"The tin which we use", to use the words of Herodotus, implies the existence of a trade in that metal at the time that historian wrote, in the 5th century B.C., as also does his direct assertion that "tin and amber do certainly come to us from the ends of the earth", of which he possessed so little knowledge. Even the existence of the Rhine (Eridanus) and of the sea into which it empties was held in doubt by Herodotus, such was the limited state of his knowledge. It is evident that the source of tin was best known to those who were engaged in obtaining that metal. Ezekiel mentions the tin trade between Tyre and Tarshish (ch. xxvii).

Diodorus of Sicily came into possession of information as to the source of tin. His description is well suited to Cornwall, where St. Michael's mount answers to his description of Ictis, whilst not far away, near the Lizard, is Polurrion, which may be the modern continuation of his Belerium:

"The inhabitants of Britain who dwell about the promontory known as Belerium are especially hospitable to strangers and have adopted a civilized manner of life because of their intercourse with merchants of other peoples. They it is who work the tin, treating the bed which bears it in an ingenious manner. This bed, being like rock, contains earthy seams and in them the workers quarry the ore, which they then melt down and cleanse of its impurities. Then they work the tin into pieces the size of knuckle-bones and convey it to an island which lies off Britain and is called Ictis; for at the time of ebb-tide the space between this island and the mainland becomes dry and they can take the tin in large quatities over to the island on their wagons. (And a peculiar thing happens in the case of the neighbouring islands which lie between Europe and Britain, for at flood-tide the passages between them and the mainland run full and they have the appearance of islands. but at ebb-tide the sea recedes and leaves dry a large space, and at that time they look like peninsulas. On the island of Ictis the merchants purchase the tin of the natives and carry it from there across the Strait to Galtia or Gaul; and finally, making their way on foot through Gaul for some thirty days they bring their wares on horse-back to the mouth of the river Rhone" (V. xxii. 1–4; G. H. Oldfather's trans.).

Strabo, who wrote during the same century as Diodorus, drew his knowledge of the location of the Cassiterides from Poseidonius, who in turn may have obtained his information from an earlier source. Strabo writes:

"Then all the rest of your voyage is eastward, thus making an obtuse angle to your former course, until you reach the headlands of the Pyrenees that abut on the ocean. The westerly parts of Britain lie opposite these headlands towards the north; and in like manner the islands called Cassiterides, situated in the open sea approximately in the latitude of Britain, lie opposite to, and north of, the Artabians" (II. v. 15).

After outlining the abundance of exports from Spain to Italy in "merchantmen of the greatest size", and describing the remarkable technicalities of metal mining in Turdetania where numerous smelters with "high chimneys" were to be found, Strabo goes on to say:

"Tin, however, is not found there on the surface of the ground, he says, as the historians continually repeat, but is dug up; and it is produced both in the country of the barbarians who live beyond Lusitania, and in the Cassiterides Islands; and tin is brought to Massilia from the British Islands also" (III. ii. 9).

Of incidental interest to our study is the emphasis of Diodorus upon the great skill of the early miners, whose workings were not as primitive as has been imagined. His description of silver-mining in Spain is perhaps somewhat applicable to the case of tin-mining in the Cassiterides, and may throw light on the long-abandoned and mysterious workings still to be seen in the Scillies and Cornwall. Diodorus says:

". . . and not only do they go into the ground a great distance, but they also push their diggings many stades in depth and run galleries off at every angle, turning this way and that, in this manner bringing up from the depths the ore which gives them the profit they are seeking" (V. xxvi. 4).

Strabo mentions metals produced in Britain, and makes no mention of tin; this may be considered as favourable to the identification of the Scillies as the Cassiterides. Of Britain's exports Strabo says:

"It bears grain, cattle, gold, silver, and iron. These things, accordingly, are exported from the island, as also hides, and slaves, and dogs that are by nature suited to the purposes of the chase; the Celti, however, use both these and the native dogs for the purposes of war too. The men of Britain are taller than the Celti, and not so yellow-haired, although their bodies are of looser build. The following is an indication of their size: I myself, in Rome, saw mere lads towering as much as half a foot above the tallest people in the city, although they were bandy-legged and presented no fair lines anywhere in their figure" (IV. v. 2).

Serial No. 92c.

A century later, the elder Pliny thought it a myth that tin was brought from the Atlantic isles (xxiv. 47), though he says lead, which he calls "black lead" to distinguish it from "white lead" or tin, was to be found in abundance in Britain: ". . . in Britannia it is found in the upper stratum of the earth, in such abundance, that a law has been spontaneously made, prohibiting any one from working more than a certain quantity of it' (xxiv. 49; Bohn). Pliny's scepticism was unjustified.

It has been observed by the writers in the *Encyclopaedia Britannica* (1946), that: "From Pliny's writings it appears that the Romans in his time did not realize the distinction between tin and lead *plumbum album* or *candidum* to distinguish it from *plumbum nigrum* (lead proper)" (art.: "Tin"). But since Roman information on the subject of tin was largely derived from the Greeks, who knew of that metal and named it *cassiteros*, it is not likely that we are here concerned with that metal's being confused with lead.

It has been pointed out by George Smith that the vague use of the name *Cassiterides* by Greek and Roman writers may be excused in view of the fact that the tin trade "opened five hundred years before Grecian history began, and still longer before the foundation of Rome was laid" (p. 50). Furthermore, Phoenician records obscured the fact of whether tin came from islands or from a mainland coast:

". . . the Hebrew, Phoenician, and cognate languages had no terms which distinctly specified islands, peninsulas, &c.; one word being used to signify islands, seacoasts, and even remote countries. In those languages, the whole coast of Cornwall and Devonshire might be termed island or islands" (pp. 52, 53).

It appears that the Phoenicians maintained a secrecy as to the location of the Cassiterides, which only complicated matters the more. Strabo says:

"The Cassiterides are ten in number, and they lie near each other in the high sea to the north of the port of the Artabrians. One of them is desert, but the rest are inhabited by people who wear black cloaks, go clad in tunics that reach to their feet, wear belts around their breasts, walk around with canes, and resemble the goddesses of Vengeance in tragedies. They live off their herds, leading for the most part, a nomadic life. As they have mines of tin and lead, they give these metals and the hides from their cattle to the sea-traders in exchange for pottery, salt and copper utensils. Now in former times it was the Phoenicians alone who carried on this commerce (that is, from Gades), for they kept the voyage hidden from every one else. And when once the Romans were closely following a certain ship-captain in order that they too might learn the markets in question, but of jealousy the ship-captain purposely drove his ship out of its course into shoal-water; and after he had lured the followers into the same ruin, he himself escaped by a piece of wreckage and received from the State the value of the cargo he had lost. Still, by trying many times, the Romans learned all about the voyage. After Publius Crassus crossed over to these people and saw that the metals were being dug from only a slight depth, and that the men there were peaceable, he forthwith laid abundant information before all who wished to traffic over this sea, albeit a wider sea than that which separates Britain from the continent" (III. iii. 11).

It will be observed that each account of the Cassiterides has its peculiarities. It has been deemed that these islands have been variously positioned by the ancients. On this particular point, a useful observation has been made by George Smith in his book *The Cassiterides*:

"Then, again, it is mentioned as contradictory, that these *Cassiterides* are by some writers placed many days' sail in the western ocean; and by others, nearly opposite to Corunna! But what is there contradictory in this statement? Let the reader look on a map of western Europe. He will find Corunna a short distance to the north-east of Cape Finisterre, on the south-west extremity of the Bay of Biscay; and the coast soon afterwards runs in a direction nearly east and west. If a vessel, therefore, was to sail from Corunna eastward, on this coast, about one hundred and twenty or one hundred and thirty miles; and then, starting exactly at right angles with the line of coast, should sail direct north, it would reach the Mount's Bay, in the south-west extremity of Britain, and the centre of the tin-mines; the distance from this point, on the southern shore of the Bay of Biscay to Cornwall, being somewhat more than four hundred miles, which would be several days' sail in the western ocean. It is not just to construe the language of ancient writers under the false impression, that the western coast of the European continent is a straight line, running from north to south, and that an island, to be opposite any given point, must lie to the west of it. To be opposite a coast, is to be in such a position, that, leaving that coast at right angles, you will reach the place so described. Cornwall is in this sense nearly opposite Corunna; that is, it is directly opposite a point about one hundred miles from Corunna, and lies in that direction, several days' sail in the western ocean'' (pp. 53, 54.).

It will be of interest to consider the impressions of a Greek on seeing a Phoenician ship. The *Oeconomicus* of Xenophon (born about 430 B.C.), contains the following description:

"Once I had an opportunity of looking over the great Phoenician merchantman, Socrates, and I thought I had never seen tackle so excellently and accurately arranged. For I never saw so many bits of stuff packed away separately in so small a receptacle. As you know, a ship needs a great quantity of wooden and corded implements when she comes into port or puts to sea, much rigging, as it is called, when she sails, many contrivances to protect her against enemy vessels; she carries a large supply of arms for the men, and contains a set of household utensils for each mess. In addition to all this, she is laden with cargo which the skipper carries for profit. And all the things I mentions were contained in a chamber of little more than a hundred square cubits. And I noticed that each kind of thing was so neatly stowed away that there was no confusion, no troublesome untying to cause delay when anything was wanted for immediate use. I found that the steersman's servant, who is called the mate, knows each particular section so exactly, that he can tell even when away where everything is kept and how much there is of it, just as well as a man who knows how to spell can tell you how many letters there are in Socrates and in what order they come. Now I saw this man in his spare time inspecting all the stores that are wanted, as a matter of course, in the ship. I was surprised to see him looking over them, and asked what he was doing. 'Sir,' he answered, 'I am looking to see how the ship's tackle is stored, in case of accident, or whether anything is missing or mixed up with other stuff. For when God sends a storm at sea, there's no time to search about for what you want or to serve it out if it's in a muddle. For God threatens and punishes careless fellows, and you're lucky if He merely refrains from destroying the innocent; and if He saves you when you do your work well, you have much cause to thank heaven'' (viii. 11–16; Loeb).

Possibly it was in such a ship that the Carthaginian commander Himilco sailed to Britain in the course of a voyage commemorated by Rufus Festus Avienus in his *Ora Maritima* in which the Oestrymnides are described as islands from which tin comes, and are placed two days' sail from Ireland, the home of the Hibernian race (Serial No. 92 [572.94151]).

". . . Here rises the head of the promontory, in olden times named Oestrymnon, and below, the like-named bay and isles; wide they stretch, and are rich in metals, tin, and lead. There a numerous race of men dwell, endowed with spirit, and no slight industry, busied all in the cares of trade alone. They navigate the sea on their barks, built not of pines or oak, but wondrous! made of skins and leather. Two days' long is the voyage thence to the Holy Island, once so called, which lies expanded on the sea, the dwelling of the Hibernian race: at hand lies the isle of Albion. Of yore the trading voyages from Tartessus reached to the Oestrymnides; but the Carthaginians and their colonies near the Pillars of Hercules, navigated in this sea, which Himilco, by his own account, was upon during four months.'' (Extracted from A. H. L. Heeren's *African Nations*, Oxford, 1832, vol. i. pp. 503, 504).

Of this, Smith has observed, probably correctly:

"The 'bay and isles rich in metals and tin' are St. Michael's Mount, Mount's Bay in Cornwall, and its neighbouring promontories, which might be taken for islands by a stranger. What settlements were planted by the Carthaginians on the shores thus explored, we do not know; but we find it asserted in the Periplus of Scylax, that 'from the Pillars of Hercules on the European coast, there lay many settlements of the Carthaginians.' We are not informed whether they made any establishments in Britain; but Heeren regards it as 'placed beyond a doubt', that they visited the British Islands for commercial purposes'' (pp. 134, 135).

Serial No. 92d.

There is thus considerable evidence to support the opinions of historians of the past, that the products of Britain were well known to the Levant. The learned Mommsen wrote:

"The Phoenicians directed all the resources of courage, acuteness, and enthusiasm to the full development of commerce and its attendant arts of navigation, manufacturing, and colonization, and thus connected the east and the west. At an incredibly early period we find them in Cyprus and Egypt, in Greece and Sicily, in Africa and Spain, and even on the Atlantic Ocean and the North Sea. The field of their commerce reached from Sierra Leone and Cornwall in the west, eastward to the coast of Malabar. Through their hands passed the gold and pearls of the East, the purple of Tyre, slaves, ivory, lions' and panthers' skins from the interior of Africa, frankincense from Arabia, the linen of Egypt, the pottery and fine wines of Greece, the copper of Cyprus, the silver of Spain, tin from England, and iron from Elba" (*The History of Rome*, 1913 ed., vol. II, Bk. iii. ch. 1, pp. 131, 132).

Professor Rawlinson has observed that:

"Without a chart, without a compass, guided only in their daring voyages by their knowledge of the stars, these bold mariners penetrated to the shores of Scythia in one direction; to Britain, if not even to the Baltic, in another; in a third to the Fortunate Islands; while, in a fourth, they traversed the entire length of the Red Sea, and entering upon the Southern Ocean, succeeded in doubling the Cape of Storms two thousand years before Vasco di Gama, and in effecting the circumnavigation of Africa" ("*History of Phoenicia*, p. 57).

Behind all this, as has been pointed out, lies the fact that under the name "Phoenician", Greek and Roman writers embraced the people of Canaan and coastal districts of Syria. These regions were largely dominated and to some extent settled by Israel, especially under David and Solomon. In the absence of references to pre-captivity Israel (though her land is frequently called Phoenicia and its inhabitants Phoenicians in classical literature) it is clear that Israelites themselves were embraced by the Phoenician name, and that under this appellation, their mariners maintained sea-communications with the British Isles and the Atlantic coast of Europe. This, when considered in conjunction with what has been established in an earlier study on the subject of the comprehensive surveying of the British Isles, the Hebrides, Orkneys, and Iceland (Serial No. 74 [912.30]), demonstrates with reasonable certainty the fact that the Hebrews in general were fully conversant with those regions.

Serial No. 92e
Published by *The National Message* Ltd.,
6 Buckingham Gate, London, S.W.1.
Copyright.

Authority: ISAAK DA COSTA
Israel and the Gentiles

"Da Costa, Isaak (1798-1860), Dutch poet and theologian, was born at Amsterdam on Jan. 14, 1798. His father was a Jew of Portuguese descent, and claimed kindred with the celebrated Uriel D'Acosta. He studied at Amsterdam and at Leiden, where he took his doctor's degree in law in 1818, and in literature in 1821. In 1814 he wrote *De Verlossing van Nederland*, a patriotic poem, which placed him in line with the contemporary national romantic poets in Germany and in France. . . . In 1822 he became a convert to Christianity, and towards the close of his life was a director of the seminary established in Amsterdam in connection with the mission of the Free Church of Scotland. He died at Amsterdam on April 28, 1860. Da Costa ranked first among the poets of Holland after the death of Bilderdijk . . ." (*The Encyclopædia Britannica*, 14th Edition.)

The Sephardic Jews

SPANISH and Portuguese historians—both Jewish and non-Jewish—have accepted the strong tradition that the Sephardim, or 'Spanish', Jews are Judahites. Some of their noble families are regarded by their co-religionists as having strong claims to descent from the House of David. Ancestors of these Sephardim migrated to the Peninsular during the period following the destruction of the first Temple; some of them possibly as early as the time of Solomon.

POINTS OF SPECIAL INTEREST

1. This authority inclines to the view that Spain is the Tarshish mentioned in Scripture as a country which had contact by sea with Palestine from the time of Solomon.

2. He quotes the following Spanish names as being obviously of Hebrew origin: Yepez (Joppa); Tavora (Tabor); Avila (Abila); Gaona (Gaon); Correa (Core); Zachute (Zachut); also Meneses, Calatayud, Geremias, Salema, Curiel, Bazan, and many others.

3. In visiting Spain, with its large Israelite community, St. Paul (Romans xv) was obviously carrying out his own acknowledged precept of delivering the message of the New Covenant "to the Jew first".

4. The lion rampant, so confidently displayed on the coat of arms of the Abarbanel family, points undeniably to royal lineage. In this stronghold of Judah he would have been bold indeed who used this emblem lightly.

5. Günther, in his *Racial Elements of European History* (p. 75), estimates that the Sephardim and Ashkenazim constitute about one-tenth and nine-tenths respectively of modern Jewry; the *Universal Jewish Encyclopædia* (New York, 1939, article 'Ashkenazim') states, "about 92 per cent of all Jews or approximately 14,500,000 are Ashkenazim''. These figures may need some revision since the terrible campaign of extermination carried out by Hitler against European Jewry.

6. The statement that the Sephardic speech is much less corrupt than the Ashkenazic is useful evidence that the former also retained their racial purity in a higher measure. This is borne out by the fact that formerly they did not intermarry with the more mixed Ashkenazim.

7. It is illuminating to note that Sephardic Jewry furnished such stalwarts of the Christian Church as the Gideons, Eardleys, Seniors, da Costas, Capadoses, etc. (Brewster, pp. 142 ff.), and that—disdaining 'chaffering occupations'—they achieved such high office in many western countries.

8. Da Costa makes interesting reference to a project to found a new Order among Spanish nobility—the Order of St. James of the Bare Sword—to which no Jew or Moor might be admitted. So high was the percentage of these races, however, that "out of the thousand noble families of Spain no more than eight and forty could be found willing to enter the ranks of the new Order" (p. 123).

Thus the hidalgos were, many of them, of Israelite descent. Those who acknowledged the Roman Catholic faith avoided the banishment imposed upon the Jews in the fifteenth century. There can be little doubt that many of the leading sailors and explorer-adventurers of Spain and Portugal derived their seafaring skill from the far-off ancestors who went with the 'king's ships' to Tarshish (II Chronicles ix, 21).

9. It is remarkable that both Jews and Moors were present together in Spain. The former were descendants of Joshua's conquering Israelites, whilst the latter sprang from the very Canaanite tribes who fled before them to find refuge in North Africa, as far west as the Atlantic Coast. (Procopius, *History of the Wars*; Book IV, Cap. x.)

10. The Judahites resident in the Peninsula at the time of the Crucifixion could not be held blameworthy for the death of Israel's Redeemer.

ISAAK DA COSTA, LL.D.: EXTRACTS FROM HIS *ISRAEL AND THE GENTILES*
(English translation by M. J. Kennedy; James Nisbet & Co., London, 1850).

(P. 211.) Without enlarging upon the hypothesis, that King Solomon possessed both colonies and jurisdiction in Spain (supposed to be the Tarshish of Scripture), tradition on every side agrees in fixing the establishment of Jews in this country at a date soon after the destruction of the first temple. This tradition . . . informs us, that . . . many families of the tribe of Judah, and of the house of David, established themselves in the country, and built cities, the names of which still recall localities and reminiscences of Palestine . . .

(Pp. 213-215.) The groundwork in the present instance is, the simple fact that the Jews were settled in Spain long before the destruction of the second temple; and this many circumstances prove. We may mention, among others, the coincidence in name of several places in Spain with those of Palestine, a coincidence which no hypothesis of a Phœnician or Arabic derivation could account for. Another circumstance which helps to fix the date of their settlement at a period previous to the Christian era is, that the names of Philip, Alexander, Mark, &c.,

Serial No. 30a.

though in general use among the Jews of all parts of the world, were never borne as their Jewish appellations by those of Spain and Portugal. These names were first introduced into Palestine when that country was under the dominion of the Greeks and Romans. If, then, they are not to be met with among the Sephardim, may we not naturally conclude that their ancestors were at that time already established in Spain? We may consider the existence of synagogues in Spain more than probable when calling to mind the passage in the Epistle to the Romans, in which St. Paul announces his intention of visiting Spain also (Romans xv, 24-28). We know it was generally the practice of the Apostle to the Gentiles to make use of the synagogue as his means of communication, and thus to act upon the principle he so often inculcates, of preaching the Gospel to the Jew *first*, and *also* to the Gentile. We may add another circumstance, mentioned by Josephus (Joseph. de Bell.

Jud., ii. 9, sec. 6) as bearing upon this point. He says that Herod Antipas was banished, by order of the Emperor, to Spain. The Emperor Adrian also, after quelling the revolt of Bar Cochab, permitted the Jews who had escaped, or were made prisoners, to establish themselves in Spain.

The result of these various traditions seems to prove that the Jews were already established in the Peninsula before the time of the Roman emperors; whether they arrived there by way of Alexandria and Cyrene, or at once from Palestine, and the more distant parts of Asia. It is interesting to notice the claim made by this portion of the dispersed of Judah to belong to the house of David. It is evident that this claim cannot be supported by any historical document; for the Israelites, formerly the people of genealogies *par excellence*, have not, since their dispersion continued their genealogical tables . . .

EXTRACTS FROM THE 1876 DUTCH EDITION OF THE SAME WORK, first translated into English by B. Brewster, under the title *NOBLE FAMILIES AMONG THE SEPHARDIC JEWS* (Oxford University Press, 1936).

(Pp. 123-124.) The wholly exceptional standing of these Sephardim (South-European) Jews is explained by both Jewish and Spanish writers of the Peninsula as being due to the ancient tradition of their descent from the house of David, or from the royal stem of Judah at any rate. The persistent maintenance of this tradition even by Spanish authors, who are by no means to be accused of partiality to the Jews (at least in regard to faith), is certainly most remarkable. Don Jose Amador de Los Rios, in his important work *Estudios Historicos, Politicos. Literarios sobre los Judios de Espana* (Madrid, 1848), . . . constantly refers to the Spanish Jews as being descended from David and the house of Judah. The only actual gulf between the different populations was naturally that of religion . . . The entire congregations of synagogues sometimes were converted at once. In this manner many Spanish Jews became the progenitors of a multitude, mostly nobles and grandees, de-

scended from those converts either through the male or female line. Before the introduction of the Inquisition, and the subsequent expulsion of the Jews, this connexion was publicly recognised.

(P. 142.) Abarbanel. An old Spanish and Portuguese family, which, with the Jachias, claims to be descended from David, a claim generally supported by or on behalf of the Jews of the Peninsula. This family, which is unquestionably of great antiquity in the Spanish Peninsula, lived at Seville for a considerable time and afterwards at Lisbon. The name, perhaps originally a sobriquet (Abarbanel, Abrabanel, Abrabaniel, and later in the Netherlands also abbreviated to Barbanel), was, in 1368 at any rate, already used by D. Samuel Abarbanel. The family arms, as found, amongst others, on the title pages of books published at Venice by R. Don Isaac Abarbanel, consists of a lion rampant turned toward a castle.

(P. 148.) That the Jachias, together with the Abarbanels, amongst the Sephardim especially prided themselves upon their descent from David, is a fact which has already been mentioned here.

(P. 154.) It is therefore small wonder that a body such as the emigrant Jews from Spain and Portugal, particularly in the capitals of the regions where they settled, such as the Netherlands, England, Hamburg, Tuscany, etc., considered themselves—we think, too, had the right to consider themselves—and were considered by their brethren from Poland and Germany as the nobility of the Jewish people in their exile (Galuth, in Spanish *destierro*, and in Portuguese *desterro*).

(P. 157.) As a nation within a nation the Sephardic Jews are especially remarkable for the early date of their settlement in the Peninsula. The time of the first settlement was formerly reckoned by both Jewish and Christian authors as belonging to the period of the Babylonian exile. We do not wish to enter here into a discussion of the pros and cons of this chronology. The fact, however, that the Jews were settled in those parts in the time of the Apostles is probable enough from the passage in the Epistle to the Romans (xv, 24-28). One of the most recent historians of Spain does not hesitate to record as a fact that fifty thousand Jews were transferred by the Emperor Vespasian to that country. (Rosseeuw St. Hilaire, *Historie d'Espagne* (Paris, 1844; i, 304, 305).)

(P. 158.) So the Jews who live in Castile, as far as may be determined regarding such matters, reckon their lineage from King David. The lion, even though suffering from fever, does not cease to be a lion . . . The continuance of the house of David, in Babylonia, and from thence in the Spanish Peninsula, has always been maintained by the Jews . . .

(Reproduced by kind permission)

EXTRACT FROM *JEWISH ENCYCLOPÆDIA* (1925 Edition)

SEPHARDIM (called also Spagnioli, Spaniols, or, more rarely, Franconians): Descendants of the Jews who were expelled from Spain and Portugal and who settled in southern France, Italy, North Africa, Turkey, Asia Minor, Holland, England, North and South America, Germany, Denmark, Austria, and Hungary . . . they considered themselves a superior class, the nobility of Jewry, and for a long time their co-religionists, on whom they looked down, regarded them as such . . .

The Sephardim never engaged in chaffering occupations nor in usury, and they did not mingle with the lower classes. With their social equals they associated freely, without regard to creed, and in the presence of their superiors they displayed neither shyness nor servility. They were received at the courts of sultans, kings, and princes, and often were employed as ambassadors, envoys, or agents. The number of Sephardim who have rendered important services to different countries is considerable, from Samuel Abravanel (financial councillor to the viceroy of Naples) to Benjamin Disraeli. Among other names mentioned are those of Belmonte, Nasi, Pacheco, Palache, Azevedo, Sadportas, Costa, Curiel, Cansino, Schonenberg, Toledo, Toledano, and Teixeira . . . It must be remembered that Judæo-Spanish, or Ladino, is in no wise as corrupt a language as is the Judæo-German . . .

Although the Sephardim lived on peaceful terms with other Jews, they rarely intermarried with them; neither did they unite with them in forming congregations, but adhered to their own ritual, which differed widely from the Ashkenazic . . .

Authorities: Various

The Karaites and the Ten Tribes of II Esdras xiii : 40-45

ONE of the most interesting Jewish communities is that of the Karaites, a comparatively unknown body deserving much closer attention by the scholarly world.

The Karaites cherish only the Mosaic *Law*, the *Prophets*, and the *Writings* as the Word of God; but reject the Talmud as of merely human origin, therefore as of no authority, and go so far as to show that its writings are contradictory.

Although they have long formed a more or less scattered but world-wide community, the Karaites were for long settled in strength along the northern coasts of the Black Sea. Though followers of the Old Covenant religion, their history and traditions connect them not only with Judah, but with the Ten Tribes of Israel. That they could be so descended is quite possible; in fact II Esdras xiii. 40-45 indicates in no uncertain manner that at least a proportion of the Ten Tribes removed from the region of their captivity into another land where they returned to the law of Moses:

Those are the ten tribes, which were carried away prisoners out of their own land in the time of Osea the king, whom Salmanaser the king of Assyria led away captive, and he carried them over the waters, and so came they into another land.

But they took this counsel among themselves, that they would leave the multitude of the heathen, and go forth into a further country, where never mankind dwelt,

That they might there keep their statutes, which they never kept in their own land.

And they entered into Euphrates by the narrow passages of the river.

For the most High then shewed signs for them, and held still the flood, till they were passed over.

For through that country there was a great way to go, namely, of a year and a half: and the same region is called Arsareth.

The Karaites: A People Apart

A profound gulf has ever separated the Karaites from the orthodox Jewish religion, by reason of the fact that they have steadfastly refused to recognize as inspired writings anything other than the *Law*, the *Prophets*, and the *Writings*, which alone they consider to be the canon, which was closed by Simon the Just. They consider that the Old Testament Scriptures provide their own sufficient interpretation, within which they may live actively and intelligently with great freedom. They are, in consequence, much less bound by tradition, and have much more in common with the world, than have orthodox Jews.

The Karaite name derives from that of "reader", that is, of the holy law; and although it does not appear until about the middle of the eighth century A.D., the community to which it applied was much older and not restricted to any specific geographical location. In effect, the distinguishing feature of the Karaites throughout the world was both their rigid adherence to the holy law and their uncompromising attitude to the traditions of men, among which they class the Talmud. They were not a new sect; rather, the Sadducees, Talmudists, and others were the schismatics and heretics.

Esdras on the Return to the Law

The quoted extract from *Esdras* shows that a portion, at least, of the Ten Tribes, decided to migrate to an isolated region and there keep the Law which their forefathers had forsaken. The whole of the Ten Tribes are not specifically mentioned in this connection, but only those who are said to have suffered deportation by Shalmaneser, who neither began nor ended the removal of the Ten Tribes (see *Serial No.* 29 [572.9353]).

The direction of movement of this body of ten-tribed Israelites is but vaguely indicated by Esdras; but a passage of the upper reaches of the Euphrates seems to be implied. Such a movement would be in the general direction of Asia Minor, which in turn may have been left in the course of an eighteen months' trek to the region of Arsereth, a district not definitely known.

It may not be without significance that both in and beyond the Caucasus we find Israelitish communities traditionally connected with the Ten Tribes (see also *Serial No.* 104 [572.936314]). As having some connection with these (see *Serial No.* 105 [572.933]), the Karaites once settled extensively along the northern coasts of the Black Sea; and in the western part of their territory is to be found the River Sereth, which enters the Danube at Galatz, in Roumania. Within the region settled by the Karaites, the Crimean gravestone-inscriptions, in Hebrew, were long ago brought to public notice as belonging to the old Karaite community.

Serial No. 119a.

The return of part of the Ten Tribes to the Mosaic law may be regarded as a natural result of repentance and conversion. It will be recalled that even in the darkest days of northern Israel's apostasy, there remained "seven thousand in Israel, all the knees which have not bowed unto Baal, and every mouth which hath not kissed him" (I *Kings* xix. 18); and that it was at this time, a century and a half prior to their removal into captivity, that the multitudes of the nation had been gathered together to witness the futility of the Baal-worshippers, and the triumph of Elijah over the pagan priesthood (I *Kings* xviii. 19-45). A national reformation was prevented, however, by the machinations of Jezebel and Ahab, and by a succession of apostate rulers after them. But the achievements of Elijah, of his successor Elisha, and of other prophets who followed, may not have been without lasting effects upon large numbers of the masses, who, in due course led into captivity, found themselves free to follow whatsoever religion they desired. Some of them, evidently desirous of returning to the worship of Jehovah, moved to new regions. That descendants of some of the erstwhile ten-tribed followers of Elijah eventually settled in the Caucasus is reasonably certain (*Serial No.* 104 [572.936314]). In due course some lapsed into paganism, but others, such as their Karaite descendants, doubtless after the times of Ezra and Nehemiah, established contacts with the faithful in Jerusalem and thereby became part of the widely scattered Jewish community, using their Scriptures, language, and writing, and possibly borrowing a Levitical priesthood for the maintenence of religion.

So strong was the Karaite faith that it remained untainted by the rise of the "traditions of men": in fact it has been implied that Karaite influence may be detected in the edict of Justinian against the Talmud. Although not given to Christianity, the Karaites possess an Order of Common Prayer which is unique in that while the orthodox Jewish Order clearly proscribes belief in Jesus Christ, the Karaite does not. In common with the Christian liturgy, that of the Karaites is traced to the time of the men of the Great Synagogue: Ezra, Nehemiah, and the High Priests until Simon the Just.

The known existence of faithful claiming descent from the Ten Tribes in apostolic times offers a reasonable explanation of the meaning of St. Paul's words to Agrippa concerning "the hope of the promise made of God unto our fathers: unto which promise our twelve tribes, instantly serving God day and night, hope to come" (*Acts* xxvi. 7). The Ten Tribes, even in dispersion, were accomplishing the divine purpose concerning the calling of the gentiles; and some, at least, of all the tribes, as in the case of the Karaites, had returned to the Old Covenant religion, though as Paul put it: "I bear them record that they have a zeal of God, but not according to knowledge. For they being ignorant of God's righteousness, and going about to establish their own righteousness, have not submitted themselves unto the righteousness of God. For Christ is the end of the law for righteousness to every one that believeth" (*Rom.* x. 2). Re-covenanting of cast-off Israel was not to be by returning to the Mosaic Law via the ordinances of the Old Covenant worship, but in Christ according to the terms of the New Covenant (*Rom.* ix. 25-26; *Heb.* viii. 6-13).

EXTRACTS FROM *THE HISTORY OF THE KARAITE JEWS*, by William Harris Rule, D.D. (London, 1870).

RULE, WILLIAM HARRIS (1802-1890), divine and historian, born at Penrhyn. . . . Early in 1822 he left the Church of England for the Wesleyan body. . . ordained a Wesleyan preacher on 14 March 1826. . . acted for more than a year as resident missionary in Malta. . . sent in November 1827 by the Wesleyan Missionary Society to the island of St. Vincent . . . Wesleyan pastor at Gibraltar, where he founded the first charity school, besides four day and evening schools. . . . A Wesleyan mission established by Rule at Cadiz was suppressed by the Christinist government in 1839 . . . he obtained a royal order repealing the edicts which prohibited foreigners from taking part in Spanish education. . . . From 1842 till 1868 he undertook ministerial duty in England . . . a scholarly preacher and a prolific writer, and is said to have been master of ten languages. He received the degree of D.D. from Dickenson College (Methodist episcopal church), Ohio, in July, 1854 (*The Dictionary of National Biography*).

By whomsoever written, the history of the Kara-ites is comparative. They are a people honorably known by faithful maintenance of the principle of submission to acknowledged authority, and also by firmness in exercising their own reason in order to ascertain the sufficiency of that which claims to be authoritative. Nothing with them is authoritative which is not Divine—God only is to them the fountain of authority. They profess willingness to submit to Him, and to submit at any cost. This is the normal principle of Karaism. Submission to human authority in matters of faith and religious duty, unless that authority be manifestly supported by Divine Revelation, they justly consider to be no better than blind and servile superstition.

They pay unbounded reverence to the Written Law of God, contained in the Old Testament. They utterly reject what is called the Oral Law, and is now contained in the Talmud—at least, so far as it can be made out by those who spend their life learning. (Pp. vi, vi.)

* * *

So far as I can ascertain, the name of Karaite does not yet occur in history, but first comes to view about the middle of the eighth century, in connection with the Chozars, a rude but powerful nation north of the Caucasus, among whom the Karaite Jews must have been for a long time previously known. . . In the history of Russia, the Chozars are described as having possessions on the sea of Azof, and they also appear with the Petchnigans, or tribe of Patzinak, on the western side of the Black Sea. They dwelt also along the Volga, which river they called Atel, and extended their conquests to the North Sea. . . . They were conquered in the year 945 by King Sviatoslaf, and their name, otherwise almost forgotten, was preserved in the archives of the Muscovite. (Pp. 79, 80.)

* * *

There can be no doubt that they had been settled in those northern regions long enough to be known and compared with other Jews. They were not immigrants and strangers, but a distinct class of persons of established reputation; and this is quite consistent with what the Karaites in the Crimea tell of a grant, or *Privilegium*, as Köhl the German traveller in South Russia calls it, given them by Mohammed. Now Mohammed died in the year 632, and this alleged grant would have been more than a century later than the edict of Justinian against the Talmud, which is so worded that a Karaite might have dictated it, yet without the *name*.

The ancient residence of Jews in that part of the world is attested by existing monuments. Since the last war with Russia, several of the most ancient gravestones in the burial-ground of Djufut Kalé, in the Crimea, have been examined; the tracings are preserved, and some of them were early published in St. Petersburg.* If the Hebrew antiquarians are

* *Mélanges asiatiques*, Tom. v; livraisons 2 et 3.

not mistaken, one of them bears date of a death in the 702nd year of the "Captivity", and others also are dated in the same style; all such inscriptions having been cut before the era of the Creation was adopted by the Jews. Now if the Captivity be, as is believed, that of Sennacherib, the year 702 answers to the *sixth* of the Christian era, according to the common computation. The gravestone so dated, and others after it, may or may not have been those of persons holding the Karaite doctrine, nor does the fact of a mere corpse being buried in that ground at any time prove that the deceased was a Karaite, for even R. Isaac Sangari, who argued against them, was buried with their dead in the Crimea. But there is not the same uncertainty at later dates, and the inscriptions which may, with very rare exceptions, be pronounced Karaite, date so early as A.M. 4090, answering to A.D. 330. (Pp. 82, 83.)

* * *

With regard to Christianity, a few discriminative observations may be offered further on, but we must first examine the Articles of Faith professed, respectively, by the Jews in general, and by the Karaites in particular, setting down first the *Thirteen Articles* of the Common Creed, and then the *Ten* of the Scripturist. The *Thirteen*, as I find them in an edition of the Liturgy of the Sephardim used in England, read thus:

1. The Living God shall be exalted and praised: He is, and there is no period to His existence.

2. He is One, and there is no unity like His unity: He is invisible, and yet there is no bound to His one existence: He has no corporeal resemblance, nor has He a body: we cannot express to Him His holiness.

3. He is before every created thing: He is the First, and there is no beginning to His beginning.

4. Behold Him Lord Eternal of the whole creation: Displaying His majesty and His dominion.

5. The abundance of prophecy is His gift: To men of His own treasure, and His glory.

6. There hath not arisen in Israel one like Moses yet: Nor a prophet that looketh upon His likeness.

7. A law of truth God gave to His people: By the hand of His prophet, faithful in His house.

8. God will not change, nor will He alter: His decree is for all ages, for Himself alone.

9. He spieth out and knoweth our secrets: He foresaw the matter to the end in His eternity.

10. He recompenseth the good man according to his works: Giving to the wicked evil according to his wickedness.

11. He will send our Messiah at the end of days: To redeem them that expect the end of His salvation.

12. God will revive the dead in the abundance of His goodness: Blessed for ever and ever be the name of His praise.

13. These thirteen are to be as roots: The decree of God and His Law.

The *Ten* fundamental Articles of the Karaites, I find in their own liturgy, and translate as follows:

1. That all this bodily (or material) existence, that is to say, the spheres and all that is in them, are created.

2. Tha. they have a Creator, and the Creator has His own soul (or spirit).

3. That He has no similitude, and He is one, separate from all.

4. That He sent Moses, our Master, upon whom be peace.

5. That He sent with Moses, our Master, His Law, which is perfect.

6. For the instruction of the faithful, the language of our Law, and the interpretation, that is to say, the Reading (or Text), and the division (or vowel-pointing).

7. That the Blessed God sent forth the other prophets.

8. That God—blessed be His name—will raise the sons of men to life in the Day of Judgment.

9. That the Blessed God giveth to man according to his ways, and according to the fruits of his doings.

10. That the Blessed God has not reprobated the men of the captivity, but they are under the chastisements of God, and it is every day right that they should obtain His salvation by the hands of Messiah, the Son of David.

We may now compare these two confessions. The former is full and clear; there is much verbal diversity in its form in the various editions, but it will be acknowledged that the one now before the reader is very beautiful as a piece of Hebrew composition. The latter is not to be regarded as a perfect creed, but a confession of Karaism. While the former, as a summary of Jewish faith, has the merit of completeness, it is unquestionably composed with the view of conveying, in every synagogue, a direct protest against Christianity, which the eighth Article is intended to condemn, as if God were *changed* in the Incarnation, or *altered* in the Gospel. The sixth and eleventh Articles, if true, would annihilate the New Testament.

The latter document does not contain any such anti-Christian protest, and the tenth Article, read hastily, might even seem to have been framed for the purpose of leaving a way open at any time for an express acceptance of the Saviour. But in reality, the Karaite creed harmonizes with the other, and differing only in so far as was thought necessary for the profession of the distinctive principles of Karaism. (Pp. 126-129.)

EXTRACT FROM AN ARTICLE ENTITLED *ON THE DATE OF THE FALL OF NINEVEH*, by J. W. Bosanquet; published in the *Transactions of the Society of Biblical Archaeology*, Vol. II (1873).

BOSANQUET, JAMES WHATMAN (1804-1877), a partner in the banking-house of Bosanquet, Salt, & Co., and a writer on biblical and Assyrian chronology . . . educated at Westminster . . . a generous contributor to the *Transactions of the Society of Biblical Archaeology*, not merely in word but in deed, for besides writing papers, he paid nearly half the expenses of publication, and bore a considerable share in the cost of bringing out other works on Assyriology, insomuch that the president of the society, in pronouncing his éloge, described him as "the Mæcenas of Assyriology" (*Dictionary of National Biography*).

Now, according to Demetrius, the ten tribes were carried away from Samaria 473 years and 9 months before Ptolemy IV, that is in February 695 B.C., the capture of Samaria having taken place in 696 B.C. And this year agrees, as I have elsewhere shown, with the date of the captivity long preserved by the descendants of the ten tribes, that is by the Caraite Jews of the Crimea, as witnessed by several ancient tombstones found at Tschufukale, which have been carried up to St. Petersburgh, and which are now in the library of the Academy, bearing by computation the date 696 B.C. (Pp. 160, 161.)

EXTRACT FROM AN ARTICLE ENTITLED *SYNCHRONOUS HISTORY*, by the same author; *ibid.*, Vol. III (1874).

"The old gravestones in the Crimea", writes Neubauer,* "which are now recognized as genuine by all men of learning, attest that there were Jewish communities in the Crimea as early as the year A.D. 6"—"and that the Jews there held themselves to be descended from the ten tribes." Three different eras are recorded on these monuments, as well as in many ancient manuscripts of the Karaites. First, the era of the captivity of the ten tribes, 696 B.C. . . . Second, the Karaite era of the creation . . . 3911 B.C. Third, the era according to the reckoning of the inhabitants of Metarcha, that is, the common Rabbinical era of creation, 3760 B.C. Facsimiles of three of the gravestones, out of several which have been carried up to St. Petersburg, will be sufficient to certify the date of Shalmanezer's capture of Samaria, or the commencement of the era Ligalu-thenu.

* *Geschichte des Karaerthums*, p. 29.

No. 1

This is the tombstone of Buki, the son of Izchak, the priest; may his rest be in Eden, at the time of the salvation of Israel. In the year 702 of the years of our Exile (=A.D. 6).

No. 2

Rabbi Moses Levi died in the year 726 of our Exile (=A.D. 30).

No. 3

Zadok the Levite, son of Moses, died 4000 after the creation, 785 of our Exile (=A.D. 89).

Shanim Ligaluthenu

Years of our Exile from 696 B.C.,

as in itself an interesting fact in Biblical Archaeology, and as confirmatory of the new reckoning at several later dates, in addition to its special bearing on the matter in hand, the date of the fall of Samaria. For it appears to me sufficiently clear that this era must have been made use of by the writers of two books appertaining to the ten tribes of Israel, viz., the Book of Tobit and the Book of Judith. When the writer of the first of these books relates, according to the Greek translator, that Tobias died at Ecbatana at the age of 127 (which is absurd), "and before he died he heard of the destruction of Nineveh which was taken by Nabuchodonosor and Assuerus", that is by Nebuchadnezzar and Cyaxares, in 583 B.C. new reckoning, we can hardly doubt that the words in the original, derived either from his tombstone or from some family document, were written "shenath 127, shanim Ligaluthenu" (=569 B.C.), as on the tomb of Buki son of Izchak. And again, when Judith is said to have lived to the age of 105, the words on her monument originally ran "moth 105, shanim Ligaluthenu" (=591 B.C.), that is twelve years before Jehoiakim first became subject to Nebuchadnezzar. (Pp. 28-30.)

TRANSLATION OF A CRIMEAN EPIGRAPH: from A. E. Harkavy's German text published in *ACADEMIA SCIENTIARUM IMPERIALIS, MEMOIRES*, etc., St. Petersburg, Vol. 24, No. 1, 1863, p. 9; translated by the Rev. C. Coffin.

(1) I Jehuda ben Mose ha-Nagolon

(2) of the East country, ben Jehuda ha-Gibbor

(3) of the tribe of Napthali, of the generation

(4) Schillem, who went into the exile with

(5) the exiles, who were driven away with

(6) Hosea, the king of Israel, together with

(7) the tribes of Simeon and Dan and some of the

(8) generations of the other tribes

(9) of Israel, which (all) were led into exile by the enemy

(10) Shalmanesser from Schomron and their cities

(11) to Chalach, that is, Baclack and to Chabar, that is,

(12) Chabul and to Hara, that is, Herat

(13) and to Gosan, that is, Gozna, the cities

(14) of the exiled tribes of Reuben, Gad and the half of

(15) Manasseh, which Pilneser drove into exile

(16) and settled there (and from there they scattered themselves

(17) over the whole land of the East as far as

(18) Sinim)—when I returned from wandering

(19) in the land of their exile and from journeying

(20) in the dwelling places of the descendants of their generations

(21) in their resting places of the Land of Krim. . . .

Reduced facsimiles of the accompanying translated texts. From D. A. Khvol'son's *Achtzen Hebraische Grabschriften aus der Krim*; St. Petersburg, 1865.

Authority: PROCOPIUS OF CAESAREA
'History of the Wars'

"Procopius, Byzantine historian, was born at Caesarea, in Palestine, towards the end of the 5th century A.D. . . . and was in 527 appointed secretary and legal adviser to Belisarius, who was proceeding to command the imperial army in the war against the Persians . . . As an historian Procopius is of quite unusual merit . . . industrious in collecting facts, careful and impartial in stating them: his judgment is sound, his reflections generally acute; his conceptions of the general march and movement of things not unworthy of the great events he has recorded." (*Encyclopaedia Britannica*, 13th Edition.)

A Summary of the Facts Established

THE Moors migrated to North Africa from the coastlands of Palestine between Sidon and Egypt. They included the Gergasites, Jebusites and other Canaanite tribes who fled before the victorious Israelites after their Exodus from Egypt.

These refugees journeyed by way of Egypt and Libya as far west as Tangier, establishing numerous cities. A later wave came with (Queen) Dido and these were accepted as kinsmen, being allowed to found and hold Carthage. After a period of Roman domination the Moors won many victories over the Vandals, gaining possession of almost the whole of North Africa.

Procopius relates that, in his day, there were at Tigisis (Tangier) two columns of white stone upon which—in the Phoenician language—appeared the inscription:

"We are they who fled before the face of Joshua,

the robber, the son of Nun."

POINTS OF SPECIAL INTEREST

1. Procopius' record of the Tigisis columns confirms the Old Testament narrative of the Israelite conquest of Canaan.

2. The Moors were Canaanites.

3. Joshua's campaign produced a migration of peoples reaching as far west as the Atlantic coast of North Africa.

PROCOPIUS: EXTRACTS FROM HIS *HISTORY OF THE WARS, Book IV, Cap. X,* (Loeb Class. with Eng. trans. by H. B. Dewing (HEINEMANN, London, and HARVARD UNIVERSITY PRESS, Camb., Mass.), 1916., Vol. II., pp. 286-291)

And now, since the narration of the history has brought me to this point, it is necessary to tell from the beginning whence the nations of the Moors came to Libya and how they settled there. When the Hebrews had withdrawn from Egypt and had come near the boundaries of Palestine, Moses, a wise man, who was their leader on the journey, died, and the leadership was passed on to Joshua, the son of Nun, who led this people into Palestine and, by displaying a valour in war greater than that natural to a man, gained possession of the land. And after overthrowing all the nations he easily won the cities and he seemed to be altogether invincible. Now at that time the whole country along the sea from Sidon as far as the boundaries of Egypt was called Phoenicia. And one king in ancient times held sway over it, as is agreed by all who have written the earliest accounts of the Phoenicians. In that country there dwelt very populous tribes, the Gergasites and the Jebusites and some others with other names by which they are called in the history of the Hebrews. Now when these nations saw that the invading general was an irresistible prodigy, they emigrated from their ancestral homes and made their way to Egypt, which adjoined their country. And finding there no place sufficient for them to dwell in, since there has been a great population in Egypt from ancient times, they proceeded to Libya. And they established numerous cities and took possession of the whole of Libya as far as the pillars of Heracles and there they have lived even up to my time, using the Phoenician tongue. They also built a fortress in Numidia, where now is the city called Tigisis. In that place are two columns made of white stone near by the great spring, having Phoenician letters cut in them which say in the Phoenician tongue: "We are they who fled from before the face of Joshua, the robber, the son of Nun." . . . And in later times those who removed from Phoenicia with Dido came to the inhabitants of Libya as to kinsmen. And they willingly allowed them to found and hold Carthage. . . . Later on the Romans gained the supremacy over all of them in war and settled the Moors at the extremity of the inhabited land of Libya and made the Carthaginians and the other Libyans subject and tributary to themselves. And after this the Moors won many victories over the Vandals and gained possession of the land now called Mauretania, extending from Gadira as far as the boundaries of Caesarea, as well as the most of Libya which remained.

Authorities: Various

Modern Israel—Still One Family

It has been shown that the bulk of ancient Israel was carried captive and deported to the Caspian territories, which once formed part of the indeterminate region to the north and east of the Black Sea, once known as *Scythia*. It is recognised that most of the original Celto-Saxons roamed and sojourned in that vast area before they were finally forced westwards to the countries of the North Sea Fringe.

Opposition has frequently been raised to the view that the Celto-Saxons of to-day are the descendants of the Israelites of old, on the ground that they are a 'mongrel' people, deriving from several racial types.

Authoritative evidence shows this contention to be fallacious. Far from being 'mongrels', the peoples who formed the broad base of Celto-Saxondom—the Celts, Angles, Saxons, Jutes, Danes, Normans, Flemings and Huguenots—are now known to have derived from one original parent stock.

POINTS OF SPECIAL INTEREST

1. The tribes of Celto-Saxondom arrived in western Europe comparatively late in history. Archaeological discovery, racial unity, language similarities, manners and customs all point in the direction of an eastern origin.

2. Evidence of their racial affinity indicates that the origin of the Celto-Saxons is to be found among the families of Shemite stock. (See Ser. Nos. 55 [572.9353], 57 [572.9394], 60 [572.9394], 70 [572.9335].

3. The deportations of the Israelites from Palestine to *Scythia* are dealt with in Ser. Nos. 29 [572.9353], and 32 [572.935].

EXTRACT FROM *NATIONALITY AND RACE FROM AN ANTHROPOLOGIST'S POINT OF VIEW,*
by Sir Arthur Keith; being the Twenty-first Robert Boyle Lecture, delivered before the Oxford University
Junior Scientific Club, 17 Nov. 1919.

KEITH, SIR ARTHUR (1866-   ); born in Aberdeen; "a
leading authority on anthropology, and an expert on the reconstruction of prehistoric man from fragments or fossil
remains". Educated: Aberdeen University; University College,
London; Leipzig University. Secretary, Anatomical Society of
Great Britain, 1899-1902; later President of the same; President,
Royal Anthropological Institute, 1912-14; Fullerian professor
of Comparative Anatomy at the Royal Institution, 1917-23.
Secretary, Royal Institution, 1922-26; Treasurer of same, 1926-
29; President, British Association, 1927; Rector, University of
Aberdeen, 1930-33. Author of several books on anthropology
and anatomy; edited *Hughes' Practical Anatomy,* 1902; Assist.
Editor of Treves' *Surgical and Applied Anatomy (Encyclopaedia
Britannica,* 1946, and from *Who's Who,* 1950).

At the outset of our inquiry we are met by the
ancient belief that the British Isles are divided by a
racial frontier which separates the western or Celtic
peoples from the eastern inhabitants of Saxon
origin. It was my fortune to be born on the border
of the Celtic fringe, and no one growing up under
these circumstances can fail to realize that the
Celtic spirit is a real live force. Is it a racial antagonism which is elicited when Celt and Saxon are in
conflict? What is the physical difference between a
Celt and a Saxon? That is a matter to which I have
given my attention for some years, and the results
of my inquiries I will place before you as briefly as
I may. In the audience now before me there are
certain to be pure representatives of all our four
nationalities; Celts and Saxons as pure as any in
the country are sure to be present in any university
audience. But except for a trick of speech or a local
mannerism, the most expert anthropologist cannot
tell Celt from Saxon or an Irishman from a Scots-
man. There are, to be sure, certain physical types
which prevail in one country more than in another.
But I do not know of any feature of the body or
any trait of the mind, or of any combination of
features or traits which will permit an expert, on
surveying groups of university students, to say this
group is from Scotland, that from Wales, the third
from Ireland, and the fourth from England. In
stature and in colouring, in form of skull and of
face, elaborate trials have revealed national difference only of the most minor kind. Nay, we know
very well the physical features of the Saxon pioneers
who became the masters of England and dominated
the lowlands of Scotland. Their graveyards have
been examined by the score, but it is not by the
form of the skulls and the strength of their limb bones
that we know we are dealing with the graves of
ancient Saxons, but by the implements, ornaments,
and utensils, which were buried with them. As
regards shape of skull or form of bones, I do not
think a practised craniologist could distinguish the
skulls and bones found in an ancient Saxon ceme-
tery in Surrey from the remains of a Celtic grave in
Connemara, so much are Celtic and Saxon types
alike. Were we to dress one group of fishermen from
the coast of Norfolk and another from the shores
of Connaught in the same garb, I do not think
there is an anthropologist in Europe who by mere
inspection could tell the Irish from the English
group. From a physical point of view the Celt and
Saxon are one; whatever be the source of their
mutual antagonism, it does not lie in a difference of

race. It is often said that we British are a mixed and
mongrel collection of types and breeds; the truth is
that as regards physical type the inhabitants of the
British Isles are the most uniform of all the large
nationalities of Europe.

The statement which I have just made, that
Britons are really a uniform folk, seems altogether
at variance with the teaching of history. What I am
to say now will explain a discrepancy which, in its
essence, is only superficial. Our written history
opens with the Roman invasion and occupation of
Britain; it was an "occupation" or "plantation",
not a true colonization. On the other hand, the
Saxon and Danish invasions ended in widely spread
and true colonizations of Britain. The Norman
invasion, on the other hand, was of the nature of a
plantation. I will make the difference between the
various forms of invasion apparent presently. There
have been, too, flocks of immigrant refugees at
various times. We have the most positive evidence
that long before the dawn of written history the
processes of invasion and colonization had been
going on in Britain. In all these invasions, historic
and prehistoric, with one important exception, no
strange or new racial stock was added to the British
Isles; all were apparently branches of the human
stock which still occupy the northwest of Europe—
—men of the Nordic type—or as I should prefer to
call them, the North Sea breed . . . (pp. 22-24).

. . . In all these invasions and colonizations there
is only one which was not drawn from the North
Sea stock. That invasion took place in the second
millennium before Christ, when the round-headed
stock of Central Europe broke through the Nordic
belt, reached the shores of the North Sea, and invaded Britain on a scale which has never been
equalled before or since save in Saxon times. That
invasion of round-heads broke first on England and
Scotland, but Wales and particularly Ireland received in time a full share of the fresh arrivals. With
this one exception all the invaders and settlers of
the British Isles were waves derived from the same
prolific source—the North Sea breed. We see, then,
why there should be little physical difference between
Celt and Saxon. The one was an earlier wave, the
other a much later wave of the same stock. But each
wave brought its own mode of speech and its own
tribal spirit. Of all the inhabitants of the British
Isles the Irish may be regarded as the purest representatives of the North Sea or Nordic stock (pp. 25,
26).

Serial No. 90a.

EXTRACT FROM *ARE WE COUSIN TO THE GERMAN?*, by Sir Arthur Keith, in *The Graphic* Dec. 4 1915, p. 720.

In their standard atlases and school geographies the Germans colour Great Britain, Holland, Denmark, Norway and Sweden with the same tint as their own empire, to indicate that all those lands are inhabited by branches of the great Teutonic family. Our best historians are inclined to admit the German claim; we cannot deny, even if we had the desire, that English and German are cousin tongues. It is an historical fact that the Anglo-Saxons came from lands lying on the western shores of the present German empire. Those, however, who have studied the modern populations of Britain and Germany have reached a very definite and very different conclusion, namely, that the Briton and German represent contrasted and opposite types of humanity. In this war Britain and Germany are fighting not only for opposite ideals of life; it is a life-and-death struggle between two contending types of physical manhood.

On this page are shown the prevalent British and the prevalent German forms of skull. The radical differences in the two forms leap to the eye. In the majority of Britons—English, Welsh, Scottish and Irish—the hinder part of the head, the occiput, projects prominently backwards behind the line of the neck; the British head is long in comparison with its width. In the vast majority of Germans the occiput is flattened as if the hinder part of the head, when still young and plastic, had been pushed forwards and upwards. The peculiarity of the German skull is due to no artificial means; we know that the prominent occiput and flattened occiput are characters that breed true over thousands of years, and that they are characters which indicate a profound racial difference. Even in the sixteenth century, Vesalius, who is universally regarded as the "father of anatomy", regarded the flat occiput as a German characteristic; but seeing that he was born in Brussels in 1514, it is possible that Teutonic anatomists may now impugn his veracity. We have, however, the evidence of Virchow—the greatest of German anthropologists. He came, rather unwillingly, to the conclusion that the vast majority of modern German people differed from British, Dutch, Dane and Scandinavian in form of head.

It is fit and proper from an anthropologist's point of view that Marshal Hindenburg should have become the national hero of Germany. He represents the physical type of manhood now struggling for the dominance of Europe; he is a concrete embodiment of the German ideal of manhood and *Kultur*. We see the British ideal in the portrait of an English gentleman, placed side by side with Marshal Hindenburg's portrait for comparison. In these two portraits we have brought before us

opposite racial types; it rests with the manhood of this country to prove which is to be the dominant type in the world.

How are we to reconcile history with actual facts —for it is undeniable, from an anthropologist's point of view, that British and Germans belong to opposite European types? The explanation is easy. With the exodus of the Franks to France and the Anglo-Saxons to Britain in the fifth, sixth, seventh, and eighth centuries of our era, Germany was almost denuded of the long-headed elements in her population. These were concentrated in the eastern shorelands, and in modern Germany it is only in these same lands, forming less than one-fifth of the total Empire, that we find a good proportion of "long-heads" amongst the German people. When the Franks and Anglo-Saxons were moving into France and England the great area now covered by the German Empire had been invaded from the east—from the regions now occupied by Russians, Poles and Czechs—by swarms of people with flat occiputs and round heads—men of the Hindenburg type. History relates that by the end of the sixth century this type had overrun all the area of modern Germany, except the lands along the western shores. We now know, however, that the permeation of Germany by men of the Hindenburg type did not begin with the break-up of the Roman Empire. In ancient graves of the early iron, bronze and neolithic ages we find the Hindenburg type, showing that the western movement of the flat occiputs had set in thousands of years before the days of the Roman Empire.

With the exit of the Franks and Anglo-Saxons the short-headed ancestors of modern Germany were left as the dominant type of Germany. The famous French anthropologist, de Quatrefages, regarded the cruelties practised by the Germans in 1870-71 as attributable to their racial origin. Modern anthropologists are not inclined to regard any mental character which can be eradicated by education as a racial trait. The practice of a codified system of "Frightfulness" is due to the vicious method of education, not to a vicious racial origin. Yet there can be no doubt that certain aptitudes do belong to certain races and breed true from generation to generation. The flat occiput has never shown any aptitude for the sea. All the races which have commanded the sea—the Portuguese, Spaniards, Dutch, Norwegians and British—have long heads with prominent occiputs. It is remarkable that even at the present day the German navy recruits its crews from the western shores, where a long-headed element still manages to survive.

EXTRACT FROM AN ARTICLE by Sir Arthur Keith, in *The Daily Mail*, Feb. 26, 1931, p.10.

The British Isles are supposed to be inhabited by a mongrel people—the most mixed in Europe. We are the descendants of Celts, Saxons, Angles, Jutes, Danes, Normans, Flemings and Hugenots. As dressed up in a Lord Mayor's Show we recognise each of these faces without difficulty. But suppose we return to the crowd which deploys into the city every morning—can we recognise Celt from Saxon, Angle from Dane, Irishman from Scot? I confess that I cannot.

"Of course you cannot", my critic replies, "because in these recent centuries all our original races have become mixed up by intermarriage and migration." The mixture is older than critics suppose. We know many burial places where early Saxon settlers laid their dead; we know English cemeteries of pre-Saxon date—cemeteries in which Celts were buried. We know well the facial features and shapes of the head of the original Danish and Norman invaders.

Yet the expert craniologist, when he examines a mixed collection of skulls, obtained from the Celtic, Saxon, Danish, and Norman graveyards of England, has the same difficulty as the ordinary man has when he seeks to separate the descendants of these races in the morning crowd which emerges from Liverpool-street Station.

In facial feature and cranial shape all these invaders of England were of the same general conformation. Celt, Saxon, Dane, and Norman, although they came at different times, bringing with them peculiarities in speech, manners, and customs, were not, in a physical sense, different peoples; one and all they were offshoots of the same great parent stock of North-West Europe. They were cousin peoples.

It is true today, just as it was in the time of Tacitus, that a dark-haired people of Mediterranean origin lives in Southern Wales; there are dark-haired people of similar origin in Southern Ireland. Notwithstanding these exceptions we may rightly look upon the British people as the least mongrel, the most uniform, to be found in any country of Europe.

Thus the reader will see that dead bones can speak; what they tell us is that we are a less diverse people than we thought, and that although civilisation is altering us, yet not to a degree which need give us any uneasiness.

EXTRACT FROM *THE RACIAL ELEMENTS OF EUROPEAN HISTORY*, by Hans F. K. Gunther, English transs. by G. C. Wheeler; Methuen & Co.; London 1927.

GUNTHER, HANS; Doctor of Philosophy; born in Freiburg, Breisgau, 1891. Studied at Universities of Freiburg and Paris, and in the Department of Anthropology of the Dresden Museum of Zoology and Ethnology. Became professor at Berlin University, 1935. No religion; specialty, racial investigation.

Author of books on ethnology and other subjects, including *Racial Studies of the German People, Racial History of the Greek and Roman Peoples, Racial Study of the Jewish People*, etc. (*Compiled from the German 'Who's Who', etc*).

The Mediterranean race and isolated Alpine settlers in England had been driven into the south and west by the invading Kelts. The Kelts brought the first heavy invasion of the Nordic race into all the British Isles. They may have carried with them from the Continent a certain number of Alpine bond-men, whose bones then will necessarily be found earlier and oftener in certain layers of the Bronze and the Hallstatt period than Nordic bones; for the Nordic class in the European peoples of that time had already taken to body-burning. But the Alpine lower orders among the Kelts who invaded England cannot have been numerous. As the Nordic upper class, therefore, disappeared among the Kelts the aboriginal Mediterranean characteristics must have made their appearance again in the population, which now spoke Keltic dialects. A further Nordic invasion of England came about through the Anglo-Saxons. It brought with it the thorough nordicization of England. But the Anglo-Saxon states were shattered by the hard Normans. (Were they the creations of a people with a rather soft disposition? Anglo-Saxon poetry would seem to point to this.) The Normans, who, like the Anglo-Saxons, were of Nordic blood, and left behind them on the map of France for all to see the districts in Normandy with light colouring, and the strip along the coast of Brittany, became the masters of England. Their conquest was the third invasion in historical times of Nordic blood. Whatever peoples, whatever individual Viking bands may have trodden English ground—Kelts, Angles, Saxons, Jutes, Danes, Norwegians and Icelandic Vikings, Normans—they were always predominantly Nordic peoples. It is a mixture of *peoples* that marks English history; it was only in the south and west that a mixture of *races* took place from time to time, whither each new conquest by Nordic peoples had driven back the Mediterranean and Alpine men. English history is rich in movements of peoples; in movements of races it has little to show (pp. 228, 229).

EXTRACTS FROM *THE RACES OF EUROPE*, by Professor W. Z. Ripley; Chicago, 1900.

RIPLEY, WILLIAM ZEBINA, 1867-1941, Assistant Professor of Sociology, and Professor of Economics, Massachusetts Institute of Technology; lecturer on Anthropology at Columbia University in the City of New York.

The most remarkable trait of the population of the British Isles is its head form; and especially the uniformity in this respect which is everywhere manifested. The prevailing type is that of the long and narrow cranium, accompanied by an oval rather than broad or round face. This cephalic uniformity throughout Britain makes the task of illustrating types by means of portraits peculiarly difficult; for distinctions of race are reduced mainly to matters of feature and relative blondness, instead of the more fundamental characteristics. . . .

Measured by cephalic index . . . the uniformity in cranial type all through the British Isles is so perfect that it cannot be represented by shaded maps as we have heretofore been accustomed to do. Wherever heads have been measured, whether in the Aran Islands off the west coast of Ireland, the Hebrides and Scottish Highlands, Wales and Cornwall, or the counties about London, the results all agree within a few units.

It will be observed at once that the indexes all lie between 77 and 79, with the possible exception of the middle and western parts of Scotland, where they fall to 76.

What do these dry statistics mean? In the first place they indicate an invariability of cranial type even more noticeable than in Spain or Scandinavia. Compared with results elsewhere in central Europe, they are remarkable. On the continent nearby, the range of variation of averages of cephalic index in a given country is never less than ten points; in Italy and France it runs from 75 to 88. Oftentimes within a few miles it will drop five or six units suddenly. Here in the British Isles it is practically uniform from end to end. Highland and lowland, city or country, peasant or philosopher, all are practically alike in respect of this fundamental racial characteristic (pp. 303-305).

The Romans came in considerable numbers; they walled cities and built roads; they introduced new arts and customs; but when they abandoned the islands they left them racially as they were before. For they appear to have formed a ruling caste, holding itself aloof in the main from intermarriage with the natives. Not even a heritage of Latin place names remains to any considerable degree. Kent and Essex were of all counties perhaps the most thoroughly Romanized; and yet the names of towns, rivers, and hills were scarcely affected. The people manifest no physical traits which we are justified in ascribing to them.

The Teutonic invasions, however, were of a different character (i.e. from the Roman). The invaders, coming perhaps in the hopes of booty, yet finding a country more agreeable for residence than their barren northern land, cast in their lot with the natives, in many districts forming the great majority of the population. We find their descendants all over Britain today.

The Teutonic invaders were all alike in physical type, roughly speaking. We can scarcely distinguish a Swede from a Dane today, or either from a native of Schleswig-Holstein or Friesland, the home of the Jutes, Angles and Saxons. They are all described to us by the chronicles, and our modern research corroborates the testimony. . . . The Danes are somewhat broader headed than the Hanoverians perhaps; but in all other respects they are tall and blond Teutons.

Since we cannot follow these invaders over Britain by means of their head form, they being all alike and entirely similar to the already prevailing type in the British Isles previous to their advent, we must have recourse to a contributory kind of evidence (p. 311).

EXTRACTS FROM *THE RACES OF EUROPE*, by C. S. Coon, Assistant Professor of Anthropology, Harvard University; Macmillan, New York, 1939.

It can be shown that Sumerians who lived over five thousand years ago in Mesopotamia are almost identical in skull and face form with living Englishmen, and that predynastic Egyptian skulls can be matched both in a seventeenth-century London plague pit, and in Neolithic cist graves in Switzerland. Modern dolichocephalic whites or browns are very similar in head and face measurements and

form. The Nordic race in the strict sense is merely a pigment phase of the Mediterranean (p. 83).

The Long Barrow population formed a distinct, homogeneous type; one different from any which, to our knowledge, had previously inhabited the British Isles since the days of Galley Hill; and one which cannot be duplicated, except as an element in a mixed population, anywhere on the western European continent. One is, therefore, led to conclude that the Megalithic cult was not merely a complex of burial rites which diffused without visible carriers; and also that the bearers of this complex avoided mixture by coming by sea (pp. 110-111).

In looking for related populations of equal age, we may eliminate at once the smaller, less dolichocephalic branches of the Mediterranean race proper, including the Danubian. A few individual crania in Neolithic Spain and Italy would qualify, but none of the series from these countries. The standard Egyptian crania, as groups, are all too small, as is the single lady from Greece. In one particular feature, the nasal index, the Long Barrow people resemble the Egyptians more than most of the more northerly Mediterraneans, for the Long Barrow crania are leptorrhine . . . (p. 111).

A true and valid similarity, however, may be found between the English Long Barrow series and the early skulls from el'Ubaid in Sumeria, which, whether belonging to the fourth or the third millennium B.C., are in either case older than their British counterparts. The only difference which prevents identity is that the Mesopotamian faces and noses are somewhat longer (p. 112).

EXTRACT FROM *UR OF THE CHALDEES*, by Sir Leonard Woolley; Scribner's, New York; 6th ed. p. 117.

. . . I have already said that we do not quite know who the Sumerians are; tradition would make them come from the East; the study of their bones and skulls shows that they were a branch of the Indo-European stock of the human race resembling what is called Caucasian man, a people who in stature and in appearance might pass as modern Europeans rather than as Orientals.

Serial No. 90c.
Published by *The National Message*, Ltd.
6 Buckingham Gate, London, S.W.1.
Copyright.

Authority: Professor A. D. Peacock, Natural History Department, University
College, Dundee, in his Address to the Belfast (1952) Meeting of the
British Association for the Advancement of Science.

Virgin Birth: Not an Impossibility

FOR a century past, unbelievers have derided or discounted the Bible
theme of the Virgin Birth of Jesus Christ, on the premise that such a
phenomenon is biologically impossible.

The Scriptural basis of this fundamental tenet of the Christian faith is
unmistakable. The prophet's momentous announcement: ''A virgin shall
conceive'', though confirmed in the New Testament, has often been
waved aside by the sceptic on the ground that the Hebrew word used by
Isaiah can also mean ''unmarried female''. Relevant passages, however,
are so positive that no other meaning but *virgin*, as the term is generally
understood, can possibly be assigned. The Angel of the Lord comforted
the troubled Joseph with the assurance that blessing and not shame
attached to Mary's condition and that "that which is conceived in her is
of the Holy Ghost''. St. Matthew adds the important testimony that
Joseph "knew her not'' until after Jesus was born. St. Luke records
that the bewildered Mary enquired of the Angel: ''How shall this be, seeing I know not a man?'' From its inception, the Christian Church, with
its early testimony to guide it, has held steadfastly to this teaching of
Scripture.

In recent years the complacency of the atheist and the agnostic has been
rudely shaken by the revelations of Science that virgin birth in human
beings is not outside the bounds of possibility. This view has now been
clearly stated before so modern a body as the British Association for the

Advancement of Science. In a recent address to the Association, Professor A. D. Peacock put forward the view that the fundamental possibility of virgin birth has been established.

Most Christians are content to believe that "with God all things are possible" and biological consideration of this sacred theme may seem as repugnant to them as the doubts cast by the unbeliever. Nevertheless, it would surely be lamentable to miss the opportunity of using a view, which Scientists now acknowledge, to rebut the attacks of the sceptics. There will be many whose wavering faith may be strengthened by such secular testimony.

SOME PROBLEMS OF PARTHENOGENESIS

An address by Professor A. D. Peacock, to a Meeting of the British Association for the Advancement of Science—At Belfast, 4th September 1952.

Extract from a reprint in THE ADVANCEMENT OF SCIENCE—No. 34, 1952. (By kind permission of the Author.)

Parthenogenesis, virgin birth, means the production of offspring from a reproductive cell, usually the female gamete, without the concurrence of a gamete of the opposite sex (p. 134).

Female parthenogenesis is of two distinct types, one resulting in male-production (arrhenotoky) and the other, in general, female-production (thelytoky) (p. 134).

Arrhenotoky occurs in wheel animalcules, sawflies, bees and their allies, thrips, mites, scale insects and a Micromalthus beetle (p. 134).

Despite the many difficulties inherent in the living material, experimenters have not been deterred from attempting to obtain parthenogones from mammalian eggs, and astonishing results have been obtained at the hands of Pincus (1936, 1951a) and co-workers (1951b) in the U.S.A., using rabbits, and of Thibault (1948-49) in France, using rabbits, rats and sheep (p. 143).

The most extraordinary achievement of the Pincus school (1951b) has been the development of seven rabbit parthenogones, all female, one of which produced a litter of nine after mating . . . (p. 143).

Despite all the aforementioned curious and interesting things about parthenogenesis its biological significance should not be over-stressed. . . . Certainly parthenogenesis is very widespread but as the sole method of reproduction its extent is generally limited. For instance, it is of no account in the vast group of vertebrates while among invertebrates it is chiefly found among rotifers and insects. . . . (p. 146).

Finally, a natural question. Of what possible import is parthenogenesis to mankind? Pincus (1950) gives a part-answer: "Parthenogenetic reproduction in mammals would have the extraordinary advantage of the production of females only whose gene complement is exclusively that of the mother supplying the eggs. . . . It is interesting to note that the bee produces males by a natural parthenogenesis. If, by superovulation, egg transfer and artificial parthenogenesis, the desirable milk cow could be made to yield a large offspring of females like herself the land flowing with milk and honey will be available. Its economy will be based on parthenogenesis."

Applying the matter to mankind itself, the biologist speaking objectively, would say that though some may hold that there have been mammalian and human parthenogones in the past and, for all we know, may walk unsuspected in our midst today, there is no scientific evidence of such. . . (p. 148).

Serial No. 107.

Published by The National Message, Ltd.
6 Buckingham Gate, London, S.W.1.

Authorities: Various.

Geography in Old and New Testament Times   .

NUMEROUS geographical references in both the Old and New Testaments indicate something of the extent of the knowledge of geography
of those times. Mesopotamia, Egypt, Babylonia, Assyria, Media, Sinim,
India, Persia, "Asia", Greece, Rome, Spain, Cyrenaica, the "isles of the
sea", "the ends of the earth", are all mentioned in various Bible passages.
From such texts alone it is certain that by New Testament times the known
world extended at least from India and possibly China, to the Atlantic
coast of Europe.

From secular sources it can be demonstrated that detailed maps of the
known world, which extended from south-eastern coasts of Asia, Ireland,
the Orkneys, Shetlands, and Iceland, existed centuries before the Christian
Era, and were possibly well known in the times in which the Old
Testament prophets lived.

The knowledge that the earth is spherical, and of its circumference,
can be traced to earlier than two centuries before the Christian era, and
the practice of dividing maps of the earth's surface into degrees of latitude
and longitude would appear to be no less ancient. It is not at all improbable that the writers of the New Testament, and even of the Old, and
numerous others, possessed a surprisingly accurate knowledge of physical
geography from the Pacific to the Atlantic and from the Equator to the
Arctic Circle. A realisation of this is of great help in bringing the events
described in Scripture into proper focus.

THE EARLIEST KNOWN MAPS OF THE WORLD

It is not commonly known that centuries before the Christian era it had been determined that the earth was a sphere, and its circumference had been computed with commendable accuracy. Eratosthenes (276-196 B.C.) had given the circumference of the earth as 250,000 stadia, which is very nearly 25,000 miles (*vide Encyclopaedia Britannica*, art.: "Ptolemy"). Hipparchus (*c.* 150 B.C.) had divided the equatorial circle of the earth into 360 parts (our degrees). It has been pointed out by E. Lynam, of the British Museum, in his book, *The Cosmographia of Claudius Ptolemaeus* (1941), that the stadium of Eratosthenes was "between 512 and 520 English feet long", which gave 700 such stadia to 1° of equatorial longitude; and that the unit used by Poseidonius was the Philetarian stadium, which was somewhat longer, there being 500 such stadia to 1°. Poseidonius thus gave the earth's circumference as 180,000 stadia. In later years, both figures were used without regard to the fact that they were in different units; and eventually the earth's circumference was erroneously accepted as 180,000 of Eratosthenes' stadia, or 18,000 miles, a figure much too small.

The earliest known atlas of the world was handed down to us by Ptolemy, the Alexandrian geographer, mathematician, and astronomer, born, we are told, at Ptolemais Hermii, a Grecian city of the Thebaid, in Egypt. "All that is known for certain about him is that he observed at Alexandria during the reigns of Hadrian and Antoninus Pius, between the years A.D. 127 and 141 or 151" (*Encyclopaedia Britannica*, 1946).

In the present state of knowledge it is difficult, if not impossible, to say how much of the earliest atlases that have come down to us originated with Ptolemy. Much of his information was derived from the works of the geographer, Marinus of Tyre (A.D. 70-130). "The greater part of Marinus' treatise was occupied with the discussion of his authorities, and it is impossible, in the absence of the original work, to decide how far his results attained a scientific form. But Ptolemy himself considered them, on the whole, so satisfactory that he made his predecessor's work the basis of his own in regard to all the Mediterranean countries, that is, in regard to almost all those regions of which he had definite knowledge. In the more remote regions of the world, Ptolemy availed himself of Marinus' information, but with reserve, and he explains the reasons that induced him sometimes to depart from his predecessor's conclusions. Among other things, Ptolemy's work shows the increased knowledge of Asia and Africa acquired since Strabo and Pliny" (*Encyclopaedia Britannica*, 1946).

It has been pointed out by Mr. Lynam that Ptolemy was an expert in mathematical geography, but that he never either attempted descriptive geography or observations of latitude and longitude of various places. What Ptolemy did attempt, and succeeded in doing, was to make maps of the known world "upon a projection of his own devising, which would show the sphericity of the earth" (Lynam, p. 3). " . . . in Book I of his text he described two projections, the first conical with one standard parallel, the second pseudo-spherical, all of his maps are drawn upon a modified form of Marinus' projection in which, while the parallels and meridians are all straight, the resultant rectangles differ in height, apparently in an attempt to bring the latitude into correct ratio to the longitude" (*ibid.*). It appears that we cannot attribute the whole of the first atlas of the world or even the first maps to Ptolemy, but that he may have been the originator of certain projections devised to improve upon those of earlier geographers in certain respects.

Serial No. 74a

It should be observed in passing, that from the foregoing description of the features of Marinus' projection, it anticipated that of the famous Mercator by over a thousand years, and that its great advantage to navigators lies in the fact that any straight line drawn on it between two points gives a constant bearing whereby the one point may be reached from the other. Although the distance travelled along that line is greater than along a Great Circle route, which gives the shortest distance between two points, the navigational problems are much simpler, for in following a great circle over long distances, a succession of alterations of course must be performed. Although the sailing vessels of the ancients might not always be able to hold a constant course from place to place, it is of interest that the projection seemingly used by Marinus is still a basis for modern sea and air navigation.

Marinus, in turn, may not have been the originator of the maps and projections available to Ptolemy; and certainly his information came from earlier sources; but where? This is a problem that cannot be answered in detail, but certain things point to some very interesting conclusions. Within the comparatively narrow limits of the "known" world of the Mediterranean countries—the Greek, Persian, and Babylonian empires—there must have been numerous sources upon which to draw for materials to make maps. But in the case of lands beyond the limits of these empires and yet for which there are numerous and surprisingly accurate details in the so-called Ptolemy's maps, the problem of sources of information is much more complex. Ptolemy's maps cover regions which, so far as we know, were never visited by the Romans: distant parts of India, Ceylon, Burma, Malaya, and China on the one hand, and northern Scotland, Ireland, the Orkneys, Hebrides, Norway, Sweden, and possibly even Iceland, on the other. If Roman forces never set foot in Ireland, for instance, how is it that Ptolemy's maps portray with reasonable accuracy the shape of that island, and locate such places as Eblana, early Dublin, and tribes such as the Brigantes? It is clear that the maps were made by someone with a knowledge of the island, or from accurate accounts of it, and that they were of pre-Roman origin. This receives confirmation in an observation made long ago by Thomas Moore, the poet, in his *History of Ireland* (1835), in which he wrote:

"It is worthy of remark, too, that while of the towns and places of Britain he has in general given but the new Roman names, those of Ireland still bear on his map their old Celtic titles. . . . When it is considered that Ptolemy, or rather Marinus or Tyre, the writer whose steps he implicitly followed, is believed to have founded his geographical descriptions and maps on an ancient Tyrian atlas, this want of aboriginal names for the cities and places of Britain, and their predominance in the map of Ireland, prove how much more anciently and intimately the latter island must have been known to the geographers of Tyre than the former." [1]

Greek writers have left accounts of Ireland, which might indicate a possible source for such maps. On the other hand, the fact that Ptolemy's maps and information were at least in part derived from a Tyrian might be taken to indicate a Phoenician origin; which would harmonise with the accounts of Herodotus, Diodorus, and Strabo concerning the voyages of the Phoenicians to, and their trade with, the distant west. Herodotus mentions the British Isles by name (Albion and Ierne—the Britannic Isles); he also mentions the existence of Ceylon (Taprobane), and relates that the Phoenicians had circumnavigated Africa.

Although none of Ptolemy's original maps is known to exist, reasonably exact copies have been handed down to us in two series. The A Group, consisting of one map of the

_____
[1] Vol. I, p. 9.

world and twenty-six countries, is fairly well known, for the most frequently reproduced copies belong to this series. Some fifty editions were published between 1477 and 1730. Group B, of one map of the world and sixty-four maps of provinces, is little known to the average student, as they have not been published.

The authenticity of Ptolemy's maps is supported by Mr. Lynam, who writes:

"While it has often been argued that Ptolemy's maps as they first became known to Europeans as Greek manuscript maps were not authentic' but revisions by a later hand, Father Fischer has now shown that this is true only of the map of the world' and that others, in spite of minor differences between them due to errors by copyists, are undoubtedly copies of Ptolemy's originals" (*ibid.*, p. 4).

Ptolemy treated the earth as a sphere, and divided it into 360 degrees of latitude and longitude. Latitude was measured over the known world from the Equator to the Pole through 90°; South of the Equator, in latitude 16°, 25' S., Africa became *Terra Incognita*. Longitude was measured from the most western part of the known world, the Fortunate, or Canary, Islands, which served as his "Greenwich", which were placed 2½° instead of 9° 20' west of the Sacred Promontory. The present coast of what appears to be Indo-China reached 180° under Ptolemy's system, which, as we have seen, was based on an erroneous use of the stadia. Hipparchus had early divided (*circa* 126 B.C.) the globe into 360 degrees of latitude (*Encyclopaedia Britannica*, 1946, art.: "Ptolemy"). This may have an earlier astronomical association, based on the ancient Mesopotamian, Hebrew, Egyptian, and Greek calendars, representing the circle of the year of 360 days, with its four quarters between the equinoxes and the solstices; the twelve months of thirty days each would be parallel to the twelve signs of the zodiac; while in Egypt in particular the remaining five whole days of the solar year were termed "over and above the year".

It is interesting to speculate as to whether earlier geographers, such as Eratosthenes, whose computation of the circumference of the globe was correct, actually had drawn up maps accurate in their proportions: a thing that seems far from improbable, in which case Ptolemy's work only represents a stage in the decay of the learning of his predecessors—a decay which continued until in the Middle Ages scientists like Galileo were forced to recant their teachings that the earth was round. Marinus of Tyre (from whom Ptolemy obtained much of his geographical information) obtained his data from earlier sources, and although he seemingly used the erroneous calculation of Poseidonius, he appears to have retained the latitude of certain earlier and correct geographical accounts, for we find that he places Thule, or Iceland, in 63° N. or 66° if Eratosthenes' reckoning for the angle of the tropic be used. This is correct in theory. It therefore appears that Ptolemy realised he must place Thule on the Arctic Circle, as we now call it; so that while he used a globe of too small dimensions, he nevertheless placed that island on its correct latitude. Ptolemy's, or rather Marinus', maps of Europe are thus distorted not so much in a northerly direction as to the west, due to his attempt to place distances for a globe of 25,000 miles on projections for one of 18,000 miles. Of Ptolemy's and Marinus' errors in this respect, the *Encyclopaedia Britannica* (1946) states:

"But at the very outset of his attempt he fell into an error vitiating all his conclusions. Eratosthenes (*c.* 276-196 B.C.) was the first who had attempted scientifically to determine the earth's circumference, and his result of 250,000 (or 252,000) stadia, i.e. 25,000

(25,200) geographical miles, was generally adopted by subsequent geographers, including Strabo. Posidonius, however (c. 135-50 B.C.), reduced this to 180,000, and the latter computation was inexplicably adopted by Marinus and Ptolemy. This error made every degree of latitude or longitude (measured at the equator) equal to only 500 stadia (50 geographical miles), instead of its true equivalent of 600 stadia. The mistake would have been somewhat neutralized had there existed a sufficient number of points of which the position was fixed by observation; but we learn from Ptolemy himself that such observations for latitude were very few, while the means of determining longitudes were almost wholly wanting. Hence the positions laid down by him were, with few exceptions, the result of computations from itineraries and the statements of travellers, which, owing to the want of instruments, etc., were liable to much greater error in ancient times than at the present day. But, great as were the errors resulting from such imperfect means of calculation, they were increased by the permanent error arising from Ptolemy's system of graduation. Thus, if he concluded (from itineraries) that two places were 5,000 stadia distant, he would place them 10° apart, and thus in fact separate them by 6,000 stadia.''

If, as seems likely, there was a time before Ptolemy in which accurate knowledge of the distant world prevailed, it would seem to have been in the age either of Greece or Phoenicia, perhaps both; and rough dates may be set as limits. Alexander's destruction of the island fortress of Tyre, which city had been greatly reduced by the thirteen-year siege of Nebuchadnezzar in which the mainland fortification had been destroyed, ended that great power's maritime supremacy. The destruction of Carthage by Rome in 163 B.C. ended Phoenician colonial power in the Mediterranean. There is no tradition of Phoenician supremacy in the western Mediterranean prior to the founding of Carthage, some time about or after 1000 B.C., by the legendary Dido of Tyre. We are thus left with an era of Phoenician supremacy covering approximately 1000-600 B.C., and in which it may be possible to place the sources from which the earliest maps of the world were made. This period, singularly enough, embraces the history of the northern Kingdom of Israel, and for the adjacent tribes of which (Asher, Dan, Naphtali, Zebulon and Issacher—the latter two also using Accho) Tyre must have been an important port. It is singular that classical writers never refer to the northern Kingdom of Israel by name, either before or after the captivities; the implication of this is that their use of the name ''Phoenician'' embraced that kingdom, and that the maritime achievements of the so-called Phoenicians may not be dissociated from an active participation by Israelites themselves, for the era of Phoenician power is that of Israelitish prosperity. Thus, when ''Phoenicians'' are known to have reached the ends of the earth, there is good reason to believe that Israelites did also.

Finds of Baltic amber along the long sea-route to Palestine; of Irish gold in Gaza; and a long trail of Megalithic monuments along the coastal route from Palestine to Britain, support such a belief (see Serial Nos. 45 [386.0936]; 49 [571.3]; 60 [572.9394].

Our study of ancient geography thus shows with certainty that long before the time of our Lord's ministry, and possibly as early as the times of the Prophets, the distant coastlands of Europe and Asia, from Iceland to Malaya, had been portrayed on maps with a remarkable degree of accuracy. No doubt such maps were available to the Phoenician mariners, whose ''glory'' was portrayed by Ezekiel (xxviii: 13) as that of being adorned by nine of the precious stones of the high-priest's breastplate which represent the tribes of Israel whose seaborne trade brought great prosperity. The familiarity of the Greeks with the spherical shape of the earth, and their accurate computation of its circumference in the third century B.C., strongly support the view that they too possessed a detailed knowledge of geography. The absence of any indication that the Greeks themselves had prepared maps of the world, further supports the view that such maps, which must have been in existence and must have formed the basis of such computations, belonged to an earlier people. There is no indication that the maps were of Egyptian origin. We are thus left with strong support for the presumption that, since Ptolemy obtained his data from Marinus of Tyre, they were of Tyrian origin, and attributable to the great age of Phoenician prosperity that extended from the times of David and Solomon to the period of Nebuchadnezzar. There is thus a distinct possibility, if not probability, that the Prophets of the Old Testament uttered their predictions with an excellent background of geographical knowledge.

The accompanying reproductions of Ptolemy's maps belong to the A Group, prepared in 1482, now in the British Museum (ref. IC. 9303), and represent the British Isles, Germania, European Sarmatia, Asiatic Sarmatia, western Scythia, eastern Scythia, ''India'' west of the Ganges, ''India'' (Burma, etc.) east of the Ganges. These plates cover a continuous area from Iceland to Malaya, and show something of the ancients' geographical knowledge concerning what were to them some of the remote parts of the world.

Illustrations are by courtesy of the British Museum.

Serial No. 74c.
Published by *The National Message Ltd.,*
6 Buckingham Gate, London, S.W.1.
Copyright.

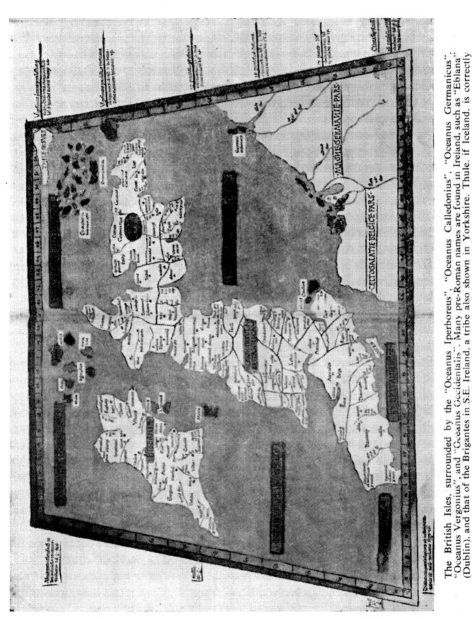

The British Isles, surrounded by the "Oceanus Iperboreus", "Oceanus Calledonius", "Oceanus Germanicus", "Oceanus Vergonius", and "Oceanus Occidentalis". Many pre-Roman names are found in Ireland, such as "Eblana" (Dublin), and that of the Brigantes in S.E. Ireland. a tribe also shown in Yorkshire. Thule. if Iceland, is correctly placed on the latitude of the Arctic Circle.

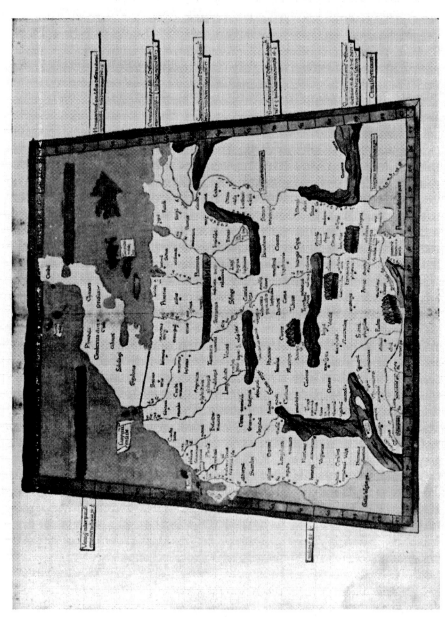

Germania. The Cimbri are shown in northern Denmark, the "Cimbricus Chersonesus". To the south of Denmark are shown the Saxones. The Rhine (Renus) and Vistula (Istula) lie to the west and east of Germania respectively.

Serial No. 74d

European Sarmatia, lying between the "Oceanus Sarmaticus" (Baltic), the "Paludes Meotides" (Sea of Azov), the Istula (Vistula), and the Tanais (Don).

Asiatic Sarmatia, lying between the Tanais (Don), the Rha (by which it would seem that the Volga was intended, but which name is more like that of the Ural), the Caucasus, and the watershed which divides the rivers flowing into the Arctic and Baltic from those flowing into the Black and Caspian Seas.

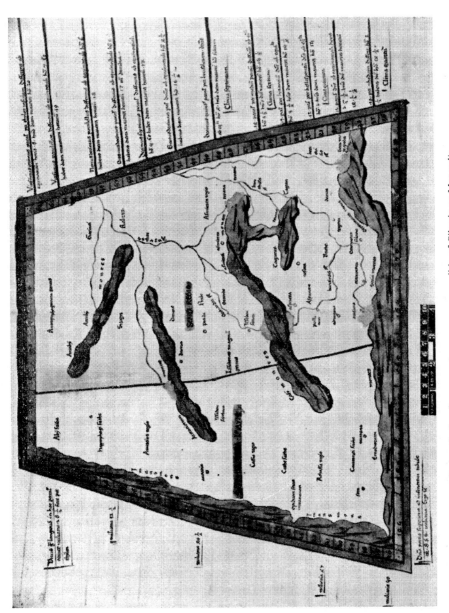

Serica, the less-known eastern expanses, possibly of Siberia or Mongolia.

Serial No. 74

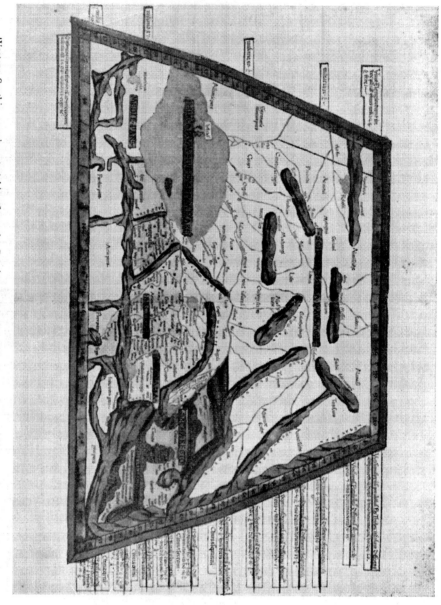

Western Scythia, a region stretching from the Caspian, seemingly to the mountains of Eastern Turkestan, where lies the "Sacha Regio", and northwards from Bactriana. The identification of the Imaus mountains is doubtful, but they may be the Altai, Sayan, and Yablonoi ranges.

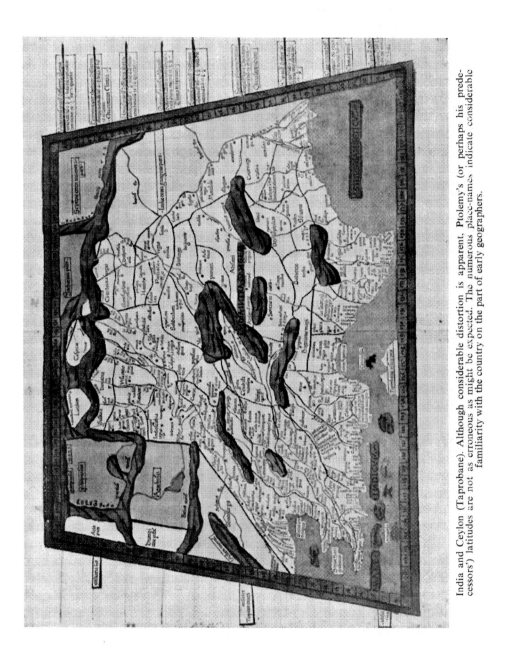

India and Ceylon (Taprobane). Although considerable distortion is apparent, Ptolemy's (or perhaps his predecessors') latitudes are not as erroneous as might be expected. The numerous place-names indicate considerable familiarity with the country on the part of early geographers.

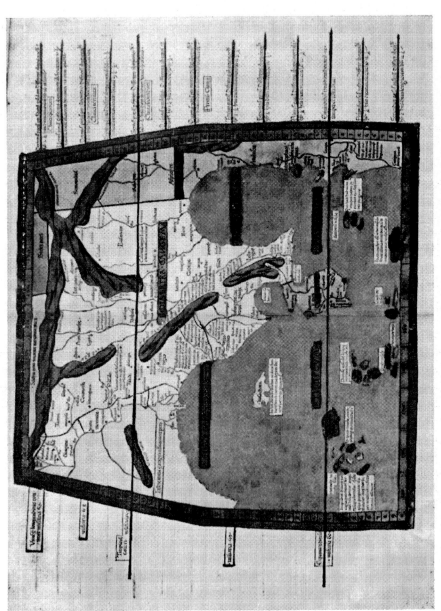

"India" east of the Ganges, showing the modern Assam. Burma. Thailand ("Sina Regio"), and, if Ptolemy's latitude may be used as a guide. the Malayan Peninsula reaching. as he shows not quite accurately, to the Equator and beyond.

Serial No. 74g

Authority: P. A. O. NEYMO, *Similitudes*

The Irish and Scottish Customs akin to Israelitish

IT is not generally realized that there is a marked similarity between the ancient manners and customs of the Irish and Scottish people and those of both the ancient Israelites and the modern orthodox Jews. These similarities a century ago attracted the attention of an acute observer whose name is no longer remembered in literary circles, but whose book, from which the following information is drawn, deals with this subject and has preserved some most useful information.

Although time has modified a number of the ancient Irish and Scottish customs, their Hebrew connections clearly are not derived from Christian sources, but from something much older and deeper than mere social contact of unrelated peoples.

The "similitudes" here reproduced from our author are by no means all that he has shown, and their number might be increased, as by considering the ancient Celtic (and for that matter also, Anglo-Saxon and other related) legal systems, which would reveal further likenesses to the Biblical system, as in the case of the laws concerning gavelkind (a system that began to disappear under feudalism); in the restricting of kingship to members of a single family recognized as the blood-royal; in blood feuds; etc.

EXTRACTS FROM *SIMILITUDES; OR, THE ISRAELITES, THE SCOTCH, AND THE IRISH*, by P. A. O. NEYMO; printed at the office of the *Galway Express*; 2nd edition. A first edition only of this work is listed in the British Museum catalogue: 10390.aaaa.14 (1850?).

The houses belonging to the poor in Palestine, travellers inform us, are generally built of mud, thus becoming appropriate images of the frailty of human life. The walls are easily broken through, or rather "dug" through by robbers, and it was this fact to which our Saviour referred when He exhorted His disciples not to lay up treasures where thieves could break through and steal. He was speaking, be it remembered, to the poor.

The doors of these houses move on pivots, and are secured by bars or wooden bolts with notches, which can be withdrawn from the outside by passing through a hole in the door, a wooden pin made to fit the notches of the bar. On the door posts are written portions of the law. The windows have no glass, and in winter are covered with wooden shutters, having holes sufficient to admit light. There are no chimneys, and the smoke of the fires kindled on flat stones or hearths escapes through a hole in the roof. The furniture is extremely simple, consisting but of a few articles, and these, such as are absolutely necessary. The interior of the cabin is furnished with large nails, having square heads, which are fixed in the walls while they are still soft, since, as they are built altogether of clay, they are too frail to admit of being struck with the hammer. On these nails are hung their kitchen utensils or other articles. Instead of chairs they generally sit on straw mats, which at night serve as beds, while their upper garments are used for covering; sometimes you will see low-legged stools, and at others you will find a room or kitchen full of people sitting cross-legged or with their knees bent under them.

The domestic utensils are of earthenware, copper, wood and leather. For instance a few plates, a pot or two, an oven which is only a metal pot with a lid, wooden bowls, known as kneading-troughs, a querns or handmill, and leathern bags; these, with a few chests or boxes, supply the place of many articles with which the houses of the rich are crowded.

How far this "house of the Israelite" bears any similitude to the "cabin of the Irish" the reader shall judge.

The cabins of the labourers are built of yellow clay and mud with stone foundations, or of mud and stone mixed, or of mud alone. The best cabins have large open chimneys, a common one only a hole in the roof. There are no grates, and the fire is kindled on the hearth. The windows are small, unglazed, except in cabins near towns or villages; while in the country they generally have wooden shutters, in which there are round or heart-shaped holes to admit the light. The doors are fastened by wooden bolts or wooden latches, which may be opened from the outside by means of a wooden pin,

suspended by a bit of twine from a nail in the door. These cabins usually contain a rough bedstead or frame, propped up on blocks of wood or stones, for the man and his wife; the elder children sleeping on mats or on a bundle of loose straw spread on the ground, while a piece of sacking or an old cloak, or the man's big-coat, constitutes the covering. The best cabins have two or three chairs, or low stools, a table and dresser, with a little stock of plates, cups, and saucers, a pot or two, a griddle, a few wooden bowls, a chest or box, and a querns.

A description of the house of a Scotch shepherd or farmer would be simply a repetition of either of the foregoing (pp. 6–9).

I remember one evening shortly after my return to my home in the West of Ireland, standing in the bay window of a pretty sitting-room, gazing on a glorious sunset, when an athletic young farmer suddenly presented himself, and invited me to be present at his marriage the next evening at four o'clock. I had no choice but to consent, such invitations in Ireland being as imperative as any dated at St. James's, or any other royal court (p. 10).

While these and other like thoughts were passing through my mind, the moon rose calm and clear over the distant woods of Ross-hill, motling "with mazy shade", the beautiful landscape; and at the same instant, an earnest voice, half suppressed, sounding close to me, I turned round and saw my old servant, who had come into the room with candles and to close the shutters, in the act of putting the sign of the cross on her forehead—the usual custom of the Irish of her class, on first seeing a new or full moon. When her eyes met mine I saw the deep blush mount even to her grey hair, yet with great self possession, she finished the act which she conscientiously believed to be right, then in a still lower tone, adding something to the effect that she hoped for protection from all harm, and the charms and spells of evil spirits, concluded with the words, "O Moon! may thou leave us safe as thou hast found us."

Had she been young, instead of an old maiden "past forty", she would have tripped off to the nearest gate or style, and abjuring the moon to be propitious to her "love", would have returned home with closed lips and gone to bed without speaking, in the fond hope of dreaming of her lover.

In the middle and higher classes it is customary for young girls to gather roses and lavender, wet with dew on the first night of a moon, in the belief—and what Irish girl does not believe—that the perfume of those floating about her, will secure to her the affections of her lover. Not dissimilar to this is the Jewish maiden's custom of gathering "buds o'er which the moon has breath'd", to weave into chaplets for her hair, by wearing which she hopes to bind, in "Love's gentle chains", her lover's heart to her own for ever; and the wreath of Moore's Nourmahal, which was woven "beneath the moonlight's hallowing beams", by the enchantress Namouna, is not merely a dream of the poet's own, but was suggested by this beautiful superstition common amongst the Israelites, and not unknown in any part of the East.

The Scottish maidens also, as well as the more imaginative daughters of Israel and Ireland, sometimes seek amusement in watching at the new and full moons, for revelations connected with their courtships; and not many years have passed since the canny Highland farmers observed the phases of the moon for the time of sowing their fields, believing as implicitly as our Connemara-men do still, that the fulness of the harvest depends on whether the moon was favourable at seed-time.

Neither the Israelites, however, nor the Celts— Scotch or Irish—ever worshipped the moon, as some have imagined, though these latter, up to the present day, observe many traditional superstitions in connection with it, . . . (pp. 14-16).

In former times the age of the moon was studied with regard to its influence in almost all the affairs of life by the inhabitants of Scotland and Ireland, and England too: the superstitious custom being a remnant of that study known as "Judicial Astronomy" which the Jews learned from the Babylonians and Chaldeans who practised it two thousand years before Christ. The avowed reason for assigning such properties to the planetary bodies was, that the heavens are one great book, in which God has written the history of the world, and in which every man may read his own fortune and the transactions of his time.

Proceeding on this doctrine, the study of the planets, and their various movements in reference to each other, became one of the most imposing superstitions of the East, extending its delusive influence even down to a comparatively late period of history, and to this day many of the Jews, particularly those who live in Cracow and its neighbourhood, will not perform the most ordinary duty without assuring themselves by a reference to either the moon or stars that the hour is propitious.

It is only about fifty years since both the Scotch of the Highlands, and the Irish of the South and West— even those of the higher and better educated class— deemed it of the utmost importance that a child should be born on a lucky day, the whole tenor of his life being supposed to depend on the influences of the heavenly bodies at the time of his birth.

It is of course perfectly needless to state that no shadow of reason exists for believing that either stars or planets possess the smallest influence over human affairs, and even the moon, which was long supposed to exercise some peculiar power over the seasons, and certain mental affections, is now declared by scientific men to have no effect whatever.

In the reign of James I, however, the English outstripped both the Scotch and Irish, and went near even to surpassing the Israelites themselves in their belief in, and practice of "Judicial Astronomy". Previously to this period Alfonso, King of Castile surnamed the Astrologer, had assembled the Arabic and Jewish sages of his empire and had sat in consultation with them five years, drawing up the Alfonsine Tables which gave to Europe all the mysteries of the Arabic and Hebrew astrology.

These tables, or rather copies of them, were obtained by an imposter named William Lilly, whose supposed powers made him a most important actor in the civil wars, and in the politics generally of his time (pp. 23-26).

At the door of a cottage, the walls of which were of snowy whiteness, though its surroundings were none of the neatest, I was met by the mother of the bride elect, who received me with a salutation equally Jewish as Celtish, "God save you. You are welcome." Admiring her national dress, which was Eastern as her greeting, I followed her into the house and was introduced to the bride, of whom, however, I shall not make further mention until I have described the dress of the mother.

She had on a flannel under-skirt of bright scarlet, blue stockings, and strong leather shoes, while the tight bodice of brown camlet or flannel which she usually wore, was replaced in honour of the occasion by a full loose jacket descending almost to her knees, of showy printed cotton, and confined at the waist by the string of a linen-gingham apron. Her head was covered by a snowy muslin cap, close to the ample borders of which was pinned a large shawl folded corner-ways, which hung down her shoulders.

This shawl, without which, or some equivalent, you never see a Western peasant-woman, is supposed by many to resemble Ruth's veil which held six measures of barley, both in its size, in the strength of its texture, and in the uses to which it is applied.

Calmet describes four sorts of veils, for three of which we find perfect similitudes amongst both Scotch and Irish. The first is a kerchief doubled and tied under the chin. It is almost unnecessary to say that the commonest head-dress worn by the married peasant women in the Highlands of Scotland and Ireland is a "little hood", which is simply a folded handkerchief put on over a muslin or linen cap and tied under the chin. The second veil described by the historian, is a large kerchief which covers the head, and hangs down over the bosom. This is the shawl as worn by our farmers' wives on Sundays and holidays, and all other days requiring a careful toilet. The third is the veil like Ruth's, enveloping the whole figure, and for which we find parallels in the mantles and hooded cloaks of the women West of Ireland, as well as in the tartan plaids of the inhabitants of the North of Scotland.

Peculiar to the Connemara district, however, there is another wrap or covering, which, perhaps, more nearly than any other resembles Ruth's veil.

It consists of a piece of coarse woollen cloth or flannel, of about three yards in length and two in breadth, either white or dyed scarlet. This, without in anyway folding it, the women put on their heads, allowing it to hang in front down to their toes. If the wearer of one of these has a bundle to carry, she takes up one corner and ties it into it; or she spreads it out on her arm, and has meal or potatoes poured into it; or should she have a heavy burden to carry, or an infant, she stoops her head while some one places the load between her shoulders, and then turns up over it the wrap or veil, which she draws tightly in front, and walks as easily under her burthen as we may suppose the Children of Israel did when they hastened out of the land of Egypt, laden in the same manner, "their kneading troughs being bound up in their cloths on their shoulders" (pp. 52–55).

. . . Heaped on the bed in this little room were the treasures which caused the light of inward gladness to look out through the beautiful eyes of the bride, like a living star at the edge of a cloud. All this she had with her own hands accomplished, and now her task was done, and his love was the reward; and more than enough for her happiness appeared that prize as with voiceless lips she breathed, "How proud he'll be to see all this!"

"And no wonder he should," I replied, as I handled and admired pieces of broad blanket-cloth, and pieces of fine linen, and pieces of scarlet flannel, all of which she had spun with her own hands; and gingham quilts, and a piece of gingham for curtains, and coarse diaper, and yarn stockings in endless varieties of blue and grey. These were all to be packed by *his* hands, after the marriage, into a large new deal-box standing in a corner, and in which were lying some sprigs of thyme and lavender—the present of a young gardener—to preserve the clothes from moths, and give them a sweet perfume.

Just such, and similar almost in quality and quantity, would have been the result of a Hebrew peasant maiden's strivings to make herself a comfortable home. The domestic duties of the woman whose price was "above rubies", were enumerated by Solomon, and he said, "she seeks wool and flax, and worketh willingly with her hands . . . She layeth her hands to the spindle, and her hands hold the distaff. She reacheth out her hand to the poor; yea, she reacheth forth her hands to the needy. She is not afraid of the snow for her household, for all her household are clothed in scarlet . . . She maketh fine linen and selleth it."

A great portion of the wealth of an Israelitish husband consisted in the goods manufactured by his wife and her assistants; and even men of rank owed no inconsiderable share of their treasures to the industry of the women of their households. Raiments of needlework are mentioned with silver and gold as of equal value, both by Zecharia and the Apostle Paul, and David alludes to garments being perfumed with "myrrh, aloes and cassia". Solomon figuratively mentions garments having "the smell of Lebanon"; and when Isaac blessed Jacob, he "smelled the smell of his raiment", and compared it to a "field which the Lord had blessed". That the embroidery of these garments ornamented with "needlework", and the care of them afterwards (which included perfuming them, to preserve them from moths, and laying them up in boxes made of cedar wood, sometimes poetically called "ivory palaces"), was more particularly the occupation of young women of rank, than either spinning or weaving, we may easily infer from the amount of skill, taste and perseverance which were required for the task (pp. 57–60).

To this day the Jewish maidens are as anxious to have an abundance of apparel laid up in chests, with myrrh and other sweet herbs, as either the maids of Scotland or Ireland are to store into "kists" and boxes fine linen, and flannel, and patch-work, with thyme, lavender, and lemon peel. Neither will the young lover of any of the three nations ever forget to enquire concerning the extent of his intended wife's wardrobe; and, by the way, this reminds me that at one time English ladies, even those of high rank, rarely thought of marrying until they had spun as much flax as was required for bed furniture, and were therefore till their marriage called "spinsters", an appellation which is still preserved in all proceedings at law, and in bans of marriage, as published in Church (pp. 61–62).

But to return to my interesting companion, who while we had remained together in the little room, had contrived to tell me a portion of the history of her love. She and Willy had, it appeared, been engaged when little more than children. . . (p. 65).

Until within a comparatively short period, young people had no voice in the selection of their partners. In the middle and lower classes the parents made the choice, and in the upper the right to do so was frequently usurped by the king (p. 167).

It is the custom of the Israelites as well as the Scotch and Irish to send a friend to demand the hand of the bride, ever since the time when Abraham said to the man who ruled over his house, "go unto my country and to my kindred, and take a wife unto my son Isaac". This man is termed "Scatchan", and he is master of the ceremonies during the revels. When these are over his duties close in a significant yet graceful little ceremony. He goes to the bride and bridegroom presenting some wedding gifts intended for each, bound firmly together, and addressing them for the first time as "husband" and "spouse", he wishes they may make a happy, or "blessed" household, and then retires (p. 66).

. . . The hour appointed for the coming of the bridegroom had arrived. Presently a horseman appeared in view, closely followed by several others, and all the young men who were friends of the bride, at once hastened out, using at the same time, the words, ''Hello! the bridegroom's coming!'' almost literally the Eastern exclamation, ''Behold the bridegroom cometh, go ye out to meet him.''

With every demonstration of joy young O'Donnell was led into the house, and when the bride came forward to meet him, he smiled to perceive that she had already concealed her rich black hair beneath a matron's cap. Previously he had seen her beautiful and abundant tresses gathered into a knot, confined by a comb at the back of her head, or occasionally even ''sthreeling'' about her shoulders, but now only the front locks were visible beneath the pretty lace borders.

Covering the head on the wedding day is also customary amongst the Israelites. Formerly a sort of crown formed of a gold or gilt rim, and large puffings of gauze intermingled with flowers, was placed on the bride's head by her mother, or some other near relative, her hair having been previously cut off; but of late years the young maidens of Israel, on becoming matrons, merely confine their tresses in nets of pearl or coral, while in Ireland, even in the far West where I dwell, and in Scotland as far north as John O'Groat's, the young wife thinks a net of brown silk or black chenile a sufficient covering for her head.

Immediately on the arrival of the bridegroom he was handed a glass of whisky ''heaped''. This is called the ''cup of blessing'', and while he drinks it, his friends, all standing around him, each holding a glass, wish that his ''life may be long and happy''. ''That his wife and himself may live to see their children's children.''

This is just what takes place among the Israelites, on the entrance of the bridegroom, except that instead of whisky, wine is poured to overflowing into his cup; and it seems to me that it was familiarity with similar manifestations of hospitality which caused David, when wishing to illustrate the Lord's gracious dealings with him, to say, ''My cup runneth over.''

As soon as the bridegroom had drank the ''cup of the blessing'', the best man touching him significantly on the shoulder, drew his attention to the preparations in the inner room, where a clergyman, wearing a robe of fine transparent-worked muslin, and a stole of white silk, richly embroidered in coloured and silver threads, stood before a table, which had been converted into a temporary altar, by covering it with a white cloth, and placing on it seven lighted candles.

The preparation for a Jewish marriage would not be very dissimilar. The altar would have a rich covering of needle-work, and amongst its ornaments would stand a seven-branched candlestick, with tall, lighted tapers. Burning candles or lamps during all religious ceremonies is a Jewish custom to this day; first, because the Divine presence was symbolized by a bright glory; and, secondly, because God commanded the Israelites to keep a light and fire always burning in the tabernacles, in opposition to the darkness in which the mysterious rites of the Egyptians were celebrated. At marriage feasts, however, there were always an unusual number of lamps. The ceremony generally took place in the evening, and every invited guest was provided with a lamp called a massal or mashal, which was a little copper vessel stuffed with linen rags, into which oil from a bottle was poured from time to time. As soon as the bridegroom's approach was announced by the person whose duty it was to watch for his coming, all the company lighted their lamps and ran joyfully to meet him, exclaiming, ''Behold, the bridegroom cometh.'' The moment he entered, the doors were shut, and a brimming cup of wine was handed to him. He took it in silence, but with joybeaming eyes. His friends stood around him in silence, too, yet sympathizing heartily in his joy. . . . While he drinks, the friends who had gone out with shouts of welcome to meet him, extinguish their lamps; henceforth his path is to be illumined by no stranger's hand, the voice of gladness and the light of love in which his spirit is to rejoice is to come from the ONE, who is now, mysteriously, to glide into his own being, and become interwoven with his life (pp. 69–73).

While the ceremony proceeded I observed that when the bridegroom was asked for the ring, he placed with it on the open book which the clergyman held in his hand, a small purse, containing gold, silver, and copper coins, and immediately after, while repeating, ''with this ring, etc.'', he retook both, placing one on the fourth finger of Mary's left hand, and the other in her right hand, gently closing her fingers round it.

The ring is used by many people as well as the Israelites and the Irish, in marriage ceremonies, but the custom is not universal, not even amongst Christians; though ladies generally wear one of plain gold after their marriage, as emblematical of their position. By those, however, who receive it with the plighted troth of their husbands, it is regarded with a feeling of holy affection, as a symbol of the intention of both parties to keep for ever the solemn covenant of which it is the pledge. The purse containing coins, is, as far as I am aware, now used only at the marriages of the Israelites and the Irish: the latter present it as the first fruit of the promise, ''with all my worldly goods I thee endow'', while the Jew merely shows it for a moment as he names the sum he has agreed to give his wife in the event of his divorcing her; the purse, or other present, which is emblematical of her right to share with him all his possessions, is presented before the marriage commences, and instances have occurred of the nuptials being deferred, or wholly broken off, owing to the insufficiency of the bridegroom's gift (pp. 74–75).

At these betrothals, the historian tells us, the bridegroom gave to the parents a "security", or "wed", from which is derived our term "wedding". Part of this "wed" always consisted of a ring, placed upon the maiden's right hand, and there religiously kept until transferred to the other hand at the later nuptials. Then, also, were repeated the marriage vows and other ceremonies, out of which those now prevailing have grown. The bride was taken "for fairer for fouler, for better for worse, for richer for poorer", and promised "to be buxom and bonny" to her future husband. At the final ceremony the bridegroom put the ring upon each of the bride's left-hand fingers in turn, saying, at the first, "in the name of the Father", at the second, "in the name of the Son", at the third, "in the name of the Holy Ghost", and at the fourth, "Amen". Then, also, the father gave to his new son one of his daughter's shoes, in token of the transfer of authority which he effected, and the bride was at once made to feel the change by a tap or a blow on her head given with the shoe. The husband, on his part, took an oath to use his wife well. If he failed to do so, she might leave him, but by law he was allowed considerable license.

The next day the husband presented his bride with a gift, and from the moment she received it, his power to separate from her, or return her to her parents, ceased.

At first this gift was altogether optional, the husband gave anything or nothing, as he pleased. But as women grew in influence (and at some time prior to the period of King Alfred), it was always expressly agreed that the husband should bestow a gift upon his wife, as he thereby relinquished his right to return her. Its value however, was allowed for a considerable time to depend entirely on his generosity and affection, but ultimately it was settled by law, and depended on his rank and wealth.

After Mary had received the ring and purse, the bridal veil (in this instance a small square of damask linen), was handed to the priest, who threw it over the heads of the married pair: the bridegroom then kissed his bride, and flinging off the veil they received the congratulations of their friends; and once more the overflowing glasses were circulated freely.

A Jewish bride has two veils. Enveloped in one, from her head to her feet, she is led to the bridegroom by her handmaidens. The texture of this first one is so heavy as to preclude the possibility of distinguishing her features, and thus affords to modern Labans an opportunity for a similar deception as was practised on Jacob. The second veil is a large shawl, which is thrown over her head as a mark of subjection (just as the square of damask was thrown over Mary's), and after the ceremony, when the bridegroom draws it over his own head also, and salutes his bride, the Rabbi gives them the wine cup, saying, "Blessed art thou, O Lord our God, king of the world, who hast created all things for thy glory.

Blessed art thou, O Lord our God, king of the world, who hast created man in thy likeness, and hast prepared for him, and from him, a house for ever and ever" (pp. 78–81).

When every one had congratulated the bride and bridegroom, and "drank their health", we were all summoned to the kitchen to partake of dinner. The table reached from the front or entrance door quite to the opposite wall, so that, of course, no one sat at either end. The priest took a position towards the middle of the table, the bride on one hand and the bridegroom on the other. I was placed opposite, between the bride's mother and brother. No precedence was accorded to, or sought for, by any other of the guests: a seat near a pretty "colleen" being the highest honour wished for by the young farmers, while the women dropped down naturally "just anywhere". The fare provided was most abundant, and not badly cooked. Down the centre of the board there was a double row of dishes, containing roast and boiled meats, potatoes and bread. Everything which had been prepared was placed on the table at once, a great portion if not all of which had been brought by the guests. This also is a common custom amongst the Israelites, and it is not more than a century since the practice ceased in Scotland, even amongst people of rank. As a proof of this we may venture to give Mr. Barclay's account of the Cummerfalls, or supper before a baptism in the house of one of the Dalrymple family (pp. 82–83).

The supply of knives and forks at the wedding feast was small, and almost confined to those sitting at the centre of the table, while the other guests managed to divide their meat and convey it to their mouths with their fingers.

Habit enables the Irish peasant to do this without being in the least disagreeable, and it renders necessary amongst them the observances of the Jews' custom of washing the hands before and after meat—their manner of performing the ablution, however, is different. An Irishman dips his hands into any vessel standing outside the door under the eave of his house; or he plunges them into any stream, or even pool, if more convenient, and then an apron serves him for a towel; or he just shakes the drops from his fingers, and lets the air dry them; while the Jew has water poured on his hands by some member of his family, who goes round from one to the other, carrying a basin, a ewer of water, and a towel. The Jews' reason at the first for these frequent washings was the same which actuates the Irish, namely, cleanliness; but as in several other instances, they have suffered a necessary duty to degenerate into a superstitious observance; and to eat with unwashed hands is now deemed sinful (pp. 85–86).

When dinner was over, the priest hushed, in an instant, all the gay clamour by slightly elevating his hand and looking sharply around. In a few Latin sentences he then returned thanks, each of the Roman Catholics present "making", at the same time, the "sign of the cross", by putting the right hand to the forehead, then to the breast, and then to the left and right shoulder, repeating, "In the name of the Father, and of the Son, and of the Holy Ghost. Amen." This form of "grace" is never neglected by the lower class, and though it is rather inappropriate and inexpressive as a thanksgiving, it is to be preferred before the practice of rising from table to pursue the common business of life, after having partaken of a "graceless meal".

The Israelites are also strict observers of this duty: their grace after meat is short, but beautiful and expressive. The head of the family, when the meal is finished, rises, all the others following his example, and in a low, solemn voice repeats, "Let us bless Him of whose benefits we have been partaking"; the others respond, "Blessed be He who has heaped favours on us, and by His goodness has now fed us." A short prayer follows, in which all unite, thanking God for His many benefits to Israel, beseeching Him to have pity on Jerusalem and the temple, to restore the throne of David, to send Elias and the Messiah, and to deliver the Israelites, wherever they may be found, from their low estate.

The thanksgiving of the Scotch is pure, voluntary heart-praise offered up in no set of words. Out of the abundance of his gratitude the father or minister pours forth thanks for God's gifts, and a fervent prayer for a continuance of them (pp. 89–90).

In less than an hour after we had risen from the hospitable board, the cottage had assumed quite another appearance. The temporary altar, removed from the room in which the marriage ceremony had been performed, was replaced by a table, from which bright glass and pretty delf reflected back the light of tall candles, in highly-polished brass candlesticks. Around this table the elder portion of the guests were seated. The kitchen had also undergone a transformation, the long table had disappeared, and the forms were ranged close by the wall all round; the rafters were ornamented with green branches, and several sconces, each having a candle, were hung on various parts of the wall. At the upper end of the room were seated the musicians—a harper, a piper, and a violin player.

At the lower end of the room blazed a turf fire, beside which a huge kettle, borrowed at the nearest way-side inn, was singing. While the young people were in groups and little knots, here and there, arranging the programme, the musicians played one of these exquisite national airs for which Ireland is famous. I stood near them, won to their side by the strangely wild, yet perfect harmony, produced by the combined sounds of the three instruments, and I thought of the Israelites, in whose feasts were "the harp and the viol, the tabret and the pipe" (pp. 91, 92).

Of both the Israelites and the Irish, the harp is peculiarly the national instrument; and as emblematical of their present condition, the poets of both nations have apostrophized it: to one it is the silent harp on the willows, whose tuneful strings may not breath their sweetness in a strange land; to the other it is the mute and broken harp on the walls of Tara, whose last passionate strains melted in the murmur of its dying notes. In form, the ancient Eastern harp very much resembled that in use amongst us, but though it was of solemn sound and wonderful power, the Irish harp excelled it, as it excels all other harps in the world . . .

The astonishing effects of the music of David's harp when he played before Saul to allay his stormy passions, are recorded in the sacred writings; and in ancient Irish history we find the story of Fionbelle, or the "Sweet-voiced", who, seeing two chieftains engaged in deadly combat, entered the field with his harp, filling the air with such sweet sounds that the startled knights let their weapons fall, and grasping each other's hands, renewed the friendship of their early youth. The power of David's harp was miraculous, but the success of Fionbelle was the simple, natural effect, of soothing music on the mind. An old poet who wrote in praise of the harp declared it to be an instrument "too good to be profaned in taverns, and fit only to be used by knights, esquires, clerks, persons of rank, and ladies with plump and beautiful hands; and that its courteous and gentle sounds should be heard only by the elegant and good". Formerly a harper was to be found amongst the retainers of every family of rank. Both in Scotland and Ireland, and until very lately, the wandering harpist might be met with any day passing along the highways, followed by a stout youth, bearing the harp on his shoulders. But now the race has become almost extinct, and the few who remain may mourn in the words of Scott's "Last Minstrel", that:—

" . . . their date is fled;
Their tuneful brethren all are dead."

The harp, however, though one of the instruments once common in Scotland, was never regarded as the national instrument, an honour which belongs to the "pipes", known to the Israelites as the "sacbut", and to us as the "bagpipes" (pp. 100–102).

The bagpipe, of a rude and discordant construction is still in common use thoughout the East; and that it continues the popular instrument of the Italian peasant is well known (p. 103).

But while the national instruments were engaging my attention, the bride and bridegroom had stood up to open the evening's amusements by dancing a "jig", and as I watched them, merrily, laughingly, without order, plan, or arrangement, changing places, joining hands, turning and pirouetting, I felt convinced that I need not try to find amongst the Terpsichorean acquirements of the Israelites, any similitude for a wild Irish jig, though I could, without difficulty, find its counterpart in the "fling" of the Highlanders.

Dancing has been at all time an ordinary accompaniment of music amongst the Celts, and that the same is true of the Israelites we learn from numerous records in Holy Writ. Miriam and her women glorified God in dances and songs; David danced before the ark; the daughters of Shiloh were dancing when the sons of Benjamin took them wives according to the number of them that danced. The only child of Jepthah went to meet him, after his victory, with timbrel and with dances; and, lastly, the profligate daughter of Herodias received, as the reward of her attainments in dancing, the head of John the Baptist. On each side, however, there is one exception to this rule; the Celts have never made dancing a portion of their religious worship, as did the ancient Israelites; nor have the latter ever introduced it into the house of mourning, as the Scotch did formerly, and as our Irish peasantry sometimes do still. In former times this "death dance" consisted of a mournful kind of movement. The nearest relative of the deceased often commenced the ceremony weeping, yet did begin it, to give as it were, an example of fortitude and resignation (pp. 106, 107).

In a few moments I found myself in the crowded sanctum, seated near two young peasants, whom I knew were lovers. They were both very young, but want of age and experience are never regarded as obstacles to a marriage by either the Israelites or the Celts: the age prescribed to men by the Rabbins, is eighteen years, and the number allowed to the women is still less, while in the Highlands of Scotland and Ireland, though there is no especially appointed age, it is no uncommon circumstance to see a man of about thirty and a woman of five-and-twenty the parents of six or seven children.

I knew by the coy laughter and the half startled exclamations of the young girl beside me, that he was whispering to her the hopes which were swelling up in his own heart; the thousand joys of the future; the new home. When she had partaken of tea he playfully forced the cup from her hand and giving it to a comely pleasant-looking matron who was sitting near us, desired her to "read Sarah's fortune", which simply meant to predict the future events of her life, by the accidental arrangement of the grounds in the cup. Here, again, is a superstition derived from the customs of the Israelites. "Is not this," exclaimed Joseph's steward, as he drew the priceless goblet from Benjamin's sack, "Is not this it in which my Lord drinketh, and whereby indeed he divineth?" Some doubt that Joseph ever made use of his cup for the purposes of divination, but whether he did so or not, the words of his servant prove that the art was practised, if not by him, by others amongst the Israelites, and that the sons of Jacob understood the allusion. The divination by the cup in the East at the present day is by fluids, or what is usually termed a "fluid mirror". Perhaps it was the same of old, and we know that for some centuries past it has become a popular form of amusement amongst young people

both in Ireland and the North of Scotland. The lamented Hugh Miller has given a graphic description of it (pp. 110–112).

He bent his head close to hers, and then I saw him take from his vest a morsel of folded paper, instantly and almost simultaneously both stood up and moved into a corner, as if desirous to escape observation, and, except to myself, no one appeared to notice them. He opened the paper: he was smiling, and yet he looked as if a solemn feeling was, in spite of himself, stealing over him. I knew I was witnessing a betrothal. I saw that her hand trembled, nor was his steady, as he took from the paper the half of a broken sixpence and placed it on her open palm. The lips of both moved: no doubt they were promising to be faithful unto death; and judging by the expressions of their faces, as for one moment her mild eyes were raised to his kindling orbs, the blest assurance of mutual attachment at that moment shut out from their hearts all fears for the untried future. They were to share it together, and this thought, the only one they gave it, lay nestling in the innermost core of their hearts.

Could I help it, as I gazed on them, so young, betrothed, and after such a fashion, and not think of similitudes, and drawing comparisons, even if not so prone to it as I am? Espousing or betrothing as already noticed, usually precedes marriage, both amongst the Israelites and the Celts. Amongst the former it is a ceremony in the presence of many witnesses, while none may hear the whispered words which bind two Irish lovers to remain through all years, and all ills, changeless in affection till they die. Sometimes, but not often, a written paper is given by the young Jew to his betrothed, recording the terms of the matrimonial contract, but the usual token of his affections and his faithfulness is a small coin, which he places in her hand, saying, "Receive this piece of silver as a pledge that you shall become my spouse."

Sarah, blushing, concealed the precious token in her bosom, and returned to the kitchen, where a young farmer was busy taking up a collection for the priest, while the rest of the company amused themselves proposing riddles. Just as I entered, the priest, who was standing with his back to the fire, set them all thinking and smiling by asking, "What are the lonesomest things you meet on a journey, boys?" The guesses were numerous, mirthful, and ludicrous; laughter and the clinking of coin on the willow-pattern plate mingled together and made a cheerful noise, filling the cabin, and stimulating, no doubt, the generosity of the people. Exactly such a scene would a Jewish marriage amongst persons of the same class have presented; the plate handed round to collect coins for the musicians, while the guests proposed curious questions, which must be "honoured with a forfeit", if not answered. Sampson put forth a riddle to those who came to his marriage—"Out of the eater came forth meat, and out of the strong came forth sweetness''—and he allowed them the seven days of the feast to declare it, or else to forfeit to him thirty sheets and thirty changes of raiment. Most likely they made marvellously odd guesses, and amidst laughter and mirth, Sampson, with ludicrous gravity, would shake his head and utter his "Noes" like our priest on the present occasion, who at last increased the merriment tenfold by giving the solution in a manner full of droll, rich humour, "Milestones, honeys; because you never see two of them together."

A few minutes later the bridegroom was seen moving amongst the guests; he was giving to each one separately an invitation to the "hauling home" on that day week, the custom being, that the bride and bridegroom remain in the house of her parents for seven days, unless in cases of great poverty, when they remove on the evening of the marriage. The same practice is observed by the Israelites, and has descended to them from the days when Jacob, according to the usage then established, was constrained to persevere in the wedding festivities of his marriage with Leah, for a "week", before he was given the beloved Rachel, for whose sake he served Laban fourteen years (pp. 115–119).

On the day after the wedding I went to the cottage occupied by Jem's parents. On my way I met numerous peasants, it being market day in the neighbouring town of Ballinrobe, and each in passing uttered some holy aspiration, or endearing expression, as "God save you", "God be with you", "God speed you safe home." Just such are the forms of salutation used by the Israelites, and such they have been from time immemorial. "The Lord be with thee", was the greeting of Boaz to his reapers, and they answered him, "The Lord bless thee." At this day the address and the rejoinder would have been the same.

As I approached my destination I observed two women coming towards me; one wore a hooded cloak, like the burnoose of the Israelites, and carried her shoes in her hand. She looked travel-stained, weary, sad: the other was wrapped in a scarlet "broth", resembling Ruth's veil, or hyke: it was drawn over her head, almost concealing her face. She was weeping bitterly, and as she was passing with a murmured "God save you", I stopped her and heard her tale of sorrow. Her only brother had died the previous evening, and his widow had sent her to Cong to tell his sister, who was now with her, of his death, and to procure from the abbot blessed clay to put on his coffin. She hurried on her way almost while she was speaking, and I pursued mine, thinking of the Israelites and of this new similitude. They, too, use "blessed clay", or "Jerusalem earth", in the coffins of their dead, purchasing it at a high price from the rabbins who have made pilgrimages to Jerusalem (pp. 120, 121).

When I entered the cabin I found Jem talking earnestly to his mother, no doubt telling her of his betrothal. Both saluted me, using the same expression, "God save you", to which one of their own class would have replied, "God save you, kindly"; while, if the meeting had been between two Israelites, the greeting would have been, "Sholam Alicham", Peace be unto thee, and the answer, "Alicham Sholam", Unto thee be peace. An out-door salutation and that used on entering a house differs both amongst the Israelites and the Irish, and that one just quoted has long been the most general form used by the Israelites, who profess Christianity, because our Lord, when he called together His disciples, giving them the most minute directions for their guidance in the narrow way, evidently recommended it when He desired them to salute a house on entering, "And if the house be worthy, let your peace come upon it; but if it be not worthy, let your peace return to you."

Jem had placed a chair for me, while his mother, with a bustling kindness peculiar to the Irish, whose eager attentions, however, are never troublesome, dusted it with her apron. I thanked her, and sitting down looked round in delight on a room, or kitchen, which might have belonged to an Israelite, so thoroughly were all its belongings Jewish. I had often before been in huts which forcibly reminded me of the description given of the chamber into which the Shunamite had put a "table, and a stool, and a candlestick", and now I was in a cabin which, though it contained more then these specified articles, might have stood on the banks of the Jordan, and been as adapted to the tastes and the habits of the people, as it was in Ireland, where it overshadowed a foetid duck-pool (pp. 123–125).

Bridget at once drew her querns to the door, and, by a peculiar undulating cry, summoned a neighbour to help her to grind. Before this person had arrived, however, Bridget put a portion of the corn into an iron pot, which she hung over a fire of furze. The quick blaze and the crackling noise attracted my attention, from the sapient observations of the husband on the crops and the weather, to watch the operations of the wife. We all know that the fuel commonly used in Ireland and in the North of Scotland is turf, but there are districts where turf is scarce and dear, and where farmers collect heath and furze which they cut on the mountain, while the wives of the labourers gather sticks by the road side, and the dung of animals, which they dry and pile up in the corner of a shed. All these kinds of fuel were common amongst the Israelites. The "crackling of thorns" must have been a familiar sound in the ears of the people, or Solomon would not have referred to it as an illustration, when condemning the "laughter of fools". It was from a "fire of sticks" the viper darted which fastened on Paul's hand; and dung fuel, as all travellers bear witness, is, at the present, as much used by the Israelites as by the Irish or the Scotch (pp. 125–127).

Whilst Bridget and her neighbour continued singing and grinding, it occurred to me that just such a tableau must our Saviour have had before Him when, eighteen hundred years ago, He illustrated by the two women grinding at a mill, of whom one was to be taken and the other left, the thoughtless gaiety with which people will pursue their wordly affairs up to the very moment when the Son of Man will come suddenly to judge the earth.

The Israelites were not allowed to take querns in pledge from a debtor. The command is, "No man shall take the nether or the upper millstone to pledge: he taketh a man's life to pledge." These "primeval mills of the world", as Dr. Clarke calls them, are still found amongst the Celts, though many centuries ago the legislature of Scotland endeavoured to discourage these mills, and it was decreed that "nae man sall presume to grind quekit, maish-lock, or rye, hand-mylne except he be compelled by storme, or bein lack of mills, quihilk soulde grinde the samen; and in this case, gif a man grindes at hand-mylnes, he sall gif the threllin measure as milture; gif any man contraveins this, our proclamation, he sall tyne his mill perpetuallie". This was signed by Alexander III, almost six hundred years ago; and until about one hundred years ago there was a similar prohibition against the use of them in Ireland . . .

When the corn was ground, Bridget took a wooden bowl, using it as a kneading trough, so far as mixing in it the flour, water, and salt, which she afterwards spread into a cake on the corner of the dresser. I had no doubt that Bridget's "bowl" and the "kneading troughs" which the Israelites bound up in their clothes on their shoulders, when they fled out of Egypt, were very similar, if not quite alike, while the cake which she baked on the griddle or flat iron plate, having first placed it on some turf embers, was no doubt similar to the cakes "quickly baked on the hearth" which Sarah made ready for the angels whom her husband entertained. The usual form into which dough is worked by the Irish is that known as the "cake" and when a griddle is not at hand this may be baked on a hot flag, or is laid down on the embers; or the tongs being laid across the coals, the cake is placed on it. I was obliged to wait and partake of some of the cake: hospitality being deemed as much a sacred duty by the Irish as it is by the Israelites.

The operation of grinding by the females was always accompanied, as it still is in the East, with melodious and shrill-trilled ditties, sung in chorus, which sounded strong enough to be heard out of doors throughout all the lanes and streets; the pleasant jollity of which, associated as it was with the just-apparent brightness of dawn, and announcing the approaching activity of village or city population just awaking to their daily labour, gave to this simple domestic operation a peculiar character of happiness, peaceful industry, and tranquillity. The Hebrew writers, accordingly, always connect the sound of the morning mill with prosperity and repose, coupling it, in its degree of vivacity, with "the voice of harpers and musicians"; its cessation they associate with the presence of melancholy, trouble, and adversity. Thus, when the wise man wishes to describe the dreary melancholy of old age, he expresses it by the "sound of the grinding" being "low". "I will take away the sound of the mill-stone", says Jeremiah, to express utter desolation.

That women or maid-servants generally performed this piece of domestic labour, we learn from the first mention made of grinding with mills. "All the first-born in the land of Egypt shall die, from the first-born of Pharaoh that sitteth upon the throne, even unto the first-born of the maid-servant that is behind the mill": in which passage, from the contrasted states of dignity and meanness, it is plain that, in Egypt at least, the drudgery of grinding was deemed the lowest possible. Two women were generally employed; they sat fronting each other, with the mill-stone between them, which was kept whirling by alternate impulsions of the hand. Slaves taken in war were frequently doomed to undergo this tedious penance; Samson "did grind in the prison-house of the Philistines"; The Hebrews, in their Babylonish captivity, were subjected to its degradation; "they took our young men to grind", says Jeremiah in his Lamentations; and Isaiah, in his prophetic declaration to Babylon of her impending state of captivity, bids her, as a proper badge of her servile subjection, "take mill-stones and grind meal". The piece of a mill-stone whereby Abimelech was slain, when he was attacking the tower of Thebez, was cast upon his head "by a certain woman", whom it befitted to wield as a weapon the humble utensil of her daily occupation (pp. 130–135).

The day appointed for conducting the bride to the house of her husband, and generally called the "hauling home", arrived in due course, and accompanied by a friend I set out early . . . (p. 136).

As we drove along towards the cottage on the cliff, we overheard many fervent ejaculations from the passers by in praise of our "kind hearts" and our "good hearts", and our "humble hearts".

It is strange that both the Israelites and the Irish regard the heart as the source of pleasure, grief, love, hate, wit, understanding, and courage; and hence are derived the many figurative expressions of both nations. "An honest and good heart" is mentioned by Luke, and we read also of a "broken heart", a "clean heart", an "evil heart", a "liberal heart", a "stony heart", of "loving with all one's heart", of "turning the hearts of the fathers to the children, and the hearts of the children to their fathers"; of the "want of heart": "Ephraim is like a silly dove without heart". "O fools and slow of heart"; that is, ignorant and without understanding. "This people's heart is waxed gross, lest they should understand with their hearts"; and, "the prophets prophesy out of their hearts"—that is, according to the thoughts of their hearts. The Israelites speak of the heart as being dilated by joy, broken by sorrow, growing fat and hardened in prosperity, melting under discouragement, forsaking one in terror, fluctuating in doubt, and being desolate in trouble.

In such beautiful though hyperbolical expressions the Irish language is rich, for with us, according to the poet, "the heart is all" . . .

We speak of a "heart killed with grief", and a "heart broken", and a "brave-heart", and of a "bruised heart," and of an "aching heart". . . .

And then we have many allusions to "liberal hearts", and "open hearts", (and I praise God while I say it, that neither are few in dear Ireland), and many to "loving hearts" and "fond hearts", and "faithful hearts", while the endearing expressions as "The secret treasure of my heart", "the darling of my heart", "the pulse of my heart", "the light and joy of my heart"; pour from the inexhaustible kindness of "Irish hearts", like water from the gushing spring.

The friends of both bride and bridegroom were all assembled by the time we reached the cottage, and almost all of them were in the yard and on horseback, a woman being seated behind each man on the pillion. The bride and bridegroom were mounted like all the others. The mother, with two or three matrons stood at the door, giving to each of the party the "parting cup", or, as it is sometimes called, "the stirrup cup", or "cup at the door". When all had partaken of it the bridal pair were the first to turn the horse's head towards the new home, and immediately on moving an old shoe was thrown after them for good luck by some one in the cottage.

At a Scotch wedding the very same scene would have occurred, while at the marriage of an Israelite the old shoe or slipper is always used symbolically, conveying a most serious signification.

We fling it after a bride when she is leaving her childhood's home, sportively, with blessings, wishing that her step may be ever gladsome; but when a Jewish bride is touched with it, it serves only as an ungraceful reminder of her new ties and obligations. Just as she crosses the threshold he stoops down, and slipping off his shoe, which had been previously unloosed, he strikes her with the heel on the nape of the neck, in token of his supremacy, and of the reverence and duty which he expects. In the East generally, the slipper is taken off in-doors, and is not unfrequently used to administer correction. When a Persian presumes to speak his mind unreservedly, or

should he be in disgrace, to utter anything in his own defence, the king orders him to be smitten on the mouth with a shoe or slipper; and so frequently is this disgraceful punishment inflicted, that the common phrase, "you have eaten the shoe", may be addressed to almost every man in the kingdom.

This shameful custom reminds us of St. Paul's being smitten on the mouth by the command of the high priest, when he spoke in his own defence; and his indignation on the occasion shows that it was felt by him as a peculiarly insulting demonstration of power (pp. 153-158).

Like the Scotch and the Irish it is customary amongst the Israelites also for the bridegroom to conduct his spouse from her friends to his own home with all the brilliancy and joy that could be crowded into a procession. All his young female friends and relatives are invited to grace this procession and to add numbers to his cavalcade; and these, adorned in robes suitable to the occasion, take lamps, and wait in a company near the house, till the bride and bridegroom, with their friends, issue forth, whom they welcome with the customary congratulations, then join in the train, and with songs and acclamations and every demonstration of joy advance to the bridegroom's house where an entertainment is provided according to the circumstances of the united pair.

It occurred to me, while looking on the several happy groups assembled in this lowly cottage kitchen, that one reason why there was less of the riotous amusement of dancing, was that it was a "housewarming" as well as a "hauling-home", and strange as it may appear, a sort of mysterious solemnity always mingles with this latter festival, which, we find, is observed by the Israelites to this day, under the title of "dedication", and which God himself commanded the Israelites to observe, saying, "What man is there that hath built a new house, and hath not dedicated it? Let him go and return to his house, lest he die in the battle field, and another dedicate it." The Israelites commenced the dedication festivals with prayer and praise, but they concluded them as the Scotch and Irish do, with feasting, music and dancing.

Just as the rosy light appeared at the edge of the horizon, the guests departed, and if fervently-uttered blessings could secure the earthly happiness of the young pair, then was their life one of perfect peace (pp. 160-162).

Serial No. 110*f.*
Published by *The National Message* Ltd.,
6 Buckingham Gate, London, S.W.1.
Copyright.

Authorities:

(*a*) *The Geographical Journal,* Vol. LXI, No. 6, June 1923. A paper read before the Royal Geographical Society by Mr. Wilfred Irwin.

(*b*) *Encyclopædia Britannica* (14th Edition).

(*c*) *Production of Minerals from the Waters of the Dead Sea: Reports relating to pre-liminary investigations,* 1923-1925; published on behalf of the Government of Palestine, by the Crown Agents for the Colonies.

(*d*) Extract from Official Report of a House of Lords' speech by the Rt. Hon. Viscount Templetown on the Dead Sea Salts Concession.

The Mineral Wealth of the Dead Sea

"For the Lord thy God bringeth thee into a good land, a land of brooks of water, of fountains and depths that spring out of valleys and hills; A land of wheat, and barley, and vines, and fig trees, and pomegranates; a land of oil olive, and honey; . . . a land whose stones are iron, and out of whose hills thou mayest dig brass" (Deut. viii. 7-9).

ALL students of Scripture are familiar with Palestine as the land "flowing with milk and honey" which passed into the possession of the people of Israel, following their exodus from Egypt; and all interested in Palestine have watched the modern transformation in the Holy Land, which is restoring much of its ancient fertility, to the standard enjoyed by the Israelites of old. Thousands of square miles of what for centuries has been arid waste, are now yielding to modern methods of irrigation.

Not many people, however, are aware of the mineral position in Palestine; particularly as to the wealth which lies in solution in the waters of the Dead Sea. Reports of chemical analysts show clearly that a stupendous accumulation of mineral salts is available; indeed, extraction of these on a commercial basis is already in process of serious development by using the high rate of atmospheric evaporation which exists in that region for the purpose of dehydration, leaving the residual solids ready for appropriate treatment.

POINTS OF SPECIAL INTEREST

1. The enormous quantity of mineral salts which have accumulated is almost too great to be imagined. It would require a vessel of four cubic miles volume to contain them. The experts compute the main content to be as follows:

Potassium chloride	. .	2,000 million metric tons
Magnesium bromide	. .	980 ,, ,, ,,
Sodium chloride .	. .	11,900 ,, ,, ,,
Magnesium chloride	. .	22,000 ,, ,, ,,
Calcium chloride .	. .	6,000 ,, ,, ,,

2. The location of this great mineral wealth in the world-centre of Palestine enhances its value very greatly. It is inevitable that a great volume of world traffic will, in the future, focus on that country as transport facilities by land, sea, and air continue to develop.

3. Control of the Dead Sea concession to extract the salts was secured by Mr. Moses Novomeysky, a Russian Zionist. Extraction of the salts is now in progress on a commercial scale by Palestine Potash Ltd.

4. The Jordan alone carries 6,000,000 tons of water daily into the Dead Sea. Apart from the fact that this means a further annual accretion of about 300,000 tons of mineral salts, a vast volume of water will be available for irrigation purposes when the necessary engineering works are in full operation. Great schemes for hydro-electric power are already in preparation.

Extract from the *GEOGRAPHICAL JOURNAL*, Vol. LXI, No. 6, June 1923

A paper read by Mr. Wilfred Irwin

. . Many references to the Dead Sea are to be found in Jewish and classical literature. Pausanias and Galen both mention it, and Tacitus and Josephus note the fact that boats navigated it. During the Crusades a considerable revenue was received from navigation dues. In more recent times this has all disappeared, and a solitary boat was the only craft left before the war when the Sultan claimed the sea as his personal property.

The River Jordan supplies almost the whole of the water received by the Dead Sea, to which there is no outlet. The principal sources of the Jordan are two immense springs near the foot of the snow-clad Mount Hermon, Ain Banias and Ain el Leddan. A longer tributary but of much less volume comes down from Lebanon, the Nahr el Hasbani, and another little tributary is the Nahr Bareighit. These unite to form the river, which soon widens into a swampy expanse which is very fertile, and at the lower end is Lake Huleh or "Waters of Merom", 4 miles long and 2½ broad, but shallow, and even now, though so near the source of the river, only 7 ft. above sea level. The water here holds in suspension a brownish flocculent precipitate which does not improve its appearance.

On leaving the lake the river runs as a "below sea level" torrent forming one cascade after another through a 10-mile course in which the fall is 687 ft., after which it widens out into the Sea of Galilee, 14 miles long and 7 miles broad, area about 65 sq. miles, and greatest depth 150 ft. according to Merrill and Barvis, though earlier authorities give it as much as 800 ft. Two miles south of Tiberias is a hot spring which in Roman times had a great reputation for its curative powers. The water feels quite hot to the hand. I had not a thermometer when I visited it, but I understand it has a temperature of 137°-140°F. The temperature of the lake below a depth of 50 ft. is 59°F., showing that the water retains some of the coolness it receives in the internal reservoirs of Mount Hermon, though the climate is sub-tropical.

The river, which is brown on entering the lake, is clear on leaving it, as the precipitate has had plenty of time to settle. Assuming the average depth of the lake to be 80 ft. and the flow of the river 1,000 million gals. per day, it would take 2½ years for the water of the Jordan to pass through it.

From its outlet from the Sea of Galilee the river commences its zigzag course to the Dead Sea 60 miles south, but in its windings it actually traverses three times that distance. Five miles from the lake it is joined by its largest tributary, Nahr el Yarmuk, rising in the Hauran. This river, after flowing for some distance at an elevation of 2,000 ft. above the Mediterranean, falls down a series of grand cascades through 2,000-3,000 ft. before it reaches the Jordan. Owing to the soft calcareous strata over which the Jordan after leaving the Sea of Galilee, flows, and the tributaries which join it, it soon develops a milky appearance like most of the other streams of Palestine. Naaman the Syrian, we may remember, made the observation in his day, "Are not Abana and Pharpar rivers of Damascus better than all the waters of Israel?" The former were clear, the latter milky streams. In its course of 180 miles to the Dead Sea the Jordan falls another 610 ft., on its way receiving two other tributaries of some size, the Wadi Farah from the west, and the Wadi Zerka from the east, both entering it about 25 miles north of the Dead Sea.

Captain Lynch made a careful survey of the Dead Sea in 1860. He found the length 47 miles, breadth 9½ miles, area 340 sq. miles, greatest depth 1,279 ft.

I calculate the area of the catchment at about 10,000 sq. miles, but the rainfall in it varies enormously. In Hermon and among the mountains to the north it is extremely heavy. In Galilee it is given as 66 cms. or 26 in.; then it diminishes all the way to the Dead Sea. After the confluence of the Jordan with the Farah, the land not irrigated is practically barren, and at the Dead Sea the rainfall is very slight. With the exception of a few oases due to the presence of springs, all the land from the Farah to the rising ground south of the Dead Sea is wilderness.

The average depth of the Dead Sea will be 400-500 ft., and taking the former figure as a basis we may work out the total quantity of water in it as 23.7×10^{12} gals. In the northern part the water is clear down to the stones on the bottom, but further south where the solution is more concentrated, the floor of the sea is all solid salt mixed with sulphate and carbonate of lime. The southern end is very shallow, and round the southern banks are great masses of solid salt. This may be due to the land at the south of the sea having risen owing to the same influence which caused the elevation of the land between the Dead Sea and the Gulf of Akaba. The peninsula "El Lisan" is chiefly composed of sulphate of lime interspersed with beds of salt. In certain parts in thundery weather a quantity of asphaltum rises to the surface. Hence the ancient name "Lacus Asphaltites". The colour at the time of my visit was bottle green. . . . The most exhaustive analyses of the Dead Sea water have been made by Terriel (see *Comptes Rendus*, 62,1329) . . . . . . The principal constituents, it will be seen, are magnesium and sodium chlorides . . . The following is an analysis which I made some time ago of a sample taken by myself from the north end of the lake:

Chlorine, Cl	.	.	.	66.46
Bromine, Br	.	.	.	—
Sulphate, SO₄	.	.	.	0.46
Sodium, Na	.	.	.	14.41
Potassium, K	.	.	.	1.48
Calcium, Ca	.	.	.	4.26
Magnesium, Mg	.	.	.	12.29
Silica and carbonic acid	.		.	Trace
				99.36

Sodium chloride	.	.	7.17
Magnesium chloride		.	9.50
Calcium chloride	.	.	2.18
Potassium chloride	.		0.55
Calcium sulphate	.	.	0.13
Total solids	.	.	19.53
Water by difference	.		80.47
			100.00

Taking the figure 23.7×10^{12} as representing the number of gallons of water in the Dead Sea, and the average total salinity at 24 parts per 100, or 2.4 lb. per gal., a figure below rather than above the mark, then the total solids in solution will be 56.8×10^{12} lb. Of this, magnesium may be taken to average 16 per cent or 9.1×10^{12} lb., and the sodium in the total solids at 10 per cent, or 5.7×10^{12} lb. These metals are both present as chlorides, which will then amount to:

$MgCl_2$, magnesium chloride 36.0×10^{12} lb. or 16.1×10^9 tons.
NaCl, sodium chloride 14.5×10^{12} lb. or 6.5×10^9 tons.

. . . Infiltration from the Mediterranean is not a probable source of salt in the Jordan, because the Waters of Merom are above the level of the sea, and because the proportion of magnesium to sodium is much greater in the Jordan water than in the Mediterranean Sea water. The greater part of the salt in the Jordan as it enters the Dead Sea must therefore have come all the way down from its home in the subterranean recesses of Hermon, and possibly Lebanon.

. . . Seeing that the life of the Dead Sea is probably short compared with that of the Jordan gorge, it is not likely that there has been any great change in the volume or composition of the river since it first began to form.

Then there is the question of the accuracy of figures for flow of the Jordan. I do not know who was the first to suggest 6 million tons as the daily average flow, but all writers on Palestine appear to accept it. McIntyre, geologist to the Palestine Exploration Fund, says it is at least 6 million tons. Now, taking Captain Lynch's figure

340 sq. miles as the area of the Dead Sea, it means an evaporation of 99 in. per annum plus any little actual rainfall into the sea. In this country the average evaporation amounts to 16 in. per annum. . . . My general conclusion from these investigations is that the Jordan and Dead Sea together form a gigantic piece of natural apparatus for taking the mixed chlorides of magnesium and sodium from their home in the recesses of Mount Hermon and the hills further south, dissolving them, and recrystallising the sodium chloride in the enormous evaporating pan of the Dead Sea, leaving the magnesium chloride in solution . . .

Before the paper the President said: The paper this afternoon, by Mr. Wilfred Irwin, deals with the question of the composition of the Dead Sea. As we all know, the Dead Sea contains a very large amount of salt. I have been trying to visualise the amount which Mr. Irwin has concluded that it contains—an amount in figures, I think, of 39,000,000,000 tons—and in order to assist me to visualise that amount, Mr. Irwin tells me that it would form a solid mass four cubic miles in extent. One of the interesting features which Mr. Irwin will bring out in the course of his paper will be that the greater part, if not the whole, of this vast amount of material has been brought down by the Jordan river, and that the period of time which he estimates has been necessary for the river to bring down this salt is something like 50,000 years. He will give you many more details with regard to this matter, and I will ask him to read his paper.
(*Reproduced by kind permission of the "Geographical Journal".*)

Extract from the *ENCYCLOPÆDIA BRITANNICA* (14th Edition), article "Dead Sea"

DEAD SEA, the lake in Southern Palestine in which the River Jordan terminates. It is bounded on the north by the Jordan valley —at that point broad, arid and forbidding, on the east by the escarpment of the Moabite plateau, on the south by the desert of the Arabah, and on the west by the mountains of Judæa. It has a length of

47 m. and a breadth of 10 m., a superficial area of 360 sq. m., and a mean depth of 1,080 ft. Its surface level, which has a seasonal variation of 10-15 ft., lies about 1,300 ft. below that of the Mediterranean, and is the lowest sheet of water on the earth's crust. The Jordan alone pours into the Dead Sea on a daily average a volume of water

estimated at 6 million tons, and in the winter season torrents—very few of which are perennial—from the hills to the east and west add their contribution. . . .

Salinity.—The water of the Dead Sea is intensely saline. Whilst ocean water has a salinity of 4-6 per cent, Dead Sead water contains 23-25 per cent of salts. Exhaustive analyses of water taken from different parts and at different depths have been made . . .
. . . Magnesium, sodium, calcium, and potassium are present as chlorides. The chloride of magnesium, largely held in solution, gives the water its nauseous taste, and chloride of calcium its smooth, oily feeling. The brine, as can be seen, is a commodity of great economic and commercial value . . . and applications have recently (1926) been invited by the Government of Palestine for the monopoly right for developing the mineral resources of the Dead Sea . . .

(Reproduced by kind permission of the "Encyclopædia Britannica".)

Extract from *PRODUCTION OF MINERALS FROM THE WATERS OF THE DEAD SEA*, Reports, etc., relating to preliminary investigations, 1923-1925; published on behalf of the Government of Palestine by the Crown Agents for the Colonies (4 Millbank, S.W.1), p. 2

. . . From the foregoing figures the quantities of salts in the Dead Sea are therefore approximately:

(in million metric tons)

Potassium chloride	.	2,000
Magnesium bromide	.	980
Sodium chloride .	.	11,900
Magnesium chloride	.	22,000
Calcium chloride .	.	6,000

For practical purposes, the supply of potash may be considered inexhaustible.

DEAD SEA SALTS CONCESSION

Extract from Official Report, printed by H.M. Stationery Office, of a speech by the Rt. Hon. Viscount Templetown in the British House of Lords on 20th March, 1929

Viscount Templetown rose to move to resolve, That a Permanent British Control be established on the Dead Sea, and the subsidiary industries arising therefrom; and that any group to whom the concession is granted shall be required to have British finance and British control and have no connection, direct or indirect, with the German potash monopoly. The noble Viscount said: My Lords, I should like to say at the beginning that in bringing this matter forward it is not my intention to attack races, nationalities or individuals, or their religious beliefs. As your Lordships are aware, the Dead Sea is to-day the centre of a drama destined to rivet the attention of nations. Situated in the world's most historic land, it has been for many years a magnet for chemists, whose labours have now revealed great potential powers, which, allied with the enterprise of science and civilisation, will transform a place of desolation into beneficent activity; and Palestine, which once lay at the crossroads of ancient civilisation, becomes anew the highway between east and west.

There is potash, magnesium, bromine, in millions of tons. From the waters of the Dead Sea alone the amount of potash, so essential both to agriculture and to war, would supply the world with one million tons a year for 2,000 years. The values are enormous, and enormous still, were they (to suit the matter-of-fact British imagination) reduced a thousandfold. The Dead Sea has no outlet, and lies in a cleft 1,300 ft. below sea level. Six million tons of water pour into it every day, and a fierce sun has promoted the process of evaporation through countless years. Great subsidiary fertiliser and chemical industries will arise. Soap and glass industries will flourish, railways will be built, and potash can be brought to London at £4 10s. a ton, to bring a renaissance to revive our British agriculture, which, due to the German monopoly and government neglect, has been the Cinderella of English industrial life. "Whoever holds the Dead Sea holds the Key of the Middle East." It might be said that the Haifa Harbour, and the electrification and irrigation of the Jordan Valley, and the Dead Sea, constitute a unique industrial Trilogy which can unlock to the world great beneficent powers and revive again an active civilisation from the River of the Nile to the River of the Euphrates.

These long vistas of development lay a heavy responsibility upon England as the Mandatory Power, and much interest naturally exists as to how the sacred trust to civilisation for the well-being and development of Palestine is to be fulfilled. It has to be remembered that the boundary line between Palestine and Transjordania runs through the middle of the Dead Sea, and that half the Dead Sea, therefore, belongs to Transjordania . . .

Authorities:

(*a*) Dr. Adam Clarke's 'Commentary on the New Testament' (1817 ed.).

(*b*) The Venerable Lord Arthur C. Hervey, M.A., in 'A Dictionary of the Bible', edited by William C. Smith, D.C.L., LL.D. (3 vols., 1863 ed.).

The Importance of the Genealogy of Jesus Christ

THE Genealogy of Jesus Christ is of the utmost importance in view of the many texts in the Bible which assert His royal descent and His right to succeed to the throne of Israel. Christians generally accept our Lord's right to kingship because of His divinity alone; but a careful examination of the Scriptures shows that it was clearly foretold that the Messiah, though born of a virgin, should possess lineal descent from Abraham through David, to whose throne over Israel He should succeed.

It was therefore essential for the fulfilment of prophecy that our Lord should have been born within the House of David, that His genealogy should be known, that such descent be legitimate according to the holy law, and that His right to succession be clearly demonstrated by that same law.

The New Testament genealogies of Jesus Christ supplied the evidence necessary to establish according to the law that He indeed fulfilled all the requirements of prophecy concerning His royal descent and rights.

The Importance of Biblical Genealogies Generally

Hereditary succession and inheritance are known to have existed among the Egyptians and Semites from a very early period and to have continued in later centuries among the Greeks, Romans, Celts and Saxons. The preservation of such practices naturally fostered the keeping, in either oral or written form, of genealogies which might be recited or produced as evidence of descent.

Genealogies held a special significance for the Israelites, for the promise of the land of Canaan was specifically made to Abraham, Isaac, Jacob and the children of Israel; the promised Messiah was to be of Judah, and He was to be a descendant of David, from whom should also come everlasting kingship without a break in earthly succession; and an exclusively hereditary priesthood was to descend from Aaron. The division of the Land was to be preserved upon a genealogical basis through the tribes, families and *Houses* of the fathers. The preservation of comprehensive genealogical records was regarded as guaranteeing a measure of protection for legitimate succession and inheritance against false claimants. Failure to produce a valid genealogy rendered all claims to succession and inheritance of no account.

Numerous genealogical notices appear in the Scriptures; and several references show that what might be termed national archives were preserved until the time of our Lord. Genealogies appear to have been kept even before the Flood, as is evident from *Genesis*, etc. Moses assembled all Israel, "and they declared their pedigrees after their families, by the house of their fathers . . ." (Num. i. 18). The census taken on this occasion was repeated thirty-eight years later (Num. xxvi). The camp of Israel pitched and marched according to genealogical divisions. Achan, the troubler of Israel, was discovered after a search by families. David divided the priests, Levites, musicians and singers into "courses" and family groups.

Iddo kept genealogical records in the time of Rehoboam (II Chron. xii. 15). When Hezekiah restored the temple worship he reckoned the whole nation by genealogies (I Chron. ix. 1; II Chron. xxxi. 16-19); and writings of the time of Solomon were copied by his scribes (Prov. xxv. 1). A genealogy of the Reubenites was in existence in the time of Jotham (I Chron. v. 17). Zerubbabel preserved the genealogies of those who returned from Babylon (I Chron. iii. 19; ix; Neh. vii. 5; xi; xii). Nehemiah also "reckoned by genealogy" the nobles and rulers (Neh. vii. 5; xii. 26; Ezra ii; I Chron. iii. 21-24).

Evidence of the preservation of genealogies in later times is found in Neh. xii. 22; I Macc. ii. 1-5; viii. 17; xiv. 29; and perhaps Judith viii. 1; Tobit l. 1; etc.

Augustus ordered a census of the Jews, which caused each to go to his ancestral city; thus Joseph and Mary went to Bethlehem, the City of David. The Gospels mention Zacharias "of the course of Abia"; Elizabeth "of the daughters of Aaron"; and Anna "of the tribe of Aser".

Josephus, the Jewish historian, in the opening of his 'Life', tells how he came to be of both royal and priestly descent, adding, "I have thus traced my genealogy, as I have found it recorded in the public tables". Since Josephus' genealogy is thus connected with that of Christ, it is valuable evidence to the effect that the latter's descent was fully r ecorded in official documents.

Josephus, as mentioned in Wm. Smith's *Dictionary of the Bible*, also adds that after the wars of Antiochus Epiphanes, Pompey, and Q. Varus, new genealogical tables had been made by the priests.

Serial No. 65a.

According to Africanus, Herod the Great ordered the destruction of all Jewish genealogies in order to conceal his own ignoble origin, and that after that time only a few privately-owned genealogies remained, among them those of the Desposyni, or brethren of our Lord. Modern authorities hold Africanus' statement in doubt on the basis of Josephus' references to then existing genealogies, but agree that records certainly perished in the destruction of Jerusalem in A.D. 70.

Prophecies that Declared Details of our Lord's Descent

Infallible tests were given long beforehand to identify the Messiah when He came. Not only should He live a holy and perfect life in full accordance with the Law, but He should fulfil the following prophetic utterances regarding His descent after the flesh, as distinct from His divine origin, of which there are also many prophecies. The following prophecies apply to either our Lord or to the Royal House from which He came:

The Seed of the Woman (Gen. iii. 15).
The Root of Jesse (Isa. xi. 10).
A Rod out of the stem of Jesse (Isa. xi. 1).
A Branch out of his roots (Isa. xi. 1).
The Branch (Zech. vi. 12).
My Servant, the Branch (Zech. iii. 8).
The Branch of the Lord (Isa. iv. 2).
The Branch of Righteousness (Jer. xxxiii. 15).
A Righteous Branch (Jer. xxiii. 5).
The Messiah the Prince (Dan. ix. 25).
The Prince of Peace (Isa. ix. 6).

The Prince of Princes (Dan. viii. 25).
A Prince (Ezek. xxxiv. 24).
A Ruler (Micah v. 2).
A Sceptre (Num. xxiv. 17).
The King's Son (Ps. lxxii. 1).
King over all the Earth (Zech. xiv. 9).
The King of Glory (Ps. xxiv. 10).
The King in his beauty (Isa. xxxiii. 17).
King for ever (Ps. xxix. 10).
Crowned with a Crown of pure Gold (Ps. xxi. 3).
Born in Bethlehem of Judah (Mic. v. 2).

The Jews were meticulously careful in preserving all these scriptural details of the Davidic descent of the Messiah. Ironically, despite the fact that many thousands of them recognised and accepted Christ as such, officially their people rejected, and continue to reject Him.

The modern Jewish prayer book still proclaims the descent of "Messiah the son of David thy servant" (Morning Service).

The writers of the New Testament, who were all drawn from the ranks of Jewry, repeatedly emphasised the fact of our Lord's descent from David in fulfilment of prophecy, and their references to His descent are more numerous than in the Old Testament itself. The frequency with which such references appear in the New Testament is in itself impressive and shows something of the importance attached to the matter. The following references from the New Testament bear upon the subject of Christ's genealogy; they affirm that He was:

The Son of Abraham (Matt. i. 1).
The Son of David (Matt. i. 1).
Of the House of David (Luke i. 69; ii. 4).
The Son of Mary (Mark vi. 3).
The Son of Joseph (reputed) (Jno. i. 45).
The Seed of Abraham (Gal. iii. 16, 19).
Of the Seed of David (Jno. vii. 42;
    Acts ii. 30; Rom. i. 3; II Tim. ii. 8).
The Root of David (Rev. v. 5).
The Root and Offspring of David
    (Rev. xxii. 16).

The King of Israel (Jno. i. 49).
King of the Daughter of Zion (Jno. xii. 15).
The King of the Jews (born) (Matt. ii. 2; Mark xv. 2).
The King of the Jews (crucified) (Jno. xix. 19).
The King of Saints (Rev. xv. 3).
The King of Righteousness (Heb. vii. 2).
The King of Peace (Heb. vii. 2).

The Lion of the Tribe of Judah (Rev. v. 5).
Lord of Lords (Rev. xvii. 14).
King of Kings (Rev. xvii. 14).
The Prince of Life (Acts iii. 15).
A Prince and a Saviour (Acts v. 31).
The Prince of the Kings of the earth (Rev. i. 5).

Crowned with a Crown of Thorns (Jno. xix. 2).
Crowned with Glory and Honour (Heb. ii. 9).
Crowned with many Crowns (Rev. xix. 12).
Born in the City of David, Bethlehem (Matt. ii. 6; Luke ii. 4; Jno. vii. 42).

Perhaps the most emphatic of all New Testament references is from Peter's speech at Pentecost (Acts ii):

"Men and brethren, let me speak freely unto you of the patriarch David, that he is both dead and buried, and his sepulchre is with us unto this day.

"Therefore being a prophet, and knowing that God had sworn with an oath to him, that of the fruit of his loins, according to the flesh, he would raise up Christ to sit on his throne . . ."

Details of the Laws of Succession and Inheritance

In full keeping with the requirements of the Law, genealogical evidence of the continuity of at least one branch of the Davidic family was preserved by the Jewish people. The technicalities of the Law of succession in general were of a complicated nature, so it will be well to examine a few of its details before commencing a study of our Lord's genealogy itself:

1. An original patrimony must not pass to another family or tribe so long as members of the original family remained with just claims to it (Num. xxxvi; Lev. xxv. 10; and c.).

2. In the event of legitimate freeborn male issue failing, a freeborn daughter might transmit an inheritance to her legitimate offspring providing she married one of her own house or tribe (Num. xxxvi).

3. Under the terms of a levirate marriage, the first son of the next-of-kin who married the childless widow concerned was named after the deceased and accounted as his legal heir (Deut. xxv. 6); sons born after this were reckoned as the next-of-kin's own.

4. Arising out of the above, as a result of levirate marriage, inheritance might be transmitted to either natural or putative descent.

5. Individuals might be deprived of rights of primogeniture on moral considerations: Reuben forfeited his rights; Jeconiah's wickedness deprived him and his successors of the throne of David (Jer. xxii. 30).

6. Rights of freemen might be denied offspring of certain unions until the third (fourth if parents were counted) or even the tenth generation (Deut. xxiii. 3, 8).

Technicalities such as the above enter into the recorded genealogies of Jesus Christ; and unless the student is aware of their existence it will be impossible to appreciate how certain connections can be perfectly correct legally. Thus, while prophecy declared that the Messiah should be born of a virgin, the law required that He be born in wedlock, and be registered as the son of His mother's husband as proof of His mother's having been a married woman at the time of His birth. This seeming paradox was entirely satisfied by the circumstances of the Nativity, for although He was not Joseph's *natural* son, He was *legally* accounted as his heir.

Serial No. 65b.

The Validity of our Lord's Genealogy

It must be admitted that a number of factors, now unknown, but which were doubtless fully and widely known at the time of the birth of our Lord, prevent us from explaining the full relationships between individuals whose names appear in the genealogy of Christ. We can be certain, however, that any contest of the validity of His descent from David would certainly have been preserved by the legal experts of Jewry if the slightest weakness had existed in His title. The only passage which might possibly be construed as a taunt, that our Lord was of illegitimate origin (Jno. viii. 41), was clearly made by those who had no regard for the law or the prophecies that He should be born of a virgin (Gen. iii. 15; Isa. vii. 14) and who were thus heretics.

In the absence of any known official objection to the validity of Christ's genealogy, it would therefore appear that the record of His descent from David was unassailable in official circles. The charges made against Jesus, while they *concerned* His descent, were never a denial of it, even during His trials, for they were of blasphemy and treason, not of being a pretender to the throne of David. The treason was that of claiming rights of kingship when one, Herod, the Idumean, a descendant of Esau, not David, was already acclaimed.

The Unknown Factors in Christ's Genealogy. The Loss of the Original Records

As already indicated, we may not now be able to reconstruct with certainty the complete background of the genealogy of Christ as given in the New Testament; this is probably due to the destruction of official records in the disastrous siege of Jerusalem in A.D., 70 when the city was sacked and burnt, and to the similar fate of centres of learning generally, such as in the case of the burning of the world's then greatest library in Alexandria in A.D. 640. There can be no reasonable doubt that in the days of our Lord accurate records existed by means of which all the details of His genealogy were explained.

From the time of the early Christian Fathers up to the present, attempts have been made to explain the complexities of Christ's genealogy. *Some most capable and learned ecclesiastics have asserted, like the great Dean Alford, that a solution is impossible without further knowledge than we possess* (*vide* Wm. Smith's *Dictionary of the Bible*). It is perhaps not too much to hope that time will yet reveal further data which will enable us to establish, with positive proof, the intricacies of our Lord's descent. In the meantime we are left with various suggested solutions from which in due course a comprehensive exposition may emerge in full keeping with the requirements of the Mosaic law.

The Davidic Covenant

Divine promise of an unconditional nature was given to the House of David that it should never lack a member to sit upon the throne of Israel and that that throne should remain for ever. A progressive revelation, through the Prophets, shows that the Davidic covenant was part of a sequence of prophecies which declared beforehand many details of the everlasting dynasty that should be established on the Throne of the Lord over Israel. The following data are from that sequence:

The sceptre should not depart from Judah (Gen. xlix. 10).

The covenant with David was everlasting (II Sam. xxiii. 5).

The throne of David was to be remarkable for its peacefulness (I Kings ii. 33).

There should always be a successor to the throne of Israel of the House of David (I Kings viii. 22-25; Jer. xxxiii. 17).

An everlasting throne should pass down from David's son Solomon (II Sam. vii. 12-16; I Chron. xvii. 7-14; xxii. 8-10).

Solomon's house should be liable to punishment for disobedience (I Kings ix. 1-9).

A righteous Branch should be raised up in the House of David to execute judgment and
   justice in the earth (Jer. xxiii. 5, 6).
The righteous Branch should be raised up on the restoration of Israel and Judah (Jer.
   xxxiii. 10-16).
Israel and Judah should be restored to their land under the Davidic throne (Jer. xxx. 1-11).
Government under the throne of David should increase for ever (Isa. ix. 7).
The covenant with David is as enduring as day and night, and as heaven and earth (Jer.
   xxxiii. 20-26).

It stands to reason that the promises concerning the Davidic throne are to be fulfilled
in harmony with the Law given by God to Israel, of which certain requirements and per-
missions have been cited. According to this law, for instance, a family or dynasty might
continue in a legal sense, despite failure of male issue, provided that certain procedure,
already indicated, was observed. In reading these promises it is therefore necessary to
distinguish carefully between those made concerning the continuity of the throne of David
and those made concerning the continuity of *natural* offspring from David and his sons;
for a promise of the one does not of itself ensure the other. The foregoing and following
lists, when examined in this light, seem to show a number of definite and indefinite factors:

	PERPETUITY OF:—			
	THRONE	ISSUE		
			Putative (reputed) (Son failing)	
		Natural	Through a daughter marrying within her tribe or house	Through Levirate marriage
JUDAH	(a) Yes	(b) Yes	(c)	(d)
DAVID	Yes (unconditional)	Yes (unconditional)	Possibly in addition	Possibly in addition
SOLOMON	Yes	Yes, but conditional on obedience	Possibly in event of disobedience	Possibly in event of disobedience
NATHAN	No	Yes (Zech. xii. 12, and Luke iii.)		
JECHONIAS	No			

Several important points arise out of a comparison of the promises made to the House
of David and of the History of Israel, chief among which are the following:
   (a) The Davidic throne did not continue in the Holy Land after the time of Zedekiah.
      Therefore it must have continued in another land. The problem of where the ever-
      lasting throne removed to is not the subject of this investigation, but its transferal
      to another land is clearly indicated in *Ezekiel* xvii. Its restoration to Palestine is also
      promised.
   (b) The seed of David continued in the Holy Land without a throne from the return of
      the remnant of Judah under the decree of Cyrus (520 B.C.) until the time of Christ.
   (c) The throne of David and our Lord's family were therefore two independent but
      co-existent entities in different places.

Serial No. 65c.

(*d*) The throne of David, in the line of Solomon, still continues, if not in a natural, at least in a fully legal, that is to say, putative sense.

(*e*) Our Lord was at all times obedient to the Law; and since the line from Nathan, who was Solomon's brother, from whom it appears He was descended, has not reigned and therefore has not been disqualified by disobedience, we must consider the possibility that He possesses rights of precedence over the seed of Solomon whose issue might be set aside at any time because of the clause stipulating that its perpetuity is conditional on obedience. But the *throne* of the Lord, on which Solomon sat in succession to David must, by virtue of the promises quoted, continue for ever. That it would be occupied for ever by the sons of David is also assured; but the survival of the Solomonic line depended upon the faithfulness of his materialistic institutionalism to the law of God, and, as we know, this began to fail even in his own reign, and culminated in the prohibition and disinheritance of the *seed* of Jechonias, and the abolition of the kingdom and hence of the throne in *Judah*. The keeping of the promise to David, therefore, requires that there should be a monarch descended from his sons (not excluding Solomon's line, but with due regard to the clause relating 'o Jechonias) reigning over *Israel* elsewhere. That this was so at the time of the pronouncement to Mary appears evident (Luke i. 32, 33).

(*f*) Various possibilities arise for the future, for prophecy assures us that not only shall our Lord be King of Israel, but King of Kings. David's throne will therefore become a more glorious monarchy.

Authoritative Opinions on our Lord's Genealogy

It is helpful to learn something of the views of learned and devout scholars who have investigated our Lord's genealogy in detail. While their findings are at times in opposition, it will be seen that they agree in one most important thing: that originally there was no known dispute concerning its validity, and that the ravages of time on the ancient records have been so complete that there is now no extra-biblical material of known value in reconstructing the full details of that genealogy.

The points of difficulty are too numerous to deal with them at length in a treatise of this nature; but briefly they concern the technicalities of individual relationships; added to which are problems to be found in the names themselves, which vary greatly when compared, even when allowance has been made for translators' difficulties, as in the case of rendering Hebrew names into Greek, for certain sounds in the former have no equivalent pronunciation in the latter.

Seeming gaps in the lists also constitute problems requiring satisfactory explanations not always agreed upon by scholars.

By way of illustrating the difference of interpretation by recognised expositors of the Scriptures, we may point out that the view of Adam Clarke and the learned Dr. Barrett whom he cites, that Christ had to be descended from Solomon, is quite at variance with that of Lord Hervey, who holds that our Lord was not descended from Solomon, but from Nathan. Again, Lord Hervey assumes that Eleazar was childless, when *Matthew* clearly states that this individual "begat" Matthan; he implies that this descent was putative rather than natural, the latter, on the contrary, being accepted by Clarke.

Dr. Clarke accepts the descent given in Matthew as from father to son, while Lord Hervey accepts it as a list of successors and legal heirs not always consisting of fathers and sons.

Lord Hervey takes the pronouncement against Jehoiachin (Jechoniah, or Coniah) (Jer. xxii. 30) in its fullest sense, that is to say that he died childless, or that any of his sons died young, or that they were eunuchs (I Chron. iii. 17; Isa. xxxix. 7). Adam Clarke, on the other hand, seems to think the utterance to be qualified by the clause: ''for no man of his seed shall prosper, sitting upon the throne of David, and ruling any more in Judah''; thus his view is that the prohibition might be interpreted to mean only that any issue that he might have had was debarred from kingship in Judah. This latter view would create several possibilities; according to rabbinical traditions, as mentioned by Clarke, the Apocryphal daughter of Neri, Susanna, was wife of Jehoiachin, and of this union came Salathiel, father of Pedaiah, and grandfather of Zerubbabel; but this in turn appears contrary to the Apocrypha, where she is stated to have been a daughter of Chelcias.

Africanus, as quoted by Eusebius in his ecclesiastical history, stated that according to an account he received from the relatives of our Lord, the Jews accepted either natural or putative descent, (the latter being used in the case of offspring of a levirate marriage, when next-of-kin married a childless widow and the first son of that widow was named after the deceased and accounted as his legitimate heir and successor). This, according to Africanus, explains why Joseph's father is stated to have been Jacob, son of Matthan, in *Matthew*, while in Luke the father is given as Heli and grandfather Melchi; for Estha, widow of Matthan, of the line of Solomon, married Melchi, of the line of Nathan, and had sons, Jacob by her first marriage, and Heli by the second. Heli married but died childless, so his half-brother Jacob married his widow and had a son Joseph who, according to the Mosaic law, was accounted ''son'' of the deceased, which explains why *Matthew* says Jacob begat Joseph, and *Luke* says he was *son* of Heli.

This explanation is not considered trustworthy by many authorities because the early Christian Fathers were not consistent in their views. Further, Africanus has omitted Levi, son of Melchi, which indicates an imperfection in his treatment.

Irenaeus, Africanus and Ambrosius assert, as we are informed by Dr. Clarke, that Luke has interpolated some names; but we are assured by later commentators that there is no evidence of such interpolation.

Dr. Adam Clarke, who followed the learned Dr. Barrett, supposed that in effect *Matthew* gives the genealogy of *Joseph*, and *Luke* that of Mary; and he assumed that according to the divine promise of II Sam. vii. 12-16, Christ must be a descendant of Solomon, a point that is not insisted upon in Scripture. The Venerable Lord Hervey has expressed the strong conviction that only a single genealogy is to be found: that *Matthew* contains a list of successive kings and *legal* successors (which did not always pass from father to son) in Palestine, while *Luke* gives an actual line of descent from father to son, with both lines converging to show that our Lord possessed both unbroken natural descent from David and full *legal* claims to succession. This view is well worth our consideration.

In view of the fact that great contradiction exists between even the most capable of scholars who have attempted to show the exact relationships of all the individuals mentioned in Christ's genealogy, the reader may realise that the whole problem is beset with what may well be, for some time to come, insurmountable difficulties. At this time we can only bring forward some of the more judicious and helpful general remarks of some authorities. The student will have accomplished something if he does no more than to learn of the difficulties involved and to be guarded against making hasty pronouncements on the subject.

The main defence of the validity of the genealogy of Jesus Christ is not in our present ability to explain its detail, but in the fact that the recorded descent was not questioned by the Jewish authorities of His period. Most of them were His bitter enemies, who would undoubtedly have seized upon any error in so vital a matter.

Serial No. 65d.

EXTRACT FROM Dr. ADAM CLARKE'S *COMMENTARY ON THE NEW TESTAMENT* (London, 1817, edition).

"CLARKE, ADAM (1762?-1832), theologian; educated at Kingswood School, near Bristol; a methodist, 1778; preacher on the Wiltshire circuit, 1782; lived near London from 1805; LL.D. Aberdeen, 1808; published bibliographical works, 1803-6, and a scriptural commentary, 1810-2 gan to edit Rymer's 'Fœdera' 1818.''(*The Concise Dictionary of National Biography*.)

(On Matthew, chap. i.)

St. Matthew took up the genealogies just as he found them in the public Jewish record, which, though they were in the main correct, yet were deficient in many particulars. The Jews themselves give us sufficient proof of this . . . and although we learn from the Jews that great care was taken to separate the spurious from the true born Israelites, and Canons were made for that purpose, yet it so happened that sometimes a spurious family had got into high authority, and therefore must not be meddled with. See several cases in *Lightfoot*. On this account, a faithful genealogist would insert in his roll such only as were indisputable. "It is therefore easy to guess", says Dr. *Lightfoot*, "whence Matthew took the last fourteen generations of this genealogy and Luke the first forty names of his: namely, from the genealogical rolls, at that time well known and laid up in the public repositories, and in the private also. And it was necessary indeed in so noble and sublime a subject, and a thing that would be so much inquired into by the Jewish people, as the lineage of the Messiah would be, that the Evangelists should deliver a truth not only that could not be gainsaid, but also might be proved and established from certain and undoubted rolls of ancestors."

(On Luke, chap. iii.)

Perhaps few questions have occasioned more trouble and perplexity to the learned than that which concerns the genealogy of our blessed Lord as it is given by the Evangelists St. Matthew and St. Luke. The tables found in these writers are extremely different, or as some think, contradictory. Allowing the divine inspiration of the authors, we must grant that they could make no mistakes in any point, and especially on a subject where the truth of the gospel history and the fulfilment of the ancient prophecies are so nearly concerned. The expression of Le Clerc, however, *Universam antiquitatem exercitam habuere*, is not strictly true. In *later* times the difficulty has certainly excited much discussion; but it is worthy of remark that while the archives of the Jews remained entire, the accuracy of the Evangelists was never called in question. Hence it follows, either that some corruptions have since that time crept into the text, or that the true method of reconciling the seeming inconsistencies was then better understood. The silence of the enemies of the gospel, both Heathen and Jewish, during even the *first* century, is itself a sufficient proof that neither inconsistency nor corruption could be *then* alleged against this part of the evangelical history. If a charge of this nature could have been supported, it unquestionably would have been made. The Jews and Heathens who agreed in their hostility to the religion of Christ, were equally interested in this subject; and could they have proved that a single flaw existed in these genealogical tables, they might at once have set aside the pretensions of our Lord and his disciples; for if the lineal descent of Jesus from David were not indisputable, he could not possess the character essential to the Messiah, nor any right to the Jewish throne. If his title in this respect were even questionable it is impossible to suppose that the Jews would have withheld an allegation which must fully vindicate them in denying his Messiahship and in putting him to death as an impostor. We may confidently assert, therefore, that his regular lineal descent from David could not be disproved, since it was not even disputed, at a time when alone it could have been done successfully, and by those persons who were so deeply interested in the event. The sincere believer may consequently be assured that whatever difficulties appear at present had formerly no existence, and are even now of such a nature as cannot be allowed to shake the faith of any reasonable man. I would not, however, be understood to intimate that these difficulties are now insuperable; on the contrary, I am satisfied that the real difficulties are few, and that these have, for the most part, been satisfactorily explained by most of the Evangelical Harmonists.

•   •   •   •   •

I have said that the peculiar manner used by some of the Eastern nations in recording their genealogies is one cause of their present obscurity: on this subject the late ingenious Mr. Harmer refers to a case in point, which I shall give in his own words: "Genealogical tables were kept among the Jews with great exactness. Every person of learning, however, knows that the great difference in this point between St. Matthew and St. Luke, who have each of them given us a genealogy of our Lord, has greatly embarrassed the curious, and did so early (see Aug. Retract. l. ii. c. 7); but as in other cases, what was at first thought an objection against the sacred writer has turned out in his favour; so doubly will this, when it shall be thoroughly cleared up. Time may perhaps do it: all I would attempt to shew here is that there has been lately discovered an inscription at Palmyra, which has just the same difficulty. He that clears up the Syrian difficulty will, I presume, clear up the *Sacred*. To which I would add that it is to be remembered that Palmyra was in the neighbourhood of Judea, and the inscriptions that are found there are about the apostolic age. As to the *Inscription* I refer to, Mr. Wood, the ingenious editor of those ruins, who has observed that it was more difficult to understand than translate it. This, says he, will appear by rendering it literally, which is easiest done into Latin, thus: *Senatus populusque Alialamenem, Pani filium, Mocini nepo-tem, Aeranis pronepotem, Mathae abnepotem, et Aeranem patrem ejus, viros pios et patriae amicos, et omni modo placentes patriae patriisque diis, honoris gratia. Anno 450, Mense Aprili.* Our difficulty is, continues he, that Aeranes is called the *father* of Alialamenes, who is himself called the son of Panus, just in the same manner as St. Matthew tells us that *Jacob begat Joseph*; and St. Luke calls Joseph *the son of Heli.* There is something without doubt in these affairs peculiar to the East, which, however unknown to us, was common to the Jews and the people of Palmyra, and will, when properly ex-plained, be a proof of the authenticity of these genealogies, instead of an objection . . .'' (Harmer's *Observations*).

. . . From a very particular acquaintance with this subject, I think I have sufficient ground to state that, through the ignorance and carelessness of *transcribers*, innumerable mistakes have been made in ancient *names*. These also have suffered very greatly in their transfusion from one language to another, till at last the original name is almost totally lost. Examples might be multiplied without end; a very few will suffice: . . . *Yehoshua* (according to the Masoretic punctuation) of the Hebrew Bible, is changed into *Joshua* and *Jesus*; . . . *Yeshayahoo* into *Isaiah* and *Esaias*; . . . *Eliyahoo* into *Elijah* and *Elias*; the Persian *Darab* into *Darius*; *Ardsheer* into *Ahasuerus*; *Artachshasta* into *Artaxerxes*, and even *Darius*; and . . . *Yahchanan* into . . . *Johannes*, and *John*! Besides, neither the Greeks nor Romans could pronounce either the Hebrew or Persian names; and when engaged in the task of transcribing, they did it according to their own manner of pronuncia-tion. It is notorious that all the Greek and Latin historians have committed innumerable blunders of this kind in their accounts of foreign nations. St. Jerome loudly complains of the ridicule which those Christians who were accustomed only to a Greek or Latin mode of pronunciation endured continually from the Jews because they could not pronounce the Hebrew *proper names*, particularly the gutturals.

EXTRACT FROM THE VENERABLE LORD ARTHUR G. HERVEY'S ARTICLE IN *A DICTIONARY OF THE BIBLE*, edited by Wm. Smith, D.C.L., LL.D. (John Murray, London, 1863 edition).

HERVEY, LORD ARTHUR CHARLES (1808-1894), bishop of Bath and Wells; fourth son of Frederick William Hervey, first marquis of Bristol; educated at Eton and Trinity College, Cambridge; B.A., 1830; ordained priest, 1832; rector of Horringer and Ickworth, 1856; archdeacon of Sudbury, 1862; bishop of Bath and Wells, 1869-1894; on committee of revisers of authorised version of Old Testament, 1870-74; published 'Genealogies of our Lord', 1853.

The New Testament gives us the genealogy of but one person, that of our Saviour. The priesthood of Aaron having ceased, the possession of the land of Canaan being transferred to the gentiles, there being under the N.T. dispensation no difference between circumcision and uncircumcision, Barbarian and Scythian, bond and free, there is but One whose genealogy it concerns us as Christians to be acquain-ted with, that of our Lord Jesus Christ. Him the prophets announced as the seed of Abraham, and the son of David, and the angel declared that to Him should be given the throne of His father David, that He might reign over the house of Jacob for ever. His descent from David and Abraham being therefore an essential part of his Messiahship, it was right that His genealogy should be given as a portion of Gospel truth. Considering, further, that to the Jews first He was manifested and preached, and that His descent from David and Abraham was a matter of special interest to them, it seems likely that the proof of his descent would be one especially adapted to convince them; in other words, that it would be drawn from documents which they deemed authen-tic. Such were the genealogical records preserved at Jerusalem. And when to the above considerations we add the fact that the lineage of Joseph was actually made out from authentic records for the purpose of the civil census ordered by Augustus, it becomes morally certain that the genealogy of Jesus Christ was extracted from the public registers. Another consideration adds yet further conviction. It has often excited surprise that the genealogies of

Christ should both give the descent of Joseph and not Mary. But if these genealogies were those con-tained in the public register it could not be other-wise. In them Jesus, the son of Mary, the espoused wife of Joseph, could only appear as Joseph's son (comp. John i. 45). In transferring them to the pages of the Gospels, the evangelists only added the qualifying expression ''as was supposed'' (Luke iii. 23, and its equivalent, Matt. i. 16) . . .

. . . But it is not too much to say that, after all, in regard to the main points there is no difficulty at all, if only the documents in question are dealt with reasonably, and after the analogy of similar Jewish documents in the O.T.—and the clues to a right understanding of them are so patent and so strongly marked, that it is surprising that so much diversity of opinion should have existed. The following proposition will explain the true construction of these genealogies:

1. They are both the genealogies of Joseph, i.e. of Jesus Christ, as the reputed and legal son of Joseph, and Mary. One has only to read them to be satisfied of this. The notices of Joseph as being of the house of David, by the same evangelists who give the pedigree, are an additional confirmation (Matt. i. 20; Luke i. 27, ii. 4, etc.), and if these pedigrees were extracted from the public archives they must have been Joseph's.

2. The genealogy of St. Matthew is, as Grotius most truly and unhesitatingly asserted, Joseph's genealogy as legal successor to the throne of David, i.e. it exhibits the successive heirs of the kingdom

Serial No. 65e.

ending with Christ, as Joseph's reputed son. St. Luke's is Joseph's private genealogy, exhibiting his real birth, as David's son, and thus showing why he was heir to Solomon's crown. This is capable of being almost demonstrated. If St. Matthew's genealogy had stood alone, and we had no further information on this subject than it affords, we might indeed have thought that it was a genealogical stem in the strictest sense of the word, exhibiting Joseph's forefathers in succession, from David downwards. But immediately we find a second genealogy of Joseph—that in St. Luke's Gospel—such is no longer a reasonable opinion. Because if St. Matthew's genealogy, tracing as it does the successive generations through the long line of Jewish kings, had been Joseph's real paternal stem, there could not possibly have been room for a second genealogy. The steps of ancestry coinciding with the steps of succession, one pedigree only could in the nature of things be proper. The mere existence therefore of a second pedigree, tracing Joseph's ancestry through private persons, by the side of one tracing it through kings, is in itself a proof that the latter is not the true stem of birth. . . .

. . . It must be added that not only does this theory explain all the phenomena, but that that portion of it which asserts that Luke gives Joseph's paternal stem receives a most remarkable confirmation from the names which compose that stem. For if we begin with Nathan, we find that his son, Mattatha, and four others, of whom the last was grandfather to Joseph, had names which are merely modifications of Nathan (Matthat twice, and Mattathias twice); or if we begin with Joseph we shall find no less than three of his name between him and Nathan: an evidence, of the most convincing kind, that Joseph was lineally descended from Nathan in the way St. Luke represents him to be (comp. Zech. xii. 12).

3. Mary, the mother of Jesus, was in all probability the daughter of Jacob, and first cousin to Joseph her husband. So that in point of *fact*, though not of *form*, both the genealogies are as much hers as her husband's. . . .

Authorities: Various.

.

PERPETUAL succession to the Throne over Israel was promised to the Royal House of David. Our Lord's earthly title to the Throne is firmly asserted in both Old and New Testament Scriptures.

In addition to His kingly office, the Bible declares that Jesus is also "High Priest after the order of Melchisedec", of whom all Israelitish high priests were but types. In His perfection He thus combines the duties of chief ruler and leader of worship. Though the time has not yet arrived for Him to take over "the throne of His father David" He has, for nineteen centuries been "Advocate with the Father" for Israelites by race and by Grace having, by His sacrifice, fulfilled and thereby terminated the Aaronic ritual.

In His office of High Priest Jesus fulfils the "covenant of everlasting priesthood" promised to Phinehas, of the Aaronic family, mentioned in the 25th chapter of the Book of Numbers. Several sources indicate that—in addition to being a lineal descendant of David—our Lord was also descended from the line of high priests which sprang from Aaron, through Phinehas and Eleazar. Both as King and High Priest, the ancestry is traceable through the family of the Virgin Mary.

Thus the promises of perpetual succession made to the Davidic and Aaronic families are secure for all time.

The Cessation of the Aaronic Priesthood as a Separate Entity

With the murder of Aristobulus, the last of the Asmonians, by Herod the Great, the separate Aaronic succession of High Priests gave way to men of ignoble estate. "Herod made men of low birth high-priests, deposed them at his will, and named others in their room" (Wm. Smith's *Dictionary of the Bible*, art. "High Priest"). Prior to this time members of the Aaronic family had united in marriage with the House of David, as in the case of the families of John the Baptist and of our Lord. John's father was the priest Zacharias, of the course of Abia, or Abijah, of the eighth course of the priesthood (I Chron. xxiv. 10; Luke i. 5); his mother was "of the daughters of Aaron, and her name was Elisabeth" (Luke i. 5). Elisabeth was also cousin to the Virgin Mary (Luke i. 36), who was descended from the House of David. It is therefore clear that the two families had inter-married; but the Scriptures do not reveal the specific details of the connection.

The Continuity of the Line of Phinehas in Post-Captivity Times

The destruction of the Aaronic priesthood as a separate family by Herod must be considered in relation to the promise of everlasting priesthood to the lineage of Phinehas: "Wherefore say, Behold, I give unto him my covenant of peace: And he shall have it, and his seed after him, even the covenant of an everlasting priesthood; because he was zealous for his God, and made an atonement for the children of Israel" (Num. xxv. 12, 13). The complete destruction of the Aaronic succession would have to be regarded as nullifying this promise. If, however, the Aaronic family had joined with that of our Lord, which was of David, the continuation of the succession to the high-priesthood of Phinehas would be realised in the family of Mary.

That Phinehas' succession continued in post-captivity times is evident in the lists of the "sons of Phinehas" in Ezra viii. 2, and I Esdras v. 5. Phinehas is also commemorated by the psalmist, who wrote: "Then stood up Phinehas, and executed judgment: and so the plague was stayed. And that was counted unto him for righteousness unto all generations for evermore" (Psa. cvi. 30, 31). The Apocrypha also refers to the everlasting "covenant" made with Phinehas: "Therefore was there a covenant of peace made with him, that he should be the chief of the sanctuary and of his people, and that he and his posterity should have the dignity of the priesthood for ever: According to the covenant made with David the son of Jesse, of the tribe of Juda, that the inheritance of the king should be to his posterity alone: so the inheritance of Aaron should also be unto his seed" (Ecclesiasticus xlv. 24, 25).

Jesus Christ the High Priest

The role of the Aaronic high priest was indeed assumed by our Lord in His Ministry, who fulfilled all that was typified in the first Tabernacle: "But Christ being come an high priest of good things to come, by a greater and more perfect tabernacle, not made with hands, that is to say, not of this building; Neither by the blood of goats and calves, but by his own blood he entered in once into the holy place, having obtained eternal redemption for us" (Heb. ix. 11, 12). This and related texts might be thought to infer the Aaronic descent of Christ, especially in view of St. Paul's plain statement that an element of "change" (not cessation) had been introduced into the high-priesthood by joining it to another tribe of which "Moses spake nothing" concerning that office: "If therefore

Seriol No. 86a

perfection were by the Levitical priesthood, (for under it the people received the law,) what further need was there that another priest should rise after the order of Melchisedec, and not be called after the order of Aaron? For the priesthood being changed, there is made of necessity a change also of the law. For he of whom these things are spoken pertaineth to another tribe, of which no man gave attendance at the altar. For it is evident that our Lord sprang out of Juda; of which tribe Moses spake nothing concerning the priesthood. And it is yet far more evident: for that after the similitude of Melchisedec there ariseth another priest, Who is made, not after the law of a carnal commandment, but after the power of an endless life. For he testifieth, Thou art a priest for ever after the order of Melchisedec. For there is verily a disannulling of the commandment going before for the weakness and unprofitableness thereof'' (Heb. vii. 11-18). The ''disannulling of the commandment going before'' was not to the effect that the Aaronic succession should cease, for it should last for ever according to the covenant with Phinehas and his seed, but to the effect that priesthood and kingship should no longer be separate, and should form the order of Melchisedec, in which the ''weakness and unprofitableness'' of the former separation would be overcome.

The view that the Aaronic priesthood ended for ever before the time of Christ is contrary to the promise to Phinehas. But the cessation of the Aaronic priesthood as a separate entity only, and its absorption in the House of David through marriage would account for the ''change'' in the priesthood in a manner harmonious with all Scripture. As legitimate successor to both the Davidic kingship and the office of high priest, our Lord might be appropriately described as having been ''after the similitude of Melchisedec'', or ''righteous king''.

The Fusion of the Davidic and Aaronic Families

The relationship of John the Baptist to the Aaronic priesthood is highly pertinent to our Lord's descent. John, whose mother was cousin to the Virgin Mary, was son of ''Zacharias, of the course of Abia'' (Luke i. 5), or Abijah, a name which means ''my father is Jah'' (Young), and which is perfectly descriptive of Jesus' paternal ancestry. It was highly appropriate that the family of the priesthood from which Jesus' forerunner came was so named; and it would be even more so if Jesus was of this course. Symbolically, the number of this course, the eighth (I Chron. xxiv. 10), may be taken as typical of the commencement of a new octave, or order, as in the eighth and fiftieth years, the times of release and rest; and eighth time, which, by implication follows the ''seven times'' of punishment; the eighth day of our Lord's circumcision; the eighth day on which Jesus appeared after the Resurrection; the eighth day, holy to Christians; the fiftieth day (the eighth after the seventh week) of Pentecost; etc. In a parallel sense it is fitting that our Lord commenced the new order of combined kingship and priesthood, that of Melchisedec.

Legally there would appear to be no obstacle to the joining of the Aaronic priesthood to the House of David. Inter-tribal marriages were forbidden where loss of landed inheritance to the tribe might be involved (Num. xxvii. 8; xxxvi. 1-12). In the case of Levi, from which tribe the Aaronic priesthood was drawn, there was no tribeship of land (Num. xviii. 20; Deut. x. 9; xviii. 2), although there were Levitical cities (Josh. xxi. 19, etc.). In any case, at the time in question, after the Captivities, the twelve tribes were no longer confined to their allotted boundaries. Levi's inheritance (Num. xviii. 20; Deut. x. 9; xviii. 2), the Lord, was a spiritual one, but was in fact by far the greatest, incorporating all. The raising of the whole twelve tribes to a priestly status, in which no distinction is made, is assured in prophecy (Ex. xix. 6; I Pet. ii. 9; Rev. vii. 4-8; see also Ser. No. 84 [(228)], so that, in effect, all the tribes become Levitical and indistinguishable in that capacity.

Details of the connections between our Lord's family with the line of Aaron are not complete in the sacred canon—the origins of the parents concerned in the link between Mary and Elisabeth not being stated; but apocryphal and extra-Biblical materials throw light on the subject, although their authenticity is admittedly open to question.

The Gospel of the Birth of Mary, part of the *Apocryphal New Testament*, a series of documents known to have been preserved by the Christians prior to the fifth century A.D., tells us that: "The blessed and ever glorious Virgin Mary, sprung from the royal race and family of David, was born in the city of Nazareth, and educated at Jerusalem, in the temple of the Lord. Her father's name was Joachim, and her mother's Anna. The family of her father was of Galilee and the city of Nazareth. The family of her mother was of Bethlehem" (chap. i. 1, 2).

The Protevangelion, a work of the same collection, also refers to Joachim (ch. i. 1) and to "his wife Anna" (ch. ii. 1), and states "when nine months were fulfilled to Anna, she brought forth . . . and called her name Mary" (ch. v. 6-9).

According to the *Koran*, as supported by Mohammedan commentators, Mary's father was called Imrân, who, besides Mary, had a daughter Ishá (or Elisabeth), who married Zacharias, and was mother of John the Baptist (The *Koran*, ch. III: "The Family of Imrân"). According to the *Koran*, Imrân also had a son named Aaron (The *Koran*, ch. XIX). Commentators on the *Koran*, as cited by Sale in his notes to his translation, say that Imrân's wife was named Hannah, or Ann, the daughter of Fakudh. These authorities also relate that when a dispute arose among the priests as to who should have charge of the education of Mary, "Zacharias insisted that he ought to be preferred, because he had married her aunt" (Sale, notes to The *Koran*, ch. III: "The Family of Imrân).

Ethiopian Christian liturgies, believed to have been written in the XVth century and based on or copied from earlier sources, state that the name of the Virgin Mary's mother was Hanna, and that she was "the daughter of noble parents who offered up offerings before God Almighty, and who were Levites belonging to the priesthood" (*Legends of Our Mary the Perpetual Virgin and her Mother Hanna*, translated from the Ethiopic Manuscripts collected by King Theodore at Makdalâ, and now in the British Museum, by Sir E. A. Wallis Budge, M.A., Litt.D., D.Litt., Lit.D., F.S.A., Keeper of the Department of Egyptian and Assyrian Antiquities in the British Museum; 1922; p. 13). But in another place the liturgies trace both Hanna's parents to the House of David (pp. 5, 6). The name of Hanna's mother, say these liturgies, was Faustina; and of John the Baptist's mother's mother was Sophia, daughter of Matthat (Luke iii. 24), of the House of David, which seems to contradict Scripture.

The Book of the Cave of Treasures, attributed to Ephraim the Syrian (*c.* 306-373 A.D.), but believed to be not older than the VIth century in its present form, contains a genealogy of Christ in which it is stated that "Abiud (Matt. i. 13) took to wife Zakhyath, the daughter of Joshua, the son of Yozadak (Josedec, I Esdras v. 5, 48, 56; vi. 2; ix. 19; Ecclesiasticus xlix. 12; father of Jeshua, Joshua, or Jesus the high priest of Josephus), the priest, and begot by her Eliakim" (Sir Wallis Budge's translation, 1927, p. 194). The antiquity of this text increases the probability of its accuracy, which admittedly is not established.

Serial No. 86b.

It was long ago accepted (*vide* James Anderson's *Royal Genealogies*, 1732 and 1736 editions, table LXVI) that a daughter of the high priest Simon the Just married Mattathias II (Tobias), whose son by her was Joseph (Luke iii. 24, 25). This construction would appear to be based on Josephus' *Antiquities*, XII, iv. 1, 2, where we are informed that the high priest Simon, called "The Just", brother of Eleazar, was father-in-law to Tobias, and through him, grandfather of Joseph, who was "young in age, but of great reputation among the people of Jerusalem, for gravity, prudence, and justice. His father's name was Tobias; and his mother was the sister of Onias the high priest" (*Ant.* XII. iv. 2).

Thus from such sources it is indicated that Jesus was of Aaronic as well as of Davidic descent, and that in a genealogical sense the description of Him as High Priest would be . fully justified.

Genealogically it may be that Jesus, in being entitled to hold the offices of both King and High Priest, was truly "after the similitude of Melchisedec", and was the first in Israel to be fully qualified to hold the two dignities. Hitherto the Davidic kings are not known to have possessed Aaronic blood; and the attempt of the Asmonians to elevate their Aaronic high priests to kingship, although abortive in the end, was based on impudence, for their priests were not descended from the House of David. This Jewish endeavour to confer upon the priesthood the office of kingship was the reverse of what had been divinely ordained—that the royal family of David should be elevated to the priesthood after the order of Melchisedec, i.e. "Righteous King".

The Flight of Our Lord's Family after the Resurrection

Persistent continental traditions, the testimony of the early fathers of the Christian Church, and local historical remains, ably presented and discussed by J. W. Taylor in his *The Coming of the Saints* (Methuen & Co., 1906, 1911, 1923) may be considered as fairly conclusively establishing that in addition to the journeys of St. Paul to Rome and "Spain", St. Mary (wife of Cleopas), St. Salome (Mary Salome), St. Mary Magdalene, St. Martha and her maid Marcella, Lazarus, Trophimus, St. Joseph of Arimathea, and others, arrived at Arles, in the south of France, and from thence dispersed to spread the Gospel. St. Martha and Marcella went to Tarascon and Avignon; St. Mary Cleopas and Sarah their maid to the Camargue; while St. Joseph proceeded up the Rhone valley and on to Britain.

According to Cornish and other local British traditions also, St. Joseph, together with his son Josephus and other Israelites, are stated to have come to Britain after the Crucifixion. Joseph's son is stated to have married into the family of the British kings or chieftains. In *The High History of the Holy Graal*, compiled about A.D. 1220, purportedly from an older MS. of the clerk Josephus of Glastonbury, King Arthur, Galahad and Lancelot are said to have been descended from this union of the family of St. Joseph of Arimathea and the British Royal House. The story is much more fully given, together with extracts from *The High History of the Holy Graal* and other sources in *The Coming of the Saints; St. Joseph of Arimathea at Glastonbury*, by the Rev. Lionel Smithett Lewis, M.A., Vicar of Glastonbury (Mowbray's, Oxford, 1922, etc.); *Glastonbury*, by A. E. Webb (Avalon Press, Glastonbury, 1929); *The Central Somerset Gazette Illustrated Guide to Glastonbury* (Glastonbury, 1936, etc.); *Two Glastonbury Legends*, by the Rev. J. Armitage Robinson, D.D., F.B.A., Dean of Wells (Cambridge University Press, 1926); *A Guide to The Glories of Glastonbury*, by A. Le Strange Campbell (Sheed & Ward, London, 1926); etc.

The Genealogy of the Tudors

In the uniting of the royal and sacerdotal offices in Christ there stood in Israel for the first time One ''after the similitude of Melchisedec'', that is to say, One Who was both ''King'' (*melek*) and ''Righteous'' (*zadok*) Priest. Not only were the regal and sacerdotal families joined in Himself, but in His next-of-kin, some of whom reputedly came to Glastonbury and joined with the ancient British king-line, to infuse into it both Davidic and Aaronic blood which descended into the Tudors.

Among the oldest documents in British literature is the genealogy of Owain Tudor, here illustrated, which traces his descent from Anna, cousin of the Virgin Mary. This genealogy is found in MS. No. 3859 of the Harleian collection now in the British Museum. We are informed in *Annales Cambriae*, edited by the Rev. John Williams ab Ithel, and published under the authority of the Lords Commissioners of Her Majesty's Treasury, under the direction of the Master of the Rolls, 1860 (Longman), that this MS. is probably a work by Owain's personal scribe in the tenth or eleventh century (pp. x, xi). A second line of this genealogy ascends through Owain's mother Elen, up to Constantine the Great and his Royal British mother, the Empress Helena, descended from Bran the Blessed, son of Lear and Penardim the sister of Beli, whose mother was Anna, cousin of the Virgin Mary (*vide The Royal House of Britain*, by the Rev. W. M. H. Milner, M.A., §8; and the Rev. R. W. Morgan's *St. Paul in Britain*). Owain is thus doubly connected with this Anna. A Jesus College, Oxford, manuscript (No. 20) supposed to be of the thirteenth century, refers to ''Beli the Great, son of Anna'', and states that ''That Anna used to be said by the men of Egypt to be cousin to the Virgin Mary'' (*The Welsh People*, 3rd, ed., 1902, by J. Rhys and D. Brynmor-Jones, p. 42; Unwin, London).

A genealogy preserved by John of Glastonbury shows King Arthur's descent from Joseph of Arimathea as follows: ''*Helaius, nepos Joseph, genuit Josue. Josue genuit Aminadab, Aminadab genuit Castellors, Castellors genuit Manael, Manael genuit Lambord & Urlard. Lambord genuit filium, qui genuit Ygernam, de qua rex Uterpendragun genuit nobilem & famosum regem Arthurum; per quod patet, quod rex Arthurus de stirpe Joseph descendit*'' (Thomas Hearne's edit., 1726, pp. 56, 57.) This Helaius is none other than Beli the Great, whose name is given as Hely by Geoffrey of Monmouth (*d.* 1154 A.D.) in his *Histories of the Kings of Britain*, Bk. III, ch. 20, and is stated to have been grandson (*nepos*) of Joseph of Arimathea. Since Anna was Beli's mother, she was also evidently daughter of Joseph of Arimathea, who was therefore an uncle of the Virgin Mary.

Anna, according to sources already mentioned, was the name of the mother of the Virgin Mary, as also of the prophetess of the tribe of Asher (Luke ii. 36), so that it was by no means uncommon. The Ethiopic liturgies state that Hanna was the name of one of Matthat's three daughters, the other two being Mary, mother of Salome, and Sophia the mother of Elisabeth, who was the mother of John the Baptist; this may, however, be in error, for Elisabeth was ''of the daughters of Aaron''.

This alleged descent of Arthur from Joseph of Arimathea is supported by the several obviously Hebrew names in the genealogy. Had there been *no* Israelitish contacts in so early a period in the history of the British church, and had there been *no* intermarriage of the House of David with the Early British royal line, which at least in part had not accepted Christianity, according to native records, this feature would be most difficult to explain.

Serial No. 86c.

A second genealogy in John of Glastonbury's writings derives the husband of Arthur's sister from a *"Petrus"*, who was *"consanguineus Joseph ab Armathea"* *"Petrus consanguineus Joseph ab Armathea Rex Organiæ, genuit Erlan. Erlan genuit Melianum, Melianus genuit Arguth. Arguth genuit Edor. Edor genuit Loth, qui duxit in uxorem sororem regis Arthuri, de qua genuit quatuor filios, scilicet Walwanum, Agraneyns, Gwerehes, & Czheries"* (Hearne, p. 57).

Heraldic Coincidences

The badge of the Tudors was the "portcullis", which, with its twelve squares, bears a remarkable resemblance to the golden breastplate of the high priest which bore the twelve jewels representing the tribes of Israel. The accompanying illustrations of the high priest and the Arms of the City of Westminster, which carry the Tudor portcullis on shield with supporters, are shown in accompanying illustrations. These Arms also bear the cross, which according to legend, was the badge of Joseph of Arimathea, and which was adopted by King Arthur in honour of "Our Lady and her Son our Lord Jesus" as superior to his Trojan arms which were, according to John of Glastonbury, "silver, with three lions red, turning their heads to their backs, from the time of the coming of Brutus even until this change of King Arthur" (*Two Glastonbury Legends*, by the Rev. J. Armitage Robinson, D.D., F.B.A., 1926, p. 22; see also extracts from *The High History of the Holy Graal*, in *The Coming of the Saints*, by J. W. Taylor, pp. 319, 320). The legendary Trojan origin of the Early British kings, from whom descended the Tudors, is more fully dealt with in Ser. No. 83 (572.942).

Head of Church and State

The support given to the Glastonbury legends from continental sources, so fully and ably presented and discussed by Taylor, indicates that by reason of intermarriage, the descent of the Tudors from the Royal House of David, from which our Lord was descended, may be accepted with a high degree of confidence. The implications of such a combined descent are of the highest significance, for thus the Tudors were traditionally descended not only from the most ancient line of British kings of Judahite origin (Ser. No. 81 [572.93918]; 83 [572.942]), but also from the House of David, and from the high priests of the line of Aaron. From a genealogical standpoint this is a most appropriate connection for the first family that came to head both church and state in England. This uniting of church and state under a single head who derived from both the House of David and the House of Aaron is all the more remarkable when it is realised that long prior to this event the Roman church, after the manner of the Jewish state in the time of the Asmonians, had exerted the greatest efforts to elevate its non-Davidic priest to the office of kingship in an unsuccessful attempt to make him the head of both the Catholic church and the world-state.

The Tudors joined with the Stuarts, of the Scottish and Irish royal lines; and thus Davidic and Aaronic descent has come into our present Royal House of Britain, which so appropriately provides the head of both church and state in the United Kingdom.

From the earliest years of the Christian era our British Royal Family descended from Glastonbury has protected and championed the Christian church. In its long history no charge of having persecuted Christianity can be laid to its door, excepting in the time of Mary, who obeyed the dictates of the foreign papacy. Under this family Christian government has steadily increased in the world, and under its benevolent attention it may be said that Isaiah's glorious prophecy has witnessed steady fulfilment: ''Of the increase of his government and peace there shall be no end, upon the throne of David, and upon his kingdom, to order it, and to establish it with judgment and with justice from henceforth even for ever. The zeal of the Lord of hosts will perform this'' (Isa. ix. 7). In this transferal of the Davidic family to the British Isles after the Crucifixtion may also be seen something of the fulfilment of the cryptic prophecy by our Lord: "The kingdom of God shall be taken from you, and given to a nation bringing forth the fruits thereof" (Matt. xxi. 43).

EXTRACTS FROM *ANNALES CAMBRIAE*, edited by the Rev. JOHN WILLIAMS AB ITHEL, M.A., published by the authority of the Lords Commissioners of Her Majesty's Treasury, under the direction of the Master of the Rolls; Longman, Green, Longman, and Roberts; London, 1860.

The result of the present volume which, though of small dimensions, is nevertheless highly interesting, and of considerable value, as being, perhaps, the oldest chronicle of Welsh affairs that we possess. It is derived from three different copies which, for the purpose of reference, we have distinguished respectively by the letters A, B, C . . .

A is a manuscript in the Harleian Collection, No. 3,859, on vellum, in octavo, of the latter part of the tenth or beginning of the eleventh century, inserted without title or introduction in the body of a manuscript of Nennius. It is followed immediately by the pedigree of Owain, son of Howel the Good, and his mother Elen, which gives us reason further for supposing the chronicle in question to have been originally compiled during the sway of that prince. Howel died A.D. 948, when his sons, four in number, Owain, Rhun, Roderic, and Edwin, divided among them the kingdom of South Wales, and Powys; North Wales being ruled over by Ieuav and Iago, sons of Idwal Voel. Between the two families there was a very severe struggle for supremacy, and several bloody battles were fought with various results. Under these circumstances it was very natural that publicity should be given to Owain's regal claims, as genealogically derived through both his parents from the ancient monarchs of the land. The officer, whose province it was to keep a register of births, marriages, and deaths, was the bard, who, being already in possession of a maintenance of five free acres of land in virtue of his profession, received, moreover, in consideration

of this special act, a pecuniary fee according to the social position of the head of the household which he visited. As the bard was an officer of the court, it is but fair to suppose that the genealogist was Owain's own bard, one who enjoyed a more honourable post than fell to the lot of the itinerant Clerk; a supposition further corroborated by the knowledge of Latin which he evidently possessed.

Now if this manuscript is not a mere transcript, which there is no reason to suspect, inasmuch as both the chronicle and the pedigree are written in the same hand, it follows that the genealogist was also the compiler of the chronicle; and with propriety would he be so; for, as we learn from the ancient laws of Wales, "the three records of the bards of the Isle of Britain are the genealogy of descent by marriages, territorial divisions, and praiseworthy acts and sciences."

The family registers of the princes and other great men of the land would naturally form the basis of a national chronicle, such as the *Annales Cambriae.*

It is very possible, moreover, that the compiler was also an ecclesiastic, for men in holy orders were frequently found to be members likewise of the bardic profession. But we can hardly suppose that he was an Englishman, because Owain had, for some reason or other, a great antipathy to the Saxon clergy and monks, which he carried out to such lengths as even to destroy the Welsh colleges which harboured them (pp. ix-xii).

This pedigree is as follows:

Yv'e Map Iguel	M. Mailcun	M. Anquerit
Map Catell	M. Catgolaun Iauhir	M. Onmum
Map Rotri	M. Einiaun girt	M. Duvun
Map Mermin	M. Cuneda	M. Brithguein
Map Ethil	M. Oetern	M. Eugein
Merch Cinnan	M. Patern Pesrut	M. Aballac
Map Rotri	M. Tacit	M. Amalech, qui
M. Tutgual	M. Cein	fuit Beli Magni filius
M. Catgualart	M. Guoicein	et Anna mater ejus,
M. Catgollaun	M. Doli	quae dicitur esse con-
M. Catman	M. Guordoli	sobrina Mariae Vir-
M. Jacob	M. Dumn	ginis matris Domini
M. Beli	M. Gur dumn	nostri Jesu Christi.
M. Run	M. Amguoloyt	

Serial No. 86d.

Yvein Map Elen	M. Guortepir	M. Constans
Merch Loumerc	M. Aircol	M. Constantini Magni
Map Hymeyt	M. Trifun	M. Constantinii et
Map Tancoyst	M. Clotri	Helen Luiedauc quae
Merc Ovei	M. Gloitguin	de Britannia, exivit
Map Margetiut	M. Nimet	ad crucem Christi
M. Teudos	M. Dimet	quaerendam usque
M. Regin	M. Maxim Gueletic	ad Jerusalem, et
M. Catgocaun	M. Ytec	indi attulit secum
M. Cathen	M. Ytector	usque ad Constanti-
M. Cloten	M. Ebiud	nopolim, et est ibi
M. Nougoy	M. Eluid	usque in hodiernum
M. Arthur	M. Stater	diem.
M. Petr	M. Pircsmisser	
M. Cincar		

(From footnote 1, p. x)

[Concluding portions of the Latin texts of the foregoing genealogy, as translated *ad sensum* by the late Rev. J. Courtenay James, M.A., B.D., Ph.D.:

"Amalech, who was the son of Belus the Great and Anna his mother, who is said to be the cousin of the Virgin Mary the mother of our Lord Jesus Christ."

"Constantine the Great (son) of Constantius and Helena Luiedauc, who went from Britannia seeking the Cross of Christ all the way to Jerusalem, and thence bore it with her all the way to Constantinople and it is there right up to the present day."]

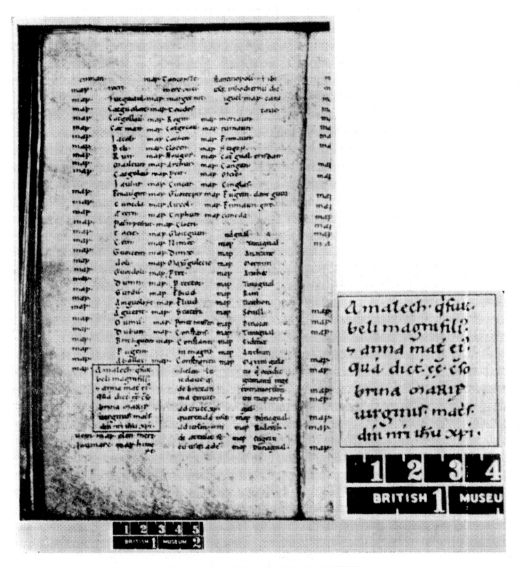

THE GENEALOGY OF OWAIN TUDOR

(MS. No. 3859 of the Harleian Collection now in the British Museum; folio 193, reverse).

THE HIGH PRIEST

(from *The Tabernacle, Priesthood, and Offerings of Israel,*
by the Rev. F. Whitfield, 1875.)

THE ARMS OF THE
CITY OF WESTMINSTER

in which appears the Portcullis, the Badge
of the Houses of Tudor and Beaufort.

Serial No. 86*f*
Copyright.

Authority: Viktor Rydberg, *Teutonic Mythology.*

RYDBERG, ABRAHAM VIKTOR (1828-1895), Swedish author and publicist; editorially connected with Göteborgs Handels-ochsjöfartstidning from 1855-76. Having become a leading contemporary novelist, he turned to theology and wrote *The Bible's Teaching about Christ* (1862), and on aspects of modern Bible criticism; wrote a series of archaeological essays on Italy entitled *Roman Days* (1876); was elected to the Swedish Academy in 1877, after he had "long been the first living author in Sweden". He also wrote poems, collected in 1882, a version of *Faust*, and in 1884 was appointed professor of ecclesiastical history at Stockholm. (Compiled from the *Encyclopaedia Britannica*, 1946.)

The Judaic and Trojan Origin of the Frankish and Swedish Kings

The varied collection of sagas, poetry and prose which comprises the early literature of the northern nations of Europe contains much valuable historical material, although it is often difficult to separate the fanciful from the factual. The repeated assertions and implications that the families descended from Odin derive from the ancient Trojan kings (often thought to belong to the "fanciful" category) may indeed prove to have firm foundation in truth. Several factors provide evidence which is harmonious with such a claim.

Ancient classical and extra-Biblical sources indicate that the Trojan kings were of the royal line of Judah and that they were closely related to other royal families in Ionia, Greece and Crete. The Early British king-line is traditionally descended from the Trojans; and the kings of Ireland are stated to have sprung from the Milesian royal family in Ionia into which "Pharaoh's daughter" married. According to such sources, therefore, the royal families of the northern nations of Europe—Irish-Scottish, Early British, Frankish, Swedish, etc.—are all of the sceptre tribe of Judah; and the many intermarriages of these regal lines would thus all be within the one great royal family of which so much is prophesied in Scripture.

The Heimskingla Saga

The sources of the Troy Saga are to be found mainly in 13th-century Icelandic literature, according to the Swedish scholar Rydberg, who, like so many historical critics, is sceptical of the accuracy and value of the story, for he rejects the legends and attributes them merely to pious desires on the part of scholars of the Middle Ages to ascribe a known origin to a hitherto unknown people. If erroneous, his argument is at least ingenious. Mere piety on the part of his clerics would hardly suffice to create a story so in harmony with anthropological, philological, and other data revealed by modern sciences.

Rydberg states that, according to the Heimskringla Saga (which is an account of the lives of the Kings of Norway, compiled by Snorri Sturluson in the early 13th century A.D. from earlier materials), the Swedes are descendants of Odin, who came to their country about a hundred years before Christ from a country called Asaland, or Asaheim, east of the Tanakvisl (Tanais or Don), a river that separated Asia from Europe. The chief town or citadel of Asaland was Asgard; here Odin ruled, and "under him ruled twelve men who were high priests and judges" (p. 23). His wife was Frigg, and his brothers Vile and Ve. Odin made war on his neighbours the Vans, but they proved to be very powerful, so a friendly alliance was concluded: Njord and his son Frey, of the Vans, were made priests by Odin.

Odin had possessions in Tyrkland, which was separated from Asaland by high mountains. Tyrkland, says Rydberg, is Asia Minor, where Troy was the chief city.

The Prose Edda

The Younger, or Prose Edda, also the work of Snorri Sturluson, contains another form of the story, in which the influence of mediaeval Biblical scholars is evident, for the tale begins with the account of the Flood (Rydberg, p. 25); and Zoroaster is said to have participated in the building of Babel by the sons of Ham; the people speaking Hebrew are stated to have come from this region. The chronological discrepancy is all too evident, but to continue with the Prose Edda:

In Crete was born Saturnus, of whose ancestry the Edda says nothing. He had three sons: Jupiter, Neptunus and Pluto. Saturnus divided his kingdom between them—to Jupiter went heaven, but since he wanted earth too he contested with his father, who fled to Italy and changed his name to Njord. Pluto received as his share the dog named Cerberus and hell (in the *Odyssey* this is Pluto's dread realm, where darkness prevailed, indicating northern regions). Jupiter had many sons, one of whom was Dardanus; in the fifth generation descended from him was Priamus of Troy, whose son was Hektor. The Romans were descended from the Trojans. (It may be recalled that Virgil's *Aenead* commemorates the belief that the Julian family was so descended.)

Under Priamus were twelve tributary kings speaking twelve languages: "from them all European chiefs are descended" (p. 26). One of these twelve was Memnon, who married a daughter of Priamus; their son was Tror, called Thor, who took his father's kingdom in Thracia. "In the twentieth generation from this Thor, Vodin descended, 'whom we call Odin' " (p. 26). "At that time the Roman general Pompey was making war in the East" (p. 27). Odin therefore left Tyrkland and migrated to Saxland, over which he made his son Veggdegg king; another son, Beldegg, he made king of Westphalia; a third, Sigge, king of Frankland; while Odin himself "came to Svithiod" (p. 27), that is to say, Sweden. Odin later made his son Saeming king of Norway, and left Svithiod to his son Yngve, "from whom the race of Ynlings are descended" (p. 27). The Asas married native women, but the speech of Troy displaced the old language of the lands, "and became the speech of Svithiod, Norway, Denmark, and Saxland, and thereafter also England" (p. 27).

Serial No. 88a.

Other Sources

The writings of Saxo Grammaticus (c. 1150-c. 1206 A.D.) are earlier than those of Snorri Sturluson (1179-1241 A.D.), who has passed the Troy Saga to us, and who was only eight when the former began to write his *Historia Danica*. Saxo makes no mention of the Troy story, but says that Odin came from the East, having come from Byzantium (not Asgard, as noted earlier, pp. 23, 33). Byzantium, however, is on the opposite side of the Hellespont.

Fredegar, a chronicler of 650 A.D., half a millennium before the Heimskringla and the Prose Edda, stated that Priam was a Frankish king ruling Troy, that the Franks were emigrants from that city, and gives as his sources the Church father, Hieronymous, and the poet Virgil (Rydberg, p. 34).

About seventy years after Fredegar, the *Gesta Regum Francorum* gives the following details of the Troy story: Aeneas ruled in Ilium (Troy); after its fall two parties fled, one to Italy under Aeneas, the other, numbering 120,000 men, sailed to the Tanais, and to Pannonia, near the Moeotian marshes, where they founded the city of Sicambria (p. 35). When the Roman emperor Valentinianus drove the Alani into the marshes and offered a reward to any who would follow them and drive them out, the Trojans did so, and in return received the name of *Franks*, which in Attic means "savage", "for the Trojans had a defiant and indomitable character". They became free from taxes for ten years; but after this the Roman emperor demanded tribute. They then proceeded to the Rhine under Markomir, Priam's son, and Sunno, son of Antenor (p. 35).

About 787 A.D. Paulus Diaconus, the Langobardian historian, wrote a history of the bishops of Metz. One of the Frankish bishops, Arnulf, from whom Charlemagne was descended in the fifth generation, had a son Ansgisel, or Ansgis in shortened form. Paulus says it was thought that this name was from Anchises, father of Aeneas, and that the Franks were believed to have come from the Trojans (p. 36).

Great care must be exercised in making use of all such historical material. The descent of a royal line from the Trojans does not necessarily imply also the descent of its tribe or nation from the same source. To illustrate this it may be observed that the establishment of a Norman line in England does not mean that the people of England are Normans. The study may be more closely connected with royal genealogies than with tribal ethnology. Danes, Norwegians, Swedes and others may have come to accept the rule of the family of Odin, though the tribes themselves may not have been of Trojan origin. On the other hand, the people of the Franks may well have been Trojans originally, though eventually the name embraced an empire. "The name Franci gradually absorbed the names of the separate tribes forming the confederation, which, however, is sometimes designated by the name of the leading people, the Sigambri. . . . These Franci, or Franks, as they are commonly called, conquered the northern parts of Gaul; and having amalgamated with the Romanised Celts of that country, they adopted the civilisation of the conquered peoples and soon acquired such power that, under their great king Clovis, A.D. 496, they returned and subdued their own kinsmen in the north and south of Germany, and thus established the great Frankish empire" (Wm. Smith's *Dictionary of Greek and Roman Geography*). The distinction between tribes and their royal families must always be born in mind.

Rydberg's observations on the Saxons, Normans, and Danes, are of interest. He points out that Widukind, the Saxon chronicler of the tenth century, gives two stories of the origin of the Saxons, one of which makes them to be a remnant of the army of Alexander the Great, and of Macedonian descent (p. 36). The evidence upon which Widukind's statement is founded is not clear, but it may be based on an attempt to derive the Saxons from the

Sacae who served in Alexander's army. The belief that the Saxons were descended from the Sacae has been mentioned in an earlier [serial No. 70 (572.9335)].

Dudo of St. Quentin, whose chronicle goes down to A.D. 996, is quoted by Rydberg, to the effect that the "Norman men regarded themselves as Danai, for Danes (the Scandinavians in general) and Danai was regarded as the same race name" (Rydberg's parenthesis, p. 38).

These records do not equate the Franks with Saxons, Normans or Danes in origin. It may be true that Normans, moving south, settled among the Franks and became known as such; and although of the same stock in remote times, their more immediate origins were different. Danes may well be Danoi of Greece or Danites; Saxons, the Sacae from Persia, and Franks the Phrygians of Dardanian Troy.

When considered in the light that the Trojan war was a struggle between Danaans of Greece and Dardanians of Phrygia, the rhymed chronicle of Robert Wace, entitled *Roman de Rou*, may be found to express some historic truth:

> "When the walls of Troy in ashes were laid,
> And the Greeks exceeding glad were made,
> Then fled from flames on the Trojan strand
> The race that settled old Denmark's land;
> And in honour of the old Trojan reigns
> The people called themselves the Danes" (Ryberg, p. 38).

Many details of circumstantial evidence are entirely in harmony with the Trojan and therefore Judahite [ser. No. 81 (572.93918)] origin of the royal family of Odin. The badge of the royal families of the northern nations is the lion, the symbol of Judah. That Danites moved in the same general direction as this royal family is severally indicated.

The eagle, the emblem of *Dan*zig, is the symbol of the tribe of Dan [ser. No. 53 (929.9)]; [ser. No. 41 (572.938)]. Place names, from Jor*dan* of the Holy Land, and the Jar*danus* river of Crete, to the Dar*dan*ians of Troy, the *Dan*aans of Greece, the Dar*dan*elles separating these two, the *Dn*iester, *Dn*ieper, *Don*, Eri*danus* (Rhine), Rho*danus* (Rhone), *Den*mark, Scan*dina*via, and hundreds of other place-names bearing this root, especially in Ireland (*Dun*lewy, Killy*don*nell, Lon*don*derry, etc.) are evidence of the movement of a people who made constant use of it. The badge of the clan *Don*nachaidh, the oldest Scottish clan, is a serpent and a so-called *dove*.

Ethnically also, there is strong evidence to show that Israelites, Greeks, Anglo-Saxons, Danes, etc., were of the same stock [ser. No. 57 (572.9394)]. The construction of megalithic monuments was also common to these people [ser. No. 60 (572.9394)]; [ser. No. 76. (572.9394)].

From such considerations it becomes more and more evident that the legend of the Trojan, and thence Judahite, origin of the royal families descended from Odin may be founded on truth.

For further study of an attempted reconstruction of the genealogies of these families from various historical sources the reader is referred to *The Royal House of Britain; an Enduring Dynasty* (with chart), by the late Rev. W. M. H. Milner, M.A. (Covenant Publishing Company).

There is a widespread tendency to regard Odin as a mythical deity instead of a person of remarkable prowess who was after his death so closely identified with the deity he

Serial No. 88b

worshipped that a confusion of the two resulted. Several renowned scholars have defended the existence of Odin as a historical character, among them being Sharon Turner, author of *The History of the Anglo-Saxons*, Du Chaillu, author of *The Viking Age*, etc., and the French scholar, M. Mallet, author of *Northern Antiquities*.

Mediaeval writers accepted the descent of the royal families of the Swedes, Norwegians, Franks, etc., from Odin, and, as is evidenced in the genealogies preserved in the *Langfedgatal*, his descent from the Trojan kings. In their endeavours to trace the Trojan kings to an earlier origin, these scholars agreed in tracing them through the Cretan kings, but beyond this they differed, some deriving them from Japhet, and some from Shem, as is clear from a footnote to the *Langfedgatal* in Jacob Langebek's *Scriptores Rerum Danicarum Medii Aevi* (1772), Vol. I, p. 8, note i, where, against a genealogy deriving Odin from the Cretan kings and in turn from Japhet, we read: ''Ailredas Abbas Rievall. ap. Twysden, p. 351. de Odino ita scribit: 'A Sem genealogia ducitur usque ad Woden . . .' ''

Extract from *NORTHERN ANTIQUITIES, or, AN HISTORICAL ACCOUNT OF THE MANNERS, CUSTOMS, RELIGION AND LAWS, MARITIME EXPEDITIONS AND DISCOVERIES, LANGUAGE AND LITERATURE OF THE ANCIENT SCANDINAVIANS (DANES, SWEDES, NORWEGIANS AND ICELANDERS) WITH INCIDENTAL NOTICES RESPECTING OUR SAXON ANCESTORS*, translated from the French of M. Mallet, by Bishop Percy; New Edition, Bohn's *Antiquarian Library Series*, London, 1847.

Before I describe the state of ancient Scandinavia I must stop one moment. A celebrated tradition, confirmed by the poems of all the northern nations, by their chronicles, by institutions and customs, some of which subsist to this day, informs us, that an extraordinary person named Odin, formerly reigned in the north: that he made great changes in the government, manners, and religion of those countries; that he enjoyed there great authority, and even had divine honours paid him. As to what regards the origin of the man, the country whence he came, the time in which he lived, and the other circumstances of his life and death, they are so uncertain, that the most profound researches, the most ingenious conjectures about them, discover nothing to us but our own ignorance. Thus previously disposed to doubt, let those ancient authors I have mentioned relate the story: all their testimonies are comprised in that of Snorri, the ancient historian of Norway, and in the commentaries and explications which Torfæus added to his narrative.

The Roman Commonwealth was arrived to the highest pitch of power, and saw all the then known world subject to its laws, when an unforeseen event raised up enemies against it, from the very bosom of the forests of Scythia, and on the banks of the Tanais. Mithridates by flying, had drawn Pompey after him into those deserts. The king of Pontus sought there for refuge, and new means of vengeance. He hoped to arm against the ambition of Rome, all the barbarous nations his neighbours, whose liberty she threatened. He succeeded in this at first; but all those people, ill united as allies, ill armed as soldiers, and still worse disciplined, were forced to yield to the genius of Pompey. Odin is said to have been of this number. He was obliged to withdraw himself by flight from the vengeance of the Romans; and to go and seek in countries unknown to his enemies that safety which he could no longer find in his own. His true name was Siggi, son of Fridulph; but he assumed that of Odin, who was the Supreme God among the Teutonic nations: either in order to pass among his followers for a man inspired by the Gods, or because he was chief priest, and presided over the worship paid to that deity. We know that it was usual with many nations to give their pontiffs the name of the God they worshipped. Sigge, full of his ambitious projects, we may be assured, took care to avail himself of a title so proper to procure him respect among the people he meant to subject.

Odin, for so we shall hereafter call him, commanded the Æsir, whose country must have been situated between the Pontus Euxinus, and the Caspian Sea. Their principal city was Asgard. The worship there paid to the supreme God was famous throughout the circumjacent countries. Odin having united under his banners the youth of the neighbouring nations, marched towards the north and west of Europe, subduing, we are told, all the people he found in his passage, and giving them to one or other of his sons for subjects, Many sovereign families of the north are said to be descended from these princes. Thus Horsa and Hengist, the chiefs of those Saxons, who conquered Britain in the fifth century, counted Odin, or Wodin, in the number of their ancestors; it was the same with the other Anglo-Saxon princes; as well as the greatest part of those of Lower Germany and the north. But there is reason to suspect that all these genealogies, which have given birth to so many insipid panegyrics and frivolous researches, are founded upon a mere equivoque, or double meaning of the word Odin. This word signified, as we have seen above, the Supreme God of the Teutonic nations; we know also that it was customary with all the heroes of these nations to speak of themselves as sprung from their divinities, especially their god of war. The historians of those times, that is to say, the poets, never failed to bestow the same honour on all those whose praises they sung: and thus they multiplied the descendants of Odin, or the Supreme God, as much as ever they found convenient.

After having disposed of so many countries, and confirmed and settled his new governments, Odin directed his course towards Scandinavia, passing through Cimbria, at present Holstein and Jutland. These provinces, exhausted of inhabitants, made him no resistance; and shortly after he passed into Fünen, which submitted as soon as ever he appeared. He is said to have staid a long time in this agreeable island, where he built the city of Odensee, which still preserves in its name the memory of its founder. Hence he extended his arms all over the north. He subdued the rest of Denmark, and made his son Skjöld be received there as king; a title, which according to the Icelandic annals, no person had ever borne before, and which passed to his descendants, called after his name Skjöldungians; if this name was not rather given them on account of the shield, which they were accustomed to bear, for this is called Skjöld in the Danish language to this day. Odin, who was apparently better pleased to give crowns to his children, than to wear them himself, afterwards passed into Sweden, where at that time reigned a prince named Gylfi, who persuaded that the author of a new worship consecrated by conquests so brilliant, could not be of the ordinary race of mortals, paid him great honours, and even worshipped him as a divinity. By favour of this opinion, which the ignorance of that age led men easily to embrace, Odin quickly acquired in Sweden the same authority he had obtained in Denmark. The Swedes came in crowds to do him homage, and by common consent bestowed the regal title and office upon his son Yngvi and his posterity. Hence sprung the Ynglingians, a name by which the kings of Sweden were for a long time distinguished.

Gylfi died, or was forgotten. Odin governed with absolute dominion. He enacted new laws, introduced the customs of his own country; and established at Sigtuna (a city at present destroyed, situate in the same province with Stockholm) a supreme council or tribunal, composed of twelve pontiffs or judges. Their business was to watch over the public weal, to distribute justice to the people, to preside over the new worship, which Odin brought with him into the north, and to preserve faithfully the religious and magical secrets which that prince deposited with them. He was quickly acknowledged as a sovereign and a god, by all the petty kings among whom Sweden was then divided; and he levied an impost or poll-tax upon every head through the whole country. He engaged on his part to defend the inhabitants against all their enemies, and to defray the expense of the worship rendered to the gods at Sigtuna.

These great acquisitions seem not, however, to have satisfied his ambition. The desire of extending farther his religion, his authority and his glory, caused him to undertake the conquest of Norway. His good fortune or address followed him thither, and this kingdom quickly obeyed a son of Odin named Sæming, whom they have taken care to make head of a family, the different branches of which reigned for a long time in that country.

After he had finished these glorious achievements, Odin retired into Sweden; where, perceiving his end to draw near, he would not wait till the consequences of a lingering disease should put a period to that life, which he had so often bravely hazarded in the field; but assembling his friends and companions of his fortune, he gave himself nine wounds in the form of a circle with the point of a lance, and many other cuts in his skin with his sword. As he was dying, he declared he was going back to Asgard to take his seat among the other gods at an eternal banquet, where he would receive with great honours all who should expose themselves intrepidly in battle, and die bravely with their swords in their hands. As soon as he had breathed his last, they carried his body to Sigtuna, where, conformably to a custom introduced by him into the north, his body was burnt with much pomp and magnificence (pp. 79-82).

Note: Adon, in Hebrew, signifies *Lord, sir, or master*.

EXTRACTS FROM *THE HISTORY OF THE ANGLO-SAXONS, FROM THE EARLIEST PERIOD TO THE NORMAN CONQUEST*, by Sharon Turner, F.A.S., R.A.S.L.; 7th ed., London, 1852.

Without imitating those who have lately fancied that there never was an Odin, and that he is merely a mythological personage, the name of a deity, we may remark, that the date of Odin's appearance in the North cannot be accurately ascertained. This difficulty has arisen partly from the confusion in which, from their want of chronology, all the incidents of the North, anterior to the eighth century, are involved, and partly from the wild and discordant fictions of the scalds, who have clouded the history of Odin by their fantastic mythology. The same obscurity attends the heroes of all countries who have been deified after death, and upon whose memory the poets have taken the trouble to scatter the weeds as well as the flowers of their fancy. The human existence of Odin appears to me to be satistactorily proved by two facts: 1st. The founders of the Anglo-Saxon Octarchy deduced their descent from Odin by genealogies in which the ancestors are distinctly mentioned up to him. These genealogies have the appearance of greater authenticity by not being the servile copies of each other; they exhibit to us different individuals in the successive stages of the ancestry of each, and they claim different children of Odin as the founders of the lines. These genealogies are also purely Anglo-Saxon. 2nd. The other circumstance is, that the Northern chroniclers and scalds derive their heroes also from Odin by his different children. Snorre, in his Ynglinga Saga, gives a detailed history of Sweden regularly from him; and though the Northerns cannot be suspected of having borrowed their genealogies from the Anglo-Saxons, yet they agree in some of the children ascribed to Odin. This coincidence between the genealogies preserved in their new country of men who left the North in the fifth and sixth centuries, and the genealogies of the most celebrated heroes who acted in the North during the subsequent ages, could not have arisen if there never had been an Odin who left such children. (Note 5, Appendix to Bk. II, chap. iii.)

One of the most ancient Icelandic documents that now exist is the *Langfedgatal*. It was used both by Ara Frode and by Snorre. It calls Odin the king of the Tyrkia, who are supposed to be Turks, and gives him the following ancestry, deducing him from Thor;

Japhet	Einridi
Japhans	Vingethorr
Zechim	Vingener
Ciprus	Moda
Celius	Magi
Saturnus of Krit,	Seskef, or Sescef
Jupiter	Bedwig
Darius	Athra
Erichhonius	Itormann
Troes	Heremotr
Ilus	Scealdna
Lamedon	Beaf
Priam, King of Troy	Eat
Minon, or Memnon,	Godulf
who married Pri-	Finn
am's daughter.	Frealaf
Their son was Tror	Vodin, whom we call
whom we call Thor,	Oden
the father of	
Hloritha	

"From him descended most of the kingly races in the north part of the world. He was king of the Tyrkia. He fled from the Romans to the north."

It then deduces, through two lines of descendants from him, by two other sons than those who head the Anglo-Saxon dynasties, the kings of Norway and Denmark. (Bk. III, chap. ii, pp. 240, 241.)

The Heraldry of Israel

ALTHOUGH heraldry, as we know it, was not codified until feudal times, the adoption of heraldic symbols by ruling families goes back to remote antiquity. In the Wilderness the Israelites pitched camp "Every man . . . by his own standard, with the ensign of their father's house." Although the Bible itself does not specify the particular tribal crests it is clear that there was a distinctive ensign for each tribe. Traditional Jewish information shows that the emblems adopted had reference to the cryptic blessings which Jacob pronounced upon his twelve sons and also—in a lesser degree—to the blessing which Moses laid upon the tribes just before his death. The traditions imply that certain tribes used more than one heraldic device. A most interesting feature is that the 'four beasts'— living creatures: lion, ox, man, and flying eagle—of Ezekiel and Revelation are found to be the emblems of the leading tribes (Judah, Ephraim, Reuben, and Dan) in each of the four 'brigades' of Israel in the four-square Wilderness Camp, thus symbolising all Israel in perpetual remembrance before the Throne of God.

THE WILDERNESS CAMP AND ORDER OF MARCH
Numbers ii, 2-34

"EVERY man of the children of Israel shall pitch by his own standard, with the ensign of their father's house . . . on the east . . . shall they of the standard of the camp of Judah pitch . . . next unto him shall be the tribe of Issachar. . . . Then the tribe of Zebulun. . . . On the south side shall be the standard of the camp of Reuben. . . . And those which pitch by him shall be the tribe of Simeon. . . . Then the tribe of Gad. . . . Then the tabernacle of the congregation . . . with the camp of the Levites in the midst of the camp . . . every man in his place by their standards. On the west side shall be the standard of the camp of Ephraim. . . . And by him shall be the tribe of Manasseh. . . . Then the tribe of Benjamin. . . . The standard of the camp of Dan shall be on the north side. . . . And those that encamp by him shall be the tribe of Asher. . . . Then the tribe of Naphtali. . . . They shall go hindmost with their standards. These are those which were numbered of the children of Israel by the house of their fathers . . . so they pitched by their standards . . . according to the house of their fathers."

THE BLESSINGS OF JACOB UPON HIS SONS
Genesis xlix

Reuben	"Unstable as water, thou shalt not excel."
Simeon } Levi	"I will divide them in Jacob, and scatter them in Israel."
Judah	"Is a lion's whelp."
Zebulun	"Shall dwell at the haven of the sea."
Issachar	"Is a strong ass couching down between two burdens."
Dan	"Shall be a serpent by the way, an adder in the path, that biteth the horse heels."
Gad	"A troop shall overcome him: but he shall overcome at the last."
Asher	"Shall yield royal dainties."
Naphtali	"Is a hind let loose."
Joseph	"Is a fruitful bough . . . by a well; whose branches run over the wall."
Benjamin	"Shall ravin as a wolf."

THE BLESSING OF THE TRIBE BY MOSES
Deuteronomy xxxiii

Reuben	"Let not his men be few."
Levi	"Let thy Thummim and thy Urim be with thy holy one."
Zebulun	"Rejoice, Zebulun, in thy going out."
Gad	"He dwelleth as a lion."
Joseph { Ephraim / Manasseh	"His glory is like the firstling of his bullock, and his horns are like the horns of unicorns . . . of Ephraim, and . . . of Manasseh."

NOTE: The blessings on the remaining tribes are not here recited, as they would appear to have no bearing on any of the devices ascribed to the tribes.

THE 'CHIEF RULER'—JESUS CHRIST
Revelation v. 5.

". . . the Lion of the tribe of Juda, the Root of David, hath prevailed to open the book . . ."

THE TRIBAL EMBLEMS

Information as to the tribal emblems is tablulated below. The first column gives information taken from the *Jewish Encyclopædia* (article 'Flag'). Thomas Fuller, B.D., wrote a remarkably comprehensive work on Israel (*Pisgah Sight of Palestine*, 1869), in which he describes the various devices attributed to the tribes. He also quotes the records of Aben Ezra—the learned Jewish scholar of the Cromwellian period.

	'Jewish Encyclopædia'	*Fuller*	*Aben Ezra*
Reuben	Mandrake	Mandrake, or man with mandrakes in hand	Man or male child
Simeon	City (Schechem)	Sword	—
Levi	Urim and Thummin	—	—
Judah	Lion	Lion couchant	—
Issachar	Sun and moon	Ass between two burdens	—
Zebulun	Ship	Ship	—
Dan	Snake	Adder biting horse heels	Eagle
Gad	Camp	Lion rampant	—
Naphtali	Hind	Hind	—
Asher	Female figure and olive tree	Covered cup	—
Ephraim	Bullock	Ox	—
Manasseh	Unicorn	Tree by a well	—
Benjamin	Wolf	Wolf	—

POINTS OF SPECIAL INTEREST

1. Adam Clarke, in his commentary on Numbers ii, refers to both the eagle and the serpent as being emblems of Dan (Vol. I, p. 631, 1836 ed.).
   The Lacedæmonian Greeks (known to be of Israelite stock and probably of the tribe of Dan) used a seal in communications of national import which depicted "an eagle holding fast a serpent" (Josephus, *Antiquities*, Book XII, iv, sec. 10).

   Homer recites that the 'eagle and serpent' emblem appeared—a sign of ill omen to the Trojans—over the contesting armies at the siege of Troy (*Iliad*, Book XII, lines 216-249).

2. "The Jews have a tradition that the ensign, carried in the standard of Judah, was a lion; in that of Reuben, a man; in that of Ephraim, an ox; and in that of Dan, an eagle. St. John seems to allude to this in Rev. iv" (*Notes, Explanatory and Practical*, to the Authorised Version of the Holy Bible, by the Rev. George D'Oyly, D.D. and the Rev. Richard Mant, D.D., Lord Bishop of Down and Connor, on Numbers ii—S.P.C.K., 1840).

   The same four 'living creatures' are described in the vision of Ezekiel (ch. i, 10). The position in which the prophet describes them compares perfectly with the positions assigned to the tribes of Judah, Ephraim, Reuben, and Dan in the Wilderness Camp.

DAN
"The face of an eagle"

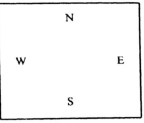

EPHRAIM
"The face of an ox on the left side"

JUDAH
"The face of a lion on the right side"

REUBEN
"The face of a man"

3. The Midrash (Num. R. ii), on the passage "Every man of the children of Israel shall pitch by his own standard, with the ensign of their father's house," explains that the emblems and colours corresponded with the twelve precious stones set in the breastplate worn by the high priest.

   The Targum Yerushalmi says that the flag of Judah bore, over a roaring lion, the inscription "Rise up, Lord, and let thine enemies be scattered . . ." (*Jewish Encyclopædia*, 1925, art. 'Flag').

4. The mandrake root has always been regarded as roughly conforming to the shape of a man's figure. The incident of the mandrakes and the mother of Reuben is narrated in Genesis xxx.

"The Banners of the Tribes", from *The Tabernacle, Priesthood and Offerings of Israel*, by the Rev. Frederick Whitfield, M.A., Vicar of St. Mary's-in-the-Castle, Hastings (1875); facing p. 261. Variations are found in different authorities; but there is general agreement concerning the leading tribes. Thus the Jewish *Encyclopædia* says: "Ephraim's banner was painted black, and bore the picture of a bullock (Num. R. ii); Moses alluded to it when he said of Joseph: 'The firstling of his bullock, majesty is his' (Deut. xxxvii, 17, R.V.)." ". . . the Talmud mentions that Manasseh's tribal banner, during the journey to the Promised Land, consisted of a black flag with the embroidered figure of a unicorn" (Arts: "Ephraim" and "Manasseh").

BIBLE RESEARCH HANDBOOK INDEX FOR SERIAL Nos. 1-100

(This replaces all previous Indexes, which may be destroyed.)

BIBLE RESEARCH HANDBOOK SUPPLEMENTARY INDEX FOR
SERIAL Nos. 101-124

(This, with Index for Serial Nos. 1–100 comprises complete index.)

NOTES ON ARRANGEMENT OF SERIAL NUMBERS 1-100

(Destroy all previous lists)

MANY subscribers prefer to have their serials arranged in order of subject, and the Dewey Decimal Classification (as printed on the top right-hand corner of each serial) was adopted for that purpose. When serials are arranged in accordance with this classification it will be found that all references to Migrations will be together, all Old Testament references will be together, and so on.

If you wish to have your Handbook serials arranged according to subject, put them in this order (reading from top to bottom):

Serial No.		Decimal No.	Serial No.		Decimal No.
1	(Title page; serial No. omitted in 1st edition)		36		222.5
			27		222.5
54	(Mr. Churchill and the Bible)	—	39		222.5
2	(Foreword; serial No. omitted in 1st edition)	—	98		222.5
3	(Introduction; serial No. omitted in 1st edition)		99		222.5
			42		222.6
			43		222.6
—	*Index here or at end, as desired*	—	35		222.7
94		220.6	38		222.94
82		220.8	80		223.2
62		221.4	15		224.1
50		222.1	63		224.2
67		222.1	91		224.2
96		222.1	73		224.4
4		222.11	75		224.4
14		222.11	97		224.4
16		222.11	48		224.5
19		222.11	31		224.92
51		222.12	59		225.4
68		222.12	95		226.
69		222.12	78		226.7
71		222.12	84		228.
100		222.15	79		263.
			72		270.
5	(The Crossing of the Jordan; serial No. omitted in 1st edition)	222.2	52		274.4201
20		222.2	87		340.3
77		222.4	89		340.3
			45		386.0936
6	(II Kings: xvii; serial No. omitted in 1st edition)	222.5	66		389.
10		222.5	85		415.
11		222.5	33		492.4
12		222.5	46		492.4
22		222.5	49		571.3
23		222.5	7	(Chief Rabbi's letter; serial No. omitted in 1st edition)	572.933
24		222.5			
25		222.5	17		572.933

Serial No.		Decimal No.	Serial No.		Decimal No.
26		572.933	58		572.93944
28		572.933	18		572.93951
40		572.933	21		572.93951
56		572.933	61		572.941
64		572.933	93		572.94151
70		572.9335	83		572.942
32		572.935	92		572.942
29		572.9353	30		572.94601
55		572.9353	9	(Procopius on Moors; serial No.	
37		572.9355		omitted in 1st edition)	572.961
47		572.9355	90	(Misprinted as 273)	573.
41		572.938	74		912.30
8	(On Lacedemonians; serial No.		44		915.569
	omitted in 1st edition)	572.9389	65		929.2
81		572.93918	86		929.2
13		572.93934	88		929.2
57		572.9394	34		929.9
60		572.9394	53		929.9
76		572.9394			

When ordering further copies of separate serials please quote serial number only.